T0220774

Lecture Notes of the Institute for Computer Sciences, Social Informatics and Telecommunications Engineering 323

More information about this series at http://www.springer.com/series/8197

Henrique Santos · Gabriela Viale Pereira ·
Matthias Budde · Sérgio F. Lopes ·
Predrag Nikolic (Eds.)

Science and Technologies for Smart Cities

5th EAI International Summit, SmartCity360
Braga, Portugal, December 4–6, 2019
Proceedings

 Springer

Editors
Henrique Santos 🆔
Information Systems Department
University of Minho
Guimaraes, Portugal

Matthias Budde 🆔
Karlsruhe Institute of Technology
Karlsruhe, Germany

Predrag Nikolic 🆔
ShanghaiTech University
Shanghai, China

Gabriela Viale Pereira 🆔
Department of E-Governance
and Administration
Danube University Krems
Krems an der Donau, Niederösterreich
Austria

Sérgio F. Lopes 🆔
University of Minho
Guimarães, Portugal

ISSN 1867-8211 ISSN 1867-822X (electronic)
Lecture Notes of the Institute for Computer Sciences, Social Informatics
and Telecommunications Engineering
ISBN 978-3-030-51004-6 ISBN 978-3-030-51005-3 (eBook)
https://doi.org/10.1007/978-3-030-51005-3

This Springer imprint is published by the registered company Springer Nature Switzerland AG
The registered company address is: Gewerbestrasse 11, 6330 Cham, Switzerland

Preface Smart City 360°

Our civilization is changing rapidly. Forecasts point to a rise in megacities, pushing population density, and putting some pressure on governments, municipalities, private and public organizations, and citizens to maintain the quality of life (but, of course, to improve it, if possible). However, the challenges to accomplish such a simple goal are enormous. Technology evolution plays a vital role but, as usual, also introduces some risks. Human behavior needs to adapt, as well as social habits, and, more than ever, professional activities, following the tendencies of the so-called fourth industrial revolution, mostly based on digital transformation, demanding for a more enlightened society. Environmental aspects are also critical, but social indicators are not less important, as demonstrated in the recent pandemic crisis. The only way to embrace such a challenge is by working together (all society agents), sharing ideas and experiments, discussing alternatives openly, making science, in its fundamental aspects, the leading guide to our path towards a healthy and pleasant society, living in really Smart and Sustainable Cities.

The Smart City 360° Convention is an annual event providing a proper forum to pursue such a vision. This year (in its 5th edition), the event included four co-located conferences from which we selected 33 papers. Furthermore, we added five papers from excellent keynote presentations, ending up with the present volume as a valuable contribution to the area.

The selected co-located conferences were as follows:

- The 4th International Conference on IoT in Urban Space (Urb-IoT 2019), focused on the impact of new technologies on the recreation of the urban spaces and the environment (nine papers)
- The First International Conference on Smart Governance for Sustainable Smart Cities (SmartGov 2019), focused on all aspects of urban smart governance issues, from planning, managing, transforming, and monitoring cities' governance, to improving decision-making processes (eight papers)
- The 10th Sensor Systems and Software (S-cube 2019), focused on all aspects of state-of-the-art engineering for artifacts based on wireless sensors networks and fostering system and software techniques to fulfill the evolving requirements of Smart Cities (six papers)
- The 11th International Conference on Intelligent Technologies for Interactive Entertainment (INTETAIN 2019), focused on intelligent technologies for interactive entertainment, in the emerging and demanding context of Smart Cities (ten papers)

Lastly, we thank all participants, authors, keynote speakers, the Municipality of Braga (kindly supported the venue), the chairs of all conferences, and the incredible teams they manage to put together, the local collaborators, and the EAI staff (we would like to name all involved, but space do not allow it). It was an honor and a pleasure to organize and host the 5th Smart City 360° International Summit in Braga, Portugal.

May 2020   Henrique Santos

Preface Urb-IoT 2019

We are delighted to introduce the proceedings of the 4th edition of the European Alliance for Innovation (EAI) International Conference on IoT in Urban Space (Urb-IoT 2019), co-located with the Smart City 360° Summit 2019, which took place in Braga, Portugal. This conference brought researchers, developers, and practitioners around the world together who are exploring the urban space and its dynamics within the scope of the Internet of Things (IoT) and the new science of cities.

The technical program of Urb-IoT 2019 consisted of eight full papers, which were distributed by two sessions: Session 1 – Sensing Methods; and Session 2 – Environmental Sensing.

Coordination with the steering chairs, Prof. Imrich Chlamtac and Prof. Fahim Kawsar, as well as with the general chair of Smart City 360° Summit, Prof. Henrique Santos, was essential for the success of the conference. We sincerely appreciate their constant support and guidance. It was also a great pleasure to work with such an excellent Organizing Committee and we thank them for their hard work in organizing and supporting the conference. In particular, the Technical Program Committee (TPC), led by our TPC co-chairs, Dr. Philipp M. Scholl and Dr. Matthias Budde, and all the additional reviewers, who completed the peer-review process of technical papers for the Urb-IoT 2019 technical program. We are also grateful to conference managers: Kristina Lappyova, Andrea Piekova, and Karolina Marcinova for their support.

Finally, a special mention to all the authors who submitted their work to the Urb-IoT 2019 conference. We strongly believe that the Urb-IoT conference provides a good forum for all researcher, developers, and practitioners to discuss all science and technology aspects that are relevant to Smart Cities. We are now even more confident that future Urb-IoT conferences will be as successful and stimulating as suggested by the contributions presented in this volume.

May 2020

Philipp M. Scholl
Matthias Budde
Helena Rodrigues
Rui José

Organization (Urb-IoT 2019)

Steering Committee

Imrich Chlamtac	University of Trento, Italy
Fahim Kawsar	Bell Labs, Belgium

Organizing Committee

General Co-chairs

Helena Rodrigues	University of Minho, Portugal
Rui José	University of Minho, Portugal

TPC Chair and Co-chair

Matthias Budde	Karlsruhe Institute of Technology, Germany
Philipp M. Scholl	University of Freiburg, Germany

Local Chair

César Analide	University of Minho

Publicity and Social Media Chairs

Joaquín Torres-Sospedra	Universitat Jaume I, Spain
Fábio Silva	Polytechnic Institute of Porto, Portugal

Publications Chair

Filipe Meneses	University of Minho, Portugal

Web Chair

Vítor Santos	New University of Lisbon, Portugal

Posters and PhD Track Chair

Maria João Nicolau	University of Minho, Portugal

Technical Program Committee

Adriano Moreira	University of Minho, Portugal
Akhul Mathur	Nokia Bell Labs, UK
António Luis Duarte Costa	University of Minho, Portugal
Christopher Bull	Lancaster University, UK
Florian Michahelles	Siemens Corporation, USA

Preface SmartGov 2019

It is a pleasure to introduce the proceedings of the first edition of the 2019 European Alliance for Innovation (EAI) International Conference on Smart Governance for Sustainable Smart Cities (SmartGov 2019). This conference focused on all aspects of urban smart governance, broadly understood as the intelligent use of digitization and their technologies (e.g. data-driven, cognitive, cyber-physical, etc.) in planning, managing, transforming, and monitoring cities' governance instances and improving decision-making through enhanced collaboration among different stakeholders.

The technical program of SmartGov 2019 consisted of eight full papers, which were presented in two sessions at the main conference track. The conference tracks were: Track 1 – Framing and measuring Smart Cities chaired by Lorenzo Madrid; and Track 2 – Smart Governance applications chaired by Luís Soares Barbosa. Aside from the high-quality technical paper presentations, which is empathized by the acceptance rate of 37%, the technical program also featured one keynote speech by Soumaya Ben Dhaou, Research Coordinator at UNU-EGOV, Portugal. The keynote speech discussed how the emerging/frontier and disruptive technologies leveraged in smart city initiatives could be oriented towards sustainable public value generation.

The conference organization was supported by UNU-EGOV, the Operational Unit on Policy-driven Electronic Governance of the United Nations University. Coordination with the steering chairs, Imrich Chlamtac and Henrique Santos, was essential for the success of the conference. We sincerely appreciate their constant support and guidance. It was also a great pleasure to work with such an excellent Organizing Committee and we thank them for their hard work in organizing and supporting the conference. In particular, the Technical Program Committee (TPC), led by the TPC co-chair, Prof. Luís Soares Barbosa, who, together with myself, have completed the peer-review process of technical papers and made a high-quality technical program. We are also grateful to the conference manager, Karolina Marcinova, for her support, to the local chair, Dr. Teresa Pereira, and all the authors who submitted their papers to the SmartGov 2019 conference.

I strongly believe that the SmartGov conference provides a good forum for all researchers, policy makers, and practitioners to discuss all science and technology aspects that are relevant to smart governance. I also expect that future SmartGov conferences will be as successful and stimulating, as indicated by the contributions presented in this volume.

May 2020   Gabriela Viale Pereira

Organization (SmartGov 2019)

Steering Committee

Chair

Imrich Chlamtac   University of Trento, Italy

Organizing Committee

General Chair

Luis Soares Barbosa   United Nations University, Portugal

General Co-chair

Gabriela Viale Pereira   Danube University Krems, Austria

Technical Program Chair

Luis Soares Barbosa   United Nations University, Portugal

Web Chair

Guillermina Cledou   University of Minho, Portugal

Publicity and Social Media Chair

Luís Barreto   The Polytechnic Institute of Viana do Castelo, Portugal

Publication Chair

Teresa Pereira   The Polytechnic Institute of Viana do Castelo, Portugal

Local Chair

Teresa Pereira   The Polytechnic Institute of Viana do Castelo, Portugal

Conference Manager

Karolina Marcinova   EAI

Technical Program Committee

Adegboyega Ojo   Galway University, Ireland
Alejandro Sanchez   UN San Luis, Argentina
Alexandre Barbosa   NIC.br, Brazil
Alexandre Madeira   Universidade de Aveiro, Portugal
Cyril Velikanov   The Memorial Society, Moscow, Russia

Dmitri Trutnev	ITMO University, Russia
Elsa Estevez	Universidad de La Plata, Argentina
Enzo Falco	Delft University of Technology, The Netherlands
Jill Tao	Incheon National University, South Korea
Gabriela Viale Pereira	Danube University Krems, Austria
Gianluca Misuraca	European Commission, JRC, Spain
Harekrishna Mishra	Institute of Rural Management, Anand, India
Luis Barreto	IPVC, Portugal
Luis Soares Barbosa	UNU-EGOV, UN
Luis Teran	University of Fribourg, Switzerland
Leonidas G. Anthopoulos	University of Thessaly, Greece
Lorenzo Madrid	Smart City Business Institute, USA
Manuel Pedro Rodríguez Bolívar	Universidad de Granada, Spain
Maria Guillermina Cledou	University of Minho, Portugal
Miguel Sopas Bandeira	CMB, University of Minho, Portugal
Peter Kimpian	Council of Europe, France
Peter Parycek	Danube University Krems, Austria
Ralf-Martin Soe	Tallinn University of Technology, Estonia
Reinout Kleinhans	Delft University of Technology, The Netherlands
Renato Neves	INESC TEC, Portugal
Soumaya Ben Dhaou	UNU-EGOV, United Nations University, Portugal
Teresa Pereira (OC chair)	IPVC, Portugal
Theresa Pardo	University at Albany - SUNY, USA
Vinod Kumar	School of Planning and Architecture, Delhi, India
Yuri Misnikov	ITMO University, Russia

Preface S-cube 2019

We are delighted to introduce the proceedings of the 10th edition of the European Alliance for Innovation (EAI) International Conference on Sensor Systems and Software (S-cube 2019). This conference has brought researchers, developers, and practitioners from around the world together who are leveraging and developing state-of-the-art work in the areas of system development and software support for wireless sensors networks.

Integrated in Smart City 360° Summit, the technical program of S-cube 2019 consisted of six full papers, in an oral presentation session at the main summit track, which represents an acceptance rate of 50%. Aside from the high-quality technical paper presentations, the papers approached a wide range of topics, with some prevalence in the monitoring and predictive maintenance issues, which are becoming more relevant with the technological advancements and the application of sensor networks to critical infrastructures, like water quality management, urban air quality, and electric motors-based equipment. Notwithstanding, there are also important contributions centred on the human side of the IoT revolution, both concerning tracking in dense industrial environments (using video images), and the quality of the working environment as perceived through building management systems. Data analysis is also a fundamental function linked to sensor networks and in particular with the spread of sensor technologies. No surprise, the smart aspects of sensors are also addressed, this time connected to an irrigation system, contributing to optimise agriculture-related activities.

Coordination with the Smart City 360° Summit was essential for the success of the conference. It was a great pleasure to work with such an excellent Organizing Committee and we thank them for their hard work in organizing and supporting the conference. In particular, the Technical Program Committee, who carried out a high-quality peer-review process of the technical papers. We are also grateful to conference managers, Karolina Marcinova and Barbora Cintava, for their support from the beginning to end of the conference, and EAI publications coordinator, Martin Karbovanec, for his help in validating the camera-ready versions of the papers and preparing the publication. We also thank all authors who submitted their papers to the S-cube 2019 conference and especially those who presented them and contributed to make S-cube 2019 an interesting and fruitful exchange of ideas.

May 2020

António Costa
Henrique Santos
Sérgio F. Lopes

Organization (S-cube 2019)

Steering Committee

Chair

Imrich Chlamtac   University of Trento, Italy

Organizing Committee

General Chair

Paulo Freitas   International Iberian Nanotechnology Laboratory,
                                    Portugal

General Co-chair

João Piteira   International Iberian Nanotechnology Laboratory,
                                    Portugal

Technical Program Committee Chairs

Andrei Utkin   Instituto De Novas Tecnologias, Portugal
João Ferreira   Instituto De Novas Tecnologias, Portugal

Publications Chair

Sergio Lopes   University of Minho, Portugal

Local Chair

Antonio Luis Duarte Costa   University of Minho, Portugal

Conference Manager

Karolina Marcinova   EAI

Technical Program Committee

Henrique Santos   Centro Algoritmi Universidade do Minho, Portugal
Sérgio Lopes   Centro Algoritmi Universidade do Minho, Portugal
António Duarte Costa   Centro Algoritmi Universidade do Minho, Portugal
Óscar Gama   Centro Algoritmi Universidade do Minho, Portugal
Pedro Nuno Sousa   Centro Algoritmi Universidade do Minho, Portugal
Bruno Dias   Centro Algoritmi Universidade do Minho, Portugal
Joaquim Henriques Macedo   Centro Algoritmi Universidade do Minho, Portugal
Sérgio Monterio   Centro Algoritmi Universidade do Minho, Portugal
José Augusto Afonso   Centro Algoritmi Universidade do Minho, Portugal

José Carlos Metrôlho	Instituto Politécnico de Castelo Branco, Portugal
Luís Gonçalves	CMEMS Universidade do Minho, Portugal
Paulo Mendes	CMEMS Universidade do Minho, Portugal
Andrei Utkin	Instituto de Novas Tecnologias, Portugal
Habtamu Abie	Norwegian Computing Centre, Norway
Antonio J. Jara	Universidad de Murcia, Spain
Zhijun Yang	Middlesex University London, UK

Preface INTETAIN 2019

We are delighted to introduce the proceedings of the 11th edition of the 2019 European Alliance for Innovation (EAI) International Conference on Intelligent Technologies for Interactive Entertainment (INTETAIN 2019). This conference has brought researchers, developers, and practitioners from around the world together who are leveraging and using intelligent technologies for interactive entertainment. The theme of INTETAIN 2019 was "New Frontiers for Intelligence Technologies in Society of Future."

The technical program of INTETAIN 2019 consisted of 10 full papers, including oral presentation sessions at the main conference tracks. The conference tracks were: Track 1 – Technology as Tool for New Sensory Experiences; Track 2 – Opportunities for Artificial Intelligence in Society of Future. Aside from the high-quality technical paper presentations, the technical program also featured two keynote speeches. The two keynote speeches were presented by Prof. Mohd Shahrizal Sunar from the Institute of Human of Centered Engineering (iHumEn) Universiti Teknologi Malaysia, Malaysia, and Prof. Dagmar Caganova from Institute of Industrial Engineering and Management, Faculty of Materials Science and Technology, Slovak University of Technology, Slovakia.

Coordination with the steering chair, Imrich Chlamtac, was essential for the success of the conference. We sincerely appreciate his constant support and guidance. It was also a great pleasure to work with such an excellent Organizing Committee and we thank them for their hard work in organizing and supporting the conference. In particular, the Technical Program Committee (TPC) and publication chair, Prof. Mohd Shahrizal Sunar, workshop chair, Prof. Andy Pusca, poster and PhD chair, Ruhiyati Idayu Abu Talib, and TPC co-chairs, Prof. Dagmar Caganova and Prof. Alessandro Simeone, who completed the peer-review process of technical papers and made a high-quality technical program. We are also grateful to conference managers, Barbora Cintava and Kristina Lappova, for their support, and to all the authors who submitted their papers to the INTETAIN 2019 conference and workshops.

We strongly believe that the INTETAIN conference provides a good forum for all researcher, developers, and practitioners to discuss all science and technology aspects that are relevant to usage of intelligent technologies for interactive entertainment. We also expect that future INTETAIN conferences will be as successful and stimulating, as indicated by the contributions presented in this volume.

May 2020

Predrag K. Nikolic

Organization (INTETAIN 2019)

Steering Committee

Imrich Chlamtac   University of Trento, Italy

Organizing Committee

General Chair

Predrag K. Nikolic   ShanghaiTech University, China

General Co-chair

Hua Yang   ShanghaiTech University, China

TPC Chair and Co-chair

Alessandro Simeone   Shantou University, China
Dagmar Caganova   Slovak University of Technology, Slovakia

Sponsorship and Exhibit Chair

Yan Feng   Chinese National Academy of Art, China

Local Chair

Lin Wen   Shantou University, China

Workshops Chair

Andy Pusca   Danubius University, Romania

Publicity and Social Media Chair

Feng Yuan   Sun Yat-sen University, China

Publications Chair

Mohd Shahrizal Sunar   Universiti Teknologi Malaysia, Malaysia

Web Chair

Yujin Wang   Cheung Kong School of Art and Design,
Shantou University, China

Posters and PhD Track Chair

Ruhiyati Idayu Abu Talib   Media and Game Innovation Centre of Excellence, Institute of Human Centered Engineering, Universiti Teknologi Malaysia, Malaysia

Panels Chair

Stahl Stenslie   Kulturtanken – Arts for Young Audiences, Norway

Demos Chair

Mohd Razali Md Tomari   Universiti Tun Hussein Onn Malaysia, Malaysia

Technical Program Committee

Predrag K. Nikolic	ShanghaiTech University, China
Andy Pusca	Danubius University, Romania
Mohd Shahrizal Sunar	Universiti Teknologi Malaysia, Malaysia
Ruhiyati Idayu Abu Talib	Media and Game Innovation Centre of Excellence, Institute of Human Centered Engineering, Universiti Teknologi Malaysia, Malaysia
Mohd Razali Md Tomari	Universiti Tun Hussein Onn Malaysia, Malaysia
Alessandro Simeone	Shantou University, China
Dagmar Caganova	Slovak University of Technology, Slovakia
Hua Yang	ShanghaiTech University, China
Stahl Stenslie	Kulturtanken – Arts for Youn Audiences, Norway
Feng Yuan	Sun Yat-sen University, China
Lin Wen	Cheung Kong School of Art and Design, Shantou University, China
Yan Feng	Chinese National Academy of Art, China
Jyunjye Chen	Shantou University, China

Contents

Smart Governance for Sustainable Smart Cities

Keynotes

Tech and the City: Axialization, Institutionalization and Disruption

Bud Mishra$^{(\boxtimes)}$

Courant Institute, New York University, New York, USA
mishra@nyu.edu,
https://cs.nyu.edu/mishra/

Abstract. "Something, something big, was happening in multiple places along the axis running from China to the Mediterranean [and beyond] in the first millenium BCE..." That axial age spurred by urbanization and with guidance from axial sages invented modernity (logic and institutions, rationality and strategic interactions and education and participatory civic society.) How should the smart cities of the future reaxialize to withstand deceptive interference, isolation against pandemics, cellularized instituions, etc.?

Keywords: Causality and probabilistic temporal logic · Deception and signaling games · Safety · Verifiers · Liveness and recommenders

1 Introduction

Ruminating on and off about relocating elsewhere, I have been wondering since 2016 what our new (smart) home cities could resemble. Athens or Sparta? Kapilavatsu or Rajagriha? Qufu or Jinan? These are the home towns of the Axial age (600-350 BCE) philosophers: Socrates, Buddha and Confucious. As Karl Jaspers [1] recounted in his description of the Axial Age: "*Confucius and Lao-Tse were living in China; India produced the Upanishads and Buddha; Greece witnessed the appearance of Homer, of the philosophers. Everything implied by these names developed during these few centuries almost simultaneously in China, India and the West.*"

It has been speculated that the Axial Period coincided with the rise of Mega Cities, whose survival depended on human reciprocal altruism, empathy and logic - but were plagued by tyranny, suffering and demagoguery. My talk at $SC360°$ in Braga (Portugal) focused on these ingredients for smart cities: **Deductive Logic** of the west, **Samsaric Game Theory** of India and **Junzi Data Science** of China – which shape our Privacy and Trust, (Cyber) Security, Smart/Safe Households via Cellularization, Hastily Formed Networks and Identity Management.

Supported by and Army Research Office Grant: W911NF-18-1-0427.

© ICST Institute for Computer Sciences, Social Informatics and Telecommunications Engineering 2020
Published by Springer Nature Switzerland AG 2020. All Rights Reserved
H. Santos et al. (Eds.): SmartCity 360 2019, LNICST 323, pp. 3–12, 2020.
https://doi.org/10.1007/978-3-030-51005-3_1

There are two recent developments along these lines, namely, (1) Perhaps Jaspers' Axial Age theory is largely incorrect (Seshat History of the Axial Age [8]). The standard assumptions of Axialization – its specific temporal boundary, its specific geographic boundary, its critical transformation in culture, ideology and religion, its spread by diffusion, and its identifiable "sages" rooted in the major largely imperial polities of Eurasia – have begun to be questioned. (2) Even though the Axialization narrative may be wrong in details, the process lifting tribal humans into "modernity" is largely captured by Jaspers' observation [3], and very relevant to the emerging cyber-physical societies, to which the smart cities and their "digital modernity" must adapt. The emerging digital-physical technologies for IoHT (Internet of Humans and Things) seem to be spiraling in to an amalgamation of Logic (Smart Contracts and Verification), Game Theory (Signaling Games with Costly Proof-of-work Signaling to maintain consistent consensus Digital Ledgers) and Statistical Inference aware of Privacy and Security (Explainable AI to maintain Recommenders and Verifiers). Thus the digital civil polities (e.g, governance) will be central to the mega-cities of the future as much as energy efficiency, supply chains, pollution control, environmental concerns, driver-less transportation, and electronic commerce. We propose a design around the technolgies of Probabilistic Temporal Logic (e.g., PCTL), Model Checking, Signaling Games, Digital Ledgers and Reinforcement Learning and Bandit Problems.

2   Logic: Models and Model Checking

In logic, temporal logic refers to a system of rules and symbolism for representing, and reasoning about, propositions qualified relative to various "modes" of time (for example, "I am always shopping," "I will eventually Uber to a shop," or "I will be shopping until I am dropping of exhaustion;" time is treated in terms of its topology). Given a Kripke Structure model, there are efficient decision processes to "check" if a certain temporal property (expressed in the logic) holds true. How can smart urban societies deploy dynamically emerging (social) contracts and their rigorous logical verification via data and technology recording interactions over time?

Thus not just *relations* – neither genetic (e.g., possibly, leading to nepotism) nor reciprocation-based trust (e.g., possibly, leading to tyranny and demagoguery) – provide a good foundation for the establishment of a complex cosmopolitan urban society and the evolution of social contracts needed to glue together the strategic, shrewd and selfish members of a complex system. Such an evolving dynamic structure must introspect its inner working and understand the causes and effects in order to create robust and stable social contracts, constitutions and laws, which must be recommended, executed, recorded and verified using the best technologies available to a smart urban society and its governing body.

The mathematical/logical underpinnings of Probabilistic Causation are easily expressible in the logic below, which also allows efficient model checking in general. Thus enumerating complex *prima facie* causes from data or probabilistic state transition models becomes feasible. Thus, starting with a discrete time

Markov chain (DTMC) – a directed graph with a set of states, S, it is endowed (via labeling functions) with the atomic propositions true within them.

It is then possible to make the labeling probabilistic, so that one may express that with some non-negligible probability, one's (e.g., Athen's) "optimistic views of democrcacy" may be false and may not suffice to harmonize other neighboring cities (e.g., Sparta) into a better governance – thus, "truthiness" of such a statement could have been used to avoid long and devastating wars. A city's laws, logic and λογος could create its cosmos, ordering it and giving it form and meaning!

The states of the underlying (Kripke structure) model are related pairwise by the transition probability. We also have an initial state from which we can begin a path (trajectory) through the system. Each state has at least one transition to itself or another state in S with a non-zero probability. A general framework for causality analysis is provided by model checking algorithms in PCTL (Probabilistic Computational Tree Logic) and has been explored in details elsewhere [9]. We have shown there how Suppes' prima-facie causality can be formulated in PCTL, and also suggested developing an efficient, albeit simplified, approach to testing contracts using Kripke-models and SBCN (with pair-wise causality represented as edges in a graphical model) – originally introduced elsewhere. See [4,7].

Definition. *Probabilistic Computational Tree Logic, PCTL.* The types of formulas that can be expressed in PCTL are path formulas and state formulas. State formulas express properties that must hold within a state, determined by how it is labeled with certain atomic propositions, while path formulas refer to sequences of states along which a formula must hold.

1. All atomic propositions are state formulas.
2. If f and g are state formulas, so are $\neg f$ and $f \wedge g$.
3. If f and g are state formulas, and t is a nonnegative integer or ∞, then $fU^{\leq t}g$ is a path formula.
4. If f is a path formula and $0 \leq p \leq 1$, then $[f]_{>p}$ is a state formula.

□

The syntax and the logic builds on standard propositional Boolean logic, but extends with various modes: the key operator is the metric "until" operator: $fU^{\leq t}g$: here, use of "until" means that one formula f must hold at every state along the path until a state where the second formula g becomes true, which must happen in less than or equal to t time units. Finally, we can add probabilities to these "until"-like path formulas to make state formulas.

Path quantifiers analogous to those in CTL may be defined by: $Af \equiv [f]_{\geq 1}$ [*Inevitably f*]; $Ef \equiv [f]_{>0}$ [*Possibly f*]; $Gf \equiv fU^{\leq \infty}$false [*Globally f*], and $Ff \equiv$ true $U^{\leq \infty}f$ [*Eventually f*]. Formal semantics of the PCTL formulæ may be associated in a natural manner. One can then say event f "probabilistically causes" g, iff f is temporally prior to g and f raises the probability of g

$$f \mapsto^{\leq t}_{\geq p} g \iff AG[f \to F^{\leq t}_{\geq p}g],$$

for some suitable hyper-parameters $p > 0$ (for probability raising) probability and $t > 0$ duration (for temporal priority). Additional criteria (e.g., regularization) are then needed to separate spurious causality from the genuine ones.

SBCN, thus, provides a vastly simplified, and yet practical, approach to causality, especially when explicit time is not recorded in the data. There are efficient algorithms to ensure that smart contracts in PCTL facilitate a future, thus keeping the city's activities *alive*, and to ascertain *safe* behavior in the past by model checking specifications in PCTL.

3 Games: Signaling and Deception

Urban societies of the future will be structured around anonymous citizens interacting rationally (e.g, Dharma) and strategically (e.g., Karma) to improve their utilities, even though other individuals' "types," identity and personal information must be allowed to remain private. Deceptive behavior in the cities could be rampant and must be tamed. Safe house-holds in the city will protect the citizens by a "cellularization-process," which must include (in a cell) humans, pets and things associated by familial relations. Multi-cellular neighborhoods may emerge, experiment, persist and extinguish by "hastily formed networks," and more permanent Intra- and Internets – some explorable and some dark! Game theory – be it evolutionary, or epistemological – provides a forum in which such dynamics may be studied and moulded.

Game theory involves the study of the strategies followed by individuals, and organizations, in situations of conflict and cooperation. A Nash equilibrium refers to a certain mixture of strategies where a unilateral change in strategy by one player will not bring any benefit to it [2]. Maynard Smith pioneered the use of game theory in evolutionary biology, developing the concept of the evolutionarily stable strategy (ESS). An ESS is a form of Nash equilibrium in a population where a mutant with a variant strategy cannot successfully invade. Replicator dynamics addresses the dynamics of fitter players (which possess superior utility) that preferentially replicate within a population [cccc]. An important contribution in these types of evolutionary games was the recognition that there is no need for epistemologically aware agents given that the players could be non-human Bots which may use black-box AIs, unable to consciously adopt strategies.

Signalling game theory is a branch of game theory that was developed concurrently in both economics and organismal evolutionary biology in the 1970s, and it involves the sending of signals, honest or deceptive, from a sender to a (possibly, many) receiver(s) [10]. Information asymmetry occurs when the sender possesses information about its type, that is not available to the receiver, thus the sender can choose whether or not to reveal its true type to the receiver. In comparison to organismal evolutionary biology, cyber-physical evolution has made lesser use of concepts from game theory, but with a growing number of contributions (e.g, cyber security), for example [6]. In addition, microbial ecology has made use of evolutionary game theory to explain cooperative interactions where metabolites are public goods shared between microbes. Not unlike in the Buddhist axialization (evolving a Samsara created by a deceptive Mara/Maya), one can build technologies founded upon signalling game theory that has great explanatory power for a range of social processes, by pinpointing the 'strategies' of humans and things in their interactions with other humans and things. In doing so, we also wish to highlight commonalities between signalling behaviour at the device, organismal, human and social levels.

To understand whether in a city – smart or otherwise – undesirable outcomes may arise in the form of deception, we may call upon the theory of information-asymmetric signaling games, which unify many of the adversarial use cases under a single framework. In particular one may be interested in situations when adversarial actions may be viewed mathematically as rational (i.e., utility-optimizing agents possessing common knowledge of rationality). The simplest model of signaling games involves two players (e.g, a Uber driver and a passenger). They are asymmetric in information (driver may not be told passenger's destination until they agree to engage in a ride). They are called S, sender (informed passenger), and R, receiver (uninformed driver). A key notion in this game is that of type, a random variable whose support is given by T (known to sender S). Also, we use $\pi_T(\cdot)$ to denote probability distribution over T as a prior belief of R about the sender's type (e.g., a Uber driver may guess a possible destination based on the source and time of the journey). A round of game proceeds as follows:

- Player S learns $t \in T$;
- S sends to R a signal $s \in M$; and
- R takes an action $a \in A$.

Their payoff/utility functions are known and depend on the type, signal, and action:
$$u^i : T \times M \times A \to \mathbb{R}, \quad \text{where } i \in \{S, R\}.$$

In this structure, the players' behavior strategies can be described by the following two sets of probability distributions: (1) $\mu(\cdot|t)$, $t \in T$, on M and (2) $\alpha(\cdot|s)$, $s \in M$, on A. For S, the sender strategy μ is a probability distribution on signals given types; namely, $\mu(s|t)$ describes the probability that S with type t sends signal s. For R, the receiver strategy α is a probability distribution on actions given signals; namely, $\alpha(a|s)$ describes the probability that R takes action a following signal s. A pair of strategies μ and α is in Nash equilibrium if (and only if) they are mutually best responses (i.e., if each maximizes the expected utility given the other):

$$\sum_{t\in T, s\in M, a\in A} u^S(t, s, a)\pi_T(t)\mu^*(s|t)\alpha(a|s)$$

$$\geq \sum_{t\in T, s\in M, a\in A} u^S(t, s, a)\pi_T(t)\mu(s|t)\alpha(a|s); \tag{1}$$

and

$$\sum_{t\in T, s\in M, a\in A} u^R(t, s, a)\pi_T(t)\mu(s|t)\alpha^*(a|s)$$

$$\geq \sum_{t\in T, s\in M, a\in A} u^R(t, s, a)\pi_T(t)\mu(s|t)\alpha(a|s); \tag{2}$$

for any μ, α. It is straightforward to show that such a strategy profile (α^*, μ^*) exists. We conjecture that the natural models for sender-receiver utility functions could be based on functions that combine information rates with distortion, as in rate distortion theory (RDT). For instance, assume that there are certain natural connections between the types and actions, as modeled by the functions f_S and f_R for the sender and receiver respectively:

$$f_S : T \to A; \quad f_R : A \to T. \tag{3}$$

Then the utility functions for each consist of two weighted-additive terms, one measuring the mutual information with respect to the signals and the other measuring the undesirable distortion, where the weights are suitably chosen Lagrange constants

$$u^S = I(T, M) - \lambda_S d^S(f_S(t), a), \quad \& $$
$$u^R = I(A, M) - \lambda_R d^R(t, f_R(a)), \tag{4}$$

where I denotes information and d^R, d^S denote measures of distortion.

This definition also captures the notion of *deception* as follows. Note that the distribution of signals received by R is given by the probability distribution π_M, where

$$\pi_M(s) = \sum_{t \in T} \pi_T(t)\mu(s|t), \tag{5}$$

and the distribution of actions produced by R is given by the probability distribution π_A, where

$$\pi_A(a) = \sum_{s \in M} \pi_M(s)\alpha(a|s). \tag{6}$$

Clearly π_T and π_A are probability distributions on T and A respectively. If $\hat{\pi}_T$ is the probability distribution on T induced by π_A under the function f_R, then

$$\hat{\pi}_T(\cdot) := \pi_A(f_R^{-1}(\cdot)). \tag{7}$$

A natural choice of measure for deception is given by the relative entropy between the probability distributions π_T and $\hat{\pi}_T$:

$$\text{Deception} := \text{Rel. Entropy}(\hat{\pi}_T | \pi_T)$$
$$= \sum_{t \in T} \hat{\pi}_T(t) \log_2 \frac{\hat{\pi}_T(t)}{\pi_T(t)}. \tag{8}$$

This definition describes deception from the point of view of the receiver. To get the notion of deception from the point of view of the sender, one needs to play the game for several rounds. The equation implies that deception can be both defined as the sending of misleading information, or the witholding of information, both in order to manipulate the receiver. The Shapley value describes the distribution of utility to different players in a cooperative game. In a signaling game where deception occurs the value is skewed towards the sender.

4   Institutions: Recommenders and Verifiers

It is inevitable that predictive learning systems (ML, Machine Learning and AI, Artificial Intelligence and Formal Methods) will play an important role in the urban societies of the future. The inferences obtained by these systems will manifest themselves in social networks induced by "trust" relations, where trust may be measured by a "correlation of encounter." In other words, if one selects to rationally (but, possibly, information asymmetrically) and strategically interact with another individual, how likely would it be to choose to interact with the same individual repeatedly – in other words how trustworthy is the other individual thus encountered? There have been growing interest in distributed permissionless and trustless systems supported by distributed ledgers (e.g., Kripke Structures) and non-strategic verifiers (e.g., miners with costly signaling supported by proof-of-work), the technology still remains in its infancy. Not unlike Confucian "scholars," and "state officials," we may envision machine learning to produce a system of "recommenders," and "verifiers," – duals *yin* and *yang* serving negative and positive aspects of aspirational and traditional values – said differently, the evolutionary (replicator) dynamics set forth by variations and selections. Recommenders and verifiers are non-strategic, perform costly signaling to display trustworthiness and augment intelligence of the cities' humans and things, who are nonetheless strategic; they thus, rationally optimize their individual utilities. Agents (e.g., humans and things) then "virtualize" themselves by selecting a tribe of suitable recommenders and verifiers, while maintaining their privacy and strengthening their trust relations; possible distributed algorithms and policies, for this purpose, may be built upon adversarial bandits (with interpretations).

One may be inspired by the Chinese Axial Sage, Kong Qiu (a name confusingly translated as Confucius by Matteo Ricci [1552–1610], a Jesuit Minister). Confucius assumed (1) humans' (and things') ability to develop "morally," (2) using self-cultivation (by rationally modeling utility sought), (3) thus perfecting the world (state, city, or cell), (4) for which purpose, examples of "sages" (data, recommenders and verifiers) may be used. Thus ultimately, cellularization, and supporting institutions, for developing and evaluating recommenders and verifiers would be AI's main contributions to the cities of the future.

Returning back to the framework of signalling games, one notes that the Nash equilibria of these signaling games fall into few classes: (1) desirable separating equilibrium, albeit conventional or (2) uninteresting pooling equilibrium [or combinations there of, in partial pooling equilibrium].

- *Separating Equilibrium*: Each type t sends a different signal M_t.

$$f^S : t \mapsto a[M_t].$$

- *Pooling Equilibrium*: All types t send a single signal $s*$, almost surely.

Thus in order for the Internet of the future to be relevant to physical smart urban societies, it (e.g., hyper-visor on a cloud) must be aware of the (partially) observed data and meta-data involved in signaling on the Internet and the underlying inter-twined sender-receiver games. For example, highly relevant to the Internets' revenues and returns-on-investment are signals involved in Google Search queries (with the users' state of ignorance remaining private), key-words (private to Google) and advertisement selected by auction in an Ad-exchange (private to product developers) – utilities respectively being: page relevance for the user, return on investment for the advertisers, and customer satisfaction and retention for the publishers. A key proposal to tame deception in these systems would be to control them by non-strategic Recommenders and Verifiers.

- Recommenders ensure *Liveness*: $\forall_A \exists_T \exists_S U_S(T, M, A) \geq \theta^*$;
- Verifiers ensure *Safety*: $\forall_T \exists_A \exists_R U_R(T, M, A) \geq \theta^*$.

thus acting as correlating devices helping the entire system to evolve towards good separating equilibria, albeit conventional.

5   Cities and The Techs: Internet of Humans and Things

The technologies must be built around various Cyber-physical Games important to urban societies: e.g., Cellularization, Kripke-ledgers, model-checking and ZK (Zero Knowledge). In summary, following protocols may be devised to play a role to organize safe households in the cities.

1. *Game Protocols.1*
   - S = Sender (Informed) $\mapsto$ R = Receiver (Uninformed)
   - The game may reach a Nash equilibrium that permits deception, but in this scheme it is tamed by Checkers. The checkers verify
     • Local (Propositional Logic Properties) [*using CRYPTO*]
     • Global (Modal Logic Properties) [*KRIPKE-LEDGER*]
   - The system uses asymmetric cryptography:
     • Public/Verification Key: VR_S and VR_R
     • Private/Signature Key: SG_S and SG_R
     • Keys are linked via *COMPUTATIONALLY-ONE-WAY-FUNCTIONS*: e.g., McEliece scheme.
2. *Game Protocols.2*
   (a) S generates SG_S and VR_S, and publishes only VR_S.
   (b) S detects (i) type/state $t \in T$, (ii) message $m \in M$ and (iii) a time stamp τ.
   (c) S sends an augmented message
   $$C \equiv (VR_S, VR_R, m, \#\langle t, m \rangle, \tau) \| SG_S$$
3. *Game Protocols.3*
   (a) R ensures that S sent the message $C \|_{VR_S} \mapsto VR_S, VR_R$, etc.
   (b) Check Local properties ... e.g., m is consistent with t: $\mathbf{F}(t, m)$.
   (c) Check Global properties [using model checking and ZK SNARKs] ... e.g., $t_{\tau_1}, t_{\tau_2}, \cdots$ satisfy some modal properties: $\mathbf{G}(t, m)$.
   (d) R performs an action a consistent with m:

– S gets utility $U_S(t, m, a)$

– R gets utility $U_R(t, m, a)$

4. *Game Protocols.4*

(a) To check the global properties and to be strategic, the players need access to the records of t's, $\#\langle t, m \rangle$'s and $U^{S,R}(t, m, a)$'s over time.

(b) For this purpose one creates a *KRIPKE-LEDGER*: a distributed database that maintains a continuously-growing list of data records hardened against tampering and revision.

(c) KRIPKE-LEDGER is maintained by *MINERS* who are subject to costly-signaling via proof-of-work or proof-of-space related to certain intractable computational problems.

5. *SPVs, Coalitions and Intermediaries*

(a) An intermediary (e.g., a House Holder) may be interested in only a particular group of players/humans/things (senders and receivers).

(b) The intermediary must not reveal membership information.

(c) The intermediary checks certain local and global properties about the players and publishes the results.

(d) The intermediary convinces a member that he is truthful. (Using zk-SNARK's for Propositional Modal Logic).

(e) Trivial Corollary: *The players can make smart contracts with one another: Futures, Derivatives, Bonds subject to Positive and Negative Covenants, etc.*

5.1   Example: A Library

One may cellularize a subset of households to create a safe and secure ways of sharing data, files (e.g., books and music), computation and things (e.g., childrens' toys) where families can get together for community and civic activities without leading to security problems or lack of fairness (e.g., tragedy of the commons)[1]. The process begins with many households joining to create a hastily formed (ephemeral) network and may use Bare Metal as a Service; in other words, user (e.g., each household) gets a physical machine, can install (open source) firmware, hypervisor, OS, etc. All communications are performed encrypted. It may require that providers controlling the network can only deny service, but not snoop. Furthermore, results of computation may be hidden, and computation obfuscated (further incorporating Differential Privacy, Multi-Party Computing, Erasure Coding – data makes sense only when k out of n pieces come, etc.) The participants (humans and things) interact subject to enforceable smart contracts.

6   Conclusion

Smart Mega Cities of the future require novel philosophical bases, computation and governance. If Axial Age Sages can be our inspiration; our urban societies

---

[1] Jointly with Larry Rudolph, VP TwoSigma and MIT.

will use logic, game theory and data science; model checking, credible and non-credible threats (with costly signaling) and reinforcement learning (with capabilities for intervening and interpreting regularly); central governance (monarchy and tyranny, critically analyzed by Qufu's Confucius), rank-based governance (oligarchy and aristocracy, critically analyzed by Shakya-tribe's Buddha from Lumbini) and decentralized governance (politiae and democracy, critically examined by Athenian Socrates). With new technologies (based on data sharing, crowd sourcing and gig economy) these questions have now come to forefront, but we seem to be " weeping and wailing from being united with the unloved [deception] and separated from the loved [honesty][2]," not able to foresee how the Internets could be rescued from fragmentation and collapse. Are we then building a city of logos, logic and lawfulness or just another fortified favela of mis-communicated signals, waiting to collapse like a modern day Tenochtitlan?

References

1. Assmann, A.: Jaspers' Achsenzeit, oder Schwierigkeiten mit der Zentralperspektive in der Geschichte. In: Karl Jaspers: Denken zwischen Wissenschaft, Politik und Philosophie, pp. 187–205 (1989)
2. Binmore, K.: Game Theory: A Very Short Introduction. Oxford University Press, Oxford (2007)
3. Black, A.: The "Axial Period:" what was it and what does it signify? Rev. Polit. **70**(12), 23–39 (2008)
4. Bonchi, F., Gullo, F., Mishra, B., Ramazzotti, D.: Probabilistic causal analysis of social influence. In: Proceedings of the 27th ACM International Conference on Information and Knowledge Management, CIKM 2018, Torino, Italy, 22–26 October 2018, pp. 1003–1012 (2018)
5. Byrom, T.: Dhammapada: The Sayings of the Buddha, Shambhala pocket classics (1993)
6. Casey, W., Kellner, A., Memarmoshrefi, P., Morales, J.A., Mishra, B.: Deception, identity, and security: the game theory of sybil attacks. Commun. ACM **62**(1), 85–93 (2019)
7. Gao, G., Mishra, B., Ramazzotti, D.: Causal data science for financial stress testing. J. Comput. Sci. **26**, 294–304 (2018)
8. Hoyer, D., Reddish, J.: Seshat History of the Axial Age (2019)
9. Kleinberg, S., Mishra, B.: The temporal logic of causal structures. In: Proceedings of the Twenty-Fifth Conference on Uncertainty in Artificial Intelligence, UAI 2009, Montreal, QC, Canada, 18–21 June 2009, pp. 303–312, AUAI Press (2009)
10. Skyrms, B.: Signals: Evolution, Learning, and Information. Oxford University Press, Oxford (2010)

---

[2] Cited from the Buddhist Text Dhammapada [5].

MegaSense: 5G and AI for Air Quality Monitoring

Sasu Tarkoma$^{(\boxtimes)}$, Xiaoli Liu, Andrew Rebeiro-Hargrave, and Samu Varjonen

Department of Computer Science, University of Helsinki,
Pietari Kalmin katu 5, 00560 Kumpula, Finland
{sasu.tarkoma,xiaoli.liu,andrew.rebeiro-hargrave,
samu.varjonen}@helsinki.fi

Abstract. Air pollution has become a global challenge during the growth of megacities, which drives the deployment of air quality monitoring in order to understand and mitigate district level air pollution. Currently, air pollution monitoring mainly relies on high-end accurate reference stations, which are usually stationary and expensive. Thus, the air quality monitoring deployments are typically coarse grained with only a very small number of stations in a city. We propose scalable air quality monitoring by leveraging low-cost air pollution sensors, artificial intelligence methods, and versatile connectivity provided by 4G/5G. We describe pilot deployments for testing the developed sensing technologies in three different locations in Helsinki, Finland.

Keywords: Internet of Things · Air pollution sensing · Smart cities

1 Introduction

In recent years, we have witnessed unprecedented growth of urban areas. Future smart cities are characterized by high density, versatile connectivity requirements, localized processing, and mobile sensors. Citizens are expecting to experience personalized, anticipatory, real-time, clean and safe city services supported by digital services, autonomous vehicles, Artificial Intelligence (AI), and robots. Hundreds of thousands of smart street lights, base stations, and sensors support near real-time decision making and optimization.

During the growth of urban areas, we have also witnessed the degradation of air quality in developing countries. Urban air pollution has become a global challenge for human health, ecosystem, and the climate. The recent study by the Global Burden of Disease (GBD) project reported 5.5 million people worldwide are dying prematurely each year as a result of air pollution [1]. Air pollutants are conventionally measured by expensive high-end stationary stations. However, high cost and needs for constant maintenance of such stations prevent large-scale dense deployments. The recent advances in sensing technologies and wireless communications enable a complementary approach with large scale sensing solutions with low-cost sensors.

© ICST Institute for Computer Sciences, Social Informatics and Telecommunications Engineering 2020
Published by Springer Nature Switzerland AG 2020. All Rights Reserved
H. Santos et al. (Eds.): SmartCity 360 2019, LNICST 323, pp. 13–19, 2020.
https://doi.org/10.1007/978-3-030-51005-3_2

In the MegaSense research program, we introduce a scalable and intelligent real-time air pollution monitoring system by developing and deploying a hierarchical sensing architecture with low-cost sensors and leveraging machine learning for sensor calibration and versatile connectivity provided by 4G/5G. Our goal is to achieve near real-time air quality sensing with high spatial resolution. We propose calibration of a large number of low-cost sensors with a small number of accurate reference stations by using machine learning techniques. 5G offers unification by supporting versatile connectivity options and a framework for managing smart city deployment. Scalable real-time air quality sensing is expected to enable many applications.

We present pilot deployments carried out in the EU UIA HOPE project [2] in Helsinki, Finland. The experimental results from three large urban test areas indicate that crowd sourcing of air quality measurement is feasible, data validity can be significantly improved through calibrating the low-cost sensors with higher quality stations, and crowd-sourced air quality data can serve as a basis for new applications, such as green path routing.

The chapter is organized as follows: Sect. 2 presents the vision of the scalable air pollution sensing in megacities. We describe the low-cost sensors used in our sensing platform in Sect. 3 and present our pilots currently running with these sensors in Sect. 4. Section 5 concludes this chapter with discussing future research.

2   Spatio-Temporal Air Quality Sensing

In this section, we present the vision of the scalable spatio-temporal air quality sensing.

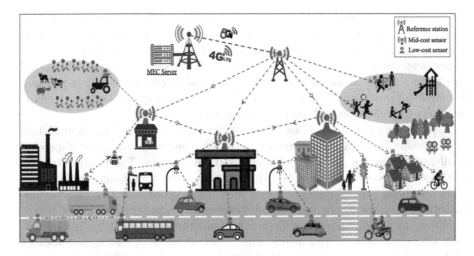

Fig. 1. Vision of spatio-temporal air quality sensing.

Figure 1 gives an outline of our vision of spatio-temporal air quality sensing. A number of different types of sensors are deployed for monitoring the air quality, including low-cost mini-sensors, middle-cost sensors, and high-cost reference stations. The low-cost and medium-cost sensors can be mobile and can be integrated into vehicles or carried by citizens [3].

The emerging 5G-based technologies are expected to enable efficient data collection, reliable sensor connection, less energy consumption, and intelligent sensor management. Building on massive connectivity, sensing and distributed data processing capabilities, the next-generation air quality monitoring networks can automatically identify the operational environment of each sensor and optimize sensor parameters in order to minimize errors and sensor drift.

Air quality sensors are hindered by many environmental factors and need to be placed in suitable locations, where network connectivity and power supply issues are taken into account. We introduce flexible and short-term placement of the mini-sensors to optimize the coverage and accuracy of the pollution detection process and study urban mobility patterns to improve coverage using portable micro-sensors carried by citizens. We envisage that multi-vendor and open-source sensor devices of different accuracy and capabilities can form a self-optimizing mesh network. In our current work, we investigate the integration of low-cost (tens to hundreds of euros) air pollution sensors, mid-cost sensors (thousands of euros), and the high accuracy Measuring Earth Surface-Atmosphere Relations (SMEAR) [4] stations that monitor a high number of pollutants every second.

Low-cost sensors are typically limited in accuracy compared with city monitoring reference stations. We have designed a calibration model that maps the measurements of low-cost sensors to measurements of reference stations using machine learning algorithms to improve the performance of the low-cost sensors. The low-cost sensors are co-located near to the reference station for a sufficient period of time to collect the data for performing the sensor analysis and calibration. This corresponds to other research work related to sensor calibration [5–7]. Periodic re-calibration of sensors is necessary during the air quality monitoring process due to its high instability, sensor drift phenomenon [8], and other errors that reduce the accuracy.

The current solutions for sensor calibration have limited support for large-scale and very dense deployments. It is not practical to bring thousands of sensors to the reference stations for performing the calibration. Our key insight is to support calibration through a hierarchical mesh of sensors with both stationary and mobile sensors (Fig. 1). We are exploring the possibility of using opportunistic re-calibration, collaborative re-calibration, and transfer re-calibration [9] with hierarchical sensor mesh networks.

Near real-time wide-area air quality sensing is expected to support the development of many applications. Reliable and fine-grained air quality data and insights are helpful in pinpointing pollution hot-spots and gaining understanding of the root causes of the identified pollution problems [10]. The insights can then help in mitigating pollution. For example, a smartphone map and navi-

(a) Portable low-cost device.

(b) Device attachment.

(c) Measurement application.

Fig. 2. Pilot devices.

gation application provide suggestions and directions regarding the paths and routes with the best estimated air quality.

The MegaSense system is designed to provide information on multiple levels from the city and district levels to the level of personal exposure to pollution. On the city and district levels, it is possible to detect pollution sources and provide suggestions for stakeholders to take actions for mitigating pollution. Such information can be used to improve fitness and health applications as well as control air ventilation systems. For example, the car ventilation system can be controlled based on the current and predicted outside air quality to maximize indoor air quality. The air quality information can also be used for building a predictive model for early warning, which is very important especially for people with respiratory problems.

3 Low-Cost Sensors

To evaluate the capabilities of low-cost crowd-sourced micro-sensors, we designed a portable air quality sensing platform based on a BMD-340 system on a module and mobile phone application (Fig. 2c). The portable platform connects to the citizen's Android smartphone over Bluetooth Low Energy, and the smartphone reports the readings and GPS location to a collecting server. The measurements are calibrated using the data from reference stations and machine learning techniques before being displayed in the mobile app. The mini-sensor platform component for measuring the Particulate Matter (PM) is a Sensirion SPS30. Table 1 presents a list of all the sensor components available on the portable device. The platform is powered with a 3500 mAh battery and enclosed in a 3D-printed case made of ESD-PETG filament. The form dimensions are: width 75 mm, depth 33 mm, height 127 mm, with weight 165 grams. The front is protected by an aluminum mesh. General battery life before recharging via micro USB interface:

26 h. Figure 2a presents a portable low-cost sensor that was carried by one of the voluntary citizens in his bag for tracking the measurements of air pollutants (Fig. 2b).

Table 1. Sensor types available in the low-cost portable device.

Sensor	Type
BME-280	Temp, Humidity, Air Pressure
Battery	Voltage
Sensirion SPS30	PM
SI1133-AA00-GM	UV
MiCS-4514	CO, NO_2
MQ-131	O_3

To evaluate the practicalities of low-cost mini air quality sensors, we designed a Raspberry Pi HAT with the same sensors (Table 1) with Nb-IoT modem encased in water-proof rugged casing suitable for fixed outdoor stationary locations having constant power. This allows us to experiment with edge computing as we can have more computation power with the sensors in comparison to the portable sensor.

4   Pilot Deployments

We are running multiple pilot deployments with the university designed sensors, including three pilots with portable micro-sensors and one pilot with stationary mini-sensors in Helsinki, Finland.

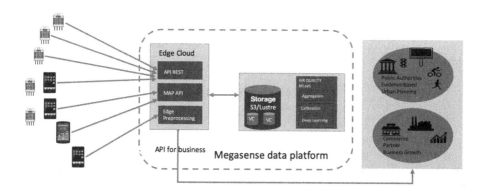

Fig. 3. The MegaSense platform architecture.

One hundred portable micro-sensors are loaned to voluntary citizens in the UIA HOPE project [2] for measuring their own daily air pollution exposure using the HOPE mobile application and crowd-sourcing data gathering. The citizen exposure readings are based on measurements from the portable sensors, city reference stations and an air quality model. The mini-sensors are deployed in a small Nb-IoT network as part of a 5G testbed at the Kumpula area with support from the City of Helsinki.

Both the portable micro-sensors and stationary mini-sensors upload air quality measurements and download data to/from the MegaSense Edge/Cloud data services. This is aligned with the MegaSense research program focuses on addressing significant challenges towards scalable air quality sensing using low-cost sensors with 5G technology and realizing big data analytics with machine learning for supporting wide-area air quality monitoring applications. As presented in Fig. 3, sensors and mobile devices are connected to Edge/Cloud with available 5G/4G connections via Rest API. Air quality MLaaS (machine learning as a service) offers machine learning tools as a part of Edge/Cloud services to support business analytics. Specifically, low-cost sensors are periodically calibrated to provide reliable air quality data, data can be saved and processed on Edge/Cloud depending on the application purposes.

 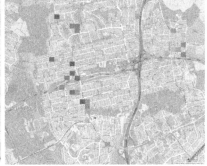

(a) Pilot monitoring areas in Helsinki, Finland. Top-down: Pakila, Vallila, and Jätkäsaari.

(b) Pollution hotspot map created from Pakila using portable low-cost sensors.

Fig. 4. Monitoring areas.

Early results from the UIA HOPE monitoring areas support the MegaSense approach for optimising the spatial coverage and accuracy of the pollution detection through loaning citizens portable low-cost micro-sensors living in three districts of Helsinki for a period of 3 months, and each district having a different source for the emitted air pollutants (Fig. 4). Jätkäsaari is a new maritime inner city district with a busy passenger port in the area which has high levels of traffic pollution (see Fig. 4a). Pakila is an old suburban housing area and has mostly been single-family housing burning wood which had lead to high black carbon emissions. Vallila is an old densely built residential district at the edge of the inner-city with major traffic routes and street canyons recycling high street dust pollution. An example of citizen crowd-sourcing data is the pollution hotspot map presented in Fig. 4b based on the measurements from Pakila. The emissions data on the map consist readings for one day. On the map the PM2.5 scale ranges from light red $(2.5 \mu g)$ to dark red $(25 \mu g)$.

5 Conclusion

MegaSense addresses significant challenges pertaining to scalable air quality sensing by developing and using low-cost sensors with 5G technology in a hierarchical mesh network environment, and implementing big data analytics with machine learning. MegaSense utilizes the designed sensing data platform and reliable atmospheric data from SMEAR reference stations to field calibrate low-cost sensors that can be integrated into vehicles or carried by users for scalable and near real-time air pollution monitoring. In future research, we will continue to explore runtime calibration of the hierarchical sensor mesh as well as investigate approaches for processing real-time image and video data from hyperspectral cameras for air pollutant detection.

References

1. http://www.healthdata.org/gbd. Accessed 20 Feb 2020
2. https://www.uia-initiative.eu/en/uia-cities/helsinki. Accessed 24 Mar 2020
3. Motlagh, N.H., et al.: Toward massive scale air quality monitoring. IEEE Commun. Mag. **58**(2), 54–59 (2020)
4. https://www.atm.helsinki.fi/SMEAR/. Accessed 24 Mar 2020
5. Spinelle, L., Gerboles, M., Villani, M.G., Aleixandre, M., Bonavitacola, F.: Field calibration of a cluster of low-cost commercially available sensors for air quality monitoring. Part A: Ozone and nitrogen dioxide. Sens. Actuators B: Chem. **215**, 249–257 (2015)
6. Spinelle, L., Gerboles, M., Villani, M.G., Aleixandre, M., Bonavitacola, F.: Field calibration of a cluster of low-cost commercially available sensors for air quality monitoring. Part B: NO, CO and CO2. Sens. Actuators B: Chem. **238**, 706–715 (2017)
7. Lin, Y., Dong, W., Chen Y.: Calibration low-cost sensors by a two-phase learning approach for urban air quality measurement. In: Proceedings of the ACM on Interactive, Mobile, Wearable and Ubiquitous Technologies, 18 March 2018
8. Jiao, W., et al.: Community Air Sensor Network (CAIRSENSE) project: evaluation of low-cost sensor performance in a suburban environment in the southeastern United States. Atmos. Measur. Tech. **9**(11), 5281–5292 (2016)
9. Cheng, Y., He, X., Zhou, Z., Thiele L.: ICT: in-field calibration transfer for air quality sensor deployments. In: Proceedings of the ACM on Interactive, Mobile, Wearable and Ubiquitous Technologies, 6 March 2019
10. Lagerspetz, E., et al.: MegaSense: feasibility of low-cost sensors for pollution hotspot detection. In: 17th IEEE International Conference on Industrial Informatics, Helsinki, Finland, 22–25 July, pp. 1083–1090 (2019)

Potentialities of the Internet of Things in the Health Area in Brazil

Ana Lídia Corrêa da Silva Moreira[1,2]([✉]), Marcelo Archanjo José[2],
and Roseli de Deus Lopes[1,2]

[1] Departamento de Engenharia de Sistemas Eletrônicos,
Escola Politécnica, Universidade de São Paulo (PSI-EP-USP), São Paulo, SP, Brazil
lidialenzi@alumni.usp.br
[2] Centro Interdisciplinar em Tecnologias Interativas, Universidade de São Paulo (CITI-USP),
São Paulo, SP, Brazil

Abstract. Brazil is the ninth economy and seventh-largest health market in the world, currently accounting for more than 9% of the Gross Domestic Product (GDP). In addition, the country ended 2019 with more than 400 startups working in the health area, demonstrating the maturity of the market and the ability to foster innovation. In this scenario, the Internet of Things (IoT) emerges as a technology with a revolutionary potential to bring significant progress to the health area in Brazil. The Brazilian national IoT plan includes health as one of its strategic areas and is promoting a solid structural base, through a set of centers of excellence and initiatives, supporting research, development, and innovations. However, encouraging and training of qualified professionals and facing challenges related to infrastructure and connectivity are decisive factors for Brazilian success in the IoT area.

Keywords: Healthcare · Brazil · Internet of Things

1 Introduction

Health Units are complex environments where information plays a fundamental role. It is crucial that professionals have access to information about patients, procedures performed, or complications. It is also necessary to know about stocks of medicines, supplies, and conditions of the equipment used. Ensuring adequate and optimized processes for collecting, storing and disseminating information to team members who need to access it, while preserving patient privacy and maintaining data quality, integrity and consistency are major challenges [1].

Tools such as electronic medical records and mobile solutions for patient's interaction with institutions already save time and resources, even if implementation in Brazil is limited in scope. However, the Internet of Things represents the potential to promote a revolution in the sector, precisely because this technology redefines these processes. It is possible, for example, to send information about the vital signs of the patient directly

H. Santos et al. (Eds.): SmartCity 360 2019, LNICST 323, pp. 20–26, 2020.
https://doi.org/10.1007/978-3-030-51005-3_3

from the equipment that collects the information to the electronic medical record in real-time, without human interference.

Brazil understands the potential that IoT represents for several sectors, including health. In this article, we show how the country is preparing to foster the development of IoT solutions and how it is creating an environment favorable to entrepreneurship and innovation.

2 Brazil Overview

First, it is necessary to reveal some information about Brazil. It is a country with an extensive area, with a large and heterogeneous population of more than 211 million people, according to the Brazilian Institute of Geography and Statistics (IBGE) [2]. In addition, the country is the ninth-largest economy in the world (International Monetary Fund for 2018 and 2020 (estimates) and the leading economy in Latin America, with a Gross Domestic Product (GDP) of approximately USD 2 trillion, assuming regional leadership in the dissemination of new technologies and market trends [3]. Moreover, Brazil ended 2019 in the third place in the ranking of countries with the largest number of new unicorns, which are, according to the definition of Aillen Lee (2013), startups that reached a market value above USD 1 billion (Fig. 1), behind the USA and China, both

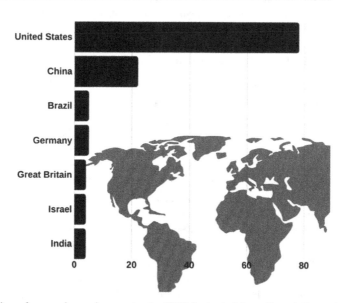

Fig. 1. Number of new unicorns by country for 2019 (extracted from Crunch Base. Available at https://news.crunchbase.com/news/the-new-unicorns-of-2019/)

showing more expressive numbers [4–6]. This ranking show that our innovation ecosystem is undergoing maturation, and opening space for technology-based entrepreneurship in most diverse areas.

3 The IoT Plan in Brazil

The National Internet of Things Plan is a broad initiative that mobilizes members of the public, private sectors and the academy, provides investments in infrastructure and the promotion of entrepreneurship [7], whose main objectives are [8]:

- improve the quality of life of the Brazilian population through efficiency gain in the services offered;
- promote professional qualification and generate new jobs for a growing up IoT market;
- increase the productivity and competitiveness of companies developing IoT solutions in Brazil;
- establish partnerships between the public and private sectors;
- improve the country's integration in the international scenario.

The national plan started in 2017, and the first step involved a survey on diagnosis and aspirations. In other words, what would be the potential of Brazil to be a regional reference, the objectives to reach, the position Brazil intended to occupy in the international scenario, and the internal problems it could solve with this technology. Therefore, based on the conclusions built during the stage of diagnosis and aspirations, four verticals were listed: cities, health, agribusiness, and industry. Also, Ministry of Science, Technology, Innovation and Communications (MCTIC) recently announced the creation of eight Artificial Intelligence laboratories in Brazil. The laboratories will operate as a network, and four of them will be focused on IoT [7, 9].

4 The Healthcare Market in Brazil

According to the World Health Organization (WHO), Brazil is the seventh-largest health market in the world, with health expenses representing about 9% of GDP, including public investments and private spending, which means a total amount per year exceeding USD 160 billion and per capita spending per year of USD 929.00 [10]. The public system serves free of charge 75% of the population, while 25% of Brazilians use private health [11]. The country has 6,702 hospitals, of which 4,267 are private [12]. The Healthcare Information and Management Systems Society (HIMSS) offers certification according to the degree of hospital digitalization, with 7 being the highest score. Brazil has only nineteen institutions certified at level 6 and seven institutions at level 7, which suggests that most hospitals in the country are still behind in the digital transformation process [13]. Although the technologies are not present in hospitals as they should, organizations show an active interest in modernizing and overcoming this delay. It should be emphasized that the country currently has more than 400 startups seeking to offer innovative solutions for the health market [14].

5 The Internet of Things and the Health Context in Brazil

According to a recent survey, only 8% of hospitals adopt an Internet of Things (IoT) solution in their operation, and 70% of the Chief Information Officers (CIO's) report the intention to implement IoT solutions in their institutions in the next two years [15]. The research also mentions that the intention is to adopt IoT, in the first moment, to solve problems or improve operational efficiency, but they do not intend to put the technology in direct contact with the patient. However, there is openness for mobile solutions for patients, inside and outside the hospital environment. Costs, mainly with integration, were mentioned as the main entry barrier to be overcome [15]. It is a vast market, which will actively seek IoT solutions in the coming years.

The National Bank for Economic and Social Development (BNDES), in partnership with the MCTIC, estimates that gains from the Internet of Things in the Brazilian health market by 2025 may reach USD 39 billion [7]. In a survey carried out in 2017, about 50 companies in the state of São Paulo and a few in the states of Minas Gerais, Rio de Janeiro, and Rio Grande do Sul, declared themselves ready to offer IoT solutions for the health area. Therefore, on the one hand, we have a demand that will undergo a sharp growth in the next two years, and on the other hand, we still have a small number of institutions able to absorb this demand across the country, concentrated in the Southeast and South regions [7].

Several institutions are mobilizing around a series of actions to be taken so that opportunities are not lost, and the potential of IoT in Brazil is realized. Today, Brazil counts on the Brazilian Association of Internet of Things (ABINC - Associação Brasileira de Internet das Coisas), which is a non-profit organization and, according to its creators, arose from the "need to create an entity that was legitimate and representative, nationwide, and that would act on different fronts of the Internet of Things sector." According to the entity's website, its main objectives are: to disseminate relevant information about new technologies and the Brazilian market; promote commercial activities among members; promote research and development activities; act with government authorities and regulatory bodies and seek international partnerships [16].

In addition, Brazil also presents relevant research and development initiatives. It is valid to highlight the Integrated Systems Laboratory (LSI - Laboratório de Sistemas Integráveis) and the Interdisciplinary Center for Interactive Technologies (CITI - Centro Interdisciplinar de Tecnologias Interativas). Both are at the University of São Paulo, which is among the most important institutions in Latin America [17, 18].

LSI works on applied research and cutting-edge technology to offer innovative solutions that prioritize public interest, as well as the country's development. The laboratory was founded in 1975, has seven research groups, and a Digital Health and Assistive and Rehabilitation Technologies among its subjects of expertise. In addition, the LSI objectives are aligned with Brazilian ambitions in the field of IoT, as the laboratory has one among its objectives to work in technology transfer to the national industry [17].

CITI is a platform for multidisciplinary projects available to the scientific community. In this center, the "Caninos Loucos" project is underway, aiming to form a community of IoT developers in Brazil and, in addition, develops Single Board Computers with national technology and open structure, including hardware and software. The center also has a digital health center and works with the concepts of Think-tank and FabLab

(Factory-Laboratory) to enable projects that have an impact on human problems, such as health and accessibility [18, 19].

6 Challenges and Opportunities for IoT in the Health Area in Brazil

According to the National IoT Plan, Brazil has three main health challenges that can be overcome with solutions involving IoT [7]:

Improvement of the general health of the population: Eating habits are bad, and people are less active. These two factors have a negative impact on the health system.

Improve patient care: Only 25% of patients trust the health system and, among health professionals, only 35% trust the system. There are reasons to believe that the lack of confidence is related to the long waiting times for care. A problem that has the potential to be mitigated through efficiency gains that technology brings.

Financial sustainability of the system: There are two main factors adding pressure to the system: population aging and growing medical inflation, that is, the increase in health costs related to new treatments or procedures that are available to the population [20]. Both issues are not restricted to Brazil and have been discussed globally. Brazil's population is aging at an impressive rate. In 2030, we will see a reduction in all age groups below 40 years and accelerated growth in groups above that age. And this growth is more pronounced at the top of the age pyramid. Estimates indicate that, in 2030, the age group over 60 years old will be 3 times larger than it is today (Fig. 2) [2]. According to the "Instituto Coalizão Saúde," [21] it is estimated that only 10% of the elderly population will have access to private health services, that is, 90% will depend on the public system. Thus, an urgency to develop plans to meet the needs of this growing part of the population is enormous.

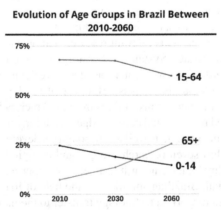

Fig. 2. Projection of the evolution of different age groups in Brazil until 2060 (extracted from IBGE - Brazilian Institute of Geography and Statistics: Projections and estimates of the population of Brazil and of the Federation Units. Rio de Janeiro: 2010 available at https://www.ibge.gov.br/apps/populacao/projecao/).

In addition to the three challenges that receive special attention, solutions to improve the use of resources, facilities, professionals, and pieces of equipment will similarly be well accepted. Innovations related to schedule control, stocks, and availability of hospital beds. Confronting epidemics, as the country has faced severe problems with dengue, zika virus, and chikungunya. Finally, it is also worth highlighting the management of patient data because a large amount of information is still on paper, and this is a limiting factor when we think about using this data as a planning tool.

For Brazil to take full advantage of the expansion of IoT solutions, it is essential that efforts be allocated to overcome challenges, such as regulatory issues. The draft General Data Protection Law already exists, so this issue should be mitigated soon [22].

Furthermore, Brazil is a country of continental proportions and very heterogeneous. In this scenario, connectivity is quite challenging, which is why investments in infrastructure and training of human resources are part of the National Internet of Things Plan. Brazil has 0.9% of its workforce in telecommunications, and for the European Union, this number is close to 4%, which reinforces the indication that it is essential to invest in the training of these professionals [23].

7 Conclusion

As discussed above, we can conclude that Brazil government understands the strategic role of IoT in the health area, enabling technologies with revolutionary potential and capability to bring significant progress to the Brazilian health market and health benefits for the population. Precisely for this reason, Brazil actively seeks to create strategies to develop its own solutions and achieve a higher degree of autonomy and a guiding role. Several efforts are taken in public investments and partnerships with the academy and the private sector. It is, therefore, a window of opportunity to leverage research, developments, projects, initiatives, and startups interested in innovation in the health area.

References

1. Adamer, K., et al.: Developing a wearable assistant for hospital ward rounds: an experience report. In: Floerkemeier, C., Langheinrich, M., Fleisch, E., Mattern, F., Sarma, S.E. (eds.) IOT 2008. LNCS, vol. 4952, pp. 289–307. Springer, Heidelberg (2008). https://doi.org/10.1007/978-3-540-78731-0_19
2. Instituto Brasileiro de Geografia e Estatística: Projeções e estimativas da população do Brasil e das Unidades da Federação. https://www.ibge.gov.br/apps/populacao/projecao. Accessed 09 Feb 2020
3. International Monetary Fund: Gross Domestic Product. https://www.imf.org/external/datamapper/NGDPD@WEO/OEMDC/ADVEC/WEOWORLD. Accessed 09 Feb 2020
4. Fan, J.S.: Regulating unicorns: disclosure and the new private economy. Bost Coll Law Rev. 57(2), 583–642 (2016)
5. Teare, G.: Crunch Base. https://news.crunchbase.com/news/the-new-unicorns-of-2019/. Accessed 09 Feb 2020
6. Lee, A.: Crunch Base. https://techcrunch.com/2013/11/02/welcome-to-the-unicorn-club/. Accessed 09 Feb 2020

7. Banco Nacional de Desenvolvimento Econômico e Social. Internet das Coisas: um plano de ação para o Brasil Produto 7B: Aprofundamento de Verticais – Saúde. https://www.bndes. gov.br/wps/wcm/connect/site/9e481a5b-a851-4895-ba7f-aa960f0b69a6/relatorio-aprofunda mento-das-verticais-saude-produto-7B.pdf?MOD=AJPERES&CVID=m3mTltg. Accessed 09 Feb 2020
8. BRASIL. Constituição (2019). Decreto nº 9854, de 2019. Brasília, 2019. Disponível em: http://www.planalto.gov.br/ccivil_03/_Ato2019-2022/2019/Decreto/D9854.htm. Accessed 09 Feb 2020
9. Peduzzi, P.: Agência Brasil EBC. https://agenciabrasil.ebc.com.br/geral/noticia/2019-11/min istro-anuncia-criacao-de-8-laboratorios-de-inteligencia-artificial. Accessed 09 Feb 2020
10. World Health Organization: Global Health Expenditure Database. http://apps.who.int/nha/database/country_profile/Index/en. Accessed 09 Feb 2020
11. Agência Nacional de Saúde Suplementar: Mapa da Assistência Saúde Suplementar (2017). http://www.ans.gov.br/images/Mapa_Assistencial_2017.pdf. Accessed 09 Feb 2020
12. Ministério da Saúde: Datasus – Departamento de Informática do SUS. Cadastro Nacional de Estabelecimentos de Saúde (CNES). http://cnes2.datasus.gov.br/. Accessed 09 Feb 2020
13. Healthcare Information and Management Systems Society. https://www.himssanalytics.org/stage-6-7-achievement. Accessed 09 Feb 2020
14. Startup Base. https://startupbase.com.br/home/startups?q=&states=all&cities=all&seg ments=Sa%C3%BAde%20e%20Bem-estar&targets=all&phases=all&models=all&bad ges=all. Accessed 09 Feb 2020
15. Sartor, V.: Grupo Mídia. https://grupomidia.com/hcm/estudo-sobre-o-uso-da-tecnologia-nos-hospitais-brasileiros-pela-frost-sullivan-e-abcis-e-o-destaque-do-direto-da-redacao/. Accessed 09 Feb 2020
16. Associação Brasileira de Internet das Coisas. https://abinc.org.br/. Accessed 09 Feb 2020
17. Laboratório de Sistemas Integráveis. https://sites.usp.br/lsi/. Accessed 09 Feb 2020
18. Centro Interdisciplinar de Tecnologias Interativas. http://www.lsi.usp.br/citi/. Accessed 09 Feb 2020
19. Projeto Caninos Loucos. https://caninosloucos.org/pt/. Accessed 09 Feb 2020
20. Dhaene, J., Godecharle, E., Antonio, K., Denuit, M., Hanbali, H.: Lifelong health insurance covers with surrender value: updating mechanisms in the presence of medical inflation. ASTIN Bull. **47**, 803–836 (2017). https://doi.org/10.1017/asb.2017.13
21. Instituto Coalizão Saúde: Coalizão Saúde Brasil Uma agenda para transformar o sistema de saúde. http://icos.org.br/wp-content/uploads/2017/04/Relato%CC%81rioNet.pdf. Accessed 09 Feb 2020
22. BRASIL. Constituição (2018). Lei nº 13709, de 2018. Disponível em: http://www.planalto.gov.br/ccivil_03/_ato2015-2018/2018/lei/L13709.htm. Accessed 09 Feb 2020
23. Marques, F.: Brazil's Internet of Things. Revista Pesquisa FAPESP **259**, 18–23 (2018)

An Omitted Cross-Border Urban Corridor on the North-Western Iberian Peninsula?

Valerià Paül[1]([envelope]), Juan-M. Trillo-Santamaría[1], and José-I. Vila-Vázquez[2]

[1] Departamento de Xeografía, Universidade de Santiago de Compostela,
Praza da Universidade 1, 15703 Santiago de Compostela, Galicia, Spain
{v.paul.carril,juanmanuel.trillo}@usc.es
[2] Université Paris Est, LATTS, 14-20 Boulevard Newton, 77420 Champs-sur-Marne, France
jivilavazquez@gmail.com

Abstract. The alleged North-Western Iberian urban corridor, mainly covering Northern Portugal and Galicia, is examined. The international boundary between Portugal and Spain is assumed to have a role in the analysis of such a corridor. The theoretical section reviews the literature on urban systems and corridors and shows how they are commonly conceived under a nation-state framework. Some of the international literature on urban corridors has been criticised given that it is not based on actual inter-urban links. The results are based on the analysis of the literature about the North-Western Iberian urban corridor developed in Portugal and in Galicia. The intention is to grasp to what extent the corridor has emerged as an academic spatial category in both countries. The paper concludes by discussing the results and by providing some final remarks regarding inter-urban and inter-regional cross-border governance and the relevance of other scales rather than individual cities for the development of smart city agendas.

Keywords: Urban corridor · Urban system · Smart city · Cross-border · Portugal · Galicia (Spain)

1 Introduction

One of the most currently popular urban scholars has defined the so-called "mega-regions" as "a new, natural economic unit that results from city-regions growing upward, becoming denser, and growing outward and into one another" (Florida 2008: 42). However, most of the literature about smart cities deals with individual cities and, in practice, neglects to consider that cities do not work in isolation and can amalgamate into "mega-regions". In this sense, when there is a discussion about smart principles applied to a particular city, quite commonly the debate is focused on this city in itself, understood as autarkical, paying limited attention to its relationships with other neighbouring cities. This, quite often, may imply that the scale for developing smart and other relevant urban policies is miscalculated.

Florida (2008: 54) included a map of Europe, where the Iberian Peninsula western coastal region appears mapped as a single "mega-region" named after its alleged main

H. Santos et al. (Eds.): SmartCity 360 2019, LNICST 323, pp. 27–35, 2020.
https://doi.org/10.1007/978-3-030-51005-3_4

city: Lisbon. Importantly, this "mega-region" goes beyond Portugal and includes Galicia, located on the North-Western Iberian Peninsula and politically pertaining to Spain. Beyond the fact that this map is not pertinently justified from a scientific perspective, this "mega-region" is striking, given that it extends into another country. In fact, when dealing with urban systems, scholars tend to reproduce the understanding of the "state as a container" as defined by Taylor (1994), thus working inside the bounded territories of their countries, with limited attention given to the dynamics which cross nation-state boundaries.

In this context, this chapter tries to examine the literature on the urban system of the North-Western Iberian Peninsula—namely Northern Portugal and Galicia—, by discussing its main urban corridor (usually called "Atlantic axis" in Galicia)[1], trying to elucidate to what extent the existence of the international boundary between Portugal and Spain has motivated it being disregarded. According to Marques (2004) and other relevant Portuguese urban scientists who will be mentioned below, Lisbon and Porto are quite detached as they do not work in an integrated manner. For this reason, Florida's (2008: 54) proposal of considering an urban corridor from Lisbon to the north as a single "mega-region" is not followed here. In fact, his methodology, based on employing "the satellite images of the world at night [...] to identify mega-regions as contiguous lighted areas" (Florida 2008: 47) seems inaccurate; indeed, subsequent studies, such as Nel·lo et al. (2017), have methodologically improved the use of this data source.

Accordingly, the hypothesis here stands that Porto is the main metropolitan area of the North-Western Iberian urban corridor, including cities outside Portugal. There is evidence that this is the case. Firstly, Porto airport (Sá Carneiro) is self-promoted as "the airport of all Galicians"[2]; in fact, the available statistics show that more than 12% of the total users come from Galicia, accounting for more than one million Galician passengers, roughly the same figure that Vigo or A Coruña airports achieve all year round, including passengers of all nationalities (Suau 2020). Secondly, a map of densities and volumes at municipal level of the North-Western Iberian Peninsula makes an urban corridor apparent, from Aveiro to Ferrol, approximately accounting for 4.9 million inhabitants, with 2.5 million residents in the—broadly understood—Porto metropolitan region (see Fig. 1). Thirdly, when comparing the average daily traffic (ADT) of all the cross-border roads between Spain and Portugal, 38% was recorded in 2016 at the bridges crossing the Minho River (where the international boundary is set just in the middle of the studied urban corridor). The most intense cross-border pass between both countries is the highway which is the axis of the urban corridor (AP9 in Galicia/A3 in Portugal), with an ADT of 15,015 vehicles per day (2016) crossing the border (OTEP 2018).

---

[1] "Atlantic Axis" is a common concept in the urban studies literature developed in Galicia since the 1990s. It refers to the urban corridor extending from Ferrol, in the north-west of Galicia, to the border with Portugal, in the south-west of Galicia (Fig. 1). However, the same name is used by a voluntary inter-municipal association currently consisting of 35 municipalities in Galicia and Northern Portugal (https://www.eixoatlantico.com/), not all of them in the urban corridor studied here and some of them are not even strictly urban. All this leads to a vagueness in the use of "Atlantic Axis", so we prefer to use North-Western Iberian urban corridor.

[2] Advertisement placed in the airport premises.

This clearly shows that mobility is higher at this point—where the corridor crosses the boundary—than anywhere else along a boundary of more than 1,200 km in length.

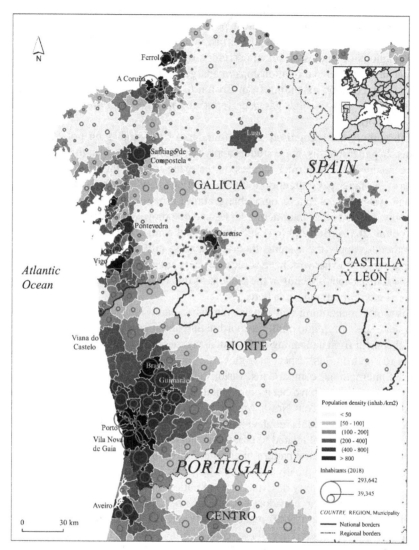

Fig. 1. Population per municipality on the North-Western Iberian Peninsula (2018). Sources: https://www.ine.pt/, https://www.pordata.pt/ and https://ine.es/ (last accessed 2020/02/25).

This chapter begins by reviewing the literature on urban systems and corridors, usually conceived under a nation-state framework. Then, the analyses already carried out on the Northern Portugal-Galicia coastal corridor are expounded. This consists of a systematic attempt to examine the Portuguese and Galician scientific literature available on this corridor. Finally, this research is discussed and some final remarks are made.

2 Conceptualising Urban Systems and Corridors

Geddes (1915) is recognised as one of the first authors to give a scientific interpretation of cities' coalescence into the so-called "conurbations". To define them, this author made use of the urban physical development process by means of the increasing mobility linked to the improvement of transport infrastructure. Afterwards, Gottmann (1962) laid the foundations of studies on urban corridors, by combining analyses on morphology and inter-urban functional relationships in a large US north-eastern urbanised region—the BosWash corridor, extending from Boston to Washington—, which he labelled as "megalopolis". This research has been replicated in other large metropolitan regions across the world.

Both authors are recognised as the founders of the studies on polycentric urban systems. In general terms, these studies apply two main approaches: the morphological and the functional. The former focuses on the extension and the shape of urban built-up areas. The latter pays attention to the interactions between cities. Be that as it may, an urban system refers to a recognisable group of urban settlements of different sizes, commonly understood as inter-acting nodes and creating a particular hierarchy of levels (Zoido et al. 2013). Berry (1964) and Bourne and Simmons (1978) were some of the first authors to apply the systems theory to analyse city interaction. Interestingly, the concepts *system* and *network* have sometimes been interchangeably used, in a profound discussion that is out of remit in the context of this chapter. In this sense, we prefer to employ *system* for our purposes here.

It is worth mentioning that urban systems research is commonly carried out at a nation-state scale, trying to confer a coordinating and organising role to each city in its national context from a planning and political perspective (Zoido et al. 2013). However, there is research in this respect at a global level. For instance, different authors have proposed international comparisons, various contiguous nation-states have been studied together and there have been continental and/or macro-regional investigations, in particular in Europe and in North America (Cattan 1999; Taylor 2004; Simmons and Kamikihara 2006; Rozenblat et al. et al. 2018; Vives-Miró and Paül 2019).

Lastly, a key concept related to urban systems is urban corridors. An urban corridor refers to a particular spatial pattern of cities conforming the urban system, which holds a linear configuration, typically following a transport infrastructure corridor. Urban corridors have been commonly described within nation-states (for instance, in the case of Spain, the Mediterranean corridor) but can also be international if they cross boundaries. In Europe, Brunet (1989) made an early attempt at drawing continental urban corridors, such as the subsequently so-called "blue banana", from London to Milan, and the Mediterranean corridor from Madrid to Rome, which to some extent extended the traditional Spanish Mediterranean corridor, embracing France and Italy. All of them have received considerable criticism. Indeed, Williams (1996) and Cattan (2007) have labelled these urban corridors (sic) as "spatial metaphors", stating they are images that do not necessarily reflect actual inter-urban links. As mentioned above, the same might be applicable to the urban corridors (sic) drawn by Florida (2008).

3   Reviewing the North-Western Iberian Urban Corridor

3.1   Portuguese Perspectives

The Portuguese urban system has been analysed following functionalist approaches since the 1980s. Salgueiro (1992) and Guichard (1995) referred to the primacy of the Lisbon metropolitan region, followed by the metropolitan region led by Porto, and describing a south-north corridor between them. Ferrão and Marques (2003) concurred, pointing out that beyond Lisbon and Porto there are only several small-sized cities in Portugal, thus causing an imbalanced and uneven urban system that lacks a layer of cities positioned at an intermediate level.

This chapter deals, obviously, with the Porto metropolitan region, which the available literature describes as polycentric, especially when compared to Lisbon, which is clearly monocentric. However, there is a widespread discussion about its extension: while some research considers the region limited to the contiguous built-up area of Porto and some neighbouring municipalities, other authors point out that the functional metropolitan region may include Braga, Guimarães, Aveiro and/or other urban nodes of Northern Portugal (Salgueiro 1992; Ferrão 2002; Ferrão and Marques 2003; Fernandes 2014).

There are scant mentions of Galicia and of the North-Western Iberian urban corridor by Portuguese urban scientists. One of the early scholars to show a Galician connection in this respect was Guichard (2000), who mapped western coastal Galicia as part of the area influenced by Porto. Moreover, as a cartographic representation, Portas et al. (2011) mapped the continuity between Porto and the western Galician coastal cities, using a morphological method.

However, Ferrão and Marques (2003: 17) highlighted that "[t]here is still relatively little cross-border interaction by comparison [with] existing growth potential, even in […] Northern Portugal/Galicia". Indeed, these authors forecast four scenarios for the future of the Portuguese urban system, one of them expressively labelled as "fragmentation": "Portugal's urban system most at risk of being subject to outside influence, particularly from Spain. Portugal would lose out both from a hierarchical point of view […] and from a proximity point of view (the increased influence of Spanish cities located along the border)" (p. 48). Interestingly, it can be interpreted that these scholars are concerned about a potential breakdown between Lisbon and Porto, which might be associated with strengthening the links of the latter with Galicia.

In a similar direction, Marques (2019) has recently demonstrated that the functional relations, measured by the number of commuters according to the 2011 Census, between Lisbon and Porto is higher than between Porto and Galician cities. In short, Portuguese researchers have not evidenced the North-Western Iberian urban corridor from a functional perspective.

3.2   Galician Perspectives

A systemic approach has been used to analyse Galician cities since the 1970s. The Galician urban system is usually considered an autonomous sub-system of the Spanish urban system. In this regard, Precedo (1974) identified two main metropolitan areas—Vigo and A Coruña—, working quite autonomously. He also pointed out that a future scenario might imply the structuration of an urban "development axis" between Ferrol (located north of A Coruña) and Vigo, connecting both metropolitan areas. The notion of "axis" was imported from regional economic analysis theories that established a direct connection between infrastructure development and the emergence of economic and population growth corridors.

However, this scenario became a self-fulfilling prophecy: Pérez Vilariño (1990), Precedo (1990) and Alonso and Lois (1997), among others, described the emergence of the "Atlantic urban axis" associated with the final work on the AP9 motorway structuring the corridor (initiated in the late 1970s, it was finished in 2000, when it reached Ferrol). Beyond the obvious increase of inter-city traffic flow that was experienced in the 1990s, the development of manufacturing activities operating at this urban system scale was also noticed.

Since the 1990s, this urban corridor has been studied under different lenses, combing both functional and morphological approaches as well as from other perspectives (sociological, imageries, planning, etc.). The increasing integration between cities has been extensively reported, including the inauguration of the high-speed train between A Coruña and Vigo in 2015. In addition, several researchers have shown how urban sprawl has affected the corridor area, evidencing a low-density pattern of suburban development, mostly contiguous along the highway structuring the corridor and its main perpendicular extensions towards the coast. A recent synthesis of most of the research carried out is provided by Lois and Pino (2015).

Lois (2004a) was possibly the first scholar to refer to the alleged Portuguese counterpart of this Galician urban corridor. He characterised the North-Western Iberian urban corridor as follows: (i) consisting of several urban areas with significant population, relevant at both the Iberian and European contexts; (ii) noticing its economic relevance, especially in terms of the concentration of manufacturing companies; and (iii) showing increasing economic exchanges and mobility. Lois (2004a) described this urban corridor extending to Aveiro (located 50 km south of Porto). However, Lois (2004b) also added that, due to the already described urban system in Portugal, the corridor should be seen as reaching Setúbal, located south of Lisbon, which is geographically coincident with Florida (2008).

4   Discussion and Conclusion

The North-Western Iberian urban corridor has been researched in several studies in the last three decades. It seems that Galician scholars (e.g. Lois, 2004a, b) have been more attentive to its configuration, with more enthusiasm about a possible integration of western Galician cities into the dynamics of Northern Portugal, especially those exercised by the metropolitan area of Porto. In contrast, we have found in Ferrão and Marques (2003) a Portuguese narrative assuming that if the linkage between Portuguese and Galician cities gains momentum, there is a potential risk for the integrity of the Portuguese urban system. We interpret this as a prevalence of methodological nationalism as described by Schiller and Glick (2002).

When dealing with this corridor, the dominant perspective exploring its scope has been morphological, while the functional approach has been widely critical of its presence. A case in point is Marques (2019), who states that the North-Western Iberian urban corridor is not proved by commuting data, while recognising that "a more complex analysis might involve a wider variety of indicators" (p. 27–28; own translation). In this sense, they could make use of the available series from Eures (2002–2019). This source shows that factual transboundary employees between Galicia and Northern Portugal exceeds 13,000 annually, a figure that is recovering from the post-2008 GFC years (before the GFC the figure was more than 20,000 commuters). This type of indicator should be considered when trying to elucidate to what extent there is a functional urban corridor on the North-Western Iberian Peninsula. As explained by Taylor (1994), the existence of a nation-state boundary is a powerful mental barrier, mostly unconscious, that leads to disregarding particular spatial processes.

The widespread use of "Atlantic Axis" does not equal the North-Western Iberian urban corridor, because the former sometimes refers to an association of municipalities, but on many occasions, especially in Galicia, it equals the latter. Interestingly, this association has funded academic publications (e.g. Souto 1999; Souto et al. 2005) where the affiliate cities are described as an actual or potential single urban system, on the basis that the persisting boundary made its articulation impossible until the consolidation of the four EU "free freedoms" of the single market, including the free movement of persons, in the early 1990s. This "Atlantic Axis urban system" might embrace the North-Western Iberian urban corridor and other municipalities in inland areas. In this sense, and contrary to the analysed works in this chapter, Souto (1999) and Souto et al. (2005) seem to respond to the need to integrate all the municipalities gathered in the association rather than to accurately characterise an urban system.

That is possibly a local manifestation of the common confusion between images and actual functional links reported in the theoretical section. Nevertheless, the image of a corridor (or axis) has had a powerful effect, impelled by the Atlantic Axis association itself. Urban cross-border integration is quite often aspirational and prospective rather than a matter of fact. Indeed, when Williams (1996: 96) analysed the "blue banana" corridor as proposed by Brunet (1989) he indicated that "this metaphor creates a memorable image which simplifies and structures people's thinking about the spatial structure". This is consistent with other notions which emerged when dealing with planning devices such as "anticipatory geographies" (Sparke 2000: 187), "imagined geographies" (Häkli 2004: 62) and "aspirational spaces" (Deas and Lord 2006: 1863).

Beyond the Atlantic Axis Association, other governance structures have been created between Galicia and Northern Portugal. A case in point is the intergovernmental Galicia-Northern Portugal (G-NP) EGTC[3]. Ironically, the G-NP EGTC region can also create a confusing "container" in the sense given by Taylor (1994) when analysing the urban corridor: Aveiro does not administratively belong to the Portuguese Northern Region, and that has led to understand this city to be more connected to the Portuguese Central Region, thus disconnected from Porto.

The G-NP EGTC covers a wider region beyond the North-Western Iberian urban corridor. However, in 2018 an EGTC was created for the strictly cross-border region of this corridor: the Rio Minho. This EGTC has an odd spatial extension as it covers the

---

[3] Since 2008, the European Grouping of Territorial Cooperation (EGTC) is the EU legal device created to propel inter-administrative cooperation, mainly among local and regional levels.

Southern-most municipalities of the metropolitan area of Vigo—without Vigo itself—
and the urban area of Viana do Castelo—very dependent on Porto. However, the Rio
Minho EGTC has designed an intense smart urban agenda that deals, amongst other
issues, with setting shared services for the citizens of both sides of the boundary and
the development of sustainable cross-border local mobility (Paül et al. 2019). To sum
up, smart strategies are applicable beyond the edges of a particular city, its scope being
apparently pertinent in complex urban systems as well. The discussion carried out here
about a cross-border urban corridor is a particularly challenging arena in this respect.

References

Alonso, M.P., Lois, R.C.: Proceso de industrialización y organización del espacio en un territorio
   periférico: Galicia. Boletín de la Asociación de Geógrafos Españoles **14**, 147–168 (1997)
Berry, B.J.L.: Cities as systems within systems of cities. Pap. Reg. Sci. **13**, 147–163 (1964). https://
   doi.org/10.1111/j.1435-5597.1964.tb01283.x
Bourne, L.S., Simmons, J.W. (eds.): Systems of Cities: Readings on Structure, Growth and Policy.
   Oxford University Press, New York (1978)
Brunet, R. (dir.): Les villes «européennes». La Documentation Française, Paris (1989)
Cattan, N. (ed.): Le système des villes européennes. Anthropos, Paris (1999)
Cattan, N. (ed.): Cities and networks in Europe. A critical approach of polycentrism. J. Libbey
   Eurotext, Montrouge (2007)
Deas, I., Lord, A.: From a new regionalism to an unusual regionalism? the emergence of non-
   standard regional spaces and lessons for the territorial reorganisation of the state. Urban Stud.
   43(10), 1847–1877 (2006). https://doi.org/10.1080/00420980600838143
Eures. https://www.eures-norteportugal-galicia.org/. Accessed 25 Feb 2020
Fernandes, J.A.: Muitas vidas tem o centro e vários centros tem a vida de uma cidade. In: Lois,
   R.C., Miramontes, Á. (eds.) Reflexiones sobre las ciudades y el sistema urbano en tiempos de
   crisis, pp. 131–146. Grupo ANTE, Santiago de Compostela (2014)
Ferrão, J.: As regiões metropolitanas portuguesas no contexto ibérico. DGOTDU, Lisboa (2002)
Ferrão, J., Marques, T.S.: National Urban System, Overview. DGOTDU, Lisboa (2003)
Florida, R.: Who's Your City? How the Creative Economy Is Making Where to Live the Most
   Important Decision of Your Life. Basic Books, New York (2008)
Geddes, P.: Cities in Evolution. An Introduction to the Town Planning Movement and to the Study
   of Civics. Williams & Norgate, London (1915)
Gottmann, J.: Megalopolis: The Urbanized Northeastern Seaboard of the United States. Twentieth
   Century Fund, New York (1962)
Guichard, G.: Le Portugal au défi de l'urbain: enjeux et périls de la métropolisation. Méditerranée
   (81), 5–10 (1995)
Guichard, F.: O Porto no século XX. In: História do Porto, pp. 524–637. Porto Editora, Porto
   (2000)
Häkli, J.: Governing the mountains: cross-border regionalization in Catalonia. In: Kramsch, O.,
   Hooper, B. (eds.) Cross-Border Governance in the European Union, pp. 56–69. Routledge,
   London/New York (2004)
Lois, R.C., Pino, D. (eds.): A Galicia urbana. Xerais, Vigo (2015)
Lois, R.C.: A model of Spanish-Portuguese urban growth: the Atlantic Axis. Dela **21**, 281–294
   (2004a). https://doi.org/10.4312/dela.21.281-294
Lois, R.C.: Galice-Portugal: des rélations transnationales privilegiées dans la Peninsule Iberique.
   Sud-Ouest Européen **18**, 31–40 (2004b)

Marques, T.S.: Portugal na transição do século. Retratos e dinâmicas territoriais. Afrontamento, Santa Maria da Feira (2004)

Marques, T.S. (coord.): O papel dos sistemas urbanos na caracterização do território nacional no contexto ibérico e europeu. Universidade do Porto/CEGOT, Porto (2019)

Nel·lo, O., López, J., Martín, J., Checa, J.: Energy and urban form. the growth of European cities on the basis of night-time brightness. Land Use Policy **61**, 103–112 (2017). https://doi.org/10. 1016/j.landusepol.2016.11.007

OTEP.   https://www.mitma.gob.es/informacion-para-el-ciudadano/observatorios/observatorios-de-transporte-internacional/observatorio-transfronterizo-espan%CC%83a-portugal. Accessed 25 Feb 2020

Paül, V., et al.: Estratexia do Río Miño Transfronteirizo 2030=Estratégia do Rio Minho Transfronteiriço 2030. Deputación de Pontevedra, Pontevedra (2019)

Pérez Vilariño, J.: As cidades alineadas do Atlántico e a economía política metropolitana en Galicia. Revista Galega de Economía 159–176 (1990)

Portas, N., Domingues, A., Cabral, J.: Políticas Urbanas II: Transformações, Regulação e Projectos. Fundação Calouste Gulbenkian, Lisboa (2011)

Precedo, A.: Galicia: red urbana y desarrollo regional. Boletín de la Real Sociedad Geográfica **110**, 161–220 (1974)

Precedo, A.: La Coruña metrópoli regional. Fundación Caixagalicia, A Coruña (1990)

Rozenblat, C., Pumain, D., Velasquez, E. (eds.): International and Transnational Perspectives on Urban Systems. AGES. Springer, Singapore (2018). https://doi.org/10.1007/978-981-10-7799-9

Salgueiro, T.B.: A cidade em Portugal: uma geografia urbana. Afrontamento, Porto (1992)

Schiller, A., Glick, N.: Methodological nationalism and beyond: nation-state building, migration and the social sciences. Glob. Netw. **2**(4), 301–334 (2002)

Simmons, J., Kamikihara, S.: The North American urban system: the limits to continental integration. In: Lois, R.C. (ed.) Urban Changes in Different Scales: Systems and Structures, pp. 287–296. Universidade de Santiago de Compostela, Santiago de Compostela (2006)

Souto, X.M. (coord.): Xeografía do Eixo Atlántico. Eixo Atlántico do Noroeste Peninsular, Vigo (1999). http://www.eixoatlantico.com/eixogal/paxinas/publicac/xeograf/creditos.htm. Accessed 27 Apr 2000

Souto, X.M., Bouzada, X., Figueirido, A.: Segundos Estudos Estratéxicos do Eixo Atlántico. Eixo Atlántico do Noroeste Peninsular, Vigo (2005)

Sparke, M.: "Chunnel Visions": unpacking the anticipatory geographies of an Anglo-European borderland. J. Borderlands Stud. **XV**(1), 187–219 (2000). https://doi.org/10.1080/08865655. 2000.9695547

Suau, P.: Plan Estratégico para la Conectividad del Aeropuerto de A Coruña 2020–2021. Aviation Data Works, Barcelona (2020)

Taylor, P.J.: The state as a container: territoriality in the modern world system. Prog. Hum. Geogr. **18**, 151–162 (1994). https://doi.org/10.1177/030913259401800202

Taylor, P.J.: World City Network. A Global Urban Analysis. Routledge, London/New York (2004)

Vives-Miró, S., Paül, V.: Las transformaciones de los sistemas y de los espacios urbanos europeos. In: López Palomeque, F., Plaza, J.I. (coords.) Geografía de Europa. Estructuras, procesos y dinámicas territoriales, pp. 205–271. Tirant Humanidades, València (2019)

Williams, R.H.: European Union Spatial Policy and Planning. Paul Chapman, London (1996)

Zoido, F., et al.: Diccionario de urbanismo, geografía urbana y ordenación del territorio. Cátedra, Madrid (2013)

Intelligent Playful Environments in New Urban Social Landscape

Predrag K. Nikolić[(✉)]

School of Creativity and Art, ShanghaiTech University, 393 Huaxia Middle Road, Pudong,
Shanghai 201210, China
predragnikolic@shanghaitech.edu.cn

Abstract. The concept of Smart Cities are giving lots of opportunities for using technology to make citizens heathier and happier in the future cities. Recent development of artificial intelligence and its capacity to support people in creative and learning processes can be crucial factor in changing social landscape and lead to novel social innovations. In this paper, we are presenting art/research projects, and design experiments of interactive designer Predrag K. Nikolic exposed in various public spaces within the period of last ten years. The conceptual idea behind the projects has been to affect human behavior through novel interactions within playful mix realities and lastly in artificial reality (AIR) as new user experience phenomena in a new urban social landscape.

Keywords: Smart Cities · Playful environment · Smart living environments · Intelligent interface design · User experience design · Mix reality · Artificial Intelligence Reality · Robot-robot interaction · Robot creativity

1 Introduction

Smart Cities as a concept for better quality of citizens' life is facing lots of challenges and has many different aspects to encompass to offer sustainable solutions in the future. One of the most important issues to consider is happiness of the people who are living in the cities. Interactive media art and design together with the uprising sensor and detection technologies, vast data collection and artificial intelligence, could give significant contribution to social development and innovation in smart living environments. Moreover, robot creativity development can encounter humans with the intelligent entities who will not be only replacement for human tasks but rather equally important for social interactions, beside human to human, in the urban social landscape [1].

In his design experiments and interactive media artworks, Predrag K. Nikolic focus is on how to offer to the citizens' playful environments where they can experience new interactions and establish communication between each other, machines and responsive public spaces in more engaging way. Through his creative practice, he found that artistic pretenses and context can have a crucial role in developing pleasurable feelings, spontaneous reactions and more intensive effect on participants' behavior during the engagement.

© ICST Institute for Computer Sciences, Social Informatics and Telecommunications Engineering 2020
Published by Springer Nature Switzerland AG 2020. All Rights Reserved
H. Santos et al. (Eds.): SmartCity 360 2019, LNICST 323, pp. 36–45, 2020.
https://doi.org/10.1007/978-3-030-51005-3_5

In the background section of the paper, we are going to present eight interactive media artworks relate to different research topics he intended to explore within the project agenda. We will describe the type of the interactions investigated, desirable experience intended to trigger and conceptual decision which was made to achieve that. Then we will present the concept of the Artificial Intelligence Reality (AIR) through description of three related art/design projects. Lastly, we will conclude and specify potential directions of using Artificial Intelligence Reality (AIR) concept to design intelligent, playful interfaces for better citizens' quality of life in future cities.

2   Background

For the last ten years, Predrag K. Nikolic is actively investigating new techniques and interaction design methods which could contribute to the smart cities concept development. In his art and design works he is using playful environments to provoke human behavior changes and offer new approaches to social innovation in urban communities. In this section, we will describe eight interactive media art/design artefacts with different user experience design approach and used interactive tactics. The aim was to trigger various participants' reactions which will eventually lead to long lasting behavioral changes and improve of a social well-being.

2.1   MindCatcher

The MindCatcher is an interactive installation where the central part for interaction and playful experience is floor interface. Users are using their body movements to step on and interact with sensitive floor switches. The visitors were stepping on coloured circles switches and creating so called audio-visual sentences projected on a wall in front of the floor interface (see Fig. 1).

The users created the patterns of the audio-visual sentences, but the author of the installation defined the basic rules (grammar). That gave us possibility to change the visualisations and challenge the participants' creativity and abstraction more intensively. Special attention was given to multiple meanings of the visual images generate as result of synergy between the humans and the system. We wanted to arouse intrinsic and emotional triggers which will entice creative immersion and temporary release of repressed emotions [2].

2.2   Ciklosol

In the interactive installation Ciklosol exercise bicycle is used as medium between participants and the dynamic visualisation projected on the screen (see Fig. 2). The speed of paddling is in direct correlation with the movement of the screen projected animated sunflower.

The conceptual idea for this public installation was routed into environmental message intended to be communicate with the visitors and affect their behavior. Furthermore, to emphasise importance of human role and invested energy in preservation of

Fig. 1. Mother and daughter in the collective creative session, interacting together on the floor interface. (© Predrag K. Nikolic. Photo: Predrag K. Nikolic)

Fig. 2. The Ciklosol Bike Interface where paddling is trigger to the system (© Predrag K. Nikolic. Photo: Predrag K. Nikolic)

Earth resources and living environment. The important issue was to extend existing functions and embed additional meanings to the used object for the interface, fitness bicycle. Additionally, to make possible effective transmission of ideas implemented in installation narrative, educate users and enhance their experience. Hence, we used paddling as a trigger for the system input-output communication [3].

2.3 Vrroom

The installation Vrroom is playing with the childhood memories to provide immersive mix reality experience and trigger suppressed emotions. In particular, an experience is built upon sonic interaction between visitors and the system by mimicking sounds of various vehicles to simulate movement like we used to do during our childhood. Visitors are invited to simulate sound of car engine in the microphone and start moving on the road projected on the screen. Depending on sound intensity, they were able to regulate their speed along the road (see Fig. 3).

Fig. 3. Interacting with the road in virtual environment and controlling movement by making sound of car engine and modulating its intensity. (© Predrag K. Nikolic. Photo: Predrag K. Nikolic)

Metaphors related to the road signs and arrows, in the context of decisions and choices we are making in our life, we used as genuine narrative language. As such, visitors are not exposed only to experience of virtual road trip controlled by the intensity of their voice but also they are in the middle of the visual story which goes on the road surface [4].

2.4 Before & Beyond

In the installation, Interactive Before & Beyond visitors are having physical interactions which are stimulating their internal processes such as motivate them to collaborate, interact with bodies and communicate. The installation space is enhanced with the Kinect and location based sensors which are tracking visitors' body movements, direction of walking and interpersonal distance. After entering the installation, participants are getting visual representation of their presence in the virtual world as audio-visual "String of Energy" projected on the screen in front of them. Every string has a characteristic color and sound which are used to induce feeling of personal attachment between visitors and the generated string. To increase tracking accuracy and level of intimate relationship between participants and the projected strings we are using sensory based technologies,

Fig. 4. After entering the installation space, every participant gets his String of Energy projected on the screen (© Predrag K. Nikolic. Photo: Predrag K. Nikolic)

Kinect movement detection placed on the wall and beacons integrated in the medallion around the neck of the participants (see Fig. 4).

With interactive installation Before & Beyond the aim was to challenge visitors to contemplate about their virtual existence and the way they share it with others. In the playful integrative environment, they are enhanced with new personal properties such as colour, shape and sound attached to their string. With those features, they can interact with other in novel way, such as making group composition, which allows them to enjoy in authentic experiences and novel multisensory communication with others. Physical and virtual space of the artwork are becoming a place for body and social interactions as well as the place for establishment of a new relationships between participants [5].

2.5 InnerBody

InnerBody is an interactive installation where visitors are interacting with the human-heart look like the interface to take a fake medical exam. The visitors are exposed to life-threatening diagnosis to provoke positive health related behavioral changes. The installation was set in public spaces. The central space of the installation consisted of the tactile human heart-shaped interface, the audio-visual projection of vital human functions and the odor made of iodoform and coal tar, typical smells we are experiencing in hospitals (see Fig. 5). Intention was to use expressive metaphorical and sensory stimulation to impact the experience of death anxiety by exposing them to fake medical exam with life treating results as the outcome [6].

To avoid potential ethical consideration, after the completion of the fake exam session, the visitors were informed that projected data were not real either related to them. The look and feel of the "Human Heart Interface" has been one of the crucial elements used to design visitors' experience in a way to trigger desirable health concerns.

In the installation, interactive media artists and designer Predrag K. Nikolic is using multisensory model of digital storytelling where the sound of heartbeats, textual messages, and visual representation of the human body vital functions, are all together part

Fig. 5. The Inner Body installation space and set up. (© Predrag K. Nikolic. Photo: Predrag K. Nikolic)

of the narrative employed to achieve desired behavior change. The installation positive and educational role starts with the textually introduced which describes the nature of a so-called Preventive Diagnosis by an Infrared Scanner and ends with the explanatory message on the which we both used as instrumental to design behavioral change.

3   Artificial Intelligence Reality (AIR)

The concept of Artificial Intelligence Reality, presented by Predrag K. Nikolic at the Smart360 Summit 2019, is novel reality paradigm designed with robot creativity and artificial intelligence processed data, collected via sensors from the environment. Beside textual, numeric and sound analysis, we are using users' facial recognition features and emotional data as inputs for artificial intelligence to design new reality and immerse users in it. Eventually based on their features, they are becoming part of the artificial intelligence created reality.

In the first part of our investigation of AIR systems, we are using independent neural networks to create machine made content and arouse robot creativity. As part of that, four artificial intelligence philosopher clones (Aristotle, Nietzsche, Machiavelli and Sun Tzu) are created till now as part of the installations Robosophy Philosophy and Botorikko, Machine Created State. Besides that, with inclusive game In_Visible Island, we explored potentials of using AIR, multisensory and intelligent interfaces to join together sighted and visually impaired children in playful experience. Further, we will describe in more details all mentioned projects and core conceptual ideas.

3.1   Robosophy Philosophy

The artwork Robosophy Philosophy is authentic example of using robot-robot interaction as novel interactive design technique worth of exploring further in AIR contexts.

The installation is conceptualized as philosophical discussions between two artificial intelligence philosopher clones, Aristotle and Nietzsche. The content they are creating is generated based on the initial algorithm, which triggers the conversation and artificial intelligence internal processes. As result, we are getting completely genuine machine-made content, with minimum of human interference and maximum employment of robot creativity. The installation has two aims, to setting up a model for future content creation based on machine mindfulness and to question ongoing cultural and social changes which are results of interactions between people and technology [7].

The Aristotel's Ethical Robot is fed with knowledge collected from Aristotle's Nicomachean Ethics, Poetics, Politics, Metaphysics and Nietzsche's Overman Robot from Nietzsche's Thus Spoke Zarathustra, The Antichrist, Beyond Good and Evil, The Guy Science, The Birth of Tragedy and Ecce Homo [8]. The two robots are pseudo-robots and they do not have movable part for any assistance in human tasks as we wanted to emphasise potentials of their mental processes (see Fig. 6).

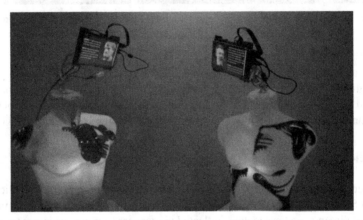

Fig. 6. Aristotel's Ethical Robot and Nietzche's Overman Robot (© Predrag K. Nikolic. Photo: Predrag K. Nikolic)

3.2   Botorikko: Machine Created State

The Botorikko, Machine Created State [9] is an interactive installation made of two to bicycles construction, two computer monitors and two pseudo robot manikin figures. For this artwork, we developed two artificial intelligence philosopher clones representing Machiavelli and Sun Tzu. They are discussing about social, historical and philosophical standpoints related to politics, diplomacy, strategy, wars and conflicts. Furthermore, we designed sentiment analysis algorithm capable to interpret sentiment from the authentic machine-created content and move the robots' head accordingly. The sentiments analysis algorithm is using typical human head-movement behavior based on six basic emotions anger, happy, sad, fear, surprise, disgust.

By pedaling bicycles, visitors are starting sword fight between Machiavelli and Sun Tzu manikin figures look robots, placed at the front part of the bicycles (see Fig. 7).

The installation is a unique example of human-robot-robot interaction which tends to become genuine social phenomena of our and future time. Moreover, sentiment analysis of the authentic machine made content is giving us opportunity, based on multiple data types used in AIR, to follow AI agent interpretations of given knowledge and emotional gesture based data.

Fig. 7. Interactive Installation Botorikko, human-robot-robot interaction (@ copyright photo: Predrag K. Nikolic)

3.3   In_Visible Island

In_Visible Island is smart, collaborative platform where visually impaired children can play with their normal peers [10]. It is AIR based platform which consist of multisensory storytelling system made of multilayered main board, central computer powered by artificial intelligence agent and multisensory disks with the story characters placed on its top. Participants are choosing the characters and place them into three different environments on the main board (see Fig. 8). Based on those choices, the artificial intelligence agent is choosing piece of the predefined narrative content based on the designed software criteria and creates storyline which will fit the players' decisions during the creative session. The platform is supporting multisensory experience (visual, audio and tactile). Players can touch the grace, rocks, water, cuddle the animal character and hear their specific sounds as well as feel shaking vibration if they are afraid of something. None visible experience is specially created for the visual impaired children so they can be equal in perception of that part of the platform with sighted kids during the play. By doing that we gave them multiple options for interactions and social relationship development between each other, and the most important is that they can play together and override physical differences.

Fig. 8. In_Visible Island, three different environments placed on the main board (forest, river, and mountain) and placements for the multisensory disks (@ copyright photo: Predrag K. Nikolic)

The central artificial intelligence unit is collecting various types of external data related to players' sensibility and choices such as animal character or environment and generates audio-tactile responses and authentic narrative in artificial intelligence generated reality (AIR).

4   Conclusions and Future Directions

In the presented projects we are trying to employ together smart environments, multisensory interaction, intelligent interfaces, concept of playful cities and artificial intelligence toward idea of novel social landscape where humans and robots will coexist and share the same reality.

In our further research and development of the Artificial Intelligence Reality (AIR) systems, we will focus on emotional and machine created content analysis toward a better understanding of robot data interpretations and achieved abstraction. Moreover, to find opportunities to increase variety of data categories collected and implement it in new urban reality created by artificial intelligence agent.

Acknowledgement. We thank Marko Jovanovic, Software Engineer, who did programming for all the presented projects.

In_Visible Island is an ongoing joint project with Media and Game Innovation Centre of Excellence, Institute of Human Centered Engineering Universiti Teknologi Malaysia.

We thank Dr Mohd Razali Md Tomari from Universiti Tun Hussein Onn Malaysia for designing the robotic head for the installation Botorikko, Machine Created State.

Great thanks to Cheung Kong School of Ar and Design, Shantou University for supported inicial development of the ongoing art/research project Botorikko, Machine Created State.

References

1. Shabbir, J., Anwer, T.: Artificial Intelligence and its role in near future. arXiv preprint arXiv: 1804.01396 (2018)
2. Nikolic P.K.: Measuring creative experience from visitors' paths and abstract multi-sensory artefacts. Mob. Netw. Appl. J. 1–10 (2019). https://doi.org/10.1007/s11036-019-01317-4
3. Nikolic, P.K.: Multimodal interactions: embedding new meanings to known forms and objects. In: Mandler, B., et al. (eds.) IoT360 2015. LNICST, vol. 170, pp. 107–121. Springer, Cham (2016). https://doi.org/10.1007/978-3-319-47075-7_13
4. Nikolić, P.K., Hua, Y.: Designing playful cities: audio-visual metaphors for new urban environment experience. Mob. Netw. Appl. (2020). https://doi.org/10.1007/s11036-020-015 14-6
5. Nikolic, P.K., Cheok, A.D.: Designing behavioral changes in smart cities using interactive smart spaces. In: Cagáňová, D., Balog, M., Knapčíková, L., Soviar, J., Mezarcıöz, S. (eds.) Smart Technology Trends in Industrial and Business Management. EAISICC, pp. 367–382. Springer, Cham (2019). https://doi.org/10.1007/978-3-319-76998-1_27
6. Nikolic, P., Cheok, A.D.: InnerBody: using interactive and multisensory interfaces to design behavioral change. LEONARDO J. **53**, 128–134 (2018)
7. Nikolic, P.K., Yang, H.: Artificial intelligence clone generated content toward robot creativity and machine mindfulness. Mob. Netw. Appl. 1–10 (2019). https://doi.org/10.1007/s11036-019-01281-z
8. Nikolic, P.K., Yang, H., Chen, J., Stankevich, G.P.: Syntropic counterpoints: art of ai sense or machine made context art. In: Proceeding SIGGRAPH 2018 Poster, Article no. 18. ACM, New York (2018)
9. Nikolić, P.K., Yang, H.: Syntropic counterpoints: philosophical content generated between two artificial intelligence clones. In: Cortez, P., Magalhães, L., Branco, P., Portela, C.F., Adão, T. (eds.) INTETAIN 2018. LNICST, vol. 273, pp. 3–13. Springer, Cham (2019). https://doi.org/10.1007/978-3-030-16447-8_1
10. Talib, R.I.A., Nikolic, P.K., Sunar, M.S., Prada, R.: Smart collaborative learning environment for visually impaired children. In: Cagáňová, D., Horňáková, N. (eds.) Mobility IoT 2018. EICC, pp. 485–496. Springer, Cham (2020). https://doi.org/10.1007/978-3-030-30911-4_34

IoT in Urban Space

RnMonitor: An IoT-Enabled Platform for Radon Risk Management in Public Buildings

Pedro Martins[1], Sérgio I. Lopes[1,2(✉)], Felisberto Pereira[2],
and António Curado[3]

[1] ARC4digIT - Instituto Politécnico de Viana do Castelo, Viana do Castelo, Portugal
`sil@estg.ipvc.pt`
[2] Instituto de Telecomunicações, Campus Universitário de Santiago, Aveiro, Portugal
[3] Prometheus - Instituto Politécnico de Viana do Castelo,
Viana do Castelo, Portugal

Abstract. Radon is a naturally occurring radioactive gas that can easily
accumulate in indoor environments, being classified by the World Health
Organization (WHO) as the second most important cause of lung cancer after tobacco, negatively impacting public health. The presence of
this gas indoors tends to increase in regions were the subsoil presents
a higher granitic prevalence, such as the northern and central interior
regions of Portugal. The paper introduces RnMonitor, a Cyber-Physical
System (CPS) with humans-in-the-loop specifically designed for online
monitoring and active mitigation of radon risk in public buildings. The
system takes advantage of an IoT device specifically designed to acquire
radon concentration and other relevant Indoor Air Quality (IAQ) and
consequently transmit the collected data, using a low-power wide-area
network (LPWAN), to a cloud-engine for reasoning and therefore trigger
specific mitigation actions, e.g. manual ventilation.

Keywords: Cyber-Physical Systems · IoT · Radon

1 Introduction

Radon is a naturally occurring radioactive gas classified by the World Health
Organization (WHO) as the second most important cause of lung cancer after
tobacco [1,2]. Its presence tends to increase in regions where the subsoil has
granitic prevalence, such as the northern and central interior regions of Portugal. In poorly ventilated indoor environments it can easily accumulate, which
negatively impacts the Indoor Air Quality (IAQ). Recently, several studies have
been carried out in the Minho region, northwest of Portugal, and evidences
that the Portuguese Legal limit was being largely exceeded, have been found in
several samples, cf. [3–6]. In order to mitigate the associated human exposure
risk, the design and development of the RnMonitor platform, hereby presented,

© ICST Institute for Computer Sciences, Social Informatics and Telecommunications Engineering 2020
Published by Springer Nature Switzerland AG 2020. All Rights Reserved
H. Santos et al. (Eds.): SmartCity 360 2019, LNICST 323, pp. 49–55, 2020.
https://doi.org/10.1007/978-3-030-51005-3_6

was put forward in late 2017 with the main goal of designing a Cyber-Physical System (CPS) with humans-in-the-loop to enable online monitoring and active mitigation of radon risk in public buildings. The developed system includes an IoT edge device specifically designed to collect several IAQ parameters and a LoRaWAN radio link to transmit the data to a cloud-engine for reasoning and to trigger specific mitigation actions.

2   Architecture Design and Implementation

The RnMonitor system's conceptual design can be inferred through the observation of Fig. 1. The figure depicts the three main blocks along with one use case example that includes buildings with regular human occupation. The RnMonitor platform is composed of three main building blocks: 1) IoT Edge Devices and LoRaWAN, 2) Cloud/Analytics Engine and 3) Client App/Dashboard, that will be described in more detail in the following subsections.

Conceptually, the proposed system takes advantage of IoT-based devices installed in several rooms of distinct buildings. These IoT-based devices were designed to measure, not only, the radon gas concentration, but also, other relevant IAQ parameters, such as CO_2, temperature, relative humidity and atmospheric pressure.

In the illustrated use case example, several rooms in distinct buildings are equipped with IoT-based devices that include long range and low power connectivity by means of using the LoRaWAN communications network technology. This use case contains three main events:

- **Event 1)** a specific room of Building 2 has been identified with a poor indoor air quality for a given occupation profile in a specific time interval;
- **Event 2)** following Event 1, and based on the overall building management context, the analytics engine dispatches an alarm notification to the Building Administrator;
- **Event 3)** since Building 3 has no HVAC and no active ventilation system installed, a manual ventilation action is carried out by the building administrator.

2.1   IoT Edge Devices and LoRaWAN

The IoT edge device is shown in Fig. 2a, having been designed to measure IAQ parameters, such as CO_2, temperature, relative humidity, atmospheric pressure and radon gas concentrations, cf. [7,8]. Connectivity is made available through LoRa, a Sub-GHz technology that can be used with the LoRaWAN stack to enable long range and low power networking. Moreover, by using LoRaWAN we are not depending on local and specific infrastructures, such as Wi-Fi or Ethernet, that due to security issues are normally closed for third party applications. Figure 2b illustrates estimated LoRaWAN coverage in Viana do Castelo, the city where this technology demonstrator is being put forward.

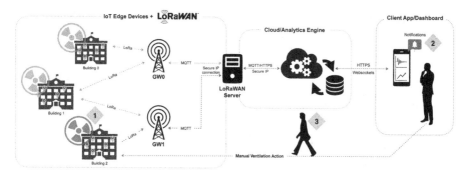

Fig. 1. Concept specification with three events: *Event 1)* a specific room of Building 2 has been identified with poor indoor air quality for given occupation profile in a specific time interval; *Event 2)* following Event 1, an alarm notification is sent to the Building Administrator; *Event 3)* since the building has no HVAC and no active ventilation system installed, a manual ventilation action is carried out by the building administrator. Image from [9].

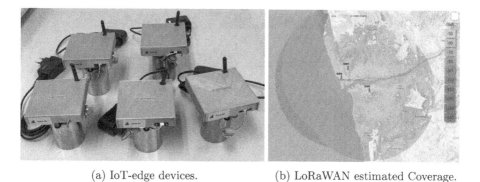

(a) IoT-edge devices.   (b) LoRaWAN estimated Coverage.

Fig. 2. IoT Edge Devices and LoRaWAN estimated Coverage in Viana do Castelo [9].

2.2   Cloud/Analytics Engine

This block stores the data collected by the IoT edge devices. It is responsible for the reasoning and data analytical processing, implemented by an Extract, Transform and Load (ETL) process that computes a set of metrics and indicators for distinct time periods: Real-Time (last hour), Very-Short-Term (last day), Short-Term (last 7 days) and Long-Term (last year), based on a specific building/compartment occupancy profile.

The usage of Occupation Profiles provides a better Radon Risk Assessment in metrics computation because it only uses radon concentration data that are inside the time periods associated with the occupancy profile. It also provides the system API and notification services. To generate the dashboard for an easy user interface, Grafana as-a-service was used, which is directly connected to the time-series database.

The GIS services are available via Geoserver with the integration of the geospatial collections of the MongoDB, which contain a "2dsphere" index that calculate geometries on an earth-like shape. Detailed information of the platform architecture can be found in [9].

2.3   ClientApp/Dashboard

RnMonitor is a web-based application designed for high-level building management. The main purpose of the ClientApp is to provide data visualization that allow users to quickly view dashboards and receive real-time notifications. The application is map-centered and has GIS techonolgies integrated, i.e. OpenLayers and Geoserver, which provide a better visual data analysis enabling the establishment of native and geo-referenced hierarchies between entities, cf. Fig. 3, which can be buildings, rooms or devices. Selecting an entity will render a customized dashboard, showing metrics and indicators that were previously defined for radon management according to the occupation profile.

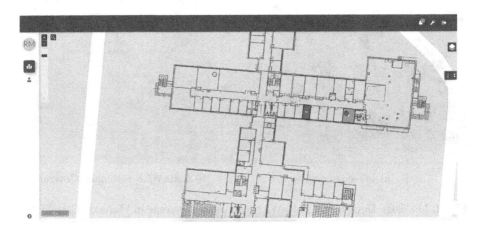

Fig. 3. Building view with distinct compartments identified.

3   Case Study - Demonstration

Figure 4a shows the map-centered interface. This is what the user is prompted after he logs in. The map changes the zoom and centroid based on the polygons that the user is managing. The map has two types of features defined as layers - Sensor and Polygon. Each feature is represented by a color which is associated with the Radon Risk Indicator, in case of polygons, and by the radon legal limit, in case of a sensor. The colors go from a range of Green - Safe, to Yellow - Warning, Orange - Alert, and Red - Critical, which change in real-time, triggering notification alerts to the sensor/polygon owner.

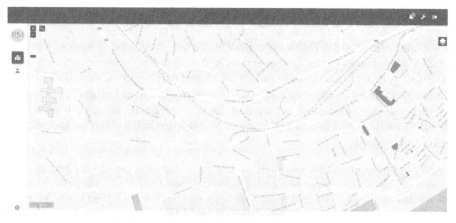

(a) City view with distinct buildings identified.

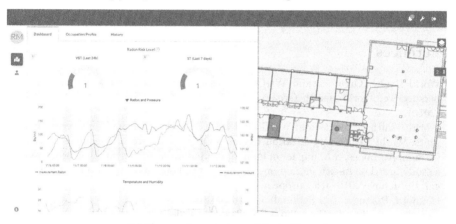

(b) Compartment view with dashboard.

Fig. 4. Client application views. a) City level and b) specific building/compartment with dashboard. (Color figure online)

If the user selects a feature, a new tab opens up as shown in Figure 4b, displaying three tabs corresponding to Dashboard, Occupation Profile and History. In the Dashboard tab, charts are displayed with data of 7 days and indicators corresponding to three periods of data range - Very-Short-Term (VST) for periods of 24 h, Short-Term (ST) for periods of 1 week to 3 months and Long-Term (LT) for periods higher then 3 months.

The Occupation Profile tab displays a form with data from the occupancy period of the polygon. For example, a public building has an occupation period of Monday to Friday, from 9 a.m. to 5 p.m. Using occupancy profiles, the system is able to compute effective Radon Risk Indicators. The History tab allows the user to search and view data on a specific time-range.

4   Conclusions and Future Work

This paper presents the RnMonitor platform, part of a Cyber-Physical System (CPS) with humans-in-the-loop specifically designed for online monitoring and active mitigation of radon risk in public buildings, with focus on its main features and functionalities. Future work will include the expansion of LoRaWAN network coverage and the long-term evaluation of the proposed platform with several IoT edge devices deployed in a set of potential problematic buildings in the Minho region in Portugal.

Acknowledgements. This contribution has been developed in the context of the Project "RnMonitor - Online Monitoring Infrastructure and Active Mitigation Strategies for Indoor Radon Gas in Public Buildings on the Northern Region of Portugal (Ref. POCI-01- 0145-FEDER-023997)" funded by FEDER (Fundo Europeu de Desenvolvimento Regional) through Operational Programme for Competitiveness and Internationalization (POCI).

References

1. World Health Organization: WHO handbook on indoor radon - a public health perspective. World Health Organization Regional Office for Europe, Copenhagen (2010)
2. World Health Organization: WHO guidelines for indoor air quality: selected pollutants. World Health Organization Regional Office for Europe, Copenhagen (2010)
3. Curado, A., Lopes, S.I.: impact of human occupation on indoor radon concentration: a study based on in-situ measurements for a set of households in Alto-Minho, Portugal. In: Behave 2016–4th European Conference on Behaviour and Energy Efficiency, Coimbra, Portugal, 8–9 September 2016 (2016)
4. Curado, A., Silva, J., Carvalho, L., Lopes, S.I.: Indoor Radon concentration assessment in a set of single family houses: case study held in Barcelos, North of Portugal. Energy Procedia **136**, 109–114 (2017). ISSN 1876–6102. https://doi.org/10.1016/j.egypro.2017.10.295
5. Lopes, S.I., Silva, J.P., Antão, A., Curado, A.: Short-term characterization of the indoor air radon concentration in a XII century monastery converted into a school building. Energy Procedia **153**, 303–308 (2018). ISSN 1876–6102. https://doi.org/10.1016/j.egypro.2018.10.036
6. Curado, A., Silva, J.P., Lopes, S.I.: Radon Risk Management in public buildings in northwest Portugal: from short-term characterization to the design of specific mitigation actions. Int. J. Recent Technol. Eng. 8(1), 90–96 (2019). ISSN 2277–3878
7. Lopes, S.I., et al.: On the design of a Human-in-the-Loop Cyber-Physical System for online monitoring and active mitigation of indoor Radon gas concentration. In: 2018 IEEE International Smart Cities Conference (ISC2), Kansas City, MO, USA, pp. 1–8 (2018). https://doi.org/10.1109/ISC2.2018.8656777

8. Lopes, Sérgio I., Pereira, Felisberto, Vieira, José M.N., Carvalho, Nuno B., Curado, António: Design of compact lora devices for smart building applications. In: Afonso, João L., Monteiro, Vítor, Pinto, José Gabriel (eds.) GreeNets 2018. LNICST, vol. 269, pp. 142–153. Springer, Cham (2019). https://doi.org/10.1007/978-3-030-12950-7_12

9. Lopes, S.I., Moreira, P.M., Cruz, A.M., Martins, P., Pereira, F., Curado, A.: RnMonitor: a WebGIS-based platform for expedite in situ deployment of IoT edge devices and effective Radon Risk Management. In: 2019 IEEE International Smart Cities Conference (ISC2), Casablanca, Morocco, pp. 451–457 (2019). https://doi.org/10.1109/ISC246665.2019.9071789

Air Quality Monitor and Forecast in Norway Using NB-IoT and Machine Learning

Andreas Lepperød[1], Hai Thanh Nguyen[1,2(✉)], Sigmund Akselsen[2],
Leendert Wienhofen[2], Pinar Øzturk[1], and Weiqing Zhang[2]

[1] Norwegian University of Science and Technology, Trondheim, Norway
`hai.nguyen@ntnu.no`
[2] Telenor ASA, Fornebu, Norway

Abstract. In recent years, air quality has become a significant environmental and health related issue due to rapid urbanization and industrialization. As a consequence, real-time monitoring and precise prediction of air quality gained increased importance. In this paper, we present a complete solution to this problem by using NB-IoT (Narrowband-Internet-of-Things) sensors and machine learning techniques. This solution includes our own compiled cheap micro-sensor devices that are planned to be deployed at stationary locations as well as on the moving vehicles to provide a comprehensive overview of air quality in the city. We developed our own IoT data and analysis platform to support the gathering of air quality data as well as weather and traffic data from external sources. We applied seven machine learning methods to predict air quality in the next 48-h, which showed promising results. Finally, we developed a mobile application named Lufta, which is now available in Google play for testing purposes.

Keywords: Air quality · Internet of Things · Machine learning

1 Introduction

Air quality has increasingly attracted attention from environment managers and citizens all over the world. New tools continue to emerge to raise air quality awareness worldwide. Continuous improvements in air quality monitoring are occurring along with the advancements of smart cities and with the rapidly increasing deployment of internet-of-things sensor devices. As a natural consequence, air pollution forecasting has become a hot topic, aiming the prediction of the atmospheric composition of pollutants at a given time and location. With an accurate air quality forecast, individuals can take action to reduce the possible adverse effects of air pollution on their health, such as choosing the cleanest routes for the commute or the best time for outdoor activities. From the

© ICST Institute for Computer Sciences, Social Informatics and Telecommunications Engineering 2020
Published by Springer Nature Switzerland AG 2020. All Rights Reserved
H. Santos et al. (Eds.): SmartCity 360 2019, LNICST 323, pp. 56–67, 2020.
https://doi.org/10.1007/978-3-030-51005-3_7

policy-making perspective, accurate forecasting contributes to better planning and establishment of procedures to reduce the severity of local pollution levels.

Much effort has already been made by researchers to create accurate forecasting models capable of fitting the underlying time series, which is challenging for various reasons. Often, air quality prediction involves a noisy and limited amount of historical data, mainly due to the poor quality of sensors used. Furthermore, the prediction of a single observation usually depends on many factors, such as weather conditions, traffic flow, time of the week, and so on. Besides, the air changes rapidly in short time frames, with hourly data being more uncertain compared with monthly and yearly trends and seasonality. These problems make it hard to generalize a created model to be transferable to other locations.

We studied air quality monitoring and forecasting in Trondheim, one of the largest cities in Norway. Typically, and similar to many other cities in Scandinavia, the air quality in Trondheim is on average at a healthy level but has periods with severe pollution, especially in the winter months. This is mainly because people drive a lot and use wood-burners during wintertime. Also, municipalities often put sand on the roads to make them less slippery under conditions with snow and ice.

We developed a complete solution for air quality monitoring and forecasting using Narrowband IoT (NB-IoT) and machine learning. Our holistic IoT solution contains self-compiled micro-sensor devices, IoT data platform, and analytics tools [1]. The solution aggregates different data sources and performs air quality prediction by using machine learning methods. We also developed a mobile application named Lufta [2] to visualize the air quality data as well as to give users forecast information.

Our study demonstrates the benefits of machine learning for predicting general patterns of air pollutants and foresees sudden spikes of a high pollution level. The study has tested seven different machine learning algorithms for modeling and forecasting the pollution of $PM_{2.5}$, PM10, and NO2. The data of pollutants, and meteorological and traffic data with statistical temporal-spatial feature engineering were taken into account to build models for multi-step-ahead air quality forecasts for 24 and 48-h. Results express that ensemble techniques could significantly improve the stability and accuracy of the prediction of the general trends of air quality. Among the ensemble techniques, gradient boosting with dropouts resulted in prediction errors with the lowest deviation. For the prediction of sudden changes in air pollution, using a recurrent neural network with a memory unit provided the highest accuracy of classified spikes. Lastly, the machine learning results were compared with that of the national air quality services, which uses a knowledge-driven model. The predictions of general patterns and anomalies are shown to be superior for 24-h, and more comparable results for the 48-h forecasts. The data-driven approach is considered to be an excellent complement for the knowledge-driven model.

2   State of the Art on Air Quality Prediction

Air quality prediction methods can be split into two main categories: classical deterministic models and data-driven models [3]. The traditional dispersion models consist of heavy domain knowledge of air quality behavior with expertise from multiple areas among other on chemical, emission, and climatological processes. These factors help to create complex numerical models to predict the future. However, these dispersion models are computationally heavy and expensive in maintenance. The second category refers to data-driven models, where various machine learning methods have been applied to predict air pollution.

2.1   Influential Variables

Due to the complexity of air quality behavior, it is crucial to include multiple influential variables. In recent studies, several pollutants and meteorological variables have been included. The different pollutants are often PM_x, NO_x, SO_x, CO_x, Ozone, and VOC. Meteorological variables are those which describe the weather and the atmospheric composition. The most common meteorological variables are temperature, pressure, humidity, and surface wind with speed and direction. The meteorological variables vary from location to location and affect air pollution differently. Various air pollutants and meteorological variables have been extensively studied in the literature [4,6–8,12,13,15]. Other variables such as traffic [5] and weather forecast [4,6,11,16] have been investigated to find their relations with air quality changes.

2.2   Air Quality Prediction Methods

Multiple research studies apply variations of Recurrent Neural Networks (RNN) to capture temporal dependencies. [6] includes an LSTM model to learn short-term and long-term temporal dependencies by using the weather forecast. [9] adopts an LSTM solution on IoT sensor data to perform short-term prediction. [12] provides a performance overview of different RNN cells and concludes that GRU cell has a slightly higher accuracy of learning PM10 concentration. [13] consists of an LSTM model that considers spatio-temporal relations for predicting air quality concentrations. From their results comparing an extended LSTM to SVR, deep learning-based models exhibit better prediction.

Multiple specialized multilayer perceptron (MLP) networks [11] were implemented for each weather class, determined by clustering. They further learn the relation between a high concentration of air pollutants and different weather classes to improve the classification of sudden spikes. In [17], they show how a deep learning regression model can learn patterns of pollutants and weather data collected from 449 sensors all around Aarhus city in Denmark. Their DNN model can outperform SVM in predictions of the next hour.

In [10], they use fuzzy inference of the results from an ensemble of random forest (RF) and feed-forward neural network. They combine the power of a non-linear relationship in a neural network and the averaging strategies of an ensemble approach to generalize the results. [14] predicts daily NO2 exposure and compares an RF model with an LR model at a national scale. [15] also applied an RF model to predict $PM_{2.5}$ with features including other pollutants and meteorological variables. Their RF model shows better performance than their implementation of a generalized additive model.

2.3 Norwegian Air Quality Service

A new nationwide air quality information service was launched on December 18th, 2018 in Norway, by the Norwegian Environment Agency, which will be referenced in this paper as MET [18]. Their urban EMEP (uEMEP) model is a downscaling model of EMEP, a knowledge-driven model that calculates the transboundary transport of air pollutants [19]. uEMEP initiates with low spatial data (10 km-2.5 km resolution) from the EMEP model, which is scaled down to an approximately 50 m grid resolution based on proxy data from each grid. The proxy data consist of meteorological forecasts, historical emissions and traffic volume, and geographic variables. Each grid calculates its local contribution of emissions and with a Gaussian model to find non-local concentrations.

Notable strengths of uEMEP are its consideration of all primary sources of air quality pollution with a direct connection to weather forecasts and geographical terrain. Although adding weather forecasts into the model is a strength, it can also be a weakness if the forecasts deviate from the real values and thereby induce warnings of too high or low air pollution levels.

3   Complete Solution

This section introduces the complete solution we developed for air quality monitoring and forecasting using NB-IoT and machine learning. The overall architecture is presented in Fig. 1.

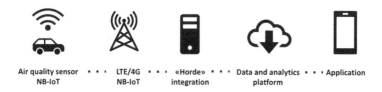

Fig. 1. IoT pipeline.

3.1   Air Quality NB-IoT Sensor Device

Recent progress in sensory and communication technologies has made the development of portable air-quality micro-sensing devices feasible. For our project, a device consisting of a board with sensors and a communication modem was compiled[1]. The initial price of this device was around EUR 100, excluding costs tied to writing software for the integration of parts. The sensors report levels of particle dust ($PM_{2.5}$ and PM10), temperature, humidity, CO2 equivalents, and VOC equivalents. The communication modem includes a GPS module, and it supports both LTE-M and NB-IoT connectivity[2]. So far, only off-the-shelf low-cost micro-sensors have been used in these designs. In the first version, a particle sensor made by Honeywell was used[3].

The quality of data from micro-sensors has been questioned, and there is a need for assessment of the sensors' performance in varied applications and environments. This need has been addressed by [20]. An initial test of the data quality from the device compiled in this project (compared to an industrial sensor of particle dust in the same location) was made, indicating that the measurements were influenced by variations in temperature, humidity, and pollutant levels. A thorough and systematic testing of the differences in performance between our micro-sensor devices and the standardized industrial equipment over time remains to be done. Based on the initial test, we decided to use data only from the standardized industrial equipment for training the machine learning models (see Chap. 4). The plan for this project includes systematic testing of micro-sensor devices with more expensive components and various designs, e.g., positioning and structure of the inlet which tends to have a big impact on the measurement quality of PM devices. Depending on the results of these tests a number of micro-sensor devices will be deployed throughout the city and on vehicles. The initial plan is in the range of 25–50 devices.

3.2 IoT Data Platform and Analytics

The Lambda Architecture [21] is used in the design of the air quality data platform. The architecture is a data-processing architecture designed to handle massive quantities of data by taking advantage of both batch-processing and stream-processing methods. It attempts to balance latency, throughput, and fault-tolerance by using batch processing to provide comprehensive and accurate views of batch data, while simultaneously using real-time stream processing to provide views of online data. The IoT data platform adopts the Lambda Architecture in its design to build a robust system that is fault-tolerant and able to serve a wide range of workloads and low-latency reads and updates.

---

[1] https://blog.exploratory.engineering/post/where-the-air-is-crisp/.

[2] The modem is based on Nordic Semiconductor technology, see https://www.nordicsemi.com/Products/Low-power-cellular-IoT/nRF9160 and had an indicative price of USD 45, see https://shop.exploratory.engineering/.

[3] Honeywell HPM Series, Particle Sensor, 32322550, Issue E, using a light scattering method. The price of this sensor measuring both $PM_{2.5}$ and PM10 was less than 40 USD as of November 2018.

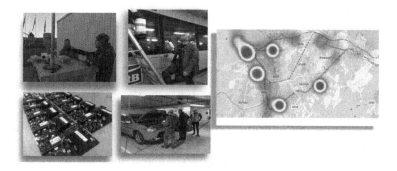

Fig. 2. Air quality micro-sensor devices mounted to buses and stationary locations

In this project, we use the Horde IoT data platform [1] (beta version) from Telenor Exploratory Engineering team to support running NB-IoT devices experiments quickly and efficiently. Horde handles data encryption and provides backend services to manage IoT devices, inspect payloads, share devices between team members, and send data from the devices. Through Horde, users are able to get data online quickly either as a WebSocket (for a simple single-page web apps) or WebHooks (for a quick demo service), and into IFTTT (known as IF This Then That [23], a free web-based service to create chains of simple conditional statements, for quick prototypes and hackathons) or MQTT (Message Queuing Telemetry Transport [22], for flexible and reliable delivery) (Fig. 2).

3.3   Mobile Application for Air Quality Monitoring and Forecasting

The mobile application we developed, named Lufta, is now available in Google Play for testing purpose [2]. The app analyses the aggregated data provided by both sensors in stationary locations as well as sensors mounted to moving vehicles. That gives users the possibility to have a better and real-time monitoring of air quality in the areas where they live. In the app, users can also see recommendations or set up to get notifications about the level of air quality, whether it is good, moderate, or bad. We plan to provide the forecast information to users in the app as well through APIs to third parties.

4   Experiment for Exploring Air Quality Prediction

This section describes the experiments performed in the project. First, in Subsect. 4.1, we introduce the experimental setting, including the description of datasets, extracted features, machine learning methods used, and the evaluation metrics. Next, the experiment results are presented in Subsect. 4.2.

4.1 Experimental Settings

Dataset. Because of the unstable data provided by our micro-sensors during the testing phase, we decided to do our experiments with the data from expensive sensors given by the Norwegian Institute for Air Research through open APIs [24]. Four air quality stations are used in this research. Air quality in Trondheim has improved due to initiatives taken by the municipality, such as road cleaning and dust suppression. Thus the data analysis and machine learning models utilized data from January 2014 to April 2019 to avoid learning on too old data with unrelated distributions.

The weather dataset consists mainly of the hourly data recorded at a station at Voll in Trondheim, which includes features like temperature, precipitation, humidity, pressure, wind speed, and wind direction. The traffic data consists of traffic information on the road network in Trondheim. The traffic information was included by taking the mean of the closest three traffic stations for each of the locations predicted. The recorded variables are hourly vehicle count in both driving directions. This paper uses the sum of the numbers of passing vehicles in both driving directions and assumes that this sum of recordings is sufficient for analyzing the relationship between traffic and air pollutants (Fig. 3).

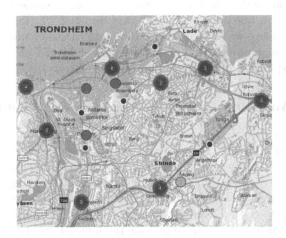

Fig. 3. Map of the data stations in Trondheim where red marks show air quality stations, pink is a weather station, and blue (small and large) is traffic stations. The numbers within the circles are indicators of the total number of stations in that area. (Color figure online)

Extracted Features. The extracted features are divided into different categories. See Fig. 4 for an overview of all with their shorthand ID, type, feature, and a short description. In this paper, we deal with three kinds of features that measure some qualities in nature (meteorological, air quality, and traffic). We also identify three types of features (temporal, statistical, and spatial). In total, we have used 655 high-level extracted features.

ID	Type	Feature	Description
M	Meteorological	humidity	Hourly average relative humidity (%)
		pressure	Hourly average surface pressure (Pa)
		temperature	Hourly average air temperature (°C)
		wind direction	Hourly average wind direction (degrees)
		wind speed	Hourly average wind speed (m/s)
		precipitation	Hourly measured sum of precipitation (mm)
O	Air Quality	PM2.5	Hourly measured particular dust below 2.5 $\mu g/m$
		PM10	Hourly measured particular dust above 2.5 $\mu g/m$
		NO2	Hourly measured ($\mu g/m$)
		NO	Hourly measured ($\mu g/m$)
		NOx	Hourly measured ($\mu g/m$)
V	Traffic	Traffic volume	Hourly traffic count
T	Temporal	hour	Hour of the timestamp (0-23)
		month	Month of the timestamp (1-12)
		day of week	Day of week of the timestamp (0-6)
		day of month	Day of month of the timestamp (0-30)
		holiday	Is the day of the timestamp a Norwegian holiday
		season	The timestamp season (1-4)
		N lagged of X	X parameter during the past N hours
C	Statistical	Moving Average	Moving average, $n = [3, 6, 12]$
		Difference	Difference between previous values, $n = [3, 6, 12]$
		Deviation	Deviation from previous values, $n = [3, 12, 24]$
		Minimum	Minimum of previous values, $n = [24, 48]$
		Maximum	Maximum of previous values, $n = [24, 48]$
S	Spatial	PM2.5	Mean value of neighbouring stations
		PM10	Mean value of neighbouring stations
		NO2	Mean value of neighbouring stations
		NO	Mean value of neighbouring stations
		NOx	Mean value of neighbouring stations

Fig. 4. The final set of extracted feature

The temporal features are mainly generated by the use of the timestamp of the measurement. The timestamp includes information of the hour of the day, the day of the week, the day of the month, the month, and the season of the year. The Norwegian holiday calendar is matched against the date to see if it is a day off. The last temporal feature is created out of the historical values of the parameter. The spatial features contain properties from neighboring stations. These are calculated from the mean of the nearby stations. These features are included to help the models capture spatial relations of the air quality.

The statistical features are produced by applying a set of mathematical functions to the time series to derive unique properties, such as lagged value difference, moving average, moving standard deviation, moving minimum, and moving maximum, as shown in Fig. 4. The goal of statistical features is to add a more general and broader temporal dependency by including historical values. The statistical functions will consist of a smarter relation of the past, that the models will easier learn. The statistical features will provide reliable and more straightforward ties between the past and the forecasts. Statistical feature engineering can help smooth the raw values of the time series to decipher the complexity. The functions minimum, maximum, and moving average are used to capture trends in the series. The difference and deviation can help to detect sudden changes by learning what happened just before the change.

Machine Learning Models. It was decided to implement seven forecasting techniques, each with its unique trait, and identified as potentially advantageous approaches for air quality prediction. Autoregressive Integrated Moving Average

(ARIMA) and Ridge Regression (Ridge) had been applied to time series problems with reliable results in the past. Multilayer Perceptron (MLP) and Random Forest (RF) had been used in the recent literature with reliable results within air quality prediction problems. A version of Recurrent Neural Network with Gated Recurrent Unit cells (GRU) was included due to its predicting powers of time series problems. Finally, because of the ability of gradient boosting to minimize error in complex problem domains, and because it is less used in the literature, two unique variations of gradient boosting were implemented, Gradient Boosting Decision Tree (GBM) and Dropouts meet Multiple Additive Regression Trees (DART).

Gradient Boosting implemented with Microsoft's version of LightGBM [25]. It is an optimized version of gradient boosting and is faster with the same accuracy than its competitors XGBoost and Scikit Learns version. In this paper, we use the implementation of the traditional GBM, and DART. PyTorch is used to implement the Recurrent Neural Network (RNN) model. The implementation can utilize either GRU or LSTM cells. Several model hyperparameters were optimized using randomized search; the RNN cell (LSTM or GRU), number of layers, number of RNN cells, learning rate, sequence length, dropout rate, and batch size.

Evaluation Metrics. In the literature of air quality, there is no single superior evaluation method. For our experiments, we have used the set of multiple performance metrics, including Mean Absolute Error (MAE), Relative Absolute Error (RAE), and Root Mean Squared Error (RMSE). However, because of the limitation on the number of pages in this paper, we chose to present the RAE results only. Other evaluation metrics provided consistent results.

In addition to regular air quality patterns, it frequently occurs sudden changes in the pollution concentration, which are essential to predict for real-time monitoring as they can have more impact on the daily life of most people. While the evaluation metrics defined in the previous section cover the total error and how good the model fit the actual values, they are not suitable metrics for anomaly prediction. Instead, we used the F1-Score as the evaluation metric for anomaly prediction. The predicted anomalies are matched against the real observed time series and are counted as hits if they were in the span of 1 h into the past and 1 h into the future. The smoothing and interval calculation will then account for a range of 4 h that needs to overlap. The interval of 4 h is fine since a typical sudden change lasts for about 4–6 h, and there are few partial overlaps of lengthy anomalies in the time series dataset. This straightforward approach for anomaly prediction ignores the residuals of the predicted spikes, but it related well to classifying the specific warning levels. These warning levels (good, OK, or bad) are a simple indicator for the city populations to grasp the air quality at their location.

4.2   Experimental Results

The models are trained on data from 1. January 2014, to 30. November 2018, and tested on data until 30. April 2019. The results are split up into two evaluations where the first concerned with the model's regression error for general air quality pattern, while the second for its classification accuracy toward anomaly prediction of sudden changes and spikes. All results are shown in Fig. 5. As we can see, the DART model performed the best in terms of predicting the ordinary situations of air quality whereas the GRU model provided the best results in predicting spikes in air quality pollution.

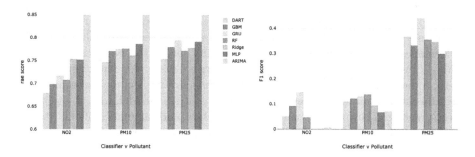

Fig. 5. Models performance RAE (left chart) and anomaly prediction F1-score (right chart) with different pollutants.

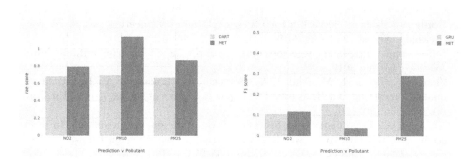

Fig. 6. Results of regression error RAE (left chart) and anomaly prediction F1-score (right chart) grouped by pollutant type.

We compared the results of machine learning predictions with the Norwegian national air quality service, a knowledge-driven model described in Sect. 2. The evaluation of the results is presented in two parts in Fig. 6: The first includes the RAE regression error of 24-h predictions. The second evaluation shows the results of the accuracy of classifying anomalies found. Our tested machine learning models DART and GRU outperformed the MET expert-based forecast model in both ordinary situations and in case of sudden changes in the air quality.

5 Conclusion

We have developed a complete solution for air quality monitoring and forecasting, which contains the holistic IoT pipeline with our own developed micro-sensors, IoT data platform, data analytics, machine learning for prediction, and mobile app for visualization. The goal of this study is to evaluate the performance of machine learning methods for air quality prediction in Trondheim. We started with an analysis of datasets of Trondheim, including air pollutants, historical weather observations, traffic volume count, and wood burners. Further, we created more features with statistical feature engineering and tested multiple state-of-the-art machine learning techniques. Seven machine learning models were implemented, optimized, trained, and tested to determine the strengths and weaknesses of air quality prediction. The results showed that DART has the best performance of predicting the overall air quality for all the pollutants studied ($PM_{2.5}$, PM10, NO2). We found that GRU can classify sudden changes better than the other methods. Lastly, the machine learning results were compared with the national air quality service, a knowledge-driven model, to evaluate real-world practice. The predictions of general pattern and anomalies of this study are shown to be superior for 24-h, and more comparable for the 48-h forecast.

Acknowledgements. This work is part of the AI4EU project (https://www.ai4eu.eu/) which has received funding from the European Union's Horizon 2020 research and innovation program, under the Grant Agreement No 825619.

References

1. Horde IoT Backend Service. https://blog.exploratory.engineering/post/horde-iot-backend/. Accessed 13 Aug 2019
2. Lufta app. https://play.google.com/store/apps/details?id=com.luftaapp.lufta. Accessed 13 Aug 2019
3. Zhang, Y., Bocquet, M., Mallet, V., Seigneur, C., Baklanov, A.: Real-time air quality forecasting, part I: history, techniques, and current status. Atmos. Environ. **60**, 632–655 (2012a)
4. Yi, X., et al.: Deep distributed fusion network for air quality prediction. In: Proceedings of the 24th ACM SIGKDD International Conference on Knowledge Discovery & Data Mining (KDD 2018), pp. 965–973. ACM, New York. https://doi.org/10.1145/3219819.3219822
5. Chen, L., et al.: Spatially fine-grained urban air quality estimation using ensemble semi-supervised learning and pruning. In: International Joint Conference on Pervasive and Ubiquitous Computing, pp. 1076–1087. ACM (2016)
6. Wang, J., Song, G.: A deep spatial-temporal ensemble model for air quality prediction. Neuro Comput. **314**, 198–206 (2018)
7. Qi, Z., et al.: Deep air learning: interpolation, prediction, and feature analysis of fine-grained air quality. IEEE Trans. Knowl. Data Eng. **30**(12), 2285–2297 (2018)
8. Lin, Y., et al.: Exploiting spatiotemporal patterns for accurate air quality forecasting using deep learning. In: Proceedings of the 26th ACM SIGSPATIAL International Conference on Advances in Geographic Information Systems, pp. 359–368 (2018)

9. Kök, İ., et al.: A deep learning model for air quality prediction in smart cities. In: IEEE International Conference on Big Data, pp. 1983–1990 (2017)
10. Bougoudis, I., et al.: HISYCOL a hybrid computational intelligence system for combined machine learning: the case of air pollution modeling in athens. Neural Comput. Appl. **27**(5), 1191–1206 (2016)
11. Tamas, W., et al.: Hybridization of air quality forecasting models using machine learning and clustering: an original approach to detect pollutant peaks. Aerosol Air Qual. Res. **16**, 405–416 (2016)
12. Athira, V., et al.: DeepairNet: applying recurrent networks for air quality prediction. Procedia Comput. Sci. **132**, 1394–1403 (2018)
13. Li, X., et al.: Long short-term memory neural network for air pollutant concentration predictions: method development and evaluation. Environ. Pollut. **231**, 997–1004 (2017)
14. Zhan, Y., et al.: Satellite-based estimates of daily NO2 exposure in China using hybrid random forest and spatiotemporal Kriging model. Environ. Sci. Technol. **52**(7), 4180–4189 (2018)
15. Chen, G., et al.: A machine learning method to estimate $PM_{2.5}$ concentrations across China with remote sensing, meteorological and land use information. Sci. Total Environ. **636**, 52–60 (2018)
16. Zheng, Y., et al.: Forecasting fine-grained air quality based on big data. In: Proceedings of the 21th ACM SIGKDD International Conference on Knowledge Discovery and Data Mining, pp. 2267–2276. ACM (2015)
17. Ghoneim, O.A., Manjunatha, B., et al.: Forecasting of ozone concentration in smart city using deep learning. In: 2017 International Conference on Advances in Computing, Communications and Informatics (ICACCI). IEEE, pp. 1320–1326 (2017)
18. Denby, B.R., et al.: The norwegian air quality service: model forecasting (2018). https://www.met.no/
19. Tørseth, K., et al.: Introduction to the European monitoring and evaluation programme (EMEP) and observed atmospheric composition change during 1972–2009. Atmos. Chem. Phys. **12**(12), 5447–5481 (2012)
20. Fishbain, B., et al.: An evaluation tool kit of air quality micro-sensing units. Sci. Total Environ. **575**(1), 639–648 (2017). https://doi.org/10.1016/j.scitotenv.2016.09.061
21. Kiran, M., Murphy, P., Monga, I., Dugan, J., Baveja, S.S.: Lambda architecture for cost-effective batch and speed big data processing. In: 2015 IEEE International Conference on Big Data (Big Data), Santa Clara, CA, pp. 2785–2792 (2015)
22. Singh, M., Rajan, M.A., Shivraj, V.L., Balamuralidhar, P.: Secure MQTT for Internet of Things (IoT). In: 2015 Fifth International Conference on Communication Systems and Network Technologies, Gwalior, pp. 746–751 (2015)
23. Kauling, D., Mahmoud, Q.H.: Sensorian Hub: an IFTTT-based platform for collecting and processing sensor data. In: 2017 14th IEEE Annual Consumer Communications & Networking Conference (CCNC), Las Vegas, NV 2017, pp. 504–509 (2017)
24. Norwegian Institute for Air Research. https://www.nilu.no/en/
25. Ke, G., et al.: LightGBM: a highly efficient gradient boosting decision tree. In: Advances in Neural Information Processing Systems, vol. 30, pp. 3146–3154. Curran Associates Inc. (2017)

Challenges and Limitations for the Systematic Collection of Cycling Data from Bike Sensors

Miguel Costa and Rui José[(⊠)] [iD]

Centro Algoritmi, University of Minho, Guimarães, Portugal
rui@dsi.uminho.pt

Abstract. Information and Communication Technology is increasingly recognised as a key element for the ability of cycling mobility initiatives to create real, profound, incremental and measurable impact. Even though previous work has extensively explored many applications of smart cycling data, the first challenge is to actually produce consistent cycling data in a systematic way. In this research, we explore the range of sensors which could be more relevant to integrate into urban bicycles to support the systematic collection of data about cycle routes. To gain a deeper insight into the real-world challenges of systematic cycle-based sensing, we conducted an experimental data collection. We equipped a bicycle with a diverse set of low-cost sensors, and we collected data in a pre-defined route, in which it was possible to experience very diverse environmental circumstances regarding road surface or the level of surrounding traffic. The results highlight some of the practical challenges that can be faced by systematic sensing for urban cycling, suggesting that not all sensors might be appropriate for this type of large-scale deployment on bicycles. The main contribution is a set of design implications, which should help to inform the design of novel sensing systems for bicycles.

Keywords: Bicycle sensing · Smart cycling · Mobility data

1 Introduction

Cycling is becoming a key element in smart mobility policies [1]. This new reality is emerging in a context of sustainability agendas, but also as a fundamental path towards more liveable cities, where public space is rescued from cars and given back to citizens. Information and Communication Technology (ICT) is expected to play a key role in this transition. ICT is already a dominant factor for the successful adoption of shared bicycles [2], but we can expect this trend to extend to all others forms of cycling.

Despite the wide consensus about the key role of ICT on new soft mobility paradigms, there are still no clear views on how exactly that potential can be realised. There are major challenges to be addressed, such as limited availability of data sources, their strong dispersion among multiple stakeholders and the lack of clear value propositions to help prioritizing data needs. As a consequence, the lack of systematic and consistent monitoring processes remains one of the obstacles towards more sustainable development of

© ICST Institute for Computer Sciences, Social Informatics and Telecommunications Engineering 2020
Published by Springer Nature Switzerland AG 2020. All Rights Reserved
H. Santos et al. (Eds.): SmartCity 360 2019, LNICST 323, pp. 68–79, 2020.
https://doi.org/10.1007/978-3-030-51005-3_8

cycling mobility policies [3]. This lack of information tools for soft mobility modes is a systemic problem and is also a huge challenge for municipalities and other entities, who need this type of information for their decision-making processes.

1.1 Objectives

In this research, we explore the range of sensors which could provide a systematic source of in-bike sensing data. Our main concern is the instrumentation of bicycles with sensors and the identification of any sort of constraints associated with the data collection process itself.

For this work, only bicycle embedded sensors are being considered, which excludes for example, mobile phones or wearables. Even though we consider any type of bicycle, we will use electric bicycles as our key reference to assess the viability of new sensing possibilities, as they seem to offer the most suitable context for the initial large-scale deployment of this type of embedded sensors. They already have a higher cost, meaning that the added cost of sensors can more easily be diluted within the total cost of the bicycle. Even more importantly, they already have electric power and other electronic equipment, allowing these additional sensors to benefit from the technology already present in the bicycle. Regarding sensor viability, our key assumption is that only low-cost sensors should be considered, and that their total cost should have no significant impact on the production cost of a low-end electric bicycle.

Regarding data needs, we are mainly considering the multi-dimensional character-ization of cycle routes. Data collected during a cycle route can offer multiple insights about the route, which can be valuable to the cyclist, but also to all the others cyclists and the city itself. In particular, such data could significantly help cyclists to select their routes. Those decisions can involve complex combinations of criteria and a rich charac-terization of routes could significantly the decision process. This same information could also be valuable for urban planners and particularly for assessing the cycling potential or the safety risks of existing city streets.

Our research question is about the types of sensors that could be more relevant to integrate in urban bicycles to support this type of systematic and automated collection of data about cycle routes. To seek an answer to this broader question, we need to address two more concrete objectives: The first objective is to identify a set of low-cost sensors that could provide relevant data to monitor phenomena of interest to the characterization of cycle routes. This requires a through exploration of the various types of sensors available and the analysis of their potential to help to categorize cycle routes according to the many criteria that can be used to support route choice. The second objective is to assess the implications of using those sensors in real-world cycling situations. This involves experimenting with the data collection process to access the quality and relevance of the data which can effectively be obtained within the many constraints of real-world cycling situations.

2 Related Work

Cycling is a very personal and circumstantial experience, and cyclists can consider a broad range of factors when selecting the best route to a given destination. Understanding these factors is crucial for route planning, but indirectly it is also a way to understand the vital factors which influence cycling preferences and consequently understand how cities can be enhanced to become more cycling friendly. Previous studies have identified many factors which influence route choice, including dependent attributes (e.g. trip distance, travel time, network characteristics, etc.) and generic trip attributes (e.g. socio-demographic characteristics of the cyclists, trip purpose and weather conditions) [4]. While distance and travel time are regularly mentioned as top factors, cyclists are also particularly sensitive to variables which are related to their perceived risk, such as traffic volume, road types or speed limits. A study in Minneapolis [5] analysed over 1000 rides and concluded that the chosen routes were not always the shortest, most of which included the presence of bicycle paths. A survey in the city of Vancouver, based on paper, web and phone questionnaires, has identified that cyclists prefer to ride away from the noise of car traffic and pollution, by routes with beautiful landscapes separated from traffic, by dirt-free roads and finally by streets without high-speed or heavy-haul vehicles [6]. According to Felix [7], the shortest route is not always the most attractive for cyclists, because there are other relevant factors, such as slope of path, distance or safety perception. However, the decision always depends on the rider, and can be strongly situated. Hochmair defined a set of classes of route decision criteria [8]. The best rated were Time, Safety, Simplicity and Attractiveness. Multiple factors can be associated with each class. Examples include distance, crossings, reduced light traffic, cycle paths, night time brightness, floor conditions and avoid heavy-duty traffic.

Smart phones are increasingly seen as a platform for large-scale data collection [9]. They already integrate a very vast range of sensors, enabling the collection of substantial data about people and their movements. Using the smartphone sensors of urban cyclists, the data transmitted by them can enable the generation of collective knowledge in order to improve the quality of cycling mobility. BeCity [10] is an example of a mobile application that allows all riders to share their tracks and comments, working as a distributed data collection system. It also includes the ability to recommend routes, considering factors such as distance, presence of bike paths and even the attractiveness of those paths. Another example is the BikeNet mobile application, which gathers data about the rides to provide cyclists with a general perspective of their experience and performance. This system is able to obtain information about the environment and the entire experience along the way, such as pollution levels, noise and floor condition [11].

Data gathered from sensors is often used to estimate more subjective factors, such as the quality of the road or the comfort it can provide to cyclists. Verstockt et al. [12] combined data from GPS, accelerometers and web-based geographic API's to classify the terrain type (asphalt, mud, earth, parallel). Biketastic [13] also uses smartphone's sensors to access information about location as well as an accelerometer and a microphone, capable of measuring the state of the floor and the noise level all the way. Cyclists can also provide feedback about the routes using written comments, voice clips or photos. This information can then be used to help to choose routes which are more aligned with user preferences. Aeroflex uses bicycles in an urban environment to make measurements about air quality [14]. The information captured by the system is meant to support the identification of pollution hot spots, e.g. major car intersections or industrial zones, classify streets according to their air quality and determine the exposure level to which cyclists are exposed. In our work, we are exploring which of these many forms of data collection could become a common expectation for urban cycling.

3 Experimental Data Collection

A key part of this research involved the collection and analysis of diverse forms of cycling data to gain a deeper insight about the real-world challenges of systematic cycle-based sensing. The objective is to understand the viability of the sensor deployment on the bicycle as well as the quality of the data generated.

Sensor Selection and Deployment
For this study, we considered a very diverse set of low-cost sensors, which could, as much as possible, address the very broad set of criteria which have been referred in the literature as route choice criteria. Table 1 identifies the selected sensors.

Table 1. Sensor types and corresponding route choice criteria.

#sensors	Sensor type	Route choice criteria
1	GPS	Route trace
2	Accelerometers	Road surface quality, ride smoothness
4	Distance	Number of nearby obstacles, surrounding traffic
1	CO2/VOCs	Exposure to pollution
1	Sound level	Exposure to noise
1	Light level	Sunny/shady routes
1	Environmental	Weather conditions (humidity, temperature, pressure)

To control the system, we used an Arduino UNO unit with a Qwiic card to connect to most sensors and a micro SD card to store the collected data. A LED light was also added to signal when the system is in operation. A 12 V battery was used to power the whole system.

An important element for assessing the viability of the whole approach was to analyse the implications of deploying these sensors in a bicycle for real-world usage. In this work, we only considered the implications of sensor position and connection. We did not consider other issues such as protection against theft, vandalism or exposure to environmental elements. The deployment of the sensors was made easier by the existence of a front basket in the bicycle. The basket provided a natural and valuable context for placing the Arduino Unit and its battery, which were both placed inside the basket. Many sensors were also attached to the basket to facilitate the cable connections with the Arduino unit. In a production bicycle, these devices would have to be embedded within the bicycle itself, which could produce additional deployment constraints.

Fig. 1. Prototype bicycle for data collection

Sensor deployment had to be made according to the particular properties of each sensor. Placement was absolutely critical for some of those sensors, while largely irrelevant for others. In Fig. 1, we can visualize the prototype for data collection, with the various sensors placed at key locations according to their properties.

We had to consider the specific placement requirements associated with distance and light sensors, which were meant to assess proximity to obstacles or moving vehicles or people. They were placed pointing at four distinct directions: forward, right, left and rear. For the placement of the first three, we took advantage of the existence of the bicycle basket, where it was easier to accommodate them all, while complying with directional requirements. The fourth sensor, on the rear, was attached directly to the bicycle frame underneath the seat. The light sensor was also placed facing up in the same basket to maximise exposure to light. It was also placed as far as possible from the cyclist, in this case at the front of the bicycle basket, to reduce the interference of the cyclist's shadow in the collected data. With accelerometers, we considered the need to support slightly different sensing goals. A first sensor was attached to the bicycle frame to maximise the sensing of vibrations. This should be the key data source to assess the smoothness of the road, as well as the use of brakes. A second accelerometer was placed on the handlebar and could serve mainly to assess the smoothness of driving and possibly assess the frequency and intensity of turn movements.

Data Collection Route
To optimize data collection, we defined a specific route, which included streets with various levels of traffic, different road surfaces, areas with natural shade and potentially more polluted areas. The data collection involved 3 rides conducted by two distinct cyclists on three different occasions. As a complement to the sensors, we also used an action camera. This camera was attached to the bicycle and facing forward. Its purpose was to serve as a source of ground truth data to help with the interpretation of the sensor data. Likewise, we also used the MapMyRide mobile application, to register the track and later export it as a GPX file with longitude and latitude data.

Data Analysis
While previous work has already proposed a broad range of data analysis techniques for route characterisation from raw sensor data, the shortage of data remains a major

problem for a more systematic use of those techniques. Consequently, our assessment of the data collected was mainly focused on the perspective of its quality and its viability to support common use cases of automated route characterisation.

To support this type of analysis, we developed a set of python scripts to process the data and produce relevant visualizations. For each source, we produced a set of quantitative indicators, mainly in the form of common summary statistics, such as the count, mean, standard deviation, minimum value, maximum value, and quadrant distribution (25%, 50%, 75%). This was complemented with graphic visualizations of the respective time series, which provided important insights into outliers and other abnormal cases. Additionally, we also used the ELAN tool [15] to synchronize the various data sources and link them with the video feed captured by the action camera (c.f. Figure 2).

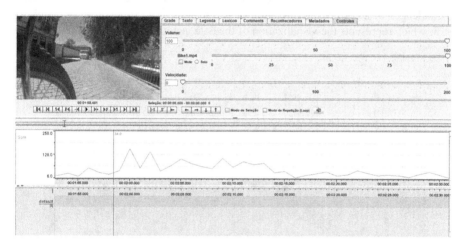

Fig. 2. Elan displaying the video feed and the sound data capture

Even though the video feed was not explored as a data source on its own, it played an important role in this study as a ground truth source. More specifically, it allowed us to explore the concrete situations in which data had been generated and seek to understand the connection between data variations and specific events.

4   Results

The assessment made for the various types of sensors in this study has shown interesting insights about the potential of the various sensors for systematic sensing in a cycling context. The sensors for pressure, humidity and temperature have all behaved as expected, but they did not seem to be the most relevant. Given the relatively low spatial resolution of these data, it can be efficiently obtained through a smaller number of sensors, possibly more reliable ones, at fixed locations around the city.

Regarding accelerometers, we also obtained the type of results which was expectable. This type of sensor is known to be reliable and even low-cost sensors seem to provide a robust data source for most of the more common use cases, e.g. inferring road conditions or level of driving smoothness. We will now focus the analysis on the cases where we were able to uncover more meaningful insights.

4.1 Distance Sensors

In our data collection prototype, we included 4 IR distance sensors, which were supposed to provide data to access the level of obstacles within a short range of the bicycle. These could be buildings, walls, people, parked cars, or traffic in general. The sensors had a 4 meters range and they were placed on the bicycle to cover all the surroundings of the bicycle, at the front, right, left and rear sides. In this case, the data produced has shown multiple incoherences, which might mean that these low-cost sensors were not the most suitable for this task. To better understand the nature of the data produced and the challenges of a correct interpretation of its meaning, we can analyse the graph in Fig. 3, which represents the visualization of the data generated by the front sensor.

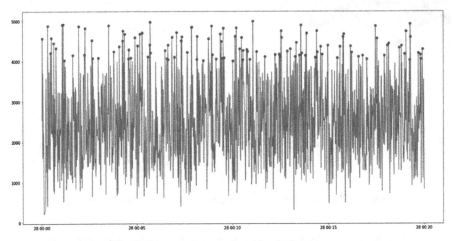

Fig. 3. Distance data produced by the front sensor

The red dots in the graph are signalling the cases where the distance produced exceeded the maximum sensor range of 4 meters (4000 mm). This data seems to suggest the very frequent presence of all sorts of obstacles in front of the bicycle. Data is quickly changing from just about 50 cm to more than 4 meters. However, by comparing this data with the video stream, we were able to confirm that only very rarely there was actually any obstacle within the 4 meters in front of the bicycle. This suggests that the operational requirements for this type of sensing context are not compatible with the type of low-cost distance sensor used in our study. Very similar results were obtained with the other distance sensors, as shown in Fig. 4, which represents right and left sensors.

Once more we can observe an extreme and frequent variation of the data. The first graph represents the data from the right-side sensor and the second from the left side sensor. In this case, the apparently closer distance to objects observed in the right-side sensor seems to be aligned with the intuitive idea that there are normally closer objects

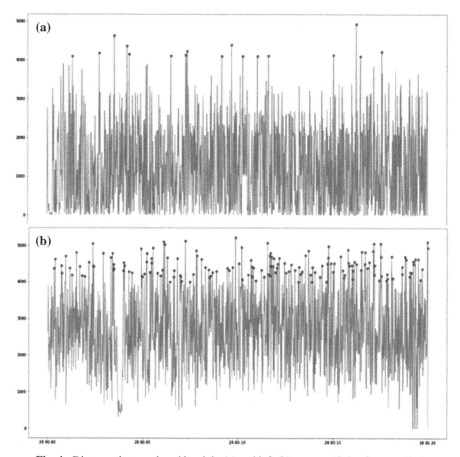

Fig. 4. Distance data produced by right (a) and left (b) sensors (Color figure online)

on that side, such as buildings or parked cars. However, while this was true for some route segments, it was far from being the general rule, as suggested by the graphs. When we used the video to compare the data capture situations, we observed that significant parts of the route were very uncluttered streets without any near obstacles on any side and very low traffic.

4.2 Air Quality Sensors

Air quality sensors can be very relevant to assess the level of exposure to pollutants faced by cyclist. This can help with route selection, especially for commuters, who may take the same cycle route every day and may want to improve the quality of their daily ride. This type of data may also be useful as a new generic source of data about urban pollution. Leveraging bicycles for this particular purpose could be interesting because they are not polluters themselves and collectively they would have the capability to collect large sets of samples every day at multiple location across the city.

The broader concept of air quality can be assessed by measuring some of the specific elements which more commonly correlate with reduced air quality. Carbon Dioxide (CO2) sensors are particularly efficient as a sign of high emissions of pollutant levels and the presence of the others types of pollutants associated with combustion sources, such as traffic or industry. Additionally, Carbon Dioxide sensors are known for being reliable and accurate, even without any type of calibration. In our data collection prototype, we included a carbon dioxide sensor, which measured the concentration of carbon dioxide particles along the selected route, as shown in Fig. 5.

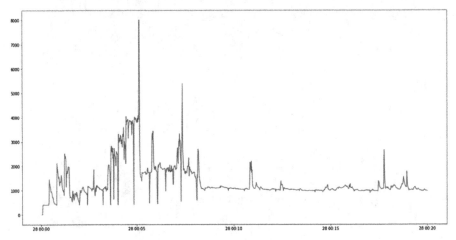

Fig. 5. Data from carbon dioxide sensor

We also included a sensor for Volatile Organic Compounds (VOCs), which could sense a much broader variety of particles. While a VOC sensor may complement Dioxide Carbon sensors, the results we obtained were very similar for both sensors and suggest that a single CO2 sensor may provide a suitable indicator of higher pollution levels.

Given the low-cost nature of these sensors, they should not be seen as a replacement for the more reliable sensors used in official air quality control systems, which many cities have in operation. Still, "peaks" observed in the Fig. 5 were confirmed to correspond to streets where the concentration of pollutants was expected to be higher due to heavy traffic.

4.3 Sound Level Sensors

Figure 6 is a graphical representation of the sound volume level in decibels registered in by the sound sensor during the data collection.

The average sound value was about 46 decibels, a value considered tolerable and normal by human hearing. However, we also identified several outliers were the sound level was above 120 decibels, which even exceeds the human hearing capacity. The video stream allowed us to confirm that no sound of that nature had ever been experienced by riders.

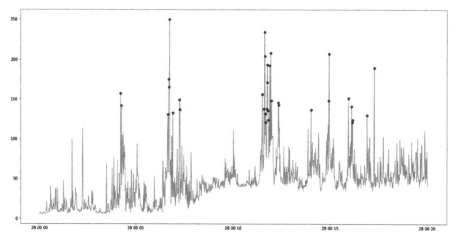

Fig. 6. Data from the sound volume sensor in decibels

4.4 Luminosity

Regarding light sensors, the most striking results is the almost permanent saturation of the data, which seems to indicate that the sensor reached its range limit. Rather than measuring the various levels of light, this data can only allow us to identify occasional situations where the buildings, trees, the cyclist or other sources of shadow covered the sensor. One possible explanation is that this type of low-cost sensor is actually designed to identify these extreme situations of whether or not there is light, rather than accurately measuring the level of light.

5 Discussion

The results have shown some of the practicalities associated with bicycle sensing, allowing us to identify some important design implications for any forms of systematic in-bike sensing.

The first implication to is the huge differences in accuracy, precision and reliability which seem to exist for some sensor types between those normally used for scientific data collection and those which one can reasonably expect to have embedded on any bicycle. In particular, the data produced by a significant set of sensors did not seem to have a plausible alignment with the perception of the concrete situations in which data was captured. Distance sensors seemed to have failed to produce data which is aligned with the reality of the cycle routes in which it captured. They did not seem to be suitable for this role, possibly because their operation properties may not be suitable for the continuously fast changing dynamics around a moving bike. This suggest that a realistic collection of data about the surroundings of a moving bicycle may require much better distance sensors or even more sophisticated techniques, such as Light Detection And Ranging (LiDAR)-based sensor systems [16], similar to those used in drones or autonomous cars. Likewise, sound level sensors have also failed to produce a reliable account of the level of noise experienced by riders during data collection. They have produced unrealistic maximum levels of noise and they have even failed to signal the phases during which the riders were crossing what should be noisier areas. A partial explanation may be associated with the noise produced by the bicycle itself, especially in certain road surfaces. Other sensors, such as light, have given contradictory signs. Even if they have failed to produce an account of the level of light across the route, they were still able to distinguish extreme situations and signal passage through shady areas.

This apparent lack of basic reliability is particularly negative, as it may jeopardize the viability of using some of these sensors. Among the possible reasons is the selection of low-cost sensors, most of which were not designed to be operated under the challenging circumstances of in-bike sensing. They are very sensitive electronic devices, which have been optimised for measurements in controlled and stable situations. They may not be able to cope with a moving bicycle, with its speed, vibrations and quickly changing environment. While this does not necessarily dismiss the use of low-cost sensors, it represents an additional challenge in regard to the cost/benefit equation.

A second implication concerns the positional requirements of some of the sensors. For example, distance sensors can have very stringent requirements about where they should be and where they should be pointing. Small variations in position, may affect the results produced by different bicycles, and the additional complexity brought by this type of requirement, may negatively impact bicycle production costs.

The final implication is to acknowledge that that the range of sensors deployed across bicycles does not need to be uniform. Ultimately, they will be determined by the value propositions that they can offer to cyclists or to a bicycle operator, e.g. in shared bicycles schemes. Still, collectively they should be able to complement each other and benefit from the fact that for some data needs even occasional samples by a reduce subset of the cyclists could still be enough to provide valuable data. Likewise, some key factors can be extrapolated from different types of data. For example, the general riding comfort offered by a particular route may be indirectly estimated from very different sources such as accelerometers, average speed or distance sensors.

6   Conclusions

The contribution of this work is to highlight some of the challenges that can be faced by systematic sensing for urban cycling. Even though previous work has extensively explored the use of various type of data to infer road conditions or traffic situations, this work highlights how the first challenge is actually to produce consistent data in a systematic way. In particular, it seems that the ability to select sensors with operational properties which are suitable for the specificities of their on-bike deployment will play a crucial role in the viability of the whole process. Together with emerging initiatives on standards for cycling data, this type of systematic data collection could significantly impact the ability of cycling ecosystems to really make use of data as a central element for new mobility paradigms. The set of design implications emerging from this work should help to develop new approaches for the systematic integration of sensors in urban bicycles.

Acknowledgements. This work has been supported by national funds through FCT, Fundação para a Ciência e Tecnologia, within the Project Scope: UID/CEC/00319/2019, and also by the European Structural and Investment Funds in the FEDER component, through the Operational Competitiveness and Internationalization Programme (COMPETE 2020) [Project n° 039334; Funding Reference: POCI-01-0247-FEDER-039334].

Development of the Arduino code was made by André Torrinha, Marcelo Alves, Pedro Lobo and Rui Almeida as part of a Masters' Project.

References

1. Violeta Bulc: Cycling: green and efficient transport for the future. European Commission (2016). https://ec.europa.eu/commission/commissioners/2014-2019/bulc/blog/cycling-green-and-efficient-transport-future_en. Accessed 31 Oct 2019
2. Lee, J., Leem, Y.T., Lee, S.H.: Categorizing U-Bike service and assessing its adoptability under it-. In: 12th World Conference for Transportation Research, pp. 1–10 (2010)
3. Ricci, M.: Bike sharing: a review of evidence on impacts and processes of implementation and operation. Res. Transp. Bus. Manag. **15**, 28–38 (2015)
4. Li, S.: Cycling in Toronto: route choice behavior and implications to infrastructure planning. Master thesis. University of Waterloo (2017)
5. Harvey, F., Krizek, K.: Commuter bicyclist behavior and facility disruption. Transp. Res. Board **60** (2007)
6. Winters, M., Davidson, G., Kao, D., Teschke, K.: Motivators and deterrents of bicycling: comparing influences on decisions to ride. Transportation **38**(1), 153–168 (2011)
7. Félix, R.: Gestão da Mobilidade em Bicicleta Master thesis, Engenharia do Território. Universidade Técnica de Lisboa (2012)
8. Hochmair, H.: Decision support for bicycle route planning in urban environments. In: 7th AGILE Conference on Geographic Information Science, pp. 697–706 (2004)
9. Srivastava, M., Abdelzaher, T., Szymanski, B.: Human-centric sensing. Philos. Trans. R. Soc. A: Math. Phys. Eng. Sci. **370**(1958), 176–197 (2012)
10. Torres, S., Lalanne, F., Del Canto, G., Morales, F., Bustos-Jimenez, J., Reyes, P.: BeCity: sensing and sensibility on urban cycling for smarter cities. In: Proceedings - International Conf of the Chilean Computer Science Society, SCCC 2016 (2016)
11. Eisenman, S.B., Miluzzo, E., Lane, N.D., Peterson, R.A., Ahn, G.-S., Campbell, A.T.: BikeNet. ACM Trans. Sens. Netw. **6**(1), 1–39 (2009)
12. Verstockt, S., Slavkovikj, V., De Potter, P., Van De Walle, R.: Collaborative bike sensing for automatic geographic enrichment: geoannotation of road/terrain type by multimodal bike sensing. IEEE Signal Process. Mag. **31**(5), 101–111 (2014)
13. Reddy, S., Shilton, K., Denisov, G.: Biketastic: sensing and mapping for better biking. In: Proceedings of the 28th International Conference on Human factors in Computing Systems, pp. 9–12 (2010)
14. Elen, B., et al.: The Aeroflex: a bicycle for mobile air quality measurements. Sens. (Switz.) **13**(1), 221–240 (2013)
15. Auer, E., et al.: ELAN as flexible annotation framework for sound and image processing detectors. In: Proceedings of the Seventh Conference on International Language Resources and Evaluation (LREC 2010), European Language Resources Association (ELRA), pp. 890–893 (2010)
16. Zhao, M., Stasinopoulos, S., Yu, Y.: Obstacle detection and avoidance for autonomous bicycles. In: IEEE International Conference on Automation Science and Engineering, 2017 August, pp. 1310–1315.1 (2018)

Short-Term Indoor Radon Gas Study in a Granitic School Building: A Comparative Analysis of Occupation Periods

Rolando Azevedo[1], Joaquim P. Silva[1], Nuno Lopes[1(✉)], António Curado[2,5], and Sérgio I. Lopes[3,4]

[1] Escola Superior de Tecnologia, Instituto Politécnico do Cávado e do Ave, Barcelos, Portugal
rolandoazevedo@gmail.com, {jpsilva,nlopes}@ipca.pt
[2] proMetheus, Instituto Politécnico de Viana do Castelo, Viana do castelo, Portugal
acurado@estg.ipvc.pt
[3] ARC4digiT - Instituto Politécnico de Viana do Castelo, Viana do Castelo, Portugal
sil@estg.ipvc.pt
[4] Instituto de Telecomunicações, Campus Universitário de Santiago, Aveiro, Portugal
[5] CONSTRUCT-LFC, Faculty of Engineering (FEUP), University of Porto, Porto, Portugal

Abstract. Granite territories continuously release radon, a radioactive gas that can be very harmful to human health. The assessment of radon gas indoor concentration is relevant for granitic buildings that lie over this substrate. In this work we use a sensor system to study the variation through time of indoor air quality (IAQ) parameters like radon concentration, temperature, and humidity following the occupation pattern of a school building made of granite. We identify distinctive radon concentration patterns that can be related with the time of day and week days that result from human occupation of the building and establish a basic indicator for radon exposure risk. The results of this analysis identify critical periods during the day that should be the subject of future mitigation strategies through an actuator system in order to improve the IAQ.

Keywords: Radon gas · Indoor Air Quality · Public granitic buildings · Public health

1 Introduction

Granite territories continuously release radon, a radioactive gas that can be harmful to human health. According to World Health Organization (WHO) indoor radon gas is the second largest risk factor associated with lung cancer [1]. The assessment of radon gas indoor concentration is relevant for granitic buildings that lie over this substrate. Several studies have been carried out, in the North of Portugal, to perform a short-term characterization of indoor radon gas showed evidence of high indoor radon gas concentration in several public buildings with granite construction [2]. In European Union (EU) countries, according to Council Directive 2013/59/Euratom, the reference

H. Santos et al. (Eds.): SmartCity 360 2019, LNICST 323, pp. 80–89, 2020.
https://doi.org/10.1007/978-3-030-51005-3_9

levels for the annual average radon activity concentration in air shall not be higher than 300 Bq.m^{-3} [3].

This work is part of a research project for developing a Cyber-Physical System (CPS) for continuous and online monitoring of the radon concentration and other relevant Indoor Air Quality (IAQ) parameters like temperature, relative humidity, and air pressure. The goal of this study is to identify radon concentration patterns according to the time of day and week days that result from human occupation of the building and to estimate the radon exposure risk. The use of a sensor system will enable the environmental safety assessment for radon concentration inside buildings and to deploy on premises a permanent monitoring system that consists of multiple remote sensors and a centralised control station with a web interface [4].

This paper is organized as follows. In the next section, we present relevant studies about indoor radon gas concentration in public buildings and the measurement equipment used on it. The third section describes the data analysis approach, including the sample characterization. The results from the study are discussed in the fourth section. The last section refers to the final conclusion.

2 Related Works

Several studies have been carried out to evaluate the influence of occupation on indoor radon concentration in public buildings. In 1996, a team of researchers analysed the radon concentration in a public school of a small village, next to Barcelona, Spain, including some dwellings [5]. The indoor radon concentration values obtained in the buildings were comparable to the mean world values. In [6], Madureira et al. assessed radon concentration in 45 classrooms from 13 public primary schools located in Porto, Portugal, and observed that in 92.3% and 7.7% of the measurements, the limit of 100 and 400 Bq.m^{-3}, established by WHO IAQ guidelines and in the national legislation, respectively, was exceeded.

The radon concentration in a centenary monastery recently converted to a polytechnic school building in an inner village in the Northwest region of Portugal was assessed in a recent study [7]. The in situ campaign involved a set of radon concentration short-term measurements in 17 rooms during 2 different time periods. The study reinforced the ventilation influence on the radon concentration reduction and stressed the year season influence in which the monitoring campaign is carried out, on the radon concentration performance.

A study for the assessment of the radon concentration, performed in 19 school buildings in a city located in the Midwest of Italy, obtained the minimum, median and maximum (interquartile range—IQR) values of 45.0, 91.6 and 140.3 Bq/m3 [8]. The authors of the study found evidences that radon concentration was significantly correlated with the number of students and teachers, foundation wall construction material, and with the absence of underground floors.

In [9], Gordon et al. examined the regulations and statutes in all US states concerning radon exposure in schools. The main goal was to identify key features of policies and discrepancies among states that may have public health implications. The study concluded that US state regulations related to the testing, mitigation, and public dissemination of radon levels in schools are inconsistent and the lack of nationwide indoor radon policy for schools may result in unacceptably high radon exposure levels in some US schools.

Currently, radon concentration assessment can be performed with active radon detectors that enable continuous monitoring. In [10], Baskaran et al. present a recent survey that compiles and compares several offline fast responding, highly sensitive radon air probes.

The use of sensor systems to monitor Indoor Air Quality was already proposed by multiple authors, like Schieweck et al. [11] and Cociorva et al. [12] among others. The use of gas sensors to control both the IAQ and the energy efficiency is reviewed by Guyot et al. [13]. In particular, the work Chao et al. already takes in consideration the use of a radon sensor for a dual goal actuator system for maintaining IAQ and energy consumption [14]. Lopes et al. introduce the design a Human-in-the-Loop Cyber-Physical System for online monitoring and active mitigation of indoor radon gas concentration in public buildings [4]. The proposed technology allows, not only a continuous and online monitoring of the radon gas concentration, but also the implementation on time of active mitigation strategies to reduce the indoor radon gas concentration.

3   Analysis Approach and Data Characterisation

The analysis approach adopted for this study is illustrated in Fig. 1. The measurements took place over a period of 41 days in 2018 from May 16 to June 25 at a school in Viana do Castelo in northern Portugal. The school selected for the measurements is running in a hundred years old granite building. The public building is used from 8:00 to 18:00 during working days, from Monday to Friday. The building is closed during the weekends and holidays.

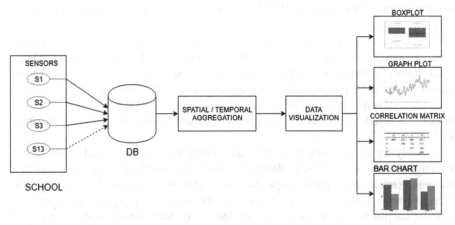

Fig. 1. Adopted analysis approach

The data measurements used in this study were obtained by 13 portable devices Airthings Corentium Plus that were placed inside different divisions on the two floors of the building. The data was gathered and stored into each devices' internal memory hourly during 41 days. The sample rate of the device is hourly. Each record has a timestamp in the Date ISO8601 standard and includes the parameters: radon, temperature, relative humidity, and atmospheric pressure. We did not consider the (indoor) atmospheric pressure as it was measured on the sensor itself. We found no direct relation with the remaining parameters. We plan to study the indoor and outdoor atmospheric pressures in a future work. Table 1 presents these parameters and its related aggregation types.

Table 1. Parameters and aggregation types

	Radon concentration	Temperature	Humidity
Measurement unit	Bq/m^3	°C	%RH
Data type	Floating point	Floating point	Floating point
Aggregation type	Spatial/hourly/daily	Spatial/hourly/daily	Spatial/hourly/daily

A data spatial/temporal aggregation was made afterwards, combining the data from the sensors and integrating it within a single aggregated view. The aggregation function used was the average of the measurements grouped by the hour which is the smallest temporal granularity available. Finally, after performing the aggregation, three techniques have been used to visualize the data (graph plot, boxplot, and bar chart), so that a graphical representation of the data facilitates the extraction of useful information. The different techniques are described in more detail below:

- **Boxplot:** This standardized type of figure shows the variation in samples of statistical population as a graphic representation of five numbers (minimum, first quartile(Q1), median, third quartile(Q3) and maximum). Outliers can also be displayed on the same figure. The first quartile (Q1) leaves 25% of the observations below while the third quartile (Q3) leaves 25% of the observations above.
- **Graph Plot:** This type of data visualization, allows the graphic representation of a dataset and shows the relation of a variable in function of another one, being possible to represent several variables in the same figure.
- **Bar chart:** This type of data visualization presents data with rectangular bars with heights proportional to the values they represent. Several bar charts can be overlapped to represent different measures. In our study, data is represented using a vertical bar chart.

Figure 2 depicts the radon concentration during the five consecutive weeks, with an average hourly graph plot. An initial observation reveals a possible repeating pattern in the radon concentration during the week and during each day.

The normalized radon concentration, temperature and humidity during the 41 days are presented in Fig. 3. All the measurements have been first aggregated hourly and then normalized to get a common representation scale. A first look at the graphic does not reveal any visible strong correlation between radon and the other two parameters. The

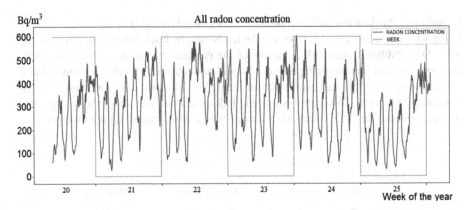

Fig. 2. Radon concentration during five consecutive weeks.

Fig. 3 shows that radon concentration seems to follow humidity variation and to change inversely with temperature. In the following section, we will look in more detail to the correlation between these parameters.

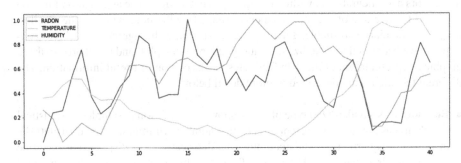

Fig. 3. Normalized radon concentration, temperature and humidity over a 41 days period

4   Discussion

In order to study with deeper detail the data collected, and without any visible relation among the values, we analysed the temporal variation of the radon throughout the day of the week. First, we performed a spatial aggregation, already described above, and then grouped the data by the day of the week. The result is the boxplot depicted on Fig. 4.

The results highlight a clear difference of the boxplots for weekdays and weekends. On Saturday and Sunday, the mean and minimums are higher when compared to week-days and the variation interquartile is much lower. It therefore seems appropriate to carry on with a separate analysis for weekdays and weekends since the variation seems to be different.

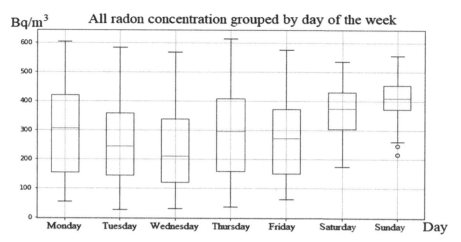

Fig. 4. Radon concentration boxplot aggregated by day of the week

4.1 Concentration Values for Weekday Versus Weekend Periods

An initial characterisation of the data was made by evaluating the mean and standard deviation for all the measurements, measurements during the week days and finally during weekends. The values obtained on Table 2 reveal that when considering only weekends, the mean concentration is higher than both all data and weekdays. Furthermore, the weekdays reveal a smaller mean and higher std. dev., indicating that the concentration is more stable and higher on weekends and more volatile during the weekdays.

Table 2. Radon concentration mean and standard deviation values (units $Bq.m^{-3}$)

Measure type	All days	Weekends & holidays	Weekdays
Mean	307	395	264
Standard deviation	137	83	138

Based upon a loose visual correlation between the concentration and the humidity, and an inverse correlation with the temperature for both parameters, we proceed to study the correlation values among the three parameters for the weekdays (Table 3) and weekends (Table 4). The Table 3 reveals a correlation between the radon concentrations and the humidity by 0,44 and an inverse correlation between the temperature with the radon concentration by $-0,49$ and between the temperature and the humidity by $-0,67$, being the last one an already known correlation result. The Table 4 shows that the correlations are weaker for the samples taken on weekends and holidays.

Table 3. Weekdays correlation matrix.

	Radon concentration	Temperature	Humidity
Radon concentration	1.00	−0.49	0.44
Temperature	−0.49	1.00	−0.67
Humidity	0.44	−0.67	1.00

Table 4. Weekend and holiday correlation matrix

	Radon concentration	Temperature	Humidity
Radon concentration	1.00	−0.26	0.31
Temperature	−0.26	1.00	−0.57
Humidity	0.31	−0.57	1.00

4.2 Variation of the Concentration During the Day

We proceed to study the variation of the radon over the hour of day. To do so, data was grouped by hour, thus obtaining measurements that go from 0 o'clock to 23 o'clock. As in the first approach, we analysed the data in two different cases. First for all the weekdays and then for weekends and holidays. The Fig. 5 depicts a boxplot for the hourly concentration on a) weekdays and b) weekends. The occupation time frame is represented in Fig. 5 a) during the hours where the building is occupied by people.

The hourly evolution during the weekdays (Fig. 5a) reveals a clear higher values during the early morning, up to the moment the building is opened to the public (8:00), a clear tendency for the concentration to decrease during the day gradually up to the end of the working day (18:00) where it reaches the lowest concentration. Then, when the building is closed, the concentration increases again until reaching its highest peak again. This variation pattern was not clearly observed during the weekends (Fig. 5b), where the mean variation is smaller. This might be explained by the fact that the building is always closed and ventilation barely exists during this period.

4.3 Risk Factor: Total Time Versus Occupation Period

Ultimately, it is necessary to quantify the people's exposure to radon, by calculating the mean radon concentration only during human presence. Although the mean concentration for all measurements exhibits a high value, in fact, the mean exposure to humans should only consider the opening hours of the building. First, radon concentration was aggregated daily in order to obtain the daily mean value, and then the mean exposure value was calculated considering that the school is open from Monday to Friday, from 8:00 to 18:00, resulting on the bar chart depicted on Fig. 6.

The Fig. 6 shows that the mean concentration value for the entire day is much higher than the value for only the opening hours of the building which is when people are

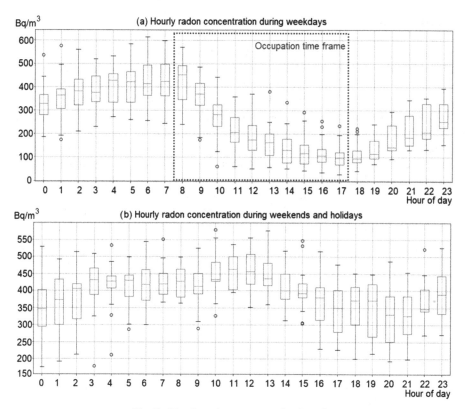

Fig. 5. Hourly radon concentration boxplot

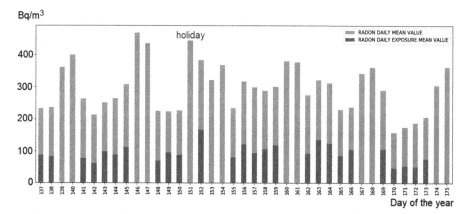

Fig. 6. Radon concentration daily mean value and mean exposure value

exposed to the gas. On day 151 in the Figure, one can see that the daily mean value is one of the highest, despite being a week day. This day is a holiday, and hence the building was closed in this day.

5 Conclusions

The analysis of the data shows that the average radon concentration measured is high, on average 306 Bq.m^{-3}, which is above the WHO guidelines, but below the legal limit in Portugal. A correlation with other air quality parameters like temperature and humidity were not relevant, with values of $-0,49$ for the temperature and $0,44$ for the humidity.

Despite the lack of correlations, a variation pattern was identified with weekly and daily cycles. A more detailed look at the variation of the radon concentration during weekdays (usually working days) and weekends (usually days where the building is closed) revealed a cyclic behaviour. The concentration is lower during working days than during weekends. Within working days, it is higher during the early morning, and lower at the end of the working day (around 18:00). We conclude that this pattern is caused by the human presence and use of the building, which follows the working timetable of the public school. The use of the building implies some kind of ventilation, arising from people entering and leaving the rooms and the building in itself. When a building is ventilated and the air is refreshed, the radon gas concentration drops. Furthermore, an exception was found in day 151, that while being a weekday, it was a holiday, which made the building be closed and exhibited the same pattern observed on weekends. During the weekends, when the building is closed, the variation of the concentration was smaller and had a consistent higher mean.

Although the global average concentration of the radon gas was high, the risk of a high gas concentration exposure to people is lower, because during working hours, the average concentration is smaller.

We conclude that, while on average the radon gas concentration is higher than desirable, in practice the exposure to the gas to people is not as high as the global mean and is diminished by the usage of the building in itself. Nevertheless, the initial evaluation of this sensor system reveals a case of public attention that should be continuously monitored and acted upon, in order to ensure that the gas concentration values are permanently within desirable limits through a mitigation system. The design of a mitigation system that automatically controls and limits the gas concentration is the focus of future work.

Acknowledgements. This contribution has been developed in the context of the Project "Rn-Monitor - Online Monitoring Infrastructure and Active Mitigation Strategies for Indoor Radon Gas in Public Buildings on the Northern Region of Portugal (Ref. POCI-01- 0145-FEDER-023997)" funded by FEDER (Fundo Europeu de Desenvolvimento Regional) through Operational Programme for Competitiveness and Internationalization (POCI).

References

1. World Health Organization: WHO handbook on indoor radon – a public health perspective. World Health Organization (2009). ISBN 978 924 154 767 3
2. Curado, A., Silva, J., Carvalho, L., Lopes, S.I.: Indoor Radon concentration assessment in a set of single family houses: case study held in Barcelos, North of Portugal. Energy Procedia **136**, 109–114 (2017)
3. European Union: Council Directive 2013/59/Euratom. E.U. Official Journal, 5 December (2013)

4. Lopes, S.I., et al.: On the design of a Human-in-the-Loop Cyber-Physical System for online monitoring and active mitigation of indoor Radon gas concentration. In: 2018 IEEE International Smart Cities Conference (ISC2), Kansas City, MO, USA, pp. 1–8. IEEE (2018)
5. Baixeras, C., Font, L.L., Fernandez, F., Domingo, C.: Indoor radon levels in a public school and some dwellings from the village of Teià, Catalonia, Spain. In: Proceedings of the 1996 International Congress on Radiation Protection. Vienna, Austria (1996)
6. Madureira, J., Paciência, I., Rufo, J., Moreira, A., de Oliveira Fernandes, E., Pereira, A.: Radon in indoor air of primary schools: determinant factors, their variability and effective dose. Environ. Geochem. Health **38**(2), 523–533 (2015). https://doi.org/10.1007/s10653-015-9737-5
7. Lopes, S.I., Silva, J., Antão, A., Curado, A.: Short-term characterization of the indoor air radon concentration in a XII century monastery converted into a school building. Energy Procedia **153**, 303–308 (2018)
8. Azara, A., et al.: Indoor Radon exposure in Italian schools. Int. J. Environ. Res. Public Health **15**(4), 749 (2018)
9. Gordon, K., et al.: Radon in schools: a brief review of state laws and regulations in the United States. Int. J. Environ. Res. Public Health **15**(10), 2149 (2018)
10. Baskaran, M.: Radon: A Tracer for Geological, Geophysical and Geochemical Studies. Springer, Basel (2016). https://doi.org/10.1007/978-3-319-21329-3
11. Schieweck, A., et al.: Smart homes and the control of indoor air quality. Renew. Sustain. Energy Rev. **94**, 705–718 (2018)
12. Cociorva, S., Iftene, A.: Indoor air quality evaluation in intelligent building. Energy Procedia **112**, 261–268 (2017)
13. Guyot, G., Sherman, M., Walker, I.: Smart ventilation energy and indoor air quality performance in residential buildings: a review. Energy Buildings **165**, 416–430 (2018)
14. Chao, C., Hu, J.: Development of a dual-mode demand control ventilation strategy for indoor air quality control and energy saving. Building Environ. **39**(4), 385–397 (2004)

A Visual Analytics Approach for Effective Radon Risk Perception in the IoT Era

Sérgio I. Lopes[1,2(✉)], Sanne Bogers[3], Pedro M. Moreira[1], and António Curado[4]

[1] ARC4digiT - Instituto Politécnico de Viana do Castelo, Viana do Castelo, Portugal
sil@estg.ipvc.pt
[2] Instituto de Telecomunicações, Campus Universitário de Santiago, Aveiro, Portugal
[3] HAS - University of Applied Sciences, 's-Hertogenbosch, The Netherlands
[4] Prometheus - Instituto Politécnico de Viana do Castelo,
Viana do Castelo, Portugal

Abstract. Radon gas is one of the most relevant indoor pollutants in areas of slaty and granitic soils, and is considered by the World Health Organization (WHO) as the second-largest risk factor associated with lung cancer. In the IoT era, active radon detectors are becoming affordable and ubiquitous, and in the near future, data gathered by these IoT devices will be streamed and analyzed by cloud-based systems in order to perform the so-called mitigation actions. However, a poor radon risk communication, independently of the technologies and the data analytics adopted, can lead to a misperception of radon risk, and therefore, fail to produce the wanted risk reduction among the population. In this work we propose a visual analytics approach that can be used for effective radon risk perception in the IoT era. The proposed approach takes advantage of specific space-time clustering of time-series data and uses a simple color-based scale for radon risk assessment, specifically designed to aggregate, not only the legislation in force but also the WHO reference level, by means of a visual analytics approach. The proposed methodology is evaluated using real time-series radon data obtained during a long-term period of 7 months.

Keywords: IoT · Visual analytics · Radon risk

1 Introduction

Along with other indoor air pollutants (smoke produced from solid fuel combustion, volatile organic compounds, etc.), radon gas is responsible for the degradation of air quality in enclosed rooms. However, the World Health Organization (WHO) considers indoor radon exposure as one of the most important causes responsible for lung cancer, right after tobacco smoking [1].

Regarding radon exposure in enclosed environments, the 2013/59/Euratom Directive imposes the so-called reference level of $300\,\mathrm{Bq.m}^{-3}$ for the occupational exposure limit value [2]. All European legislation concerning ionizing radiation

Published by Springer Nature Switzerland AG 2020. All Rights Reserved
H. Santos et al. (Eds.): SmartCity 360 2019, LNICST 323, pp. 90–101, 2020.
https://doi.org/10.1007/978-3-030-51005-3_10

exposure protection goes in the same direction as a result of the transposition of the referred Directive. Furthermore, in [1], the WHO recommends that countries adopt reference levels of $100\,\mathrm{Bq.m^{-3}}$ and if this level cannot be implemented under the prevailing country-specific conditions, WHO recommends that the annual average limit for indoor radon concentration in dwellings, offices, and workplaces must stay below the reference level of $300\,\mathrm{Bq.m^{-3}}$ otherwise, mitigation actions are required to remediate the non-regulatory rooms [2].

Nevertheless, the reference level of $300\,\mathrm{Bq.m^{-3}}$ is the base value to set off some remediation actions in order to reduce indoor radon concentration in a given room, the period of occupancy is a key variable. By way of example, an office where occupants stay on a daily basis for 8 working hours, exposed to an indoor radon level of $300\,\mathrm{Bq.m^{-3}}$, results in a higher risk than a technical room, with the same average level, where workers go there by one hour per day for maintenance purposes. In summary, it can be said that the indoor radon concentration taken in isolation cannot assess radon risk exposure since variables like buildings occupancy, the period of occupation and type of building are of vital importance on radon risk assessment.

Recently, several IoT-based radon detectors have been proposed, cf. [3–5], and in the near future, data gathered by these devices will be streamed and analyzed by cloud-based systems in order to perform the so-called mitigation actions. Having in mind that a poor radon risk communication can lead to a misperception of radon risk, and therefore, fail to produce the wanted risk reduction among the population. Given this, in this work we propose a visual analytics approach that can be used for effective radon risk perception when data is streamed continuously by these IoT radon detectors.

The remainder of this paper is organized as follows, in Sect. 2 a discussion about related works is undertaken, in Sect. 3 the visual analytics approach used for effective radon risk perception is introduced, in Sect. 4, the case study is presented in detail, and finally in Sect. 5, conclusions are pointed out and discussed.

2   Related Works

Recently, due to the rapid growth of IoT and Big Data technologies, large amounts of data from distinct varieties (timestamps, geolocations, sensor data, images, audio, video, etc.) have been produced. However, such data are not useful without analytic power [6]. Other analytics approaches, notably visual analytics methods, have been explored with success in the IoT and Big Data domains. Visual analytics methods aim to assist users in gaining insights, and therefore to extract knowledge from the data, by means of visual interpretations and interactions in the data analysis process [7]. Note that, an insight, can be seen as the ability of a user to understand a specific cause and effect within a specific context.

In [7], Keim et al. define visual analytics as the combination of automated analysis techniques with interactive visualizations for an effective understanding, reasoning and decision making on the basis of very large and complex data sets, that enable people to i) synthesize information and derive insights; ii) detect the expected and discover the unexpected; iii) provide timely, defensible, and understandable assessments and iv) communicate assessment effectively for action.

In this context, several recent works have been addressing the topic of IoT visual analytics, cf. [8–10], in order to assist users in the knowledge extraction process. In [8], the authors present the Virtual Open Operating System (vf-OS) approach to IoT Analytics, and describe its main components. The proposed approach can be used to capture data from IoT devices to generate and run machine learning models to perform data analytics, not only in the cloud but also on the edge. In [9], Lee et al. present a study that introduces a holistic perspective of storing, processing, and visualizing IoT-generated contents to support context-aware spatio-temporal insight. The study focus on the combination of deep learning techniques with a geographical mapping interface. Visualization is provided under an interactive web-based user interface to enhance the visual data exploration process, by means of a spatio-temporal query-based interface. In [10], the authors propose a framework for visual analytics of geospatial, spatio-temporal time-series data to handle multivariate, multiscale, and time-series data visualization. In the adopted design model they concluded that the most useful patterns are those that show relationships and aggregations of the data in both space and time domains.

3   Visual Analytics for Effective Radon Risk Perception

In order to extract knowledge from radon concentration data, first we need to understand the data under analysis in a space-time context, cf. Fig. 1. Understanding the data will help in the process of selection of appropriate data analysis models, and therefore assist in gaining insights, knowledge generation, and knowledge communication about the data [10].

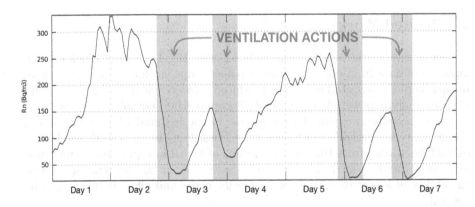

Fig. 1. Indoor radon fluctuation over a week with ventilation actions identified.

Indoor radon levels fluctuate over time depending on the building occupancy and the number of ventilation actions undertaken, cf. [11–13]. Commercial active radon detectors can perform continuous measurements in periods from 10 to 60 min. These detectors normally use an internal averaging mechanism to reduce data dispersion and therefore improve data quality. Figure 1 illustrates the variation over one week of the indoor radon concentration in a room with regular ventilation actions performed.

Moreover, indoor radon concentration is also affected by the space dimension, i.e. the soil composition and the building construction materials. Granitic soils and granitic construction materials both contribute, 80% and 20% respectively [1], to high indoor radon levels.

In our case it is expected that users can easily, and based on visual analytics, gain insights about radon risk exposure and the relations of practical situations such as building occupation and ventilation actions in the overall radon risk perception. Figure 2 depicts the proposed visual IoT analytics model that will be used in the visual analytics process.

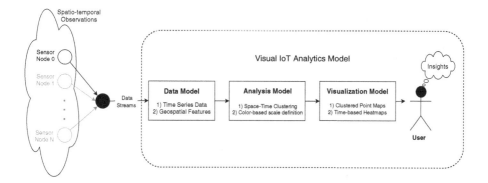

Fig. 2. Visual IoT Analytics Model: from spatio-temporal observations to user insights.

3.1   Data Model

Given the fact that multiple IoT devices can be used in distinct rooms and/or buildings, spatial context is key for radon concentration data exploration, and therefore, spatial-based clustering must be performed having in mind the relation of geographical entities, i.e. District > County > Building > Room > Device, as defined in [3], each having a specific set of geospatial features, such as soil composition, architectonic style, construction materials, etc. Moreover, time-series modeling is appropriate for radon concentration data when multiple devices geographically distributed are considered, not only for temporal clustering, but also for short-term prediction of indoor radon concentration.

3.2   Analysis Model

In [1], short-term measurements are defined as radon concentrations measurements that takes place over a period of not more than 3 months, and long-term measurements as radon concentrations measurements that take place over periods of 3 months up to 1 year. This definition was used as our baseline for clustering IoT time-series radon concentration data when multiple devices geographically distributed are considered. Multiple devices will generate time-series radon concentration data that will be difficult to analyse if no time clustering is performed. Given this, and having in mind the definitions previously introduced for short-term and long-term data clustering, we opted to use a more refined granularity containing five distinct time-based clustering approaches:

1) **RT** - Real Time (Hour);
2) **VST** - Very Short Term (Day);
3) **ST** - Short Term (Week);
4) **LT** - Long Term (Year), for periods always greater than 3 months.

In this analysis, the Euratom reference level of $300\,\mathrm{Bq.m^{-3}}$ [2] and the WHO reference level of $100\,\mathrm{Bq.m^{-3}}$ [1] were considered in the analysis model for scale definition and color selection, cf. Fig. 3, and therefore to enhance the visual analytics process.

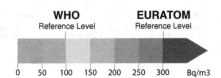

Fig. 3. Scale definition based on seven distinct colors mapped to the WHO [1] and Euratom [2] reference levels.

3.3   Visualization Model

Based on the geographical hierarchy introduced in Sect. 3.1, clustered point maps can be used and controlled by simple user-interface actions, such as zooming in to break a cluster (one point) in a subset of clusters (a group of new points), or zooming out to aggregate a set of clusters (a group of points) in a new cluster (one point).

To visualise radon concentration data in the time domain we opted to perform Very Short Term (VST), Short Term (ST) and Long Term (LT) time-based clustering through a heatmap visualization approach, were data is visualised through color variations in cells, enabling the easy assessment of its variance using distinct time-based clusters and the identification of relevant patterns.

4   Case Study

In this section, we present the evaluation of the proposed methodology using real data obtained with a certified Airthings Plus Radon detector, between 12/11/2018 and 30/06/2019 in the Lab.1.11 of the School of Technology and Management of the Polytechnic Institute of Viana do Castelo, cf. Fig. 4. The Lab is occupied regularly between 9h00 am and 5h00 pm. Radon concentration data is clustered in time, horizontally, using the periods defined in Sect. 3.2, VST, ST and LT. Vertically, and aligned from top to bottom is presented the evolution in time, week-by-week, with seasons identified.

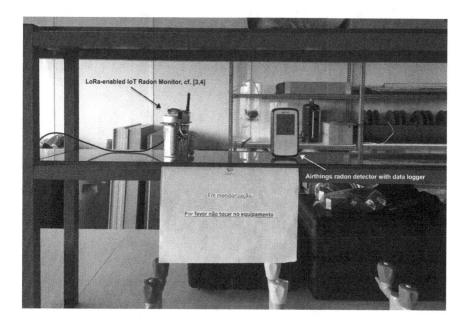

Fig. 4. The placement of the radon detectors in the Lab.

When occupancy is considered, radon concentration time-series data should be considered for particular time schedules, i.e. when users are effectively exposed to the pollutant. Since that, in public buildings, offices, schools, kindergartens, etc, occupancy is normally restricted to regular schedules during working days, many of the time-series data values must not be considered in the computation of related radon risk metrics and indicators. Common time-series models (e.g. averaging/smoothing models) are inadequate in the case of intermittent time-series because many of the series values must not be considered. Since these models are based on weighted-summations of all past time-series data, they negatively bias the calculus of, not only radon concentration exposure metrics, but also, effective radon risk exposure indicators.

The evaluation is presented based on two time aggregation criteria, i) Very-Short Term (Day) and ii) Short-Term (Week). Additionally, two distinct data visualization approaches were produced, one considering the effective room occupancy and the other considering all the data gathered by the sensors.

4.1 Time-Based Heatmap Data Visualization

Figure 5 illustrates the variation of the radon concentration during 33 consecutive weeks. The data presented was acquired in the Lab and is used here for methodology validation based on two distinct scenarios: a) no occupation considered and b) with occupation considered. The Lab under analysis is a ground-floor office regularly occupied by three people, between 9h00 am and 5h00 pm, during working days. Figure 1 b) illustrates the average radon concentration is obtained directly from the occupancy profile previously defined.

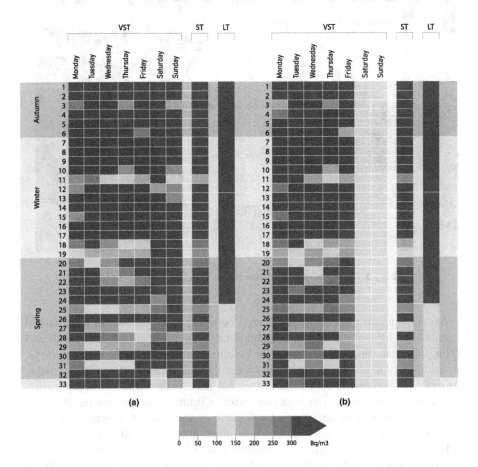

Fig. 5. Time-based Heatmap Visual Analytics: a) no occupancy considered; b) with occupancy considered.

Table 1 presents four evaluation metrics for easy comparison of the two scenarios introduced in Fig. 5. One observation is that scenario B regarding radon concentration data with occupancy considered between 9h00–17h00, results in a variation increase of metrics A and D which reveals that, the number of days below the WHO reference level [1] increased, and the number of days bellow the Euratom reference level [2] also increased. This observation also reveals that the risk perception tends to be overestimated if we look to the heatmap that considers all data, cf. Fig. 5a.

Table 1. Visual analytics performance metrics.

Metric	All data	Occupancy data	Variation	Reference level
	24 h	9h00–17h00		
A = $\sum$ Green cells/$\sum$ All cells	2.6%	4.2%	↑ 1.6%	$\leq 100\,\text{Bq.m}^{-3}$ (WHO [1])
B = $\sum$ not(Green cells)/$\sum$ All cells	97.4%	95.8%	↓ 1.6%	$> 100\,\text{Bq.m}^{-3}$ (WHO [1])
C = $\sum$ Red cells/$\sum$ All cells	72.7%	70.9%	↓ 1.8%	$> 300\,\text{Bq.m}^{-3}$ (Euratom [2])
D = $\sum$ not(Red cells)/$\sum$ All cells	27.3%	29.1%	↑ 1.8%	$\leq 300\,\text{Bq.m}^{-3}$ (Euratom [2])

4.2 User Evaluation

In order to validate the proposed approach, a set of user evaluation tests were conducted. The main goal of this evaluation test was to understand how users would read and perceive the proposed data visualization approach, and therefore, their ability to effectively perceive risk.

The evaluation protocol was based on the methodology presented in [14]. The evaluation protocol was based in two distinct documents: A) document used to introduce users to the Radon exposure problem, our case study and the main guidelines of WHO and the Portuguese legislation; and B) document with 11 questions, cf. Table 2 in which users have to answer about the visual analytics approach followed in this work, cf. Fig. 5. The questions were split in three main topics regarding Fig. 5 by considering heatmaps a), and b) alone, and considering both heatmaps at the same time.

Before the tests were conducted, the document A) was given to the users to explain the concept of the project to users. After this, the users had 3 min to look at the data visualizations and try to extract knowledge from them. Then, the questionnaire B), cf. Table 2, was handed to the participants. Subjects were then informed that, for each question, while reading the question until an answer was given, an independent observer would collect metrics on time duration and number of errors made. Finally, users were ensured that the evaluation process was about testing the visualizations and not themselves, giving them more confidence and comfort to freely answer the questions.

Table 2. Set of user evaluation questions.

ID	Heatmap	Question
1	a)	Give an example of a day where the Radon concentration was considered good by the WHO
2	a)	Indicate (one of) the best weeks regarding Radon concentration level
3	a)	Indicate the interval of the Radon concentration level observed on Thursday, week 18
4	a)	Indicate the interval of the Radon concentration level observed in week 20
5	a)	Indicate a week where the Radon concentration was better than the three months average
6	b)	Indicate the interval of the Radon concentration level observed on Wednesday week 11
7	b)	Indicate the interval of the Radon concentration level observed in week 19
8	a)+b)	Indicate one day in which the Radon concentration level was above the WHO recommendation level but below the same level, when occupation is considered
9	a)+b)	Indicate the day or days of the week for which the overall Radon Risk is considered higher
10	a)+b)	From all available data, what is the week with less Radon Risk exposure for the workers and what are the less risky days of that week?
11	a)+b)	What is the season with less Radon Risk exposure associated?

4.3 Results

The user evaluation was performed with 10 subjects aged between 22 and 48 years old, and was based on the protocol introduced in Sect. 4.2. Figure 6 depicts the statistical results regarding the users' response time through a standardized box plot representation. Additionally, in the same figure at right, the percentage of wrong answers was added. From the results presented in Fig. 6, one can observe that the spreading of the response time regarding questions 4, 6, 7 and 10B are the smallest. The results also show that most of the participants needed more time to answer question 8, with an average response time of 106 s. As shown in Fig. 6, this is the first question that regards both heatmaps. In this question, the user was asked to make connections between both heatmaps which naturally took more time to relate and gain an insight. It seems that this question was quite hard for the majority of the users, due to the fact that only half of the users answered this question correctly. Question 6 and 7 were answered rather quickly, i.e. all users answered this question in less than one minute. This relative quick response can be due to the fact that both questions are similar to question 3 and 4, which also resulted in a better success rate. Question 6 was even better understood by the users than question 3, i.e. every user answered question 6 correctly while 2 users answered question 3 wrongly. This shows that users were generally able to answer more quickly because previously gained insight earlier questions. While the users were conduction the test, it was observed that the difference between the time scales were sometimes unclear (VST-ST-LT) and it took the user some time to figure out which time scale was relevant for the question.

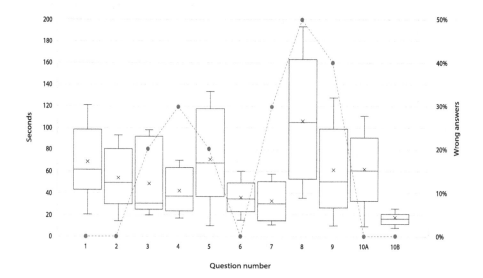

Fig. 6. User evaluation results, response time and percentage of wrong answers.

5   Conclusions

In this work, we proposed a visual analytics approach that can be used for effective radon risk perception in the IoT era. The proposed approach took advantage of specific space-time clustering of time-series data and used a simple color-based scale for radon risk assessment, specifically designed to aggregate, not only the legislation in force but also the WHO reference level.

The field results obtained after evaluation with users show that 83% of the overall questions were answered correctly with an overall average response time of 49 s. Another relevant observation was regarding similar questions made intermittently, resulting in a considerable reduction of the response time and also in a better success rate. Moreover, this study revealed that the performance of the proposed visual analytics method increases when occupancy is considered because when considering the heat map with all data available, we are inducing users to overestimate radon risk, and therefore emphasize their risk perception.

The study allowed to conclude that a proper radon risk communication is key for an effective radon risk perception, which results in a natural increase of the radon risk awareness among the population. As a consequence of this awareness increase, an overall radon risk reduction can be achieved based on these two main factors: i) increase of regular ventilation actions and ii) performing proper building occupancy management.

Acknowledgements. This contribution has been developed in the context of the Project "RnMonitor - Online Monitoring Infrastructure and Active Mitigation Strategies for Indoor Radon Gas in Public Buildings on the Northern Region of Portugal (Ref. POCI-01- 0145-FEDER-023997)" funded by FEDER (Fundo Europeu de Desenvolvimento Regional) through Operational Programme for Competitiveness and Internationalization (POCI).

References

1. WHO - World Health Organization: Handbook on Indoor Radon: A Public Health Perspective. World Health Organization (2009). ISBN 978-92-4154-767-3
2. European Union 2013: Council Directive 2013/59/EURATOM. E.U. Official Journal, 5 December 2013
3. Lopes, S.I., et al.: On the design of a Human-in-the-Loop Cyber-Physical System for online monitoring and active mitigation of indoor Radon gas concentration. In: 2018 IEEE International Smart Cities Conference (ISC2), Kansas City, MO, USA, pp. 1–8 (2018). https://doi.org/10.1109/ISC2.2018.8656777
4. Lopes, S.I., Pereira, F., Vieira, J.M.N., Carvalho, N.B., Curado, A.: Design of compact LoRa devices for smart building applications. In: Afonso, J.L., Monteiro, V., Pinto, J.G. (eds.) GreeNets 2018. LNICST, vol. 269, pp. 142–153. Springer, Cham (2019). https://doi.org/10.1007/978-3-030-12950-7_12
5. Blanco-Novoa, O., Fernández-Caramés, T.M., Fraga-Lamas, P., Castedo, L.: A cost-effective IoT system for monitoring indoor radon gas concentration. Sensors **18**, 2198 (2018). https://doi.org/10.3390/S18072198
6. Marjani, M., et al.: Big IoT data analytics: architecture, opportunities, and open research challenges. IEEE Access **5**, 5247–5261 (2017). https://doi.org/10.1109/ACCESS.2017.2689040
7. Keim, D., Andrienko, G., Fekete, J.-D., Görg, C., Kohlhammer, J., Melançon, G.: Visual analytics: definition, process, and challenges. In: Kerren, A., Stasko, J.T., Fekete, J.-D., North, C. (eds.) Information Visualization. LNCS, vol. 4950, pp. 154–175. Springer, Heidelberg (2008). https://doi.org/10.1007/978-3-540-70956-5_7
8. Anaya, V., Fraile, F., Aguayo, A., García, O., Ortiz, Á.: Towards IoT analytics. A vf-OS approach. In: 2018 International Conference on Intelligent Systems (IS), Funchal, Madeira, Portugal, pp. 570–575 (2018). https://doi.org/10.1109/IS.2018.8710476
9. Lee, J., Kim, K.-S., Lee, R., Lee, S.-H.: Visual insight of spatiotemporal IoT-generated contents. In: Proceedings of the 2018 International Conference on Advanced Visual Interfaces (AVI 2018), vol. 70, p. 3. ACM, New York (2018). https://doi.org/10.1145/3206505.3206575

10. Sibolla, B.H., Coetzee, S., Van Zyl, T.L.: A framework for visual analytics of spatio-temporal sensor observations from data streams. ISPRS Int. J. Geo-Inf. **7**(12), 475 (2018). https://doi.org/10.3390/ijgi7120475

11. Curado, A., Silva, J.P., Carvalho, L., Lopes, S.I.: Indoor Radon concentration assessment in a set of single family houses: case study held in Barcelos, North of Portugal. Energy Procedia **136**, 109–114 (2017). https://doi.org/10.1016/j.egypro.2017.10.295

12. Lopes, S.I., Silva, J.P., Antão, A., Curado, A.: Short-term characterization of the indoor air Radon concentration in a XII century monastery converted into a school building. Energy Procedia **153**, 303–308 (2018). https://doi.org/10.1016/j.egypro.2018.10.036

13. Curado, A., Silva, J.P., Lopes, S.I.: Radon Risk Management in public buildings in northwest Portugal: from short-term characterization to the design of specific mitigation actions. Int. J. Recent Technol. Eng. **8**(1), 90–96 (2019)

14. Nascimento, T., Gama, S.: FishEye: marine species' recognition and visualization: 24o Encontro Português de Computação Gráfica e Interação (EPCGI). In: Guimaraes 2017, pp. 1–8 (2017). https://doi.org/10.1109/EPCGI.2017

On the Use of Smartphone Sensors for Developing Advanced Driver Assistance Systems

Nuno M. Santos[1], André L. Ferreira[1,2](✉), and João M. Fernandes[2]

[1] Bosch Car Multimedia, S.A., Braga, Portugal
{Nuno.Santos,Andre.Ferreira2}@pt.bosch.com
[2] University of Minho, Braga, Portugal
{alferreira,jmf}@di.uminho.pt

Abstract. Technological evolution impacts several industries, including automotive. The combination of software with advancements in sensory capabilities results in new Advanced Driver Assistance System (ADAS). The pervasiveness of smartphones and their sensory capabilities makes them an solid platform for the development of ADAS. Our work is motivated by concerns on the reliability of data acquired from such devices for developing ADAS. We performed a number of controlled experiments to understand which factors impact the collection of accelerometer data with smartphones. We conclude that the quality of data acquired is not significantly affected by using different smartphones, car mounts, rates of sampling, or vehicles for the purpose of developing ADAS. Our results indicate that smartphone sensors can be used to develop ADAS.

Keywords: Advanced Driver Assistance Systems · Smartphones · Inertial sensors · Vertical acceleration · Controlled experiments

1 Introduction

Hi-tech features in cars have increased in recent years as a direct result of software-enabled solutions. Advanced Driver Assistance Systems (ADAS), like automatic parking or lane departure warning system, are examples of such advancements resulting from the combination of sensory capabilities and software.

Smartphones are an interesting platform for the development of ADAS, due to their sensory capabilities. However, concerns emerge on the adequacy of these devices when developing ADAS. An assessment on the reliability of data acquired from such devices motivates our work before using their sensors for developing ADAS. There is insufficient knowledge on the extent to which data from smartphones can be used to develop ADAS.

Research sponsored by the Portugal Incentive System for Research and Technological Development. Project in co-promotion no. 002797/2015 (INNOVCAR 2015–2018).

H. Santos et al. (Eds.): SmartCity 360 2019, LNICST 323, pp. 102–114, 2020.
https://doi.org/10.1007/978-3-030-51005-3_11

A considerable number of ADAS rely on inertial data and cameras as the basis for their functionalities. There are inertial sensors embedded in the majority of smartphones available today. In addition, the idea of retrofitting ADAS to existing vehicles fuels some of the smartphone-based ADAS available today.

Obtaining inertial data from these mobile devices is easy. It now becomes relevant to understand which variables impact the quality of data collected. This knowledge is needed to decide to which extent can smartphones support the development of ADAS. Our objective is to clarify which factors may impact the collection of accelerometer data when using a smartphone with the purpose of developing ADAS. We accomplish this by performing controlled experiments where a predefined set of variables are identified and controlled and by analyzing their impact on the quality of sensory data retrieved.

2   State of the Art

ADAS are electronic systems that improve road traffic safety, supporting the driver when driving. Such support ranges from simple information presentation, through advanced assisting, to taking over the driver's tasks in critical situations [6]. A vehicle equipped with an ADAS is referred to as a *smart car*. ADAS aim to provide a fully autonomous vehicle with self-driving capabilities and to guarantee an accident-free driving experience. Most ADAS functionalities exist in independent systems and combining different sensors leads to better decisions, higher system performance, and lower power consumption [14].

Smartphones offer new capabilities, some of them provided by their sensors. With every other person owning one, smartphones can fill in the gap for the vast amount of vehicles without sensory capabilities. This same argument was echoed in research targeting the smartphone as a sensing device for the development of ADAS motivated by the cost of vehicles equipped with sensors [4].

Eriksson et al. produced Pothole Patrol, one of the first road condition monitoring systems, using high-end accelerometer sensors and Global Positioning System (GPS) devices attached to a taxi probe car to collect data [3].

Mohan et al. describe Nericell, a system that uses smartphones to monitor road and traffic conditions [7]. They report experiences as if they were using smartphones to collect acceleration data. However, the description of the implementation reveals the use of special-purpose Sparkfun WiTilt units, which sent acceleration data to the mobile devices for further computation. Other shortcomings in Nericell is the lack of explanations about the selection of thresholds [15], lack of clarification about the labeling technique used [12], and no disclosure of the chosen approach to synchronize data from different devices.

To compare data acquired from multiple sensors, it is crucial to make sure that their readings are synchronized—or, at least, to be conscious of existing skews. As opposed to work previously discussed [3,7], other authors either acknowledged synchronization issues or tried to mitigate them in diverse ways.

Examples include manually shifting labels [13], combining interpolation and shifting of data, and using devices with real-time operating systems [2].

A distinct approach is to use statistical methods to compute data read from different sensors and prepare it for feature extraction. Linear [3,4] or polynomial interpolation [8], and moving average [12,15] are common techniques.

A contrasting method is Dynamic Time Warping (DTW), which provides the possibility to align two time series even if they are out of phase [9]. It achieves an optimal solution in quadratic time and space complexity. This is impractical for dealing with large volumes of data, with memory requirements in the order of a tebibyte (TiB) to handle time series of ~100 000 measurements [10]. Fast-DTW [10] solves this difficulty by providing a DTW algorithm with linear time and space complexity, while ensuring a nearly optimal solution.

3   Experiment Planning

During experiment planning, we focused on meeting expectations set by our objectives. A reasonable effort to mimic real world usage was carried out to ensure that knowledge drawn could be used for practical products. Major constraints were identified to prevent them from becoming a risk to the experiments' validity.

The experiments occurred on roads of Braga around Bosch plant and around University of Minho Campus.

3.1   Hypothesis Formulation

Following are the hypotheses tested during our controlled experiments. For each identified variable, a null and an alternative hypothesis was established.

Smartphones—and the inertial sensors embedded within—are very diverse, be it in size, materials, or software version. We anticipated that such differences could have an impact on acceleration values reported by those devices.

Hypothesis 1_0: *Using different smartphone models to record accelerometer data does not yield similar measurements of vertical acceleration.*

Hypothesis 1_1: *Using different smartphone models to record accelerometer data yields similar measurements of vertical acceleration.*

The car mount holding the smartphone affects the acceleration sensed by it, since the car mount acts as a proxy between the device and the vehicle.

Hypothesis 2_0: *Using different car mounts to hold the smartphone does not yield similar measurements of vertical acceleration by a smartphone.*

Hypothesis 2_1: *Using different car mounts to hold the smartphone yields similar measurements of vertical acceleration by a smartphone.*

Other authors have demonstrated the importance of the sampling rate on the quality of information collected [5,12], so we studied the result of varying it.

Hypothesis 3_0: *Setting different sample rates to acquire the data does not yield similar measurements of vertical acceleration by a smartphone.*

Hypothesis 3_1: *Setting different sample rates to acquire the data yields similar measurements of vertical acceleration by a smartphone.*

Vehicles might have influence on the acceleration. Differences in the levels of comfort experienced during a trip in different vehicle models were a good indicator of this effect.

Hypothesis 4_0: *Using different vehicles to travel along the same itinerary does not yield similar measurements of vertical acceleration by a smartphone.*

Hypothesis 4_1: *Using different vehicles to travel along the same itinerary yields similar measurements of vertical acceleration by a smartphone.*

3.2   Variables and Subjects Selection

Both the dependent and independent variables emerged from the examination of our formulated hypotheses. We selected two subjects for each independent variable, with one of them being used in the standard setup. We also identified extraneous variables and assessed their impact on the experiment.

Dependent Variable – Vertical Acceleration: Accelerometer data from each device was collected in $m\,s^{-2}$. With the geographical globe as referential, the vertical acceleration axis points towards the sky and is perpendicular to the ground plane. To collect acceleration data, one axis of the smartphone was aligned with the vertical acceleration axis.

Independent Variable – Smartphone (Inertial Sensor): We performed experiments with two smartphones from different manufacturers. They were from two different price categories to amplify differences in the quality of their components. Three Nexus 5X were used in this study. This model is fabricated by LG since 2015 and incorporates a BMI160, an inertial measurement unit (IMU) manufactured by Bosch. This was the device used in the standard setup. A Samsung Galaxy S Duos, released in 2012, was also used in the experiments. Its accelerometer data is provided by an MPU-6000, an IMU from Invensense.

Independent Variable – Car Mount: Two iOttie Easy One Touch 3 were used to hold the smartphones during the experiments. This model was chosen for the standard setup because empirical evidence has shown it to be very stable. An unbranded car mount was used to contrast. Empirical evidence demonstrated this unbranded car mount to be very unstable, wobbling a lot even when traveling on itineraries with good pavement conditions.

Independent Variable – Rate of Sampling: The choice of sampling rate for the standard setup was quite pragmatic. Both chosen smartphones reported being capable of sampling data at no more than 200 Hz, so that value was selected. A study regarding road roughness condition proposed the frequency range of 40 Hz to 50 Hz as the best solution to sample smartphone acceleration sensors [1]. Supported in it, the rate of 50 Hz (period of 20 ms) was used to compare.

Table 1 summarizes how the chosen rates of sampling compare to related studies. The standard rate (200 Hz) falls short only to systems where special purpose accelerometers were used. The alternative rate (50 Hz) is in line with other smartphone-based systems.

Table 1. Distance between consecutive accelerometer measurements at different speeds for different systems.

System	Rate (Hz)	Distance (cm) traveling at		
		$25\,\mathrm{km\,h^{-1}}$	$50\,\mathrm{km\,h^{-1}}$	$75\,\mathrm{km\,h^{-1}}$
P^2 [3]	380	1.8	3.7	5.5
Nericell [7]	310	2.2	4.5	6.7
RoADS [12]	93	7.5	14.9	22.4
Tai [13]	25	27.8	55.6	83.3
Our std. setup	200	3.5	6.9	10.4
Our alt. setup	50	13.9	27.8	41.7

Independent Variable – Vehicle: We tried to conduct experiments with two cars representative of the vehicles in operation and having a significant difference in their price points and age. The first car was a Mazda 3 from 2007, chosen for the standard setup since it was always available to us. The second was a Volkswagen Polo from 2016, a rented car available during a single day.

Other Variables: Each experiment testing a hypothesis varied just one of the described independent variables. The influence of a vehicle's speed on information sensed by an accelerometer has been demonstrated [1,2,4,15]. Because of this, speed was categorized as an extraneous variable. Ideally, the speed of vehicles used in the experiments should have been constant during the entire trip, making it a controlled variable. To minimize its impact on the dependent variable, the driver tried to maintain the vehicles' speed at 30km $\mathrm{h^{-}1}$. Traveling at such speed would mean that collected acceleration data could later be analyzed to identify road anomalies as small as 4.2 cm (see Table 1).

3.3 Experiment Design

During each experiment, a vehicle performed a set of maneuvers on a predefined itinerary to capture data within a city environment. This vehicle was equipped with Android smartphones, each running an app created for this purpose. Car mounts kept the smartphones stable. The Android app had capabilities to acquire, present, and export sensors data from the smartphone. This application collected data from the accelerometer, gyroscope, GPS coordinates, and speed. To annotate the experiment, a co-driver used a second Android application, capable of storing the type of anomaly detected and a timestamp of its occurrence.

Each experiment tested one hypothesis using two setup configurations. One configuration remained the same (same smartphone, car mount, rate of sampling, and car) across every experiment, acting as a control setup. The alternative setup changed only one variable. Every experiment was performed five times.

To ensure a rich diversity of pavement anomalies to be detected on the experiments, we surveyed potential itineraries in Braga. To identify these itineraries, we considered the number of pavement anomalies, the types of anomalies, the itinerary's size, and the possibility to make a full travel with the same speed.

Collection Process Definition: Experimental data was collected by a team of 3 researchers and were performed during periods less prone to traffic congestion. Every repetition of an experiment started with the vehicle stopped but having its engine running for 5 seconds to record accelerometer data, collecting reference values that represent noise caused by the engine. Those values were used to calibrate the smartphone accelerometers. Upon completion of this phase, the Android app started collecting and storing sensors data. The researcher in the co-driver position used the annotations application to mark the start of a recording session and commanded the driver to start moving the vehicle.

While the vehicle was moving, the co-driver made annotations of the pre-determined pavement anomalies as they were experienced. The driver drove through the road without avoiding the anomalies, keeping a constant speed. Reaching the finishing position, the driver stopped the vehicle. After that, the co-driver used the annotations application to label the end of the session and the sensors data application to stop collecting data. Finally, if there were more repetitions of the experiment to perform, the team of researchers moved to the starting point of the itinerary to restart the procedure here described.

Analysis Techniques: A suitable method to test the hypotheses formulated on Sect. 3.1 is to compute the sample correlation coefficient between vertical acceleration collected by the pair of smartphones used in each experiment. This coefficient determines the similarity of reported accelerometer data from distinct devices and how strong that similarity is. It yields a normalized result between -1 (inversely correlated) and 1 (perfectly correlated), with 0 meaning entirely uncorrelated.

Difficulties were anticipated in using this technique. For instance, correlation between raw data is expected to be low due to the noise associated with measurements provided by IMUs embedded in smartphones. Also, since Android is not a real-time operating system (OS), it is difficult to ensure that two different measurements happened at the same time. Lastly, an equal number of data points for both time series is an imperative to compute the correlation between the analyzed datasets.

DTW aims to solve the problem of data sets having different lengths and being out-of-sync, while also reasonably dealing with noise. Given the tendency of DTW to bias the correlation for higher values, a randomization significance test was performed instead of a parametric significance test.

Instrumentation: To assist the operation during experiment execution and data analysis, three special-purpose tools were identified as in need. Smartphones required an Android application to collect and export their sensors data. After testing existing applications with similar features we found that none satisfied our requirements, so we developed a new one—*Bumpr*.

A second smartphone application was needed to assist the researcher's job of annotating recording sessions. With the number of features being rather low, the development of this application—*TapEvents*—was focused on non-functional requirements, namely, on building an efficient user interface that could be used while navigating through the itinerary.

To automate data analysis, a desktop application (1) computes the correlation coefficients of vertical acceleration and (2) statistically validates the results. This application, *TimeWarper*, uses FastDTW [10], an open implementation of the DTW algorithm, to prepare the streams of sensors data for analysis.

4   Experiment Execution

Field experiments took three months, after the procedure described in Sect. 3.3. We present details about each *run*, which refers to an instance of a field study where an experiment is being conducted. A *session* is the time window delimited by the start and end of a driving exercise, during which sensors data is being recorded. Each run aggregates a number of sessions.

4.1   First Run

The first run was carried out and data gathered from this experiment acted as a control group, setting the baseline against which future runs were compared.

A configuration (similar to configuration in Fig. 1) was prepared to accomplish this objective: two Nexus 5X, incorporating each a Bosch BMI160 accelerometer, running the same OS version, with the same recording application version sampling at 200 Hz, mounted on similar iOttie Easy One Touch 3 in identical positions and angles, and inside a single 2007 Mazda 3.

Data from early recording sessions was discarded as they were considered as being part of a warm-up stage. A couple of middle sessions were also disregarded for various reasons, c.g., trucks blocking sections of road. The first run was deemed as concluded after successfully finishing five sessions.

4.2   Second and Third Runs

In order to save time and other resources, the hardware configuration was adjusted so multiple field studies could take place at the same time (see Fig. 1).

The second run scrutinized data coming from two different smartphones with different sensors. A Nexus 5X and a Samsung Galaxy S Duos were part of the hardware configuration. These smartphones encase a Bosch BMI160 and an Invensense MPU-6000, respectively, to measure acceleration.

In the third run, two different car mounts were tested. One of them was an iOttie Easy One Touch 3 and the other was an unbranded equipment, holding the mobile devices in identical positions and angles.

(a) One annotation and three recording applications running on multiple devices

(b) Combining three smartphones and three car mounts allowed to concurrently execute two experiments

Fig. 1. Equipment setup for second and third runs

(a) Both cars in preparation for the experiment

(b) Second car tailgating the first. Photo taken during warm-up session

Fig. 2. Vehicles and setups used to perform the fourth and fifth runs

4.3   Fourth and Fifth Runs

On January 13th, 2017, the fourth and the fifth runs occurred, testing different sample rates and different cars, respectively. Once again, equipment was selected in such way to support running two experiments in parallel (see Fig. 2).

For the fourth run, two different sampling rates data were studied: 200 Hz and 50 Hz (data read each 5 ms and 20 ms, respectively). Lastly, the fifth run probed two different vehicles, a 2007 Mazda 3 and a 2016 Volkswagen Polo. Like in previous runs, all of the other setup parts were kept unchanged.

Performing both runs at the same time had different implications for these two field studies. For example, the Polo was a rented car and had no permission to travel inside University of Minho's campus. Thus, the course had to be adjusted and the portion inside the Campus of Gualtar was switched for a different path with similar length and an approximate number and diversity of anomalies.

Another issue with making an experiment with two different cars was the impossibility of traveling the road in the same exact positions, or even at the same speeds. To address these issues, the driver of the vehicle in the rear tried to keep a constant distance to the one in front of it (see Fig. 2b). We chose a car with cruise control and teams in both cars communicated via a phone call.

5   Data Analysis

We used descriptive statistics to study the central tendency and dispersion of the acceleration. In addition to the number of accelerometer observations (samples), we computed mean ($\bar{x}$), median ($\tilde{x}$), mode, minimum (min), maximum (max), and standard deviation (σ). Table 2 shows data from the first run, with each horizontal band grouping a successful session, and each of the rows in a band regarding one of the two similar Nexus 5X used. So, both setups A and B had similar configurations: the one used as the control group (see Sect. 4.1).

From these tables,[1] we confirmed that most acceleration data points were clustered around 0, with a standard deviation of about $1\,\mathrm{m\,s^{-2}}$. This fell in line with our expectations, as usually a vehicle does not accelerate in the vertical axis, apart from those brief moments when a road anomaly comes across.

The median value was consistently close to the mean, indicating that values were fairly distributed on each side of the average value. It also signals there being no outliers skewing the dataset—or, at least, that such outliers exist with approximately equal frequency on both sides of the median.

Despite the relatively small standard deviation, minimum and maximum values were quite afar from the central points, yielding a high range. We confirmed that points with values so farther apart were associated with the annotated road anomalies which provoked spikes in the monitored acceleration. Despite looking like outliers, these data points increase signal-to-noise ratio (SNR) in the datasets and were not discarded.

5.1   Data Set Reduction

We considered data recorded before (and after) the vehicle initiated (and finished) the trips as noise. To improve the SNR of the datasets, we clipped sensors data prior to (and after) the start (and end) of all sessions using the timestamps collected with the annotations application.

When analyzing Table 2, we detected incorrect data in the first session, with one of the smartphones reporting a very small number of observations (see highlighted row). We confirmed that such data was missing and could not be recovered, so first run's first session was treated as invalid.

5.2   Hypothesis Testing

We tested the hypotheses formulated in Sect. 3.1 with the techniques presented in Sect. 3.3. To assist in this effort, we designed and implemented a software tool, TimeWarper (see Sect. 3.3). Data collected in the control experiment set the baseline correlation coefficient against which the other coefficients were compared. Those comparisons allowed to decide about the proposed hypotheses.

Table 3 shows the computed coefficients for all valid sessions on every run, along with the mean value ($\bar{x}$). We use the mean values to illustrate arguments

---

[1] Due to space constraints, only first run's table is shown. For all tables, see [11].

Table 2. Descriptive statistics for acceleration data from the first run. Each horizontal band groups a successful session. Highlighted row shows incorrect data found during analysis (see Sect. 5.1). All data from first session was treated as invalid.

Setup	samples	$\bar{x}$	$\tilde{x}$	mode	min	max	σ
				$(\mathrm{m\,s^{-2}})$			
A	66 079	−0.020	−0.018	0.035	−13.255	8.758	1.051
B	3047	0.008	−0.019	−0.010	−0.393	0.388	0.146
A	65 078	−0.031	−0.032	0.009	−16.833	9.010	1.064
B	65 234	−0.021	−0.027	0.047	−19.159	15.892	1.163
A	67 326	−0.021	−0.019	0.065	−16.655	8.721	1.046
B	67 322	−0.001	−0.017	0.120	−21.392	15.189	1.098
A	65 928	−0.029	−0.022	0.045	−19.230	9.884	1.042
B	65 648	−0.012	−0.032	−0.080	−23.336	16.941	1.108
A	66 384	−0.034	−0.034	−0.055	−18.669	10.797	1.041
B	66 386	−0.029	−0.042	−0.075	−21.990	15.600	1.109

in this section, but every individual coefficient was statistically validated. As discussed before, the first session of the first run was treated as invalid, so the mean value for the first run was computed over the remaining four valid values.

We expected the correlation coefficient to be high for two similar collection setups sensing the vertical acceleration during a recording session. The control experiment tested this expectation. Running the valid sessions of the first run through TimeWarper yielded a mean correlation coefficient of 0.892, a strong positive correlation (see Table 3).

To test the statistical significance of this result, we processed each valid session using the following technique. Let us start by assuming that the result has no significance. If so, it follows that computing the correlation of data with nothing but noise would produce similar correlation coefficients.

One can produce "noised" versions of the same data by rearranging the order of their data points. Using a Random Shuffle algorithm, 100 randomized copies of each smartphone's acceleration data were produced—the surrogates. Then, each pair of surrogates was warped and its correlation coefficient computed. Lastly, the coefficients were ordered.

The original assumption can be rejected if the correlation coefficient for the original pair, r_0, is at the tails of the coefficients distribution. For a significance level of $\alpha = 0.05$, if the rank of r_0 in the ordered list of coefficients is less than 3 or is greater than 98, then we reject the assumption and consider the result as statistically significant.

Figure 3 plots the ordered lists of coefficients for the first run. For all the graphs for each session from every run, see [11]. For all sessions, the original correlation appeared at the tail of the list, ranking at the 101st position which is

Table 3. Correlation coefficients by run and session. Highlighted cell shows a session for which it was not possible to compute the correlation coefficient due to invalid data. It corresponds to the highlighted row in Table 2.

Session	Run				
	1st (baseline)	2nd (smartphone)	3rd (car mount)	4th (samp. rate)	5th (car)
1	—	0.834	0.845	0.841	0.826
2	0.889	0.828	0.843	0.831	0.835
3	0.892	0.826	0.855	0.836	0.822
4	0.892	0.831	0.852	0.829	0.825
5	0.894	0.830	0.846	0.833	0.825
$\bar{x}$	0.892	0.830	0.848	0.834	0.827

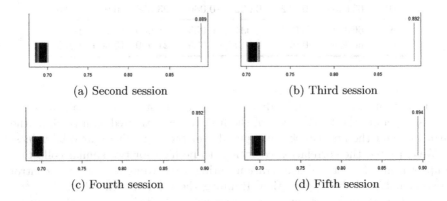

(a) Second session   (b) Third session

(c) Fourth session   (d) Fifth session

Fig. 3. Correlation coefficients for the first run, including surrogate and original pairs (highlighted). First session's data was rejected (see Sect. 5.1)

greater than required. The initial result of 0.892 was thus considered valid and used as baseline for the experiments analyzed below.

Contrasting with the control experiment, we expected that changing the independent variables would yield smaller correlation coefficients than the baseline. However, we did not have an intuition for the magnitude of the difference.

To test hypotheses 1_0, 2_0, 3_0, and 4_0, we fed into TimeWarper data from the second, third, fourth, and fifth runs, resulting in mean correlation coefficients of, respectively, 0.830, 0.848, 0.834, and 0.827 (see Table 3).

We performed statistical significance tests following the same technique as before. For every session from every run, the original coefficient ranked at 101st, validating each result. Those coefficients have shown strong positive correlations between measurements of vertical acceleration when using different smartphones, car mounts, sampling rates, and vehicles. The results refuted all proposed null hypothesis, implying a value of truth for all alternative hypothesis.

6   Conclusions

Our main contribution is an experimental study on the impact in quality of data collected by different smartphones, car mounts, rates of sampling, or vehicles when developing ADAS. This study shows that the quality of data acquired with smartphone sensors is not significantly affected by using different variations of those elements. It is thus feasible to use smartphone sensors to prototype and develop ADAS without the need to standardize the components used.

Additional studies can be conducted for any of the independent variables to strengthen the confidence on our results. Such studies should both have a greater number of repetitions and study a wider variety of subjects, e.g., by testing different types of vehicles. In particular, it would be interesting to see a further investigation on the car mounts, as their higher mean correlation coefficient seems to be counter-intuitive. A comparison of the capabilities of smartphones versus those provided by special-purpose sensor boxes could also be made. A study focused on vehicles' speed as an independent variable would be very valuable. To do so, a test track and cruise control-equipped cars should suffice.

References

1. Douangphachanh, V., Oneyama, H.: A study on the use of smartphones under realistic settings to estimate road roughness condition. Proc. Eastern Asia Soc. Transp. Stud. **9**(2007), 14 (2013)
2. Du, Y., Liu, C., Wu, D., Jiang, S.: Measurement of IRI by using Z-axis accelerometers and GPS. Math. Probl. Eng. (2014)
3. Eriksson, J., Girod, L., Hull, B., Newton, R., Madden, S., Balakrishnan, H.: The pothole patrol: using a mobile sensor network for road surface monitoring. In: Proceedings of the 6th International Conference on Mobile Systems, Applications, and Services (2008)
4. Fazeen, M., Gozick, B., Dantu, R., Bhukhiya, M., González, M.C.: Safe driving using mobile phones. IEEE Trans. Intell. Transp. Syst. **13**(3), 1462–1468 (2012)
5. Han, H., et al.: SenSpeed: sensing driving conditions to estimate vehicle speed in urban environments. In: IEEE Conference on Computer Communications, vol. 15, pp. 727–735 (2014)
6. Lindgren, A., Chen, F.: State of the art analysis: an overview of advanced driver assistance systems (ADAS) and possible human factors issues. Hum. Factors Econ. Aspects Saf. 38–50 (2006)
7. Mohan, P., Padmanabhan, V.N., Ramjee, R.: Nericell: rich monitoring of road and traffic conditions using mobile smartphones. In: Proceedings of the 6th ACM Conference on Embedded Networked Sensor Systems, p. 323 (2008)
8. Piras, M., Lingua, A., Dabove, P., Aicardi, I.: Indoor navigation using smartphone technology: a future challenge or an actual possibility? In: IEEE Position, Location and Navigation Symposium, pp. 1343–1352 (2014)
9. Ratanamahatana, C.A., Keogh, E.: Exact indexing of dynamic time warping. Knowl. Inf. Syst. **7**(3), 358–386 (2004). https://doi.org/10.1007/s10115-004-0154-9
10. Salvador, S., Chan, P.: FastDTW: toward accurate dynamic time warping in linear time and space. Intell. Data Anal. **11**, 561–580 (2007)

11. Santos, N.M.: A feasibility study on the use of smartphone sensors for development of advanced driver assistance systems. M.Sc. thesis, University of Minho, Portugal (2017)
12. Seraj, F., van der Zwaag, B.J., Dilo, A., Luarasi, T., Havinga, P.: RoADS: a road pavement monitoring system for anomaly detection using smart phones. In: Atzmueller, M., Chin, A., Janssen, F., Schweizer, I., Trattner, C. (eds.) Big Data Analytics in the Social and Ubiquitous Context. LNCS (LNAI), vol. 9546, pp. 128–146. Springer, Cham (2016). https://doi.org/10.1007/978-3-319-29009-6_7
13. Tai, Y., Chan, C., Hsu, J.Y.: Automatic road anomaly detection using smart mobile device. In: 15th Conference on Artificial Intelligence and Applications (2010)
14. Texas Instruments: Advanced Driver Assistance (ADAS) Solutions Guide. Technical report, Texas Instruments (2015)
15. Yi, C., Chuang, Y., Nian, C.: Toward crowdsourcing-based road pavement monitoring by mobile sensing technologies. IEEE Trans. Intell. Transp. Syst. **16**(4), 1905–1917 (2015)

Characterizing Air Quality in Urban Areas with Mobile Measurement and High Resolution Open Spatial Data: Comparison of Different Machine-Learning Approaches Using a Visual Interface

Yao Shen[1], Stephan Lehmler[2(✉)], Syed Monjur Murshed[2], and Till Riedel[1]

[1] KIT, Karlsruhe, Germany
`uivnz@student.kit.edu, riedel@teco.edu`
[2] EIFER, Karlsruhe, Germany
`{lehmler,lehmler}@eifer.org`

Abstract. Air quality is one of the most important topics in our urban life, as it is of great significance for human health and urban planning. However, accurate assessment and prediction of air quality in urban areas are difficult. In major cities, typically only a limited number of air quality monitoring stations are available, and inferring air quality in the un-sampled areas throughout the city is challenging. On the other hand, air quality varies in the urban areas non-linearly; it is highly spatially dependent and considerably influenced by multiple factors, such as building distribution, traffic situation and land uses.

In this research, we model air quality in the city of Augsburg using spatial features and high quality sensor data. We identify spatial features such as types and areas of different land uses, road networks with high resolution.

We integrate open available data to the air quality prediction. In this regard, we compare a simple baseline model with linear regression models (Ordinary Least-Squares and Ridge Regression) and tree-based machine-learning models (Gradient Boosting and Random Forest). In our evaluation, given the non-linearity of the data, tree-based models outperform all linear models, which are commonly used in literatures.

In addition, we created an interactive and visual dashboard. This dashboard demonstrates the analytical workflow, gives insight into model performance and uncertainty and visualizes the results.

Keywords: Air quality · Land-use regression · Dashboard · Machine-learning

1 Introduction

Smart Cities can be defined as cities that predict and accommodate citizens' needs using different types of data and sensors to provide information and applying advanced information technologies [1]. They will contribute to the efficient management of assets

H. Santos et al. (Eds.): SmartCity 360 2019, LNICST 323, pp. 115–126, 2020.
https://doi.org/10.1007/978-3-030-51005-3_12

and resources. In addition, as mentioned by [2], "all activities for a smart city related to public services can be managed by developing a platform (dashboard) for monitoring all relevant data." Visualization of data is important in Smart City applications, since it can communicate information clearly and efficiently, which supports people's decision-making process in the city planning.

In this context, advanced analysis tools have become essential for a Smart City development. Nowadays, machine-learning techniques play a key role in data analysis, predictive modeling and visualization [3]. In regard to machine-learning, one of the most complicated problems is the diverse types of input data and the amount of available data. In particular, for a smart city data analysis, spatial information of events and changes around the city is required [4].

Relevant spatial data (also known as geospatial data or geographic information) around a city is usually collected using ground surveying, remote sensing, more recently through mobile mapping, geo-located sensors, geo-tagged web contents, Volunteered Geographic Information (VGI) and so on [5]. In this study, we aim to tackle the smart city issues by using machine-learning based spatial data analysis.

Air quality information, such as the concentration of certain particulate matters like PM2.5 and PM10, is important for the quality of our urban life, as it is of great significance for human health and city management. However, in major cities, there is typically only a limited number of air quality monitoring stations. Inferring air quality in the areas not covered by measurements is challenging as air quality varies in the urban areas non-linearly, it is highly spatial-temporal dependent and considerably influenced by multiple factors, such as meteorology, traffic volume and land uses [6–8].

Compared to the previous works, the contribution of this paper lies in several aspects. We build land-use regression (LUR) models on mobile measurement data of air pollution, we can conclude that mobile monitoring data is suited for LUR modelling at a higher spatial resolution and therefore they can be used to characterize and prove the spatial variability of air quality in the complex city area. We identify more spatially related features with higher resolution, such as types and areas of different land uses, information regarding road networks. By extracting and utilizing data from VGI projects such as OpenStreetMap (OSM), we evaluate the usefulness of the crowd-sourcing data and the contribution of the open spatial data. We integrate these features to the air quality prediction; our proposed approach can be applied to assess air quality in any new urban areas. Afterwards, a visual interface is developed to demonstrate the work-flow of the analysis, including the data exploration, correlation analysis, model comparison and the inference of air quality for a new city area with a finer granularity.

2   Related Work

The LUR is one popular approach for predicting spatial variations in air pollution. As stated by [9], the general concept of a LUR is based on two steps: first, the dependencies between explanatory variables and monitored pollution levels are evaluated using ordinary least-square (OLS) regression for all measurement locations; second, the relationships found between concentrations and the explanatory variables are used to infer concentration levels at locations without measurements but with available land-use data.

LUR modeling requires air pollution measurements at multiple locations across the study area, according to a review by [10], stationary monitoring used by LUR is typically at 20 to 100 locations, spread over the study areas. [11] investigated in the effect of the number of monitoring sites on the LUR performance and their result suggested that for complex urban settings, a LUR model should be based on a large number of measurements (> 80 in their study), higher R^2 achieved from smaller number of monitoring sites for LUR models do not reflect the true predictive ability. A cost-effective alternative way to collect data at a high spatial resolution is to use mobile measurements, however, only few studies use mobile measurements as a basis for LUR modelling [12]. Based on surveyed papers [9, 12–16], the OLS regression models built on mobile measurement data explained between 0.40 and 0.60 of the observed variability in concentrations (R^2 tested on the training datasets). The time resolution of monitoring is usually 1 s.

To summarize the predictor variables used in the LUR models, frequently used data include: area of land-use, road network or traffic information, physical geography such as elevation and slope, and meteorological data. Some studies [15, 17] also used demographic data such as number of inhabitants and population density. Study of [15] brought the functions of year, day and hour into their modeling. Most studies have assessed a large number of potential predictor variables in modeling air quality concentrations and selected a smaller set of variables to the final models. Because of data availability, extraction and definition of predictor variables differ substantially between studies. For further development of LUR methods that can be transferred to other areas, open spatial data is worth getting more attention.

In addition, machine-learning approaches such as ensemble regression methods have been utilized to handle complex and nonlinear relationships that exist within data and produce forecasting models with comparable performance in practice. Based on our review of papers [6, 7, 18, 19] from the domain of spatial data analysis, since the prediction accuracy follows algorithm design, the machine-learning algorithms are crucial for building air quality prediction models, whereas statistical models have not been heavily used recently. Moreover, the random forest based approach is a prominent technique in selecting variables and inferring air pollution values.

3 Study Area and Required Data

3.1 Study Area and Description

The study site is the city of Augsburg, Swabia, Bavaria, Germany, the third-largest city in Bavaria (after Munich and Nuremberg) with a population of 300,000 inhabitants ($N48°22'$, $E10°54'$, 2000 inhabitants km^{-2}). The municipal area of Augsburg covers 147 km^2 and the city border is 78 km long. The widest point north to south is 23 km and east to west is 15.5 km. Residential and traffic areas make up only 36% of the city's land-use; one-third is devoted to agriculture and nearly 24% is forestland. The inner city of Augsburg covers approximately 6.8 km^2 and it is within the primary highway B 300 at the south and the primary highway B 2 at the east. Multiple railways locate at the west border, a tertiary highway borders the inner city at the north. The study area covers approximately 4 km^2, data was collected mostly in the inner city area of Augsburg, especially within the inner city borders at the south and east. There is no primary highway located across the study area, however, multiple railways pass through it at the southwest, shown in Fig. 1.

Fig. 1. The study area and mobile measurements during the first day of the IOP project in the city of Augsburg. To give a clear display of the data points and the buffer (50 m) around the measurements, we applied time-series re-sampling's approach to take the median PM1 value during a 5 min period (original data with 1-s resolution). The color gradient represents the height of PM1 and the data is displayed on a map, which shows different types of railways and roads extracted from OSM for the study area. (Color figure online)

3.2 Mobile Measurement Data

The mobile measurements were taken from the Intensive Operation Period (IOP) of the particulate matter measurement project SmartAQnet[1]. During the first day of the IOP, on the 26th Sep. 2018, a 11.4 km long route was done on foot 3 times in the study area. Measurements were taken from 12:16:02 to 23:10:14, about 11 h in total, approximately 4 h for each walk. The route was then repeated during the next day and one month later. The air pollution data were measured using the DustTrak DRX, which has a 1 s time resolution. The data types (unit originally in mg/m^3, multiplied by 1000 to unit $\mu g/$m^3) are: PM1, PM2.5 and PM10.

3.3 Geographic Data

The OSM project[2] is a repository that provides user-generated street maps. It is a powerful source of information that can be used free to understand and to model the built environment. OSM is available as a vector data collection comprising point features (nodes), line features (ways) and polygon features (ways and relations). Each feature has at least one "tag" (key-value-pair) describing it. See [20, 21] for more detailed description.

---

[1] https://smartaqnet.github.io/.
[2] https://en.wikipedia.org/wiki/OpenStreetMap.

The OSM data are downloaded and extracted from Geofabrik's free download server[3]. The file used for our study area is the file for Swabia, Bavaria, Germany[4]. The downloaded data is in a number of ESRI compatible shapefiles[5].

4 Implementation and Results

4.1 Aggregation of Concentrations

Following the study of [9], the measured air pollution concentrations of all three days are projected on a grid with 6100 cells, each of size 50 m * 50 m, covering the complete region of interest. For this purpose, the maximum and minimum values of the coordinates are utilized to define the bounding box for the grid building. We use this method to develop models for mean pollutant concentrations at a high spatial resolution. All measurements are performed in each cell. To assure data quality, we require the model input to be based on grid cells containing at least 50 mobile measurements, this removes approximately 4.6% of the data. Within the 6100 grid cells, 760 cells cover data points and 442 cells of them cover at least 50 measurements. The original datasets of the three days contain 131050 data points in total, 124985 data points remained for building our model after the selection of grid cells.

Considering the temporal aspect of the measurements, the information of the hour h is brought into the model to capture the temporal patterns within a day, such as the pattern during the rush hours. After the manipulation of aggregation, 3363 data points are used in the final dataset for the further analysis.

4.2 Feature Generation

We use the geographic data available from OSM, which includes land-use, buildings, traffic, railways and roads. After the aggregation of concentrations, the centroids of grid cells are used to draw 50 m buffers and to extract geographic features from OSM. Two types of features from OSM are considered: the polygon features and the line features. We generate the buffers and intersect these buffers with the OSM geographic layers. More specifically, the intersected areas for each values of keys are calculated for polygon features whereas we extract the intersected lengths for each types of the line features, such as road and railway. Based on the study of [18], we generate a vector as geographic abstraction for each aggregated mobile measurement location. In the next step, we quantify and evaluate the importance of individual components in the geographic abstraction vectors.

4.3 Preprocessing

In the experiment, we started with randomly taking left-out samples in a small size from the data and using the remaining data as the training set to predict the PM values for the

---

[3] http://download.geofabrik.de/ 2018/12/12 17:02.

[4] http://download.geofabrik.de/europe/germany/bayern/schwaben-latest-free.shp.zip.

[5] Geospatial vector data format for storing geometric location and associated attribute information.

left-out samples drawn before. That means, the model fits on the training dataset, then one uses the left-out samples as the ground truth to calculate the prediction accuracy. After we split the dataset randomly, the number of the observations in the training dataset is 2690, the percentage of data in training set is approximately 79.99%; the number of observations in the left-out set, i.e., test dataset is 673, the percentage of data in test set is approximately 20.01%.

For geographic features, we standardize them by removing the mean and scaling to unit variance, calculated from the training set. Standardization is useful when one of the variables has a very large scale, since this might lead to regression coefficients of a very small order of magnitude.

Specifically, for the sake of the interpretation of variables in linear models, the feature *hour* is one-hot encoded. They are therefore not treated as numerical but as categorical variables. This was done to improve the performance of the linear models, because air quality varies non-linear with time.

In order to assess the relative importance of the features we generated, we apply the means of importance measure based on random forest algorithm, namely Mean Decrease Impurity on the training dataset. The impurity (residual sum of squares) decreases from each feature can be averaged for a forest and the ranking of features is obtained according to this measure. Following the proposed approach of [18], we construct the weighted features by multiplying the values of all aforementioned preprocessed features by their relative importance. In this way, we can particularly penalize trivial features.

4.4 Experimental Result

To predict PM concentrations for a target location that does not have air quality measurements, we train different machine-learning models. The most commonly used LUR models in the literature apply ordinary least-square regression (OLR). We examine OLR and ridge regression. In addition, we examine two tree-based machine-learning algorithms: random forest and gradient boosting. The tree-based models are applied particularly for handling nonlinear relationships.

We tune the hyper-parameters by 5 folds cross-validated grid-search of each model to further improve their performance (tuned parameters for random forest: n_estimators = 256 for prediction on PM1 and PM2.5; n_estimators = 512 for prediction on PM10, min_samples_split = 2; for gradient boosting: n_estimators = 1024, learning_rate = 0.25; for ridge regression: alpha = 0.03125). We use the central tendency, namely, the mean of the output value observed in the training data, as a baseline to compare the results of all of our regression models.

From the Table 1, Table 2 and Table 3 we can compare the prediction's results for the three pollution types. The best prediction is achieved on the PM1. According to Table 1, gradient boosting regression generated the best training score whereas random forest performed the best on the test dataset. Tree-based models outperformed linear regression models and all the models performed better than the baseline.

Table 1. Result of prediction on PM1.

Regressors	R^2 (Train)	R^2 (Test)	RMSE	MAE	MAPE
RandomForest	0.755999	0.41941	13.013	4.61543	15.5181
GradientBoosting	0.801266	0.413835	13.0754	5.03747	17.3187
RidgeRegression	0.263594	0.177901	15.4848	7.05862	27.4429
LinearRegression	0.28177	0.190075	15.3697	6.92811	26.5321
Baseline	0.00	0.00	17.0807	9.12583	38.3164

Table 2. Result of prediction on PM2.5.

Regressors	R^2 (Train)	R^2 (Test)	RMSE	MAE	MAPE
RandomForest	0.747725	0.408235	13.3858	4.86004	16.3528
GradientBoosting	0.792927	0.399515	13.4841	5.3184	18.1369
RidgeRegression	0.244739	0.173651	15.818	7.50331	29.2644
LinearRegression	0.264099	0.187799	15.682	7.34138	28.0926
Baseline	0.00	0.00	17.4022	9.53591	39.8149

Table 3. Result of prediction on PM10.

Regressors	R^2 (Train)	R^2 (Test)	RMSE	MAE	MAPE
RandomForest	0.752592	0.299473	26.6166	7.05102	18.4924
GradientBoosting	0.849792	0.305144	26.5086	7.69487	20.9269
RidgeRegression	0.147497	0.0545743	30.921	9.5087	29.5942
LinearRegression	0.162844	0.0625943	30.7895	9.33308	28.4433
Baseline	0.00	0.00	31.811	11.2264	37.669

5 Visualization and Dashboard Development

We present an application to simplify the LUR modeling process. We develop a user-friendly dashboard using the Python (3.6) programming language, particularly, the visualizations of all parts of this application have been built with the Python package Bokeh[6] (1.0.4). This application is developed as a processing pipeline to model air quality based on sensor data and spatial information. The main goal of this dashboard is to provide an introduction of the work-flow for predicting air quality using LUR. Our model uses openly available data, which also offers the possibility to use it on other study area. The

---

[6] https://bokeh.pydata.org/en/latest/.

development of the dashboard is inspired by the Smart City applications introduced by [22] and the RLUR Shiny Dashboard [23].

To make a LUR model on the dashboard, users will need a training dataset with measured pollution concentrations and extracted geographic features, and a test dataset, which contains grid cells covering the place of interest with extracted geographic features. A sample dataset for training is provided here of PM1 concentrations in the city of Augsburg, Germany. The data description and complete approach for feature extraction is described in previous sections. A sample test dataset is provided for the whole city area of Augsburg. The bounding box of Augsburg is defined using the Nominatim API (3.2). A short description is also provided on the first page of the dashboard (Fig. 2).

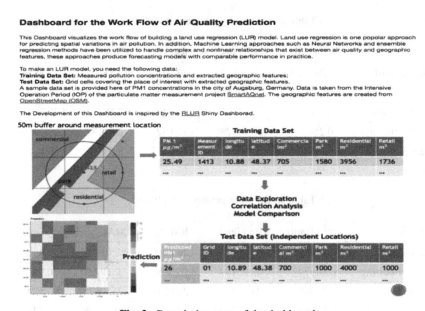

Fig. 2. Description page of the dashboard

5.1 Data Exploration

The first step of the analysis is data exploration. A sample dataset for training is provided, however, we also allow users to upload a training dataset from a local data source using Upload Training Set tool to make the dashboard more flexible to use, see Fig. 3. To do that, we utilize the CustomJS module to supply a snippet of JavaScript code that should be executed in the browser to open a file dialog. The uploaded data table should be saved as a csv text file and as another format restriction, the uploaded data table should contain two columns named as "lat" and "lon" respectively with the WGS 84 coordinates. Moreover, object data type is excluded for further development of the dashboard.

The target variable can be selected, e.g., PM1. Indexes are added to the data table as row labels. With an index slider, users can explore the data nicely, the map shows the

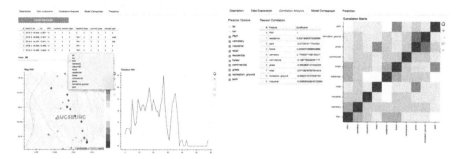

Fig. 3. Data exploration and correlation analysis (Color figure online)

location of the measurements and color code signifies the value of the target variable. In this sample dataset, the collection's time is recorded. We therefore sorted the table by time and plot the time series graph to show the temporal aspect of the data.

5.2 Correlation Analysis

As the next step, we apply correlation analysis and help users to identify which types of variables are more important for predicting the target variable. We use the function of pandas (0.23.4) DataFrame to compute pairwise Pearson correlation of columns, excluding NA/null values. As initial state, the target variable, in this case PM1 is selected automatically. The Correlation Matrix shows the correlation of all other variables except PM1 to detect the multicollinearity. As illustrated in Fig. 3, the Pearson Correlation table shows the correlation of the selected features with the target variable and this table is sorted in a descending order by the absolute value of the correlation. Selected features will be brought to the next step and will be used for training different models and comparing the model performance.

5.3 Model Comparison

The dashboard offers six different machine-learning algorithms to predict the air pollution levels using selected features from the last tab. The six algorithms are random forest, gradient boosting, extra trees, ridge, lasso and linear regression. To train the models, we build a function to execute each algorithm through a pipeline, which will fit the regressors on the training dataset, test them on the validation dataset and record performance metrics. For applying the algorithms, we use the standard methods from Python library scikit-learn (0.19.1).

As shown in Fig. 4, the Model Options is a multi-selection's tool, initially, all the models are selected for comparison. The Test Data Percentage can also be given by users. As the metrics, we record six measurements in total: Training Time, Training Score, Testing Score, RMSE, MAE and MAPE. The Training Score and Testing Score specify the R^2 on the training set and on the validation set respectively. Using the Regressor Properties table and the Model Comparison bar chart, we can get the best model according to the selected metrics. After the comparison, one can use the Model Options tool again to manually identify the best model, which will be applied for the prediction in the next step.

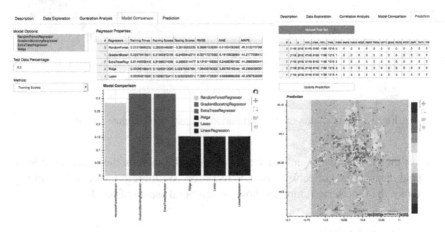

Fig. 4. Model comparison and prediction (Color figure online)

5.4 Prediction

In the last step, we visualize the prediction for the place of interest, see Fig. 4. To this end, we will need a test dataset. In the sample dataset, we built grid cells covering the city of Augsburg, each grid cell has the size 200 m * 200 m and land-use features are extracted for each grid cell. After that, we apply the model selected from last tab and predict the target variable, in this case, the PM1 value. We plot our prediction using color code on the map. The Upload Test Set button extend the flexibility of making predictions on this dashboard. We allow users to apply new test dataset for any city area. The Update Prediction button is used to make new predictions when any parameters of previous tabs have been changed, such as the target variable and the model.

6   Conclusion

6.1   Summary

This paper modeled air quality in the city of Augsburg using spatial features and mobile measurement data with high quality. We extracted and utilized data from OSM and identified spatial features such as types and areas of different land uses, road networks with high resolution. The advantages of our approach include that it used publicly available open data to construct the geographic predictor variables instead of using expensive datasets. Therefore, the built model can be easily used to infer air quality for other urban areas. In addition, our approach quantified the importance of geographic features on air quality prediction, enabled us to select features and integrate the important spatial factors automatically to the modeling, without using domain knowledge of air quality. We applied appropriate machine-learning approaches and compared the model performance using a visual interface (dashboard). A dashboard was developed at the end of this study to demonstrate the work-flow of the analysis, including the data exploration, correlation analysis, model comparison and the inference of air quality for a new city area with a fine granularity.

6.2 Limitations

The applicability of the LUR models obtained in this study is restricted by the characteristics of the input (air pollution) data, such as that the data points are collected using a single mobile sensor and they are only captured on the walked route. Due to the available data only covering 3 days, we were not able to include weather or seasonality effects into our model. Including additional measurements taken throughout the year should improve the relevance of our predictive model. Furthermore, the LUR models are only applied in a relatively small study area. How well the model would perform at a larger scale (e.g., including the peripheries and not only the city center) or even in another city area is still an open question. For instance, there is no primary highway located across the study area, however, the highway traffic could be an interesting factor to our study. As stated by [12], the generalization of the LUR model to areas where no measurements were made is limited, especially in predicting absolute concentrations. While this study showed some potential of mobile sensors and spatial features for air quality prediction, there is still more data needed for the evaluation of this approaches further applicability.

References

1. Hashem, I.A.T., et al.: The role of big data in smart city. Int. J. Inf. Manag. **36**(5), 748–758 (2016)
2. Suakanto, S., et al.: Smart city dashboard for integrating various data of sensor networks. in ICT for Smart Society (ICISS). In: 2013 International Conference (2013)
3. Gangappa, M., Mai, C.K. Sammulal, P.: Techniques for Machine Learning based Spatial Data Analysis: Research Directions (2017)
4. Bermudez-Edo, M., Barnaghi, P.: Spatio-temporal analysis for smart city data. In: Proceedings of WebConf 2018 (2018)
5. Li, S., et al.: Geospatial big data handling theory and methods: a review and research challenges. ISPRS J. Photogrammetry Remote Sens. **115**, 119–133 (2016)
6. Yu, R., et al.: RAQ–a random forest approach for predicting air quality in urban sensing systems. Sensors **16**(1), 86 (2016)
7. Zheng, Y., Liu, F. Hsieh, H.P.: U-Air: when urban air quality inference meets big data. In: Proceedings of the 19th ACM SIGKDD International Conference on Knowledge Discovery and Data Mining, pp. 1436–1444. ACM (2013)
8. Kang, G.K., et al.: Air quality prediction: big data and machine learning approaches. Int. J. Environ. Sci. Dev. **9**(1), 8–16 (2018)
9. Hasenfratz, D., et al.: Deriving high-resolution urban air pollution maps using mobile sensor nodes. Perv. Mob. Comput. **16**, 268–285 (2015)
10. Hoek, G., et al.: A review of land-use regression models to assess spatial variation of outdoor air pollution. Atmos. Environ. **42**(33), 7561–7578 (2008)

11. Basagaña, X., et al.: Effect of the number of measurement sites on land use regression models in estimating local air pollution. Atmos. Environ. **54**, 634–642 (2012)
12. Van den Bossche, J., et al.: Development and evaluation of land use regression models for black carbon based on bicycle and pedestrian measurements in the urban environment. Environ. Model Softw. **99**, 58–69 (2018)
13. Weichenthal, S., et al.: A land use regression model for ambient ultrafine particles in Montreal, Canada: a comparison of linear regression and a machine learning approach. Environ. Res. **146**, 65–72 (2016)
14. Hankey, S., Marshall, J.D.: Land use regression models of on-road particulate air pollution (particle number, black carbon, PM2.5, particle size) using mobile monitoring. Environ. Sci. Technol. **49**(15), 9194–9202 (2015)
15. Patton, A.P., et al.: An hourly regression model for ultrafine particles in a near-highway urban area. Environ. Sci. Technol. **48**(6), 3272–3280 (2014)
16. Kanaroglou, P.S., et al.: Estimation of sulfur dioxide air pollution concentrations with a spatial autoregressive model. Atmos. Environ. **79**, 421–427 (2013)
17. Habermann, M., Billger, M., Haeger-Eugensson, M.: Land use regression as method to model air pollution. Previous Results Gothenburg/Sweden. Procedia Eng. **115**, 21–28 (2015)
18. Lin, Y., et al.: Mining public datasets for modeling Intra-City PM2.5 concentrations at a fine spatial resolution. In: Proceedings of the 25th ACM SIGSPATIAL International Conference on Advances in Geographic Information Systems. ACM (2017)
19. Sun, L., et al.: Impact of land-use and land-cover change on urban air quality in representative cities of China. J. Atmos. Solar-Terrestrial Phys. **142**, 43–54 (2016)
20. Wiki, O.: Main Page – OpenStreetMap Wiki (2014)
21. Schultz, M., et al.: Open land cover from OpenStreetMap and remote sensing. Int. J. Appl. Earth Obs. Geoinf. **63**, 206–213 (2017)
22. Lehmler, S., et al.: Usability of open data for smart city applications–evaluation of data, development of application and creation of visual dashboards. In: REAL CORP 2019–IS THIS THE REAL WORLD? Perfect Smart Cities vs. Real Emotional Cities. Proceedings of 24th International Conference on Urban Planning, Regional Development and Information Society (2019)
23. Morley, D.W., Gulliver, J.: A land use regression variable generation, modelling and prediction tool for air pollution exposure assessment. Environ. Model Softw. **105**, 17–23 (2018)

NeuralIO: Indoor Outdoor Detection via Multimodal Sensor Data Fusion on Smartphones

Long Wang[✉], Lennard Sommer, Till Riedel, Michael Beigl, Yexu Zhou, and Yiran Huang

Karlsruhe Institute of Technology, TECO, Karlsruhe, Germany
{wanglong,sommer,riedel,beigl,zhou,yhuang}@teco.edu

Abstract. The Indoor Outdoor (IO) status of mobile devices is fundamental information for various smart city applications. In this paper we present NeuralIO, a neural network based method to deal with the Indoor Outdoor (IO) detection problem for smartphones. Multimodal data from various sensors on a smartphone are fused through neural network models to determine the IO status. A data set consisting of more than 1 million samples is constructed. We test the performance of an early fusion scheme in various settings. NeuralIO achieves above 98% accuracy in 10-fold cross-validation and above 90% accuracy in a real-world test.

Keywords: Indoor outdoor detection · Multimodal data fusion · Neural network model

1 Introduction

The past decade has witnessed the flourishing of the Internet of Things (IoT) and its applications in urban spaces. The widespread deployment of IoT devices and the rise of the smart cities are giving birth to an increasing number of smart applications [3,6,9,12]. Context status is critical and fundamental information for ubiquitous computing systems and context-aware IoT applications [10,25]. "Context" consists of a wide range of aspects such as location, time, surrounding environment and so on. The rapid growth of smartphones is driving the increasing interest in context-aware applications [15,16,19].

One of the most fundamental contextual information is whether the device is in an indoor or outdoor environment. It makes a significant difference if a user is standing in front of a shopping mall or in a shopping mall. Further, the availability and capabilities of different technologies vary considerably between these two environments. The knowledge about the Indoor Outdoor (IO) status enables the choice of appropriate technologies, which leads to a better user experience. For instance, the device can trigger a reminder, change the working mode, and

© ICST Institute for Computer Sciences, Social Informatics and Telecommunications Engineering 2020
Published by Springer Nature Switzerland AG 2020. All Rights Reserved
H. Santos et al. (Eds.): SmartCity 360 2019, LNICST 323, pp. 127–138, 2020.
https://doi.org/10.1007/978-3-030-51005-3_13

switch between GPS based navigation and indoor navigation schemes when the user enters or leaves an indoor environment. Further, the device can save energy by turning off the GPS module in indoor environments such as a metro station. Existing IO detection approaches commonly use GPS signal [7,8,18,26], wireless signal [5,22,27,29] and other sensor data [2,11,17,20,28,28] to determine IO status.

Due to the rich characteristics of natural phenomena, it is rare that a single modality provides comprehensive knowledge of the phenomenon of interest [13]. The increasing availability of multiple sensing modalities on smartphones offers us more freedom to recognize the context. The capability of neural network models bas been proven superior in solving increasingly complex machine learning problems, which often involve multiple data modalities [21].

We propose NeuralIO to detect the Indoor Outdoor status of smartphones through multimodal sensor data fusion using neural network models. We create a data set containing more than 1 million labelled samples by 9 users. 9 different sensing modalities are covered in the data set, which are accelerometer, GPS, light, magnetic, proximity, cellular signal strength, sound level, temperature and WiFi. We test the performance of an early fusion scheme in various settings.

To summarize, the contributions in this paper are as follows:

1. We apply neural network models to the IO detection problem and provide a comprehensive analysis.
2. We implement an Android app for data collection and conduct experiments to collect data samples in various real daily scenarios. A data set consisting of more than 1 million labeled data samples is constructed.
3. We evaluate the performance of an early fusion scheme on the data set through cross-validation and a real-world test. Above 98% accuracy is achieved in the cross-validation and above 90% accuracy is achieved in the real-world test.

The rest of the paper is organized as follows: Sect. 2 presents related work. Different fusion schemes are introduced in Sect. 3. The experiment and data collection is described in Sect. 4 and evaluation results are presented in Sect. 5. We conclude our work in Sect. 6.

2   Related Work

2.1   GPS Based Methods

GPS signal is highly dependent on the line-of-sight (LOS) paths between the device and GPS satellites. It is well known that GPS signals are poor in indoor environments as the LOS paths of GPS signals are blocked. In contrast, the LOS paths are not blocked in most outdoor scenarios. On the basis of these facts, the localization accuracy of GPS or the availability of GPS signal has been exploited to determine whether a device was in an indoor or outdoor environment [7,8,18,26].

Despite the intuitive nature and easy implementation of GPS based methods, they suffer from several disadvantages. Radu et.al. identified the GPS chipset as the sensor with the highest power consumption among the evaluated sensors [20]. The battery capacity is still limited in state-of-the-art mobile phones and most users dislike applications which drain the battery. Secondly, the intuition behind these methods is not always reliable. For instance, the GPS signal is reasonably strong if a device is in an indoor environment with large windows. In contrast, the GPS signal can be blocked by surrounding mountains if the device is in a valley. Under these circumstances, GPS based methods may give misleading results. A third disadvantage is that it normally takes around one minute to launch a GPS module, making GPS-based methods unsuitable for real-time applications.

2.2 Wireless Signals

Shtar et al. [22] presented a method for continuous indoor outdoor environment detection on mobile devices based solely on WiFi fingerprints and assumed no prior knowledge of the environment. The model trained with the data collected for just a few hours on a single device was applicable for unknown locations and new devices. WifiBoost [5] made use of a machine learning meta-algorithm that combined a sufficiently large ensemble of simple classifiers (so-called weak learners) to improve the overall performance. An average error rate of around 2.5% was achieved in the evaluation. However, a classifier needed to be created for each building and the surrounding area through measurements and labeling of each measurement point, especially in cases where there was no previous fingerprinting database. Building such a database is not a trivial task.

Wang et al. [27] applied a machine learning algorithm to classify the signal strength of neighboring cellular base stations in different environments and identified the current context by signal pattern recognition. Accuracy of 100% was reported for the identification of open outdoors, semi-outdoors, light indoors, and deep indoors.

In [29], low-power iBeacon technology was leveraged to develop an accurate, fast response and energy-efficient scheme for indoor outdoor detection. The transitions between outdoors and indoors were detected by comparing the Received Signal Strength of two pre-deployed Bluetooth beacons at two sides of each entrance.

2.3 Multiple Sensors

Since a single sensor might not be able to tackle with all application scenarios, data from multiple sensors such as accelerometer, proximity and light sensor, wireless receiver and magnetometer were exploited for IO detection [2,11,17,20, 28]. IODetector [28] combined data from three lightweight sensors (light sensor, cell tower signal strength and magnetic sensor) to develop an extensible IO detection framework which did not require a training phase. Although acceptable error rates were achieved, Radu et al. [20] criticized IODetector for its hard-coded thresholds which might not work with new devices and new environments. As an alternative, Radu et al. proposed a semi-supervised training method to improve IO detection accuracy across different devices and environments.

2.4   Other Methods

In [14], the embedded digital camera on a mobile phone was utilized for IO detection. The developed gentle boosting classifier achieved an error rates of 1.7% for indoor and 10.8% for outdoor scenes. Beside, a feed forward neural network was trained with GIST feature of images to address the IO detection problem [24]. These methods help in generating semantic IO labels for images, but do not work for tracking and other real time application cases.

Sung et al. [23] developed a sound based IO detection method using chirp signal. A simple classifier was developed with a static threshold. However, this work was rather simple and straightforward, and no comprehensive analysis was provided. Wang et al. conducted a comprehensive study on an audio based IO detection method. The method was evaluated in various scenarios with different probing signals (MLS and chirp), noise levels and device types.

3   Fusion Scheme

Neural networks offer the flexibility of implementing multimodal sensor fusion as either early, late or intermediate fusion [21].

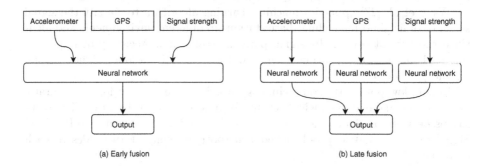

Fig. 1. Schema of early fusion and late fusion schemes based on neural networks

As shown in Fig. 1a), in early fusion scheme data from multiple sources are intergrated into a single feature vector to serve as the input of one machine learning model. In contrast, late fusion scheme aggregates decisions from multiple models which are trained separately on their own modality as shown in Fig. 1b). This fusion scheme is often favored because errors from multiple classifiers tend to be uncorrelated and the method is feature independent [21].

For traditional machine learning methods, it is typically necessary to manually extract features from each modality which is not only time-consuming but also challenging. Neural networks are known for being able to learn features automatically. In this paper we choose to use an Feedforward Neural Network (FNN) model to conduct early fusion for indoor outdoor detection problem.

4   Experiment and Data Collection

4.1   App Design and Implementation

We have developed an Android app for data collection. The app needs to access multiple sensors on the smartphone and save the sensor readings to a database. The collected data contains: battery temperature, luminance, magnetic flux density, proximity, cellular signal strength, cellular network bit error rate, an abstract level for the overall signal strength ranging from one to four number of WiFi networks around the user, the highest signal strength of the WiFi networks around the user, number of GPS satellites, GPS accuracy in meters, GPS signal-to-noise ratio, ambient noise level. Additionally, some anonymous information about the device is also recorded to distinguish different data traces.

Fig. 2. Screenshot of the developed Android app

Figure 2 shows a screenshot of the developed app. The users specifies whether they are indoor or outdoor and inputs the current weather condition. Then, they have the option to provide notes on the location and their name. The users start the logging period for either 10 min, 30 min or an unlimited amount of time. If, for example, the users walk indoors while logging data labeled outdoor they have the option to invalidate the last 5, 15 or 30 min of the collected data. The users can stop the logging process at any time.

The application collects the specified information every 200 ms as one json object. The data is then sent to an instance of the Firebase Realtime Database (DB) [1]. This ensures that every user directly writes to the same database and no data is saved locally on the user's device. From there, the data can be downloaded for further processing.

4.2 Data Collection

The smartphone application is handed out to multiple participants for data collection. The users are instructed about the application and how to use it. The data collection runs for four weeks, users are free to choose the time and environment for data logging. Figure 3 shows the typical data logging scenario.

Fig. 3. Data logging process. The picture on the left shows how a user configuring the data logging session and the picture on the right depicts data logging inside a pocket.

The resulting dataset consists of 1,038,678 samples which is around 58 h of data. 99.49% of the data is collected by four users. The remaining 0.51% of the data was collected by 5 other users. Overall, the distribution of indoor to outdoor samples is 57.61% to 42.39%. The distribution before cleaning for different smartphones is illustrated in Fig. 4. Different smartphones also represent different users.

4.3 Preprocessing

By removing the samples that were invalidated by the users themselves, 1,019,091 samples are left which is equivalent to about 56.5 h of data. However, not every collected sample is completed due to various reasons. After removing the incomplete samples, the resulting dataset includes 623,320 samples, which is equivalent to around 34.5 h of data. The balance between indoor and outdoor samples is now 43.98% to 56.02%.

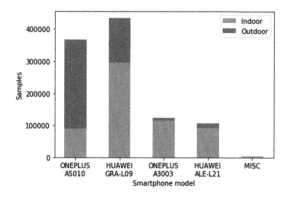

Fig. 4. Distribution before cleaning

5   Evaluation

5.1   Cross Validation

We use 10-fold cross-validation to evaluate the performance of the constructed model. We have tried various numbers of hidden units and hidden layers. Finally we got a good balance between performance and model complexity by using the architecture in Fig. 5. The input layer with 24 input nodes is omitted due to limited space. There are four hidden layers with 10, 5, 4, 3 hidden units with Relu as activation function. The output unit uses the sigmoid function as the activation function. As shown in Table 1, the results from 10-fold cross-validation demonstrate that the model performs very well in 9 out of 10 folds, in the 5th fold the model only achieves an accuracy of 0.73. This is probably due to the loss function becoming trapped at a local minimum.

Table 1. Results of 10-fold cross-validation. Precision and recall are for the outdoor label.

	1	2	3	4	5	6	7	8	9	10
Accuracy	0.98	0.99	0.99	0.99	0.73	0.98	0.99	0.99	0.99	0.98
Precision	0.98	0.99	0.99	0.99	0.73	0.99	0.99	0.99	0.99	0.99
Recall	1	0.99	0.99	0.99	1	0.99	0.99	0.99	0.99	0.98

5.2   Real-World Test

To verify the performance of the model in the real world, we tested the trained FNN model on a real-world dataset. The real-world dataset was recorded around two months later than the training dataset. During the collection of the data

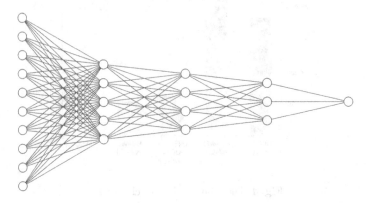

Fig. 5. FNN model architecture with four hidden layers and one output layer. Note that the input layer (with 24 input nodes) is not displayed due to limited space. The activation function of all hidden units is the Relu function. The activation function for the output node is the sigmoid function.

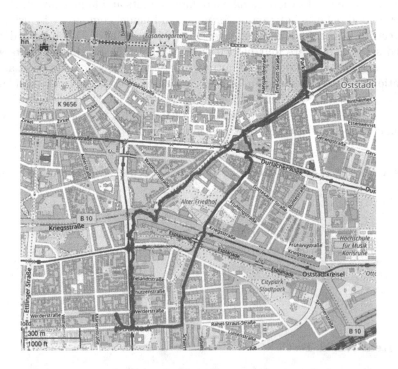

Fig. 6. Real-world test path

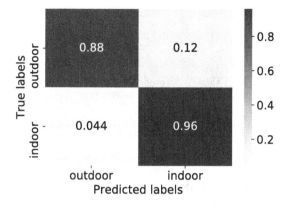

Fig. 7. Confusion matrix

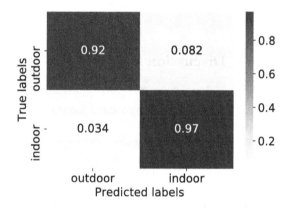

Fig. 8. Confusion matrix for model with majority voting

set, the user walked through the city as depicted in Fig. 6. The trace covers indoor environments such as campus buildings and shopping malls, and outdoor environments such as streets.

The confusion matrix is shown in Fig. 7. Generally the model perform quite well in real-world test with an overall accuracy of 91%. Specifically, the model can recognize indoor cases with a precision of 96% with only 4% falsely classified as outdoor. The model achieves a precision of 88% for outdoor cases with 12% of all outdoor cases falsely classified as indoors. The model shows good generalizability on new data set.

To investigate the cause of misclassification problem of the model, we plot the labels of all data entries against the index in Fig. 9. As shown in Fig. 9, there are some isolated misclassifications for both indoor and outdoor cases. Considering the common sense that it is very rare for people to switch between indoor and outdoor states in a short time period (for instance 2 s), we can use a majority voting strategy with a sliding window to filter out the isolated misclassification

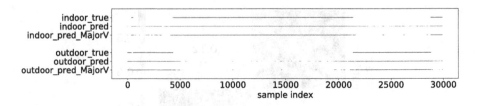

Fig. 9. Ground truth, prediction results without/with majority voting strategy.

cases. The basic idea is that the indoor/outdoor state is not only determined by the input data, but also depends on the previous predicted labels in the sliding window. As shown in Fig. 9, there are fewer isolated misclassification cases after applying the majority voting strategy with a sliding window of 10. The confusion matrix in Fig. 8 also shows an increase in the precision for both indoor and outdoor cases.

6   Conclusion and Discussion

We developed NeuralIO, a neural network based multimodal fusion method for indoor outdoor detection problem on smartphones. A data set consisting of more than 1 million data samples was constructed. 9 different sensing modalities were covered in the data set. We built a feed forward neural network model for early fusion of all available raw data. Cross-validation and real-world test have shown its feasibility for indoor outdoor detection and generalizability on a new data set.

Due the length limit, we did not investigate the late, intermediate fusion scheme and other neural network models. We reserve them as future work.

Acknowledgements. This work was partially funded as part of BMVI project "SmartAQnet" [4], grant no. 19F2003B.

References

1. Firebase realtime database documentation. https://firebase.google.com/docs/database/. Accessed 07 June 2019
2. Ali, M., ElBatt, T., Youssef, M.: Senseio: realistic ubiquitous indoor outdoor detection system using smartphones. IEEE Sens. J. **18**(9), 3684–3693 (2018)
3. Amft, O., Van Laerhoven, K.: What will we wear after smartphones? IEEE Pervasive Comput. **4**, 80–85 (2017)
4. Budde, M., et al.: SmartAQnet: remote and in-situ sensing of urban air quality. In: Proceedings of the SPIE 10424, Remote Sensing of Clouds and the Atmosphere XXII, 104240C (2017)
5. Canovas, O., Lopez-de Teruel, P.E., Ruiz, A.: Detecting indoor/outdoor places using wifi signals and adaboost. IEEE Sens. J. **17**(5), 1443–1453 (2017)

6. Chen, Y., Yonezawa, T., Nakazawa, J., Tokuda, H.: Evaluating the spatio-temporal coverage of automotive sensing for smart cities. In: 2017 Tenth International Conference on Mobile Computing and Ubiquitous Network (ICMU), pp. 1–5. IEEE (2017)

7. Chintalapudi, K., Padmanabha Iyer, A., Padmanabhan, V.N.: Indoor localization without the pain. In: Proceedings of the Sixteenth Annual International Conference on Mobile Computing and Networking, pp. 173–184. ACM (2010)

8. Cho, H., Song, J., Park, H., Hwang, C.: Deterministic indoor detection from dispersions of GPS satellites on the celestial sphere. In: The 11th International Symposium on Location Based Services (2014)

9. Franke, T., Lukowicz, P., Blanke, U.: Smart crowds in smart cities: real life, city scale deployments of a smartphone based participatory crowd management platform. J. Internet Serv. Appl. **6**(1), 1–19 (2015). https://doi.org/10.1186/s13174-015-0040-6

10. Ishida, Y., Thepvilojanapong, N., Tobe, Y.: Winfo+: identification of environment condition using walking signals. In: Tenth International Conference on Mobile Data Management: Systems, Services and Middleware, MDM 2009, pp. 508–512. IEEE (2009)

11. Jia, M., Yang, Y., Kuang, L., Xu, W., Chu, T., Song, H.: An indoor and outdoor seamless positioning system based on android platform. In: Trustcom/BigDataSE/ISPA, 2016 IEEE, pp. 1114–1120. IEEE (2016)

12. Khaled, A.E., Helal, A., Lindquist, W., Lee, C.: IoT-DDL-device description language for the "T" in IoT. IEEE Access **6**, 24048–24063 (2018)

13. Lahat, D., Adali, T., Jutten, C.: Multimodal data fusion: an overview of methods, challenges, and prospects. Proc. IEEE **103**(9), 1449–1477 (2015)

14. Lipowezky, U., Vol, I.: Indoor-outdoor detector for mobile phone cameras using gentle boosting. In: 2010 IEEE Computer Society Conference on Computer Vision and Pattern Recognition Workshops (CVPRW), pp. 31–38. IEEE (2010)

15. Maeda, H., Sekimoto, Y., Seto, T.: An easy infrastructure management method using on-board smartphone images and citizen reports by deep neural network. In: Proceedings of the Second International Conference on IoT in Urban Space, pp. 111–113. ACM (2016)

16. Maeda, H., Sekimoto, Y., Seto, T.: Lightweight road manager: smartphone-based automatic determination of road damage status by deep neural network. In: Proceedings of the 5th ACM SIGSPATIAL International Workshop on Mobile Geographic Information Systems, pp. 37–45. ACM (2016)

17. Nakamura, Y., Ono, M., Sekiya, M., Honda, K., Takahashi, O.: Indoor/outdoor determination method using various sensors for the power saving of terminals in geo-fencing. In: Proceedings of the 2015 International Workshop on Informatics (2015)

18. Okamoto, M., Chen, C.: Improving GPS-based indoor-outdoor detection with moving direction information from smartphone. In: Adjunct Proceedings of the 2015 ACM International Joint Conference on Pervasive and Ubiquitous Computing and Proceedings of the 2015 ACM International Symposium on Wearable Computers, pp. 257–260. ACM (2015)

19. Perttunen, M., et al.: Distributed road surface condition monitoring using mobile phones. In: Hsu, C.-H., Yang, L.T., Ma, J., Zhu, C. (eds.) UIC 2011. LNCS, vol. 6905, pp. 64–78. Springer, Heidelberg (2011). https://doi.org/10.1007/978-3-642-23641-9_8

20. Radu, V., Katsikouli, P., Sarkar, R., Marina, M.K.: A semi-supervised learning approach for robust indoor-outdoor detection with smartphones. In: Proceedings of the 12th ACM Conference on Embedded Network Sensor Systems, pp. 280–294. ACM (2014)
21. Ramachandram, D., Taylor, G.W.: Deep multimodal learning: a survey on recent advances and trends. IEEE Signal Process. Mag. **34**(6), 96–108 (2017)
22. Shtar, G., Shapira, B., Rokach, L.: Clustering Wi-Fi fingerprints for indoor-outdoor detection. Wirel. Netw. **25**, 1–19 (2018)
23. Sung, R., Jung, S., Han, D.: Sound based indoor and outdoor environment detection for seamless positioning handover. ICT Express **1**(3), 106–109 (2015)
24. Tahir, W., Majeed, A., Rehman, T.: Indoor/outdoor image classification using gist image features and neural network classifiers. In: 2015 12th International Conference on High-Capacity Optical Networks and Enabling/Emerging Technologies (HONET), pp. 1–5. IEEE (2015)
25. Uehara, Y., Mori, M., Ishii, N., Tobe, Y., Shiraishi, Y.: Step-wise context extraction in AoK mule system. In: Proceedings of the 4th International Conference on Embedded Networked Sensor Systems, pp. 379–380. ACM (2006)
26. Wang, H., Sen, S., Elgohary, A., Farid, M., Youssef, M., Choudhury, R.R.: No need to war-drive: Unsupervised indoor localization. In: Proceedings of the 10th International Conference on Mobile Systems, Applications, and Services, pp. 197–210. ACM (2012)
27. Wang, W., Chang, Q., Li, Q., Shi, Z., Chen, W.: Indoor-outdoor detection using a smart phone sensor. Sensors **16**(10), 1563 (2016)
28. Zhou, P., Zheng, Y., Li, Z., Li, M., Shen, G.: IODetector: a generic service for indoor outdoor detection. In: Proceedings of the 10th ACM Conference on Embedded Network Sensor Systems, pp. 113–126. ACM (2012)
29. Zou, H., Jiang, H., Luo, Y., Zhu, J., Lu, X., Xie, L.: Bluedetect: an ibeacon-enabled scheme for accurate and energy-efficient indoor-outdoor detection and seamless location-based service. Sensors **16**(2), 268 (2016)

A Low-Cost Video-Based Solution for City-Wide Bicycle Counting in Starter Cities

Eduardo Peixoto[1] , João Moutinho[2] , and Rui José[1(✉)]

[1] Centro Algoritmi, University of Minho, Braga, Portugal
eduardopeixotop@gmail.com, rui@dsi.uminho.pt
[2] Centro de Computação Gráfica (CCG), Guimarães, Portugal
Joao.Moutinho@ccg.pt

Abstract. Cycling is increasingly popular as a sustainable urban mobility mode. Data can play a key role in the success of cycling promotion initiatives, by helping to understand cycling demand and assess the real impact of investments. However, creating a global view of the cycling activity of a city can be a major challenge, as there are no obvious sources from which to obtain the necessary cycling data. While there are now many bike counters in the market, their hardware and deployment costs severely limit the number of sensors that can be deployed and consequently the spatial coverage of the city. In this work, we explore the viability of a large-scale bicycle counting infrastructure for city-wide cycling analytics, which explores the trade-off between costs and spatial/temporal coverage. The proposed solution uses a set of temporary low-cost video-based counters, which can flexibility be rotated among multiple counting locations. To understand the viability of the approach we developed a prototype counter, where we tested two video processing techniques: OpenCV and Yolo. Results suggest that the overall approach could indeed support a low-cost and universal bike counting functionality, as long as delayed access to data is acceptable. Even though this is not envisioned as a general bike counting solution, it may provide a smart way to approach the complex issue of universal city-wide bike counting.

Keywords: Smart mobility · Bike counters · Cycling data · OpenCV · Yolo

1 Introduction

Cycling and other soft mobility modes are increasingly seen as crucial for sustainable urban mobility [1]. Many cities across the world are developing cycling programmes, which may include the development of dedicated infrastructures, bike sharing services or public awareness activities. A key element for the success of those initiatives is the ability to understand their impact by measuring cycling activity [2]. The lack of systematic and consistent monitoring processes has been identified as one of the obstacles towards more sustainable development of cycling mobility policies [3]. This lack of data about cycling activity affects all elements of the ecosystem, but is particularly problematic for municipalities and other local entities who very much need concrete and actionable data

© ICST Institute for Computer Sciences, Social Informatics and Telecommunications Engineering 2020
Published by Springer Nature Switzerland AG 2020. All Rights Reserved
H. Santos et al. (Eds.): SmartCity 360 2019, LNICST 323, pp. 139–150, 2020.
https://doi.org/10.1007/978-3-030-51005-3_14

to justify investments in cycling infrastructures, to make more informed decisions and to assess the real impact of their policies. Likewise, private companies in the cycling sector also need this type of data to create solid business plans, make informed business decisions and optimize operations management.

Data is therefore critical for the ability of cycling mobility initiatives to create real, profound, incremental and measurable impact. However, creating a global view of the cycling activity of a city can be a major challenge, as there are no obvious sources from which to obtain the necessary cycling data. This is a very generic problem, which affects any city, regardless of its dimension or its level of cycling readiness. In this research, we are mainly concerned with the case of starter cities, where the first initiatives are emerging, but infrastructures and cycling adoption are still very incipient. For these cities, data can help promoting the type of societal and political transformation needed to bring cycling mobility to the centre of mobility policies. Basic data, such as the number of cycling trips at new infrastructures or the level of city-wide cycling activity are particularly crucial for sustaining a strong Return on Investment argument. Without this data, the reality of cycling mobility is largely invisible to urban planners and to society at large.

Recent years have seen the emergence of a wide range of bike counters, which can be deployed on streets to count passing cyclists. Their key advantage is the ability to continuously count the universe of cyclists at those locations, without depending on any action from cyclists themselves. Their key problem is cost, which includes not only the cost of the counting device itself, but also the often very high costs associated with deployment in public space. This severely limits the number of sensors that can be deployed and consequently the spatial coverage of the city. This is particularly severe for cities where cycling investment is still at its early stages.

In this work, we explore the viability of a large-scale bicycle counting infrastructure for city-wide cycling analytics. Rather than improving the technical performance of any particular technology, we are mainly concerned with the development of a bike counting service in the most economically efficient way and using whatever combination of technologies may be suitable for this purpose. This should allow any starter medium-size city to deploy a few hundreds of counting points, which would constitute a paradigm change for city-wide cycle sensing. Our early solution is centred on video analysis. We have developed a low-cost video-based counting device based on the Raspberry Pi platform. In this study, we analyse the ability of this low-cost platform to serve as the backbone for a city-wide bicycle counting service. The approach is based on a rotating scheme, where sensors are regularly moved to pre-defined locations and possibly combined with partial data sources to provide a global view of the city cycling activity. To understand the viability of the approach we compare the reliability and deployment flexibility of two video processing techniques. Despite using only well-known and widely available video processing techniques, this approach seems to offer enough precision to be seen as a valuable solution, in which some loss in precision may be counterbalanced by the wide spatial coverage of the counting process.

2 Related Work

A bicycle counting system can be based on manual or automated techniques, or even in a combination of both. Manual techniques involve having people manually counting passing bicycles, either physically at counting gates or by observation of videos recorded at those locations. They can offer a valuable approach for more occasional measurements or when a more thorough characterisation of cyclists is needed [4]. Still, a manual counting is a monotonous and, especially, a time-consuming task, which can only provide occasional snapshots of the cycling reality. It does not scale when a wide spatial/temporal coverage is needed.

An automated process involves placing a sensing infrastructure that is able to autonomously perform the count. A bicycle counter is normally composed by a sensor, which collects the data used for detecting the passage of bicycles, and a central apparatus, which supports any data processing needs, as well as sharing or storing the collected information. Recent years have seen the emergence of a wide range of automated bike counters, and there are now several market solutions. They explore a very broad range of bicycle detection techniques, with very different properties and performances, such as Pneumatic tubes, Inductive loop detectors, Piezoelectric Strips, Pressure or acoustic pads, Active infrared, Pyroelectric, Laser scanning, Radio Wave, Video image processing, Magnetometers or Bicycle Barometers [4]. Some of these technologies were initially developed for counting motor vehicles, but they have since been repurposed for detecting pedestrians and cyclists.

The current state of the art in commercial solutions may be exemplified by CITIX-3D by Eco-Counter [5]. This is a wide-range counter, with the capability to automatically count and classify, not just cyclists, but also pedestrians and vehicles. The technology developers claim that it offers a greater precision than traditional video analysis, requires zero calibration and can be reliably operated day or night, rain or shine. However, the very high cost of the solution and the sophistication of the data produced, make it more suitable to generate broader usage profiles of public spaces. For example, they can support the detailed study of movement patterns around specific crossings, helping planners to understand how space is used and consequently, identify the need for specific interventions. Bike counters are also often used in combination with public displays, showing daily, monthly or annual bike counts in real-time. These displays serve mainly as a public celebration of all those who already cycle and as a medium to improve the public visibility to the city's efforts to promote bicycle traffic.

While some of these techniques can be highly sophisticated and accurate, they do not seem to offer a compelling solution for a city-wide counting system. The first reason is that they typically assume that their key performance indicator is precision. This naturally favours more sophisticated and consequently more costly technologies. While precision is an obviously central criterium, the added value brought by a more complex solution may not always counterbalance the added costs, especially when considering the existence of a large number of counters. The second reason is that the viability of their deployment can be highly dependent on environmental elements, such as the possibility to physically install sensors or other hardware, the profiles of the cycling paths or even the level of cycling/pedestrian traffic. Consequently, when we consider the huge diversity of urban settings that compose any city, it becomes very difficult to identify a technique that could be the best solution for the whole city. Moreover, many of these deployment approaches may also represent significant additional costs. This severely limits the number of sensors that can be deployed and consequently the spatial coverage of the city. Large communities can sometimes afford to install two or three permanent counters at key locations, and very large communities, may reach upwards of ten permanent counters throughout the city [6]. With just a few counting devices, mobility analysis is not complete and the monitoring data is not rich enough. As a consequence, these solutions fail to provide a large scale and cost-effective solution for the problem of measuring urban cycle traffic. They are mainly deployed in very small numbers and to cover high profile locations, such as new flagship infrastructures.

3   A Video-Based Solution for Scalable Urban Bike Counting

Our exploration of this design space is driven by the need to optimize three key variables of the solution, cost, spatial coverage and temporal coverage, while also guaranteeing viable precision levels. Assuming continuous spatial and temporal coverage would always imply very high costs because a large number of devices would have to be permanently used at a very large number of locations. However, reducing costs by cutting the number of counters will have a negative impact on spatial and temporal coverage. Therefore, the fundamental design issue for this system is the optimisation of the inherent trade-off between coverage and cost.

The first and most obvious approach to address this optimisation is to simply reduce the cost of the counting devices. A solution based on low-cost counters would be more prone to be economically viable for large scale deployment across the city. For that, the cost of the counting devices should be an order of magnitude lower than current solutions. A key step to reduce costs is to focus only on concrete data needs, which in our case is information about bike passages at multiple reference locations around the city, so that we can build a global account of bike trips in that city. A clear focus on these concrete requirements should allow to reduce or eliminate any development, deployment and maintenance costs not directly related with those needs. For example, assuming that no live data is needed, the sensing device could operate without any network connectivity. It could simply store counting data, which could then be retrieved directly from the device itself, whenever there was a maintenance operation or when the device was moved to another location. For most urban planning processes, this delay in data gathering should not be a problem.

The second way to optimize the cost/coverage equation is by relaxing the requirements for continuous temporal and spatial coverage. Since we want to create a city-wide system, our approach is designed to favour spatial coverage, while relaxing time coverage. The goal is to reduce the number of bike counters that are needed, and consequently the cost of the whole infrastructure. However, since we still need to obtain data at a potentially large and representative set of collection points, we consider that the system would be based on a network of temporary bike counters to be regularly rotated across different locations. In this case, a lower number of sensors should be able to cover many counting points without compromising the essence of the data produced over time by the system.

A key requirement emerging from this approach is that a temporary counter should be very simple to deploy at multiple locations and it should not require any external energy source or cable connections. A very flexible and low-cost deployment process would be essential to reduce the cost of the overall solution, as the costs involved in the public deployment of technology can be substantially higher than the costs of the devices themselves. Flexibility is also crucial to support the deployment of bike counters into the very diverse urban spaces where they may need to be deployed.

In regard to time coverage, basic information about the number of cyclists passing by a particular counter should easily accommodate only occasional measurements. A partial temporal coverage should not be a limitation as, for most cases, bike passage numbers are essentially about trends and medium or long-term evolution, and not so much about live data. The average values are not likely to face dramatic changes, and the total number of passages over a month or a year should be easily estimated based only on samples obtained from regular, but not continuous measurements. With the proper corrections for seasonal or weather factors, it should be reasonably simple to make adequate estimations.

This process could also be improved even further by combining these video-based counters with other, more accessible, but less accurate data sources. Many of them may provide simple and reliable data about cycling activity, but they fail to provide universal counts, as they are can only count a subset of cyclists. For example, only a few cyclists will have detectable Bluetooth devices and only a few will use any particular cycling application. The complementarity between technologies may help to mitigate some of their limitations and create a view of cycling mobility that is bigger than the sum of the parts.

From this perspective, the video-based counter described in this work is mainly seen as providing the baseline data about the universe of cyclists in a particular location. When deployed alongside other sensors, they can be used to determine the percentage of passing cyclists which can be detected through other basic sensors. For example, one can estimate the percentage of cyclists using a specific cycling application from which public data can be obtained. This can then be compared against the data generated from those other sources to provide an estimate of their representativeness in regard to the universe of cyclists. With these data, it would then be possible to support dynamic and more accurate estimations of cycling counts based only on data from those partial sources. This would also reduce the need for a very complete temporal coverage of the bike counters. The process can be regularly recalibrated through the scheduled redeployment of video sensors at those locations.

3.1 A Portable Video-Based Bike Counter

We decided to focus on video analysis as the core sensing technology for this bike counting system. This decision was based on its low cost, its high reliability and the wide availability of cameras and video processing tools [7], but especially on the flexibility with which it can be deployed across many different types of city locations. Using video as a core technology does not exclude other types of sensing technology, it just assumes that video will play a central role as the source of universal counting data for direct counts and for adjusting estimation parameters.

The counting device is based on a Raspberry Pi v2 with a 900 MHz quad-core ARM Cortex-A7 CPU and 1 GB RAM. The device also includes a Raspberry Pi Camera Module 8MP V2 with auto-focus and a 10,4 mAh Power Bank. These are all simple hardware components, which are widely available on the market and should cost a total of about 100€, making it significantly less expensive than common bike counting solutions. Despite its simplicity and low performance, we have managed to use this device to run the software needed to capture and process images. Its small size and energy autonomy are also important to make it a very suitable solution for simple deployments and for regular rotation between multiple counting locations. Ideally, battery capacity should be aligned with transfer cycles, so that their charging or replacement could be made as part of that process.

The essence of our bike counting device is the ability to detect the presence of specific objects of interest, in this case, bicycles in the images captured by the camera. We explored the use of two video processing techniques which may be seen as representative of two major approaches for video processing: Background Subtraction with OpenCV and Deep Learning with YOLO.

The reason why we tested two different techniques was not to make any generic comparison between them, but to understand their implications in regard to our specific requirements of flexible usage across many different deployment locations. The software was developed using python and the respective libraries for those methods.

The OpenCV approach was based on background subtraction [8]. This method is suitable for videos, and compares each frame with the previous frames, thus allowing to distinguish background from moving objects of interest, as shown in Fig. 1.

Fig. 1. Application of background subtraction.

To extract the information of interest contained in the videos, we used multiple OpenCV library functions, including GaussianBlur, createBackgroundSubtractorMOG2, morphologyEx and connectedComponentsWithStats. This method creates bounding boxes around the white components which are attached in the mask. Bounding boxes whose area is below or above a certain threshold are peremptorily rejected.

Once the algorithm detects the object of interest, it proceeds to the bounding box design, which delimits the object in question for the study (see Fig. 2). We used a basic classification scheme where squares were classified as pedestrians and rectangles as classified as bicycles.

Fig. 2. Determining bounding box around the object of interest.

YOLO (You Only Look Once) [9] uses neural networks to detect objects in images (not taking video into account). The popularity of YOLO comes from the fact that only a neural network can describe the bounding box and classes of the objects, all at once. We used an implementation of this neural network, called DarkFlow, which implements YOLOv2 using the TensorFlow package in Python. This neural network has already been trained with bicycle and pedestrian images. For the purpose of this work, we rejected objects whose probability was less than 0.8.

4 Methodology

To evaluate and fully explore the range of design and deployment alternatives, we analysed the different possibilities associated with the application of the two presented methods (Background Subtraction and Deep Learning). For each of them, we tried to identify the operational conditions that could optimise their precision and the extent to which this could affect their viability as flexible and easy to deploy cycling sensor. The key independent variable in our study was the camera position.

The goal is to represent the diversity of scenarios that may arise when using video cameras in different urban settings. This was from the beginning an important requirement, as we wanted to guarantee that the cameras could easily be deployed across many locations in a variety of situations, which could require very diverse camera mounts. With that in mind, we defined 3 different positions for the counter device (*c.f.* Fig. 3), which we believe may be representative of most common settings:

- View 1: A vertical line pointing directly from above to the cyclist (Vertical);
- View 2: A lateral view pointing to the side of the cyclist (Lateral);
- View 3: An obliquus view with ~45° angle on passing cyclists (Obliquus).

The perspective obtained with each camera view is shown in the 3 video frames which compose Fig. 4.

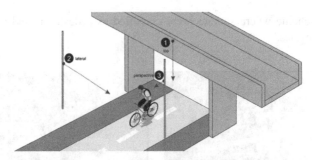

Fig. 3. Evaluation deployment with video being captured from three references angles

Vertical   Lateral   Obliquus

Fig. 4. Three video capture views used for evaluation

We collected videos at each of the three angle views and the same videos were used as input to our two video processing methods. Even though this was a cycle path, there was also pedestrian traffic and there were cyclists passing by in small groups and at various speeds. The evaluation addresses two complementary perspectives. The first was the general efficacy of the counting process, measured in terms of false positives, false negatives and the ratio between manual and automated counts, for each of the technique/angle combinations. The second was the deployment implications, assessed by the impact of different operational conditions on the efficacy of the techniques. The efficacy of the counting process is largely dependent on the deployment conditions and they both affect the final cost of the process.

5   Results

To support the evaluation process, we started by manually annotating the video streams with the events corresponding to the passage of cyclists. Each annotation corresponded to a passage event with the times of the first and last frame where the bicycle is detected. This was used as the ground truth for assessing the results of each experimental condition.

We then applied the OpenCV and Yolo techniques to automatically count the bicycles in each of the three video streams (vertical, lateral and obliquus). This was made by automatically generating a similar type of annotation where a bicycle passage event was associated with two timestamps: the time when it was first detected and the time where detection ends.

These values were compared against the begin and end times produced by manual annotations. We consider that an object had been correctly identified, whenever the absolute difference was less than two seconds. If a passage annotation is not identified by the algorithms, this was counted as a false positive. If the algorithms produced any count that did not had a corresponding passage in the video, this was counted as a false positive. Table 1 shows the results generated for the six experimental conditions.

Table 1. Results of bike counting for each experimental condition

Method	View	Man count	Auto count	False negative	False positive	Diff	%Diff
OpenCV	Vertical	177	209	3	35	32	18,1%
OpenCV	Lateral	77	82	0	5	5	6,5%
OpenCV	Obliquus	73	61	21	9	−12	−16,4%
Yolo	Vertical	177	189	6	18	12	6,8%
Yolo	Lateral	77	79	0	2	2	2,6%
Yolo	Obliquus	73	71	2	0	−2	−2,7%

A general analysis of these results shows that in general YOLO (28 false counts) seems to perform better than OpenCV (73 false counts). Also, for both techniques, the above view seems to be worst performing approach, as can more easily be perceived from Fig. 5 and Fig. 6.

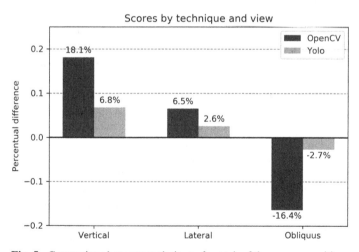

Fig. 5. Comparison between techniques for each of the camera positions

The key observation is that Yolo seems to clearly outperform OpenCV in the ability to correctly detect bicycle passages. In particular, its Deep Learning approach seems more suitable for dealing with abrupt changes in the scene caused by light variations or camera vibration.

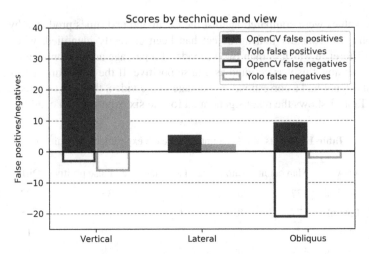

Fig. 6. Comparing false results for each of the camera positions

However, a key part of this analysis is also to identify some of the causes behind the situations where the system performed worst, mainly to understand if they were merely circumstantial and potentially easy to solve by using some different set of configurations. OpenCV scored particularly bad in Vertical or Obliquus views. This seems to have been mainly caused by the high sensitivity of this technique to variations caused by shadows and their change throughout the day. The camera focus may also have interfered, and seems the likely cause of many of the false positives that were detected with OpenCV. The key implication of these results is that OpenCV could only be considered a viable approach for side views, which would break our requirement of achieving maximum flexibility in regard to camera deployment options. However, OpenCV has a much better computational performance, which could be essential whenever there is the need for near real time data.

With YOLO, there might also be some space for improvement, particularly in regard to the less positive score in the vertical view. The YOLO package used for this work had been previously trained for bicycle recognition using mainly videos with lateral and obliquus views. This may justify the better performance of the algorithm in these cases. However, this also opens a potentially simple path for improving performance from the above view by adding new training cases using videos capture from vertical points of view. This vertical view is considered to be the most effective to properly segment bicycles when multiple cyclists are riding together in close proximity and generating occlusion situations.

The key limitation with YOLO, however, was computational performance. The Raspberry Pi device used in the experiment had very low processing power. While enough for the OpenCV approach, these devices were not able to cope with the requirements of YOLO processing. More specifically, they were not able to perform real time processing in which image capture and image processing would both be performed concurrently. A first solution would be to off-load the images to more powerful servers, which could be much more efficient in completing the task. However, this would bring connectivity requirements and increase energy demand. Also, from a privacy perspective, there is a strong argument to discard approaches where the video data leaves the counting device.

An alternative is to separate video capturing and recording from video analysis. The system could be capturing data for a certain period of time and then stop data collection to process the images. From our experience with the processing algorithms this seems to be viable and something which could potentially be aligned with day/night cycles.

6   Conclusions and Future Developments

In this study, we have analysed the conception of a low-cost, video-based and movable bike counting device for supporting large-scale counting. The approach explores the optimization of the inherent trade-off between cost and spatial/temporal coverage.

Results suggest that the overall approach could support a form of low-cost and universal bike counting functionality, providing a path to approach the complex issue of how to enable a city to understand the reality of its emerging cycling mobility. The flexibility and simple deployment that characterises this system seems well suited to the concept of intermittent counting, where sensors would be deployed for relatively short periods, i.e. 1–4 weeks, and then moved to another location, possibly returning to the original location every few months. This would provide the core data for city-wide cycling analytics, which could then be combined with other data sources to estimate a more dynamic and accurate perspective of the cycling reality.

Future work will explore the use of Bluetooth radio identification to create origin/destination matrixes. As many cyclists use Bluetooth equipment (Smartphones, wearables or speedometers), to identify their radio device while passing through a counter, this may provide partial, but very relevant, information to support the decision process in cycling mobility in municipalities. Our preliminary tests revealed that this technology is a possibility, especially considering the ever-growing number of devices that use Bluetooth. The occasional deployment of the video-based approach described in this work, would provide the data needed to estimate bicycle counts based only the percentage of users that carry detectable Bluetooth devices.

We also plan to investigate the system properties of this counting system. This may involve determining the minimum number of bike counters needed to estimate global cycling activity within particular levels of confidence. It may also involve the optimization of measurement cycles and their duration.

Acknowledgements. This work has been supported by national funds through FCT, Fundação para a Ciência e Tecnologia, within the Project Scope: UID/CEC/00319/2019, and also by the European Structural and Investment Funds in the FEDER component, through the Operational Competitiveness and Internationalization Programme (COMPETE 2020) [Project n° 039334; Funding Reference: POCI-01-0247-FEDER-039334].

References

1. Bulc, V.: Cycling: green and efficient transport for the future. In: European Commission (2016)
2. Lee, J., Leem, Y.T., Lee, S.H.: Categorizing U-Bike service and assessing its adoptability under it. In: 12th World Conference on Transport Research, pp. 1–10 (2010)
3. Ricci, M.: Bike sharing: a review of evidence on impacts and processes of implementation and operation. Res. Transp. Bus. Manag. **15**, 28–38 (2015)
4. Johnstone, D., Nordback, K., Lowry, M.: Collecting Network-Wide Bicycle and Pedestrian Data : A Guidebook for When and Where to Count (2017)
5. Eco-Counter: CITIX 3D (2019). https://www.eco-compteur.com/en/produits/citix-range/citix-3d-2/. Accessed 7 July 2019
6. Lowry, M.B.: Spatial Analysis of Bicycle Count Data: Final Project Report (2017)
7. Parekh, H., Thakore, D., Jaliya, U.: A survey on object detection and tracking methods. Int. J. Innov. Res. Comput. Commun. Eng. **2**, 2970–2979 (2014)
8. KaewTraKulPong, P., Bowden, R.: An improved adaptive background mixture model for real-time tracking with shadow detection. In: Remagnino, P., Jones, G.A., Paragios, N., Regazzoni, C.S. (eds.) Video-Based Surveillance Systems. Springer, Boston (2011)
9. Redmon, J., Divvala, S., Girshick, R., Farhadi, A.: You only look once: unified, real-time object detection. In: Proceedings of IEEE Computer Society Conference on Computer Vision and Pattern Recognition, December 2016, pp. 779–788 (2016)

Smart Governance for Sustainable Smart Cities

Assessing Urban Critical Infrastructure Using Online GIS and ANN: An Empirical Study of Bucharest City (Romania)

Adriana Reveiu[✉]

Bucharest University of Economic Studies, Bucharest, Romania
reveiua@ase.ro

Abstract. Critical infrastructure (CI) assessment is becoming a prominent topic for smart city, as it supports economic activity, governance and determines the quality of life. Due to their interdependence, the geographic location and effectiveness of CI components definitely determine the overall performance of urban system, so that any internal or external disturbance of one CI component could generate cascading failure and impact the whole urban activity. Nowadays, the explosion of urban infrastructure, the increased volume of extant data and technological advancements in ICT foster emerging smart critical infrastructure assessment solutions, adapted for various smart city requirements.

While information related to CI is heterogeneous and multi-dimensional, it is a lack of studies exploring the potential of combined data-sources in modelling and assessing urban interconnected CIs.

In this context, to better understand the holistic approach of CI and to support decision makers this paper proposes a framework for CI assessment, based on Geographic Information System (GIS) technology and artificial neural-networks (ANN) modelling. This framework envisages identifying urban sub-regions profiles as the first step in assessing resilient capacity of different urban areas.

A case study of CI assessment accomplished for Bucharest city from Romania, is included.

Keywords: Critical infrastructure · Artificial neural networks · Smart city · Geographic Information System

1 Introduction

Nowadays, the urban system is the result of complex natural, physical, social, political and economic processes and their dynamic interactions, where attributes such as urban critical infrastructure plays a major role in city activities and evolution. According to the United Nations' forecast about 66% of World's population is expected to settle in urban areas by 2050. As a consequence, the complexity of urban system and its infrastructure even high will increase more.

© ICST Institute for Computer Sciences, Social Informatics and Telecommunications Engineering 2020
Published by Springer Nature Switzerland AG 2020. All Rights Reserved
H. Santos et al. (Eds.): SmartCity 360 2019, LNICST 323, pp. 153–161, 2020.
https://doi.org/10.1007/978-3-030-51005-3_15

Cities are complex and interdependent systems, extremely vulnerable to threats, from both natural hazards and terrorism. In the recent years, the occurrence of various shocks and stressors has increased and disproportionately affected regions and cities. In this respect, identifying specific profile of various geographic areas of an urban area, from various perspectives, is a foremost subject for smart city research area.

The urban infrastructure is defined as a network of physical, cyber and organizational independent and mostly privately-owned systems and processes that collaboratively and synergistically operate to produce and distribute a continuous flow of essential products and services, to ensure citizens' protection and to support economic, social and administrative activities of the city [1, 2]. Even though it is no agreement on what components of urban subsystems infrastructure deemed to be the critical infrastructure [3], according to [4, 5] this includes those systems whose incapacity or damage would have a debilitating impact on the defense, economic security, public health and safety or any combination of these matters.

Urban infrastructure sub-systems are mutually dependent and interconnected into a network through which goods, services, people and information flow, supporting activities within the city. In this context, modeling and assessing of interdependent Cis in a holistic manner is a prominent research topic for smart city governance nowadays. Moreover, advancements in ICT support smart cities development, but withal modern solutions bring in also new risks and cyber threads.

Most of the extant papers evaluating CIs mainly focus on classic CI systems, like: telecommunications, energy systems, water supply, emergency and transportation services, but more recently [2, 6] have included economic related systems, like: banking, finance and government services in their critical infrastructure assessments as they have a major impact on smart city evolution.

As the economic related infrastructure is considered of a critical importance in mitigating and recovering from disasters [7], this paper attempts to provide a comprehensive understanding of interconnected CIs in a holistic manner.

To better understand CIs and to support decision makers, this paper proposes a new framework that combines GIS analysis with ANN to profiling and assess the available urban CIs, considering not only traditional critical infrastructure, but also economic components like: banking, financial, governmental and commercial facilities.

To exemplify the holistic approach of urban critical infrastructure assessment and proposed framework effectiveness, a case study of Bucharest city, from Romania is included. A web geographic information system has been designed to illustrate spatial distribution of some urban system assets, relevant for urban resilience assessment.

The paper is organized as follows: Sect. 2 depicts in a holistic manner, the main attributes of urban CIs to support urban policy-makers. Section 3 introduces the novel framework developed using ANN modelling for urban CIs assessment. Proposed model applied as a case study designed for Bucharest city, from Romania is presented in Sect. 4. The 5th section concludes the findings of this research and proposes future research directions.

2 Urban Critical Infrastructure Functions to Support Urban Resilience

Critical infrastructures are complex urban systems of a high importance for the quality of humans' life, for providing essential services to households and economic activities, and the functioning of which is dependent on various internal and external factors, occurring continuously or randomly, which can cause cascade failures of the interconnected assets. Traditional CIs include electricity, water, transportation, gas and waste networks. Motivated by economies of scale, digital technologies and unequal distributions of resources and economic activities, current CIs have included communication and information systems, bank and finance systems, emergency services (police, fire rescue, medical rescue) and local administration also [6]. Nowadays, CIs have been interconnected and have evolved into large spatially distributed systems, with multiple interdependencies.

From various perspectives, CIs are considered both dependently and interdependently. Whereas dependency refers to the unidirectional relationship, interdependency infers bidirectional interactions [8]. The acknowledged types of interdependency are: physical, cyber, logical, functional, spatial, geographic, informational, policy, market and economic. Such complexity provides the conditions for generating disproportionate consequences, when particular CIs asset from one location fails.

Considering this form of interdependence, the infrastructure criticality should be analyzed beyond the scale of an individual asset. Moreover, critical geographic areas of a city have to be identified.

Spatial diversity in all dimensions, including CIs diversity, is considered an important property of a city for fostering urban resilience whereas it assures risks diffusion and shapes up learning opportunities [9]. However, two apparently contradictory views that determine the role of urban infrastructure spatial diversity exist, namely: the socio-ecological view that considers diversity helpful in reorganization of processes and systems once disrupted and the socio-technical approach in which spatial diversity is seen as a costly and inefficient strategy to develop resilience, as it could affect critical infrastructure performance, but it can mitigate the risk of damaging circumstance occurrence. Since most of the urban activities are geared towards communities residing in specific geolocations, spatial diversity, spatial clusters and connectivity are considered determinants of urban infrastructure resilience [9].

Each urban community is unique and has its own local context, experiences, resources and beliefs regarding the prevention, protection, response and recovery mechanism from different types of disturbances. Function on the adopted standpoint and the strategy considered to foster urban resilience, each approach can be considered appropriate.

In addition, the amount and diversity of gathered data related to CIs have mostly increased due to advances in ICT technologies for acquiring, storing, processing and mining both spatial and non-spatial data. Since this data usually encapsulates hidden or hardly detectable relationships, using traditional statistical methods, a new appropriate approach is to apply spatial data mining methods that integrate artificial intelligence, machine learning and spatial statistics to identify and extract knowledge from large and heterogeneous datasets [10].

Additionally, Internet-of-things, cloud computing and embedded operational technologies are some of the areas which may cause serious disruptions in critical infrastructures, critical information infrastructures, and essential services for urban society.

In this context, a framework aiming to identify regional clusters, to assess urban CIs and to benchmark various resilient-specific measures is definitely valuable.

An increased number of research papers emerged in the past few years, attempting to better understand the CI systems diversity and their impact on urban activities and resilience, but as notice [11], among others, more research needs to be done in this direction. This paper aims to fill this identified gap in the smart city research area.

Furthermore, while there is a significant number of studies that model critical infrastructure system performance, due to their complexity, it is a big challenge to assess their resilience and their contribution to economic development [11]. This paper aims to fill this gap and introduces a new framework for CIs assessment, as the first step in the attempt to model CIs resilient conditions.

3 A Modelling Framework for CIs Assessment in Smart City Context

This section introduces the novel framework for assessing urban CIs that brings to light the extant cluster type agglomerations of CIs from the urban area.

The assessment of urban system infrastructure spatial diversity is not only a precondition for developing comprehensive methods of measurement and techniques for analyzing urban resilience, but also boost the understanding of society as part of the urban system resilience.

One challenge of this scientific approach is to identify spatially neighboring urban areas, characterized by similar features in respect to CIs, owing to the prominent complexity of CIs and the lack of fine-grained administrative datasets.

Clusters identification has been used in various studies related to smart city research area, such as: disaster analysis [12], criminology [13] and critical infrastructures [11], to explain reasons for occurrence of one phenomenon in a particular geographic area.

To account for spatial dependence among heterogeneous CIs related data, to extract pattern from available data and to identify homogeneous urban areas, from CIs standpoint, the following methodology has been designed:

1. All infrastructural assets were mapped and a spatial distribution of CIs has been accomplished. To reveal the geographic density of CI features a heat map was built up for each significant critical infrastructure sub-system. Relevant critical infrastructure assets considered for this study are: public transportation infrastructure, road network, emergency infrastructure: hospitals, police office, bank services: bank establishments, ATM, public administration establishments, and other point of interest: parks, schools and commercial centers.
2. To discover multivariate clusters from unstructured CIs data, a self-organizing map, namely the GeoSOM method was employed.

Self-organizing map (SOM) artificial-neural networks method uses unsupervised learning approach for training and discovering data patterns with the aim to mitigate data-dimensionality and to generate a two-dimensional representation of input datasets, while maintaining the input datasets topology. Unlike other ANN methods, which use error-correction learning approach, SOM method employ competitive learning that maintains the topological properties of the input datasets, including spatial characteristics [14].

Even there is a significant number of algorithms available for clustering analysis, only very few neural network related clustering algorithms consider spatial characteristic of data. The most prominent adaptation of self-organizing network algorithm is Geo-Self-Organizing Maps (GeoSOM) [15].

GeoSOM is a proximity-aware alternative algorithm of the standard SOM. GeoSOM uses geo-coordinates to establish the geographic tolerance parameter, which is used to maintain the geographic vicinity of similar data objects, by mapping them to neurons. GeoSOM spatial clustering method groups neighboring observations into clusters, to maximize similarity within cluster, while the similarity between clusters is minimized [14]. The method is available as part of the SPAWNN [15] toolkit.

For this research purpose, the CIs related data was mapped onto 8×12 neural network, and such generating a two-dimensional matrix of 96 neurons. Considering the observation number (3994) the resulting feature map is considered medium-size [15], and such multiple data observations could be mapped to each neuron, generating regions with more general characteristics.

The output of the GeoSOM algorithm is an attribute map that group items with similar attribute values into neighboring regions of neurons. A correlation analysis can be further performed, to identify and evaluate the associations between different attributes of the CI datasets.

As spatial distribution is a prominent characteristic of CIs components, GeoSOM method is appropriate for this research purposes.

3. Finally, the outcome of modelling process is linked back to urban geographic space providing a comprehensive understanding of the extant CIs. The pairwise difference between and within identified clusters is evaluated to ensure clusters validity. So that the identified sub-regions maintain both spatial continuity and similarity of non-spatial attributes of CIs. Modeling infrastructure allows to systematically evaluate the consequence associated with the loss of infrastructure components and to benchmark the impact of various policy measures.

4   CIs Assessment - Empirical Study of Bucharest City

The aim of this section is to evaluate Bucharest city's CIs by applying the proposed model to identify homogenous city sub-regions or clusters [16]. Data sets used for this case study were provided by ESRI Romania and include geographic coordinates of points of interest (POI).

Besides typical critical infrastructure, this case-study has considered so-called infrastructure for economic and administrative activity also. So that, a total of 3994 POIs have been included in the analysis, namely: public transportation stations (including maximum capacity in each point), bank system establishments (bank, ATM), governmental institutions (public institutions, Police office), schools, parks, hotels, hospitals and commercial centers.

Firstly, each type of critical infrastructure was evaluated considering spatial distribution of infrastructure assets. Figure 1 exemplifies public transportation infrastructure distribution for Bucharest city, where the green dots represent spatial distribution of public transportation stations considering both geo-location and the maximum capacity available in each station. The CIs features heat map presented in Fig. 4 distinguishes urban areas that holds spatial density of each CI resources.

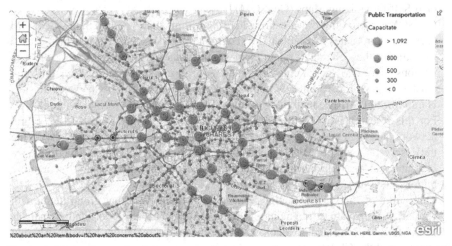

Fig. 1. Public transportation infrastructure (bus, tram and metro stations) – including available transportation capacity (Color figure online)

Secondly, ANN modelling was performed for the interconnected CI systems. Geo-SOM ANN method was applied and Fig. 2 presents the aforementioned method outcomes. The resulting output matrix reveals ten clusters of CIs, with different sizes.

Ten CIs clusters have been identified, mapped and laid out in the online GIS application, as depicted in Fig. 3. Each of the resulting urban sub-regions is characterized by internal homogeneity with regard to the non-spatial feature of CIs.

Due to the great diversity of data patters, only 501 out of 3994 CI features could be clustered. Figure 3 depicts discovered clusters in the Bucharest city and represents urban regions characterized by similar feature values across all variables of CIs, using various colors. Geo-coordinates are used to define the proximity of observations and the contiguity of urban clusters.

The largest identified cluster is figured in Fig. 3 as C1 and could be generally described as a region with a dense and high-capacity public transportation network, holding mixed points of interest like: commercial centers, public schools, hospitals, parks. The second is the cluster named C2, mainly holding both very big financial network and public transportation infrastructure. On the 3rd place is C3 cluster with numerous public and financial institution establishments. The C4 cluster is on the 4th position; it

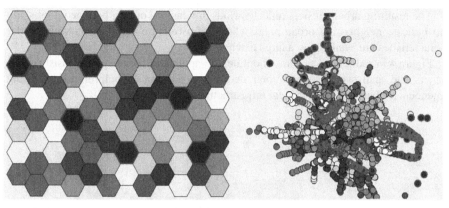

Fig. 2. Distance matrix and cartographic map of the GeoSOM algorithm and SPAWNN tool

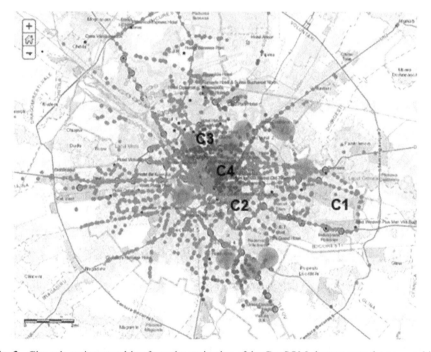

Fig. 3. City sub-regions resulting from the projection of the GeoSOM clusters onto the geographic space of Bucharest

is located in the very center of the city and it hosts mainly a combination of financial institutions, hotels and public transportation features. Definitely, future research needs to be done to determine the influence of each cluster on urban resilience and economic development of the city.

The resulting urban clusters reflect various dimensions of CIs, both geographically and indicate neighboring urban areas where infrastructure components with similar characteristics are available in a large extend.

Figure 4 introduces a snapshot of online GIS application developed to assist policy-makers and analysts to support their decisions as it can be helpful in identifying dependencies between local critical infrastructures.

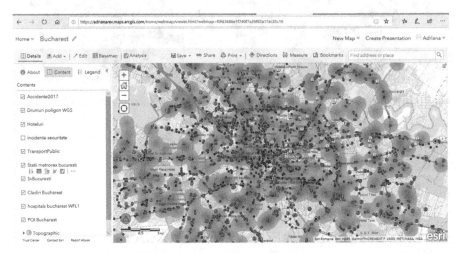

Fig. 4. A snapshot of online ArcGIS solution CIs assessment

Although the focus of this paper is on supporting interaction between local critical infrastructure within the Bucharest city this framework can be correspondingly customized and used for other urban areas.

5   Conclusion and Future Research Direction

As smart city well-being is dependent on critical infrastructure security, the subject of this paper is a prominent topic for smart city and governance research area, nowadays.

The contribution of this paper is twofold. Firstly, using the lens of GIS and ANN this paper proposes a novel theoretical model for assessing extended critical infrastructure of an urban area, using clustering modeling of spatial and non-spatial characteristics of CIs. The model can be extended and other urban resources can be included to determine the profile of urban-sub regions. This is an essential approach towards urban resilience aiming to enrich the available methods for urban resources assessment.

Secondly, this paper proposes a practical framework, including both online GIS and machine learning model techniques, to identify homogeneous sub-regions in a city.

This paper highlighted the importance of CIs clustering in heterogeneous urban areas towards setting-up appropriate resilient policy. The findings of this paper can be valuable for policy makers in their attempt to benchmark and develop appropriate resilient measures and to prioritize the financial resources available.

Further research will investigate if the identified homogeneous urban areas can be considered significant predictors of urban resilience.

Acknowledgement. This work was supported by a grant of the Ministry of Research and Innovation, CNCS - UEFISCDI, project number PN-III-P4-ID-PCCF-2016-0166, within the PNCDI III project "ReGrowEU - Advancing ground-breaking research in regional growth and development theories, through a resilience approach: towards a convergent, balanced and sustainable European Union".

References

1. EU, Green Paper on European Programmed for Critical Infrastructure Protection. EU 17.11.2005, COM, Brussels, p. 576 (2005)
2. Shen, L., Huang, Z., Wong, S.W., Liao, S., Lou, Y.: A holistic evaluation of smart city performance in the context of China. J. Clean. Prod. **200**, 667–679 (2018)
3. Procházková, D.: Principles of Management of Risks of Complex Technological Facilities. ČVUT, Praha (2017), 364 p. ISBN 978-80-01-06180-0. e-ISBN78-80-01-06182-4
4. US, Critical Infrastructure Conception. Government, Washington (2001)
5. World Economic Forum. http://reports.weforum.org/cyber-resilience/duty-of-assistance/? doing_wp_cron=1566201572.2337739467620849609375. Accessed 01 Aug 2019
6. Prochazkova, D., Prochazka, J.: Smart Cities and Critical Infrastructure, Smart Cities Symposium Prague (2018)
7. Rivera, F.I., Kapucu, N.: Disaster Vulnerability, Hazards and Resilience. EH. Springer, Cham (2015). https://doi.org/10.1007/978-3-319-16453-3
8. Rinalidi, S.M., Peerenboom, J.P., Kelly, T.: Identifying, understanding and analyzing critical infrastructure interdependencies. IEEE Control Syst. Mag. **21**, 11–25 (2001)
9. Frantzeskaki, N.: URBAN RESILIENCE A concept for co-creating cities of the future, Resilient Europe (2016). https://urbact.eu/sites/default/files/resilient_europe_baseline_study. pdf. Accessed 01 Aug 2019
10. Psyllidis, A., Yang, J., Bozzon, A.: Regionalization of social interactions and points-of-interest location prediction with geosocial data. IEEE Access **6**, 34334–34353 (2018)
11. Dunn, S., Wilkinson, S., Ford, A.: Spatial structure and evolution of infrastructure networks. Sustain. Cities Soc. **27**, 23–31 (2016)
12. van Lieshout, M.N.M., Stein, A.: Earthquake modelling at the country level using aggregated spatio-temporal point processes. Math. Geosci. **44**(3), 309–326 (2012)
13. Loo, B.P.Y., Yao, S., Wu, J.: Spatial point analysis of road crashes in Shanghai: a GIS-based network kernel density method. In: The 19th International Conference on GeoInformatics, (Geoinformatics 2011), Shanghai, China, 24–26 June 2011, pp. 1–6 (2011)
14. Jain, A.K.: Data clustering: 50 years beyond k-means. Pattern Recogn. Lett. **31**(8), 651–666 (2010)
15. Hagenauer, J., Helbich, M.: SPAWNN: a toolkit for SPatial analysis with self-organizing neural networks. Trans. GIS **20**, 755–774 (2016). https://doi.org/10.1111/tgis.12180
16. Reveiu, A., Dardala, M.: Influence of cluster type business agglomerations for development of entrepreneurial activities. Study about Romania. Amfiteatru Econ. **17**(38), 107–119 (2015)

A Unified Reference Model for Smart Cities

Nuno Soares[1,2(✉)], Paula Monteiro[1,2,3], Francisco J. Duarte[1,2],
and Ricardo J. Machado[1,2]

[1] ALGORITMI Research Centre, University of Minho, Guimarães, Portugal
nuno.soares@algoritmi.uminho.pt, paula.monteiro@ccg.pt,
{francisco.duarte,rmac}@dsi.uminho.pt
[2] University of Minho, Campus Azurém, 4800-058 Guimarães, Portugal
[3] CCG/ZGDV Institute, Guimarães, Portugal

Abstract. Smart city is a multi-faceted concept perceived in many different perspectives. Cities are multidimensional and highly complex interconnected systems of people, software, machines, and data, bringing new design, construction, and operational challenges. Work has been done on models and reference architectures for smart cities that can help to cope with those challenges. However, also because of the variability of concepts, arrangements of key components, and technology heterogeneity, a unique and universal smart city reference architecture for real world deployment is distant. This paper attempts to clarify the meaning of the concept smart cities, trying to reveal its mostly accepted dimensions and the best arrangement between them. Through an in-depth literature review of relevant studies from academia, international organizations, corporations, and standards development organizations, that gathered and analyzed contributions ranging from smart cities definition attempts and enunciations of their relevant dimensions, to already existing models and urban platforms, the paper proposes a classification for grouping the identified smart cities dimensions, exposed on a unified reference model for smart cities.

Keywords: Reference model · Reference architecture · Framework · Smart cities

1 Introduction

Cities are multidimensional and highly complex interconnected systems of people, software, machines, and data. Systems with this high level of complexity have been studied from diverse perspectives and are referred to by numerous different designations: system of systems (SoS) [1]; cyber-physical systems [2, 3]; cyber-physical-social systems [4]; socio-technical systems [5]; and multi-scale systems [6].

Besides smart cities have attracted extensive and emerging interest from both academia and industry with an increasing number of international examples emerging from all over the world, there is no unique and consensual definition for what constitutes a smart city, though the most common characteristic among all definitions is the strong recurrence to Information and Communications Technology (ICT).

H. Santos et al. (Eds.): SmartCity 360 2019, LNICST 323, pp. 162–180, 2020.
https://doi.org/10.1007/978-3-030-51005-3_16

These emerging complex, interactive systems that constitute the cities ecosystem bring new design, construction, and operational challenges. A significant challenge of these types of evolving projects related to the improvement of the quality of life for cities, is how to manage complexity, including interoperability, in a SoS with many continuously changing components.

If there is still no single definition of what a smart city is, even less is there a unified reference model, a description of the basic arrangement and connectivity of the parts of the city. Still is missing a complete broad overview and skeleton of the interlinked items, which might constitute an all-encompassing architecture that provides guidance, design patterns, common vocabulary, and enables an end-to-end information flow, lowering barriers to interoperability, thereby enabling stakeholders of smart city projects to perform more and faster implementations.

The infrastructures of a city were often developed and provided through stand-alone (silo-vertical) systems. Enhance smart service interworking across domains in combination with data analytics is required to leverage the opportunities of digitalization. Current architectural standardization efforts have not yet converged, exhibiting a lack of consensus on a common language/taxonomy and architectural principles. The interworking across multiple urban infrastructures requires a coordinated approach avoiding that the different management systems are all dealing independently.

Dedicated domain specific systems are still required to operate the related urban infrastructures, thus such urban systems need to follow an open design approach, e.g. with open interfaces, supporting open standards for exchanging urban data and supporting new urban services extending the scope of the Smart City services over time by an increased use of digitalization. To provide this SoS like approach it requires interoperability on all levels as a core principle.

A reference architecture provides this common framework around which more detailed discussions can center. By staying at a higher level of abstraction, it enables the identification and comprehension of the most important issues and patterns across its applications in many different use cases. A universal and unified model would be important to take into not only the merging of those models and architectures into a single one by eliminating overlaps and clarifying their core part, but also for combining models and architectures specialized characteristics respectively for particular domains to fulfill diversified expectations at different levels. A unified smart city reference architecture will contribute to alleviate real-world deployment of smart cities, bringing notorious advantages like interoperability assurance, integration facilitation, reuse, risk reduction, better quality, and knowledge transfer.

Besides there is no single definition for smart cities, neither a single global and unified reference model, several models for understanding and conceptualizing smart cities have been developed, which aim to define their definition, scope, objectives, benefits, and architectures.

The aim of this paper is to analyze the existing smart city modelling approaches, ranging from conceptualization to the notorious cases of realization, contributing to the definition of the components that must be part of such models. First, the benefits of a reference model for smart cities are presented; next, it describes the literature research and analyses the gathered dimensions for smart cities proposing a twofold classification for grouping the technological and non-technological dimensions; finally, it proposes a smart cities reference model based on that classification and the degree of acceptance of each dimension.

2 Reference Models, Frameworks, and Architectures

Models are abstractions of reality representing views of reality and, thus, allowing its users to focus only on the needed characteristics of the modelled reality. Models can minimize the complexity of reality they represent by including representations understandable and more easily handled by humans or machines. Models are also used to transfer pieces of knowledge between reality domains, namely from one organization into another, sharing a set of characteristics.

A conceptual model provides a common structure and definitions for describing the concepts of, and relationships among, the entities within systems.

A reference model is an abstract and easier to understand representation of a phenomenon in the world that is used or usable for reference, almost constituting a standard for. Reference models are abstract in the sense that they do not represent a particular phenomenon or organization.

An architecture is a description of the basic arrangement and connectivity of parts of a system (either a physical or a conceptual object or entity) [7]. The software engineering community considers that architecture is the fundamental organization of a system embodied in its components, their relationships to one another and to the environment and the principles guiding its design and evolution [8]. It is a set of conventions, rules, and standards employed in a system's technical framework, plus customer requirements and specifications, that the system's manufacturer or a system integrator follows in designing, or integrating, the system's various components (such as hardware, software and networks).

A reference architecture provides guidance for the development of system, solution and application architectures. It provides common and consistent definitions in the system of interest, its decompositions and design patterns, and a common vocabulary which allows to discuss the specification of implementations so that options may be compared [9].

A framework can be understood as a broad overview, skeleton, or outline, of interlinked items which supports a particular approach to a specific objective, and serves as a guide that can be modified as required by adding or deleting items.

The identification of proposed reference models for smart cities in literature, has led to consider all these terms and concepts which although conceptually can be distinguished, are closely intertwined and are together mentioned regarding the benefits and consensus around the necessity of such a definition of an all-encompassing high-level abstraction of architecture patterns and descriptions for the cities ecosystems.

The development and use of a general framework helps to identify the elements and relationships among these elements that one needs to consider for analysis [10]. A unifying high-level abstraction of these architecture patterns and descriptions has obvious benefits, since it provides common and consistent definitions, patterns, and a collective vocabulary, that facilitates easy sharing experience and know-how in designing, implementing and operating the systems [11, 12], in a way that encourages reuse of common system building blocks [11, 13], reduces the risk through the use of proven and partly prequalified architectural elements [11], provides better quality by facilitating the achievement of quality attributes [14], and contributes to the overall interoperability of the different systems [11, 13].

3   Reference Models for Smart Cities

When trying to identify proposed reference models for smart cities in literature, other terms and expressions that, more or less, refer to the same concept, must be perceived. That is the case of frameworks and reference architectures. The terms are really much intertwined as shown in the previous section.

Furthermore, they are subject to some misuse and lack of rigor. Although under the designation of architectures or models, some of the identified contributions are not proposing what can be considered an architecture, a reference architecture, a framework, or even a reference model for smart cities, but just describing an architecture of an ICT platform for cities, or the platform itself, particularly an open urban platforms (OUP), or even the simple depict of dimensions to consider in a city's ecosystem.

Rather than following a rigid systematic review methodology, this experience suggested that a more useful approach might involve a mixture of compliance and flexibility. Compliance with the broad systematic review principles of rigour, transparency and replicability, and flexibility to tailor the process towards improving the quality of the overall findings. We intended to increase the breadth of the research including urban platforms, and also works pointing out dimensions and components, most of them societal that need to be considered in a Smart City ecosystem.

Proposals of elements and their relationships to integrate on an overarching reference model for smart cities could come from diverse propositions, like obviously, already existing models for smart cities, but also from urban platforms, either working on practice or only conceptually projected, and even smart cities definition attempts, and enunciations of their relevant dimensions. Altogether, definitions of smart cities, models, and platforms, indicate the scope, the concepts, and the dimensions involved in smart cities.

Literature was surveyed not only about reference models, architectures, reference architectures, and frameworks for smart cities, but also searching for urban platforms, definitions, core concepts, attributes, indicators, key-performance indicators (KPI), and requirements for smart cities.

We surveyed literature using as sources SCOPUS and Google Scholar. Article search was performed since the year of 1997, the appearance of smart city concept, to early 2019. Works from government initiatives including EU, international organizations, corporations, and standards development organizations, were also taken into account. Screening citations on the examined articles left space for further exploration of papers missed in the initial search.

Besides recognizing that models and platforms can further contribute than the simple enunciations of dimensions, many of the latter were included on the evaluation through a selection process subject to the inherent subjectivity due to the particular appreciation we made about the validity and originality of the proposals. A total of more than forty contributions from literature were selected as proposing a reference architecture, a reference model, an urban platform, a set of KPI for cities, or at least a set of city dimensions.

3.1 Smart Cities Dimensions

Many authors dedicated work to point-out dimensions, domains, planes, process fields, viewpoints, and drivers for smart cities, in which, for standardization and simplification of concepts will be identified from now on as dimensions.

Anthopoulos [15] performed a literature review and identified seven major smart city dimensions. Giffinger et al. [16] identified six smart city characteristics. Glebova et al. [17] defend that the smart city concept can be divided into five constituent parts. Hancke et al. [18] advocate seven sensor areas in a smart city. Mahizhnan [19] identified four key dimensions of a smart city, defined for the Singapore Intelligent Island. Eger [20] defends four key dimensions of a smart community. Thuzar [21] advocates other different four key dimensions for a smart city. Barrionuevo et al. [22] identified five types of capital that contribute toward a city's intelligence. Kourtit and Nijkamp [23] argue that smart cities are based on a promising mix of four types of capital. Fromhold-Eisebith [24] based on the categorization of process fields that constitute a smart city made by several scholars and added further her own urban arenas proposing eleven fields that have the potential for CPS-driven processes. Neirotti et al. [25] advocate six smart city domains, which in turn include some subdomains. Albino et al. [26] sought the dimensions advanced by various scholars of the phenomenon and identified the four most common characteristics emerging from them.

The International Telecommunication Union (ITU) Telecommunication Standardization Sector (ITU-T) Focus Group on Smart Sustainable Cities [27] identified also another group of four core themes related to smart cities. De Oliveira Fernandes et al. [28] advocate three levels of city smartness for city authorities' actions. Lee et al. [29] conducted a research study that identified six key conceptual dimensions and 17 sub-dimensions of smart city practices that form a theoretical foundation for classification of practices. And finally, the United Nations (UN) Habitat [30] identified five dimensions of city prosperity.

3.2 Models for Smart Cities

More interlinked approaches to the smart cities core concepts and requirements can be seen in what can be considered a model or equivalent. Desouza and Flanery [31] stated a model with five city components divided between physical and social spheres. Nam and Pardo [32] introduced a representation of smart cities with the three key factors: human, institutional and technological, applied to theirs more than six, key dimensions. Chourabi et al. [33] presented a framework with five outer and three inner factors that explains the integration of technology, organization and policy.

CISCO Systems Inc. [34] envisioned a smart city framework with four layers, a decision methodology that enables both the public and private sectors to plan and implement smart city initiatives more effectively. International Business Machines (IBM) [35] introduced the technological functionalities of a smart city and highlighted the role of the ICT infrastructure and the information services stating a theory founded on two main assumptions: the city is based on nine main pillars organized in three major categories, with each category pillar being an individual system and the city seen as a SoS; and IBM's '*3 Is Equation*' where the smarter city is the result of instrumentation, interconnection of data, and intelligence brought by software. Naphade et al. [36] also have a SoS perspective with a set of seven interdependent public and private systems that the city can integrate and optimize.

Leydesdorff and Deakin [37] proposed a neo-evolutionary perspective of the Triple-Helix model for smart cities and Lombardi et al. [38] come up with also a revised version of the triple helix model, for smart cities, as always, based on networks of universities, industry, and government, that proposes a novel framework for analysis and performance measurement.

Liu et al. [39] advocate a smart city value chain model with primary and supportive activities. Edvinsson [40] envisioned the city as a knowledge tool model. Yovanof and Hazapis [41] conceptualized the digital city architectural framework for smart service provision with three main dimensions. Zygiaris [42] introduced his smart city reference model in a form of a multi-tier model with several components and entities that smart city planners could use to define the conceptual layout of a smart city and describe the smart innovation characteristics. The Spanish standard [43] has five smart cities layers in a structure devoted to assuring Open Urban Platforms (OUP) interoperability requirements. Abu-Matar and Mizouni [44] multiple-view smart city reference architecture meta-model has nine views interrelated with each other, where the cyber views run and control the physical views. Batty et al. [45] defend the structure of FuturICTs Knowledge Accelerator smart city program that organize smart cities research directions into seven distinct but overlapping areas. Anthopoulos et al. [46] propose a unified smart city model that identifies six major dimensions on literature and discovered eight conceptual models of viewpoints that address smart cities.

Yin et al. [47] state a smart city architecture proposal with four general layers and two planes based on what they observed in literature, a data-centric and multidisciplinary smart city. Santana et al. [48], based their analysis of several urban platforms and architectures and derived a novel reference architecture for software platforms for smart cities with four technological levels and an additional all-encompassing security vertical tier. Also Silva et al. [49] synthesize the commonalities of most of the works they have analyzed in a four layers architecture for a generic smart city, with a key concern on sensitive data protection.

Elhoseny et al. [50] performed an elicitation of requirements and capabilities for the ideal smart city service-oriented architecture (SOA) framework, proposing one of their authorship. Clement et al. [51] propose a reference architecture for smart cities incorporating the viewpoints of the traditional city infrastructure, services and business roles. The authors augment the traditional city architecture layers of environment, infrastructure, logistics and human elements, with a computing infrastructure based around SOA principals, traversing these computing elements and business roles across several levels of city architecture from the utilities through to the service provisions.

The smart cities model advocate by Clement et al. [51] is expected to utilize simulation so that the system can predict future outcomes and react accordingly.

ISO 37120 [52] defines and establishes methodologies for a set of indicators (a quantitative, qualitative or descriptive measure) to steer and measure the performance of city services and quality of life. The indicators are structured around seventeen themes. Recognizing the differences in resources and capabilities of cities worldwide, the overall set of indicators for city performance has been divided into core indicators (mandatory) and supporting indicators (recommended).

The ITU-T performed a components analysis for a smart sustainable city and derived a modular Smart and Sustainable Cities (SSC) ICT architecture approach [53] with six sub-systems organized in modules. For almost all the modules, a hypothetical assignment of standards is presented.

The International Electrotechnical Commission (IEC) city model presented in [54] synthesizes a set of city characteristics where smartness is applied. City subsystems surrounded by environmental context, city history and characteristics, societal context, and city governance.

ITU-T [53] and Anthopoulos [55] propose a generic multi-tier ICT meta-architecture for smart and sustainable cities (SSC) consisting of five layers (natural environment, hard non-ICT infrastructure, hard ICT-infrastructure, services and soft-infrastructure). The architecture meets existing standardization efforts [52, 56], and more specifically UN Habitat KPIs [57], can accordingly be the baseline for smart city standardization.

National Institute of Standards and Technology (NIST) and some international partners, convened an international public working group to compare and distil a consensus language, taxonomy, and framework of common architectural features for smart cities. First version of the IES-City Framework (Internet-of-Things-Enabled Smart City Framework) was recently released [58] introducing a reference framework for the development of architectures for incremental and modular smart cities. The framework provides the tools to evaluate the breadth of functional requirements, assess the readiness of the municipality infrastructure, and measure the benefits to the citizenry.

The ESPRESSO H2020 project [59] produced a smart cities reference architecture with three vertical layers formed by groups of services, and six horizontals layers topped by two services consumer layers for respectively, sectorial specific businesses and city stakeholders.

The ESPRESSO reference architecture joined with the results of the European Innovation Partnership on Smart Cities and Communities (EIP SCC) urban platform initiative, were on the basis of the German standard [60] for a reference system architecture of an open urban platform (OUP), with its multi-layered approach where each capability cluster is represented by a single layer, and three priority vertical areas.

3.3 Urban Platforms

It is also possible to identify the most recurrent components in existing OUPs. City Data and Analytics Platform (CiDAP) [61] is an analytics platform deployed into the Smart-Santander testbed. The system architecture of CIDAP has four main modules and three layers. Modules to collect, store, process, intensive process and perform analytics to data, along with a CityModel server responsible for interfacing with external applications.

OpenIoT is an IoT platform used by the Vital project, with three planes: physical, virtualized, and utility-app [62]. Sii-Mobility architecture [63] is presently in place in the

Tuscany area. Is an evolved solution of the semantic aggregator and reasoner architectural pattern with two components: a semantic aggregation & big data processing based on the Km4City Ontology, and a smart city API.

The Open Machine Type Communications (Open-MTC) platform is an IoT/M2M middleware [64] with a backend assuring several functions and several gateways for vertical domains. The Fiware platform [65] provides a set of APIs that ease the development of smart applications in multiple vertical sectors, with its library of generic enablers.

4   Discussion

From the analysis of the above contributions, it was realized that there is a great variety in the way the elements of the smart cities models and the various dimensions perceived as intervening in the complex ecosystem of smart cities, are designated, and even enunciated. E.g., all the thematic dealing with the mobility of persons and goods in a city is designated in smart cities literature in several ways, like 'transportation', 'smart mobility', 'smart transportation', 'intellectual transport system', and 'sustainable urban mobility'.

In addition to this taxonomic topic, the models do not agree on the same set of dimensions, and this is immediately visible in the more conceptual models that almost exclusively include human and institutional dimensions. If we observe the layers or tiers that constitute the more technological models, this scenario is even more evident, with a great diversity of ICT components with their functionality and designation.

Though there is abundant literature available on smart cities, there is no standardized and commonly accepted set of terminologies to aptly identify a set of univocal dimensions that a smart city must take into account. Given the lack of standardized terminologies, a comparative analysis was performed to map and compare the designations and definitions of the various smart city dimensions and organize the results to reveal commonalities and consensual dimensions. This section presents a study of the dimensions associated to smart and sustainable cities.

For this purpose, several papers were collected from academic literature, as well as reports and articles from other databases. These sources were reviewed and analyzed to help consolidate a wide range of dimensional perspectives of smart cities. These dimensions were obtained from a variety of sources comprising academic and research communities, government initiatives including EU, international organizations (like United Nations, ITU, European Commission, etc.), corporate/company profiles, and standards development organizations, briefly exposed in the previous section.

More than forty sources of proposals about the components or dimensions to be considered for a smart city were analyzed. All sources were scrutinized and a spreadsheet was used to collect the dimensions indicated by each one, what facilitated the subsequent aggregation.

The decomposition operated for the dimensions pertinent to the overall ecosystem of smart cities, showed a total of one hundred and one (101) dimensions, even after some depuration obtained from eliminating evident synonyms and aggregating obviously similar dimensions.

To sort and group all dimensions found, dimension categories have been defined. These categories were established taking into consideration the classification of Nam and Pardo [32] and Lea [66], that arranged the components of smart cities in three major aspects: institutional, human, and technological.

Some dimensions cross several boundaries just like Nam and Pardo [32] and Lea [66] conveyed in theirs overlapping classifications, so, two more categories were taken into account with purposes of univocity and intended and casuistic specialization: city component-related aspects, and environmental aspects. So, all the viewpoints of what a smart city is can be segmented into the following categories:

- **Human** viewpoint - pertains to human infrastructure and social capital, involving education and governance, lifestyle, historical legacy, culture, recreation, economics, finance, social equity, engagement, laws, division of power, and politics.
- **Institutional** viewpoint - relates to institutions, governance, government, policy, regulations/directives, planning, procurement, safety, emergency response, security, healthcare, city infrastructure.
- **Technological** viewpoint - concerns all topics related to ICT, namely software, mobile and virtual technologies, and digital infrastructure and networks.
- **City Component-related** viewpoint - is used to denote cities specific resources and processes like transportation, hard infrastructures, buildings, waste management, water, energy, and some city functions and services in general.
- **Environmental** viewpoint - indicating environmental management, protection, and sustainable usage.

This classification provided the first grouping level and more noticeable than the five categories is the underlying distinction between technological dimension and all the others. Each non-technological dimension perceived in literature was uniquely identified as belonging to one of the categories above, although ambiguity occurred for some of them.

A second grouping level would have to detail this segmentation, particularly for the yet not segment technological dimensions. TOGAF [67], the Open Group standard for enterprise architecture includes four different architectural domains, which are accepted as sub-sets of an overarching enterprise architecture. A complete enterprise architecture should address all four architecture domains: data, application, and technology architectures that build on the business architecture. An "enterprise" is any collection of organizations that have common goals. Could be partnerships and alliances of businesses working together, such as a consortium or supply chain.

The purpose of enterprise architecture is to optimize across the enterprise the often fragmented legacy of processes (both manual and automated) into an integrated environment that is responsive to change and supportive of the delivery of the business strategy [67]. An intent that is not far from the main objective of smart cities if we take strategy in a much broader sense than just the business.

This paper's proposed aggregation and classification of the technological smart cities dimensions identified in the overall literature, used the TOGAF architecture domains and influences from the OSI reference model [68] suggesting the following categories:

Type A – Consumers (include any smart city stakeholder who wishes to interact with and consume smart city services) and the business services themselves which are demanded from the non-technological smart cities dimensions. Represents the application and presentation levels of the OSI reference model and are contained in the TOGAF application architecture domain, but also in some extent, in the business architecture domain.

Type B – Includes data services for data management, processing, exploitation and dissemination capabilities, and the software applications that manipulate that data, to support the forth Type A application and business services. Modelling & Analytics, Integration, Data Management, Reporting, Visualization, Systematization, Choreography and Orchestration, Technology and Supporting Services (Transaction Management, Orchestration, BI, Collaboration). Represents the TOGAF data architecture domain.

Type V – Supporting and common services. Some layers shall be 'vertical' as they cut across various other layers within the overall architecture. E.g. sensitive data protection is a key concern, thus security modules shall be integrated into each layer.

Type C – Includes communications, network & transport capabilities. Represents the TOGAF technology architecture domain and the session, transport, and network levels of the OSI reference model.

Type D – Includes the operation and management of physical devices, sensors, actuators. Represents the TOGAF technology architecture domain and the data link and physical levels of the OSI reference model.

5   Proposed Reference Model

Given the various contributions, definitions and the 100+ dimensions or layers for a smart city, there was a need to perform some more in-depth analysis to determine what would be a comprehensive and inclusive proposal of a smart city reference architecture.

In the above literature survey, there are divergent visions of smart city architectures. Through these different expressions, we can still find some common characteristics, evidenced by the way they were grouped in the categories described above.

The need to have a second level of grouping for non-tech dimensions, such as the classification presented in the previous section for the technological ones, led to sort all these dimensions taking into account their similarity. Therefore, groups become apparent.

Excluding the technological components addressed below, we identified thirteen main dimensions in the literature (the most referred to), which although mentioned by different designations as shown in Table 1, fairly represent the same principles and seem more than consensual given the profusion of citations.

The number of times each dimension is referred to in the selected literature is presented in parenthesis and contributes to the perception of which dimensions are considered as most important and inescapable. The table shows the exact designations used by the selected scholars and professionals, to the right of the aggregating designation that represents them.

Outside of this unification attempt were placed dimensions that occurred seldom, such as innovation, only advanced by Zygiaris [42] that dedicates to the cities' fertile innovation environment with new business models and opportunities pushed by the emerging technologies, an entire layer in the top of his smart city conceptual reference model. However not itemize as an individual dimension, this aspect is not forgotten by the rest of the authors that prefer to spread it over the remaining dimensions.

Table 1. Non-technological dimensions

Dimensions	Alternative designations and sub-dimensions
Government and Governance (17 + 2)	Government [15, 25, 33, 35, 39, 42, 52, 54]; Smart governance [16, 24, 46][*][59]; Government services [36]; e-Government [53]; City governance for the smart city & decision support and participation [45][*]; sub-dimensions: Urban planning [52]; Smart procurement [39]
Economy and Business (17 + 3)	Economy [15, 25, 33, 52][*][46]; Smart economy [16]; Economic development [20][*]; Sustainable economic development [21]; Economic capital [22]; Socio-economic development [58]; Urban economics and commerce [60]; e-Business [53, 59]; Intelligent services layer [43]; Domain application layer [47]; sub-dimensions: Job growth [20]; Finance [52]; IT economy [19]
Transportation (16)	**Transportation(16):** Transportation[15, 25, 35, 36, 46, 51, 52, 58, 59]; Smart mobility[16, 24]; Smart transportation [18, 32, 53]; Intellectual transport system [17]; Sustainable urban mobility[60]
Environment (15 + 10)	Environment [25, 26, 33, 35, 38, 46, 51, 52, 54, 59]; Smart environment [16, 32]; Environmental capital [22]; Smart metabolism [24]; Green city layer [42]; sub-dimensions: Environmental protection [17]; Smart consumption [24]; Solid waste [52, 58]; Waste management [53]; Water and sanitation [52, 53]; Water and wastewater [58, 59]
People (13 + 3)	People [25, 26, 33, 46, 51, 59]; People (social) [31]; Smart people [16]; People - human factors (learning) [32]; Human capital [22, 23]; Actors [54]; Civil society [38]; sub-dimensions: Entrepreneurial capital [23]; Society and entrepreneurship [40]; Coherency [15]
Urban infrastructure (11)	Urban infrastructure [15, 33, 35, 42]; Smart infrastructure [18, 26, 39, 51]; Infrastructural capital [23]; Infrastructure [54]; Integrated infrastructure & processes [60]
Safety and Security (11)	Smart safety [32, 52, 53, 59]; Public safety [35, 36]; Public safety policing and emergency response [58]; Public security [17, 60]; Smart security [24]; Smart surveillance [18]
Smart Buildings (10)	Smart buildings [18, 25, 35, 53, 59]; Smart construction [24]; Shelter [52]; Facilities and buildings [54]; Built environment [58]; Sustainable district and built environment [60]

(continued)

Table 1. (*continued*)

Dimensions	Alternative designations and sub-dimensions
Energy (10 + 3)	Energy [25, 46, 51–53, 58, 59]; Smart energy [24, 32]; Energy consumption management and control [17]; *sub-dimensions: (paired with Water)* Smart electricity and water distribution [18]; Energy and water [35, 36]
Healthcare (9)	Healthcare [36]; Smart healthcare [18, 32, 53]; Health [46, 52, 58, 59]; Health and welfare [60]
Institutions (8)	Institutions [31]; Community - institutional factors [32]; Institutional capital [22]; Activities [54]; Social capital [22, 23]; Societal context [54]
Education (8 + 3)	Education [36, 52, 53, 58–60]; Smart education [24, 32]; *sub-dimensions:* University [38, 40] IT education [19]
Smart Living (8 + 3)	Smart living [15, 16, 25, 38, 46]; Quality of life [19–21]; *sub-dimensions:* City history & characteristics [54]; Recreation [52]; Knowledge cafes/cathedrals [40]

Almost forgotten seems to be the Industry subject. Only three works from the ones selected defend a smart industry dimension in the context of smart cities. Leydesdorff and Deakin [37] and Lombardi et al. [38] in the scope of their evolutionary perspectives for the triple-helix model for smart cities, and Fromhold-Eisebith [24] that considers the industry an obvious process field for the potential use of CPS-driven processes. Factories have their existence in cities, at least in the broader concept of cities adopted by smart cities, best embodied by regions or territory, and share many resources and restrictions with cities. ICT has the exactly same role in smart cities and initiatives aiming digital industries, conducting factories to the fourth industrial revolution, like Platform Industrie 4.0 [69], Industrial Internet Consortium (IIC) Industrial Internet [9], and NIST Smart Manufacturing [70], behaving has a key factor and acting as an enabling technology. For production and manufacturing in industry and also to assure an integrated city, ICT is a tool, not an end in itself. Noticeable key information that needs to be shared between factories and smart cities are for example traffic, energy needs, energy consumption or waste-handling. This survey shows the failure to perceive and establish an explicit link between these two domains that are not even disjointed, but overlapping.

Table 1 shows only the non-technological dimensions. ICT is one additional and inescapable dimension of smart cities. According to the particular classification of technological layers discussed in the previous section, that incorporates influences of TOGAF [67] and the OSI reference model [68], all layers proposed by the studied reference models, architectures, and platforms for smart cities were identified and organized by type in Table 2, that displays each proposed technological layer identified by its original designation and in-text citation.

Table 2. Technological dimensions grouped by type

Type A Dimensions
Applications [48], Application Layer [43, 49, 50, 59], Applications (ICT) [53], Services and Business (ICT) [53], External Applications [61], Application View (Cyber) [44]
Business Process View [44], Business Roles Viewpoint (Management, Integration, Operational) [51]
Smart City API [63], Utility-App Plane (Request Definition, Config & Monitor, Request Presentation) [62]
Stakeholder Engagement & Collaboration Capabilities [60]
City/Community Specific Capabilities [60]
User Interface [43], Presentation Layer [50]
Gateways (Protocol Adapters) for Vertical Domains [64]
Type B Dimensions
Service View [44], Middleware [48], Services Viewpoint [51], Common Data and Service Layer [47]
Open Integration Layer [42], Integration Layer [50], Integration, Choreography and Orchestration Capabilities [60], Generic City/Community Capabilities [60]
Integrated Databases Management [45], Management (ICT) [53], View Planning and Management [46]
Data [43] Data Management Layer [49], Data Services [59], View Data & Knowledge [46], Data View [44]
Data Management & Analytics Capabilities [60], Data Analysis and Modelling [45], Analytics View (Cyber) [44], Analytics and City Model Server [61]
Data Collection (IoT Broker and IoT-Agents) [61], Semantic Aggregation & Big Data Processing [63], Data Vitalization Layer [47], Data Context Broker [65]
Data Storage (Big Data Repository) [61], Big Data Management [48], Data Processing (Intensive Big Data Processing) [61]
Virtualized Plane Cloud and Big Data (Linked Stream Middleware, Scheduler, Service Deliver & Utility Manager) [62], Backend (Connectivity Management, Data Management, Authentication & Authorization) [64]
Type V Dimensions
Security [48], Privacy & Security Capabilities [60], Security Services [59], Security & Authentication [47]
Technology Services [59]
Supporting Services [43, 59], Common Services Capabilities [60]
Development Toolkit [48]
Type C Dimensions

(continued)

Table 2. (*continued*)

Interconnection Layer [42], Communications, Network & Transport Capabilities [60], Transmission layer [49], Cloud and Networking [48]
Device Asset Management & Operational Services Capabilities [60], IoT Backend [65]
Positioning Services [59]
Type D Dimensions
Sensing Layer [49], Field Equipment/Device Capabilities [60], Sensor/Actuator [43], Sensing Services [59], Physical plane IoT (Sensor Middleware) [62], Instrumentation Layer [42], IoT Edge (inc. IoT Gateways) [65]
Data Acquisition Layer [47, 50]
Infrastructure View (Physical) [44]
Place View (Physical) [44]
Participant View (Physical) [44]

After this thorough analysis of multiple existing models and architectures, we derived the unified reference architecture illustrated in Fig. 1, conjoint with a majority of proposed works. The figure illustrates the dimensions grouped in the categories human, institutional, city-component related and environmental, having a proportional dimension to their popularity in the literature studied, and supported by the ICT layers according to the classification justified above.

The non-technological dimensions appear on the top of the reference architecture as columns and in their role of consumers of the technological services provided below by the technological layers. This dimensions are grouped according to the viewpoints previously presented and which were derived and extended from Nam and Pardo [32] and Lea [66]. The chosen color gradation denotes this categorization. The number of times each non-technological dimension is referred to in the selected literature, as computed in Table 1 arises as the height of the respective column in the figure and denotes the relative importance and inescapability of each dimension.

At the bottom of the reference architecture appears the technological viewpoint. Each level or dimension provides services to the level immediately above. The exception and the reason for being a vertical and all-encompassing level in opposition to the others is the ICT Level V responsible for supporting and common services for all the remaining ICT levels.

Associated with each level is a list of the components derived from the dimensions aggregation illustrated in Table 2. Particularly, a component designation that could represent and identify the set of designations used in the literature for the similar dimensions that were arranged by row below each type. For instance, dimensions whose authors in the literature have designated as Applications, Application Layer, Applications (ICT), Services and Business (ICT), External Applications, and Application View (Cyber), are recognized as the component Applications inside ICT Level A.

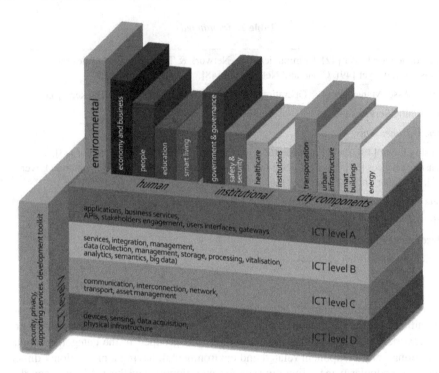

Fig. 1. Unified reference architecture for smart cities

6 Conclusion

This paper attempts to clarify the meaning of the smart cities concept, trying to reveal all its mostly accepted aspects. Researchers have been working on models and reference architectures for smart cities, in order to ease real-world deployment. However, also because of the variability of concepts and the various arrangements of key components for cities, a universal smart city reference architecture for real world deployment is far from reality, yet theoretically possible. Lack of consensus on a common language/taxonomy that begin with a multiplicity of names chosen for the dimensions involved, continues with the variety of the arrangements proposed for them, and ends in heterogeneous supporting ICT building blocks, lead to divergence on architectural standardization efforts.

This paper reviewed existing smart city modelling proposals, ranging from the more conceptual to the more technological, and synthesized them into a unified smart city reference architecture, contributing to the definition of the components that must be part of such models. The result is a set of dimensions organized by human, institutional, city-component related and environmental viewpoints, supported by a services provider five layers ICT framework.

The study shows that the overall vision of a smart city recognizes the growing importance of ICT as a core element and driver to foster smartness and the resulting sustainability and liveability of cities. ICT is inescapable in the smart cities ecosystem as services provider for the other dimensions. Although the variety of building blocks proposed to architect the overall ICT infrastructure of a city, the proper model to present these components is multi-layered, where each layer uses services from the lower level and provides services to the upper level. As an exception, some ICT supporting functions must be arranged vertically as they cut across various other layers within the architecture. The upper ICT layer must interface with the various domains of smart city stakeholders who consume these ICT services. The work presents these domains grouped in the categories human, institutional, city component-related and environmental and testifies their relative popularity and recognition, also denoting the importance that satisfying the requirements of each domain may have to achieve the ultimate goal of an increasing smart and sustainable city.

A critical remark and a perplexity when studying the contributions to this subject: a domain that, despite its importance, appears much neglected and outside the cast of the most mentioned - industry.

Although this work came to a reference architecture, the next suitable step could be to attain a truly reference model for smart cities, a yet easier to understand representation of the smart cities entire ecosystem that could be used or usable for reference, almost constituting a standard for. The reference model could extend this reference architecture providing the common semantics that can be used unambiguously across and between different implementations for the various smart cities domains.

Also as future research, we recommend studies that evaluate the incorporation of smart industry in smart cities, establishing similarities and realizing eventual common paths between smart cities and the current smart manufacturing initiatives that inhabit the same physical space and seem to have so many common purposes, resources and constraints. Moreover, an all-encompassing reference architecture is also currently pursued for digital factories.

Acknowledgments. This work is supported by national funds through FCT – Fundação para a Ciência e Tecnologia within the Project Scope: UID/CEC/00319/2019 and by the Doctoral scholarship PDE/BDE/114567/2016 funded by FCT, the Portuguese Ministry of Science, Technology and Higher Education, through national funds, and co-financed by the European Social Fund (ESF) through the Operational Programme for Human Capital (POCH).

References

1. Maier, M.W.: Architecting principles for systems-of-systems. Syst. Eng. J. Int. Council Syst. Eng. **1**, 267–284 (1998)
2. Lee, E.A.: Cyber physical systems: design challenges. In: 2008 11th IEEE International Symposium on Object and Component-Oriented Real-Time Distributed Computing (ISORC), pp. 363–369 (2008)
3. Griffor, E.R., Greer, C., Wollman, D.A., Burns, M.J.: Framework for cyber-physical systems: overview, vol. 1 (2017). https://doi.org/10.6028/NIST.SP.1500-201
4. Wang, F.-Y.: The emergence of intelligent enterprises: from CPS to CPSS. IEEE Intell. Syst. **25**, 85–88 (2010)
5. Fischer, G., Herrmann, T.: Socio-technical systems: a meta-design perspective. Int. J. Sociotechnol. Knowl. Dev. **3**, 1–33 (2011)

6. Kevrekidis, I.G., Gear, C.W., Hummer, G.: Equation-free: the computer-aided analysis of complex multiscale systems. AIChE J. **50**, 1346–1355 (2004)
7. ISO 15704: ISO 15704, Industrial automation systems - requirements for enterprise-reference architectures and methodologies. International Organization for Standardization, Geneva, Switzerland (2000)
8. ISO/IEC/IEEE 42010: ISO/IEC/IEEE 42010:2011 - Systems and software engineering - architecture description. International Organization for Standardization/International Electrotechnical Commission, Geneva, Switzerland (2011). https://doi.org/10.1109/IEEESTD.2011.6129467
9. Lin, S.-W., et al.: Industrial Internet Reference Architecture 1.8 - Volume G1: Reference Architecture. Ind. Internet Consort. (2017)
10. Ostrom, E.: Doing institutional analysis: digging deeper than markets and hierarchies. In: Ménard, C., Shirley, M.M. (eds.) Handbook of New Institutional Economics. Springer, Heidelberg (2008). https://doi.org/10.1007/978-3-540-69305-5_31
11. Cloutier, R., Muller, G., Verma, D., Nilchiani, R., Hole, E., Bone, M.: The concept of reference architectures. Syst. Eng. **13**, 14–27 (2010)
12. Muller, G., van de Laar, P.: Researching reference architectures. In: Van de Laar, P., Punter, T. (eds.) Views on Evolvability of Embedded Systems, pp. 107–119. Springer, Dordrecht (2010). https://doi.org/10.1007/978-90-481-9849-8_7
13. Galster, M., Avgeriou, P.: Empirically-grounded reference architectures: a proposal. In: Proceedings of the Joint ACM SIGSOFT Conference–QoSA and ACM SIGSOFT Symposium–ISARCS on Quality of Software Architectures–QoSA and Architecting Critical Systems–ISARCS, pp. 153–158. ACM (2011)
14. Nakagawa, E.Y., Oliveira Antonino, P., Becker, M.: Reference architecture and product line architecture: a subtle but critical difference. In: Crnkovic, I., Gruhn, V., Book, M. (eds.) ECSA 2011. LNCS, vol. 6903, pp. 207–211. Springer, Heidelberg (2011). https://doi.org/10.1007/978-3-642-23798-0_22
15. Anthopoulos, L.G.: Understanding the smart city domain: a literature review. In: Rodríguez-Bolívar, M.P. (ed.) Transforming City Governments for Successful Smart Cities. PAIT, vol. 8, pp. 9–21. Springer, Cham (2015). https://doi.org/10.1007/978-3-319-03167-5_2
16. Giffinger, R., et al.: Smart cities Ranking of European medium-sized cities **16**, 13–18 (2007)
17. Glebova, I.S., Yasnitskaya, Y.S., Maklakova, N.V.: Assessment of cities in Russia according to the concept of "smart city" in the context of the application of information and communication technologies. Mediterr. J. Soc. Sci. **5**, 55 (2014)
18. Hancke, G.P., Hancke Jr., G.P., et al.: The role of advanced sensing in smart cities. Sensors **13**, 393–425 (2012)
19. Mahizhnan, A.: Smart cities: the Singapore case. Cities **16**, 13–18 (1999)
20. Eger, J.M.: Smart growth, smart cities, and the crisis at the pump a worldwide phenomenon. I-WAYS-The J. E-Gov. Policy Regul. **32**, 47–53 (2009)
21. Thuzar, M.: Urbanization in Southeast Asia: developing smart cities for the future? Reg. Outlook 96 (2011)
22. Barrionuevo, J.M., Berrone, P., Ricart, J.E.: Smart cities, sustainable progress. IESE Insight **14**, 50–57 (2012)
23. Kourtit, K., Nijkamp, P.: Smart cities in the innovation age. Innov. Eur. J. Soc. Sci. Res. **25**, 93–95 (2012)
24. Fromhold-Eisebith, M.: Cyber-physical systems in smart cities - mastering technological, economic, and social challenges. Smart Cities Found. Princ. Appl. 1–22 (2017)
25. Neirotti, P., De Marco, A., Cagliano, A.C., Mangano, G., Scorrano, F.: Current trends in Smart City initiatives: some stylised facts. Cities **38**, 25–36 (2014)

26. Albino, V., Berardi, U., Dangelico, R.M.: Smart cities: definitions, dimensions, performance, and initiatives. J. Urban Technol. **22**, 1–19 (2015). https://doi.org/10.1080/10630732.2014.942092
27. ITU-T FG-SCC: Smart sustainable cities: an analysis of definitions. International Telecommunication Union (2014)
28. De Oliveira Fernandes, E., Meeus, L., Leal, V., Azevedo, I., Delarue, E., Glachant, J.-M.: Smart Cities Initiative: how to foster a quick transition towards local sustainable energy systems. Eur. Univ. Inst. (2011). https://doi.org/10.2870/34539
29. Lee, J.H., Hancock, M.G., Hu, M.-C.: Towards an effective framework for building smart cities: lessons from Seoul and San Francisco. Technol. Forecast. Soc. Change **89**, 80–99 (2014)
30. UN-Habitat: State of the World's cities 2012/2013 Prosperity of Cities. UN-Habitat (United Nations Human Settlements Programme) (2013)
31. Desouza, K.C., Flanery, T.H.: Designing, planning, and managing resilient cities: a conceptual framework. Cities **35**, 89–99 (2013). https://doi.org/10.1016/j.cities.2013.06.003
32. Nam, T., Pardo, T.A.: Conceptualizing smart city with dimensions of technology, people, and institutions. In: Proceedings of the 12th Annual International Digital Government Research Conference: Digital Government Innovation in Challenging Times, pp. 282–291 (2011)
33. Chourabi, H., et al.: Understanding smart cities: an integrative framework. In: Proceedings of Annual Hawaii International Conference on System Sciences, pp. 2289–2297 (2011). https://doi.org/10.1109/HICSS.2012.615
34. Falconer, G., Mitchell, S.: Smart city framework: a systematic process for enabling Smart+ connected communities (2012)
35. Söderström, O., Paasche, T., Klauser, F.: Smart cities as corporate storytelling. City **18**, 307–320 (2014)
36. Naphade, M., Banavar, G., Harrison, C., Paraszczak, J., Morris, R.: Smarter cities and their innovation challenges. Comput. (Long Beach Calif.) 32–39 (2011)
37. Leydesdorff, L., Deakin, M.: The triple helix model of smart cities: a neo-evolutionary perspective. J. Urban Technol. **18**, 53–63 (2011). https://doi.org/10.1080/10630732.2011.601111
38. Lombardi, P., Giordano, S., Farouh, H., Yousef, W.: Modelling the smart city performance. Innov. Eur. J. Soc. Sci. Res. **25**, 137–149 (2012)
39. Liu, Y., Wei, J., Rodriguez, A.F.C.: Development of a strategic value assessment model for smart city. Int. J. Mob. Commun. **12**, 346–359 (2014)
40. Edvinsson, L.: Aspects on the city as a knowledge tool. J. Knowl. Manag. **10**, 6–13 (2006)
41. Yovanof, G.S., Hazapis, G.N.: An architectural framework and enabling wireless technologies for digital cities & intelligent urban environments. Wirel. Pers. Commun. **49**, 445–463 (2009)
42. Zygiaris, S.: Smart city reference model: assisting planners to conceptualize the building of smart city innovation ecosystems. J. Knowl. Econ. **4**, 217–231 (2012)
43. UNE: UNE 178104:2017, Sistemas Integrales de Gestión de la Ciudad Inteligente. Requisitos de interoperabilidad para una Plataforma de Ciudad Inteligente, Madrid, Espana (2017)
44. Abu-Matar, M., Mizouni, R.: Variability modeling for smart city reference architectures. In: The Fourth IEEE Annual International Smart Cities Conference (ISC2 2018), Kansas City, MO, USA (2018)
45. Batty, M., et al.: Smart cities of the future. Eur. Phys. J. Spec. Top. **214**, 481–518 (2012). https://doi.org/10.1140/epjst/e2012-01703-3
46. Anthopoulos, L., Janssen, M., Weerakkody, V.: A unified smart city model (USCM) for smart city conceptualization and benchmarking. In: Smart Cities and Smart Spaces: Concepts, Methodologies, Tools, and Applications, pp. 247–264. IGI Global (2016)
47. Yin, C., Xiong, Z., Chen, H., Wang, J., Cooper, D., David, B.: A literature survey on smart cities. Sci. China Inf. Sci. **58**, 1–18 (2015)

48. Santana, E.F.Z., Chaves, A.P., Gerosa, M.A., Kon, F., Milojicic, D.S.: Software platforms for smart cities: concepts, requirements, challenges, and a unified reference architecture. ACM Comput. Surv. **50**, 78 (2017)
49. Silva, B.N., Khan, M., Han, K.: Towards sustainable smart cities: a review of trends, architectures, components, and open challenges in smart cities. Sustain. Cities Soc. **38**, 697–713 (2018)
50. Elhoseny, H., Elhoseny, M., Abdelrazek, S., Bakry, H., Riad, A.: Utilizing service oriented architecture (SOA) in smart cities. Int. J. Adv. Comput. Technol. (IJACT) **8**, 77–84 (2016)
51. Clement, S.J., McKee, D.W., Xu, J.: Service-oriented reference architecture for smart cities. In: 2017 IEEE Symposium on Service-Oriented System Engineering (SOSE), pp. 81–85 (2017)
52. ISO: ISO 37120:2014, Sustainable development of communities - indicators for city services and quality of life. Geneva, Switzerland (2014)
53. ITU-T FG-SCC: ITU-T Y.4400 series – Smart sustainable cities – setting the framework for an ICT architecture - Supplement 27. Geneva, Switzerland (2016)
54. ISO/IEC JTC 1: Smart Cities - Preliminary Report 2014. International Organization for Standardization/International Electrotechnical Commission, Geneva, Switzerland (2014)
55. Anthopoulos, L.: Defining smart city architecture for sustainability. In: Proceedings of the 14th IFIP Electronic Government (EGOV) and 7th Electronic Participation (ePart) Conference 2015 (2015)
56. BSI: PAS 180:2014 Smart cities – Vocabulary (2014)
57. ITU-T FG-SCC: Technical Report on "Overview of key performance indicators in smart sustainable cities." International Telecommunication Union, Geneva, Switzerland (2014)
58. IES-City PWG: IES-City Framework - A Consensus Framework for Smart City Architectures v1.0 (2018)
59. Cox, A., Parslow, P., De Lathouwer, B., Klien, E., Kempen, B., Lonien, J.: D4.2 - definition of smart city reference architecture. ESPRESSO systEmic Standardisation apPRoach to Empower Smart citieS and cOmmunities (2016)
60. DIN: DIN SPEC 91357, Reference Architecture Model Open Urban Platform (OUP). Deutsches Institut für Normung, Berlin, Germany (2017)
61. Cheng, B., Longo, S., Cirillo, F., Bauer, M., Kovacs, E.: Building a big data platform for smart cities: experience and lessons from santander. In: 2015 IEEE International Congress on Big Data (BigData Congress), pp. 592–599 (2015)
62. Soldatos, J., et al.: OpenIoT: open source Internet-of-Things in the cloud. In: Podnar Žarko, I., Pripužić, K., Serrano, M. (eds.) Interoperability and Open-Source Solutions for the Internet of Things. LNCS, vol. 9001, pp. 13–25. Springer, Cham (2015). https://doi.org/10.1007/978-3-319-16546-2_3
63. Badii, C., Bellini, P., Cenni, D., Difino, A., Nesi, P., Paolucci, M.: Analysis and assessment of a knowledge based smart city architecture providing service APIs. Future Gen. Comput. Syst. **75**, 14–29 (2017). https://doi.org/10.1016/j.future.2017.05.001
64. Fraunhofer FOKUS OpenMTC: OpenMTC. https://www.open-mtc.org
65. Fiware: Fiware Wiki. https://forge.fiware.org/plugins/mediawiki/wiki/fiware/index.php
66. Lea, R.J.: Smart cities: an overview of the technology trends driving smart cities (2017)
67. The Open Group: The TOGAF Standard, Version 9.2 - Reference: C182 (2018)
68. Zimmermann, H.: OSI reference model - the ISO model of architecture for open systems interconnection. IEEE Trans. Commun. **28**, 425–432 (1980)
69. Kagermann, H., Wahlster, W., Johannes, H.: Recommendations for implementing the strategic initiative INDUSTRIE 4.0. Final report of the Industrie 4.0 Working Group, Frankfurt (2013)
70. Lu, Y., Morris, K.C., Frechette, S.: Current standards landscape for smart manufacturing systems. Natl. Inst. Stand. Technol. NISTIR **8107**, 39 (2016)

A Review of Measures to Evaluate Smart Sustainable Cities

Judy Backhouse[(⊠)]

United Nations University, Guimaraes, Portugal
backhouse@unu.edu

Abstract. This paper presents preliminary results of a review of tools that claim to measure aspects of the state of a city, related to the smart, sustainable city concept. Using academic literature as well as online searches, over 50 tools were identified, including standards, indices and models, that each measure a range of city attributes. So far, detailed information about 18 of these tools has been collected from articles, web sites and correspondence. This paper analyses data from this subset, looking at the intended purpose of the tools, what they measure, the nature and transparency of the tools, who is able to use them and for what purposes. The ultimate aim is to be able to advise cities on how to choose measures that are appropriate for their circumstances.

Keywords: Smart city · Intelligent city · Digital city · Resilient city · Sustainable city · Standard · Index · Indices · Measure · Indicator

1 Introduction

Various measures have been proposed to evaluate smart, sustainable cities [1–4]. They include international standards for indicators, models of smart city performance, and composite measures that summarize city performance on a number of indicators. Such measures are of interest to city stakeholders, including city managers, businesses, non-profit organisations and city residents seeking to understand, manage, monitor and improve city performance [5].

Such measures can be used to set targets, measure performance and make management decisions. They can also be used to identify opportunities for business or social enterprise and to hold local governments accountable. Measures which define indicators for specific city dimensions can be useful for cities to identify what can be measured and how. Measures which summarize information help cities to navigate the complexity of evaluating something as multi-faceted as a city [5]. Such tools can also help cities to build capacity in monitoring over time. Well-defined city measures and the regular collection of credible data in standard formats are particularly useful for organisations at national, regional or international levels to be able to compare cities, observe their progress and better understand the relationships between inputs, outcomes and impacts.

Measures of cities have, however, proliferated. This study has to date identified over fifty multi-dimensional measures of city performance. These include international

H. Santos et al. (Eds.): SmartCity 360 2019, LNICST 323, pp. 181–191, 2020.
https://doi.org/10.1007/978-3-030-51005-3_17

standards [6–9], academic research [1–4], and measures administered by private or public organisations [10], [11]. While many of these could be helpful to cities, it is difficult for cities to navigate this wealth of choices, to know which measures are most appropriate, which will best serve their goals, how to find good data and whether to pay the consultancy fees associated with participating in regional or international indexing and ranking.

Huovila et al. [12] compared recently published indicator standards for smart sustainable cities and argue that indicators for a city should be selected depending on (1) at what phase in city development (planning or operation) the measures will be made; (2) the spatial scale (district, city, region or country); (3) the time scale of the evaluation (from real-time to annual) and (4) the purpose of the assessment (target setting, monitoring, reporting, benchmarking or marketing). They argue that, while standardized indices have benefits, they "are always a compromise for a large group of different cities with different agendas, contexts and needs" [12, p150] and that cities should select what they measure based on their needs. These compromises have been recognised by researchers who have developed indices for specific contexts in terms of city size and location [13, 14].

In trying to assist cities to navigate these choices, this research examines the purposes for which the various measures were developed, their transparency and rigour, the ease of using them, and the benefits of using them. This paper is part of an ongoing study and reports on preliminary results in answering the following research questions:

Why? What are the stated and unstated purposes of the smart city measures that have been proposed?

How? What data collection and consolidation methods are proposed and are these processes transparent and rigourous?

2   Background

The idea of a smart city or community has been around since the start of the new millennium [15], and has been variously interpreted as using networked infrastructure to make cities more competitive, urban development led by high-tech and creative businesses, using technology to improve the governance of cities and communities, and the growth of connected and inclusive communities [15–17].

A working group of the Telecommunication Standardization Sector of the International Telecommunication Union (ITU-T) analysed definitions and conceptions of smart and sustainable cities to construct a composite definition that would encompass the key elements. They define a smart, sustainable city as "an innovative city that uses information and communication technologies (ICTs) and other means to improve quality of life, efficiency of urban operation and services, and competitiveness, while ensuring that it meets the needs of present and future generations with respect to economic, social and environmental aspects" [18, p. 13]. While this type of consensus definition may not be the most nuanced approach to understanding the construct, it incorporates the key ideas of innovation, the use of information and communication technologies (ICTs), improved quality of life, urban management and competitiveness, while introducing the need for sustainability, and so provides a useful working definition in an otherwise shifting landscape.

As cities grow, and are expected to continue to grow, increased urbanisation magnifies the challenges of managing them in a manner that ensures a good quality of life, while also being sustainable. ICTs and ongoing innovation are seen as key tools for addressing these challenges by improving efficiencies and communication as well as by continually finding new ways to tackle problems [19, 20]. A city is complex, with many interacting systems and the task of keeping a city functioning is shared between city managers, businesses, non-profit organisations and, increasingly, the residents of the city, all of whom have a role to play.

All of these role-players would benefit by having information about the current state of the city and how it changes over time. Such information can inform planning, help in identifying appropriate interventions, and be used to monitor the state of the city, manage the city and to establish a common language between role-players [12]. In addition, national, regional and international bodies are interested in information that is comparable across cities so that they can understand how cities are faring and to inform policy interventions at these levels.

Measures of the state of a city, and how well it is performing, are complex because cities are multi-dimensional [21]. Cities need to function well in providing facilities, a safe environment, and services, like power, water and waste removal. They need to cater for residents with transportation, healthcare, education and leisure facilities. Cities also need to facilitate business activities and trade while preserving the environment and anticipating future change. Any attempt to understand how a city is performing, needs to examine a wide range of city dimensions and collect information about each.

Indicators are measures of specific aspects of city performance and form the basis of higher-level composite measures. Six international sets of indicators have been identified for measuring aspects of city functioning, including smartness and sustainability [12]. While indicators form the basis of measuring cities, there have been many attempts to combine sets of indicators into composite measures that summarize the performance of a city [1–4]. One way of creating consolidated measures is through the creation of city indices. Indices are commonly used to create single measures of multi-faceted constructs. Such measures simplify a lot of information and they facilitate comparisons, in the form of city rankings [5].

There has been a proliferation of studies that construct indices for smart and sustainable cities, as well as indices implemented by private companies and national, regional or international organisations. This study reports preliminary results of a review that seeks to understand this proliferation of measures, what they are being created for, their quality and uses.

3   Methods

This study began with an investigation into smart city indices, in order to understand how many there were in existence and what they were used for. Searches were made of web sites and academic literature, initially to establish what smart city measures had been proposed, by whom and for what purposes.

The initial search in the Web of Science was for journal or conference papers that included the terms "smart city" and the term "index", carried out in May 2019. This returned 100 papers. An initial search through the titles of these papers identified 41 papers that appeared to be about the construction of or evaluation of a smart city index. Reading the abstracts of these papers eliminated a further twenty-eight papers that either duplicated work reported in another paper (1 paper), or constructed indices for only one aspect of a city, such as transport, happiness or construction efficiency (14 papers). Of the remaining 26 papers, full text access was not available for ten and the authors of these papers were e-mailed to request copies.

The remaining 16 papers were downloaded and read, capturing information about the index constructed, the purpose, the geographical focus, the target cities, how many cities had been evaluated, the dimensions, indicators and data sources, as well as the methods of construction. Also noted were any references in these papers to other existing indices and these were used to expand the list. For these indices I looked for details either through any reference given or by searching online for further information.

A review done by the United Nations University [22] identified fifteen smart city measures and those were included in the list. This work made it clear that it might be necessary to look beyond indices to other measures of smart cities as that review had included standards and maturity models, so the list was expanded to include those as well. Searches were carried out using Google and Duck Duck Go, for "smart city index" and "smart city maturity model", and the first two pages of results were examined for likely web sites that provided measures for smart cities. Similar information was captured for these measures, when it was available.

The current list includes references to 57 smart city measures. Work is still ongoing to collect details about each of these and to eliminate duplicates. Not all measures identified were clearly named and some sources referred to the same measure by different names, so duplicates are still coming to light as the data collection and analysis continues. New measures also come to light as the work proceeds, so this number is expected to change over time. This preliminary paper reports on the 18 measures for which there is currently comprehensive data.

Not all of the measures analysed were, strictly speaking, measures. For example, the standard ISO37101 is a standard for city or community management systems, although it includes how to monitor these systems. The two models are frameworks that describe the characteristics of smart cities. One of them is used to evaluate city smartness, but there are no details as to how this is done. The other invites cities to apply for smart city status and access to government funding for smart initiatives, giving information about how the application will be scored. The two sets of indicators give details of indicators that can be used to measure aspects of city performance and how to calculate them. The remainder of the measures examined are consolidated indices, based on a set of city dimensions (and sometimes sub-dimensions), with each dimension being measured by one or more indicators.

The analysis of the data is informed by the research questions. To establish the intended purposes of the measures I examined stated purposes, and then looked for commonality and differences between them using thematic analysis. I also looked for unstated purposes where these could be deduced from the originator of the measure, the intended users, and the kind of relationship between the two.

The measures were evaluated for transparency based on how public the information is. Intended or reported sources of data were examined and compared. While it is not possible to evaluate the accuracy of data sources used, I did look for efforts to ensure data quality. Finally, if there was a consolidation process (as in constructing an index), descriptions of this process, the rationale for the process and indications of rigour, in the form of statistical analyses, were examined and compared.

4 Why? Purposes of City Measures

Measures of city performance are created with different purposes in mind, some more clearly expressed than others. To understand what the intended purposes of the selected measures were, this section starts by analysing the nature of the measures and where they originated. The 18 measures that were examined for this paper included two standards, one set of indicators, two smart city "models" and thirteen indices. One of the standards is for a set of indicators, so there are effectively two sets of indicators.

The measures originate from academic sources, from governments, from international bodies and from private companies and individual consultants. Eight of the measures have academic roots; five of them from groups of researchers, two from a consortium of universities and one from a research institute which is university-based, but includes local government and business partners. Five of the measures originated from international organisations, three from private companies or individuals and two from national governments. The predominance of academic measures may reflect the approach taken to sourcing the data and the full set of measures, which is still to be analysed, may reveal different proportions between these sources.

The purposes that are ascribed to the measures show some interesting themes. The predominant theme (in nine cases) is about measurement and some do not expand in any way on the purpose of this measurement. For example, one private company's index is intended to provide "balanced benchmarking" and an "objective perspective" on where cities work and where they don't. One academic index is intended to "simplify and summarize a complex concept" and another aims to "measure the intellectual capital of cities". One international organization's index is intended for "comparative ranking of cities" and another aims to "to measure prosperity and sustainability of cities".

Others are explicit about the reasons for measuring and the most common ones are to aid decision-making (four measures) and to improve conditions in cities (four measures). Purposes such as "to steer the performance of city services", to "prioritize investments" and to "manage city sustainability" suggest that the measures are useful to city authorities in making decisions. Other measures aim at "helping cities, communities and companies become smart", or to "foster smartness and resilience" and improve quality of life.

Four of the measures aim at "urban innovation" or to "develop valuable ideas and innovative tools", while another three are positioned as tools themselves, to aid learning. One index, with academic origins, is trying to "find relationships" between city characteristics and innovation and another to "assess and analyse development patterns" in cities. Other goals are competitive. One index, constructed by a private company, is "for cities to compete for companies, tourists and talent" while another government measure was designed for cities to compete for funding. Finally, two of the measures developed by international organisations are tools for achieving the sustainable development goals (SDGs) or to meet other compliance requirements.

There is a clear relationship between the origins of the measures and the cities or communities to which they are intended to be applied. Those measures with academic and government origins were looking at cities in specific geographic areas. This is unsurprising for governments which were creating measures for their own countries (India and Brazil). For academics, the choice of cities was influenced by where they were based, usually researching cities in their country, but also by the availability of data. Six of the studies were based in Europe and two in China. There appears to be good data available, at least for larger cities, in both Europe and China.

International organisations, not surprisingly, create measures that can be applied globally (all five cases), and the two standards can be applied at different scales, including "communities of all sizes, structures and types, in developed or developing countries, at local, regional or national levels, and in defined urban or rural areas". Private companies and consultants focus on their target markets with one only measuring "global or regional capitals of business and finance" and another aiming to measure smartness in "cities, communities and companies".

Observing the targets of these different measures allows some speculation about the less explicit purposes of the measures. While the explicit purposes are to measure with an eye to improving conditions in cities, academic researchers are pursuing knowledge and national governments are creating tools to measure outcomes or progress on initiatives they are implementing. International organisations are interested in creating measures that facilitate global monitoring and analysis, in pursuit of their goals for global development, while private companies are seeking to collect information that supports their business goals through its usefulness to their clients.

5   How? Data Collection and Consolidation

5.1   Indicators

The indices that were examined were based on between five and ten different city dimensions. These dimensions were then associated with between 18 and 96 indicators. The academic papers that were not from research groups tended to consider fewer indicators (between 18 and 32), but those produced by research groups considered between 81 and 96 indicators. Private companies and consultants used between 39 and 67 indicators, the one government index used 81 indicators and the one index produced by an international organisation used 72 indicators with the option to extend that, depending on budget. (The other index proposed by an international organisation was still under development, so the number of indicators was not yet fixed.)

Indicators need to be consistent across cities and across time, in order to allow meaningful comparisons. For example, city data can be affected by the selection of city boundaries [12, 23] and so need to be interpreted in their contexts. Consistency depends on having detailed definitions of each indicators, so as to avoid multiple interpretations, as well as guidance on how the data might be sourced. The two indicator sets examined for this study, ISO37120 and the ITU-T Key Performance Indicators for Smart, Sustainable Cities [9], both provide such definitions and guidance on data sources. As such they are valuable resources. Indeed, two other measures that were examined made use of the ITU-T indicators as the basis of their measures. The ISO37120 standard proposes 111 indicators and the ITU-T Key Performance Indicators for Smart, Sustainable Cities uses 55 core and 36 advanced indicators.

Most measures proposed a mandatory, common set of indicators, while two that try to be more flexible or developmental, suggest that the set could be negotiated with the cities. Clearly flexibility limits comparability, but this provision allows the wider application of the index to cities where data might not yet be available or feasible.

5.2 Data

All measures depend on some kind of data or information about the city or community being evaluated. Two of the measures did not say what the source of data was. Those that did, gave three sources of data. Either data is collected by the city itself or data is collected from the cities through an externally administered survey. In these cases, there was sometimes an external verification process. The third source of data was trusted third parties that aggregate and verify data.

Indicators depend on reliable and comprehensive data and trusted third parties seem to be the most reliable source. Some world regions are well supplied with data. For example, Eurostat is used by researchers as a reliable source of data about cities in Europe. Some countries have good national data collection points, but many parts of the world have limited data sources. This limits the number of cities that can make effective use of indicators, although, where data is not available for a particular indicator, various techniques can be used to compensate. For example, national data can be used to substitute for city data [1].

Where cities collect data themselves there is always a risk that they omit data that might show the city in a bad light or skew the data collection towards data that is easier to collect or appears more favourable. Despite this, an important discourse, present in the measures proposed by international organisations, is that of developing the capacity of cities to collect accurate data. These bodies are concerned to strengthen data collection practices at local and national levels in order to fill gaps in our knowledge of the global state of affairs and to facilitate the kind of monitoring and policy work that they undertake. Skills in data collection within cities will also strengthen the ability of national and regional bodies to provide good data.

Surprisingly, given that smart cities are strongly associated with real-time data, only one index suggested the use of real-time data "if available". Real-time data collected from city residents or sensors in the city would give accurate and timeous information that might be less open to manipulation. Researchers have argued that "smart cities need smart indicators" as people, companies and governments "generate digital data on almost all the urban activities they perform, but it is estimated that only 5% of the available digital information is currently being used" [5, p618].

5.3 Consolidation and Validation

The level of detail provided on how the measures were to be applied differed widely. In the case of the two models one provided no information and the other provided guidelines as to how the scoring of applications to be considered smart would be applied. The indicator sets and standards, however, gave detailed information about how they were to be used.

Indices are constructed from the indicators through various consolidation techniques, some more complex and rigorous than others. Again, differing levels of detail were provided on how that consolidation takes place and the rationale for using a particular method. The one government index gave no information about how the index was calculated. Of the indices developed by private companies, one gave no information about the construction, a second gave some information about a board of experts who agreed on the method and the third explained that the evaluated cities would be ranked on each sub-index and these scores totaled for the final index. Of the two indices proposed by international organisations one was similarly short on detail, explaining only that the final measure is a "weighted mean of standardized indices from each of six dimensions" and that it would be "adjusted to the priorities of the country and the availability of information". The other was still under development.

For many of the academic indices, researchers were trying to arrive at a minimal or representative set of indicators, that provide an accurate measure of city smartness or resilience. These papers focused on validating the index as an accurate measure and explained in detail the techniques used to do this. Academics explain the statistical techniques they use, the reliability of their results and they give their rationale for decisions made about the consolidation with comments like: "This approach ensures that the cities being compared have a useful amount of homogeneity and uses the underlying structure of the dataset to weight and aggregate our data while guaranteeing the consistence, coherence and reproducibility of our results." [1, p484]. They are also careful to specify where indices are constructed for specific regions, and are not applicable more broadly [24, 25].

This means that the indices produced by academic sources are the most rigourous and also the most transparent. Those produced by governments, international organisations, and private companies and consultants appear less transparent. Without transparency it is not possible to comment on their rigour.

Given the promise of new data analytical techniques one might expect to see some of these being used in the evaluation of smart cities, but that was not the case in this set of data. Chinese researchers are beginning to use such techniques. For example, Liu et al. [26] made use of an "influential network relation map (INRM)" to analyse the relationships between indicators and compare the performance of two cities.

6   Conclusion and Next Steps

This paper identified measures of city performance, including indicator sets, models and indices.

Two sets of city indicators were examined, both of which provide details of what can be measured and how. Such indicator sets are useful base measures for cities and can save cities the work of agreeing and defining indicators. Indicator sets are transparent, although not always easy to implement due to the difficulty of sourcing data, but they do serve as a development tool for cities and communities who want to improve their data collection and measurement. Some standards have to be purchased, so there may be a cost in accessing them. Standard indicators also facilitate comparisons across cities. Standards for city indicators do not necessarily improve management of cities or quality of life, but establishing good measures is a step towards those bigger goals.

This paper has not examined models in any depth. The sub-set of data examined did not give much information about how models might be used for measuring cites, although many of the indices are underpinned by models of city performance which inform the dimensions and sub-dimensions to be investigated.

Composite indices that measure city performance originate from three types of sources and these origins appear to influence the uses and usefulness of the indices.

The first source are academic researchers who construct indices either to test or illustrate technical aspects of index construction, or to support conceptual understandings of smart cities. These indices tend to be rigourous in their construction and the norms of academic publishing ensure that they are transparent. The indices are clearly associated with specific objectives and types of cities. However, except for cities that fit their criteria, they are unlikely to be useful. The academic presentation of the techniques also means that the information is not in an accessible format for cities and communities.

The second source of composite indices is private companies or consultants who use them to support customers with information about cities. Of the three examined in this paper, two were using this data to inform clients about the benefits of investing in or locating in leading cities. A different two were looking to assist cities to improve their performance. The transparency of these indices varied. They all described the dimensions they used, two listed some information about the indicators used and one described the consolidation process. Those that are only measuring leading cities are of little use to other cities and communities. The third, which purports to help cities, communities and companies, gives the least information and so would not assist a city in measuring itself.

The third source of composite indices is national or international bodies. This group were interested in national or international monitoring, comparisons and, in one case, the allocation of resources to cities. These indices were similarly mixed in terms of transparency. They all listed dimensions and indicators, but only one gave details of how all the indicators were measured. All were designed to be applied to cities with the originating body playing a consulting role. There was not enough information provided for a city to apply the process entirely independently. This configuration may relate to a desire to ensure the quality of data collected since these bodies, while supporting a capacity development discourse, seem to be motivated primarily from a desire to collect comparable data across cities. There was little information about the process adopted for consolidation or justification of the choice, missing the opportunity to raise awareness of the technical considerations in such a process. Marsal-Llacuna et al. advise that "official normalizing bodies have to take the lead in the elaboration of summarizing indices" [5, p621], and this seems to be something not yet effectively addressed.

This paper reports on preliminary results of a survey of measures of the performance of cities. Detailed information about the remaining measures is still being collected and will be reported in due course. However, patterns are already starting to emerge in the purposes, construction, transparency and potential uses of the indices. Going forward, the patterns need to be confirmed using more data. From this work, recommendations are expected for practitioners as to which measures to use and how to use them effectively.

References

1. Akande, A., Cabral, P., Gomes, P., Casteleyn, S.: The Lisbon ranking for smart sustainable cities in Europe. Sustain. Cities Soc. **44**, 475–487 (2019). https://doi.org/10.1016/j.scs.2018. 10.009
2. Giffinger, R., et al.: Smart cities: Ranking of European medium-sized cities. Centre of Regional Science (SRF), Vienna University of Technology, Vienna, Austria (2007)
3. Theng, Y.L., Xu, X., Kanokkorn, W.: Towards the construction of smart city index for analytics (SM-CIA): pilot-testing with major cities in China using publicly available data. In: The Annual Hawaii International Conference On System Sciences, pp. 2964–2973 (2016). https:// doi.org/10.1109/HICSS.2016.371
4. Shi, H., Tsai, S.B., Lin, X., Zhang, T.: How to evaluate smart cities' construction? A comparison of Chinese smart City evaluation methods based on PSF. Sustainability (Switzerland) **10**(1) (2017). https://doi.org/10.3390/su10010037
5. Marsal-Llacuna, M.L., Colomer-Llinàs, J., Meléndez-Frigola, J.: Lessons in urban monitoring taken from sustainable and livable cities to better address the Smart Cities initiative. Technol. Forecast. Soc. Change **90**(PB), 611–622 (2015). https://doi.org/10.1016/j.techfore. 2014.01.012
6. ISO: 2013a. "Smart Cities." ISO Focus + . http://www.iso.org/iso/livelinkgetfileisocs?nod eid=16193764
7. ISO: Sustainable Development and Resilience of Communities—Indicators for City Services and Quality of Life. http://cityindicators.org/Deliverables/ISO37120BriefingNote_7-9-2014-103514.pdf. Accessed 15 June 2019
8. ISO: ISO 37120:2014 Sustainable Development of Communities—Indicators for City Services and Quality of Life. https://www.iso.org/obp/ui/#iso:std:iso:37120:ed-1:v1:en. Accessed 15 June 2019
9. ITU: Overview of Key Performance Indicators in Smart Sustainable Cities (2014)
10. Cohen, B.: The smartest cities in the world (2015). http://www.astcoexist.com/3038818/the-smartest-cities-in-the-world-2015-methodology. Accessed 15 June 2019
11. IBM: How Smart is Your City? Helping Cities Measure Progress. IBM Global Business Services. https://doi.org/10.1126/science.1217637. Accessed 15 June 2019
12. Huovila, A., Bosch, P., Airaksinen, M.: Comparative analysis of standardized indicators for Smart sustainable cities: what indicators and standards to use and when? Cities **89**(January), 141–153 (2019). https://doi.org/10.1016/j.cities.2019.01.029
13. Dall'O, G., Bruni, E., Panza, A., Sarto, L., Khayatian, F.: Evaluation of cities' smartness by means of indicators for small and medium cities and communities: a methodology for Northern Italy. Sustain. Cities Soc. **34**(July), 193–202 (2017). https://doi.org/10.1016/j.scs. 2017.06.021
14. Shang, J., Wang, Z., Li, L., Chen, Y., Li, P.: A study on the correlation between technology innovation and the new-type urbanization in Shaanxi province. Technol. Forecast. Soc. Change **135**(April), 266–273 (2018). https://doi.org/10.1016/j.techfore.2018.04.029
15. Hollands, R.G.: Will the real smart city please stand up? Intelligent, progressive or entrepreneurial? City **12**, 303–320 (2008)
16. Allwinkle, S., Cruickshank, P.: Creating smarter cities: an overview. J. Urban Technol. **18**, 1–16 (2011)

17. Caragliu, A., Del Bo, C., Nijkamp, P.: Smart cities in Europe. J. Urban Technol. **18**, 65–82 (2011)
18. ITU-T: Smart sustainable cities: Analysis of definitions. ITU-T Focus group on smart Sustainable Cities. Focus Group Technical report (2014)
19. Leydesdorff, L., Deakin, M.: The triple-helix model of smart cities: a neo-evolutionary perspective. J. Urban Technol. **18**(2), 53–63 (2011). https://doi.org/10.1080/10630732.2011.601111
20. Soe, R.-M., Drechsler, W.: Agile local governments: experimentation before implementation. Govern. Inf. Q. (November), 1–13 (2017). https://doi.org/10.1016/j.giq.2017.11.010
21. Leem, C.S., Kim, B.G.: Taxonomy of ubiquitous computing service for city development. Pers. Ubiquitous Comput. **17**(7), 1475–1483 (2012). https://doi.org/10.1007/s00779-012-0583-5
22. Esteves, E., Lopes, N.V., Janowski, T.: Smart Sustainable Cities: Reconnaissance Study. United Nations University Operating Unit on Policy-Driven Electronic Governance (UNU-EGOV) (2016)
23. Kitchin, R.: Making sense of smart cities. Camb. J. Reg. Econ. Soc. **8**(1), 131–136 (2015)
24. Garau, C., Balletto, G., Mundula, L.: A critical reflection on smart governance in Italy: definition and challenges for a sustainable urban regeneration. In: Bisello, A., Vettorato, D., Stephens, R., Elisei, P. (eds.) SSPCR 2015. GET, pp. 235–250. Springer, Cham (2017). https://doi.org/10.1007/978-3-319-44899-2_14
25. Rodrigues, M., Franco, M.: Composite index to measure cities' creative performance: an empirical study in the Portuguese context. Sustainability (Switzerland) **11**(3) (2019). https://doi.org/10.3390/su11030774
26. Liu, Y., Wang, H., Tzeng, G.-H.: From measure to guidance: galactic model and sustainable development planning toward the best smart city. J. Urban Plann. Dev. **144**(4), Article 04018035 (2018)

Well-Being Indexes - Privileged Tools for Smart Cities Governance

Bruno Rebelo and Orlando Belo(⌧)

ALGORITMI R&D Centre, School of Engineering, University of Minho Campus de Gualtar,
4710-057 Braga, Portugal
bruno.f.f.rebelo@gmail.com, obelo@di.uminho.pt

Abstract. The creation of smart cities aims to improve the quality of life of people and the environment that surrounds them, ensuring a better response of the services they interact with in urban environments. The inhabitants of the cities tend to make concrete opinions about their own city. The possibility of collecting and reconciling these opinions is very interesting for those who have to govern such environments, as these can allow for the identification of some strengths and weaknesses of the various aspects of a city. With this knowledge, a manager can, in a more supported way, having information sent by the inhabitants of the city, knowing the effect of their decisions using a set of dashboards that include well-being indexes, combining the various elements collected, and reflecting people's appreciation of the city in real time. In this work, we will present how we designed and implemented a well-being urban index, applying it in a concrete application of an urban case study – a university campus.

Keywords: Smart cities · Smart governance · Quality of life · Business Intelligence · Well-being urban indexes

1 Introduction

Throughout the last years, humanity has witnessed a constant technological evolution, growing constantly at a great speed, and at the same time seeing a great development and progress of human society itself. The significant increase in human population and the high adherence to migration of a significant part of the population, from rural areas to urban areas, showed to the cities a marked decrease in their capacity for supporting such events, with the consequent emergence of problems related to the management of the city itself [1]. This increase in the population in urban areas forced the cities, and their managers, to prepare themselves in the best possible way, so they could respond quickly and effectively to such new adversities and needs. Thus, with population growth, it is crucial to evade congestion of new or existing services created in the meantime, avoiding obstacles to normal life in a city. Increasing the sustainability capacity of the cities is then essential. Cities now account for more than 50% of the world's population and it is estimated that by 2050 this figure is about 70%. Against the background of these figures, unless we adopt preventive measures for this demographic change, it can be expected that

© ICST Institute for Computer Sciences, Social Informatics and Telecommunications Engineering 2020
Published by Springer Nature Switzerland AG 2020. All Rights Reserved
H. Santos et al. (Eds.): SmartCity 360 2019, LNICST 323, pp. 192–204, 2020.
https://doi.org/10.1007/978-3-030-51005-3_18

cities will suffer even more from problems such as increased pollution, traffic congestion, or insufficient parking spaces [2–4]. In order to solve the problems related to urban management caused by this migratory flow of people and guarantee a better social order to drive economic growth in a sustainable and rapid way, the concept of intelligent cities has emerged in the last decades, using them more effectively in conjunction with the knowledge, intelligence and innovation of their citizens. This conjugation allows for helping in the construction of better solutions to problems such as those mentioned. The concept of smart city is increasingly popular in the most diverse areas. Although it has emerged in academic environments, today it can be identified in many existing real world applications, having been adopted for supporting some well-known international policies, which makes its application an unstoppable trend [1, 4]. To understand the concept of a smart city, it is essential to recognize that cities are the key elements for the future, since them promote growing at all kind of levels. Cities play a key role in terms of social and economic aspects around the world, which in turn has implications for the environment with a major impact. The concept also emerged as a response to the major economic and environmental changes recorded, as well as to the continuous acceleration of technological progress. All this created the need to find new ways for dealing with the problems of cities, such as the aging of their population, urban overcrowding, or climate changes problems [5, 6].

The aim of this work was to exploit a city-based computing infrastructure supported by a data warehousing system to support applications for monitoring various urban aspects - social, cultural, climatic, traffic, among others – in order to feed a *Well-Being Urban Index* (WBUI), having the potential for classifying a city and its environment at any given time. Taking such system as our base platform, we designed and implemented a computational platform that allowed us to set up an application case study for evaluating the quality of services provided in a university campus. This permitted to demonstrate the utility of such analytical platform for feeding the calculus of a WBUI, combining the various elements collected and reflecting student's appreciation in real time, and follow its evolution over time. In this paper, we will expose and explain the process we carried out to study, identify and characterize a WBUI for assessing the quality of service of a university campus, taken as an urban city case study. In the following sections, we will expose and discuss some related work (Sect. 2), presenting the concept of WBUI as well as some real applications cases, and reveal the process of inception and implementation of a concrete WBUI application taking a university campus and the services it provides as an application case study (Sect. 3). Finally, in Sect. 4, we present a brief set of conclusions, pointing out some working lines for future work.

2   Well-Being Urban Indexes

A smart city is an urban area highly technologically advanced as a whole, if we considered its infrastructures, means of communication, viability in the market and sustainability with respect to the goods properties. Information technology is the main infrastructure of a smart city, giving it the possibility for supporting essential services to its citizens. Usually, in smart cities there are many technological platforms involved, such as data centres and automated sensor networks, providing real-time data that can be analyzed posteriorly for improving the quality of living in a smart city [7–10]. A smart city uses modern and advanced technical means for processing information in an articulated way with transmission and communication processes, integrating urban resources, improving competitiveness and guaranteeing a more sustainable future through the symbiosis between networks of people, companies, technologies, infrastructures, consumption, energy and spaces. This connection obviously brings many benefits to all the parts involved.

A smart city can also use the most relevant information from urban operations for responding intelligently to urban management activities. Basically, a smart city has the capacity to carry out a smart management, in a way that it is possible to provide a good quality of life as well as a good working environment in different areas for the citizens in the best possible way [1, 11]. However, to analyze all this diversity of information, it is essential to identify whether the people of a given city are satisfied with the course of their life and the environment that surrounds them. Therefore, it is necessary the existence of some indicators for illustrating with accuracy the mood of the people in (almost) everything concerning their city. These indicators referred often as well-being indexes. Well-being can be seen as the presence of the best standard of quality of life, by the state of the life situation of a given individual. In other words, it is a positive outcome very significant for people and for many sectors of society. Through this concept we can understand if people perceive whether their lives are going well or not, discovering the desired state of life in a given community. However, a positive well-being result does not depend exclusively on the material conditions of life, although these are fundamental for the definition of well-being, such as housing, employment, financial conditions, among others. This is because income gains are not always proportionate to happiness, as the Easterlin Paradox [12] portrays, that people's levels of happiness seem to remain constant even in the light of the substantial increase in their income.

A *Well-Being Index* (WBI) aims to provide results that allow for following the evolution of well-being and social progress of a population, taking in consideration two main aspects: material conditions and satisfaction with life. In this way, it is possible to measure economic behaviour, for example, in a given context of sustainability, emphasizing as far as possible the well-being of people. With an indicator like this, we can monitor the main critical factors of the economic and social development of a given city or urban environment in terms of well-being, and evaluate them according to a logic of concrete results, integrating statistical information and providing useful readings to facilitate the process of decision- making. A WBI provides information on the evolution, positive or negative, of well-being of a particular area, at a defined scale. The value of a WBI always depends on several factors, such as the index periodicity, the cause for which it was developed, or the variation of its own characteristics over time. A WBI provides a one-dimensional representation of well-being, allowing for measuring it through the combination of several distinct factors that help to improve people's quality of life. Using WBI, we have access to a large set of information that reveals the strengths and weaknesses of a given population, as well as other determinants of their well-being. Usually a WBI is a composite index and not a conventional panel of indicators, since it aggregates and normalizes information in a single indicator, which may include different variables or even other indexes, providing a statistical evaluation of a given population or sector we need to analyse. A composite index has several advantages, namely: it allows for a richer reading in terms of interpretation, facilitates a systemic approach to the welfare problem, and generates a great flexibility in the analysis of the results of an index in a greater or lesser detail in different perspectives. Having an index established, we can design and set up a panel of indicators for illustrating the evolution of the index and all the information supporting it. A WBI provides information that allows for a simple and quick reading of a positive or negative index evolution in a given work area [13, 14].

Concerning WBUI as an application of WBI to urban environments, it can be seen as a weighted "average", similar to a stock exchange index, of a large set of heterogeneous aspects and characteristics of a smart city, like leisure, traffic, environment, weather, and so on. As we know, a stock index is a value that illustrates the general trend of a particular set of stocks. Its value translates into a calculated average of stock prices selected from a given market or industry, which is under analysis. We can see it as an index containing only a few actions of a given sample to explore. The collective performance of these actions is a good indicator of the trends of the market under study, be it global or local, allowing for making its monitoring in a more effective way. It represents the progression of all or part of a market in a very concentrated way, as a single measure, and provides information for analysing the history of stock events, and verifying improvements or regressions, facilitating the drawing of conclusions. The index is a good indicator of analysis for those who want to analyze the direction that a given market sector is having [14, 15]. WBUI are very useful indicators for monitoring and managing numerous aspects related to a city, and for determining which cities are more global. Over the last few years, different types of methods and measurement indexes have been developed to make this identification. However, these efforts vary according to the definition of a smart city and, consequently, produce quite different solutions and results. As such, it is quite complicated establishing a generic measurement process, without missing specific important information, given the wide variety of characteristics that cities present throughout the world. Take, for example, two very concrete cases presented by the company A.T. Kearney [16], based on a very diverse set of data related to 125 cities in the world, which the company collected since 2008. With this work, the company monitored the progress of cities considered the most important by measuring a set of indicators at the level of each of them, creating two very specialized indexes that used together, namely: *Global Cities Index* (GCI) and *Global Cities Outlook* (GCO). The first index allows making an analysis on the performance of each of the cities taking into account 27 different metrics. These metrics are grouped into five distinct dimensions, taking into account commercial activity, human capital, involvement in politics, cultural experience, and information exchange. The calculation of this index is carried out through a previous allocation of weights to each of the dimensions under consideration - for example the commercial activity and the human capital, have a weight of 30%, while the exchange of information and the cultural experience a weight of 15% in determining the final value of the index. In the second index, 13 other indicators are analysed, grouped into a set of dimensions such as personal well-being, economy, innovation or governance. In this index are measured the characteristics of long-term success, such as innovation capacity, environmental performance or safety. This index is calculated by a weighted average, where each dimension has been assigned a weight of

25%. The values of both indices vary between 0 and 100. These two cases can be analysed in more detail in the A.T. report [16]. In addition to these two cases, we found a third case, which we find very interesting and inspiring for this work. We refer to a case that was carried out in Portugal by INTELI to create a specific index for smart cities the Smart Cities Index (SCI) [17]. In order to calculate this index, another set of dimensions was used, namely: innovation, sustainability, social inclusion, governance and connectivity, each of which, in turn, is organized into sub-dimensions. For example, the innovation dimension integrates the sub-dimensions competitiveness, research and development, green economy, social economy or creative economy, while the governance dimension integrates sub-dimensions public participation, public services, transparency, or urban policies. The SCI index is a composite index that incorporates 80 indicators, summarizing the average of the results of the referred dimensions. This index was applied to 20 Portuguese municipalities, members of the *Portuguese Smart Cities Network* (RENER), which is a space for the development, testing and experimentation of intelligent urban solutions in real practical contexts [18].

3   Inception and Implementation of a WBUI

3.1   The Application Case

We designed and developed the application case having the objective of identifying and understanding the way students see the quality of some services and infrastructures of our university. To do that, we needed to conceive a system with the ability to collect in (near) real time the opinions of students about their experience when using the services or infrastructures available in one of the university's campi. Opinions should be collected according to a predefined evaluation model, and monitored for analysing students' reactions in real time in order to assess their impact on the academic community. Thus we conceived a WBUI for analysing the involvement of the various human actors (students) in the various application contexts (services and infrastructures of a university campus), as well as the variation of the several analysis metrics for allowing managers or service directors to view how services and infrastructures under their supervision are evaluated.

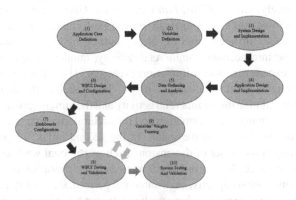

Fig. 1. An overview of the WBUI system life cycle.

In Fig. 1, we can see an overview of the WBUI system life cycle. The first thing to do is to define clearly the case study that we use to define and maintain the WBUI. As mentioned before, we decided to implement a small process of analysis applied to some services and infrastructures of one of our university's campus. We assumed that this application case fits quite well in the domain of smart cities, since our university is technologically advanced and all the people that use the campus (students, in this case) have mobile phones, which have the most typical characteristics to support an initiative for a smart city. For this, we needed to define what the target user community would be. Given the characteristics of the students of the Business Intelligence specialization profile of the Master of Informatics Engineering, it was felt that these would be the ideal community to participate in an initiative like this one. The purpose of this application case for studying the quality of the university's services and infrastructures, gathering the opinion of the target community, provided us a real situation of real world, with real data, and getting valid opinions and lessons about the university itself. In spite of being a test case, the lessons learned were important and relevant for us.

After this first part of the work, we made the definition and the choice of the analysis variables that we want to use in the evaluation carried out by the target population – students. The definition of the variables was based on the characteristics of the infrastructures and university services covered by the case study. We organized the analysis variables into two distinct categories: 1) dimensions – "Academic Services UM", "General Library UM", "Classrooms/Study", "Information Technology Department", "Bar/Restoration", "Parking Places", "Gardens/Green Spaces", and "Sports Conditions"; and 2) metrics – "Online Services", "Accessibility", "Space Comfort", "Number of Passwords" "Employees", "Waiting Time", "Time/Availability", "Air Conditioning" and "Customer Service Efficiency". After all the variables defined and analysed, we designed the system for supporting the execution of the WBUI process, from the initial phase of data gathering to the last one where we calculate it. During the design of the system, we realized that its base structure should be able to integrate new cases of study without the need to be adapted. Thus, we used a JSON configuration file for defining the incorporation of a new case study into the system, where we define the case and all the dimensions. Later, the system will import this file by during its initialization, serving as well for configuring the corresponding WBUI evaluation system, which includes system's dashboards and the data gathering application for collecting the opinions of the users.

The JSON specification presented in Fig. 2 allows for hosting a structure of analysis for each case study considered, organized in several levels of interest, according the following basic configuration: <Service>, <SubService>, <SubSubService>, <...>. One possible instantiation of this configuration could be <"UM Academic Services">, <"Accessibility">, or <"UM Academic Services">, <"Number of Passwords">, among others.

The configuration file presented in Fig. 2 contains several analysis elements and the respective specifications of its properties. Additionally, we also see the specification of other variables, namely: "application", which identifies the name of the case study; "image", which is the image of the application study case and that will function as an application logo; "dateExpiration", which is the date set by the body for the closure of

```
{
  "application": "Turras",
  "image": "Turras.png",
  "dateExpiration": "2019-06-10 20:59:59",
  "dimensions": [
    {
      "shortName": "SAUM",
      "longName": "Serviços Académicos UM",
      "imageUrl": "https://image.flaticon.com/icons/png/512/309/309264.png",
      "weight": 1,
      "metrics": [
        {
          "shortName": "Online",
          "longName": "Serviços Online",
          "imageUrl": "https://image.flaticon.com/icons/svg/235/235198.svg",
          "weight": 1
        },
```

Fig. 2. A JSON fragment of a system's configuration file.

the study; "dimensions", which includes the dimensions to be evaluated; "shortName", which is a smaller name for the dimension so that it can appear on the mobile applications display; "longName", which is the full name of the dimension; "imageUrl", which is the image of the dimension; "weight", which is the weight that the dimension in question has in the category in which it is included, which can vary between '0' and '10'; and, finally, "metrics", which is very similar to dimensions only applied to metrics. Complementarily, the system contains another configuration structure: the equalizer. This is quite similar to the previous configuration structure. However, it contains only a single variable, which varies from '0' to '1', and it is used to inform the system whether or not a given dimension or metric will be included in the calculation of the index to which it is associated. It is counted only in cases where it has a value greater than '0'.

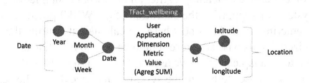

Fig. 3. The conceptual schema of the WBUI multidimensional database.

After the materialization of the data model, it was also necessary to create a data structure specially oriented to provide the data elements required by system dashboards. For this, we designed a multidimensional database (Fig. 3), with the ability to store the data about the opinions of system's users and to perform the calculations of the desired WBUI. To receive this data structure, we implemented a specific data warehouse for receive and store the votes, removing unnecessary information and consolidating the data into a single data structure. In the schema of Fig. 3, we clearly identify the fact table ("TFact_wellbeing") of the data warehouse. This table is also stored in a NoSQL database, adopted by the system in a key space named "cube_well_being", in which is store all user identifiers ("User"), metric names ("Metric"), dimensions ("Dimension"), application ("Application"), for the application case, and the value ("Value") voted by a certain user. All this information was associated with the date ("Date") of the vote and in which location ("Location") occurred. In our application case, in particular, the location refers to the campus of the university, so that one could verify if a user classified the canteen in the canteen or in a classroom, for example. The data warehouse allows for cataloguing the opinions received in the system according to the case study used, storing the data in a specific data system, organized according to the various previously identified analysis perspectives. In addition to the table "TFact_wellbeing", it was also necessary to create another table, index_table, to accept the WBUI values that were being calculated. This way, it was possible to store the WBUI history, facilitating later its calculation and analysis. After defining the main data elements for supporting the operation of the system, we implemented the WBUI management system (Fig. 4), paying particular attention how to support the application of data collection and the integration of the data collected.

Fig. 4. Functional model of the WBUI system.

In Fig. 4, we can see a sketch of the functional model of the WBUI system, having a representation of each one of its main components. The server component is responsible for providing users with references for the various dimensions and metrics they can evaluate, and processing each one of the votes in the application, together with other information relevant to the calculation of WBUI. Then, the server works the data collected by the application, producing the values for presentation in the dashboard component. This component generates several graphical elements and *key performance indicators* (KPI), revealing the various results that compose the value of the WBUI.

The application for evaluating services and infrastructures (Fig. 5) was designed especially for collecting the various data elements necessary for calculating the WBUI of the application case study we used. We transformed this tool into a mobile application, quite easy to install and use by students, so that the process of gathering opinions was easy, fast and versatile. In addition to these components, we also have another system's component: the monitor. It receives the data it works through the server, periodically revealing information for analysis, facilitating decision-making by decision-makers.

3.2 Calculating the WBUI

In order to calculate the WBUI, it was necessary to proceed gradually, adopting and adapting calculation expressions, improving them gradually to be more effective. Throughout the process we have taken into account some of the calculation models used by other systems, in particular the ones used in calculations of indexes of the so-called global

Fig. 5. Some screenshots of the application used for service evaluation.

cities. The process adopted takes place in two stages: the calculation of the index itself and its maintenance over time. First, it was necessary to calculate the value of the index of the day in question, taking into account the values obtained by the application up to the moment in which the request for calculation of the index value was registered, guaranteeing that new votes would not adulterate the result of the index calculation process.

Table 1. Dimensions and metrics relationships.

		Metrics								
		1	...	j	...	S_1	S_2	S_3	...	S
Dimensions	C_1	C_{11}	...	C_{1j}	...	C_1S_1				
	C_2	C_{21}	...	C_{2j}	...	...	C_2S_2			
	...	...	...	...	...	...	...	...	...	...
	C_i	C_{i1}	...	C_{ij}	...	...	...	...	...	...
	...	...	...	...	...	...	...	...	...	...
	C_K	C_{K1}	...	C_{Kj}	...	...	...	...	...	C_{KS}

Let us see, how is calculated the WBUI for our application case. We assumed that K is the total number of dimensions and S is the maximum number of existing metrics for all dimensions. Variable S is required since the number of metrics that a dimension has may be different from the other existing dimensions. Table 1 shows a matrix M, which illustrates the relationship between dimensions and metrics. With it, it is possible to see that each position (i, j) identifies a metric, and i identifies a dimension, where $1 \le i \le K$, $1 \le j \le S_i$ and $S_i \le S$, being S_i the maximum number of metrics of dimension i. For example, for dimension C_1 the maximum number of metrics is S_1, which is less than S, whereas for dimension C_2 the maximum number of metrics is S_2, since dimensions may not have the same number of metrics. However, when it is stated that pair (i, j) identifies a metric, this means that the value of j represents the position and not the denomination of the metric, which may be different for the same j at different i positions. As for C_{ij}, this is a trio that is in position (i, j) of matrix M, which may contain three distinct values, namely: the weight of the metric in the dimension index, p_{ij}; the value of the metric, that is, it represents the sum of all votes, v_{ij}; and the total number of votes in the metric,

n_{ij}. Only the last two are determined by voting, the first being previously defined in the configuration phase of the system. In Eq. 1, we can see the expression representing the value of the pair (i, j) in the matrix M:

$$C_{ij} = \langle p_{ij}, v_{ij}, n_{j_j} \rangle \qquad (1)$$

The process of calculating the index begins with the sum of all the values corresponding to the votes made. To do this calculation, the voting date must be lower than the date of the request – we only consider the values recorded on the day of the request. The dimension of the vote should be equal to the dimension of the metric that is under analysis. The same must succeed for metrics. Then we calculate the index for each metric (Eq. 2) and the sum of all weights of a given dimension (Eq. 3). The value of the weight $P_{i,j}$, associated with a given analysis variable, varies accordingly the value we set up previously in the system equalizer.

$$I_{ij} = \frac{v_{ij}}{n_{ij}} \qquad (2)$$

$$\sum_{j=1}^{s_i} P_{ij} = 1 \qquad (3)$$

$$I_i = \sum_{j=1}^{s_i} P_{ij} \cdot I_{ij} \cdot E_{ij} \qquad (4)$$

Then we make the sum of all the weights of the existing categories (Eq. 5), which allows for obtaining the value of the global index (Eq. 6). As for $P_{i,j}$, P_i varies accordingly the value previously defined in the system equalizer for the other dimensions.

$$\sum_{i=1}^{K} P_i = 1 \qquad (5)$$

$$I_{global} = \sum_{i=1}^{K} P_i \cdot I_i \cdot E_i \qquad (6)$$

After completing the first phase of the index calculation – the daily index, we need to calculate incrementally the index, day after day, taking into account the values we calculated before. This is done using Eq. 7, which allows us to obtain the index value for a given date. In this equation, i_h represents the actual value of the updated index, i_0 the value of the index on the previous day, $f(i_0)$ the origin of the value of the index of the previous day, and i_c the value of the index calculated for the day in question.

$$i_H \leftarrow f(i_0) + i_C \qquad (7)$$

$$i_H \leftarrow f(i_0) \cdot 80\% + i_C \cdot 20\% \tag{8}$$

When the requested index value is relative to the first day, we apply Eq. 7, since this value obviously does not exist. However, this equation does not guarantee that the index value always varies between '−1' and '1'. As such, it is necessary to define weights to the participants in the calculation of the value of the index, namely to $f(i_0)$ and to i_c, which allowed a gradual variation and ensure that the index value will be within the predefined limits. Equation 8 ensures that these limits are not exceeded. Additionally, this equation calculates the index at the level of the dimensions and metrics. For example, when we want to calculate the index value for a given metric, we apply Eq. 2 followed by Eq. 8, which allows us to obtain the trend value of the same metric. WBUI results were quite interesting, even knowing that the application case study involved only a student class. They showed us the potential of a WBUI for the evaluation of services. Just to see one of the system's dashboards, we selected to show the values of the WBUI of one of the most curious dimensions: "Parking Places" (Fig. 6). In this figure, it can be seen that the metric with the greatest positive impact on "Parking Places" is "Signalling", with a value of '1'. As already mentioned, all subcategories were "weighed" with the same value, and, as such, this conclusion holds. Conversely, the metric that most influences negatively the index of this dimension is "Number of Parking Places", with has a value of approximately '−0.3', which lowered, obviously the value of the dimension's index.

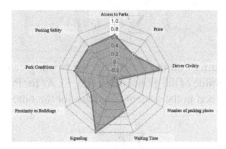

Fig. 6. WBUI results for the dimension "Parking Places".

4   Conclusions and Future Work

WBUI are very interesting and useful management tools. In fact, when properly implemented, they allow us following the behaviour of a given system, in a given application context. However, the definition of a WBUI, regardless of its nature, is very subjective, often depending on the expertise and knowledge of its designers and users, who combine their life experience with heuristics and mathematical models in a very heterogeneous "cocktail". This diversity of aspects, when transformed into a single element, an index, does not always have the desired effect or fulfil the previously established objectives.

The greatest difficulties were in the definition of the WBUI calculation process, in particular in the identification of the various relevant aspects to be included in the calculation expression, and later in the definition of its relevance, of its weights, in determining the final value of the WBUI for the case study that we considered. After that, we designed the architecture of the system and the application used for collecting opinions, a test case for WBUI. With this work, it was possible to have a rather concrete, although synthetic (an index) view on the level of satisfaction of a set of users on a set of services and infrastructures of the campus of the university. In spite of being a case we have idealized, it reflected (and reflects) a concrete opinion of a group of students, during a given period of time, revealing its behaviour and demonstrating in an unequivocal way the utility of an WBUI, as it can with the results obtained. In a near future, we intend to extend the focus of the system, enlarging and diversifying the set of dimensions, and find a real-world application case having its genesis and materialization in a recognized smart city.

Acknowledgments. This work has been supported by national funds through FCT – Fundação para a Ciência e Tecnologia within the Project Scope: UID/CEC/00319/2019.

References

1. Liu, Y., Zhu, X.: Smart city construction assessment system based on analytic hierarchy process-"quality changsha" as the case. TELKOMNIKA (Telecommun. Comput. Electron. Control) **14**(2A), 34 (2016)
2. Fallis, A.: Lisboa: indicadores de sustentabilidade. J. Chem. Inf. Model. **53**(9), 1689–1699 (2013)
3. de Notícias, D.: Migrações - Mais de metade da população mundial vive em cidades (2015). https://www.dn.pt/mundo/interior/mais-de-metade-da-populacao-mundial-vive-em-cidades-4856841.html. Accessed 15 July 2019
4. The Guardian: How to keep our cities moving in 2050—Inside SEAT—The Guardian (2016). https://www.theguardian.com/inside-seat/2016/sep/05/smart-cities-future-transport-technologies-revolution-carnet-vehicles-urban-planning. Accessed 15 July 2019
5. Albino, V., Berardi, U., Dangelico, R.M.: Smart cities: definitions, dimensions, performance, and initiatives, February 2015
6. Computer Business Review: Top 5 smartest Smart Cities in the world - Computer Business Review (2017). http://www.cbronline.com/news/internet-of-things/smart-cities/top-5-smartest-smart-cities/. Accessed 15 July 2019
7. Chennabasaveshwar: What is a 'Smart City?' All you need to know – Oneindia (2017). https://www.oneindia.com/india/what-is-smart-city-all-you-need-to-know-2476072.html. Accessed 15 July 2019
8. Government of India: What is Smart City: SMART CITIES MISSION, Government of India (2017). http://smartcities.gov.in/content/innerpage/what-is-smart-city.php. Accessed 15 July 2019
9. Mishra, N.: Smart Cities: all you need to know (2017). https://gradeup.co/smart-cities-all-you-need-to-know-i-d9f0b23a-c8e4-11e5-8447-91c9d1aed706. Accessed 15 July 2019
10. MIT201: Overview ‹Smart Cities—MIT Media Lab (2017). https://www.media.mit.edu/groups/smart-cities/overview/. Accessed 15 July 2019

11. Manville, C., et al.: Mapping smart cities in the EU. J. Chem. Inf. Model. **53**(9), 1689–1699 (2014)
12. Easterlin, R.: Well-being. My focus will be on what we are learning from the survey data on the causes of subjective well-being, and, based on this, what we might do, as individuals, to improve it. Daedalus J. Am. Acad. Arts Sci. **133**, 26–33 (1974)
13. Instituto Nacional de Estatística: O que é o Índice de Bem-estar (IBE), pp. 1–8 (2008)
14. IFC Markets: Indices de Bolsa de Valores—IFC Markets Portugal (2017). https://www.ifc markets.pt/introduction/stock-index. Accessed 15 July 2019
15. IG: Indices Trading—Online Trading Stock Indices—IG (2017). https://www.ig.com/por/ mercados/indices. Accessed 15 July 2019
16. Kearney, A.T.: Global Cities 2016 (2016). https://www.atkearney.com/documents/10192/817 8456/Global+Cities+2016.pdf/8139cd44-c760-4a93-ad7d-11c5d347451a. Accessed 15 July 2019
17. INTELI: Towards a Smart Cities Index: The Case of Portugal, November, pp. 1–10 (2009)
18. RENER: Primeiro Living Lab de Mobilidade na Europa (2019). http://www.inteli.pt/pt/go/ rener1. Accessed: 15 July 2019

Implementation of GDPR: Learning with a Local Administration Case Study

Fernando Martins[✉], Luís Amaral, and Pedro Ribeiro

Information Systems Department/ALGORITMI Research Centre, School of Engineering,
University of Minho, Guimarães, Portugal
`fernandorui@outlook.com`, {`amaral,pmgar`}`@dsi.uminho.pt`

Abstract. The General Data Protection Regulation has come into force in the European Union in May 2018 in order to meet current challenges related to personal data protection and to help harmonise the data protection across the EU. Although the GDPR was expected to benefit companies, being private or public, by offering consistency in data protection activities and liabilities across the EU countries and by enabling more integrated EU wide data protection policies, it poses new challenges to companies. However, if we take a step back and think that this regulation has been in transit for more than 2 years, and that only after the implementation of this regulation has begun the real concern is: are companies ready to make this leap?

Keywords: GDPR · Data · Data protection · Data claims · Data rights

1 Introduction

The General Data Protection Regulation (GDPR) has come into force in the European Union (EU) in May 2018 in order to meet current challenges related to personal data protection and to help harmonise the data protection across the EU.

Although the GDPR was expected to benefit companies, being private or public, by offering consistency in data protection activities and liabilities across the EU countries and by enabling more integrated EU wide data protection policies, it poses new challenges to companies [1].

The projects of implementing the GDPR have emerged with high frequency, offering new opportunities and challenges to the companies [2], being private or public. This situation led these companies to seek support from consulting firms in order to increase the likelihood of success and achieve compliance in the shortest time possible.

However, the greatest distinction between a public company and a private company is related to a lack of legal definition and public procurement that the former is obliged to follow [3], and therefore more time necessary for the implementation of these kind of efforts.

Throughout this document, it will be described the whole process followed by a local administration company in Portugal.

© ICST Institute for Computer Sciences, Social Informatics and Telecommunications Engineering 2020
Published by Springer Nature Switzerland AG 2020. All Rights Reserved
H. Santos et al. (Eds.): SmartCity 360 2019, LNICST 323, pp. 205–216, 2020.
https://doi.org/10.1007/978-3-030-51005-3_19

2 What Is GDPR?

The GDPR. was initiated, in 2012, by the European parliamentarian Viviane Reding, then the vice-president of the European Commission.

According to Viviane Reding, the main concern that led to this regulation was "the concern about the big companies, like the American GAFA—the French coinage for Google, Amazon, Facebook, and Apple" and the way they just ignored the old law [4].

A driving force behind all the arguments was the various scandals created around countless data losses, either voluntarily or involuntarily. For example, the Facebook Cambridge Analytica scandal, if it had happened after the May 26th of 2018, it would have cost billions of euros to Facebook, among others [5].

The GDPR aims to take the high ground in order protect all European citizens in the defence of their personal and sensitive data.

This is driven by philosophical thinking, and stance, as far as data protection is concerned [6]. Its core is based on the concept of privacy as a fundamental human right and seeks to extend to the whole EU [7].

This new regulation is intended to cover the personal data of all EU residents, this takes place regardless of where the data can be stored or processed.

The European Parliament and the Council of the European Union, using their legislative powers conferred under European Union law, deliberated on the subject of Data Protection, culminating, as such, in the EU General Data Protection Regulation (GDPR) of the European Parliament and of the Council of 27 April 2016) [7], which has been in force in the EU since 25 May of this year. This regulation should be considered in the practices of organisations, as it "is binding in its entirety and directly applicable in all Member States" [7].

In certain matters under the GDPR, the European legislator allows Member States to be able to specify some internal rules in certain matters within the GDPR. However, although Council of Ministers approved Law 120/XIII [8] to specify these internal rules, it has not yet been approved, so that "until there is national legislation implementing the GDPR repealing Law 67/98 on matters covered by the regulation, Law 67/98 remains in force in everything that does not contradict the GDPR.

According to Article 4 of the Regulation, personal data is information that can, directly or indirectly, identify an individual, in particular by reference to an identifier, such as a name, an identification number, location data, identifiers by electronic means (i.e. e-mail) or a more specific element of the physical, physiological, genetic, mental, economic, cultural or social identity of that individual " [7]. This is a more comprehensive regulation than its North American counterpart [6].

GDPR is often confused as one that deals only with technology, however, the GDPR protects personal data regardless of the technology used for processing that data.

The GDPR is technology neutral and considers both automated and manual processing, provided the data is organised in accordance with pre-defined criteria. It also doesn't matter how the data is stored – being in an IT system, through video surveillance, or on paper [9]. In all cases, personal data is subject to the protection requirements set out in the GDPR.

2.1 Territorial Adaptation

Despite the European regulation, there is some flexibility to adapt to the national reality of each member country of the European Union, however, until a national law to adapt this regulation comes into reality, this document comes into force on the 25th of May of 2018 [10].

This means that there is a unified and directly applicable data protection law for the European Union which replaces almost all of the existing Member States' provisions and which is applied by businesses, individuals, courts and authorities without transposition into national law [10].

Thanks to its broader territorial scope and the definition of personal data, it is a fact that the application of this regulation has a significant impact on organisations, whether private or public, and on the perceived fragility of all this information by its owner.

Regarding data processing carried out by competent authorities for the detection, prevention, investigation and prosecution of criminal offenses and for the execution of criminal sanctions, the Portuguese law 67/98 remains applicable in its entirety [11].

Thus, taking as its starting point the GDPR [7] and the Portuguese law 67/98 [11], as it remains in use at the time, this is considered as the relevant legal, statutory, regulatory and contractual requirements regarding data protection and retention periods dispersed by various normative acts.

The Portuguese law 67/98 [11] is applied to all forms of personal data processing whether resulting from the context of the business activities or the monitoring of individual activities.

Another fact that is quite relevant is the fact that the national laws that are more restrictive or impose requirements not addressed by this policy overlap with it [12].

2.2 Opportunity or Threat?

The GDPR was "the most contested law in the E.U.'s history, the product of years of intense negotiation and thousands of proposed amendments" [4].

The need to require affirmative consent, which must be freely given, specific, informed, and unambiguous [1] can be seen as an opportunity because it obtains a biddable authorization of all the treatment carried out.

It is then a determining factor the ability of each company to make the use of GDPR and turning that factor into an opportunity.

Regaining control of the data, stored and managed by the enterprises, will bring a whole host of benefits beyond compliance, demolishing the data silos and obtaining a more systemic view of all the data and processes that obtain the same data.

The need to change the way that the management of information is made will produce more accurate and useful insights [13] and a greater clarity across enterprise data.

The biggest threat, and more noteworthy, lies in the time that Portugal took to implement European legislation in which it only saw its final version adopted on June 12, 2019, which entered into force in all the member states of the European Union for more than a year [14].

3   Case Study

All companies have different scopes. Some exist in business contexts related to industry or commerce activities, others are public entities and there is still room for those that do not have any profit objective.

Despite this distinction in their scope they all have internal structures, which represent their mission, vision and strategy that serve as a foundation for all the objectives of these same companies.

Teatro Circo de Braga, EM, S.A., (see Fig. 1), is a company located in Braga, Portugal, that operates in the cultural sector, functioning in one of the most beautiful buildings of Portugal.

Fig. 1. Teatro Circo de Braga, EM, S.A.

This company is heir to a long tradition, but its ambition leads them to make future every present day through its dynamic image and continuity, looking continuously for a program that captivates and brings new audiences to its beautiful theatre room.

Nowadays, customizing the offer is always supported by a huge data processing regarding the data of its customers and possible clients.

3.1   Theatro Circo de Braga EM, S.A

In the past three years the TCB has been very involved in a process of external validation of the company, causing restrictions in the regular development of its activity and with repercussions in the programmatic and management options.

The year 2017 would mark the beginning of a new cycle through the visa awarded by the Court of Auditors to the contract programme. Thus, TCB could finally establish long-term commitments, including one to initiate the process that could lead to the compliance with GDPR, leading to several substantive changes to the day-to-day operation and processes of TCB [15].

As a local administration company, it is still imperative to mention that, in addition to the internal dynamics and TCB's willingness to reinvent itself and define new objectives every year, there are still other responsibilities resulting from the commitments made to the city's strategy are being proposed by the Municipality of Braga.

3.2 Motivation

TCB is committed to conducting its business in accordance with the European Union data protection legislation and the national data protection legislation and being in line with the highest standard of ethical conduct.

This policy establishes the principles that employees and third parties must follow in relation to collection, use, retention, transfer, disclosure and destruction of data of natural persons regarding the processing of personal data and the free movement of such data.

Personal data is subject to legislation and regulations that impose restrictions on how organisations can handle such data. An organisation that treats personal data and makes decisions about its use is designated as "controller". While being the "controller"[1], the TCB is responsible for ensuring compliance with the personal data protection requirements defined by this policy.

The top management is committed to the continuous and effective implementation of this policy and expects employees and third parties to share the same principle and the violation of this policy may result in disciplinary proceedings.

One of the great difficulties identified is the absence of standard documents and processes. By default, there was no documented process that identifies the necessary steps or a matrix of responsibilities in order to support the cycle of a said process or to sustain the decision-making process or improvements.

The absence of these processes creates a gap and therefore an opportunity of improvement in terms of management that, considering the challenge created by the implementation of the GDPR, can justify the need to create all processes, and its documentation, in order to identify the owners of the process and all the data treated and the classification of the same data according to the sensitivity that they have before this same regulation [13].

3.3 Protection of Data from Conception to Default

It is recognized that the main step towards a correct implementation of the GDPR is the involvement of all employees, the dissemination of information and the application of the various processes that are created or improved in order to dramatically improve legal certainty and coherence in the area of data protection law [10].

According to the regulation, it is recommended, and even imperative in several situations, that the organisations should have one or more Data Protection Officer (DPO) [6] in order to ensure the application of the principles of personal data protection in the institution.

---

[1] See Article 4.°, paragraph 7 of the General Data Protection Regulation.

The DPO should keep a register of all personal data processing operations in their institution [16]. Providing advice and making recommendations on rights and obligations.

This new actor is of extreme importance, for example if there are conflicts between this policy and the national legislation, the Data Protection Officer (DPO) should be consulted.

In order to increase the success rate of the implementation, the privacy value for TCB must be determined. Since the personal data of the stakeholders play a relevant role for the organisation, all the data must be treated in a way that guarantees a high level of privacy and a control by each data subject.

Therefore, all the key objectives of the privacy program must be understood in order to guarantee an adequate level of risk to the rights and freedoms of singular persons; to achieve a high level of privacy; full control by the data subject; compliance of European and national privacy rules; raising the awareness of stakeholders and continuing this process with a perspective of continuous improvement through process monitoring and metrics, and therefore, privacy by design.

3.4   The Need of Documented Processes

As stated earlier, the presence of a process that defines and helps to determine a special need in the data processing is of high importance, so a default process, as illustrated in Fig. 2, has been created in order serve as a basis for all TCB internal processes and which will ensure unprecedented control over the continuity and continuous improvement that the GDPR requires.

This way, and in order to achieve the previous objectives regarding the compliance of GDPR, TCB has developed and followed a strategic model consisting of eight steps that can be seen on Table 1:

The GDPR compliance project requires numerous changes of functions in terms of human resources, work processes and documentary.

Table 1. Strategic model of the implementation of the General Data Protection Regulation.

#	Step
1	Definition of the context of the organisation and governance
2	Classification, transfer mechanisms and inventory of personal data
3	Awareness of all the internal and external stakeholders
4	Evaluation and treatment of information security risks in the organisation (internal stakeholders) and in the relationship with third parties (external stakeholders)
5	Operational life cycle
6	Management of personal data incidents
7	Performance monitoring and effectiveness of the implementation of the Regulation
8	Conformity

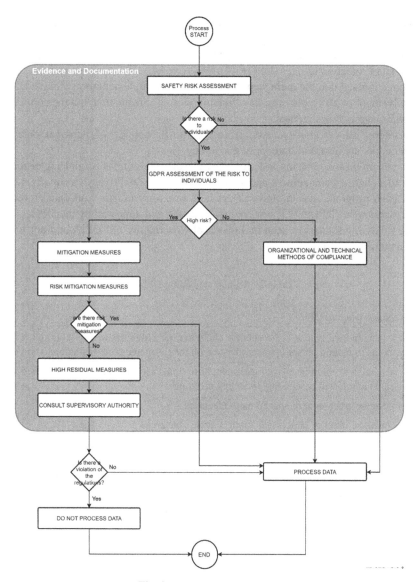

Fig. 2. Data privacy by design

4   GDPR – The Effort of Compliance

The GDPR compliance project, already completed in the TCB, required numerous changes of functions in terms of human resources, work processes and documentary.

This effort was expected to take two months of dedicated work (8 weeks), however, and as a result of an initial misidentification of the commitment of the employees, the project was extended by two weeks.

One of the main steps in the implementation of the GDPR is the commitment of the top management and the creation of a motivated team [17].

In order to demonstrate the commitment to data protection, TCB has adopted the role of Data Protection Officer (DPO)[2] [7].

It is recognized that the main step towards a correct implementation of the GDPR is the involvement of all employees, the dissemination of information and the application of the various processes created.

Therefore, all employees responsible for the processing of personal data and subcontractors are aware of and apply this policy.

All new programs, systems and processes as well as their revision and expansion are subject to a change management and approval process in the Privacy Group [7].

For each program, system and process it is necessary to carry out data protection impact assessment (DPIA)[3] [7] - in cooperation with and approved by the DPO.

The following scenarios, seen in Table 2, always require full DPIA and not just an assessment of their need:

Table 2. Scenarios needing DPIA

#	Scenarios needing DPIA
#1	New technologies whose treatments are likely to pose a high risk to the rights and freedoms of natural persons in accordance with the risk perception methodology in force
#2	Systematic and comprehensive assessment of personal aspects related to natural persons, based on automated processing, including profiling
#3	Large-scale processing of special data categories
#4	Systematic control of large-scale publicly accessible areas

As part of this process, external stakeholders who may be affected by the project (such as customers, suppliers, regulators, unions, workers' commission, lawyers or other parties who may provide a unique perspective on the privacy risks they see as which need mitigation) should be heard.

Risks that cannot be mitigated in a timely manner or that cannot be mitigated should be disclosed to regulators and stakeholders if applicable.

To ensure an adequate level of compliance by TCB to the Data Treatment Policy, the DPO must perform annually an audit of the processing of personal data on a regular basis where it should be conducted for the specific purpose of evaluating actions taken based on an external event such as a complaint, violation, inquiry or exercise of a right.

A deliverable of this kind of implementation is the adoption of the principles stated in the Table 3.

---

[2] See articles 37.°, 38.° and 38.° of the General Data Protection Regulation.

[3] See article 35.° of the General Data Protection Regulation.

Table 3. Adopted principles of the GDPR

#	Principle
1	personal data is processed lawfully, fairly and transparently in relation to the data subject[a] [8]
1	personal data is collected for specific, explicit and legitimate purposes and cannot be further processed in a way that is incompatible with those purposes[b] [8]
3	personal data is adequate, relevant and limited to what is necessary in relation to the purposes for which they are processed[c] [8]
4	personal data is accurate and up-to-date where necessary, and all appropriate measures must be taken to ensure that inaccurate data for the purpose of processing are erased or rectified without delay[d] [8]
5	personal data is stored in a way that allows data holders to be identified only for the period necessary for the purposes for which they are processed[e] [8]
6	personal data is processed in a way that ensures their safety, including protection against unauthorized or unlawful processing and loss, destruction or accidental damage by adopting appropriate technical or organisational measures[f] [8]
7	Presence of the capacity to demonstrate compliance with the six principles previously announced.

[a] See article 5°. (1) (a) of the General Data Protection Regulation.
[b] See article 5°. (1) (b) of the General Data Protection Regulation.
[c] See article 5°. (1) (c) of the General Data Protection Regulation.
[d] See article 5°. (1) (d) of the General Data Protection Regulation.
[e] See article 5°. (1) (e) of the General Data Protection Regulation.
[f] See article 5°. (1) (f) of the General Data Protection Regulation.

All the efforts made in controlling the information can not only be performed within the walls of the TCB, for example the web pages.

TCB also trails the following process in order to investigate, allegedly, improper practices performed by employees in relation to violations of established corporate rules that may result in violation or affect the rights and freedoms of natural persons, that process can be seen in the Table 4.

Upon completion of the GDPR compliance project, TCB shall initiate a process for reviewing and improving the Privacy Management System (PMS) achieved.

However, the effort made it possible to reach a risk mitigation index of around 84%, and only 15 risks remain and are expected to be solved during the first year after the closure of this project.

Table 4. Response Process to the Claim

Processes	Description
Policy	This process is tailored to the different types of allegations that may be concerned about the conduct of the employee. Other policies and procedures such as the rules of procedure and the code of conduct should be observed in addition to this process and conduct research in full respect of existing legislation
Risk	Not all alleged violations of the rules imposed constitute an adverse risk to the rights and freedoms of natural persons. The organisation's risk methodology should be followed to assess whether the risk requires treatment or whether it is likely to be classified as residual, and there is no need to take mitigation actions
Researchers	The choice of who will lead the research, one should choose someone who is independent, objective and not superior to the alleged collaborator
Plan of action	The action plan consists of the response to the claim
Evidence	These can be in the format of videos, mail exchange, interviewing witnesses among others. A signed statement from the person who reported the alleged misconduct or practice should be collected and kept as evidence. All evidence must be assigned an identification number, cataloguing and description
Report	Create a summary of the research highlighting the evidence gathered and the actions to be taken. Include evidence of support, applicable laws, regulations and internal policies that are relevant to the case, and which highlight the actions required to be taken. This report should be classified as confidential and restricted access
Corrective action	This phase may include training actions for the employee, trigger a disciplinary process, the creation of new policies or the review of existing policies. Once the correct action or actions are determined, immediate action must be taken in the implementation of the solution
Monitoring	After the implementation of the action or corrective actions, the parties involved should be monitored to evaluate the effectiveness and impact of the measures taken

5   Conclusions

It is notorious that this data protection regulation fundamentally challenges businesses that trade in personal data, however, which company does not currently handle personal data? Being this data from customers to suppliers or even employees?

Regaining control of the data, stored and managed is the main objective, and should not be a threat but rather an opportunity.

Invoking responsibility for themselves, the companies, as TCB has done, is a show of determination, responsibility and commitment to all individuals within the European community and theirs mostly unknown rights.

The fact that Portugal took too much time to implement European legislation in which it only saw its final version adopted on June 12, 2019, although it did not have a general consensus in the final document for approval, can be a demonstration that cultural factors represent an impediment in the understanding of personal rights and in the information that each one has, especially when there is a grey area between what is physical information and digital information.

Looking more closely to the case study, and upon completion of the GDPR compliance project, TCB is not looking at this regulation as a threat or a constraint, but rather looking at the broader compliance picture to find a way to focus all the efforts and make them more efficient. Turning the compliance effort, a regular business process that is in constant review and development.

This is a fine example of the opportunity and gains that the implementation of the regulation offers.

Acknowledgements. This work has been supported by national funds through FCT – Fundação para a Ciência e Tecnologia within the Project Scope: UID/CEC/00319/2019.

References

1. Tikkinen-Piri, C., Rohunen, A., Markkula, J.: EU General Data Protection Regulation: changes and implications for personal data collecting companies. Comput. Law Secur. Rev. **34**(1), 134–153 (2018)
2. Tankard, C.: What the GDPR means for businesses. Netw. Secur. **2016**(6), 5–8 (2016)
3. Martins, Fernando, Ribeiro, Pedro, Duarte, Francisco: Improving project management practice through the development of a business case: a local administration case study. In: Rocha, Álvaro, Adeli, Hojjat, Reis, Luís Paulo, Costanzo, Sandra (eds.) WorldCIST'18 2018. AISC, vol. 745, pp. 433–448. Springer, Cham (2018). https://doi.org/10.1007/978-3-319-77703-0_43
4. Powles, J.: The G.D.P.R., Europe's New Privacy Law, and the Future of the Global Data Economy. The New Yorker (2018). https://www.newyorker.com/tech/annals-of-technology/the-gdpr-europes-new-privacy-law-and-the-future-of-the-global-data-economy. Accessed 28 June 2019
5. Houser, K., Voss, W.G.: GDPR: the end of Google and Facebook or a New Paradigm in data privacy? SSRN Electron. J. **25**, 1 (2018)
6. Goddard, M.: The EU General Data Protection Regulation (GDPR): European regulation that has a global impact. Int. J. Mark. Res. **59**(6), 703–705 (2017)
7. The European Parliament and the Council of the European Union: Regulation (EU) 2016/679 of the European Parliament and of the Council of 27 April 2016 on the protection of natural persons with regard to the processing of personal data and on the free movement of such data, and repealing Directive 95/46/EC (General Data Protection Regulation)
8. Assembleia da República: PROPOSTA DE LEI N.o 120/XIII (3.a). Debate Parlam. da Assem. da República, pp. 30–48 (2018)
9. European Commission: What is personal data?—European Commission (2019). https://ec.europa.eu/info/law/law-topic/data-protection/reform/what-personal-data_en. Accessed 25 June 2019
10. Albrecht, J.P.: How the GDPR Will Change the World (2016)

11. Assembleia da República: Lei n.º 67/98 de 26 de Outubro - Lei da Protecção de Dados Pessoais (1998)
12. APOGEP: National Competence Baseline - NCB 4.0. ssociação Portuguesa de Gestão de Projetos (2017)
13. Garber, J.: GDPR – compliance nightmare or business opportunity? Comput. Fraud Secur. **2018**(6), 14–15 (2018)
14. R. do J. de Notícias: Aprovada versão final de execução do RGPD. Jornal de Notícias. https://www.jn.pt/nacional/interior/aprovada-versao-final-de-execucao-do-rgpd-11003399.html. Accessed 28 June 2019
15. Theatro Circo de Braga, "Relatório e Contas 2017," Braga, 2018
16. European Commission: The PM2 Project Management Methodology (Guide 3.0), The PM2 Gu. European Commission, DIGIT (2018)
17. Demchenko, Y., Turkmen, F., De Laat, C.: Bootstrapping GDPR: technical infrastructure requirements and architectures to implement GDPR, December 2018

A Paired Conceptual Framework Integrating Information Systems Research and Democracy Theory

Maria Anastasiadou[1]([⊠]) [iD], Vítor Duarte dos Santos[1] [iD], and Ana Maria Evans[2] [iD]

[1] Nova Information Management School, Universidade Nova de Lisboa, Campus de Campolide, 1070-312 Lisbon, Portugal
{m2016054,vsantos}@novaims.unl.pt
[2] ADVANCE, Centro de Investigação Avançada em Gestão do ISEG,
Lisbon School of Economics and Management,
Universidade de Lisboa, Rua do Quelhas No. 6, 1200-781 Lisbon, Portugal
a.evans@iseg.ulisboa.pt

Abstract. Information systems (IS) play an important role in contemporary society, but critical questions remain on their impact on democracy. This study aims to contribute to a better understanding of this phenomenon. In order to do so, the study develops an innovative methodological approach. Drawing from Design Science Research (DSR), we build conceptual pairs between core preoccupations explored by critical thought on democracy and available problem-solving information technologies. The study does not aim at an exhaustive analysis of problems and solutions; this would be unfeasible, considering the limitations of journal article format. Rather, it aims at early-stage methodology incorporation across disciplines that draw from different research paradigms. The findings will offer a preliminary probe on the analytical input of DSR conceptual artefacts in examining functional links between information systems and political outcomes.

Keywords: Information systems · Democracy · Transparency · Government · Social media · Participation · Public services

1 Introduction

Information systems are increasingly supporting modern decision-making processes and transforming communication flows and patterns of interaction in society. Over the past decade, governments have implemented innovative digital solutions, in order to provide smarter citizen-centric services, to develop more agile and resilient administration structures and, more generally, to improve effectiveness and efficiency in addressing social and political problems. The widespread use of IT instruments by public administration allows decision-makers easier and faster access to data, on the one hand, and expedites access to information by the citizens who are affected by policy decisions, on the other hand. Furthermore, it multiplies venues of citizen participation in decision-making

© ICST Institute for Computer Sciences, Social Informatics and Telecommunications Engineering 2020
Published by Springer Nature Switzerland AG 2020. All Rights Reserved
H. Santos et al. (Eds.): SmartCity 360 2019, LNICST 323, pp. 217–235, 2020.
https://doi.org/10.1007/978-3-030-51005-3_20

processes. In short, IS significantly reduce transaction costs of civic and political engagement [32, 38, 44, 45, 49, 50, 64, 82]. At the policy-level, the prevailing assumption that information systems contribute to simplifying the public decision-making process and to promote accountability and transparency in governance has led to significant structural reform: International institutions, namely the OECD, the UN and the European Commission have created policy departments dedicated to promoting ICT-led public innovation and these organizations produce a growing number of comparative surveys on e-government development at the national level[1]. New concepts such as e-democracy and digital government have emerged [43, 45]. These structural and conceptual innovations signal the advent of technology-induced paradigmatic change in long-standing models of governance.

As expected in the context of impending paradigm shift, there are growing debates on the effects of the widespread use of digital technologies in society, in general, and in politics, in particular. The current tone of public discussions is dominated by allegations on cyber interference in elections and on the spread of misinformation ("fake news") suppressing the role of established media and increasing the risk of authoritarian surveillance. In this context, there are critical questions still unanswered by previous work on information systems and democracy: How is democracy affected by information systems? Are the deliberative, representative and distributive pillars of democracy restructured by IT? If so, what are the instruments and tools that interfere with specific functions of democratic governance? Under what conditions do information systems foster citizen trust and encourage participation?

Previous studies on digital government offer important insights on the impact of ICT-enabled public governance tools for government openness, public service efficiency and user-friendliness, and for citizen political participation and societal mobilization [22, 43, 45, 52, 55]. But the literature still lacks a systematic conceptual framework mapping and assessing the role of distinctive IS instruments in democratic problem-solving and specifying functional relationships between specific technology and particular democratic outcomes. Our work aims to contribute to filling this analytical gap.

We propose to identify and pair distinctive problems of democratic governance with specific information technologies that are designed to address them. We claim that the effort to develop a paired conceptual framework tying Information Systems´ solutions with democratic problems will be useful and necessary to obtain a better understanding of the constituent elements of democracy in the digital age and to examine the factors that affect them. This will allow to improve proactive contingency planning and to design and develop more effective and efficient IT solutions, in order to target resilient domains of democratic underperformance.

Thus, we expect that our findings will encourage theory development in the field of democracy and governance and at the same time will contribute to improving technology

---

[1] See http://www.oecd.org/gov/digital-government/; http://www.oecd.org/gov/digital-govern ment/digital-government-publications.htm; https://publicadministration.un.org/egovkb/en-us/ Reports/UN-E-Government-Survey-2018; https://ec.europa.eu/digital-single-market/en/public-services-egovernment; https://ec.europa.eu/information_society/newsroom/image/document/ 2018-47/egovernment_benchmark_2018_background_report_F21FA84B-0254-F4DB-7B2 FC4567D4AA925_55487.pdf.

solutions and policy choices. On the other hand, we do not intend to be exhaustive in our mapping endeavour. Alas, this would not be possible under the space constraints of a journal article. Thus, the study aims to offer a preliminary probe on the innovative use of design research methodology to deploy conceptual artefacts that aim to operationalize interdisciplinary work integrating political philosophy and information research.

The study will be structured as follows. The next section will outline the research approach and propose the methodological claims on the use of DSR iteration for our line of investigation. In Sect. 3 we will offer a condensed review of critical thought on democracy and of the relatively recent literature on ICT and governance. Drawing from core premises of this literature, we will develop conceptual constructs identifying categories of problems in democracy and labelling IT tools, respectively in Sects. 3.1. and 3.2. We will pair those constructs in Sect. 3.3 and display the paired artefacts in Table 2. Section 4 will analyse the conceptual artefacts against the results of structured interviews with a set of experts. The study will conclude with a summary of major findings and contributions.

2 Research Approach

The research proposed here aims to develop an innovative conceptual framework that draws from findings from two disciplines that are not easily integrated methodologically, namely information systems research and democracy studies. We establish the claim that the Design Science Research (DSR) approach is ideal to pursue our interdisciplinary research effort. As defined in the Information Systems literature, the DSR approach combines the construction and analysis of innovative artefacts in view to expand knowledge on specific problem-solving [3, 4, 39, 85].

The DSR method establishes a sequential research trajectory, beginning with the identification of a problem, followed by conceptualization and development of a problem-solving artefact, and moving to assessment and refinement of the latter. The goal is to expand knowledge of a specific problem domain via an iteration process that begins, like other research methods, with a research question, and then proceeds with its characteristic trajectory of construction, evaluation, and re-dressing of design artefacts. The problem-solving artefact developed in the DSR process may not necessarily be a product. Rather, it may consist of an innovative method, technique, and/or conceptual framework [85].

In this study, the artefacts belong to the latter category: we develop conceptual pairs, with each pair identifying a problem of democratic governance and the identifiable contributions for that given problem of a specific design information system technology or platform tool. The goal is to expand knowledge on the role of IS in democracy. Mapping sets of constructs and developing analytical propositions and functional links in this complex setting involves diverse analytical domains and is a challenging scientific endeavour. The paired conceptual framework that will embody the output of the research will bring significant analytical import for the two fields of research and expand knowledge on design solutions both to long-standing and novel problems of democracy.

In adapting the DSR sequence to the tasks and goals of our research, we began our study with a comprehensive analysis of the literature that provides the analytical

Table 1. List and occupational categories of interviewees

Profile	Level of education	Current profession	Year of experience in E-government	
			Academic	Practice
Expert advisor of the special secretary of e-government in Greece	PhD	Academic – Professor assistance	7	3
Responsible for IS at a municipality. E-government services	PhD student	Software engineer e-government		20
E-government Consulate	Master	Sells director specialized in e-government segment		18
President of the Portuguese Association for the Development of the Information Society and eGov development	PhD student	Consulting partner for e-government		43
Former Director General of the DG Informatic	PhD	International consultants and E-government		40
Researcher for e-government integrability	PhD	Researcher e-governance.	8	
Senior Researcher and Project Manager at the Information Systems Laboratory of the same department, working on European and National funded research and pilot application projects	PhD	Project manager for e-government integrability	7	
Works for the Greek Parliament	Master	IS and E-government		14
Works for the Greek Parliament	Master	Computer Analyst		30

and conceptual framework for developing the paired constructs, namely classic and contemporary readings on democracy and the recent literature on ICT-enabled governance. From this literature, we deduced conceptual categories of democratic problems and identified information systems instruments targeting problem-solving in those categories. The combined analysis resulted in the development of a paired conceptual framework (see Table 2 below). The initial framework was then assessed and refined through observations gained from structured interviews with nine experts (Table 1).

3   A Critical Review of Democracy and ICT

3.1   The Resilient Problems of Democracy: Procedural Challenges and Contradictory Goals

Critical thought on democracy goes as far back as Classical Antiquity. In the long line of political philosophers' reasoning on democracy, one finds a common set of challenges persisting across time, political regimes, technological innovation, and cultural diversity. The enduring problems are largely associated with the great paradox of collective action, itself related to a procedural conundrum: historically, the processes that aggregate individual will and steer the implementation of collective policy have been inherently imperfect, subject to interference and manipulation by narrow interests, and culminate in outcomes that are inconsistent with the ideal democratic principles of freedom, equality, fairness, and accountability in political representation. Recent indicators on electoral participation and political polarization point to significant citizen dissatisfaction with democratic governance and with party politics and suggest that long-lasting problems remain unresolved [36, 61]. The gap between the functional incapacities of democratic institutions and the demands and expectations of citizens has been demonstrated by high levels of abstention and dissatisfaction with the political system [89].

Contemporary critiques of democracy argue that there is a resilient inequality problem in democratic governance. Political institutions have lost trust and legitimacy among their citizens [30]. As argued by scholars, the "one person, one vote" principle of democratic political representation implies that individuals should have equal say and influence over decisions that affect their interests [36]. However, as studies on democracy point out, distribution of influence is unbalanced: not all voices are heard and not all individuals have equal access to governance, even in mature political systems. Furthermore, political theorists claim that the combination of the principle "one person, one vote" with the procedural rule of the majority often culminates in an unwanted outcome, namely in a "tyranny of the majority" which leaves minorities unprotected [29] John Adams [2] and John Stuart Mill [48].

Scholars also point to the inherent contradictions of the principal-agent model in a representative democracy. Citizens elect representatives in the expectation that the latter will espouse their interests [88]. However, along the electoral cycle, the elected representatives have the freedom to act according to their judgment and their decisions may not be aligned with the will of those who elected them. In other words, there is a misalignment between the interests of the mass of electors and the few representatives who determine public policy outcomes. Ultimately, this contributes to dissatisfaction and people not participating, since most representatives are selected or self-selected from elites with economic power and market influence [21, 45, 53, 69, 88, 89].

Some studies also claim that the transient character of political representation may produce unwanted outcomes in democratic representation too. Accordingly, electoral cycles yield frequent government turnover and the latter induces policy instability, which plays a part in citizen dissatisfaction [19, 37, 71]. Furthermore, the electoral cycle creates incentives for politicians to sponsor interests that will support reselection.

Corruption may emerge as a result, especially in less developed political systems, under-mining effective legal systems and the protection of human and civil rights [36, 60, 71, 83]. Corruption breaks the relationship between the collective decision-making process and people's powers to influence the decision-making process, damages the culture of democracy and as a result generates inefficient public services. All this discomfort leads to a lack of participation and security with ineffective and inefficient governments, citi-zens are judging and criticizing the inefficiency of all democratic process including the bureaucratic processes [25, 30].

External factors are also pointed out as determinant of inequality in access to policy and political representation [88]. As argued by some scholars, global economic com-petition, itself an outcome of dramatic advances in communication throughout the past century, creates obstacles to fairness and equality in contemporary democracies, erod-ing trust and creates suspicion. Democracy is harmed and corruption of this sort cuts representative connections. Accordingly, multinational economic interests and global competition hold great sway over governments. More concretely, they can manipulate electoral processes and to impose a policy that undermines social rights and accentuates social, political and economic inequalities [18, 25, 88]. Other more recent outcomes of globalization, namely mass immigration and terrorism seem to have intensified citizen dissatisfaction with the social costs of unfettered market pressures. Political polarization and radical political parties and movements are the ensuing outcomes [19, 37, 71].

Studies have also pointed out the role of subjective factors in challenging democracy. In his classic writings, Dahl argued that a significant percentage of citizens are not able to participate in governance in a competent or meaningful way because they do not have the necessary experience, education or knowledge [19, 71]. Lipset's classic essay on democracy also suggested that education is a key factor for a democracy to emerge [9][2]. More generally, scholars have argued that citizen lack of information allows politicians to manipulate electors; furthermore, the lack of adequate information undermines policy [14, 16, 18, 19, 36, 88].

From these analytical premises, we establish the following conceptual constructs on the core problems of contemporary democracy:

- Globalization and unfettered market forces
- Influence of powerful economic interests
- Problems of fairness and lack of transparency
- Lack of education of citizens and representatives
- Inefficient processes
- The tyranny of the majority, which does not protect minorities and human rights
- Unequal distribution of influence, not all voices are being heard, there is no equality in access to policy-making
- Lack of participation in the political system
- Imperfect representation of social groups.

---

[2] Other authors, however, argue that education alone is not a sufficient condition to maintain democracy [13].

3.2   The Functional Ties Between Information Systems and Democracy

Studies on the relationship between information technology and politics suggest that the use of information systems and platforms in public governance and democratic practice contributes to adjust long-standing problems and imperfections of political systems, namely issues of accountability and participation, which culminate in low levels of trust. Allows governments to serve citizens in a more effective, timely, and cost-efficient way [28]. The general assumption is that, as a medium for human communication and expression, information systems have escalated knowledge sharing, have addressed resilient communication gaps between public administrations and citizens, and have facilitated public service delivery as well as citizen participation in policy [43, 45, 52].

Mark E. Warren argued in more than one paper that modern technologies and IS are the solution to more than one pathology of democracy, such as corruption, trust, security, and inefficient public services, and that the new technologies promise the power to expose those pathologies [25]. Information systems can be used to create different forms of participation in the decision-making process, including those who have little voice within electoral politics, structuring deliberation and working across and beyond jurisdictions. Information systems can enable collaborative research and form the basis for improving democratic inclusion, civic engagement, and effective public problem-solving. Information systems can enhance equality and/or inclusion in political processes, tries to improve public services and enhance public accountability [30].

More concretely, the widespread use of information systems and recent platform technology allow citizen access at any time to up-to-date information and knowledge on political and public issues, sustain public debate beyond geographical and time discontinuities, and expedite interaction with public authorities, including collaboration on resolving local issues. In other words, the use of information technology in governance has dramatically lowered the transaction costs of political communication and has vastly expanded the scale and scope of citizen engagement and opportunities for input in policy implementation. Therefore, scholars agree that information systems contribute to enhancing the core components of collaborative political participation, empowering individuals, and ultimately, advancing the common good [8, 10, 12, 51, 56, 58, 74, 81]. The literature suggests a set of functional ties between specific technologies and democratic outcomes. For a start, information systems operate at the very core of democratic procedures, namely by allowing citizen electronic participation in elections, polls, and referenda. [87] Information systems also provide electronic access to government services and information, such as electronic filing of taxes and direct deposit of government checks [6, 7, 10, 72, 86].

Moreover, the low cost and widespread use of information technology and the internet have transformed the scale of deliberative democracy: millions of voices and point of views can be shared across the world instantly and such fast and global exchange of ideas supports civil society and freedom of speech, inducing pressure on governments to become more transparent and fairer [33, 46, 47, 54, 56, 76, 78]. According to Hilbert´s study on the maturing character of e-democracy, the Web 2.0 and social media technology have spurred outright revolutionary transformation in democracy practice, suggesting it is possible to overcome the traditional problem of the size of participation in democratic processes [41][3].

Other scholars highlight the role of social media in enabling intense and sustained collaboration between citizens and governments, thus enhancing public policy and social innovation [59, 90]. And existing studies also suggest that information systems have been used to increase young people political knowledge, and awareness of processes of public choice. For example, the Highland Youth Voice in Scotland allows individuals between the age of 14 and 18 to participate in the decision-making process via websites and online fora. The goal is to involve teenagers in expressing needs and opinions via online political debate and to try out e-democratic models for online-voting [5, 17, 40][4].

Drawing from these insights, we will next label a set of IT tools and explore their respective functional role of problem-solving in contemporary democracy.

3.3 Developing Paired Conceptual Artefacts

Web 2.0 is the evolution of content platforms to focus on user-generated content, such as forums, discussion boards, social networks, wikis, collaborative platforms, knowledge sharing tools, blogs, micro-blogging, and participative budgeting platforms [57, 63, 65, 79]. It can be used to solve the problems of (see Table 2):

Table 2. Conceptual framework

		Not being fair			The problem of transparency				The imperfection of the representative political system		Inefficient government services		Lack of		Lack of education	
		No equal distribution of influence	Not all voices are heard	There are not equal rights to access Democracy	Globalization of Big Money	Influence of Big Money	Corruption	Public services	The imperfection of the representation of social groups	The tyranny of the majority, which does not protect the minorities and human rights	Inefficient bureaucratic processes	Expensive cost for public services and processes	Lack of participation of the young people	Lack of participation citizens in general	The citizens	The representation
Web 2.0	Forums, discussion boards	x	x	x				x	x	x					x	x
	Social Networks	x	x	x				x	x	x			x	x	x	x
	Wikis, collaborative platforms, knowledge sharing tools	x	x	x				x	x	x						
	Blogs, Micro blogging	x	x	x				x	x	x			x	x	x	x
	Participative budgeting platforms	x	x	x				x	x	x			x	x	x	x
Internet of things / Ubiquitous / Electronic voting	Automatic meters				x	x	x	x				x		x		
	E-voting	x	x	x				x	x	x			x	x		
	I-voting	x	x	x				x	x	x			x	x		
Artificial Intelligence / Operability	Big data analysis, Cognitive services	x	x	x	x	x	x	x			x	x				
	Textual data, Automated sentiment	x	x	x	x	x	x	x			x	x				
	Anomalies detection, Fraud detection	x	x	x	x	x	x	x			x	x				
	Web services, data standards				x	x	x	x			x	x				
Systems Integration / Operability	Public key infrastructure, smart identity cards				x	x	x	x			x	x				
	RSS feeds	x	x	x				x	x	x	x	x	x	x	x	x
Distribution of information	Portals/ websites/knowledge sharing tools	x	x	x				x	x	x	x	x	x	x	x	x
	Trivalis lists	x	x	x				x	x	x	x	x	x	x	x	x
	Mobile Computing	x	x	x				x	x	x	x	x	x	x	x	x
	Blockchain Technologies	x	x	x		x	x	x	x	x	x	x	x	x	x	x
	Peer to Peer networks	x	x	x				x	x	x	x	x	x	x	x	x
GIS operations	Geographic Information systems				x	x	x	x			x	x				

a) Not being fair: Tools provided by the web 2.0 promote the participation of individuals willing to contribute with their ideas in the democratic processes [30, 35].

---

[3] One should note that Hilbert also highlights the problematic aspect of the unstructured character of data in social media, which, in his view, can be overcome by new technologies, such as big data analytics.

[4] One should note that scholars have expressed preoccupations with the manipulation of youth participation in politics resulting from insufficient experience and knowledge [5, 17].

b) The problem of transparency: Tools provided by the web 2.0 allow greater transparency over how a consensus is reached, as contributions can be archived and remain accessible to examination. Especially useful for facilitating access to public records and information. Improve public services quality [30, 35].

c) The imperfection of the representative political system: Tools provided by the web 2.0 facilitate and expand the participation of interested parties. It is possible to measure the inclusiveness of political representation accounting for how many people participate in discussions [30, 35].

d) Lack of participation: Forums, discussion boards, social networks, wikis, collaborative platforms, knowledge sharing tools, blogs, micro-blogging, and participative budgeting platforms expand access to policy-making and increase collaboration between citizens and the public. Policy-makers can use web 2.0 to gather information about what people need and about public opinion. These tools enhance open source government and inclusive decision-making [30, 35].

e) Lack of education: Not all participants have the same level of education and understanding of issues. Easy access to prolific information sources allows citizens to increase knowledge about important policy issues [30, 35].

Internet of things/Ubiquitous Computing, such as automatic meters that support bidirectional communications to allow for accurate billing of utilities such as gas, electricity, and water [20]. This can be used to solve the following problems (see Table 2):

a) The problem of transparency: The heavy use of these tools will generate a big volume of records that can be used to audit existing bureaucratic processes and communications, resulting in more transparent processes [30].

b) Inefficient government services: IoT-enabled dynamic capabilities that can empower digital transformation and unlock the potentials of digital government into smart government and developed policies and services of public interest and public value [15, 35].

Electronic voting has been considered an inevitable development that simplifies and reduces the cost of, and speeds up processes around, elections. It also can improve the integrity of elections and can reduce the errors of the election process [1]. Scholars argue it increases the engagement and turnout of citizens and contributes to restoring relationships between citizens and political institutions [11]. E-voting systems are engineered for the specific purpose of voting and are not used online, while I-voting systems allow a voter to vote from any computer connected to the internet, even from their homes, through an online voting platform [68]. It can be used to solve the following problems (see Table 2):

a) Not being fair: Using electronic and internet voting, it is possible to provide a platform where all interested parties can express their views [1].

b) The problem of transparency: Using a voting platform, it is possible to have an auditable record of who voted and in whom, resulting in added transparency in the decision-making process [1, 25].

c) The imperfection of the representative political system: As all parties can cast their votes one can assume that all interested parties are adequately represented. Moreover, it allows the government to survey the general opinion of the population in a fast and efficient way at any time [41].

d) Lack of participation: An electronic voting system increases participation because citizens can vote from everywhere, even from their homes via a user-friendly environment implemented in cloud computing services [91].

Artificial Intelligence is the use of algorithms to obtain deeper insights into various subjects. Through the analysis of massive amounts of data, it is possible to infer useful information about trends and preferences [62, 70]. It can be used to solve the following problems (see Table 2):

a) Not being fair: If implemented correctly, artificial intelligence is not biased and not subject to corruption. Decisions are based only on the data provided. The data-driven decision-making process should allow for more effective and efficient, and fairer decisions [67].

b) The problem of transparency: Artificial intelligence will apply the set of defined rules consistently. Any decision can be traced back to the set of rules; all decisions should be able to be replicated assuming the same data and the same set of rules are used. If the rules are published, any citizen can understand why a certain decision was made. This provides a fully transparent decision-making process [30, 67].

c) Inefficient government services: Artificial intelligence is orders of magnitude faster than humans in analysing and applying a set of rules to reach a decision. This could provide nearly instantaneous decisions [67, 75].

Systems Integration/Inter-Operability, such as web services and data standards provide common sets of technologies that allow different information systems to transfer information between themselves using a standardized data format. Systems Integration/Inter-Operability can be used to solve the following problems [30] (see Table 2):

a) The problem of transparency: The ability of the various system to work together requires the use of common data formats. Common data formats allow citizens and data scientists to independently analyse data and reach their conclusions. The ability to independently replicate results or analyses data is a fundamental requirement to implement transparent systems [30].

b) Inefficient government services: Public administration services have traditionally not talked to each other and required citizens to retrieve paper records from other services. This is highly inefficient and time-consuming. Systems integration makes it possible to connect information systems of different governmental services so that they exchange information and provide citizens with a more efficient service. Most bureaucratic procedures can be automated using online platforms, thus allowing easy and quick access to governmental services. The use of national identity cards that include a digital certificate allows authenticating the citizen using a state-managed public key infrastructure. Once all citizens have digital certificates it becomes possible to benefit from advances in cryptography that allow for legally binding digital signatures and the dematerialization of most bureaucratic processes, as is the case in Estonia [24, 26, 30, 75].

Distribution of Information is the flow of data through the internet. It can be used to solve the following problems [30] (see Table 2):

a) Not being fair: Various tools for the distribution of information allow people to be informed about important policy issues, therefore improving fairness in access. Technologies such as RSS feeds allow the user to subscribe to sites and get a feed of content updates. An example is Ushahidi which is being developed by Ushahidi Inc in Nairobi, Africa. It is an application that allows users to upload real-time data, respond to issues, election monitoring, and crisis response [30, 84].

b) The problem of transparency: Tools that distribute information contribute to make decision processes more transparent and expand the number of people who have access to knowledge. Emails lists, mobile computing and P2P networks, such as the open data services cooperative developed by Tim Davies and his team in the UK help people publish and use open data to support activities that promote social impact [30, 73, 80].

c) The imperfection of the representative political system: As information about processes gets distributed, more people become aware of processes that affect their interests. Portals, websites, and knowledge sharing tools allow users and organizations to publish and share information. Most modern governments make use of this kind of portals [24, 30, 66].

d) Inefficient government services: By leveraging tools for the distribution of information it is possible to keep governmental employees aware of important information that they require to be more efficient at their job. Moreover, obtaining feedback is important to improve efficiency in governmental services. Blockchain can be used for all kinds of public services such as health and welfare payments without the need for central validation or human intervention. For example, the Dutch Government is exploring blockchain in several pilot projects, such as digital identity, income tax, autonomous vehicles, logistics, and debt counselling [23]. This redistributes power away from central decision-makers, makes service delivery more efficient, and increases transparency [11, 30, 75, 77].

e) Lack of participation: Distribution of information expands the number of individuals who obtain knowledge on processes that directly affect their interests. This stimulates participation [30].

f) Lack of education: Distribution of information using tools stimulate knowledge sharing [30].

Geography information systems applications take advantage of the recent development and general availability of online maps with high-resolution imagery of the earth to improve services provided by the state, such as land registry and other services where geographical data is relevant [27, 42]. They can be used to solve the following problems (see Table 2):

a) The problem of transparency: The use of geographical information systems allows people to visualize information. This intuitive way of looking at information makes it easier to see incorrect information and interpret it. For example, catching tax evaders by recognizing signs of wealth such as swimming pools. Another example is visualizing voting patterns by reviewing how electoral districts voted at the polls [31, 34].

b) Inefficient government services: The use of geographic information systems applications in government services allows information to be represented and displayed in a more understandable format and can improve the quality of several public services. For example, encouraging citizen involvement through web-based applications for the redistricting process (Redistricting QGIS Plugin) [31, 34].

4   Expert Assessment of the Conceptual Artefacts

In assessing the conceptual framework proposed above, experts agreed that low levels of political participation constitute a lasting and critical limitation of contemporary democracy. As argued, citizens are largely disconnected from the decision-making process, perceive government services as inefficient and ineffective and question the return on their paid taxes. Questioned if any important problems of democracy were missing from the above table, two of the nine experts mentioned the problem of accountability. Another missing problem was the lack of trust, which, according to the experts, aggravates the low levels of political participation, especially among young people.

All experts strongly agreed that information systems help to foster the elements of democracy under examination. Furthermore, they argued that IS will be a necessary venue in the future of practice and in problem-solving. However, interviewees pointed out that, when assessing the role of IS in democracy, the risk of manipulation must be considered. It is imperative to examine how and who is using information systems and what the intentions are when using IS.

All experts agreed that the proposed categorization of information systems technologies is valid but pointed out open data as an important and missing element of the conceptual framework. Accordingly, open data is a necessary condition to ensure the fairness of political systems and government services, and essential to promote transparency. One expert suggested that simulations technologies and chats bots for public services should be added to the conceptual framework (see Table 3).

All experts except one agreed that web 2.0 and the sub-categories defined above play a determining role in solving the examined problems of democracy. One expert claimed that web 2.0 has also contributed to making problems worse, as revealed for example by foreign interference in US elections. Experts also argued that social media technologies have improved the possibilities of communicating within a community, but at the same time have been misused.

According to the interviewees, crowdfunding platforms for e-government purposes have been designed to make processes faster and easier, by matching relevant problems with governmental funding. Furthermore, they have stimulated active participation. Experts also noted that participative budgeting platforms are growing in city halls and, more generally, a concept that is gaining momentum.

On electronic voting, interviewees claimed that adoption has been slow because the average voter is not fluent in the use of technology and the concept has not been adequately marketed. Accordingly, electronic voting introduces strong challenges but also great opportunities for government to increase participation by making people believe their vote is important.

Most of the experts argue that Web 2.0 technologies can also contribute to solving the problem of inefficient government services, by making public services less bureaucratic, allowing citizens to report issues and allowing public services to incorporate feedback.

Experts pointed out that the Internet of things/Ubiquitous Computing and their subcategories can be used to automate several public services processes and information dissemination processes as well. In automating decisions by measuring everything everywhere, data becomes available for decision-making. As a result, interviewees claim, transparency increases, the quality of services improves, and citizens deal with simpler procedures.

According to interviewees, artificial intelligence capabilities will be fundamental in solving problems of authentication, detecting fraud rapidly, measuring people sentiment on what the government is doing, wants to do or has done. This will ensure the participation of citizens in governmental projects. Experts also claimed that systems integration and inter-operability technologies constitute one of the most fundamental technologies - together with AI and the distribution of information - in implementing e-government solutions. Accordingly, one of the resilient challenges of e-government is to connect different services within public administration and to connect the services with citizens as well. Experts argued that the referred technologies can increase the efficiency of government services with just one click. Ultimately, interviewees claimed, this will also contribute to increase transparency and to make citizens see the value for money in government services, therefore increasing participation.

According to experts, the distribution of information technologies will be at the core of trust and security. All agreed that open data and blockchain concepts will change the way citizens think, feel and behave in online processes and services. As stated, transparency will be part of political culture, and fraud will decrease and be easier to detect. This will improve trust in e-government services and increase political participation.

To conclude, experts argued that geographic information systems can mitigate democratic problems such as not being fair. Interviews claimed that, for example, building systems that use ubiquity computing, mobile technologies, geographical information systems, and their interconnectivity, provide a workflow that follows the decision-making process and enables citizens to participate. Such systems allow citizens to find information about a specific point of interest as they pass by, and to receive data about related public decisions. Citizens can vote on a topic related to a location or point of interest and be part of the decision-making process. Furthermore, the applications can be used for fraud detection, security, and fairness: for instance, the records of the ownership of properties is fundamental for the ministry of agriculture. Police and the ministry of health use them too.

Table 3 displays the revised conceptual framework and paired artefacts resulting from the experts' assessment of our original proposal.

Table 3. Revised conceptual framework

		Not being fair			The problem of transparency			Accountability	The imperfection of the representative political system		Inefficient government services	Lack of participation		Lack of education		Lack of Trust	
		No equal distribution of influence	Not all voices are being heard	There are not equal rights to Democracy	Globally influence of Big Money	Corruption	Public services		The imperfection of the representation of minorities/groups	The tyranny of the majority: which does not protect the minorities and human rights	Inefficient bureaucratic processes	Expensive cost for public services and processes	Lack of participation of the young people	Lack of participation in general	The non-representatives		Public sector	Political system
	Forums, discussion boards																	
	Social Networks	x	x	x			x	x	x		x	x	x	x	x	x	x	
	Wikis, collaborative platforms, knowledge sharing tools	x	x	x			x	x		x		x	x	x	x	x	x	x
	Blogs, Micro-blogging	x	x	x			x	x				x	x	x	x	x	x	x
	Participative budgeting platforms	x	x	x				x	x			x	x	x	x	x	x	
	Network				x	x	x	x	x				x	x			x	x
	E-voting	x	x	x			x	x	x		x		x	x	x			
	I-voting	x	x	x			x	x	x		x		x	x	x			
	Big data analysis, Cognitive services	x	x	x	x	x	x	x	x		x	x	x				x	x
	Textual data, Automated sentiment	x	x	x	x	x	x	x	x		x	x	x				x	x
	Anomalies detection, Fraud detection	x	x	x	x	x	x	x	x		x	x	x				x	x
	Web-services, data standards				x	x	x	x	x			x	x				x	x
	Public-key infrastructure, smart identity cards				x	x	x	x	x			x	x				x	x
	RSS feeds	x	x	x			x	x	x			x	x	x	x	x		
	Portals/ websites/knowledge sharing tools	x	x	x			x	x	x			x	x	x	x	x		
	Emails lists						x	x	x			x	x	x	x	x		
	Mobile Computing	x	x	x			x	x	x			x	x	x	x	x		
	Blockchain Technologies	x	x	x			x	x	x			x	x	x	x	x	x	x
	Peer to Peer networks	x	x	x			x	x	x			x	x	x	x	x	x	x
	Open Data	x	x	x	x	x	x	x	x			x	x	x	x	x	x	x
	Geographic Information Systems	x	x	x	x			x	x			x				x	x	

5   Conclusion

Over the past decade, the spread of digital technologies and the use of social media as channels for individual expression, political debate, and social mobilization has transformed democratic practice and lowered the transaction costs of political participation. In order to understand if, how and under what conditions these new technological tools contribute to improving the historically resilient and unresolved problems of democracy, we began our research by identifying a set of challenges of contemporary democracy. Next, we examined specific applications of information systems that aim to address those problems and developed the conceptual pairs between the constructs. We then tested the resulting conceptual framework against an assessment by a set of experts.

The conceptual pairing of problems and information's systems solutions suggests that the combined adoption of artificial intelligence, systems integration, and blockchain technologies will play a determining role in the capacitating public delivery of smart, citizen-centric services, and will contribute to encouraging citizen trust and political participation. In stimulating transparency and making fraud easier to detect, open data is expected to transform the way citizens think, feel and behave while engaging in online processes, ultimately fostering citizen confidence in participatory venues. Web 2.0 technologies, geography information systems and collaboration tools are expected to stimulate information sharing and learning between public organizations that have traditionally operated in silos, as well as between public administrations and citizens.

In analysing the functional relations between specific information technologies and identifiable problems of democracy, the study aims to contribute to a better understanding of how democracy and information systems work together. The preliminary findings of the study aim open a methodological agenda that will help select effective combinations of tools to address specific problems of democracy, as well as design public policies that stimulate and coordinate the intervention of technology in society and politics. Theoretically, the study also offers contributions on how democracy is expected to evolve in the digital era.

Annex 1

(See Table 4).

Table 4. Conceptual framework

Table 4. Conceptual framework

Annex 2

(See Table 5).

Table 5. Revised conceptual framework (more details Annex 2)

Table 5. Revised conceptual framework (more details Annex 2)

References

1. Abu-Shanab, E., Knight, M., Refai, H.: E-voting systems: a tool for e-democracy. Manag. Res. Pract. **2**(3), 264–275 (2010)
2. Adams, J.: Essential Guide to Qualitative Methods in Organizational Research. Lawbook Exchange (2001)
3. van Aken, J.E.: Management research as a design science: articulating the research products of mode 2 knowledge production in management. Br. J. Manag. **16**(1), 19–36 (2005)
4. van Aken, J.E.: Management research based on the paradigm of the design sciences: the quest for field-tested and grounded technological rules. J. Manag. Stud. **41**(2), 219–246 (2004)
5. Andrew, A.M.: Cybernetics and e-democracy. Kybernetes **37**(7), 1066–1068 (2008)
6. Chadwick, A.: E-government (2016). https://www.britannica.com/topic/e-government
7. Atkinson, R.D., Castro, D.: Digital quality of life. Inf. Technol. Innov. Found. 137–145 (2008)
8. Bakardjieva, M.: Subactivism: Lifeworld and Politics in the Age of the Internet (2009)
9. Bendix, R., Lipset, S.M.: Political sociology. Curr. Sociol. **6**(2), 79–99 (1957)
10. Bertot, J.C., Jaeger, P.T., Grimes, J.M.: Using ICTs to create a culture of transparency: E-government and social media as openness and anti-corruption tools for societies (2010)
11. Boucher, P., Nascimento, S., Kritikos, M.: How blockchain technology could change our lives, Brussels (2017)
12. Caldow, J.: e-Democracy: Putting Down Global Roots (2004)
13. Caplan, B.: From Friedman to Wittman: the transformation of chicago political economy. Econ. J. Watch. **2**(1), 1–21 (2005)
14. Carter, A., Stokes, G.: Democratic Theory Today: Challenges for the 21st Century. Polity Press (2002)
15. Chatfield, A.T., Reddick, C.G.: A framework for Internet of Things-enabled smart government: a case of IoT cybersecurity policies and use cases in U.S. federal government. Gov. Inf. Q. **36**(2), 346–357 (2018)
16. Lee, C.P., Chang, K., Berry, F.S.: Testing the development and diffusion of e-government and e-democracy: a global perspective. Public Adm. Rev. **71**, 444–454 (2011)
17. Coleman, S.: Doing IT for Themselves: Management versus Autonomy in Youth E-Citizenship. The MIT Press (2008)
18. Cudd, A.E., Scholz, S.J.: Philosophical Perspectives on Democracy in the 21st Century. Springer, Heidelberg (2014). https://doi.org/10.1007/978-3-319-02312-0
19. Dahl, R.A.: Democracy and Its Critics. Yale University Press (1991)
20. O'Maley, Daniel: The Internet of Things. J. Democr. **27**(3), 176–180 (2016)
21. Romano, D.: A Very Different Ideology in the Middle East (2015). http://www.rudaw.net/english/opinion/29012015. Accessed 20 May 2017
22. Duff, A.S.: Social engineering in the information age. Inf. Soc. **21**(1), 67–71 (2005)
23. Dutch Government: Blockchain-projects, Dutch government (2018). https://www.blockchainpilots.nl/home-eng. Accessed 17 Apr 2018
24. E-Government Academy: e-Governance in Practice (2016)
25. Warren, M.E.: What does corruption mean in a democracy? Am. J. Pol. Sci. **48**(2), 328–343 (2004)
26. European Commission: eGovernment in Estonia (2016)
27. European Global Navigation Satellite Systems Agency: Galileo is the European global satellite-based navigation system, European Global Navigation Satellite Systems Agency (2018). https://www.gsa.europa.eu/european-gnss/galileo/galileo-european-global-satellite-based-navigation-system. Accessed 31 Jan 2018
28. Evans, D., Yen, D.C.: E-Government: evolving relationship of citizens and government, domestic, and international development. Gov. Inf. Q. **23**(2), 207–235 (2006)

29. Fierlbeck, K.: Globalizing Democracy: Power, Legitimacy and the Interpretation of Democratic Ideas. Manchester University Press (2008)
30. Fung, A., Warren, M.E.: The participedia project: an introduction. Int. Public Manag. J. **14**(3), 341–362 (2011)
31. Geography.com: GIS geography (2016). https://gisgeography.com
32. Gil-Garcia, J.R., Helbig, N., Ojo, A.: Being smart: emerging technologies and innovation in the public sector. Gov. Inf. Q. **31**(S1), I1–I8 (2014)
33. Gimmler, A.: Deliberative democracy, the public sphere and the internet. Philos. Soc. Crit. **27**(4), 21–39 (2001)
34. Goodchild, M.F.: Citizens as sensors: the world of volunteered geography. GeoJournal **69**(4), 211–221 (2007)
35. Gruzd, A., Lannigan, J., Quigley, K.: Examining government cross-platform engagement in social media: Instagram vs Twitter and the big lift project. Gov. Inf. Q. **35**(4), 579–587 (2018)
36. Arrhenius, G.: Democracy for the 21th Century: Research Challenges, August 2011
37. Gutmann, A., Thompson, D.F., Dennis, F.: Why Deliberative Democracy? Princeton University Press (2004)
38. Hayes, H., Sharma, O.: A decade of experience with a common first year program for computer science, information systems and information technology majors. J. Comput. Sci. Coll. **18**(3), 217–227 (2003)
39. Hevner, A.R., March, S.T., Park, J., Ram, S.: Design science in information systems research. Des. Sci. IS Res. MIS Q. **28**(1), 75–105 (2004)
40. Highland Youth: Highland Youth, Highlife Highland Youth https://www.highlifehighland.com/youth/getheard/. Accessed 27 Jan 2018
41. Hilbert, M., Hilbert, H.M.: The maturing concept of E-democracy: from E-voting and online consultations to democratic value out of jumbled online chatter. J. Inf. Technol. Polit. **6**(2), 87–110 (2009)
42. Information Analytical Centre (IAC): Russian Space Agency: Information analytical centre of GLONASS and GPS controlling, Information- analytical centre (IAC). Russian Space Agency. https://web.archive.org/web/20111020035436/, http://www.glonass-ianc.rsa.ru/en/. Accessed 31 Jan 2018
43. Jafarkarimi, H., Sim, A., Saadatdoost, R., Hee, J.M.: The impact of ICT on reinforcing citizens' role in government decision making. Int. J. Emerg. Technol. Adv. Eng. **4**(1), 642–646 (2014)
44. James, A.: O'Brien: Introduction to Information Systems: Essentials for the E-business Enterprise. McGraw-Hill, Boston (2003)
45. Janowski, T.: Digital government evolution: from transformation to contextualization. JAI (2015)
46. Jensen, M.J., Danziger, J.N., Venkatesh, A.: Civil Society and Cyber Society: The Role of the Internet in Community Associations and Democratic Politics (2007)
47. John, D., Sutter, C.: The OPEN act as an experiment in digital democracy (2012). http://edition.cnn.com/2012/01/18/tech/the-open-act-as-an-experiment-in-digital-democracy/index.html
48. Mill, J.S.: On liberty: the philosophical work that changed society for ever Harriman Economics Classics (1913)
49. Kroenke, D.M.: Experiencing MIS. Prentice Hall, Upper Saddle River (2008)
50. Lee, J., Lee, H.: Developing and validating a citizen-centric typology for smart city services. Gov. Inf. Q. **31**, S93–S105 (2014)
51. Leighninger, M.: Citizenship and governance in a wild, wired world: how should citizens and public managers use online tools to improve democracy? Natl. Civ. Rev. **100**(2), 20–29 (2011)
52. Marijn Janssen, E.E.: Lean government and platform-based governance-doing more with less. Gov. Inf. Q. **30**, S1–S8 (2013)

53. Meltzer, A.H., Richard, S.F.: A rational theory of the size of government. Source J. Polit. Econ. **89136119**(5), 914–927 (1981)
54. Merkel, W.: Is there a crisis of democracy? Can we answer the question? (2013)
55. Nam, T.: Dual effects of the internet on political activism: reinforcing and mobilizing. Gov. Inf. Q. **29**, S90–S97 (2012)
56. Norris, P.: The Worldwide Digital Divide: Information Poverty, The Internet and Development (2000)
57. Orçamento Participativo: OPP. https://opp.gov.pt/. Accessed 16 May 2017
58. Organisation for Economic Co-operation and Development: Promise and Problems of E-Democracy: Challenges of Online Citizen Engagement, Paris (2003)
59. Panagiotopoulos, P., Bigdeli, A.Z., Sams, S.: Citizen–government collaboration on social media: the case of Twitter in the 2011 riots in England. Gov. Inf. Q. **31**(3), 349–357 (2014)
60. Collier, P.: Five myths about elections' power to change nations. Washington Post (2009). http://www.washingtonpost.com/wp-dyn/content/article/2009/11/06/AR2009 110601906.html. Accessed 12 Dec 2017
61. Perry, M.S.: Four dimensions of democracy. Essays Philos. **16**(1), 3–25 (2015)
62. Perry, W.L., McInnes, B., Price, C.C., Smith, S.C., Hollywood, J.S.: Predictive Policing: The Role of Crime Forecasting in Law Enforcement Operations (2013)
63. Partei, P.: Piratenpad, Piratenpartei Deutschland (2013). https://www.piratenpad.de/. Accessed 20 May 2017
64. Polack, J.: Planning a CIS education within a CS framework. J. Comput. Sci. Coll. **25**(2), 100–106 (2009)
65. Portugal Participa: Portugal Participa. http://www.portugalparticipa.pt/. Accessed 16 May 2017
66. Portuguese Republic: Portal das Finanças. http://www.portaldasfinancas.gov.pt/at/html/index.html. Accessed 01 Feb 2018
67. Reis, J., Santo, P.E., Melão, N.: Artificial Intelligence in Government Services: A Systematic Literature Review, 16 April 2019
68. Peralta, R.: Electronic voting (2016). https://www.britannica.com/topic/electronic-voting
69. Hooker, R.: The Radical Revolution (1997). https://web.archive.org/web/19990203212816/, http://www.wsu.edu/~dee/REV/RADICAL.HTM
70. Rienks, R.: Predictive Policing: Taking a Chance for a Safer Future (2015)
71. Dahl, R.A.: Democracy (2017). https://www.britannica.com/topic/democracy
72. Rose, W.R., Grant, G.G.: Critical issues pertaining to the planning and implementation of E-Government initiatives. Gov. Inf. Q. **27**, 26–33 (2010)
73. Ross, E.: Apps for democracy – open data and the future of politics—Media Network—The Guardian, the guardian (2016). https://www.theguardian.com/media-network/2016/aug/19/apps-for-democracy-open-data-and-the-future-of-politics. Accessed 16 May 2017
74. Saglie, J., Vabo, S.I.: Size and e-Democracy: online participation in Norwegian local politics. Scan. Polit. Stud. **32**(4), 382–401 (2009)
75. Scholta, H., Mertens, W., Kowalkiewicz, M., Becker, J.: From one-stop shop to no-stop shop: an e-government stage model. Gov. Inf. Q. **36**(1), 11–26 (2018)
76. Seifert, J.W., Chung, J.: Using E-government to reinforce government–citizen relationships comparing government reform in the United States and China. Soc. Sci. Comput. Rev. **27**(1), 3–23 (2009)
77. Speech, E.C.: Speech by commissioner Gabriel on building the European digital economy and society at the DLD conference. European Commission, Munich (2018)
78. The Economist: The road to e-democracy (2008). http://www.economist.com/node/10638222
79. The Etherpad Foundation: Etherpad, The Etherpad Foundation. http://etherpad.org/. Accessed 16 May 2017

80. Davies, T.: Open Data Services, Open Data Services Co-operative Limited. http://www.ope ndataservices.coop/. Accessed 16 May 2017
81. van der Toni, G.L.A., Meer, D.G., Rotthier, S.: e-Democracy: exploring the current stage of e-Government. J. Inf. Policy **4**, 489–506 (2014)
82. Tucker, A., Deek, F., Jones, J., Hayden, C., School, H., Mccowan, D., Stephenson, C., Verno, A.: A Model Curriculum for K–12 Computer Science: Final Report of the ACM K–12 Task Force Curriculum Committee (2003)
83. United States government: Official Guide to Government Information and Services—USAGov. https://www.usa.gov/. Accessed 19 May 2017
84. Ushahidi: Ushahidi, Ushahidi (2008). https://www.ushahidi.com/. Accessed 16 May 2017
85. Vaishnavi, V., Kuechler, B., Petter, S.: Design science research in information systems. MIS Q. **28**, 75-105 (2004)
86. Zwass, V.: Information Systems (2016). https://www.britannica.com/topic/information-system
87. Vragov, R., Kumar, N.: The impact of information and communication technologies on the costs of democracy. Electron. Commer. Res. Appl. **12**(6), 440–448 (2013)
88. Warren, M.E.: A problem-based approach to democratic theory. Am. Polit. Sci. Rev. **111**(1), 39–53 (2017)
89. Warren, M.E.: Governance-driven democratization. Pract. Free. Decentred Governance, Confl. Democr. Particip. 0171 38–59 (2009)
90. Zheng, L., Zheng, T.: Innovation through social media in the public sector: information and interactions. Gov. Inf. Q. **31**(Suppl. 1), S106–S117 (2014)
91. Zissis, D., Lekkas, D.: Securing e-Government and e-Voting with an open cloud computing architecture. Gov. Inf. Q. **28**(2), 239–251 (2011)

An Investigation of Citizen's e-Participation Within Oman's Police Department Facebook Page

Tamanna Dalwai[1(✉)], Menila James[1], William Webster[2],
Abdullah Mohammed Alshukaili[3], and Arockiasamy Soosaimanickam[3]

[1] Muscat College, Muscat, Oman
{tamanna,menilajames}@muscatcollege.edu.om
[2] University of Stirling, Stirling, UK
william.webster@stir.ac.uk
[3] University of Nizwa, Nizwa, Oman
{a.alshukaili,arockiasamy}@unizwa.edu.om

Abstract. Royal Oman Police (ROP) began its virtual engagement with the citizens by enforcing its presence in social media such as Facebook and Twitter. The purpose of this paper is to explore the type of information shared through Facebook by the Royal Oman Police and analyse the extent of citizen engagement through the ROPs Facebook page. This study collected data from 1st January 2019 to 11th June 2019 from the ROPs Facebook account and supported through content analysis and statistical tests. The findings reflect that ROP had posts under 18 categories and the highest number of posts were on safety advice for the citizens, followed by the awareness sessions organized for schools, universities and other institutions. The citizens interacted virtually on the Facebook page by demonstrating likes, shares, and comments for the posts. This study contributes to providing detailed insights on the type of information exchanged between ROP and citizens. The results of this study can be used for developing strategies in increasing citizen engagement as part of Oman's development plan of building smart cities.

Keywords: e-participation · Social media · Facebook · Police

1 Introduction

Law enforcement agencies have adopted social media strategies for expanding their scope of communication and benefiting from the breadth and depth of its influence [1]. Social media is a powerful tool that provides platforms for people to establish interact and also provide information about the individual's social life. Tang and Liu [2] classify the different forms of social media as blogs (Wordpress), forum (Epinions), media

The research leading to these results has received funding from The Research Council (TRC) of the Sultanate of Oman under the Block Funding Program. TRC Block Funding Agreement No [BFP/RGP/ICT/18/172].

H. Santos et al. (Eds.): SmartCity 360 2019, LNICST 323, pp. 236–248, 2020.
https://doi.org/10.1007/978-3-030-51005-3_21

sharing (YouTube), microblogging (Twitter), social networking (Facebook), social news (Reddit), social bookmarking (Diigo) and wikis (Wikipedia). Law enforcement agencies are increasingly using social media to interact with communities and also collect information required for criminal investigation.

Social media is known for its four major strengths that include collaboration, empowerment, participation and time [3]. Organisations and local governments have been increasingly using Facebook sites for official purpose to reach out to customers as they live online [4]. Police departments acknowledge the potential of social media and are using it to enhance citizen input to police investigations, establish and strength its image, use it as a tool to control crowds and crisis and encourage input in policy-making processes [5].

Mergel [6] identifies four different social media strategies being adopted by the government agencies which include: push, pull, network and tactic strategies. Under the push strategy, the governments only broadcast information through the web content and there is no interaction. The pull strategy demonstrates the government attracts citizens to or users to provide information and usually limiting the level of interaction with them. The networking strategy exhibits high interaction whereby the government actively or passively participates in networking with the diverse constituencies. The final tactic strategy encompasses government services with actual transactions being implemented through social media applications. Thus, when government agencies choose to apply a social media strategy it also needs to anticipate citizen's social behavior and also be proactive in adopting technological trends.

Sultanate of Oman has begun its smart government initiatives under the hegemony of the Information Technology Authority. 'Omanuna' has been introduced as the official Oman eGovernment Service Portal which maintains all the eParticipation platforms for government agencies. It manages 64 social media accounts of various government entities. In comparison to the Arab region and the world, Oman is ranked 2nd and 43rd respectively in the 2018 eParticipation index [7]. The ranking was a significant improvement to the 2016 position where it stood at 33rd position in comparison to the world reflecting that the government placed a special emphasis on the effective utilization of eParticipation channels and establishing contact with the public.

Meijer and Thaens [5] point out that the police departments are distinct from the other government operations. The police are in contact with all citizens and have diversity in their communication. The use of social media has been extensively investigated however very limited research exists that explores how police use social media and interact with the public [8]. One of the noteworthy extant literature that explored the usage of Facebook and Twitter by seven police departments in the USA suggested that the contents of the information posted had an impact on how citizens interacted with them [9]. Lieberman et al. [8] investigated Facebook posts of 23 largest US police departments over three months in 2010. The findings suggested that departments with a high posting frequency shared more crime-related information whereas those with a low posting frequency shared more public relations information. Another research investigated Canadian police Twitter usage as a response to the 2011 Vancouver Stanley Cup riot [10]. The Canadian police used media to garner citizen cooperation, gather evidence and mediate communication for community involvement.

There is a dearth of research that explores the social media content from the police perspective. World over police departments are adopting social media strategies to connect with the community, thus there needs to be a systematic evaluation on the extent and purpose of why social media is being used by the police. To have a grasp on the potential of social media for the police department, this research specifically focuses on the Facebook page of Royal Oman Police. The central research question that this research investigates is: what type of information does the Royal Oman Police send through its Facebook and what is the extent of citizen engagement through the Facebook page.

The article is structured into the following sections. Section 2 addresses and discusses the literature review related to e-participation related studies for the government entities and police department. Section 3 describes the research methodology adopted to investigate the research question. This is followed by Sect. 4 that presents results and discussion of the study. Finally, Sect. 5 is on the discussion, implications, and recommendations related to the results of the research.

2 Literature Review

As the world is moving to a more internet-based environment where people are becoming more connected, the law enforcement agencies in many of the countries have started using social media as a powerful platform for interacting with communities and collecting information for criminal investigations. Social media is used frequently by police departments to interact with the public and to get and provide information. Social media is helping the police departments to gather information for the effective deployment of resources and existing practices. The police agencies can get a feel of community sentiment about their policies, procedures, and practices. Good police-community relations are vital for developing trust between citizens and police. The use of various social media helps the police departments to build community ties which in turn improves the people's trust in police.

A study was carried out by Dai et al. [9] to systematically examine and analyze the varieties in the use of social media by traditional American local police departments and their interactions with citizens. The study collected data between October 1, 2013 and March 31, 2014 from Facebook and Twitter accounts of seven city police departments in the area of Virginia in the USA. Content analysis and text mining were used to identify the patterns of social media posts by police departments, and then statistically analyzed citizen interactions on social media with the police. The authors have applied a commonly used automated text analysis approach to analyze textual contents in Facebook and Twitter posts [11]. The authors also observed that during the six-months of study there were a total of 1,293 posts and tweets on Facebook and Twitter for the seven agencies under observation and every agency had at least one post on Facebook or Twitter a day. The study used a number of Facebook likes and Twitter followers as indicators of community interaction with the police agencies. The findings of the study proved that there was a lot of variation in the way citizens interact with police on social media. It was observed that people on Facebook did more on networking as they visited the Facebook page of police agencies to like posts about the agency and police officers and provided some comments. However, people on Twitter tried to get access to information they like from the police Twitter sites such as general information required for everyday life, weather updates etc. The study finding had important implications for the police agencies to attract more citizen interaction for effective functioning. It was observed in the study that the contents of information play an important role in citizen engagement and interaction. The authors had recommended police agencies to adopt a problem-solving approach and analyze which category of information on their social media would likely to promote citizen interactions. The authors have suggested future research on how the citizen interchanges view with the police departments through social media will give more insight into the understanding of people's expectations and perceptions on policing.

Recently, the use of social media by governmental agencies has been considerably increased. For example, Mossberger et al. [12] state that 92.4% of local governments in USA has a Facebook page and 87% of the municipalities in the USA were active on Facebook by 2011. A study conducted by Bonson et al. in 2015 shows that all German local governments have a Facebook page [13]. The study by Ellison and Hardy in 2014 shows that the majority of local governments in UK uses Facebook and Twitter to interact with people [14]. Bertot et al. state that the use of social media by governments began as a way to improve transparency and openness and also highlighted collaboration, participation, empowerment and time as major potential strengths of social media [15].

Bellstrom et al. [16] conducted a study to identify the type of information exchange that happens between a local government and its citizens using social media. The research involved a qualitative single case study of the Facebook page of the Karlstad municipality in Sweden. The authors have used content analysis on Facebook data collected between May 2015 and July 2015 to find out different categories that determine the analysis. The frequency of content category proves that the municipality has used the Facebook page to promote different happenings in the municipality while the page users were asking questions to the municipality. The research involved analyzes of the type of information disseminated through the Facebook page of local government, the type of information received through the Facebook page of local government and the relation between the type of information communicated on Facebook page and the engagement between the government and citizen. The authors have suggested further study on motivational factors of posting comments and community engagement.

Al-Aufi et al. [17] examined the perceptions of Omani citizens towards the use of the government's social media for participatory and interactive relationships. Mainly the study investigated and explained the views of social media users on the transparency, engagement, responsiveness, and trust about the use of social media by the Omani Government. The study found that even though the citizens are increasingly accessing the governmental social media, governmental departments are not utilizing social media effectively and failed to engage citizens to design and deliver more collaborative and efficient services. The major emphasis of the study was to strategically frame the use of participatory social media by the governmental departments for interactive governance.

According to Warren et al. [18], the governmental departments have been obliged to listen and engage with citizens as the citizens are empowered by the use of social media. The study states that governments are now expected to regulate and professionalize their engagement with citizens through social media platforms.

Gohar Feroz et al. [19] explored Twitter usage by Korea's central government by classifying Twitter-based networking strategies into G2C and G2G which are Government to Citizen and Government to Government respectively [10]. The authors investigated the nature of networking and social media interaction strategies of the Korean government by analyzing the tweets of 32 ministries. The results found that Korean government institutions have made extensive use of Twitter in their daily interactions with the public, but their networking strategies did not necessarily motivate the public to participate in their social media activities. The research findings indicated that the ministries focused more on addressing the needs of the citizens rather than an increase in the number of followers.

Police departments in many countries have started using social media sites widely as the main method of communication with people. Liberman et al. [8] performed a study on Facebook messages posed by 23 police departments in USA over a three month period during 2010. The researchers used content analysis and the result finding indicates that the content pattern was related to the frequency of department's Facebook postings to some extent. Crime-related messages were posted by the police departments who have used Facebook more frequently and the departments who have used Facebook less frequently have posted mostly public relations messages. The researchers also analysed the policy implications of these trends in posting messages.

A study conducted by Sadulski [20] states that Twitter and Facebook are frequently used by police departments to inform the public about crime incidents. The study also informs that police department and other law enforcement agencies can improve community trust through transparency in communication with citizens. The police departments use Facebook and or Twitter for informing the public about progress in case investigations.

According to the Law Enforcement Use of Social Media Survey, Law Enforcement Agencies use social media for a wide variety of purposes [21]. The survey results show that 91% of enforcement agencies use social media for notifying the people about safety concerns, 89% use social media for community outreach and engagement with citizens and 86% use social media for public relations and managing reputation.

Unlike the developed countries, those have utilized the advantage of social media in increasing the trust and transparency of governments, the governments in Arab countries use social media mainly for news broadcasting and updating information [22].

As per the reported information from the Omani National Center for Statistics and Information [23], almost 50% of the public uses social media regularly in Oman. The report also states that people with Higher Educational Qualifications use social media more frequently than people with lower education levels. According to the report, even though the Information Technology Authority (ITA), Oman has been promoting e-government and e-services through "Digital Oman Strategy", the use of social media by Omani Governmental departments remains unregulated.

3   Research Methodology

This study uses the case study approach [16, 24] that involves content analysis of the Facebook usage of the Royal Oman Police (ROP), Sultanate of Oman. This approach is suitable as it explores the understanding of a complex and contemporary social phenomena.

3.1   Data Collection and Coding

This study uses the manual data collection of Facebook content. A web content analysis is used to explore the Facebook posts for the period 1st January 2019 to 11th June 2019. This period is chosen to investigate the communication by the ROP during the year that includes the month of Ramadan. During the holy month of Ramadan, Muslims abstain from eating and drinking from dusk till dawn. Sultanate of Oman is one of the Arab countries that has mandated reduced working hours for certain categories of employees [25]. The period of study makes it unique as the activities are different for the citizens, residents, and tourists in comparison to other times of the year.

The steps observed for investigating the posts are illustrated as follows:

1. Identification of the official Facebook page of ROP;
2. The capture of the Facebook posts in the period 1st January to 11th June 2019;
3. Codes being assigned to the posts based on the content and media type
4. Exploration of the engagement rate of the posts
5. Analysis of the post types, purpose and engagement rate

In line with the prior literature, Netvizz service is being used to collect data from the Facebook page [16, 26, 27]. Netvizz is a Facebook application that can archive the page activity by delimiting it based on the number of posts or a time interval. This research uses the latter approach to cover the specified timeframe as identified above. The page consisted of 43 posts by the ROP, 37 comments and 738 reactions. The data was collected on 13th June 2019.

The research followed the approach advised by Miles and Huberman [28] to use a 'first list' of codes generated by the extant literature [9]. The first list of codes is used before reading the actual data and is modified and expanded based on content analysis. The coding took place using seventeen classifications that included: crime information, law enforcement, asking for tips, crime prevention, safety advice, community interaction, community events, traffic updates, agency-related information, recruitment, other government services, information sharing, holiday greetings, non-police related, advertising and road conditions.

The data coding and analysis were performed using three steps. Step 1 involved coding by the first author using the first list of codes and any subsequent inductive modification. Step 2 involved coding by a second co-author and also two graduate students not affiliated with the study to ensure the reliability of the coding process. Step 3 as the final analysis led to clarification of category names. A Cohen's Kappa inter-rater reliability score of 80% was found for the co-author's results for the categorization. This reflects a substantial agreement between the two coders and is also consistent with the findings of Williams et al. [29].

The framework of Bonsón and Ratkai [30] was adopted to investigate the stakeholder engagement on the ROP's Facebook page. The framework is evaluated using three metrics that reflect popularity (P), commitment (C) and virality (V). All three metrics are aggregated to calculate the overall engagement score. The metric components are discussed in Table 1.

Table 1. Stakeholder engagement metrics for Facebook

Popularity (P)	
P1 (Percentage of posts liked)	Number of posts divided by total posts
P2 (Average number of likes per post)	Total likes divided by total number of posts
P3 (Average number of likes per post per 1000 fans)	(P2 divided by number of fans) multiply with 1000
Commitment (C)	
C1 (Percentage of posts commented)	Number of posts commented divided by total posts
C2 (Average of comments per post)	Total comments dividend by total posts
C3 (Average number of comments per post per 1000 fans)	(C2 divided by number of fans) multiply with 1000
Virality (V)	
V1 (Percentage of posts shared)	Number of posts shared divided by total posts
V2 (Average of shares per post)	Total shares dividend by total posts
V3 (Average number of shares per post per 1000 fans)	(V2 divided by number of fans) multiply with 1000
Engagement (E)	
E (Stakeholder engagement index)	P3 + C3 + V3

Source: Bonsón and Ratkai [30]

4   Results and Discussion

4.1   Classification of ROP Facebook Posts

The findings of ROP Facebook posts collected from 1st January to 11th June 2019 are presented in Table 2. The Facebook page has a total of 29,558 followers as of 11th June 2019. A total of 185 posts are found in this period and based on content analysis these were classified various categories. A total of eighteen categories were identified to capture the information posted on the Facebook page. The highest number of posts were made by the ROP under the safety advice category that accounts for 39%. This suggested that ROP is using Facebook with a community orientation tactic and disseminate related information. This is an interesting finding in comparison to the study by Williams et al. [29] that suggested its two most common categories were traffic and accidents. Table 2 highlights that the second most important category of posts was related to ROP awareness sessions for schools which accounted for 14%. Also, a cumulative of 28% is assigned to all awareness session categories (exhibition, other agency, schools and university) that reflect that ROP is continuously involved with various sections of the community to educate them.

The posts also actively gave information on law enforcement and agency-related information. On average there were at least 34 posts per month which almost accounts for one post per day. Consistent with the findings of prior studies, the ROP tended to have no postings on information that was not related to the police unless it was to do with safety advice which was driven on religious account [9].

The safety advice posts were highest during the month of Ramadan. The post included a verse from the Quran that advocated safe driving practices. This strategy by the police was being adopted to reduce the number of accidents in the month of Ramadan as fatigue is attributed during fasting and it was one of the main reasons for fatal accidents. The safety advice posts also advocated child safety belts, car maintenance checks, tips on driving at night, avoiding phones while driving and tips on driving during rainfall.

Table 2. Classification of ROP Facebook posts

S. No.	Categories	Freq	%	S. No.	Categories	Freq	%
1	Event related	10	5.41	10	Crime information	1	0.54
2	Exhibition Awareness	1	0.54	11	Holiday greetings	1	0.54
3	Other agency awareness	18	9.72	12	Information sharing	8	4.32
4	Schools awareness	26	14.05	13	Law enforcement	12	6.49
5	University Awareness	6	3.24	14	Non-police related	4	2.16
6	Advertising	3	1.62	15	Other government services	1	0.54
7	Agency related information	12	6.49	16	Road conditions	4	2.16
8	Bus driver awareness	2	1.08	17	Safety advice	72	38.92
9	Competition	2	1.08	18	Traffic updates	2	1.08

The school, university and other institution awareness posts communicated the awareness sessions conducted by the ROP to propagate traffic safety. Law enforcement category posts included information on the penalties imposed for wrongly overtaking, rash driving, speed limits, intentionally risking lives by crossing flooded valleys and allowable vehicle load. The agency-related information included information on their work timings, holidays, participation in events and meetings. The ROP posts also covered diversions on the roads and traffic updates in various other categories however at a lesser frequency.

Crime information category did not have many posts considering that it is one of the first job priority of the ROP. The avoidance of posts on crime-related information may be due to the sensitivity associated with it and a strategy to avoid creating a bad image. It might also be a source of unrest and the possibility of creating fake news in the future. This is consistent with the approach followed by the police in the USA on their social media as reported in by Williams et al. [29].

4.2 Citizens Interaction on ROP Facebook

Social media is a ubiquitous tool that allows its users to interact with one another in the virtual world. The ROPs Facebook page is also a tool for the agency to allow community interactions related to their posts. A follower gets the opportunity to 'like' the posted information, 'share' with other users or 'comment' on the posted information. Table 3 presents the citizen interaction on the ROP Facebook for the period 1st Jan to 11th June 2019.

The likes, shares and comments were classified for each of the eighteen categories. There were a total of 2506 likes, 136 shares and 127 comments (refer Table 3). The safety advice posts received the highest number of likes. This is also reflective of the fact that the highest number of posts were for safety advice. The law enforcement category received the next highest record of likes. This was followed by school awareness, agency related information and other agency-related awareness information. The findings of this study are partially consistent with Dai et al. [9] which also reported the highest number of likes for agency-related information and law enforcement categories.

Table 3 reflects the highest number of shares were again for the safety advice followed by the law enforcement categories. The remaining shares were negligible for the posts. The posts also garnered comments which were in the order of safety advice, law enforcement and crime information. In comparison to the number of followers, the citizen engagement has not been too strong with the posts on the ROPs Facebook page.

The overall engagement levels of the citizens with the ROPs Facebook post is represented in Table 4. The average number of likes per post per 1000 fans (P3) score is 0.46 which reflects on weak popularity. The average number of comments per post per 1000 fans (C3) is 0.02 considering that very few comments were made in the period of study whereas the average number of shares per post per 1000 fans (V3) was 0.02. The overall engagement level was only at 0.51. This indicator is useful to motivate the ROP in encouraging more citizen engagement.

4.3 Types of Facebook Posts

Table 5 presents the statistics on the type of posts found on ROP Facebook page. Photos were used extensively for the posts and it accounted for a total of 96% of the 185 posts found over the investigated period. There were only about six videos and two links posted on Facebook.

Table 3. Citizen interaction on ROP Facebook posts

S. No.	Categories	Likes	Shares	Comments
1	Event related	97	2	1
2	Exhibition Awareness	2	0	0
3	Other agency awareness	176	0	5
4	School awareness	223	6	4
5	University Awareness	76	2	0
6	advertising	102	1	9
7	agency related information	189	7	8
8	bus driver awareness	11	0	0
9	competition	16	5	0
10	crime information	53	0	14
11	holiday greetings	23	2	5
12	information sharing	119	2	5
13	law enforcement	300	25	24
14	non-police related	69	4	3
15	other government services	21	1	0
16	road conditions	73	2	6
17	safety advice	931	77	42
18	traffic updates	25	0	1
	Total	**2506**	**136**	**127**

Table 4. Citizens engagement

	P1	P2	P3	C1	C2	C3	V1	V2	V3	E
ROP Facebook post	1	13.54	0.46	0.10	0.69	0.02	0.17	0.73	0.02	0.51

Table 5. Types of ROP Facebook posts

Type	Link	Photo	Video	Total
Freq.	2	177	6	185
Percent	1.08	95.68	3.24	100

5 Conclusion and Recommendations

This research contributes to the scarce literature on how police are using social media strategies and interacting with the public. This study uses content analysis of ROP's Facebook page. The findings suggest that there are 18 categories under which Facebook posts can be classified.

ROP is active in posting information daily by using more photos than links or videos which is consistent with the recommendation offered by He et al [11]. The content analysis reflects that the posts were heavy titled towards the well-being of the community, therefore, there was a high percentage of posts that advocated safety. The ROP has also been active in community awareness programmes that catered to the schools, universities and other organisations. Citizens engagement in terms of (likes, shares and comments) was limited to the posts however in comparison to its followers the engagement is considered weak. Currently, the ROP Facebook posts can be termed as a push strategy as described by Mergel [6].

The practical implications of this research suggest that ROP can do better in improving its interaction with the community on social media. By reaching out to more people, the messages on public safety can be more effective. In line with the recommendation by Dai et al. [9], the ROP needs to adopt a more problem-solving approach to increase community engagement.

This study has certain limitations. The research is restricted for a few months and can be extended to cover a longer period. The investigation is limited to the Facebook account only and needs to also consider other social media such as ROPs Twitter account. The use of social media by the ROP and other government agency are set to promote Oman's commitment to building smart cities and thus it requires that strategies are set to encourage e-participation by the community.

References

1. Varano, S.P., Sarasin, R.: Use of social media in policing. In: Bruinsma, G., Weisburd, D. (eds.) Encyclopedia of Criminology and Criminal Justice, pp. 5410–5423. Springer, New York (2014)
2. Tang, L., Liu, H.: Community Detection and Mining in Social Media, 138 p. Morgan and Claypool Publishers, San Rafael (2010)
3. Bertot, J.C., Jaeger, P.T., Grimes, J.M.: Using ICTs to create a culture of transparency: e-government and social media as openness and anti-corruption tools for societies. Govern. Inf. Q. 27(3), 264–271 (2010)
4. Hanna, R., Rohm, A., Crittenden, V.L.: We're all connected: the power of the social media ecosystem. Bus. Horiz. 54(3), 265–273 (2011)
5. Meijer, A., Thaens, M.: Social media strategies: understanding the differences between North American police departments. Govern. Inf. Q. 30(4), 343–350 (2013)
6. Mergel, I.: The social media innovation challenge in the public sector. Inf. Polity 17(3, 4), 281–292 (2012)
7. United Nations: United Nations E-Government Survey 2018: Gearing E-Government to support transformation towards sustainable and resilient societies (2018)
8. Lieberman, J.D., Koetzle, D., Sakiyama, M.: Police departments' use of Facebook: patterns and policy issues. Police Q. 16(4), 438–462 (2013)

9. Dai, M., He, W., Tian, X., Giraldi, A., Gu, F.: Working with communities on social media: varieties in the use of Facebook and Twitter by local police. Online Inf. Rev. **41**(6), 782–796 (2017)

10. Schneider, C.J.: Policing and Social Media: Social Control in an Era of New Media. Lexington Books, Lanham (2016)

11. He, W., Tian, X., Chen, Y., Chong, D.: Actionable social media competitive analytics for understanding customer experiences. J. Comput. Inf. Syst. **56**(2), 145–155 (2016)

12. Mossberger, K., Wu, Y., Crawford, J.: Connecting citizens and local governments? Social media and interactivity in major U.S. cities. Govern. Inf. Q. **30**(4), 351–358 (2013)

13. Bonsón, E., Royo, S., Ratkai M. Citizens' engagement on local governments' Facebook sites. An empirical analysis: the impact of different media and content types in Western Europe. Govern. Inf. Q. **32**(1), 52–62 (2015)

14. Ellison, N., Hardey, M.: Social media and local government: citizenship, consumption and democracy. Local Govern. Stud. **40**(1), 21–40 (2014)

15. Carlo Bertot, J., Jaeger, P.T., Grimes, J.M.: Promoting transparency and accountability through ICTs, social media, and collaborative e-government. Trans. Govern. People Process Policy **6**(1), 78–91 (2012)

16. Bellström, P., Magnusson, M., Pettersson, J.S., Thorén, C.: Facebook usage in a local government: a content analysis of page owner posts and user posts. Transf. Govern. People Process Policy **10**(4), 548–567 (2016)

17. Al-Aufi, A.S., Al-Harthi, I., AlHinai, Y., Al-Salti, Z., Al-Badi, A.: Citizens' perceptions of government's participatory use of social media. Transf. Govern. People Process Policy **11**(2), 174–194 (2017)

18. Warren, A.M., Sulaiman, A., Jaafar, N.I.: Social media effects on fostering online civic engagement and building citizen trust and trust in institutions. Govern. Inf. Q. **31**(2), 291–301 (2014)

19. Feroz Khan, G., Young Yoon, H., Kim, J., Woo Park, H.: From e-government to social government: Twitter use by Korea's central government. Online Inf. Rev. **38**(1), 95–113 (2014)

20. Sadulski, J.: Why Social Media Plays an Important Role in Law Enforcement: IN Public Safety (2018). https://inpublicsafety.com/2018/03/why-social-media-plays-an-important-role-in-law-enforcement/

21. Kim, K., Mohr, A.O.-N.E.: 2016 Law Enforcement Use of Social Media Survey. Urban Institute Washington, DC (2017)

22. Schwalje, W., Aradi, W.: An Arab open government maturity model for social media engagement. Tahseen Consulting (2013)

23. National Center for Statistics and Information. Confidence in the media, NCSI. Sultanate of Oman Sultanate of Oman: National Center for Statistics and Information (2015). https://www.ncsi.gov.om/news/pages/newsct_20150519114220952.aspx

24. Yin, R.: Case Study Research: Design and Methods. Sage, Thousand Oaks (2009)

25. PWC: Ramadan in the GCC: what Employers need to know Middle East: PWC (2019). https://www.pwc.com/m1/en/services/tax/me-tax-legal-news/2019/ramadan-in-the-gcc.html. Accessed 13 June 2019

26. Lam, E.T.H., Au, C.H., Chiu, D.K.W.: Analyzing the use of Facebook among university libraries in Hong Kong. J. Acad. Librarianship. **45**(3), 175–183 (2019)

27. Rieder, B.: Studying Facebook via data extraction: the Netvizz application. In: Proceedings of the 5th Annual ACM Web Science Conference; Paris, France, pp. 346–355. ACM (2013). 2464475

28. Miles, M.B., Huberman, A.M., Huberman, M.A., Huberman, M.: Qualitative Data Analysis: An Expanded Sourcebook. Sage, Thousand Oaks (1994)

29. Williams, C.B., Fedorowicz, J., Kavanaugh, A., Mentzer, K., Thatcher, J.B., Xu, J.: Leveraging social media to achieve a community policing agenda. Govern. Inf. Q. **35**(2), 210–222 (2018)
30. Bonsón, E., Ratkai, M.: A set of metrics to assess stakeholder engagement and social legitimacy on a corporate Facebook page. Online Inf. Rev. **37**(5), 787–803 (2013)

Cognitive Systems for Urban Planning: A Literature Review

Lorena Recalde[1](✉), Jaime Meza[2], and Luis Terán[3,4]

[1] National Polytechnic School, Ladrón de Guevara E11-253, Quito, Ecuador
`lorena.recalde@epn.edu.ec`
[2] Technical University of Manabi, Avenida Jose María Urbina, Portoviejo, Ecuador
`jaime.meza@fci.edu.ec`
[3] University of Fribourg, Boulevard de P érolles 90, Fribourg, Switzerland
`luis.teran@unifr.ch`
[4] Universidad de las Fuerzas Armadas ESPE,
Av. General Rumiñahui S/N, Sangolquí, Ecuador

Abstract. The need of citizens engagement in modeling the vast amount of services provided by governments has led to mechanisms where people are seen as sensors. Development policies, processes, and aims are evolving regarding urban planning in order to use citizens-generated data as input in the intelligent systems. This data may be a rich source to mine citizens' current requirements, detect serious problems in a city and determine what is urgent and what is not. Citizens as sensors is a new paradigm that transforms the idea of *efficiency* implemented in a "smart city" into the notion of *resilience* oriented to "cognitive cities". In this regard, a systematic literature review of how intelligent systems have been employed towards modeling cognition in urban planning was conducted. This work propose a classification on how intelligent systems are being approached: Implementations in intelligent governance, big data and analytic solutions, fuzzy methods, and application scenarios toward cognitive urban planning. Moreover, this study details a comparison of the approaches mentioned above in terms of technology targeted and/or computing methods employed, as well as the advantages of the proposed works and their limitations. The results of the present review revealed that previous studies contributed with combined strategies that apply soft computing methods, but the implementation of empirical validations has not been studied in depth.

Keywords: Cognitive cities · Urban planning · Collective intelligence · Big data · Fuzzy methods · Cognitive computing · Smart cities

1 Introduction

Knowledge and the learning process that emerge from people-to-people and people-to-data interactions transform them and the social environment around.

© ICST Institute for Computer Sciences, Social Informatics and Telecommunications Engineering 2020
Published by Springer Nature Switzerland AG 2020. All Rights Reserved
H. Santos et al. (Eds.): SmartCity 360 2019, LNICST 323, pp. 249–270, 2020.
https://doi.org/10.1007/978-3-030-51005-3_22

In information applications, this social and data-oriented phenomenon is known as collective intelligence [49]. When collective intelligence serves as a baseline in information sciences, generalizations may be inferred because the system learns patterns from the behavior of the whole community. For example, the local government of certain city might propose a specific Web-based recycling program taking into account the ideas, participation and the particular conditions of the community. Then, improving the functioning of the city is an effect of self-empowering initiatives performed by heterogeneous social actors (and not as an outcome of technology companies or business strategies) [9].

People engaging in community-based platforms may offer a collective understanding of the world around them, get involved in discussions and contribute with solutions. Then, new forms of generation of knowledge are experienced. The use of intelligent algorithms to solve complex problems is extended to various domains. However, as *cognition* is recently considered in areas such as town planning, territory organization and e-participation, the application of artificial intelligence merged with collective intelligence strategies is hardly used to solve the resilience challenges of cities. Generally, collective intelligence is applied in scenarios where machines are deficient and are unable to perform a task [35]. The identification of how human factors and technology are approached together may be relevant, guide systems design and give directions for future research.

Classifying, comparing, recognizing, and explaining the social environment are cognitive factors that have proven to be useful in information systems. Then, from this arises the idea of seeing "people as sensors" in E-Government and E-Participation applications. This paper aims to survey and analyze existing cognition-based systems to detail the opportunities for innovating and supporting the progress of cities. We adopt a systematic approach to analyze and aggregate the outcomes of significant empirical studies in *Urban Planning*. Such studies may apply different methods and address various problems in the context of cognitive urban planning. Thus, our objectives are:

- Presenting a systematic review and analysis of the different domains related to the methods and strategies applied towards cognitive cities. We highlight the advantages and limitations found;
- Analyzing the main challenges in the field of cognitive cities and addressing them with options or solutions;
- Describing the key areas where future studies could change the cities while improving their resilience.

The remainder of the paper is structured as follows: Sect. 2 classifies the relevant articles in methods for cognitive urban management systematically. Section 3 discusses cognition modeling mechanisms and categorizes them; Sect. 4 reflects the results and comparison of the reviewing strategies; finally, in Sect. 5, we conclude the work done in this study.

2   Systematic Literature Review

With regard to urban management, the concept "smart cities" leaves new urban challenges out of reach. These challenges not only require improved efficiency, but also demand approaches based on sustainability and resilience [18]. To better understand how the problems related to Cognitive Urban Planning have been addressed, this section describes a *systematic literature review* (SLR) of the technological strategies applied in the domain. To provide an evidence-based transparent study, we analyzed the methods, cases and experiences gained from different research works. Then, to obtain a balanced and objective summary we formulated a question, identified the relevant studies, evaluated their quality, summarized the research evidence, and interpreted the findings [7]. We use a repeatable methodology that supports the presented SLR where the different experimental contexts may be assessed and the outcomes aggregated [3,6]. The *SLR* selection procedure is presented in the following section.

2.1   Article Selection Process

The strategy performed to select the articles have four steps: *i)* Build the search query from keywords; *ii)* Article selection based on the year of publication and its language; *iii)* Article selection based on the reputation and validity of the publisher; and *iv)* Article selection based on the content of its 'Abstract'. The first step consists of combining some keywords to formulate the search. The use of logical operators may enhance the query. We established the relevant words and noun phrases and employed them to create the query: *"cognitive cities" OR "cognitive city" urban plan citizens requirements information systems data*. This has been searched in *Google Scholar* which presented us with the related academic articles ordered according to the ranking algorithms employed by the Google search engines (a general explanation may be found in [4]). As a result, the search system extracted 135 articles from books, chapters, master and PhD thesis, journals, conferences, executive reports, working papers, notes and workshop papers. In the step *ii)*, to make sure that the most recent research works are considered, the adopted strategy was oriented to remove the articles published before 2010. Moreover, a quality criterion that we applied was to filter out the articles that were written in a language other than English. After this, we obtained a total of 105 papers. The step *iii)* was conducted with the aim of choosing only high-quality articles for their further analysis. To do so, we focused on the articles retrieved from journal publications, book chapters, and conferences published by Springer, Elsevier, IEEE, and ACM. Journals that were indexed in Scopus or listed in Scimago Journal Ranking were also included in our study. Then, reports, working papers, books, and thesis, as well as invalid journal/conference articles were excluded. The amount of the remaining articles was of 53. In last step, the 'Abstracts' of the articles were studied by the authors. If they contained a part of the keywords and were related to cognitive cities they were considered as relevant to the subject matter. In this regard, 42 academic articles were finally selected for their analysis.

2.2 Articles Classification

To have an overview of the selected articles, we classify them considering the year of publication and the publisher. The papers in our study were published in the range of 2010–2019. Figure 1 presents a matrix with the number of articles found per year and publisher. As it can be seen, before 2016 there was a small quantity of papers related to the topic (10 articles that represent the 23.81%). Besides, in 2010 and 2013 no article was presented. In the last four years (2016–2019), the interest in researching methods which involve cognitive and information systems for urban planning has increased (32 out of 42); so much so that in the first two months of 2019 there are already nine articles. In 2016, Springer stands out among the publishers with eight articles. This result was expected given that in this year the Springer book "Towards Cognitive Cities" [45] was released and most of the chapters were chosen for our study. If we consider as categories the publishers Elsevier, Springer, IEEE, and ACM, as well as the 'Other' (high-quality) indexed journals, it is shown that 45.24% of the chosen articles were published by Springer. This publisher commonly seems to lead the number of publications over the time. Moreover, it should be noted that 26.19% of the articles belong to the IEEE. Figure 2 shows that the majority of the articles are book chapters (17 papers that represent the 40.48% of the total). The presence of journal papers in our study is of 33.33% while the 26.19% belongs to the conference papers. Most of the IEEE and ACM articles are conference papers. On the other hand, only one journal article was extracted from Elsevier.

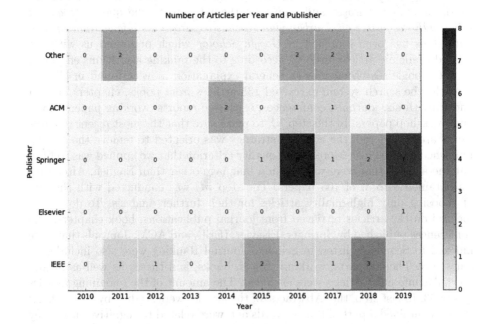

Fig. 1. Number of selected academic articles per year and publisher.

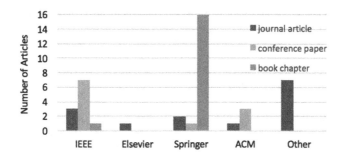

Fig. 2. Number of selected academic articles per kind of paper.

Table 1. Classification of the articles according to categories

Category	NumArticles	Percentage (%)	Articles in
Intelligent governance implementations	17	40.47	Table 2
Data-oriented problems	9	21.43	Table 3
Fuzzy models-based	9	21.43	Table 4
Application scenario solutions	7	16.67	Table 5

Based on the content of the articles, we classified them in four categories depending on their adopted strategy:

1. Intelligent governance implementations. Articles whose concerns were related to transformations in cities, theoretical contexts and the use of cognitive computing.
2. Data-oriented problems. Articles that target (big) data processing, privacy and visualization.
3. Fuzzy models-based. Articles that employed fuzzy theory as a main approach.
4. Application scenario solutions. Particular solutions to address a specific citizen/location/service problem.

According to the presented categories, Table 1 details the number and the corresponding percentage of the articles classified in each of them. Almost 41% of the articles belong to the category 'Intelligent governance implementations' (Table 2). The categories 'Data-oriented problems' and 'Fuzzy models-based' have 9 articles each (Tables 3 and 4, respectively). Finally, only 7 papers were fund as 'Application scenario solutions' (Table 5).

Table 2. Articles whose strategy is based on intelligent governance implementations

Publisher	Year	Article and reference	Journal/Conference /Book name
IEEE	2019	A Conceptual Model for Intelligent Urban Governance: Influencing Energy Behaviour in Cognitive Cities [34]	Designing Cognitive Cities
Springer	2019	Designing Cognitive Cities [50]	Designing Cognitive Cities
Springer	2019	Possibilities for Linguistic Summaries in Cognitive Cities [20]	Designing Cognitive Cities
Springer	2018	Advancing Cognitive Cities with the Web of Things [14]	New Advances in the Internet of Things
Taylor & Francis	2018	Intelligent or smart cities and buildings: a critical exposition and a way forward [19]	Intelligent Buildings International
IEEE	2018	Smart Governance for Smart Cities [47]	Proceedings of the IEEE
Taylor & Francis	2017	Computing Brains: Learning Algorithms and Neurocomputation in the Smart City [54]	Information, Communication & Society
Springer	2016	Granular Computing as a Basis of Human-Data Interaction: A Cognitive Cities Use Case [53]	Granular Computing
Springer	2016	Maturity Model for Cognitive Cities [52]	Towards Cognitive Cities
Springer	2016	From Smart to Cognitive: A Roadmap for the Adoption of Technology in Cities [40]	Towards Cognitive Cities
Springer	2016	Innovative Urban Governance: A Game Oriented Approach to Influencing Energy Behavior [33]	Towards Cognitive Cities
Springer	2016	Digital Personal Assistant for Cognitive Cities: A Paper Prototype [25]	Towards Cognitive Cities
Springer	2016	Towards the Improvement of Citizen Communication Through Computational Intelligence [44]	Towards Cognitive Cities
Inst Construction & Architecture	2016	Stratigraphy of the Smart City Concept [30]	Architektura & Urbanizmus
IEEE	2012	Intelligent Governance of Large-Scale Engineering Systems: A Sub-Systemic Approach [10]	IEEE International Systems Conference SysCon 2012
IEEE	2011	Citizens as Sensors: The Cognitive City Paradigm [38]	8th International Conference Expo on Emerging Technologies for a Smarter World
Wiley Online Library	2011	Informational Cities: Analysis and Construction of Cities in The Knowledge Society [48]	Journal of the American Society for Information Science and Technology

Table 3. Articles that offer big data and analytics solutions

Publisher	Year	Article and reference	Journal/Conference/Book name
Springer	2019	The Role of Interpretable Fuzzy Systems in Designing Cognitive Cities [1]	Designing Cognitive Cities
Springer	2018	Using Geocoding and Topic Extraction to Make Sense of Comments on Social Network Pages of Local Government Agencies [31]	Electronic Government
IEEE	2018	Enabling cognitive smart cities using big data and machine learning: Approaches and challenges [36]	IEEE Communications Magazine
Springer	2017	Managing Urban Resilience Stream Processing Platform for Responsive Cities [28]	Informatik-Spektrum
ACM	2017	City Ranking Based on Financial Flux Indicator Clustering [2]	Proceedings of the 18th Annual International Conference on Digital Government Research
Open Access Journal	2016	Data-Driven Participation: Algorithms, Cities, Citizens, and Corporate Control [51]	Urban Planning
Springer	2016	Cognitive Cities, Big Data and Citizen Participation: The Essentials of Privacy and Security [8]	Towards Cognitive Cities
Springer	2015	Big Data and Analytics for Government Innovation [37]	Big Data and Analytics: Strategic and Organizational Impacts
IEEE	2014	Visual Analysis of Public Utility Service Problems in a Metropolis [55]	IEEE Transactions on Visualization and Computer Graphics

3   Cognition Models in Urban Planning

The recent advancements in technology have made human experiences and abilities to reason be considered as part of intelligent systems' *adapting processes*. For cities that evolve quickly -and are expected to be resilient- this means to merge computing (automation) which provides a collaborative platform for discovery with the responses, actions, data and feedback of human users [21]. One of the seminal works on "Cognitive Cities" is the proposed by Novak (1997) [42]. His research provided the theoretical foundations to *invent* intelligent environments which people could interact with. Once our behavior is recognized, these real or virtual environments would know our strengths, weaknesses and needs and respond to us. Therefore, various strategies to provide these new environments (or resilient cities) with the abilities to perceive, retain, retrieve, repeat, compare, transform and generate patterns may be developed. Next, we analyze

Table 4. Articles whose strategy is based on fuzzy models

Publisher	Year	Article and reference	Journal/Conference/Book name
Springer	2019	Using Fuzzy Cognitive Maps to Arouse Learning Processes in Cities [15]	Designing Cognitive Cities
IEEE	2018	Fuzzy Reasoning in Cognitive Cities: An Exploratory Work on Fuzzy Analogical Reasoning Using Fuzzy Cognitive Maps [12]	2018 IEEE International Conference on Fuzzy Systems
IEEE	2017	Striving for Semantic Convergence with Fuzzy Cognitive Maps and Graph Databases [13]	2017 IEEE International Conference on Fuzzy Systems
ACM	2016	Synchronizing Mind Maps with Fuzzy Cognitive Maps for Decision-Finding in Cognitive Cities [17]	2017 Proceedings of the 9th International Conference on Theory and Practice of Electronic Governance
IEEE	2016	Personal Digital Assistant 2.0 – A Software Prototype for Cognitive Cities [22]	2016 IEEE International Conference on Fuzzy Systems
IEEE	2015	Enhancing Multidirectional Communication for Cognitive Cities [23]	2015 Second International Conference on eDemocracy eGovernment (ICEDEG)
IEEE	2015	Fuzzy Knowledge Representation in Cognitive Cities [24]	2015 IEEE International Conference on Fuzzy Systems
ACM	2014	Applying the Fuzzy Analytical Hierarchy Process in Cognitive Cities [27]	Proceedings of the 8th International Conference on Theory and Practice of Electronic Governance
ACM	2014	Applying Fuzzy Ontologies to Implement the Social Semantic Web [46]	SIGWEB Newsl

the 42 selected articles according to the categories explained before with the purpose of presenting an in-depth understanding. Additionally, we discuss the employed approaches, advantages and limitations, as well as differences between the articles.

3.1 Intelligent Governance Implementations

Intelligent governance allows cities' authorities to innovate their services and structures by embedding learning, memory creation and experience retrieval. In

Table 5. Articles that provide application scenario solutions

Publisher	Year	Article and reference	Journal/Conference/Book name
Springer	2019	A Dynamic Route Planning Prototype for Cognitive Cities [26]	Designing Cognitive Cities
Springer	2019	Towards Cognitive Cities in the Energy Domains [11]	Designing Cognitive Cities
Springer	2019	Extending Knowledge Graphs with Subjective Influence Networks for Personalized Fashion [5]	Designing Cognitive Cities
Elsevier	2019	A System View of Smart Mobility and its Implications for Ghanaian Cities [43]	Sustainable Cities and Society
Public Library of Science	2017	How Green are the Streets? An Analysis for Central Areas of Chinese Cities Using Tencent Street View [32]	PloS one
Springer	2016	Cognitive Cities: An Application for Nairobi [16]	Towards Cognitive Cities
SAGE Journals	2011	Spanish Cities in The Knowledge Economy: Theoretical Debates and Empirical Evidence [41]	European Urban and Regional Studies

this regard, the introduced *intelligence* through information technology improves urban governance constantly. Intelligent governance is one of the cognitive strategies that includes human beings and other cognitive entities to implement techniques that reconfigure cooperation capabilities and build a sustainable, responsible individual/collective behavior [39]. In this section, we describe and summarize the 17 articles that presented diverse intelligent governance implementations. Finally, they are compared in Table 6.

The book "Designing Cognitive Cities" (2019) gathers the most current research in the domain of cognitive urban governance. Three of these articles ([20,34,50]) address problems by proposing intelligent governance solutions. For example, in [34], Maunsouri and Khansari study the impact and use of ICTs (information and communication technologies) in urban planning regarding the efficiency of cities' energy systems. They present a government multi-layered model where human-institutional, physical, and data factors are brought together to improve sustainability. Tabacchi *et al.* focus on the design of cognitive cities [50]. They present the approaches 'Action Design Research' and 'Ontological Design' to explain how their principles can be applied in urban planning. Moreover, the authors summarize intelligent techniques that may be useful in citizen communication in a cognitive city. To communicate with citizens in comprehensible ways, in [20], the authors propose linguistic summaries based on fuzzy logic. In other words, the extracted and processed city-related data may be verbalize through linguistic summaries.

D'Onofrio *et al.* propose the use of the Web of Things (WoT) in cognitive cities [14]. WoT is the IoT extended by using Web standards and the authors present a comparison of the two technologies. Features like maintainability, privacy, programmability, security and standards are analyzed in both cases showing that the WoT has some advantages over the IoT. In [19], the difference of the meaning of 'smart city' and 'intelligent city' is established. In this article, the authors present a study of the related literature to motivate their research in intelligent buildings design. Finally, they demonstrate that the two terms complement each other and explain this with a cognitive city model. In the same way, Razaghi and Finger detail a conceptual governance approach in [47]. They offer insights about the combination of technology complex sociotechnical systems, systems theory, and governance literature for adaptation of city models. Another conceptual research is presented in [54]. Its authors analyze the new kinds of 'brain/code/spaces' where the environment is provided with brain-like functions of learning and 'human qualities' of cognition.

In [53], Wilke and Portmann study the implementation and representation of information granules for data legibility. Human-data interaction is the center of their investigation as a means to support collective decision making in pervasive computing environments. Terán et al., in [52], analyze the cognitive processes for government decision-making as well. They propose a five-layer eGovernment framework and assess its performance in three different applications. With regard to decision making for citizens' quality of life, in [40], technology infrastructure for smart cities is analyzed. Moreover, the authors propose a roadmap to a planned adoption of technology based on the detail of the different current challenges that cities face. In [33], governing mechanisms where quantitative and computational processes are included are presented as strategies for policy making. The authors employ city sensors and smart devices to create an interactive environment for collaboration.

After proposing theoretical models, in [25], the authors of the article develop and evaluate a meta-app prototype named *cogniticity*. The goal is to ensure a good work-life balance for citizens and help them to manage their time and be productive. On the other hand, to deal with the communication gap between citizens and government, [44] proposes the use of computational intelligence approaches such as CWW (Computing With Words) and Fuzzy Classifiers. In this article, collective cognitive systems are raised as a solution for social exclusion and incomprehension in terms of the efficiency of communication among the government actors. In order to understand what a green, sustainable, open, and rational city means, Legény et al. analyzes the concept of Smart City by considering several distinct layers of 'introduced intelligent components' [30]. The layer-based structure considers the 'smart people' as a core element to transform people lives and the environment. In [10], the authors implement the concept of intelligent governance in Hoboken, New Jersey following the Complex, Large-scale, Inter-connected, Open and Socio technical (CLIOS) methodology. With the aim of providing a view of its general application in large-scale urban systems, performance indicators and key subsystems are identified and interrelated. Mostashari et al., in [38], propose an architectural process approach where cognition is integrated into the urban processes. The sub-systems like energy, water, transportation, the emergency services system, and the system of information and communication were analyzed to identify their role in a cognitive city framework. In [48], the bias in informational cities is studied. The clusters and spaces for personal contacts and implicit information sharing could cause polarization.

Therefore, this conceptual article details the indicators that measure the degree of 'informativeness' of a city.

Summary of Articles Whose Strategy Is Based on Intelligent Governance Implementations. In the previous section, we analyzed 17 intelligent governance strategies. In Table 6, we compare the most important advantages and limitations of each article.

3.2 Big Data and Analytics Solutions

Technology advancements and social changes have given decision power to citizens and enhanced democracy. In this regard, online collective decision making is oriented to solve urban infrastructure problems and contribute in public policies. Therefore, governments are implementing big data applications where the huge amounts of citizen-generated data can be processed and transformed in useful information. Next, data-oriented solutions are detailed.

In [1], Alonso *et al.* present the extraction of valuable knowledge as a challenge generated in the Big Data era. In the article, it is explained how the interaction of cities' intelligent devices and people should be addressed to be effective. Besides, in order to handle (or *interpret*) large amounts of high-dimensional and heterogeneous data, fuzzy logic and its application to Cognitive Cities is presented. A more specific research is presented in [31]. To analyze the users' comments on a social network page of the local government of Rio das Ostras, Brazil, a method based on Part of speech (POS) tagging is proposed. In fact, the authors' strategy is based on the identification of mentioned locations and most frequent topics in comments to be shown for real-time decision making. Mohammadi and Al-Fuqaha study the problem of the waste of unlabeled data which is extracted from smart devices [36]. They propose a framework which employs Deep Reinforcement Learning combined with semi-supervised learning to build a Smart Agent that senses the environment. In [28], a cognitive governance framework with the name of 'Stream Processing Platform for Responsive Cities' is presented. Different applications are revised by the authors in the context of urban resilience. In [2], the authors present a method that implements clustering and regression strategies in order to group cities based on their financial features. The motivation behind this is the need for comparison of cities that are *similar* and later identifying their degree of 'smartness'. In [51], Volunteered Geographic Information (VGI) is studied as a means to enhance passive civic participation. The goal of the proposed research is to make a city truly responsive through people's data analysis. A detailed analysis of the motivations to employ VGI in local planning and citizen engagement is carried out. Cavoukian and Chibba, in [8], analyze the concerns about privacy and security in a cognitive city. They state that the 7 Foundational Principles of Privacy by Design, which are detailed, may introduce the required trust in applications of cognitive cities.

In [37], Morabito analyses the use of crowd-sourced human observation, or Crowdreporting to train artificially intelligent public systems. As a result, he

Table 6. A comparison of the most important advantages and limitations of the intelligent governance implementations in cognitive urban planning

Article	Targeted/Used Technology	Advantage	Limitation
[34]	- User Experience - Social Computing - City-Wide Sensor Network	Model enhance citizens behavioural pattern towards sustainability values	An effective education system for citizens to speed with learning capabilities should be facilitated
[50]	- Metaheuristics - Fuzzy Logic - Computational Intelligence Classifiers - Computing with Words	Emphasis on the users as active participants in the design process and design as a sociocultural process	Being able to interpret the non-verbal communication and identify the actors make the communication infrastructure a complex system
[20]	- Natural Language Processing - Big data - Fuzzy logic	No need of collecting sensitive data from citizens	Computational effort is an significant issue when calculating the summaries
[14]	- IoT - WoT - Big Data	WoT influence city development (from smart to cognitive cities)	WoT applications have not yet been applied in real-world scenarios
[19]	- Sustainability assessment tools - Health-related assessment tools	The mutual performance of smart and intelligent elements in a city impacts the potential of its services	The lack of clarity may be confusing for the professionals and stakeholders
[47]	- Parallel/Quantum computing - Mobility as a service - Fuzzy logic - Cloud computing - Machine Learning	Real-time communication and opinion sharing channels allow a better governance of urban complexity	Complex future cities require a close collaboration among interdisciplinary experts (system scientists, urbanists, mathematicians, etc.)
[54]	- Machine learning - Cognitive computing - Neurocomputational devices	Brain-inspired environments are cognitive cities with 'human qualities' and not hard-coded 'programmable cities'	Neurocomputational and the notion of the 'social life of the brain' are in their initial exploration
[53]	- Granular calculus - GIS - Granular geometry	Decision making processes can be developed in real time over maps	Though experimental technologies several tests are compulsory before it can be applied widely
[52]	- Geolocation/IoT - Recommender engines - Online Communities	Citizens participation improves government services, intelligence of the crowds for eEmpowerment	Dynamic profiles of citizens need to be updated automatically; then, strategies have to be design in advance
[40]	- Open data portals - Social Media data - Gamification	The quality of life for citizens using technology as an enabler is possible due to its growing potential	Technology is simply one part of city systems, better analysis and better delivery models are required
[33]	- Gamification - Crowdsourcing platforms - City-Wide Sensor Network	Interactive games encourage the users to participate and change their energy consumption behavior	Rely on city sensors and calibration of instruments depending on the case
[25]	- Fuzzy cognitive maps - Cognitive computing - Semantic Web	The prototype got constructive feedback, and may be helpful to develop apps and improve citizens' living	Privacy is considered as a major challenge for the meta-app users
[44]	- CWW - Metaheuristics - Geospatial Analysis - Fuzzy Ontologies	Described approaches may become useful to improve citizens-government communication	Experiments have to reach real world application and case studies from different domains need to be included
[30]	- Internet of People - Internet of Services - IoT	The components of the layer model interact to each other and integrate an intelligent combination of inputs	Smart City is a broad concept and there is no a general applicable model
[10]	CLIOS process	CLIOS is helpful in the transformation of cities and critical aspects may be modeled for governance	Key performance indicators are dependent on the city features; then, the list presented are not decisive
[38]	- Wireless sensors - Crowdsourcing platforms - Human-only sensors	In the design of the logical architecture of a Cognitive City the proposed framework may be an effective guideline	The performance of the framework need to be evaluated when large-scale information is used in cognitive responses.
[48]	- Cognitive infrastructures - Knowledge management - Information retrieval	Information science and urban informatics can contribute to the construction of digital cities	Conceptual hypotheses that need empirical studies on selected cities

details a recommendation list towards Smart City development. His study is based on the use of sources of data and their application in public engagement, in the creation of new models in public management and the challenges of big data in the public service transformation. The oldest article presented in this section was published in 2014 [55]. Here, a visual analytics process based on the main tasks of utility service management to make the related issues more understanding was implemented. The aim is to address the daily issues or emergencies related to utility services that arise due to the increasing rate of city construction, vandalism and infrastructure failures. Then, as part of their strategy, they used aggregation and clustering methods to find some patterns and events that could help administrators in making informed decisions.

Summary of Articles that Propose Big Data and Analytics Solutions. Previously, we analyzed 9 data-oriented solutions and how citizens information is employed. In Table 7, we compare the most important advantages and limitations of the seen articles.

3.3 Fuzzy Models-Based Research

Knowledge representation is required for a better understanding of the citizens' information and the data generated from urban processes. However, acquiring and processing the imprecise urban data which is mostly expressed in natural language is a challenge. Fuzzy models are employed to represent concepts or objects and establish fuzzy relationships between them [29]. Generally, when fuzzy models are used, approximation errors or strong assumptions are introduced to maintain the ability to deal with uncertainty and create soft decision boundaries. Then, by using fuzzy models it possible to represent complex urban constructs.

In [15], the authors analyze how Fuzzy Cognitive Maps (FCMs) are used in the design of a cognitive city. Based on the state-of-the-art related to the domain of FCMs and learning algorithms, [15] concludes that the implementation of FCMs facilitates the acquisition and representation of the interconnected urban data. In the same way, in [12], D'Onofrio *et al.* propose a conceptual framework based on fuzzy analogical reasoning and FCMs. Its goal is to emulate human analogical reasoning by using cognitive computing so it can be implemented in an urban dialogue system. In [13], the use of FCMs combined with graph databases as a solution for urban data management is also explored. In this research, issues about storing FCMs are analyzed; consequently, 47 graph databases employed for this purpose are evaluated and compared. D'Onofrio *et al.*, in [17], analyze the role of cognitive computing when working with FCMs to process information that was acquired using mental models (MMs).

The research presented in [22] shows a mobile application prototype of a personal digital assistant. The goal of the project is to improve calendar and mobility management in cognitive cities by implementing soft computing strategies. Likewise, in [23], Kaltenrieder *et al.* describe the technical foundations of

Table 7. A comparison of the most important advantages and limitations of the data-oriented solutions in cognitive urban planning

Article	Targeted/Used Technology	Advantage	Limitation
[1]	- Big Data - Interpretable fuzzy systems - Computational theory of perceptions	Interpretable fuzzy systems makes intelligent applications understandable and facilitates the interaction with citizens	Building interpretable fuzzy systems requires careful design
[31]	- POS tagging - Regular expressions - Social media data	The method (and developed app) allows to observe the citizens' claims that emerge in a particular city	Dictionaries such as POS and ZIP codes corresponding to locations are needed beforehand
[36]	- Semi-supervised learn - Deep Reinforcement Learning or DRL	DRL solves certain limitations of using RL alone	The model cannot reside on IoT resource-constrained devices
[28]	- Urban complexity - Cognitive design computing - Computational urban design	Urban infrastructures based on cognitive systems makes cities be responsive to changes	Responses need to be triggered in a timely fashion, then the need of distributed event stream processing
[2]	- Regression analysis - Financial data analysis - Clustering algorithms	The method allows to observe city tendencies and may guide government decisions to have a better city performance	Obtaining the particular kind of financial data may be a challenge
[51]	- VGI - Mobility as a service - Myopic algorithms - Big Data - Web 2.0 apps	Data-driven civic participation helps municipalities to engage with citizens through passive forms of interactions	Lack of control by citizens and municipalities over data-driven participation efforts (loss of empowerment, transparency and efficiency) when private corporations involved
[8]	- Big Data - Internet of Everything - Ubiquitous computing - Privacy by Design	Using a Privacy by Design framework may encourage innovative design approaches that consider both privacy and the system's goals	Privacy choices (how much and to whom share personal data) depends on the context of the citizens; so, they should have their privacy control
[37]	- Crowdsourcing - IoT - Big Data - Open government tools	People can provide real-time feedback teaching the system how to behave	Smart apps and open collaboration platform can become the critical infrastructure for the application of big data
[55]	- Clustering - Geo-spatial visual analytics - Temporal visual analytics	Visual analytics process applied for city utility service may help administrators to discover/solve problems	Various visual analytics tools, aggregation methods and interaction techniques need to be combined

a meta-app for cognitive cities in the context of e-governance. They implement the Fuzzy Analytical Hierarchy Process (FAHP) for decision making which is embedded as part of the app architecture in the data processing phase. In [24], the transition of smart cities to cognitive cities is explained through the analysis of cognitive computing. Here, also FCM is studied as a strategy to represent cities' information or knowledge and oriented to the interaction of users and technology. In [27], the Fuzzy Analytical Hierarchy Process is introduced as a method to extract cities' information. It is used as part of an interactive framework where fuzziness is present in the interactions between city entities and citizens. On the other hand, [46] shows how fuzzy ontologies may be used in Web Knowledge Management (representation, reasoning and aggregation) for cognitive cities to address the uncertainty in data. Besides, Social and Semantic Web are combined to improve human-computer interactions and enhance results of the application of digital humanities research.

Summary of Articles Whose Strategy Is Based on Fuzzy Models. In the previous section, we analyzed 9 solutions that employed fuzzy theory. In Table 8, we compare the most important advantages and disadvantages of each article.

Table 8. A Comparison of the Most Important Advantages and Limitations of the Solutions based on Fuzzy Logic

Article	Targeted/Used Technology	Advantage	Limitation
[15]	- Fuzzy logic - Fuzzy sets - Computing with words - Learning Algorithms - FCMs	Learning algorithms have the ability to enhance FCMs and together can be applied during the transformation from smart to cognitive cities	Research in this field is being recently explored
[12]	- Cognitive computing - Structure Mapping Theory - Fuzzy Analogical Reasoning - Graph data bases	Connecting large amounts of information by using FCMs, urban services might perform better and support the citizens	The development of humanistic retrieval processes in urban systems needs further research
[13]	- FCMs - Graph data bases - Cognitive Fuzzy Systems - Semantic Web	FCMs are modifiable and allow to simulate urban dynamic systems	A comparative performance analysis between graph database systems might be required depending on the context
[17]	- FCMs - Fuzzy clustering - Granular computing - Cognitive computing	Imprecise information existing in the city systems may be process by the approach because it is based on soft computing	To aggregate various FCMs, their linguistic information has to be translated into numeric values (manual process)
[22]	- FCMs - Fuzzy interval algebra - Graph databases	The combination of fuzzy grey cognitive maps with fuzzy temporal algebra may offer enhancements of the prototype	User evaluations (experts included) related to the performance of the prototype are needed
[23]	- FAHP - WebKnowARR framework - Graph databases	FAHP enables decision-making despite of the existence of uncertain knowledge	Data privacy issues arise
[24]	- NLP - Question - Answering retrieval - Knowledge graphs - FCMs	The prototype may be useful to aggregate existing knowledge about diverse topics about the city and its services	Privacy and security concerns need to be addressed
[27]	- FCMs - FAHP - Granular computing	The app improves public transportation of a city, traffic jams and accidents can be avoided	The app works properly with big amounts of data (limited to big cities, then)
[46]	- FCMs - Fuzzy ontologies - Granular computing	Social Semantic Web may be seen as a solution of cities' knowledge representation	Lack of evaluation of presented theoretical approaches

3.4   Application Scenario Solutions

The strategies to use technology, theories and data in the development of cognitive cities have been presented in the previous sections. Next, certain implementations, application scenarios and cases where those strategies have been applied are detailed. In [26], a prototype applied to dynamic route planning in the city of Bern, in Switzerland, is presented. The software prototype uses Bern's data taken from Google Maps as input and target the travel industry to improve users experience. Cuenca *et al.*, in [11], address issues like efficiency, sustainability and resilience in the *energy* domain. The use of Semantic Web and Semantic Ontologies in the management of cities energy is presented. In [5], fashion is targeted as a leisure and consumption activity in cognitive cities. The authors propose an ontological approach to model subjectivity in the domain and extract knowledge (categorizations of entities) useful in the economic development of cities.

Peprah *et al.*, in [43], target the vehicular traffic as an urbanization problem in Ghanaian cities. They propose a conceptual framework to first evaluate the mobility-smartness of Ghanaian cities and then the authors discuss how it can be operational. As conclusion, the article proposes road infrastructure investment and involvement of people in technological government solutions. In [32], Long and Liu propose a method to quantify cities greenery automatically. The authors implemented their method in 245 Chinese cities to measure how green their streets are. In [16], the authors analyze through a case study how 'smartness' and 'cognitivism' may be applied in an emerging country's city. A method for processing text messages based on cognitive computing is proposed regarding sanitation problems in slums of Nairobi, Kenya. Méndez and Sánchez, in [41], analyze the indicators that make Spanish cities join the *knowledge society*. Their findings show that cities in metropolitan areas have implemented services based on knowledge and are supported by qualified human resources. Medium-sized and small cities have made more effort than the former to introduce technology and have specialized industries.

Summary of Articles that Provide Application Scenario Solutions. In Table 9, we compare the most important advantages and disadvantages the 7 studied articles.

4   Result and Comparisons

Some of the approaches to model cognition in urban planning have been detailed in the previous section. The analyzed articles have based their proposals on diverse mechanisms in order to introduce *cognition* in urban governance ans/or government services. According to this, we considered four main categories where the authors provided *1.* intelligent governance implementations, *2.* Big Data and analytics solutions, *3.* strategies is based on fuzzy models, and *4.* application scenario solutions. Considering these categories, it was seen that each presents some challenges. For instance, there is a lack of implementation of conceptual

Table 9. A comparison of the most important advantages and limitations of the solutions presented through application scenarios

Article	Targeted/Used Technology	Advantage	Limitation
[26]	- Fuzzy logic - Fuzzy set theory - Graph databases	The prototype shows more flexibility on sightseeing trips because of the creation of dynamic routes	More research is needed to expand the prototype to other contexts different from the travel industry
[11]	- Semantic Ontology - Smart Grids - Semantic Web	Cognitive systems have a broad potential in city energy management (semantic models for representing energy data)	Cognitive cities in the energy domain face many challenges to reach mass market deployment
[5]	- Ontologies - Knowledge graphs - Subjective influence networks - Machine learning	Features generated in the influence network may be integrated into machine learning systems	Validation of the presented theoretical assumptions are needed
[43]	- IoT - Big data - Web 2.0	The framework may be used as a guide to implement the process of city smart mobility	Lack of validation and application of the proposed framework
[32]	GIS - Google Street View (GSV) image recognition - Color composition analysis	Street-view pictures are available even for developing countries and the framework allows their analysis to measure greenery	The study was limited to the analysis of urban areas
[16]	- Fuzzy logic - Fuzzy information granulation - Fuzzy clustering	Applications that are based on low-tech solutions are feasible to be used in small cities	Other problematic areas were not analyzed due to the early stage of the approach
[41]	- Urban intelligence - Urban development indicators - Knowledge-intensive business services	Recommendations from the perspectives of knowledge society and knowledge economy are proposed to improve urban development	Study oriented to city development which may not be relevant for urban planning

frameworks in real cases. In fact, many of the frameworks and/or prototypes were not validated with empirical studies.

Big data processing, analysis and visualization is one of the most relevant topics among the articles. It has been explored in research where city features like responsiveness and resilience are central. Indeed, data generated in a context of collective intelligence or extracted from crowdsourcing platforms is used in the governance of urban complexity. Computational efforts for meaningful information discovery seem to be the limitation to deal with. On the other hand, soft computing methods have been broadly used to address natural language processing. These methods include fuzzy logic, granular computing, graph databases and computing with words strategies. An entire category of articles has covered this topic and the recent research shows mature models and solutions. Mostly, proposed future work specifies the need of evaluation of theoretical approaches in diverse domains in order to generalize their application. Some of further research suggests the employment of combined solutions to cope problems like constrains regarding existent technology or devices. In this sense, experiments considering the wide variety of cities and their own cultural and societal characteristics are required to improve cognition in urban planning in future works. During this review, the researchers found that one of the open issues that stands out between the selected articles is related to the privacy of citizens. Privacy concerns are pointed out whenever citizens data is used in governance solutions. Then, it becomes the major challenge to be addressed and regulated.

5   Conclusions

Cognitive human factors such as perception, retention, retrieving, repetition, comparison, transformation and pattern generation are being modeled in machines to provide them with levels of intelligence. However, when we enhance machines' abilities with the collective intelligence of users, we are embedding cognition in the system. Given this, the active participation of the citizens in the construction and transformation of towns provide the places with degrees of resilience. The cities capability to adapt to certain circumstances and, in this case, offer a specific solution has been studied recently in order to create new opportunities. Then, we have presented a SLR of the state-of-the-art papers. Depending on the publication year, publisher and journal rank, each article was either included or excluded. To verify the relevance of these articles, their 'Abstract' and how related they were to cognitive computing and related concepts were studied. Finally, 42 academic articles have been analyzed. The first articles that talk about cognitive urban planning were published in 2011. Moreover, the largest quantity of articles in the studied topic appeared in 2016. Springer is the publisher with most articles extracted. We have compared and evaluated the content of the articles after classifying them in four main categories. The classification depended on the kind of solution or approach implemented. Furthermore, we identified the advantages of the diverse proposals and the limitations or challenges that have to be addressed in future research.

The methods and frameworks summarized in this SLR paper, show that intelligence may be embedded as a component of future cities. Indeed, the effort for combining machines, humans and communities have promoted research topics where technologies like IoT, Big Data, Semantic Ontologies, Crowdsourcing, Ubiquitous Computing and Web 2.0 are significant. Various disciplines such as urbanism, computer science, sociology, ethics require to work and converge to promote opportunities for innovating in various application areas. Specifically, Social Collective Intelligence opens research challenges and opportunities for scientists in both computer science and social sciences to tackle relevant problems. Novel approaches to benefit policy-makers, local governments and citizens will be based on understanding the ways how technological advances support the progress of society and economy.

References

1. Alonso, J.M., Castiello, C., Mencar, C.: The role of interpretable fuzzy systems in designing cognitive cities. In: Portmann, E., Tabacchi, M.E., Seising, R., Habenstein, A. (eds.) Designing Cognitive Cities. SSDC, vol. 176, pp. 131–152. Springer, Cham (2019). https://doi.org/10.1007/978-3-030-00317-3_6
2. Barcelos, M., Bernardini, F., Barcelos, A., Vaz Silva, G.: City ranking based on financial flux indicator clustering. In: Proceedings of the 18th Annual International Conference on Digital Government Research, pp. 452–460. ACM (2017)
3. Bateson, M.: Systematic reviews to support evidence-based medicine: how to review and apply findings of healthcare research. Postgrad. Med. J. **80**(940), 123–123 (2004)
4. Beel, J., Gipp, B.: Google scholar's ranking algorithm: the impact of citation counts (an empirical study). In: 2009 Third International Conference on Research Challenges in Information Science, pp. 439–446, April 2009
5. Bollacker, K., Díaz-Rodríguez, N., Li, X.: Extending knowledge graphs with subjective influence networks for personalized fashion. In: Portmann, E., Tabacchi, M.E., Seising, R., Habenstein, A. (eds.) Designing Cognitive Cities. SSDC, vol. 176, pp. 203–233. Springer, Cham (2019). https://doi.org/10.1007/978-3-030-00317-3_9
6. Brereton, P., Kitchenham, B.A., Budgen, D., Turner, M., Khalil, M.: Lessons from applying the systematic literature review process within the software engineering domain. J. Syst. Softw. **80**(4), 571–583 (2007). Software Performance
7. Budgen, D., Brereton, P.: Performing systematic literature reviews in software engineering. In: Proceedings of the 28th International Conference on Software Engineering. ICSE 2006, pp. 1051–1052. ACM, New York (2006)
8. Cavoukian, A., Chibba, M.: Cognitive cities, big data and citizen participation: the essentials of privacy and security. In: Portmann, E., Finger, M. (eds.) Towards Cognitive Cities. SSDC, vol. 63, pp. 61–82. Springer, Cham (2016). https://doi.org/10.1007/978-3-319-33798-2_4
9. Certomà, C., Rizzi, F.: Crowdsourcing processes for citizen-driven governance. In: Certomà, C., Dyer, M., Pocatilu, L., Rizzi, F. (eds.) Citizen Empowerment and Innovation in the Data-Rich City. STCE, pp. 57–77. Springer, Cham (2017). https://doi.org/10.1007/978-3-319-47904-0_4
10. Chikhale, M.M., Mansouri, M., Mostashari, A., Efatmaneshnik, M.: Intelligent governance of large-scale engineering systems: a sub-systemic approach. In: 2012 IEEE International Systems Conference SysCon 2012, pp. 1–8 (2012)
11. Cuenca, J., Larrinaga, F., Eciolaza, L., Curry, E.: Towards cognitive cities in the energy domain. In: Portmann, E., Tabacchi, M.E., Seising, R., Habenstein, A. (eds.) Designing Cognitive Cities. SSDC, vol. 176, pp. 155–183. Springer, Cham (2019). https://doi.org/10.1007/978-3-030-00317-3_7
12. D'Onofrio, S., Müller, S.M., Papageorgiou, E.I., Portmann, E.: Fuzzy reasoning in cognitive cities: an exploratory work on fuzzy analogical reasoning using fuzzy cognitive maps. In: 2018 IEEE International Conference on Fuzzy Systems (FUZZ-IEEE), pp. 1–8, July 2018
13. D'Onofrio, S., Wehrle, M., Portmann, E., Myrach, T.: Striving for semantic convergence with fuzzy cognitive maps and graph databases. In: 2017 IEEE International Conference on Fuzzy Systems (FUZZ-IEEE), pp. 1–6, July 2017
14. D'Onofrio, S., Franzelli, S., Portmann, E.: Advancing cognitive cities with the web of things. In: Yager, R.R., Pascual Espada, J. (eds.) New Advances in the Internet of Things. SCI, vol. 715, pp. 75–91. Springer, Cham (2018). https://doi.org/10.1007/978-3-319-58190-3_5

15. D'Onofrio, S., Papageorgiou, E., Portmann, E.: Using fuzzy cognitive maps to arouse learning processes in cities. In: Portmann, E., Tabacchi, M.E., Seising, R., Habenstein, A. (eds.) Designing Cognitive Cities. SSDC, vol. 176, pp. 107–130. Springer, Cham (2019). https://doi.org/10.1007/978-3-030-00317-3_5

16. D'Onofrio, S., Zurlinden, N., Gadient, D., Portmann, E.: Cognitive cities: an application for Nairobi. In: Portmann, E., Finger, M. (eds.) Towards Cognitive Cities. SSDC, vol. 63, pp. 145–164. Springer, Cham (2016). https://doi.org/10.1007/978-3-319-33798-2_8

17. D'Onofrio, S., Zurlinden, N., Kaltenrieder, P., Portmann, E., Myrach, T.: Synchronizing mind maps with fuzzy cognitive maps for decision-finding in cognitive cities. In: Proceedings of the 9th International Conference on Theory and Practice of Electronic Governance. ICEGOV 2015-2016, pp. 363–364. ACM, New York (2016). https://doi.org/10.1145/2910019.2910034

18. Finger, M., Portmann, E.: What are cognitive cities? In: Portmann, E., Finger, M. (eds.) Towards Cognitive Cities. SSDC, vol. 63, pp. 1–11. Springer, Cham (2016). https://doi.org/10.1007/978-3-319-33798-2_1

19. Ghaffarianhoseini, A., et al.: Intelligent or smart cities and buildings: a critical exposition and a way forward. Intell. Build. Int. **10**(2), 122–129 (2018)

20. Hudec, M.: Possibilities for linguistic summaries in cognitive cities. In: Portmann, E., Tabacchi, M.E., Seising, R., Habenstein, A. (eds.) Designing Cognitive Cities. SSDC, vol. 176, pp. 47–84. Springer, Cham (2019). https://doi.org/10.1007/978-3-030-00317-3_3

21. Hurwitz, J., Kaufman, M., Bowles, A.: Cognitive Computing and Big Data Analytics. Wiley, Hoboken (2015)

22. Kaltenrieder, P., Altun, T., D'Onofrio, S., Portmann, E., Myrach, T.: Personal digital assistant 2.0 - a software prototype for cognitive cities. In: 2016 IEEE International Conference on Fuzzy Systems (FUZZ-IEEE), pp. 1531–1538, July 2016

23. Kaltenrieder, P., Portmann, E., D'onofrio, S.: Enhancing multidirectional communication for cognitive cities. In: 2015 Second International Conference on eDemocracy eGovernment (ICEDEG), pp. 38–43, April 2015

24. Kaltenrieder, P., Portmann, E., Myrach, T.: Fuzzy knowledge representation in cognitive cities. In: 2015 IEEE International Conference on Fuzzy Systems (FUZZ-IEEE), pp. 1–8, August 2015

25. Kaltenrieder, P., Papageorgiou, E., Portmann, E.: Digital personal assistant for cognitive cities: a paper prototype. In: Portmann, E., Finger, M. (eds.) Towards Cognitive Cities. SSDC, vol. 63, pp. 101–121. Springer, Cham (2016). https://doi.org/10.1007/978-3-319-33798-2_6

26. Kaltenrieder, P., Parra, J., Krebs, T., Zurlinden, N., Portmann, E., Myrach, T.: A dynamic route planning prototype for cognitive cities. In: Portmann, E., Tabacchi, M.E., Seising, R., Habenstein, A. (eds.) Designing Cognitive Cities. SSDC, vol. 176, pp. 235–257. Springer, Cham (2019). https://doi.org/10.1007/978-3-030-00317-3_10

27. Kaltenrieder, P., Portmann, E., D'Onofrio, S., Finger, M.: Applying the fuzzy analytical hierarchy process in cognitive cities. In: Proceedings of the 8th International Conference on Theory and Practice of Electronic Governance. ICEGOV 2014, pp. 259–262. ACM, New York (2014)

28. Klein, B., Koenig, R., Schmitt, G.: Managing urban resilience. Informatik-Spektrum **40**(1), 35–45 (2017). https://doi.org/10.1007/s00287-016-1005-2

29. Kosko, B.: Fuzzy cognitive maps. Int. J. Man-Mach. Stud. **24**(1), 65–75 (1986)

30. Legény, J., Morgenstein, P., Spacek, R.: Stratigraphy of the smart city concept. ARCHITEKTURA & URBANIZMUS **50**(1–2), 5–17 (2016)

31. Lima, P.C.R., Barcellos, R., Bernardini, F., Viterbo, J.: Using geocoding and topic extraction to make sense of comments on social network pages of local government agencies. In: Parycek, P., et al. (eds.) EGOV 2018. LNCS, vol. 11020, pp. 263–274. Springer, Cham (2018). https://doi.org/10.1007/978-3-319-98690-6_22

32. Long, Y., Liu, L.: How green are the streets? An analysis for central areas of chinese cities using tencent street view. PLoS One **12**(2), e0171110 (2017)

33. Mansouri, M., Karaca, N.I.: Innovative urban governance: a game oriented approach to influencing energy behavior. In: Portmann, E., Finger, M. (eds.) Towards Cognitive Cities. SSDC, vol. 63, pp. 165–195. Springer, Cham (2016). https://doi.org/10.1007/978-3-319-33798-2_9

34. Mansouri, M., Khansari, N.: A conceptual model for intelligent urban governance: influencing energy behaviour in cognitive cities. In: Portmann, E., Tabacchi, M.E., Seising, R., Habenstein, A. (eds.) Designing Cognitive Cities. SSDC, vol. 176, pp. 185–202. Springer, Cham (2019). https://doi.org/10.1007/978-3-030-00317-3_8

35. Miorandi, D., Maltese, V., Rovatsos, M., Nijholt, A., Stewart, J. (eds.): Social Collective Intelligence. Combining the Powers of Humans and Machines to Build a Smarter Society. CSS. Springer, Cham (2014). https://doi.org/10.1007/978-3-319-08681-1

36. Mohammadi, M., Al-Fuqaha, A.: Enabling cognitive smart cities using big data and machine learning: approaches and challenges. IEEE Commun. Mag. **56**(2), 94–101 (2018)

37. Morabito, V.: Big data and analytics for government innovation. In: Morabito, V. (ed.) Big Data and Analytics, pp. 23–45. Springer, Cham (2015). https://doi.org/10.1007/978-3-319-10665-6_2

38. Mostashari, A., Arnold, F., Maurer, M., Wade, J.: Citizens as sensors: the cognitive city paradigm. In: 2011 8th International Conference Expo on Emerging Technologies for a Smarter World, pp. 1–5 (2011)

39. Mostashari, A., Arnold, F., Mansouri, M., Finger, M.: Cognitive cities and intelligent urban governance. Netw. Ind. Q. **13**(3), 4–7 (2011)

40. Moyser, R., Uffer, S.: From smart to cognitive: a roadmap for the adoption of technology in cities. In: Portmann, E., Finger, M. (eds.) Towards Cognitive Cities. SSDC, vol. 63, pp. 13–35. Springer, Cham (2016). https://doi.org/10.1007/978-3-319-33798-2_2

41. Méndez, R., Moral, S.S.: Spanish cities in the knowledge economy: theoretical debates and empirical evidence. Eur. Urban Reg. Stud. **18**(2), 136–155 (2011)

42. Novak, M.: Cognitive cities: intelligence, environment and space. In: Droege, P. (ed.) Intelligent Environments, pp. 386–420. North-Holland, Amsterdam (1997)

43. Peprah, C., Amponsah, O., Oduro, C.: A system view of smart mobility and its implications for ghanaian cities. Sustain. Cities Soc. **44**, 739–747 (2019)

44. Perticone, V., Tabacchi, M.E.: Towards the improvement of citizen communication through computational intelligence. In: Portmann, E., Finger, M. (eds.) Towards Cognitive Cities. SSDC, vol. 63, pp. 83–100. Springer, Cham (2016). https://doi.org/10.1007/978-3-319-33798-2_5

45. Portmann, E., Finger, M. (eds.): Towards Cognitive Cities: Advances in Cognitive Computing and its Application to the Governance of Large Urban Systems. SSDC, vol. 63. Springer, Cham (2016). https://doi.org/10.1007/978-3-319-33798-2

46. Portmann, E., Kaltenrieder, P., Zurlinden, N.: Applying fuzzy ontologies to implement the social semantic web. SIGWEB Newsl., 4:1–4:12 (2014)

47. Razaghi, M., Finger, M.: Smart governance for smart cities. Proc. IEEE **106**(4), 680–689 (2018)
48. Stock, W.G.: Informational cities: analysis and construction of cities in the knowledge society. J. Am. Soc. Inf. Sci. Technol. **62**(5), 963–986 (2011)
49. Surowiecki, J.: The Wisdom of Crowds. Anchor, New York (2005)
50. Portmann, E., Tabacchi, M.E., Seising, R., Habenstein, A. (eds.): Designing Cognitive Cities. SSDC, vol. 176, pp. 3–27. Springer, Cham (2019). https://doi.org/10.1007/978-3-030-00317-3
51. Tenney, M., Sieber, R.: Data-driven participation: algorithms, cities, citizens, and corporate control. Urban Plan. **1**(2), 101–113 (2016)
52. Terán, L., Kaskina, A., Meier, A.: Maturity model for cognitive cities. In: Portmann, E., Finger, M. (eds.) Towards Cognitive Cities. SSDC, vol. 63, pp. 37–59. Springer, Cham (2016). https://doi.org/10.1007/978-3-319-33798-2_3
53. Wilke, G., Portmann, E.: Granular computing as a basis of human-data interaction: a cognitive cities use case. Granul. Comput. **1**(3), 181–197 (2016). https://doi.org/10.1007/s41066-016-0015-4
54. Williamson, B.: Computing brains: learning algorithms and neurocomputation in the smart city. Inf. Commun. Soc. **20**(1), 81–99 (2017)
55. Zhang, J., et al.: Visual analysis of public utility service problems in a metropolis. IEEE Trans. Visual Comput. Graphics **20**(12), 1843–1852 (2014)

Sensor Systems and Software

Analysis of Building Management Systems to Ensure Optimal Working Environment

Jozef Jandačka[1], Peter Hrabovský[2(✉)], Zuzana Kolková[2], and Zuzana Florková[2]

[1] University of Žilina, Univerzitná 8215/1, 010 26 Žilina, Slovakia
[2] Research Centre, University of Žilina, Univerzitná 8215/1, 010 26 Žilina, Slovakia
peter.hrabovsky@rc.uniza.sk

Abstract. The design of an intelligent building management system is a fundamental problem in designing new modern buildings. The energy management structure is a set of main input devices and relationships between them. The paper presents the issue of thermal comfort conditions with regard to intelligent buildings. Thermal comfort describes the human satisfactory perception of the thermal environment. It refers to a number of conditions in which the majority of people feel comfortable. Thermal comfort is dependent on multiple factors such as indoor environmental conditions, user behavior and properties of building materials. For inclusion in the design process this data must first be categorized in a standardized manner. We present some aspects related with the impact of the new digital, communication and facilities technology development in the implementation of building management systems. This systems are used for monitoring, controlling and ensuring the control, comfort and efficiency in use of intelligent buildings. The integration becomes possible due to the applications of advanced IT technologies.

Keywords: Intelligent · Management · System · Building

1 Introduction

Although the successful use of advanced technologies, including information technologies, is the main feature of intelligent buildings, the implementation of technologies should not be the sole objective of intelligent buildings. Performance is definitely a key objective of intelligent buildings, although performance can be interpreted very differently as discussed above. As regards the hardware facilities, intelligent buildings cannot be separated from the architecture design, building façades and materials, which are among the essential elements of intelligent buildings note that the first paragraph of a section or subsection is not indented.

Intelligent architecture refers to build forms whose integrated systems are capable of anticipating and responding to phenomena, whether internal or external, that affect the performance of the building and its occupants. Intelligent architecture relates to three distinct areas of concern: intelligent design, appropriate use of intelligent technology, intelligent use and maintenance of buildings.

© ICST Institute for Computer Sciences, Social Informatics and Telecommunications Engineering 2020
Published by Springer Nature Switzerland AG 2020. All Rights Reserved
H. Santos et al. (Eds.): SmartCity 360 2019, LNICST 323, pp. 273–284, 2020.
https://doi.org/10.1007/978-3-030-51005-3_23

Intelligent design requires that the building design responds to humanistic, cultural and contextual issues; that it exhibits simultaneous concern for economic, political and global issues; and that it produces an artificial enclosure which exists in harmony with nature. Existing in harmony with nature includes responding to the physical laws of nature and the proper use of natural resources.

Appropriate use of intelligent technology. The mere availability of a large variety of smart materials and intelligent technologies often results in their use in inappropriate situations. Integrating intelligent technologies with an intelligent built form that responds to the inherent cultural preferences of the occupants is a central theme in intelligent architecture. As an example, in areas where people place a high premium on operable windows for conservation of electricity, the most appropriate and efficient air- conditioning strategy for a building may be the use of thermal mass and night- time free cooling instead of a high-tech air-conditioning system. In other cases, the use of carefully selected electric lighting and environmental control strategies may be more appropriate.

Intelligent use and maintenance of buildings. Truly intelligent architecture incorporates intelligent facility management processes. For a design to be intelligent it must take into consideration the life cycle of a building and its various systems and components. Although an intelligent building may be complex, it should be fundamentally simple to operate, be energy and resource efficient, and easy to maintain, upgrade, modify and recycle [1–3].

2 Energy Efficiency and Energy Management

The demand for electrical energy has increased tremendously over the last 25 years; its importance is such that it is now a vital component of any nation's economic progress. Increase in population has increased the energy requirements, coupled with the industrialization & socio-economic responsibilities; the energy supply has not kept pace with the demand. This has led to a bleak energy scenario whereby power generation and utilization from alternate energy sources has become very much a necessity.

The impact of rising energy cost has a disastrous impact on the day-today activities of industrial and domestic consumers wherein the prices of commodities, products and even essential services tend to cost more. One option is to improve the working efficiency of the process and systems. This will ensure the reduction in the product cost in addition to efficient energy management. The other option is the use of energy derived from non-conventional energy sources i.e.; ensure a balance between conventional and nonconventional energy sources in the process [4].

Energy management embodies engineering, design, applications, utilization, and to some extent the operation and maintenance of electric power systems to provide the optimal use of electrical energy [5]. The most important step in the energy management process is the identification and analysis of energy conservation opportunities, thus making it a technical and management function, the focus being to monitor, record, analyze, critically examine, alter and control energy flows through systems so that energy is utilized with maximum efficiency [1]. Every industrial facility in a particular location is unique in itself; hence a systematic approach is extremely necessary for reducing the power consumption, without adversely affecting the productivity, quality of work and working conditions [6, 13].

Building management systems is specialized software application (Sauter-Reliance) solution that enables regular energy data gathering and analysis, used as a tool for continuous energy management. The main advantage of building management application is the possibility of data collection, processing, maintenance, analysis and display on a continuous basis. A modern management system is integrated into an organization's systems for online process monitoring and control. This system provides sensitive information to manage energy use in all aspects and is therefore an important element of an energy efficiency [6–8].

3   The Building Management Systems of the Research Centre

Our building have a low-energy construction (with a heat energy consumption of less than 15 kWh/(m^2.year)) with a higher equipment level of the building (intelligent building) in terms of diversity of sources of heat, cold and energy. The main objective is to understand the functioning of all intelligent building systems and ensure optimal use of all energy sources.

The Research Centre building has intelligent control systems for lighting, exterior blinds, thermal control and air conditioning. And as separate subsystems connected similarly as the measurement of power consumption. For research activities it is equipped with a photovoltaic system on the roof - that is why it also includes a cable route to the roof. Building's Ethernet is connected by a multi-fiber cable in the date center in the basement (Fig. 1).

Fig. 1. Photovoltaic system on of the building. Last panel tracks the Sun

The whole building is functionally divided into three parts - on five floors. The first underground floor disposes of a building, technical and storage premises. At the entrance through the foyer and in the lobby there is a porter's lodge and facilities for its staff and in the hallway of the lounge. On the second to fifth floor, other research center premises.

3.1 Measurement and Regulation

The measurement and regulation systems are divided into two parts measurement and regulation of the device in technical room and measurement and regulation in rooms. Measurement and regulation in the technical room in order to control the production of heat, hot water and water for heating. It is used for radiator, floor, ceiling heating and in the summer also ceiling cooling. The source of heat and cold is preferably a group of heat pumps if the geo-drills are not sufficient, then a gas boiler and a chiller on the roof.

On the floors there is a special regulation - regulation of heat in the building by means of controlled floor heating distributors or ceiling panels with its own autonomous systems. It is also heated and cooled by air conditioning, and intelligent measurement and control system is also mounted for lighting and external blinds. And as separate subsystems connected similarly as measuring the consumption of electric power over Ethernet, with the possibility of software management on control computer in network protocol – building automation and control network.

3.2 Heating and Cooling Systems

To ensure the heat demand, the following heat sources are installed: condensation boiler, two ground-to-water heat pumps, a gas heat pump with combined air-to-water and ground-to-water operation, and a solar system for heating support, hot water and heat storage into the earth tank. For heat storage, a heat storage vessel is installed independently, in which heat is stored from heat sources - heat pumps and a solar system. The following cold sources are installed to ensure the need for cold: two ground-water heat pumps, a gas heat pump with combined air-water and ground-water operation. For cold storage, a cold storage vessel is installed independently, in which cold is stored from cold sources geo-bores and heat pumps (Fig. 2).

Fig. 2. Sources consist of heat pump for transformation heat and cold from earth and air. Left is combined heat pump of systems air-water and earth-water, middle and right is heat pump of system earth-water

The whole heating system is divided into six separate branches connected to individual pump groups: hot water heating, radiators, underfloor heating, ceiling cooling and fan coils. Each branch is controlled by equithermal control using an algorithm to calculate operating temperatures via the measurement and regulation system and a three-way valve to maintain a stable branch temperature. Each branch has a set maximum and minimum operating temperature according to the nature of the heat exchange system used.

The first prerequisite for switching the system to heating mode is to set the three-way valves to the transfer position of the heat transfer medium. This ensures that the entire system will only heat.

Solar system - when the bivalent hot water tank is heated, the three-way valve switches and the heat storage tank is heated. In case of excess heat in the solar system, the three-way valve is switched and the heat is stored in the ground tank (Fig. 3).

Fig. 3. Distributor and collector of heat and cold to heat exchanger systems of building.

When heating with a gas boiler, which is connected to the system via a hydraulic switch to the manifolds, if the heat pumps are not in operation, the solar system does not heat the storage tank, the heat transfer medium goes directly to the manifolds for hot water. The return heating water is returned through an accumulation tank in which the excess heat from the gas boiler is stored. If the temperature from the storage tank is sufficient for heating, the gas boiler is switched off if not the heat transfer medium is heated to the desired temperature. Any heat source is connected to the duct in a storage vessel and can be used for heating.

The first prerequisite for switching the system to cooling mode by automatically switching the three-way valves to the heat transfer medium passage position. This ensures that the entire system will only cool, except for the heating of the hot water, which can still be heated.

It will preferably be cooled by a passive cooling system, i.e. by cooling only from boreholes by adjusting the three-way valve. These heat transfer fluid flows will be driven by the pump groups through the exchanger. If passive cooling is not sufficient by adjusting the three-way valve, the heat pump duct will open and these will accumulate the cold of the cold storage tank (Fig. 4).

Fig. 4. Panels of solar system on the roof of building.

The hot water is heated in the bivalent hot water tank using hot primary water from the manifold so that if necessary, the hot water circulation pump blows hot water into the hot water tank. The tank is also charged from solar heating, which is automatic and independent.

If the hot water tank temperature drops below 50 °C, the circulation pump will be started and will continue to run until the hot water tank temperature reaches 55 °C. For homogeneity of hot water in the bivalent tank, a three-way regulating valve is opened a valve that returns a portion of the water from the hot water outlet to the return from the circulation circuit according to the hot water outlet reference temperature. The monitoring of the critical temperature of the bivalent storage tank is used for emergency discharge of the hot water storage tank in case of overheating (from the solar system in summer) above 75 °C. The hot water is then discharged into the drain by the solenoid valve at its outlet and the tank is cooled to 75 °C - the maximum operating charging temperature of the tank. Charging another heat storage tank from a solar unit that is connected in parallel from its output is through its pump. Thus, any excess heat from the bivalent storage tank is preferably stored therein in the event of an excess of thermal energy in the solar system, the heat is stored in the ground storage tank.

A separate autonomous measurement and regulation system is used to control the heat on the floors of the building. In addition to the function of heat and cooling (one type of its installation is distributed over the floor), in scientific experiments measurement and regulation on floors measure the consumption of single-phase electrical circuits - selected circuits of 230 V sockets, but there can also be light circuits. It is a ratio measurement that is realized by measuring transformers up to 63 A. These are simply mounted on a rail by snapping the measuring transformer circuit and around the phase conductor of the circuit under test, while this phase is also connected through the measuring module - three-circuit modules are installed by network analyzers.

The measurement can also be done in three phases on the entire sub circuit - other connection. In order to make this possible, sub-distributors have been designed for the size of the sub-distribution boards in the framework of the heavy current, where on rails a width of 50 cm is possible to install this configuration of the control information system. The connection is thus preferably close to the potential el. The measuring transformers concept enables their variable connection and disconnection either above the part of the secondary distribution lines or in a separate second switchboard for measurement and regulation, fitted next to the secondary switchboard and connected by bushings.

Installation of electrical measuring system energy is exclusively in the secondary switchboards on the floors of the building. They work autonomously on their own Ethernet connected network – building automation and control network protocol. The other polarized pair of wires is used for supplying (26 V) between the rails - through the connection modules or even in the floor space outside them. It is applied in the installation of heat and cooling - thermostats, person detectors, window contacts. Blinds and ventilation lighting - hygrometers, CO_2 sensors, luxmeters, person detectors. The installations are connected to the Ethernet within the building via communication control modules to the internet protocol - building automation and control network as transmission network.

In this way, the installations are connected within the storey and the whole building, but also between the groups of e.g. heat and cooling and electrical measurements. The program components then enable visualization, reports, statistics and control, according to access rights and the scope of installed correct and user program resources.

The regulator switches the valve circuit of the floor or ceiling wiring, as required by the thermostat. If it is lower than the equithermally set water in the heating system, the control will switch off the water supply to the zone's heating circuit. If a higher temperature is required than is sent in the form of equithermal water in the distribution, the control will switch on the supply until the temperature rise reaches the setpoint in the heating zone. The system works similarly in cooling in the summer, with the difference that the ceiling panel system is preferably used for cooling. In order for the regulation to function up to plus values, the equithermal water must be slightly elevated from the against the equilibrium curve. Heating and cooling blocks the opening of windows, or automatically the absence of people - a centrally adjustable energy saving program. On occupancy sensors, it is possible to press the upper part of the sensor to switch the presence signal to permanent, regardless of its passive infrared detector for a maximum of 4 h (then switches itself to the normal state of guarding the space). The system also allows lighting control - luxmeter controllers and dimming or switch controllers, blinds, meteo controllers as well as air controllers - controllers - humidity sensors, CO_2 (input 0–10 V, contacts) flap control output 0 (1) −10 V, contacts. Everything can be managed by an extension application in the local area network. Local area networks are interconnected into one unit.

The controller is integrated into the M&C in the technical room and proportionally controls the valve head with diameter nominal 15 kvs = 2.5 m/s^2, which is located under the ceiling on the pipe in technical room on the machine diagram room at the outlet of the common branch "cooling ceilings" - "stair" (all cooling ceilings on the floors of the stairs). The control valve is at the outlet and the mechanical return valve (which adjusts the flow rate in the staircase cooling ceiling circuit. Cooled ceilings in the staircase are connected from a pipeline which is led vertically upwards in the central pillar of the staircase. The valve is controlled by a separate new reference thermometer and hygrometer on the 1st floor (to be placed on the non-dazzling side of the pillar). If the temperature rises above 21 °C in the summer, the ceilings will start to cool to their maximum cooling capacity in this space, unless condensation occurs - according to the dew point that is still calculated, as in room configurations in rooms in the ceiling cooling section. The temperature of the cold water is the same as in the entire cooling of the ceiling in the building. From, the cold water outlet - ceiling cooling, The valve can also be operated independently according to requirements of inputs: thermometer (Nickel 1000), outputs: 0–10 V hygrometer: 0–10 V control head and valve actuator head according to implementer 0–10 V proportional, 24 V supply of valve head. Input 2 × 0–10 V and output 1 × 0–10 V in measurement and regulation configuration (Fig. 5).

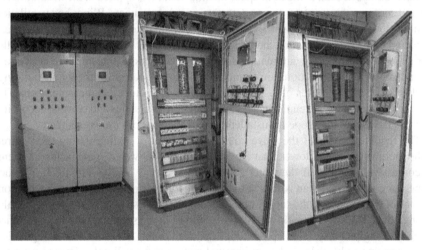

Fig. 5. Base station controlling of heating, cooling and ventilation systems.

3.3 Blinds and Lighting

These installations from distribution modules in separate switchboards are divided on floors according to the suitability of the place (for air-conditioning, blinds - actuators and their modules) or the suitability of the control points (on the wall in the box hl = 40 mm - for lux meters, hygrometers and passive infrared sensors) at a height of 120–140 cm as light switches. The connection between them and the switchboards of the installation is a four-wire cable. The routes descend from separated or safety low voltage horizontal installation routes in a double ceiling (space height approx. 50–60 cm). Connection of installation switchboards as well as local area network connections is from the closest installation point.

Lighting is chosen according to light comfort, which is continuously variable through dimmers. Dimmable elements – light-emitting diode lights are required as well as central adjustment and lighting scene programs (alternative to dimmable controls that are designed - the target is digital addressable lightning interface control of dedicated lights) as well as individual lighting. Ventilation serves as additional heating or cooling, it regulates the air quality in the building (humidity and CO_2). For scientific purposes, air flow is also measured by the measurement and regulation system. Channels. Blinds can be controlled from different places and in groups, they automatically unfold in glare, roll in windy weather, and follow the meteorology module, which is on each floor.

4 Thermal Comfort

Human thermal comfort is an important issue in the built environment. Environments either too cold or too hot can be dangerous to human life. Less satisfactory environments may lead to discomfort, resulting in a loss of productivity. When the environment is cold, the reduction of the flow of blood to the skin results in a low skin temperature. The spontaneous activity, like shivering, will occur to increase the production of heat energy. In a hot environment, large amount of heat has to be dissipated from the human body due to metabolism and physical activities. Then, blood flow to the skin is increasing and sweat is secreted from the sweat glands. When sweat evaporates, latent heat is absorbed and a thermal equilibrium can be achieved [9, 12].

Space temperature uniformity, asymmetry of the radiation temperature, and turbulence intensity of the flow air affect thermal comfort. People are capable of detecting heat and they can feel changes in temperature globally on the entire surface of the body but also locally on body parts. It has been shown that humans can acclimate to ambient temperature physiologically and psychologically. It is therefore important to address the issues of thermal comfort in the interiors (buildings) and to experimentally determine a suitable way of creating the optimal conditions of the environment.

The goal is to ensure a sense of satisfaction from the environment and also to increase work performance and a sense of comfort. We use the Dantec ComfortSense system to investigate operating conditions comply with International Standards EN 13182, ISO 7726, 7730, ASHRAE standard 113 and ASHRAE standard 55 [10, 11].

4.1 Ashrae Standard 55

ASHRAE Standard 55 (Thermal Environmental Conditions for Human Occupancy) is a standard that provides minimum requirements for acceptable thermal indoor environments. It establishes the ranges of indoor environmental conditions that are acceptable to achieve thermal comfort for occupants. Percent dissatisfied (PD) represent percentage of people predicted to be dissatisfied due to local discomfort. Predicted mean vote (PMV) is an index that predicts the mean value of the votes of a large group of persons on the seven point thermal sensation scale.

Predicted percentage of dissatisfied (PPD) is an index that establishes a quantitative prediction of the percentage of thermally dissatisfied people determined from PMV [8, 10].

Index PPD is expressed according to the relation:

$$PPD = 100 - 95.e^{-(0,03353.PMV^4 + 0,2179.PMV^2)} \tag{1}$$

PMV index predicts the mean comfort response of a larger group of people.

5 Measurement in the Building with BMS

The measurement was carried out in the Research Centre of the University of Žilina in July. The room is located on the first floor on the southwest side. The room is located in the middle of the building. The room has a rectangular floor plan with dimensions of 3.40 × 5.70 × 3.00 m.

All intelligent control systems are installed in the room. There is a room sensor - movement of workers in the room, CO_2 sensor, humidity sensor, fire sensor, open window sensor, temperature sensor and lighting sensor. The windows are fitted with external blinds with the function of shading according to the intensity of solar radiation.

Heating is provided by underfloor heating. Cooling is provided by an acoustic cooling ceiling and a central ventilation system with support for heating and cooling. The influence of intelligent control system on ensuring optimal operating conditions in space - thermal comfort has been studied. Three basic types of cooling system settings have been investigated. Setting the intelligent control system for the cooling section to 17 °C (system: −5 °C), 22 °C (home position), 27 °C (system: +5 °C).

The positions of the measuring probes are located in the living areas of the rooms. These are known places of residence of workers. These places are defined as workstations or seating positions depending on the function of the space. The measurement takes place in the center of the room or 1 m from the wall inwards from the center of the largest window. Measurements shall be made at locations where the extremely high values of thermal parameters are estimated or observed. The operating temperature is measured or calculated at 0.6 m for seated persons and 1.1 m for standing persons.

The following figure shows graphical measurement results for various settings of the building measurement and control systems (Fig. 6).

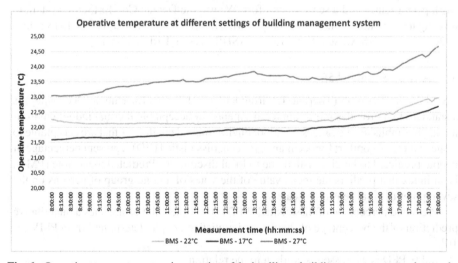

Fig. 6. Operative temperature at various setting of the intelligent building management and control system

The main parameters that were measured are the outdoor temperature, the operating temperature in the room and the setting of the intelligent control system for the cooling sections in the summer.

PPD parameters were also evaluated in the evaluation of the impact of the working environment on the thermal comfort of workers. These parameters determine the mean warmth of a group of people and the predicted percentage of dissatisfaction with the operating conditions. They are designed for each measurement day with respect to the setting of the intelligent control system (Fig. 7).

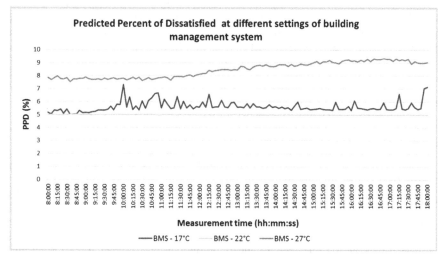

Fig. 7. PPD parameters and different settings of building management system

6   Conclusion

Our aim is to create conditions for the implementation of applied research in the field of low-energy construction and technology for the construction of low-energy buildings, high-efficiency energy sources using renewable energy sources and fossil fuels, the optimal control, optimal control of energy consumption in buildings and premises suitable choice of hot and cold sources, ensuring optimum energy consumption, safety and comfort in intelligent passive buildings, reducing the emission load environment. Our main priority is to establish a functioning, modern system and achieving economic, environmental and proper functioning of several systems.

Three different setting states have been evaluated. The position of the blinds was also evaluated in down position. The intelligent control system can adjust the blinds in seven other positions, which will be subject to further investigation. Thermal comfort is ensured in the range of optimal values of operative temperature, including the values of other microclimatic variables. The optimum temperature is the range of temperatures that the employer should strive to maintain at his workplace all year round. The permissible temperature is a limit value that the workplace temperature should not exceed even if the employer is unable to maintain optimal temperatures. The optimum operating temperature range in the office space is set at 23–27 °C. This condition was not exceeded in any of the room settings examined.

The function of the correct setting of the intelligent control system has been confirmed in every state under investigation when connected on. In all cases, the PPD parameters are comfortable - neutral. The function of the correct setting of the intelligent control system has been confirmed in every state under investigation for connecting on.

Acknowledgements. "This work was supported under the project of Operational Programme Research and Innovation: Research and development activities of the University of Zilina in the Industry of 21st century in the field of materials and nanotechnologies, No. 313011T426. The project is co-funding by European Regional Development Fund."

References

1. Shengwei, W.: Intelligent Building and Building Automation, p. 260. Spon Press. Taylor & Francis e-Library, London (2010). ISBN 0-203-89081-7
2. Garlík, B: Inteligentní budovy. BEN – technická literature, vydaní 1. české, p. 350 (2012). ISBN 978-80-7300-440-8
3. Wang, Sh.: Intelligent Buildings and Buildings Automation, 1 edn., p. 264 Routledge, Abingdon (2009). ISBN-13: 978-0415475716
4. Kini, P.G., Bansal, R.C.: Energy Management Systems, p. 288. Intech. Rijeka (2011). ISBN 978-953-307-579-2
5. Clements-Croome, D.: Intelligent Buildings: An Introduction, 1st edn, p. 232. Routledge, Abingdon (2013). ISBN-13: 978-0415531139
6. Panke, R.A.: Energy Management Systems and Direct Digital Control, p, 202. The Fairmont Press, Lilburn (2001). ISBN 0-88173-395-4
7. http://vetrani.tzb-info.cz/vnitrni-prostredi/404-tepelna-pohoda-a-nepohoda
8. http://vetrani.tzb-info.cz/vnitrni-prostredi/2650-vnitrni-prostredi-budov-a-tepelna-pohoda-cloveka
9. STN 73 0540-3:2012: Tepelná ochrana budov. Tepelnotechnické vlast-nosti stavebných konštrukcií a budov. Časť 3: Vlastnosti prostredia a stavebných výrobkov (2012)
10. http://shop.iccsafe.org/media/wysiwyg/material/8950P219-sample.pdf
11. https://www.researchgate.net/figure/282479241_fig1_Fig-1-Thermal-sensation-scale-aMCI-McIntyre-Index-b-ASH-ASHRAE-thermal
12. Cai, K.Y.: Intelligent Building Systems, p. 190. Beijing University of Aeronautics Beijing, China. Springer Science + Business Media, LLC (1999). ISBN 978-1-4613-7280-6
13. Holubčík, M., et al.: Mathematic model for prediction of heat output of small boiler depending on various aspects. In: AIP Conference Proceedings, vol. 2118, 27 June 2019 (2019). Article no. 030015

Context-Based Analysis of Urban Air Quality Using an Opportunistic Mobile Sensor Network

Xuening Qin[1,3]($\boxtimes$), Ljiljana Platisa[1,3], Tien Huu Do[2,3],
Evaggelia Tsiligianni[2,3], Jelle Hofman[4], Valerio Panzica La Manna[4],
Nikos Deligiannis[2,3], and Wilfried Philips[1,3]

[1] imec-TELIN-IPI, Department of Telecommunications and Information Processing,
Ghent University, Sint-Pietersnieuwstraat 25, 9000 Ghent, Belgium
Xuening.Qin@ugent.be
[2] imec-ETRO, Department of Electronics and Informatics, Vrije Universiteit Brussel,
Pleinlaan 2, 1050 Brussels, Belgium
[3] imec, Kapeldreef 75, 3001 Leuven, Belgium
[4] Holst Center, imec, High Tech Campus 31, 5656 AE Eindhoven, The Netherlands

Abstract. Air pollution is becoming an important environmental issue and attracting increasing public attention. In urban environments, air pollution changes very dynamically both with time and space and is affected by a large variety of factors such as road type, urban architecture, land use and variety of emission sources. In order to better understand the complexity of urban air pollution, hyperlocal air pollution monitoring is necessary, but the existing regulatory monitoring networks are typically sparse due to the high costs to cover a full city area at the necessary spatial granularity. In this paper, we use the city of Antwerp in Belgium as a pilot to analyze the temporal and spatial distribution of four atmospheric pollutants (NO_2, PM_1, $PM_{2.5}$ and PM_{10}) at street level by using mobile air pollution monitoring. In particular, we explore how the atmospheric pollutant concentration is affected by different context factors (e.g., road type, land use, source proximity). Our results demonstrate that these factors have an impact on the concentration distribution of the considered pollutants. For example, higher atmospheric NO_2 concentrations are observed on primary roads, compared to secondary roads, and some source locations such as traffic lights have shown to be hot spots of atmospheric NO_2 accumulation. These findings can be useful in order to formulate future local air quality measures and further improve current air quality models based on the observed impact of the considered context factors.

Keywords: Air pollution monitoring · Smart city · Internet of Things

1 Introduction

With industrial prosperity, urban development and growing traffic, the air pollution caused by the combustion of fossil fuels such as coal, oil and natural gas

© ICST Institute for Computer Sciences, Social Informatics and Telecommunications Engineering 2020
Published by Springer Nature Switzerland AG 2020. All Rights Reserved
H. Santos et al. (Eds.): SmartCity 360 2019, LNICST 323, pp. 285–300, 2020.
https://doi.org/10.1007/978-3-030-51005-3_24

has gradually attracted worldwide attention due to its great threat to human health and to the natural environment. On one hand, atmospheric pollutants have a significant negative impact on human health, leading to cardiovascular diseases, lung cancer and thus reducing life expectancy. On the other hand, air pollution is responsible for many environmental problems, such as eutrophication and acidification of ecosystems.

The European Environment Agency (EEA) has listed seven types of atmospheric pollutants that people may be exposed to: particulate matter (PM), ozone (O_3), nitrogen dioxide (NO_2), sulfur dioxide (SO_2), carbon monoxide (CO), heavy metals, as well as benzene and benzopyrene [3]. In Europe, the most problematic pollutants in terms of harm to human health are particulate matter (PM), nitrogen dioxide (NO_2) and ground-level ozone (O_3) [1]. In an urban environment, particularly at street level, these pollutants are directly or indirectly related to the process of burning fossil fuels such as road transport, electricity generation, industry and households [2].

Unfortunately, many European citizens live in places with serious air pollution. Air pollution monitoring is imperative to provide the government accurate data to assess air quality and the influence of counter measures such as low emission zones. It also provides the public with detailed and accurate air pollution information. This can help them plan some activities (e.g., location and time of sports activities). Nowadays, air pollution is measured by regulatory networks of static monitoring stations. Tian et al. [20] investigated the relationships between air pollution and various factors in the urban landscape including socioeconomic, urban form, and morphological characteristics based on hourly data at 35 monitoring stations in Beijing.

Although the static measuring stations are highly reliable and able to accurately measure various pollutants, the network of these stations is not suitable for street-level air pollution monitoring since the pollutants, especially traffic-related, can show high spatial and temporal variability within a small neighborhood. Their spatial resolution is typically sparse due to the high installation and maintenance costs (1–10 km [11]). For example, there are currently only 108 static measuring stations in Belgium, a country with an area of 30,688 square kilometers and a population of more than 11.4 million inhabitants [12]. Therefore, the static measuring stations may not always accurately characterize the high spatio-temporal variation in atmospheric pollutant concentration at street level and may thus not be representative for the whole city.

Meanwhile, advances in sensor technology and the emergence of portable and lower-cost sensing devices give rise to new opportunities for mobile air pollution monitoring. There have been many studies on the feasibility of mobile monitoring to measure air pollution at the high spatial and temporal resolution [23]. SM et al. [19] developed a smart personal air quality monitoring system (SPAMS) for urban air quality monitoring and personal exposure assessment. The monitoring campaign was designed to assess both pedestrian and public transport passenger exposure in Chennai city, India. The pedestrian exposure monitoring was carried out at three locations for 10 days, whereas personal exposure monitoring while travelling in bus was carried out at selected routes over a period of three months. In order to achieve fine-grained and realtime air pollution monitoring, Kaivonen et al. [10] deploy wireless sensors on public buses running on two selected routes to complement the coverage of stationary sensors in the city center of Uppsala, Sweden. McKercher et al. [14] assess the capability of low-cost mobile monitors to acquire useful data in a city without a monitoring network in place based on 30 days of data resulted from a bicycle platform along a 13.4 km fixed concentric route in Lubbock, Texas. Van den Bossch et al. [5] explored the potential of opportunistic mobile monitoring to map exposure to air pollution in an urban environment at a high spatial resolution. This was based on a total of 393 h of measurements collected by city wardens in Antwerp, Belgium. Hofman et al. [8] evaluated personal exposure to ultrafine particle (UFP), black carbon (BC) and heavy metals while cycling near Antwerp, Belgium. The mobile monitoring was performed along two commuting routes for about two months.

However, these studies are often limited in spatial and/or temporal coverage. This is because they usually choose certain locations and time periods to carry out the monitoring campaigns. For example, the studies in [10] and [14] choose to use fixed routes to move carries (buses and bicycles). The fixed and short routes obviously can not prove the impact of various context factors on atmospheric pollutant concentration. Besides, the duration of monitoring campaigns in [19], [14] and [5] is very short, ranging from ten days to several months, which ignores the effects of climate and seasonality on atmospheric pollutant concentration. In our study, we perform a one-year opportunistic mobile monitoring campaign, where the routes of mobile sensors cover almost the entire city center of Antwerp.

The main contribution of this paper is in the following aspects: (1) we provide a systematic guideline on how to process and analyze air pollution datasets with time sequence and geographic information; (2) we analyze the temporal and spatial distribution of the considered pollutants and investigate the impact of various context factors (e.g., road type, land use and different emission sources) on the atmospheric pollutant concentration, which will facilitate the construction of a new air quality model [6, 7] in the future.

The rest of the paper is organized as follows. Section 2 introduces the methods and dataset adopted in this study. Section 3 describes and discusses some results we have found in present study and Sect. 4 presents the conclusions.

2   Materials and Methods

This section firstly describes the monitoring campaign that this study used to collect air pollution data and the details of the collected dataset. Secondly, this section provides a systematic guideline on how to process and analyze air pollution datasets with time sequence and geographic information, as shown in Fig. 1.

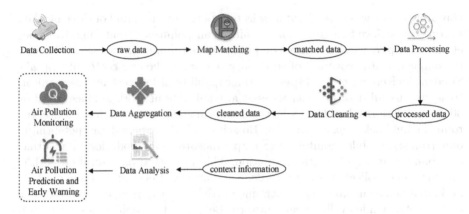

Fig. 1. The main workflow of the system

2.1   Data Collection

Opportunistic mobile monitoring is defined by [5] as a data collection method that installs the measurement devices on existing mobile sensor platforms. It differs from targeted mobile monitoring in that the measurement devices in targeted mobile monitoring follow the fixed routes designed by the researcher in advance, while the measurement devices in opportunistic mobile monitoring follow the daily routines of existing mobile sensor platforms. Therefore, opportunistic mobile monitoring enables the collection of large amounts of data at a relatively small cost.

The data used in our study has been collected as part of the opportunistic mobile monitoring campaign in Antwerp (with a population of 520,504 inhabitants, covering an area of $204.5\,\text{km}^2$), Belgium based on the City of Things (CoT) framework [18]. 20 air quality sensors were mounted on the roofs of the Bpost (Belgian Post Group, the Belgian company responsible for the delivery of national and international mail) vans since January 2018. In this paper, we use the data from January to December 2018. These sensors deliver a record every 30 s, including measurements of four pollutants (NO_2 and three particulate matters with aerodynamic diameters below $1\,\mu\text{m}$ (PM_1), $2.5\,\mu\text{m}$ ($PM_{2.5}$) and $10\,\mu\text{m}$ (PM_{10})) and meteorological information, such as temperature and relative humidity, which are linked with corresponding GPS locations and time stamps. As each Bpost car is driving around in the city, the set of sensors can cover the entire city in terms of measurements enabling the collection of real-time air quality information with broad city coverage, as opposed to an approach with static sensors, which only allows for local information. Furthermore, the number of static sensors necessary to cover the entire city is huge when compared to the needed number of cars and, thus, the installation and maintenance costs are also higher, which represent a considerable restriction when extending these kind of deployments.

2.2   Map Matching

In an urban environment, the occlusion of buildings will affect the reception of GPS signals. Coupled with the geographical error of the GPS device itself, we found that there is occasionally a big difference between the GPS location of the collected data points and their actual location.

The simplest way to improve the quality of the collected data points is to snap their locations to the nearest road segments. However, this method has great drawbacks. Without considering the consistency of the trajectories, it may lead to a point being snapped to an inconsistent road, or successive data points jumping from one road to another. Specifically, this can result in unfeasible trajectories, e.g., with unconnected roads.

To overcome this issue, Newson et al. [16] present an approach to use a Hidden Markov Model (HMM) to select the best candidate by combining the spatial and temporal component. Therefore, unconnected roads cannot be candidates and trajectories of data points must be consistent with the road network. For each GPS location, a number of map matching candidates within a certain radius around the GPS point is computed. To complement this approach, Luxen et al. [13] exploit the Viterbi algorithm to compute the most likely sequence of map matching candidates. An implementation of this approach is available in OSRM (Open Source Routing Machine) project. This framework can use a referenced road network (e.g., OpenStreetMap) to generate a hierarchical routing network. Xie et al. [22] proposed a novel approach to infer the road network by aligning the tracks for each road segment using a "stretching and compression" strategy. In this paper, we applied OSRM project to improve the data quality. Fig. 2 displays an example of the original locations and the improved locations after map-matching.

2.3   Data Processing and Data Cleaning

Further processing steps include filtering out data located outside of the study area and data not in working hours. These are described in more detail later in this section.

Step 1. Filtering Out Data Outside the Study Area. This study focuses on the city of Antwerp. To determine which measurements are located in the study area, we set two simple thresholds: $51.1430 < latitude < 51.3780$ and $4.2170 < longitude < 4.4980$. We found that more than 90% of the measurements for each pollutant were located in the city of Antwerp.

Step 2. Activity Pattern Detection and Filtering Out Off-Hour Data. Since the mobile sensors are measuring continuously day and night, we need to determine the working period to distinguish when the vehicle is on the road (working hours) and when it is parked in the garage (off-hours). We calculated

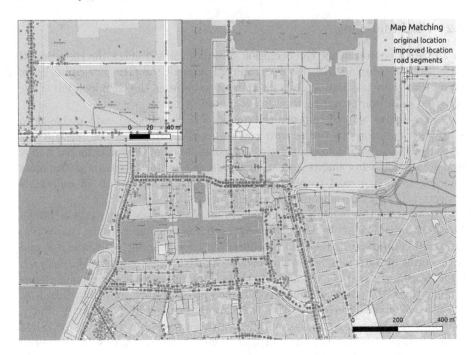

Fig. 2. Spatial data quality improvement by map matching

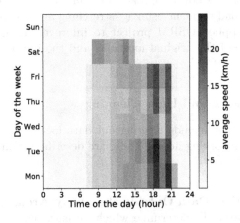

Fig. 3. The activity pattern of vehicles. It indicates the average speed (km/h) of vehicles for each hour and each day of the week.

the vehicle speed (km/h) from the geographical locations of subsequent measurements. Then, we applied the vehicle speed to detect the daily activity pattern of these devices.

As shown in Fig. 3, the daily working periods (working hours) can be defined as follows:

- Monday to Friday: 08:00–21:00
- Saturday: 08:00–15:00
- Sunday: no activity

Based on that, nearly 40% of the collected data is recorded in the streets, and is used in our analysis.

In this study, we measured, processed and analyzed four pollutants NO_2, PM_1, $PM_{2.5}$ and PM_{10}. In the following sections, we only choose one or two pollutants (e.g., NO_2 and $PM_{2.5}$) to show representative analysis results, since our main purpose is to use Antwerp as a pilot to illustrate the feasibility of the system, rather than investigating the actual urban pollution levels.

2.4   Data Aggregation

Spatial Variability. We generate the air pollution map at street level for the entire city to see if we can identify general distribution patterns of these pollutants. Figure 4 shows the resulting map of atmospheric NO_2 concentration. Different colors represent different NO_2 concentration levels. The darker the color, the higher the NO_2 concentration level and the worse the air quality. It is obvious that the concentration of NO_2 on the main roads is much higher compared to secondary roads in residential areas. We can also find that the concentration of these pollutants exhibits high spatial variability in the considered urban environment. The concentration of NO_2 in two adjacent streets may vary considerably.

Temporal Variability. All analyses of the temporal variation in atmospheric concentrations in this paper are based on the work-hour data, as defined earlier. From Fig. 5, we can observe the daily and weekly distribution patterns of the exhibited NO_2 and $PM_{2.5}$ concentrations. During the day, atmospheric concentrations of NO_2 and $PM_{2.5}$ increase during the morning and evening rush hours, especially during the morning peak (at 8 am and 9 am). This is probably because the morning rush hour is more concentrated between 9 am and 10 am, whereas the evening rush hour seems to be spread out over a longer period of time (4 am–8 am). During the week, the concentrations of NO_2 and $PM_{2.5}$ in working days are generally higher than that on Saturdays. This pronounced diurnal variation, including rush hour peaks and difference between working and weekend days is typically observed for traffic-related pollution in urban environments [8,9,15,17,21].

3   Result and Discussion

In this section, a series of data analysis tasks are conducted to understand the relationship between the considered pollutants and various context factors (e.g., road type, land use) and then find whether these context factors have an effect on the concentration of pollutants.

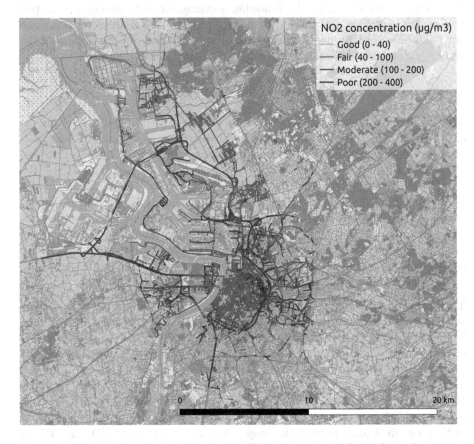

Fig. 4. Map of NO_2 concentration: average NO_2 concentration for each road segment with at least one measurement. The NO_2 concentration levels correspond to the European Air Quality Index [4].

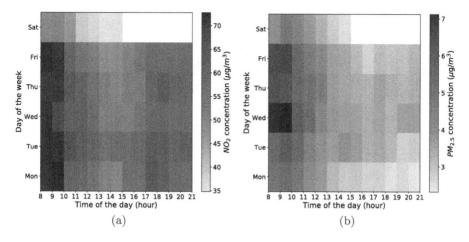

Fig. 5. The temporal pattern of (a) NO_2 and (b) $PM_{2.5}$. It indicates the average NO_2 and $PM_{2.5}$ concentrations ($\mu g/m^3$) for each work-hour of the day and each day of the week.

3.1 Road Type: Primary Roads and Secondary Roads

In this study, the primary roads refer to roads with reference number like N173 and E19, as shown in Fig. 6. In fact, these primary roads usually have high traffic flow as they connect popular regions and have higher capacity. As for secondary roads, they tend to have relatively lower traffic capacity but higher traffic density. In this paper, traffic flow refers to the number of vehicles passing a reference point per unit of time while traffic density is defined as the number of vehicles per unit length of the road. From Fig. 7(a), we can see that the NO_2 concentration on primary roads is slightly shifted towards higher values. Based on the T-test, there is a statistically significant difference in the NO_2 concentrations observed along primary roads and secondary roads ($p < 0.05$). Also, the NO_2 concentration on primary roads is always higher than that on secondary roads during most hours of the day, as shown in Fig. 7(b). This confirms that the road type has a significant impact on the distribution of NO_2 concentration. The ring road is a 6–8 lane road with a much higher capacity, when compared to a single-lane secondary road. This higher capacity (vehicles per hour per lane) will lead to the higher atmospheric NO_2 concentrations.

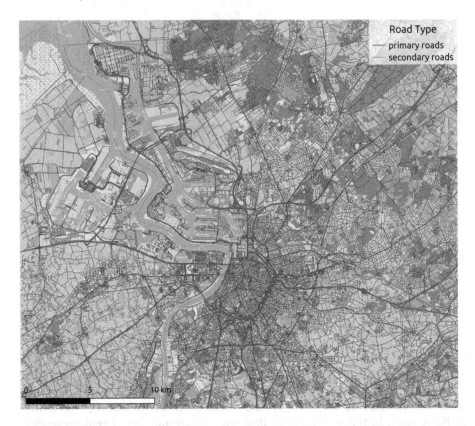

Fig. 6. Classification of road types in Antwerp, where the red lines represent the primary roads and the blue lines represent the secondary roads. (Color figure online)

3.2   Source Proximity: Traffic Signals

The reason that we are interested in the locations of traffic signals is that these locations usually have relatively high traffic density and are prone to congestion, as the vehicles stop at the traffic signals frequently and many traffic signals are deployed at road intersections. We define a threshold to determine if a measurement is close to the traffic signals. In this study, we set the threshold to 30 m. If the distance between a point and a traffic signal is less than 30 m, then the point belongs to the subset close to the traffic signals, otherwise the point belongs to the other subset. From Fig. 8(a), we can find that the NO_2 concentration close to the traffic signals is slightly shifted towards higher values. As confirmed by the T-test's result ($p < 0.05$), there is a clear difference in the NO_2 concentration close to traffic signals and others. Figure 8(b) shows the NO_2 concentration of data close to traffic signals is higher during most time of the day and shows higher temporal variability within a day.

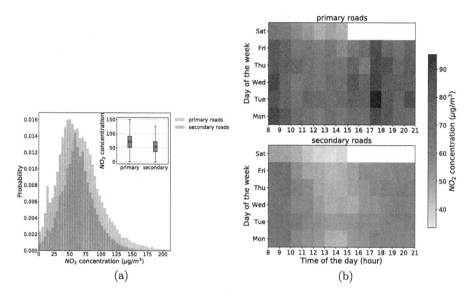

Fig. 7. (a) The normalized histogram and boxplot of the NO_2 concentration on primary roads and secondary roads: they both indicate the NO_2 concentration on primary roads is slightly shifted towards higher values; (b) The temporal distribution of NO_2 concentration on primary roads and secondary roads: it indicates the average NO_2 concentration on the two kinds of roads for each hour of the day and each day of the week.

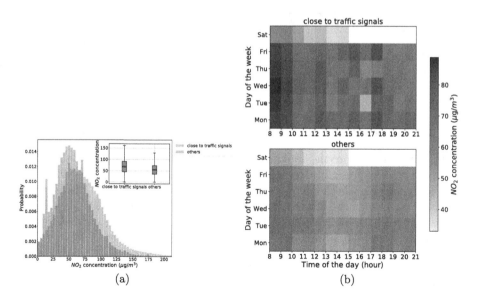

Fig. 8. (a) The normalized histogram and boxplot of the NO_2 concentration close to traffic signals and others: they both indicate the NO_2 concentration close to traffic signals and others is slightly shifted towards higher values; (b) The temporal distribution of NO_2 concentration close to traffic signals and others: it indicates the average NO_2 concentration of these two subsets for each hour of the day and each day of the week.

Fig. 9. Classification of land use types in Antwerp, where the purple polygons represent the industrial area and the yellow polygons represent the residential area. (Color figure online)

3.3   Land Use: Residential Regions and Industrial Regions

In this study, we acquire the land use types from OpenStreetMap, a collaborative project to create a free editable map of the world, as shown in Fig. 9. We define a threshold to decide whether a point belongs to the industrial region or residential region. In this study, we set the threshold to 10 m. If the distance from a point to the industrial/residential region is less than 10 m, then this point belongs to the industrial/residential region.

From Fig. 10, for both NO_2 and $PM_{2.5}$, we can observe that the concentration in residential regions is slightly shifted towards higher values compared to that in industrial regions. According to T-test's result ($p < 0.05$), there is a significant difference between the concentrations in industrial regions and residential regions. Figure 11 shows the NO_2 and $PM_{2.5}$ concentrations in residential regions are always higher than that in industrial regions during most time of the day. This is not surprising as this study focuses on urban traffic-related pollutants

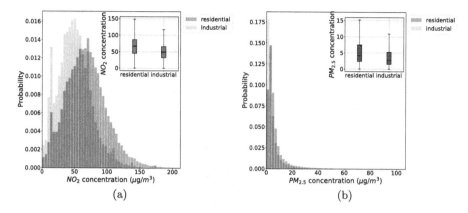

Fig. 10. The normalized histograms and boxplots of the (a) NO_2 and (b) $PM_{2.5}$ concentrations in industrial regions and residential regions: they indicate for both NO_2 and $PM_{2.5}$, the concentrations in residential regions are higher than that in industrial regions.

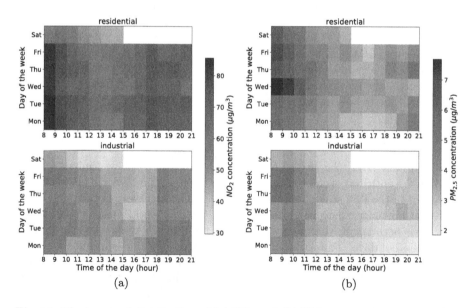

Fig. 11. The temporal distribution of (a) NO_2 and (b) $PM_{2.5}$ concentrations in industrial regions and residential regions: it indicates the average NO_2 and $PM_{2.5}$ concentrations in these two kinds of regions for each hour of the day and each day of the week.

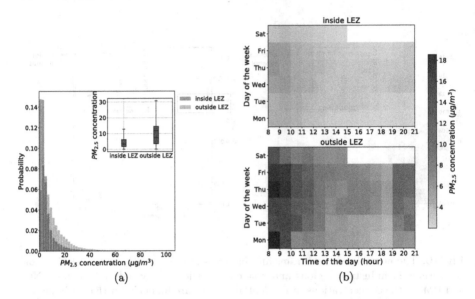

Fig. 12. (a) The normalized histogram and boxplot of the $PM_{2.5}$ concentration inside LEZ and outside LEZ: they both indicate the $PM_{2.5}$ concentration outside LEZ is slightly shifted towards higher values; (b) The temporal distribution of $PM_{2.5}$ concentration inside LEZ and outside LEZ: it indicates the average $PM_{2.5}$ concentration of these two subsets for each hour of the day and each day of the week.

(e.g., NO_2 and PM), while industry in the city of Antwerp is mainly petrochemical. Due to the obvious higher traffic density in the city center and urban architecture impeding natural ventilation, higher pollutant concentrations can be expected in the residential areas.

3.4 Low Emission Zone

Since February 2017, the city of Antwerp has introduced a Low Emission Zone (LEZ) in the entire city center. The entry restrictions of the LEZ will be gradually tightened. In the first stage between 2017 and 2020, vehicles with high pollutant levels are no longer permitted to enter the environmental zone. The LEZ of Antwerp is permanent, that means 24 h a day for 7 days a week, also on Sundays and public holidays. The environmental zone covers $20\,km^2$ and affects about 200,000 inhabitants. Figure 12(a) shows that the PM2.5 concentration outside LEZ is hugely shifted towards higher values. In addition to the T-test's result ($p < 0.05$), there is a significant difference in the $PM_{2.5}$ concentration inside LEZ and outside LEZ. As shown in Fig. 12(b), $PM_{2.5}$ concentration outside LEZ is always higher than that inside LEZ during most time of the day. This may be because in the face of additional taxes, people are more likely to choose environmentally friendly modes of travel, such as taking a bus or riding a bicycle instead of taking a private car with high emissions.

4   Conclusion and Further Steps

First of all, this study proofs the feasibility of collecting meaningful air quality data from opportunistic mobile monitoring platforms. Based on the data collected from Antwerp, we analyzed the spatial and temporal distribution of the considered pollutants (NO_2 and PM) and found that the atmospheric pollutant concentration is highly variable in both time and space. The results show the value of fine-grained air pollution monitoring. We also identified general distribution patterns of the considered pollutants. For example, the main roads are very conspicuous in the NO_2 concentration map. In particular, we investigated the impact of various context factors (e.g., road type, land use and some emission sources) on the atmospheric pollutant concentration. For example, some source locations, such as traffic signals, tend to have higher NO_2 concentration levels. We believe that these findings are of great value in assessing current air pollution control measures and formulating future air quality improvement measures.

Next, we intend to construct more effective air quality prediction and air pollution early warning models based on the context aware analysis.

Acknowledgments. This research was supported by the Internet of Things (IoT) team of imec-Netherlands under the project EI2.

References

1. European Environment Agency: Air pollution. https://www.eea.europa.eu/themes/air/intro. Accessed 24 Apr 2019
2. European Environment Agency: Air pollution sources. https://www.eea.europa.eu/themes/air/air-pollution-sources. Accessed 24 Apr 2019
3. European Environment Agency: Air quality in Europe - 2011 report. https://www.eea.europa.eu/publications/air-quality-in-europe-2011. Accessed 24 Apr 2019
4. European Environment Agency: European air quality index. http://airindex.eea.europa.eu/. Accessed 24 Apr 2019
5. Van den Bossche, J., Theunis, J., Elen, B., Peters, J., Botteldooren, D., De Baets, B.: Opportunistic mobile air pollution monitoring: a case study with city wardens in antwerp. Atmos. Environ. **141**, 408–421 (2016)
6. Deligiannis, N., Mota, J.F., Zimos, E., Rodrigues, M.R.: Heterogeneous networked data recovery from compressive measurements using a copula prior. IEEE Trans. Commun. **65**(12), 5333–5347 (2017)
7. Do, T.H., et al.: Matrix completion with variational graph autoencoders: application in hyperlocal air quality inference. In: ICASSP 2019–2019 IEEE International Conference on Acoustics, Speech and Signal Processing (ICASSP), pp. 7535–7539. IEEE (2019)
8. Hofman, J., et al.: Ultrafine particles in four European urban environments: results from a new continuous long-term monitoring network. Atmos. Environ. **136**, 68–81 (2016)
9. de Jesus, A.L., et al.: Ultrafine particles and PM2. 5 in the air of cities around the world: are they representative of each other? Environ. Int. **129**, 118–135 (2019)
10. Kaivonen, S., Ngai, E.: Real-time air pollution monitoring with sensors on city bus. Digit. Commun. Netw. (2019)

11. Karner, A.A., Eisinger, D.S., Niemeier, D.A.: Near-roadway air quality: synthesizing the findings from real-world data. Environ. Sci. Technol. **44**(14), 5334–5344 (2010)
12. Intergewestelijke Cel voor het Leefmilieu (IRCEL): Measurements - English. http://www.irceline.be/en/air-quality/measurements/measurements?set_language=en. Accessed 24 Apr 2019
13. Luxen, D., Vetter, C.: Real-time routing with OpenStreetMap data. In: Proceedings of the 19th ACM SIGSPATIAL International Conference on Advances in Geographic Information Systems, pp. 513–516. ACM (2011)
14. McKercher, G.R., Vanos, J.K.: Low-cost mobile air pollution monitoring in urban environments: a pilot study in Lubbock, Texas. Environ. Technol. **39**(12), 1505–1514 (2018)
15. Mishra, V.K., et al.: Wintertime spatio-temporal variation of ultrafine particles in a Belgian city. Sci. Total Environ. **431**, 307–313 (2012)
16. Newson, P., Krumm, J.: Hidden Markov map matching through noise and sparseness. In: Proceedings of the 17th ACM SIGSPATIAL International Conference on Advances in Geographic Information Systems, pp. 336–343. ACM (2009)
17. Pirjola, L., et al.: Spatial and temporal characterization of traffic emissions in urban microenvironments with a mobile laboratory. Atmos. Environ. **63**, 156–167 (2012)
18. Santos, J., et al.: City of things: enabling resource provisioning in smart cities. IEEE Commun. Mag. **56**(7), 177–183 (2018)
19. Shiva Nagendra, S.M., Yasa, P.R., Narayana, M., Khadirnaikar, S., Rani, P.: Mobile monitoring of air pollution using low cost sensors to visualize spatio-temporal variation of pollutants at urban hotspots. Sustain. Cities Soc. **44**, 520–535 (2019)
20. Tian, Y., Yao, X., Chen, L.: Analysis of spatial and seasonal distributions of air pollutants by incorporating urban morphological characteristics. Comput. Environ. Urban Syst. **75**, 35–48 (2019)
21. Wang, Y., Ying, Q., Hu, J., Zhang, H.: Spatial and temporal variations of six criteria air pollutants in 31 provincial capital cities in China during 2013–2014. Environ. Int. **73**, 413–422 (2014)
22. Xie, X., Philips, W., Veelaert, P., Aghajan, H.: Road network inference from GPS traces using DTW algorithm. In: 17th International IEEE Conference on Intelligent Transportation Systems (ITSC), pp. 906–911. IEEE (2014)
23. Xie, X., et al.: A review of urban air pollution monitoring and exposure assessment methods. ISPRS Int. J. Geo-Inf. **6**(12), 389 (2017)

Real-Time Monitoring of Electric Motors for Detection of Operating Anomalies and Predictive Maintenance

Luis Magadán, Francisco J. Suárez$^{(\boxtimes)}$, Juan C. Granda, and Daniel F. García

Department of Computer Science, University of Oviedo, Gijón, Spain
luis.magadan@gmail.com, {fjsuarez,jcgranda,dfgarcia}@uniovi.es

Abstract. This paper shows an implementation of an Industrial Internet of Things (IIoT) system designed to monitor electric motors in order to detect operating anomalies. This system will also be the basis for a future predictive maintenance system. The design and testing of the prototype, developed using multisensor microcontrollers and single-board computers as gateways, are presented. Each microcontroller gathers real-time data about the vibrations and temperature of an electric motor. The IIoT prototype has been designed using low-cost hardware components, open-source software and a free version of an IoT analytics service in the cloud, where all the relevant information is stored. During the development of this prototype, vibration analysis in the frequency domain was carried out both in the microcontroller and in the gateway to analyse their capabilities. This approach is also the springboard to take advantage of edge and fog computing as complement to cloud computing. The prototype has been tested in a laboratory and in an industrial dairy plant.

Keywords: Low-cost sensors and gateways · IIoT · Vibration frequency analysis

1 Introduction

Equipment maintenance is a critical aspect in industry. The correct operation of industrial equipment relies on exhaustively scheduled maintenance plans. This helps to avoid equipment failure, but some failures are inevitable.

Predictive maintenance has arisen as an ideal approach for saving costs and preventing equipment failure in industry. Traditional reactive maintenance only carries out maintenance activities after failure detection. Widespread preventive maintenance implies periodic maintenance activities based on previous experience about the periodicity of failure. The predictive approach to maintenance is the Industry 4.0 alternative, failures are predicted based on real-time information received from sensors in industrial equipment [1].

In this paper, we present a prototype of a real-time monitoring system based on wireless sensors. It will be used for detection of operating anomalies and predictive maintenance of electrical motors. The rest of the paper is organized as follows. Previous

H. Santos et al. (Eds.): SmartCity 360 2019, LNICST 323, pp. 301–311, 2020.
https://doi.org/10.1007/978-3-030-51005-3_25

works in the research context are outlined in Sect. 2. The proposed monitoring system is presented in Sect. 3. Section 4 details the experimental plan carried out. Results are discussed in Sect. 5, and finally, Sect. 6 presents conclusions and future work.

2 Background

Real-time monitoring is one of the bases of Industry 4.0 [2], and many systems have been developed to monitor currents, pressures, temperatures and other variables in industrial plants. With the advances in micro-electro-mechanical systems, it is possible to deploy myriads of low-cost sensors capable of sensing, computing and communicating wirelessly to gather information for environment and equipment monitoring [1]. These sensors are connected using wireless sensor networks. They send data to the cloud for storage or further processing using IoT protocols and technologies [4]. Many of the public cloud service providers offer IoT services using standard protocols for real-time storage and extract analytics from the data. This makes it possible to use historical data to predict future failures of equipment.

On occasions, the amount of data to be sent to the cloud or the latency of sending data to the cloud and back to the sensors/actuators is excessive. In these cases, moving part of the computation close to the sensors may alleviate the resources consumed in the network and the cloud. The fog-computing paradigm promotes the use of resources of smart sensors and gateways interconnecting sensors in conjunction with the cloud resources [3]. Fog deployments require defining the topology for interconnecting sensors among them and with the gateways providing access to the cloud. Sensors usually generate data streams that can be pre-processed, aggregated or filtered before reaching the cloud [5]. Similarly, some of the data analytics may be carried out by gateways. Thus, the organization of the fog is critical for balancing computing load and network resource consumption in order to save public cloud costs and reduce latency.

Detection of operation anomalies is the kind of predictive maintenance that can be carried out even when no data from previous failures in the equipment is available [8]. When available, machine-learning models based on binary classification are used to predict failures in the near future in order to plan repairs or substitution of equipment [7]. The prediction models are trained and tested using the historical labelled data with information about previous failures in the equipment. The amount of historical data can be huge, so real-time storage in the cloud is an effective solution, giving rise to cloud based predictive maintenance [9].

Induction electrical motors are major actuators in most industrial factories, so cloud based predictive maintenance of electric motors is of special importance. This state is supported by the amount of research work on this field in recent years [6].

Mechanical failures produce vibrations in electrical motors with different amplitude and frequency [10]. Thus, solutions monitoring the health of motors mainly focus on measuring vibrations and temperature.

An IoT solution for the monitoring of industrial machinery in an electric plant is presented in [11]. The authors use an IoT protocol stack composed of 802.15.4, 6LoWPAN, RPL and CoAP to monitor temperature and vibrations of several pumps. However, they do not analyze vibrations in the frequency domain nor include any cloud processing.

There are also solutions using the cloud as storage for further processing of the monitored temperature and/or vibration signals of inductive motors [12, 13]. The main drawback of this approach is data is rarely filtered or pre-processed taking advantage of intermediate systems between the sensors and the cloud. The authors in [18] propose sending raw data to a private cloud in order to prepare training and testing data sets to be sent to a machine-learning model in the public cloud.

Finally, there are deployments using low-cost equipment to monitor vibrations in industrial equipment [14, 16, 17]. A framework for distributing computational demanding tasks across sensors, fog nodes and the cloud is presented in [15]. Gateways at the Fog layer perform computation and classification of vibration signals coming from sensors attached to motors. However, this solution does not analyze vibrations in the frequency domain.

After this background revision, we can state that the IIoT prototype presented in this paper brings together low-cost sensors and gateways, vibration frequency analysis and fog computing to propose an innovative way towards predictive maintenance in Industry 4.0.

3 Monitoring System

The following subsections present the architecture, components and software features of the proposed monitoring system.

3.1 System Architecture

As can be seen in Fig. 1, the system architecture is composed of three layers in which the information can be processed. The first layer is the "Edge" layer, which is composed of all the IoT sensor networks. The second layer is the "Fog" layer, which is formed of the gateways. The last layer is the "Cloud", where all the relevant data is stored. visualized and analyzed.

All the layers have computing capacity. In the first one the filtering, aggregation and data transformation is carried out directly on the sensors. The Fog layer allows the gateways to collect data from multiple sensors using wireless communications (p.e. Bluetooth Low Energy, BLE) and continue processing them. Both the Edge and Fog layers help to distribute the processing of the information between sensors and cloud, improving latency and reducing the amount of data to transfer to the cloud.

3.2 System Components

The multisensor microcontroller used in the Edge layer is the low-cost SensorTag CC2650 from Texas Instruments shown in Fig. 2, which has an ARM Cortex-M3 processor, 128 KB of programmable flash memory and five integrated sensors, including movement and humidity sensors. The movement sensor is the MPU9250. It has an accelerometer, a magnetometer and a gyro, measuring vibrations with a capture frequency of 1 kHz. The humidity sensor is the HDC1000. It measures the relative humidity and also the temperature. The microcontroller support wireless communication with

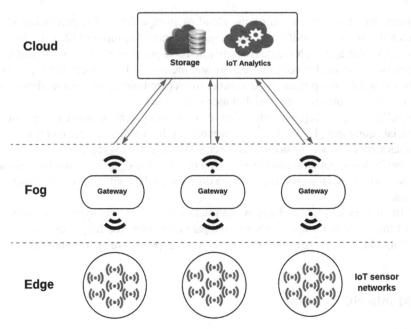

Fig. 1. System architecture

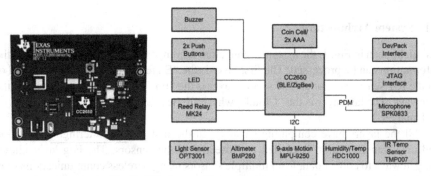

Fig. 2. Wireless multisensor microcontroller

the Bluetooth Low Energy (BLE) protocol. The wireless nature of the microcontroller allows for a very fast and economical deployment in the industrial environment.

The gateway used in the Fog layer is the low-cost single-board computer Raspberry Pi 3 Model B+, shown in Fig. 3, which has 1 GB Ram, 1 HDMI port and 4 USB 2.0 ports, as well as a CSI and a DSI port to connect a camera and a touchscreen. The Ethernet data rates up to 100 Mbps. It also allows Wi-Fi, Bluetooth 4.2 and Bluetooth Low Energy (BLE). The CPU + GPU is the Broadcom BCM2837B0, Cortex A-53 (ARMv8) 64-bit SoC @ 1.4 GHz.

Finally, the Cloud layer is implemented using a free version of ThingSpeak, an IoT analytics platform service that allows aggregation, visualization and analysis of live data

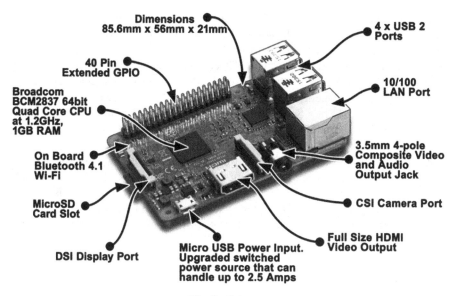

Fig. 3. Gateway

streams in the cloud (see Fig. 4). It provides instant visualizations of data posted by the system gateways and can also perform online analysis and processing of the data as it comes in. ThingSpeak is often used for prototyping and proof of concept IoT systems that require analytics.

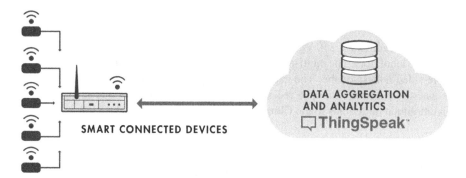

Fig. 4. IoT analytics platform

3.3   System Software

The movement sensor returns the accelerations in time domain, but this does not give enough information about the vibrations of the electric motor. It is necessary to use the Fast Fourier Transformation (FFT) over the accelerations of the vibrations measured on the motor. The output of the FFT is the vibration amplitude as a function of frequency. FFT has been computed in both multisensor microcontroller and gateway. With the microcontroller, the library used is CMSIS DSP software library, designed for use in Cortex-M processor based devices. The FFT compute using this library is done using an array of 256 continuous accelerations over time because no more accelerations could be stored in the internal memory of the microcontroller. With the gateway, the function used is FFT from the library Scipy, using an array of up to 4096 accelerations formed of 16 arrays of 256 accelerations, which are continuous over time, covering the whole dynamic behavior of the motor.

Multisensor microcontrollers and gateway are communicated with the BLE protocol, that is used to transmit small packets of data read by the sensors, while consuming less battery power than other protocols. The main drawback of this protocol is its communication range, because only about ten meters is what can be achieved between two BLE devices indoors in normal use. Finally, data is transferred from the gateway to the Cloud layer via HTTP calls from the REST API.

4   Experimental Plan

The IIoT prototype developed has been tested in two different scenarios. The first one was with a low power motor in laboratory with no workload. After performing this initial test, the prototype was installed in an industrial diary plant, where the monitored electric motors work with a real workload.

4.1   Scenario 1: Low Power Motor in Laboratory

The first scenario (see Fig. 5) corresponds to a single-phase asynchronous electric motor with a permanent condenser and a frequency of 1500 rpm. It has a power output of 0.25 kW and a voltage of 250 V/50 Hz. As indicated in Fig. 6, this motor was bolted to the floor of the laboratory. The multisensor microcontroller was fixed to the motor plate using double-sided adhesive tape. The gateway was positioned close to the microcontroller. The gateway processes the data received from the microcontroller and sends only the high amplitude harmonics to the Cloud layer.

Fig. 5. Scenario 1 in laboratory

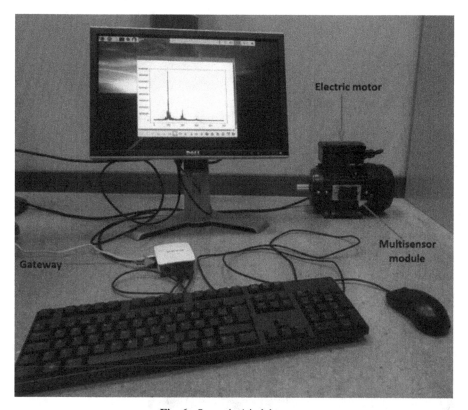

Fig. 6. Scenario 1 in laboratory

4.2 Scenario 2: Pumps in an Industrial Diary Plant

The second scenario corresponds to an industrial dairy plant. In this case, the electric motors monitored are two pumps located close to each other. These pumps have a frequency of 3000 rpm, a power output of 15 kW and a voltage of 230 V/50 Hz. Each of them works for a different sterilization line. The main difference between them is that pump 1 is in the third month of the annual maintenance cycle for changing bearings, while pump 2 is in the eleventh. Both microcontrollers have been fixed to the pumps as in scenario 1 and connected to a gateway that communicates with the Cloud layer via a WiFi Access Point (AP), as shown in Fig. 7. Figure 8 shows where the gateway and pump 1 are placed in the diary plant.

5 Results

The preliminary results presented here were obtained after computing the Fast Fourier Transformation over accelerations from the Z axis for both scenarios of the experimental plan.

In scenario 1, as seen in Fig. 9, computing the Fast Fourier Transformation in the multisensor microcontroller gives worse results than when it is computed in the gateway.

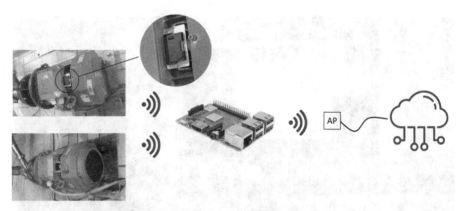

Fig. 7. Scenario 2 in an industrial dairy plant

Fig. 8. Scenario 2 in an industrial dairy plant

Both graphs show three fundamental harmonics with outstanding amplitudes of 100, 200 and 300 Hz. Those frequencies are multiples of the base frequency of the motor used in scenario 1, which is 25 Hz.

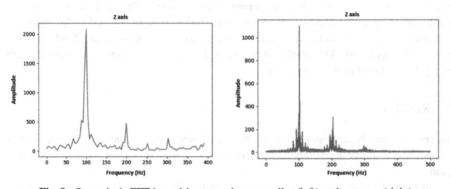

Fig. 9. Scenario 1: FFT in multisensor microcontroller (left) and gateway (right)

Figure 10 shows the amplitudes of the harmonic of 100 Hz stored in the Cloud layer after computing the FFT in the multisensor microcontroller and in the gateway. In both cases the amplitude remains stable. When computing the FFT in the multisensor microcontroller the amplitude is between 1750 and 2250, and in the case of computing it in the gateway it stays stable between 700 and 900.

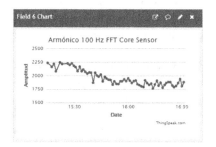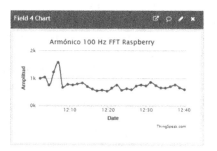

Fig. 10. 100 Hz harmonic in microcontroller (left) and in gateway (right)

In scenario 2, the FFT was computed in the gateway, as these results were more accurate. Figure 11 shows the results after computing the FFT in both pumps. Both pumps correspond to the same model, work in similar sterilization lines and are in the third and eleventh month of the annual maintenance cycle respectively. Pump 1 has some harmonics of 25 Hz, 100 Hz and some close to 300 Hz, while of pump 2 has harmonics of 25 Hz and some around 200 Hz. The biggest difference between pumps 1 and 2 is the appearance of the harmonic 200 Hz and the disappearance of those of 100 and 300 Hz. The noise level is much higher in the second scenario than in the first because the pumps were surrounded by many other vibrating motors. In both pumps, the temperature was near 40 °C.

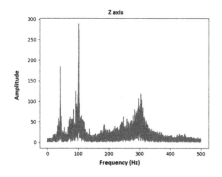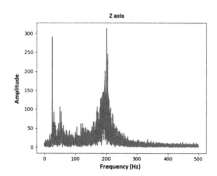

Fig. 11. Scenario 2: FFT in pump 1 (left) and pump 2 (right)

6 Conclusions and Future Work

In view of the preliminary results of the research, the IIoT prototype has demonstrated the viability of our low-cost proposal, allowing vibration frequency analysis on both multisensor microcontroller and gateway and giving results that will be readily transferable to other sensors and gateways with similar characteristics.

Current work is focused on measuring some important performance parameters as computing time of FFT function, time consumed in data transference from sensor to gateway, total latency from data capture to data transfer to the cloud and battery consumption of the multisensor microcontroller.

Future work can be classified as short term, medium term and long term. In the short term, is the development of an automatic anomaly detection system in the gateway. If this detects important changes in the amplitudes of the harmonics, the system will notify the maintenance technicians, warning that there may be a problem in one of the motors monitored and preventing unforeseen stops. Regarding wireless communications between sensors and gateway, it is necessary to explore using other protocols with longer communication range such as 6LowPan and Zigbee.

In the medium term, it is necessary to label all the data that is stored in the cloud with information about the state of the motor when the data was sent, accompanied by the qualitative status reported by technicians after preventive maintenance. This will improve the reliability of the notifications sent to the maintenance technicians and help them to take decisions about advancing or delaying the maintenance tasks.

Finally, in the long term, after having stored enough data to make a broad historical record in the cloud, a predictive model based on machine-learning will be developed and run (in the Cloud or in the gateway) to estimate the failure probability of the motor before carrying out the maintenance, thus reducing maintenance costs.

Acknowledgments. This research has been partially funded by the Spanish National Plan of Research, Development and Innovation under the project OCAS (RTI2018-094849-B-I00); the University of Oviedo under the project PAPI-19-EMERG-18; and the Asturias Institute of Industrial Technology (IUTA) under project SV-19-GIJÓN-1-18.

References

1. Gongora, V.C., Hancke, G.P.: Industrial wireless sensor networks: challenges, design principles, and technical approaches. IEEE Trans. Ind. Electron. **56**(10), 4258–4265 (2009)
2. Liu, Y., Xu, X.: Industry 4.0 and cloud manufacturing: a comparative analysis. J. Manuf. Sci. Eng. Trans. ASME **139**(3), 034701 (2016)
3. Naha, R.K., et al.: Fog computing: survey of trends, architectures, requirements, and research directions. IEEE Access **6**, 47980–48009 (2018)
4. Xu, L.D., He, W., Li, S.: Internet of things in industries: a survey. IEEE Trans. Ind. Inf. **10**(4), 2233–2243 (2014)
5. Yang, S.: IoT stream processing and analytics in the fog. IEEE Commun. Mag. **51**(8), 21–27 (2017)
6. Ajitha, A., et al.: IoT platform for condition monitoring of industrial motors. In: 2nd International Conference on Communication and Electronics Systems (2017)

7. Paolanti, M., et al.: Machine learning approach for predictive maintenance in industry 4.0. In: 14th IEEE/ASME International Conference on Mechatronic and Embedded Systems and Applications (2018)
8. Wang, J., et al.: Sensor data based system-level anomaly prediction for smart manufacturing. In: IEEE International Congress on Big Data (2018)
9. Yamato, Y., Kumazaki, H., Fukumoto, Y.: Proposal of lambda architecture adoption for real time predictive maintenance. In: Fourth International Symposium on Computing and Networking (2016)
10. Ágoston, K.: Fault detection of the electrical motors based on vibration analysis. In: 8th International Conference Interdisciplinarity in Engineering (2014)
11. Civerchia, F., Bocchino, S., Salvadori, C., Rossi, E., Maggiani, L., Petracca, M.: Industrial internet of things monitoring solution for advanced predictive maintenance applications. J. Ind. Inf. Integr. **7**, 4–12 (2017)
12. Goundar, S.S., Pillai, M.R., Mamun, K.A., Islam, F.R., Deo, R.: Real time condition monitoring system for industrial motors. In: 2nd Asia-Pacific World Congress on Computer Science and Engineering (2015)
13. Ganga, D., Ramachandran, V.: IoT-based vibration analytics of electrical machines. IEEE Internet Things J. **5**(6), 4538–4549 (2018)
14. Jung, D., Zhang, Z., Winslett, M.: Vibration analysis for IoT enabled predictive maintenance. In: IEEE 33rd International Conference on Data Engineering (2017)
15. Xenakis, A., Karageorgos, A., Lallas, E., Chis, A.E., González-Vélez, H.: Towards distributed IoT/cloud based fault detection and maintenance in industrial automation. In: Second International Conference on Emerging Data and Industry 4.0 (2019)
16. Firmansah, A., et al.: Self-powered IoT base vibration monitoring of inductive motor for diagnostic and prediction failure. In: IOP Conference Series: Materials Science and Engineering (2019)
17. Esfahani, E.T., Wang, S., Sundararajan, V.: Multisensor wireless system for eccentricity and bearing fault detection in induction motors. IEEE/ASME Trans. Mechatron. **19**(3), 818–826 (2014)
18. Wu, D., et al.: A fog computing-based framework for process monitoring and prognosis in cyber-manufacturing. J. Manuf. Syst. **43**, 25–34 (2017)

A Cost-Effective Real-Time Monitoring System for Water Quality Management Based on Internet of Things

Gonçalo Marques[1,2(✉)] ⓘ and Rui Pitarma[1]

[1] Polytechnic Institute of Guarda, Guarda, Portugal
goncalosantosmarques@gmail.com, rpitarma@ipg.pt
[2] Instituto de Telecomunicações, Universidade da Beira Interior, Covilhã, Portugal

Abstract. Water is a limited and essential resource to human existence. Furthermore, water management is not only relevant but also a complex task for several applications such as agriculture and industry. Consequently, the water quality must be monitored in real-time not only to detect water contamination scenarios in a useful time for enhanced public health in smart cities but also to improve agricultural productivity. Internet of Things is the pervasive presence of a variety of objects with interaction and cooperation capabilities among them to reach a common objective and can provide the interoperability to develop essential and cost-effective applications for enhanced smart cities and agricultural activities. This paper presents *iWater*, a cost-effective solution for water quality monitoring based on Internet of Things architecture. This solution is composed of a hardware prototype for water quality analysis and support Web compatibility for data consulting. The results show that the *iWater* provides efficient and effective water quality monitoring using integrated communication technology, combining sensitivity, flexibility, and accuracy of measurement in real-time, allowing significant evolution of the current water quality monitoring systems.

Keywords: Agriculture · Enhanced living environments · Internet of Things · Mobile computing · Smart cities · Water quality monitoring

1 Introduction

Water is a limited and essential resource to human existence. Furthermore, ensure water quality is particularly necessary for several applications such as agriculture and industry [1].

The "smart city" concept is a strategic approach to embrace new urban production circumstances in a collaborative framework and to state the significance of Information and Communication Technologies (ICTs) to promote the competitive characterisation of a city [2]. Cities meet exciting difficulties and obstacles to reach socio-economic evolution and daily life purposes. The "smart city" concept aims to be an answer to these obstacles [3]. The smart city is straightly associated with an emerging approach

© ICST Institute for Computer Sciences, Social Informatics and Telecommunications Engineering 2020
Published by Springer Nature Switzerland AG 2020. All Rights Reserved
H. Santos et al. (Eds.): SmartCity 360 2019, LNICST 323, pp. 312–323, 2020.
https://doi.org/10.1007/978-3-030-51005-3_26

to moderate the difficulties created by the urban population increase and accelerated urbanisation [4]. The smart city approach will lead to several consequences at distinguished levels such as consequences on science, productivity, technology, and culture. Moreover, it will also cause ethical issues as the smart city needs to provide correct information access which is essential when before-mentioned data is accessible at a fine spatial scale where people can be recognised [5]. Natural resources such as rivers, lakes and dams are integral to cities, and as such, the context of a smart city cannot overlook the importance of water. Contamination of such water-based resources by the dumping of industrial waste is, therefore, a relevant problem for the health and well-being of citizens. Real-time monitoring of aquatic resources provides a solution to this scenario as it presents the ability to detect possible contamination on time and enables cities to provide a better quality of life to their citizens.

Internet of Things (IoT) can be defined as a ubiquitous behaviour of material things which promote communication and collaboration abilities between them to reach a shared purpose [6–8]. The IoT implementation will produce different consequences on several perspectives of daily living and will be applied in numerous forms such as home automation, enhanced living environments and medical systems [9, 10]. IoT must be considered as a meaningful approach to the design and development of real-time water quality monitoring solutions. The most relevant issue in smart cities is the interoperability of the different technologies; the IoT can provide the interoperability to build a unified urban-scale ICT platform for smart cities [11].

On several agricultural environments, the water quality supervision is essential to ensure the right water conditions for enhanced productivity and efficiency, and it is particularly essential on aquaculture, aquaponics and hydroponics. Using real-time water quality supervision is possible to store and compare the production results with the water quality data and study their direct impact on productivity and product quality. Furthermore, it is possible to detect poor water quality patterns and plan interventions to improve productivity. Regarding the smart city context, a real-time IoT water monitoring system not only can measure the water quality levels in different places and provide data to the municipal authorities to early detect water pollution and plan interventions but also offer a space-time map of water quality evolution for public safety [12]. Therefore, the water quality must be monitored in real-time for enhanced public health and safety.

This paper presents *iWater*, a cost-effective solution for water quality monitoring based on IoT architecture. This system is based on open-source technologies with several advantages compared to existing systems, such as its modularity, scalability, low-cost and easy installation. The proposed architecture is composed of a hardware prototype for water quality analysis and support Web compatibility for data consulting. This method is based on the ESP8266 with built-in Wi-Fi 2.4 GHz compatibility and incorporates a total dissolved solids (TDS) sensor. The TDS levels are calculated based on electrical conductivity (EC). Dissolved solids are the total weight of all solids that are dissolved in the water. These solids refer to any minerals, salts, metals, cations or anions dissolved in water. In general, the total dissolved solids concentration is the sum of the cations (positively charged) and anions (negatively charged) in the water. Natural processes can originate these minerals or derived from human activities such as agricultural and urban water, which can carry excess minerals, wastewater discharges, industrial wastewater and salt that used to eliminate ice on the road. In fact, according to the World Health Organization, the high concentration of dissolved solids is not associated with health symptoms [13]. However, the analysis and assessment of TDS values evaluation can be used not only to detect in useful time possible water contamination scenarios for enhanced public health and safety in smart cities but also is extremely important to increase productivity and efficiency on agricultural environments. The TDS levels variation indicates the aesthetic characteristics of drinking water and the presence of a broad array of chemical contaminants. On agricultural environments, the TDS levels assessment is particularly relevant for the selection of the fertilisers, which have a direct impact on productivity and product quality. Moreover, both in agriculture and smart city context, the TDS levels must be monitored at least to provide alerts for possible contamination scenarios. The TDS levels supervision can be used as an essential information source to alert the authorities which can behind providing quick interventions to make further validation and tests to make sure that the increase of dissolved solids is not related with contamination scenarios and to ensure water quality.

2   Related Work

Water quality assessment is an essential topic for several agricultural environments such as aquaculture, aquaponics and hydroponics. Aquaculture refers to the cultivation of both marine and freshwater species with the primary objective being to raise fish for consumption. China is not only the world's largest producer, consumer, processor, and exporter of finfish and shellfish but also produces more than one-third of the global fish supply [14]. Hydroponics is a cultivation process where nutrients are administered as mineral nutrients. This method includes numerous benefits such as pest problem mitigation and constant feeding of nutrients while contrasted to conventional cultivation practices [15, 16]. Nevertheless, that approach is high cost, taking into account the energy expenditure contrasted to conventional soil cultivation [17]. Hydroponic cultivation can deliver a higher production rate at a more economical price; however, it additionally holds numerous covered costs [18]. Aquaponics is the symbiotic cultivation of plants and aquatic animals in a recirculating environment which depend on the fish as nutrient-generators. The fish produce waste which is converted to nitrates that are used as plant food through a nitrification process [19]. Therefore, reliable water quality monitoring systems are relevant for enhanced productivity on agricultural environments, particularly on aquaculture, aquaponics and hydroponics.

Numerous monitoring methods for environmental surveillance based on IoT, which combine open-source and mobile computing features are proposed in the state of the art [20–25]. An IoT water monitoring system that includes several sensing capabilities for temperature, light and pH supervision and supports artificial intelligence methods to provide water quality management with 88% of the accuracy is introduced by [26]. A cost-effective monitoring and control system for hydroponic environments which incorporate microcontrollers and open-source technologies for remote access is proposed by [27]. A water monitoring system to support nutrient solution temperature, EC and pH supervision capabilities for non-professional production environments is proposed by [28]. An online water quality supervision system for intensive fish culture in China is proposed by [29]. This system incorporates web-server-embedded features and includes forecast methods to predict water quality data. A wireless sensor network for water quality supervision which includes low-power methods through sleeping mode functionalities was proposed by [30]. A pilot project for water quality monitoring in smart cities was conducted by [31]. The research found positive results in high-frequency data collection and real-time data access.

Smart cities aim to ensure the sustainable use of natural resources in general and water resources in particular [32]. Additionally, with the proliferation of low-cost sensors, there is significant potential to create automated and efficient solutions for environmental monitoring, particularly in the smart city context. The development and test of a specific sensor for monitoring the groundwater salinisation process to optimise water management in smart city environments is proposed by [33].

In conclusion, there are several state-of-the-art applications for water monitoring in the agriculture and smart city context. However, there is a lack of cost-effective and easy to install solutions for enhanced water quality monitoring. The IoT architecture can be assumed as a reliable, cost-effective, easy to install and scalable approach for water quality monitoring; hence, *iWater* is proposed by the authors.

3 Materials and Methods

The proposed method is a cost-effective solution that can be easily used and installed by everyone. This solution uses an ESP8266 as microcontroller and communication unit, and a TDS sensor as a sensing unit. In this section, the hardware and software used for the system development will be discussed in detail.

The proposed system aims to provide a valuable tool for water quality monitoring to promote public health and safety in smart cities and improve productivity in agricultural environments. The authors developed a Wi-Fi system using the ESP8266 module, which implements the IEEE 802.11 b/g/n networking protocol. This microcontroller with built-in Wi-Fi capabilities is used both as the processing and communication unit. In the case of agricultural fields without a Wi-Fi connection, a 3G/4G wireless router can be used to provide Wi-Fi availability. The 3G/4G wireless routers are commonly used for several applications and achieve the system communication requirement where broadband cellular network technology is available. The monitored data is stored in a Microsoft SQL Server database using Web services. For data consulting a Web portal named *iWaterWeb* has been developed using ASP.NET C# (Fig. 1). The *iWaterWeb* and the. NET Web Services are hosted at the same Windows Server instance.

The proposed solution is based on open-source technologies and is a wireless system, with several advantages compared to existing systems, such as its modularity, scalability, low-cost and easy installation. The *iWater* incorporates a microcontroller with native Wi-Fi support, a FireBeetle ESP8266 (*DFRobot*) and the TDS sensor module (*DFRobot*) is connected using analogue interface. Figure 2 represents the prototype developed by the authors. A short description of the components used in the development of the *iWater* prototype is presented below:

- **FireBeetle ESP8266:** is a wireless board with unified antenna switches, power and low noise amplifiers which is compatible with 802.11 b/g/n protocols. Additionally,

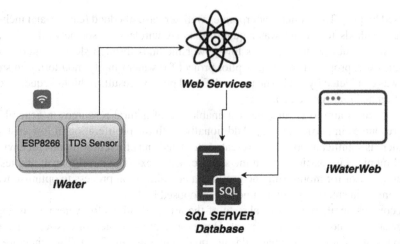

Fig. 1. *iWater* architecture.

this board is WPA/WPA2 compatible and includes a 32-bit MCU and 10-bit ADC. The selected board includes a 16 MB SPI flash memory.

- **DFRobot TDS module:** is a TDS sensor that provides reliable readings, supports AC excitation source to prevent the probe from polarisation effectively, and a waterproof probe. The module size is 42 × 32 mm. The operating voltage range is 3.3 V–5 V, and the analogue interface output voltage is 0–2.3 V. The TDS range us 0–1000 ppm and accuracy of ±10% FS (25 °C). The operating power consumption is 3–6 mA.

The sensor module includes an AC signal as an excitation source. The excitation source is able to efficiently block the probe from polarisation, increase the lifetime of the module, and enhance the stability of the sensor output. The sensor probe can be covered in water for extended analysis periods. The sensor module has been selected according to the cost of the system. The main goal of the research study is to test the functional architecture of the proposed method. Nevertheless, a stable and precise sensor module has been selected and supports 10% full scale (FS) accuracy. Additional sensors modules can be combined to control different water conditions.

The proposed method provides easy network configuration procedures. The system is by a standard in client mode. Only if it remains incapable of connecting to any network, it changes the working mode to a hotspot mode. At this moment, the created hotspot can be used to introduce the credentials of the wireless network for Internet access. Figure 3 shows the network configuration method.

The firmware of the *iWater* is implemented using the Arduino Core that is an open-source platform that aims to enable the use of standard Arduino functions and libraries directly on the ESP8266 without an external microcontroller. The *iWater* is a cost-effective system for enhanced water quality monitoring, which costs an estimated 30.99 USD (Table 1).

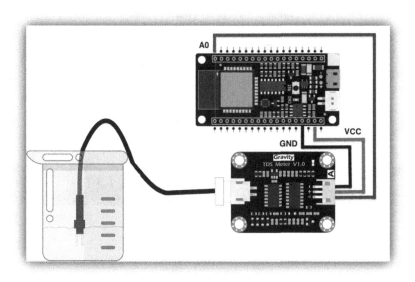

Fig. 2. *iWater* component diagram.

The Web application is denominated by *iWaterWeb* was developed with C# programming language in Visual Studio. The *iWaterWeb* provides real-time water quality monitoring data access using a Web browser. Figure 4 shows the *iWaterWeb* application.

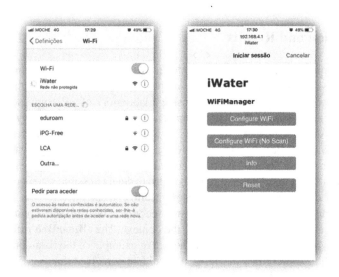

Fig. 3. *iWater* Wi-Fi network configuration process.

Table 1. Cost of the *iWater* system.

Component	Cost
FireBeetle ESP8266	7.50 USD
DFRobot TDS module	12.90 USD
Cables and box	10.59 USD
Total	30.99 USD

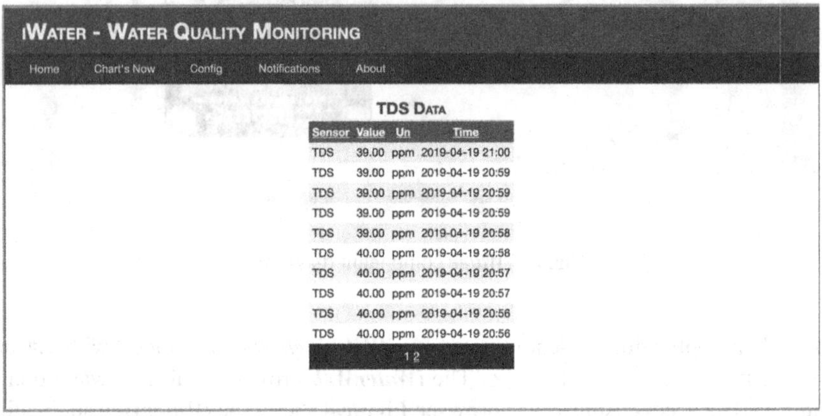

Fig. 4. *iWaterWeb* application.

4   Discussion and Results

For testing purposes, the *iWater* was mounted inside a glass laboratory volumetric flask. The system was tested with several water samples with different salt concentration. The experimental activities were conducted inside a laboratory of a Portuguese University. Figure 4 presents the water quality supervision experiments conducted by the authors. The module is powered using a 230 V–5 V AC-DC 2 A power supply. The tests show that the proposed water quality monitoring system can be used to detect poor water quality at low-cost. Furthermore, the proposed system can provide TDS monitoring for enhanced productivity in agricultural environments but also to detect possible water contamination by wastewater discharges to promote citizens health and safety.

The information is gathered every thirty seconds; however, this condition can be modified concerning the requirements of the context. The *iWaterWeb* offers information access as graphical or statistical methods. An example of the data obtained by the proposed method is presented in Fig. 5. It should be perceived that Fig. 5 presents the results achieved in the physical context with produced simulations. The response time and effectiveness of the proposed method have been tested with different samples of water with distinct salt concentrations. The outcomes assure the capacity to identify TDS levels changes in real-time and confirm a fast sensor response time (Fig. 6).

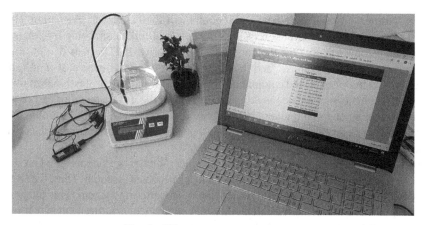

Fig. 5. *iWater* system prototype tests.

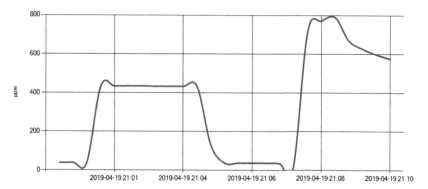

Fig. 6. TDS data collected in the tests performed.

The graphics displaying the TDS levels provide a better perception of the behaviour of the monitored parameters than the numerical format. On the one hand, the *iWaterWeb* provides easy and quick access to collected data and enables a more precise analysis of water quality temporal evolution. Thus, the system is a powerful tool for water supervision and to support decision making on possible interventions to increase productivity but also to detect contamination scenarios. On the other hand, the proposed IoT approach provide temporal water quality data for visualisation and analytics, which are particularly relevant to detect unproductive situations and plan interventions to promote a productive agricultural environment.

At present, water monitoring solutions are expensive and are based on random sampling. However, these procedures are limited by providing only information related to a specific sampling and being devoid of spatiotemporal behaviour. Most of the professional solutions available on the market are portable and compact, offering data logging on the equipment itself. However, these solutions do not support real-time data availability for city authorities or agricultural managers in order to enable rapid and efficient intervention to improve people health and productivity, respectively. For example, TDS pens are low-cost, easy to use and widely used equipment for TDS levels evaluation. However, TDS pens do not offer data transmissions and real-time monitoring for enhanced water quality supervision. One the one hand, the majority of TDS pens do not offer a history data consulting features, and the user can only be consulted in real-time values using an LCD interface on the equipment. On the other hand, the professional solutions which offer a history of data consulting are limited to the device memory and require data downloading and manipulation procedures with specific software. Additionally, a limited number of professional instruments have high accuracy and can send data to the control system, but the cost is expensive.

In this way, the development of innovative water monitoring systems based on state-of-the-art technologies that allow real-time analysis becomes essential. Thus, the *iWater* was developed in order to provide water quality monitoring system with integrated technology, combining sensitivity, flexibility, and accuracy of measurement in real-time, allowing significant evolution of the current water quality monitoring systems. The results are favourable as the proposed system can be used to provide a correct water monitoring assessment at low-cost. The proposed system can be used to support advanced agricultural methods but also to early detect possible contamination scenarios in smart cities. Furthermore, in the agricultural environments, the effective productivity results can be compared with the monitored data, which is particularly valuable for a correct evaluation and study of the cultivation methods used. Another significant improvement of the presented monitoring system is the scalability and modularity of the proposed method. The installation can begin applying one system, and other modules can be installed according to the necessities of the environment.

As future work, the main goal is to make technical improvements, including the development of essential alert methods such as SMS or e-mail to advise the user when TDS levels meet some parametrised values. The authors also plan to develop a mobile application for water quality analytics and notifications. Infrared thermography (IRT) technology is an appropriate method for plant disease supervision [34]. The authors plan to correlate the proposed system results in the context of the studies being carried out on the IRT technology applied to the monitoring of plants. Moreover, the results achieved will support the correlation between poor water quality effects on plants supported by IRT technology.

5 Conclusions

With the proliferation of IoT and mobile computing technologies on the smart city and agricultural context, it is relevant to develop automatic water monitoring systems. Therefore, this paper presents a cost-effective solution for water quality monitoring composed by a hardware prototype for water quality analysis and Web compatibility for data consulting. On the one hand, this solution can be used for enhanced water management at low-cost for enhanced productivity and quality in the agricultural environment context. Using *iWater*, the collected data can be especially valued to investigate and store the temporal changes of the water quality in order to guarantee that they are established in the course of all the agricultural process. On the other hand, rivers, lakes, and dams are integral to cities. Furthermore, the contamination of these natural resources by wastewater discharges and salt that is used to eliminate ice on the road is a relevant problem for the health and well-being of citizens. The *iWater* provides real-time monitoring of aquatic resources in order to address a solution to this scenario as it presents the ability to detect possible contamination scenarios on time and enables cities to provide a better quality of life to their citizens.

At present, water monitoring solutions are expensive and are based on random sampling. However, these procedures are limiting by providing only information related to a specific sampling and being devoid of spatiotemporal behaviour. The results achieved are promising; the *iWater* indicates a significant contribution to cost-effective water quality supervision solutions based on IoT and open-source technologies. Compared to existing systems, the *iWater* allows the access to the history of the water quality in the graphical representation in real-time but also provides other relevant advantages such as its modularity, scalability, low-cost and easy installation.

Although the suggested method has constraints, the *iWater* requires additional laboratory validation procedures to increase calibration and precision. Moreover, quality assurance and quality control have also been intended to increase product quality traceability. Technological enhancements include the addition of fundamental warning techniques such as SMS or e-mail when a TDS levels reach predefined values are also projected as future work.

References

1. Ballance, R., Bartram, J.: Water Quality Monitoring: A Practical Guide to the Design and Implementation of Freshwater Quality Studies and Monitoring Programmes. CRC Press, Boca Raton (2002)
2. Caragliu, A., Del Bo, C., Nijkamp, P.: Smart cities in Europe. J. Urban Technol. **18**, 65–82 (2011). https://doi.org/10.1080/10630732.2011.601117
3. Schaffers, H., Komninos, N., Pallot, M., Trousse, B., Nilsson, M., Oliveira, A.: Smart cities and the future internet: towards cooperation frameworks for open innovation. In: Domingue, J., et al. (eds.) FIA 2011. LNCS, vol. 6656, pp. 431–446. Springer, Heidelberg (2011). https://doi.org/10.1007/978-3-642-20898-0_31
4. Chourabi, H., et al.: Understanding smart cities: an integrative framework. In: 2012 45th Hawaii International Conference on System Sciences, pp. 2289–2297. IEEE, Maui (2012). https://doi.org/10.1109/HICSS.2012.615
5. Batty, M., et al.: Smart cities of the future. Eur. Phys. J. Spec. Top. **214**, 481–518 (2012). https://doi.org/10.1140/epjst/e2012-01703-3
6. Giusto, D., Iera, A., Morabito, G., Atzori, L. (eds.): The Internet of Things: 20th Tyrrhenian Workshop on Digital Communications. Springer, New York (2010). https://doi.org/10.1007/978-1-4419-1674-7
7. Marques, G.: Ambient assisted living and internet of things. In: Cardoso, P.J.S., Monteiro, J., Semião, J., Rodrigues, J.M.F. (eds.) Harnessing the Internet of Everything (IoE) for Accelerated Innovation Opportunities, pp. 100–115. IGI Global, Hershey (2019). https://doi.org/10.4018/978-1-5225-7332-6.ch005
8. Marques, G., Pitarma, R., Garcia, N.M., Pombo, N.: Internet of things architectures, technologies, applications, challenges, and future directions for enhanced living environments and healthcare systems: a review. Electronics **8**, 1081 (2019). https://doi.org/10.3390/electronics8101081

9. Gubbi, J., Buyya, R., Marusic, S., Palaniswami, M.: Internet of Things (IoT): a vision, architectural elements, and future directions. Future Gener. Comput. Syst. **29**, 1645–1660 (2013). https://doi.org/10.1016/j.future.2013.01.010

10. Marques, G., Pitarma, R.: mHealth: indoor environmental quality measuring system for enhanced health and well-being based on internet of things. JSAN **8**, 43 (2019). https://doi.org/10.3390/jsan8030043

11. Zanella, A., Bui, N., Castellani, A., Vangelista, L., Zorzi, M.: Internet of things for smart cities. IEEE Internet Things J. **1**, 22–32 (2014). https://doi.org/10.1109/JIOT.2014.2306328

12. Talari, S., Shafie-khah, M., Siano, P., Loia, V., Tommasetti, A., Catalão, J.: A review of smart cities based on the internet of things concept. Energies **10**, 421 (2017). https://doi.org/10.3390/en10040421

13. World Health Organization: Total dissolved solids in Drinking-water: background document for development of WHO guidelines for drinking-water quality. World Health Organization (2003)

14. Cao, L., et al.: China's aquaculture and the world's wild fisheries. Science **347**, 133–135 (2015). https://doi.org/10.1126/science.1260149

15. Jung, D.-H., Kim, H.-J., Cho, W.-J., Park, S.H., Yang, S.-H.: Validation testing of an ion-specific sensing and control system for precision hydroponic macronutrient management. Comput. Electron. Agric. **156**, 660–668 (2019). https://doi.org/10.1016/j.compag.2018.12.025

16. Marques, G., Aleixo, D., Pitarma, R.: Enhanced hydroponic agriculture environmental monitoring: an internet of things approach. In: Rodrigues, J.M.F., et al. (eds.) ICCS 2019. LNCS, vol. 11538, pp. 658–669. Springer, Cham (2019). https://doi.org/10.1007/978-3-030-22744-9_51

17. Gomiero, T.: Food quality assessment in organic vs. conventional agricultural produce: findings and issues. Appl. Soil Ecol. **123**, 714–728 (2018). https://doi.org/10.1016/j.apsoil.2017.10.014

18. Zanella, A., et al.: Humusica 2, article 17: techno humus systems and global change – three crucial questions. Appl. Soil. Ecol. **122**, 237–253 (2018). https://doi.org/10.1016/j.apsoil.2017.10.010

19. Maucieri, C., Schmautz, Z., Borin, M., Sambo, P., Junge, R., Nicoletto, C.: Hydroponic systems and water management in aquaponics : a review (2018). https://doi.org/10.21256/zhaw-3671

20. Marques, G., Pitarma, R.: Agricultural environment monitoring system using wireless sensor networks and IoT. In: 2018 13th Iberian Conference on Information Systems and Technologies (CISTI), pp. 1–6. IEEE, Caceres (2018). https://doi.org/10.23919/CISTI.2018.8399320

21. Pitarma, R., Marques, G., Ferreira, B.R.: Monitoring indoor air quality for enhanced occupational health. J. Med. Syst. **41** (2017). https://doi.org/10.1007/s10916-016-0667-2

22. Marques, G., Ferreira, C.R., Pitarma, R.: Indoor air quality assessment using a CO_2 monitoring system based on internet of things. J. Med. Syst. **43** (2019). https://doi.org/10.1007/s10916-019-1184-x

23. Marques, G., Roque Ferreira, C., Pitarma, R.: A system based on the internet of things for real-time particle monitoring in buildings. Int. J. Environ. Res. Public Health **15**, 821 (2018). https://doi.org/10.3390/ijerph15040821

24. Marques, G., Pitarma, R.: An internet of things-based environmental quality management system to supervise the indoor laboratory conditions. Appl. Sci. **9**, 438 (2019). https://doi.org/10.3390/app9030438

25. Marques, G., Pitarma, R.: A cost-effective air quality supervision solution for enhanced living environments through the internet of things. Electronics **8**, 170 (2019). https://doi.org/10.3390/electronics8020170

26. Mehra, M., Saxena, S., Sankaranarayanan, S., Tom, R.J., Veeramanikandan, M.: IoT based hydroponics system using deep neural networks. Comput. Electron. Agric. **155**, 473–486 (2018). https://doi.org/10.1016/j.compag.2018.10.015

27. Palande, V., Zaheer, A., George, K.: Fully automated hydroponic system for indoor plant growth. Procedia Comput. Sci. **129**, 482–488 (2018). https://doi.org/10.1016/j.procs.2018.03.028

28. Ruengittinun, S., Phongsamsuan, S., Sureeratanakorn, P.: Applied internet of thing for smart hydroponic farming ecosystem (HFE). In: 2017 10th International Conference on Ubi-media Computing and Workshops (Ubi-Media), pp. 1–4. IEEE, Pattaya (2017). https://doi.org/10.1109/UMEDIA.2017.8074148

29. Zhu, X., Li, D., He, D., Wang, J., Ma, D., Li, F.: A remote wireless system for water quality online monitoring in intensive fish culture. Comput. Electron. Agric. **71**, S3–S9 (2010). https://doi.org/10.1016/j.compag.2009.10.004

30. Wang, Z., Wang, Q., Hao, X.: The design of the remote water quality monitoring system based on WSN. In: 2009 5th International Conference on Wireless Communications, Networking and Mobile Computing, pp. 1–4. IEEE, Beijing (2009). https://doi.org/10.1109/WICOM.2009.5303974

31. Chen, Y., Han, D.: Water quality monitoring in smart city: a pilot project. Autom. Constr. **89**, 307–316 (2018). https://doi.org/10.1016/j.autcon.2018.02.008

32. Pellicer, S., Santa, G., Bleda, A.L., Maestre, R., Jara, A.J., Skarmeta, A.G.: A global perspective of smart cities: a survey. In: 2013 Seventh International Conference on Innovative Mobile and Internet Services in Ubiquitous Computing, pp. 439–444. IEEE, Taichung (2013). https://doi.org/10.1109/IMIS.2013.79

33. Parra, L., Sendra, S., Lloret, J., Bosch, I.: Development of a conductivity sensor for monitoring groundwater resources to optimise water management in smart city environments. Sensors **15**, 20990–21015 (2015). https://doi.org/10.3390/s150920990

34. Mahlein, A.-K., Oerke, E.-C., Steiner, U., Dehne, H.-W.: Recent advances in sensing plant diseases for precision crop protection. Eur. J. Plant Pathol. **133**, 197–209 (2012). https://doi.org/10.1007/s10658-011-9878-z

Person Tracking in Heavy Industry Environments with Camera Images

Nico Zengeler$^{(\boxtimes)}$, Alexander Arntz, Dustin Keßler, Matthias Grimm,
Ziyaad Qasem, Marc Jansen, Sabrina Eimler, and Uwe Handmann

Hochschule Ruhr West, Lützowstraße 5, 46236 Bottrop, Germany
{nico.zengeler,alexander.arntz,dustin.kessler,matthias.grimm,
ziyaad.qasem,marc.jansen,sabrina.eimler,uwe.handmann}@hs-ruhrwest.de
https://www.hochschule-ruhr-west.de/

Abstract. In this paper, we propose a method to localise and track persons in heavy industry environments with multiple cameras. Using the OpenPose network, we localise the persons feet points on each cameras image individually and perform according 3D transformations. With prior knowledge about the camera settings in the environment, we use a rule-based system to assess which sensor detections to fuse. We then apply Kalman filtering in order to stabilise the tracking. Due to a variable image stack size, our method may increase accuracy if provided with additional computational resources by processing more frames in realtime. We have simulated a heavy industry scenario and use the recorded video material and position data as a basis for our evaluation.

Keywords: Heavy industry · Industry 4.0 · Person tracking · Artificial intelligence · Image processing

1 Introduction

Industry 4.0 requires software to support and enhance existing heavy industry structures. Digital facility management systems help to increase productivity, work safety and the production process transparency [2,10,12,14]. For example, concerning work safety, in a case of emergency, workers may want to follow the shortest route to the exit. In a steel industry site, this route may lead across a potentially dangerous area, for example a freshly rolled, hot sheet steel. Moving on that sheet would cause the worker's boots to melt with the hot steel, which causes a high impact on the workers health and high costs for the corporation. An intelligent work safety system may prevent such a situation by providing the right warning at the right time using appropriate means.

Such a system may use cameras and mobile devices to locate and identify persons in dangerous situations. To do so, such systems need to gather and analyse as much information about the production process as possible in realtime, put them into context and perform the right actions. The project *DamokleS 4.0* [5]

© ICST Institute for Computer Sciences, Social Informatics and Telecommunications Engineering 2020
Published by Springer Nature Switzerland AG 2020. All Rights Reserved
H. Santos et al. (Eds.): SmartCity 360 2019, LNICST 323, pp. 324–336, 2020.
https://doi.org/10.1007/978-3-030-51005-3_27

aims to develop a system to support employees in heavy industry using modern hardware and software. In this particular contribution, we use camera images to perform human foot point localisation and provide these detections to a rich context model. Knowing the worker's locations and roles within the production process allows the context model to display valuable, individual information. In our scenarios, augmented reality (AR) devices poll the context model in order to show supportive advises to their current user. For example, an information service provides relevant data about the workers current task to his or her augmented reality device, as shown in Fig. 1. This way a worker receives context-sensitive and role-specific information, for example the state of a machine, a concrete work instruction or an evacuation route in case of emergency.

Fig. 1. Exemplary augmented reality information depending on the workers current position. Left: an instruction to check a serial number. Right: displaying an evacuation route in case of emergency.

In this paper we describe a holistic software approach to localise and track workers in heavy industry settings, solely on the basis camera images, using methods of artificial intelligence. We begin this paper by delineating this contribution within the context of the project *DamokleS 4.0* and presenting the current state of the art. In Sect. 3, a description of our software implementation explains the workflow of our program in detail. Then we present the setup of our laboratory experiments and examine how we have collected our data in Sect. 4. We also statistically evaluate the accuracy of our system compared to ground truth data, as provided by the augmented reality devices positioning. In the last section we conclude with a short discussion of our final results, the pros and cons of our implementation and possible future work.

2   State of the Art

Current state of the art research investigates person tracking techniques under various points of view with different approaches. For example, [20] proposes a person tracking algorithm for an autonomous unmanned aerial vehicle. In this approach, a drone with a surveillance camera follows individual persons, which allows for a very flexible surveillance system with the benefit of easy face recognition. Compared to a stationary camera-based approach, the aerial vehicle seems impractical for an industrial application, as the flying drone may collide with moving objects like cranes, vehicles or even other persons. Considering person identification techniques, state of the art researchers focus on methods of deep transfer learning [4,7]. These methods allow for single-shot person re-identification and prove that transfer learning may increase detection performance in that domain using very little training data. For our heavy industry application, we chose to identify workers via their wearable smart devices instead of face recognition. To handle the problem of tracking multiple persons, [9] utilise slow feature analysis [23]. [1] presents a computational framework for interpreting person tracking data, which consists of four modules for tracking instantaneous and short-time features as well as unsupervised and supervised machine learning techniques for higher levels of abstraction.

Concerning the *DamokleS 4.0* project [5], [17] describes the overall software architecture underlying our context model [6]. Also, [17] sketched the essential ideas that drive our test scenarios as well as the associated processes for implementation in mobile devices. The suggested scenarios concern workplace safety as well as production and maintenance applications. The proposed approach provides context-based support for factory employees during all these scenarios. For context recognition, [17] proposes the usage of mobile device sensors and external sensors devices mounted in the factory building, for example cameras and beacons. [24] evaluated a variety of human detection methods and concluded that the OpenPose system [3,18,21] suits our purpose best as it provides a most reliable foot point detection, even under challenging image conditions.

In a related project we developed a video surveillance system to protect critical infrastructures [8]. In this project we designed a software architecture that supports human operators to detect, track and recognize suspicious subjects in case of an alert. The human operator may sort video frames by personally selecting important features. He or she may flag suspicious subjects and reidentify them in a video database. The camera-based data analysis consisted of several image processing modules like a salient-based people detection and a histogram of oriented gradients (HOG) algorithm based on the implementation of [16]. We decided to use a GPU-based implementation to speed up the HOG algorithm and fulfill our realtime requirements. The scenarios described in [8] resemble those in the context of heavy industries with respect to challenges introduced by different light conditions and the high need for fast algorithms.

On the basis of the referenced developments, we can state that the interaction of the collected data and the constantly evolving algorithms holds a great potential for the improvement of industrial processes and the everyday working life.

3   Implementation

Our software architecture consists of three different modules, which operate on a live video stream of multiple cameras in real-time. Fig. 2 shows the program flowchart of the single processing steps. Starting with a human foot point detection system, for which we have used the OpenPose architecture [3,18,21], a coordinate transformation from image coordinates into world coordinates provides input to the second module, a rule-based sensor fusion approach. The rule-based system also prepares the trajectories for the third module, a Kalman filter, by assigning them to linear tracks. All processing steps take place on the same stack of images, guaranteeing real-time capability in a trade-off between stack size and available computing resources. The more images the software sees, the more accurate it gets. Maintaining real-time capability only depends on the available computing resources. As input we present a stack of k images per camera and choose k such that the program runs as fast and as accurate as possible. Increasing k leads to more accurate detections at the cost of higher computation time. As output we obtain current person locations in world coordinates, which we may send to a remote context model. The context model may relate the locations with other data, for example to identify persons via smart devices.

3.1 Foot Point Detection and Coordinate Transformation

Before performing the foot point detection, we improve the camera images by performing an adaptive histogram equalisation with a tile grid size of eight by eight pixels [15]. We then localise the person's foot points in camera image coordinates using the corresponding foot keypoints of the COCO model as provided by OpenPose [3,18,21]. Our calibration process assumes that the person moves on a flat plane, so we use a temporary constant height coordinate $z = 1$, which we simply discard after transformation. To transform the camera coordinates $(x, y, 1)^T$ into world coordinates $(p_x, p_y)^T$, we use the intrinsic camera matrix M, the rotation matrix R and the translation vector d, which we have obtained via a standard calibration process using chessboard patterns [11,13]. Constructing an auxiliary matrix

$$R' = \begin{pmatrix} R_{0,0}, R_{0,1}, R_{0,2} \\ R_{1,0}, R_{1,1}, R_{1,2} \\ d_0, d_1, d_2 \end{pmatrix} \tag{1}$$

leads to a coordinate transformation that reads as follows:

$$\begin{pmatrix} p_x \\ p_y \end{pmatrix} = \begin{pmatrix} x \\ y \\ 1 \end{pmatrix} (R'M)^{-1} \tag{2}$$

The resulting world coordinates relate to the origin of the chessboard pattern. For multiple cameras, which observe distinct parts of the environment, we perform multiple extrinsic calibrations and then translate the world coordinates by the distance vectors between the different coordinate origins.

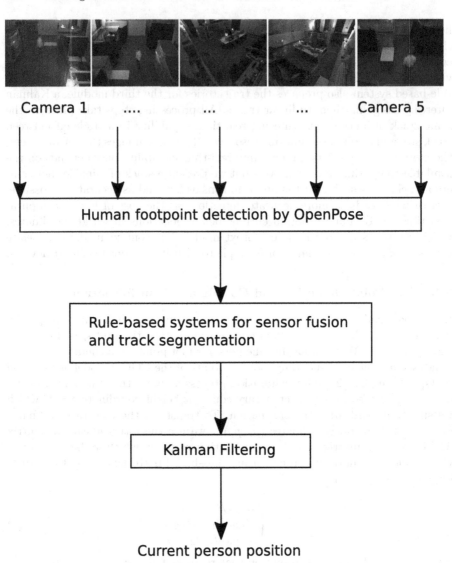

Fig. 2. The program flowchart of our person tracking procedure. The top row shows example frames, taken from the same trial at the same time. From left to right: cameras $C1$ to $C5$ as shown in Fig. 3. The person currently moves within sight of cameras $C1, C2, C5$ but out of sight for cameras $C3$ and $C4$.

3.2   Sensor Fusion and Track Separation

The second module consists of rule-based systems, that start by fusing the detections from the localisation module using prior knowledge about the camera setup. To solve the problem of missing detections by noise, we perform an autocompletion within the k frames: if in a frame we find no detection, but in the previous and following frame we do, we replace the missing detection with the geometric mean between the two successful detection. This way, we complete the detections within k frames and maintain real-time applicability for an optimal value of k. Knowing on which frame we have a detection, we put these detections into a two-dimensional boolean matrix, which tells us about which camera yields a coherent detection within the real-time window. Using this matrix, we apply a rule-based system that decides which detections to fuse together. To do so, a hard coded rule set reflects our prior knowledge about the concrete camera setup in the environment. Upon this knowledge, we apply a set of conditional clauses to decide the world coordinate fusion. If, for example, $C3$ and $C4$ detect the same person, we calculate a geometric mean of the two proposed world coordinates. To prepare the position data for Kalman filtering, we apply a rule set that assigns each position to a unique track. Each track features a steady motion, which simplifies the Kalman filtering procedure.

3.3 Kalman Filtering

In order to smooth the resulting trajectory, we employ a Kalman filter [22] on each of the separated tracks, as shown in Fig. 5. To initialize the Kalman filter, we use a four-dimensional steady motion dynamics, capturing the persons position $(p_x, p_y)^T$ as well as the persons current velocity $(v_x, v_y)^T$ with respect to a fixed time step dt as given by the camera recording frequency:

$$F = \begin{pmatrix} 1 & 0 & dt & 0 \\ 0 & 1 & 0 & dt \\ 0 & 0 & 1 & 0 \\ 0 & 0 & 0 & 1 \end{pmatrix} \tag{3}$$

such that:

$$\begin{pmatrix} p_x \\ p_y \\ v_x \\ v_y \end{pmatrix}_{t+1} = F \cdot \begin{pmatrix} p_x \\ p_y \\ v_x \\ v_y \end{pmatrix}_t \tag{4}$$

We use a unit matrix to initialise the Kalman filter covariance matrix. For the estimation process, we iterate over k subsequent positions, thus maintaining real-time applicability.

4 Evaluation

We use the recordings of a laboratory study to evaluate our person tracking approach in a simulated industrial environment. In this study, as part of the *DamokleS 4.0* project [5], the test persons wear augmented reality glasses which guide them through a parcour. During this course, they have to solve three tasks and, for the last part, follow an evacuation route to the exit, as depicted in

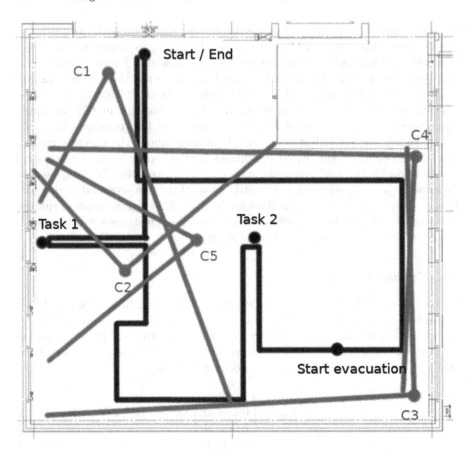

Fig. 3. The test parcour of our simulated industrial environment. The test persons follow a route (blue) and solve a number of tasks. Five cameras (green) record video footage. (Color figure online)

Fig. 3. The original user study featured two different navigation modalities and corresponding questionnaires, which aimed to evaluate the test person's feelings and attitudes towards this technology from a psychological point of view. For our person tracking study, we discard this information and merely use the collected video recordings.

4.1   Setup

Figure 3 shows the setup of our test course and the camera positions. As shown in the example frames in Fig. 2, the test persons wear safety vests and move in sight of a certain subset of our cameras. As shown in Fig. 3, the camera sets

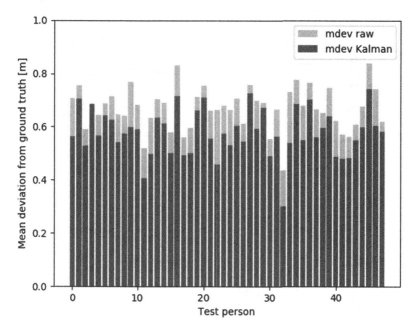

Fig. 4. The mean deviation in meters between the estimated camera positions and the ground truth positions from the augmented reality device for each test person. The red bars show the mean deviations for the raw camera estimations, and the blue bars show the mean deviations for the Kalman filtered positions. (Color figure online)

$(C1, C2, C5)$ and $(C3, C4)$ observe distinct parts of the environment. Each set has a unique calibration origin, which we relate to the parcour starting point by a translation vector which we have measures using a scale.

4.2 Results

Our cameras recorded video footage with eight to twelve frames per second, so we have used a stack size of $k = 4$ frames to maintain real-time applicability with our hardware. As the augmented reality device recorded positions with a rate of two positions per second, the cameras yield more data in the same time as they record with a higher frame rate. Figure 5 shows the complete trajectories for the ground truth data as provided by the augmented reality device, the raw camera position estimations after sensor fusion, the separated tracks and the final positions after Kalman filtering. The statistics about the travelled distances, durations and velocities, as shown in Fig. 6, ignore the different temporal resolutions induced by different recording rates. In order to compare the mean deviations between the estimated camera positions and the ground truth trajectories, as shown in Fig. 4, we solve the problem of the different temporal resolutions by searching the nearest point in the ground truth positions for each camera position.

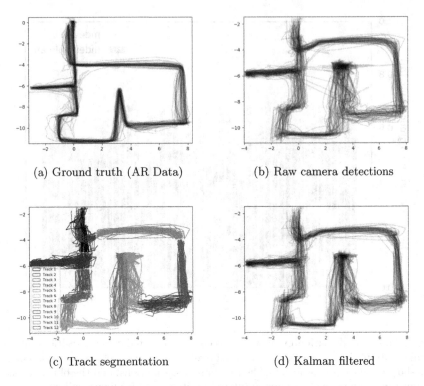

(a) Ground truth (AR Data) (b) Raw camera detections

(c) Track segmentation (d) Kalman filtered

Fig. 5. Resulting trajectories, all scales in meters. The top left figure shows the ground truth as provided by the augmented reality device, the top right plot demonstrates the trajectories after the detection of foot points and the appliance of the first rule-based system. In the bottom left plot we visualise the results after track separation. As shown in the bottom right plot, the trajectories after Kalman filtering closely resemble the positions from the ground truth data.

The average of the mean deviations between the raw camera position estimates and the ground truth data evaluates to about $0.6\,m$, while the average of the mean deviations between the Kalman filtered final positions and the ground truth positions lies slightly lower at about $0.59\,m$. This corresponds to the trajectories, which come closer to the ground truth after Kalman filtering. Looking at the trajectories in Fig. 5, we find a slight metrical distortion in the start and end region, as only camera $C2$ observes this region. Analysing the histograms in Fig. 6, we can state that both the travelled distances and the average velocities come closer to the original distribution after Kalman filtering. Furthermore, we can see that in the evacuation tracks, tracks number nine to twelve, the average velocities show higher values.

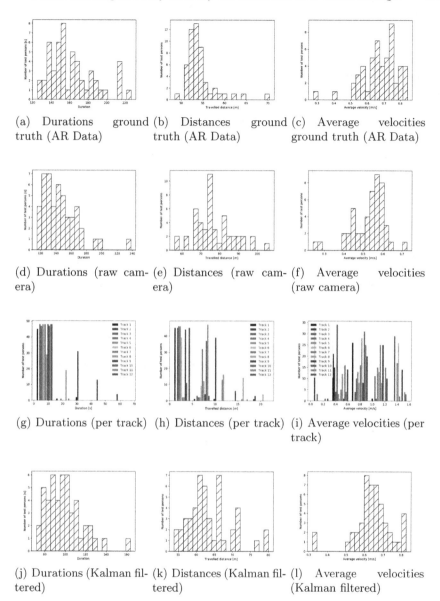

(a) Durations ground truth (AR Data)

(b) Distances ground truth (AR Data)

(c) Average velocities ground truth (AR Data)

(d) Durations (raw camera)

(e) Distances (raw camera)

(f) Average velocities (raw camera)

(g) Durations (per track)

(h) Distances (per track)

(i) Average velocities (per track)

(j) Durations (Kalman filtered)

(k) Distances (Kalman filtered)

(l) Average velocities (Kalman filtered)

Fig. 6. The histograms showing overall statistics about the results after our image processing procedure. From left to right: duration in seconds, travelled distances in meters, average velocities in meters per second. From top to bottom: ground truth data from the augmented reality (AR) device, raw camera detections, statistics per individual track and the final Kalman filtered results.

5   Conclusion

We have contributed a method to evaluate person detection models for heavy industry environments and published our source code, raw data and results under [19]. From the metrical distortion that we have observed and described in Sect. 4.2, we conclude that for a reliable location estimation a person must move in sight of at least two calibrated cameras. To obtain accurate tracking results on camera images, we strongly recommend the usage of additional means like Kalman filters. For reasons of data protection, we decide to identify persons via their smartphones in a context model instead of using face recognition on camera images.

5.1   Discussion

In our evaluations we used the default parameters for of all our third party software, like the OpenPose framework and the Matlab camera calibration toolbox. Changing these hyper parameters may improve results. More computational resources allows our approach to deliver better tracking results while maintaining real time capability by increasing a single parameter, the image stack size. The sensor fusion in form of a rule-based system relies on previous knowledge but allows for easy changes due to its transparent rule set. Our model assumes that the persons move on a flat plane, so it can't tell different height levels from each other. The rule-based systems, although transparent to the user and easy to change, miss the flexibility to simply work for other setups. The same problem arises for our rather static track segmentation. Our laboratory study only provided video material containing one single person in the parcour, so we did not evaluate our system for multiple persons. Our systems makes no assumptions on the number of persons, which we leave for future investigations.

5.2   Future Work

To further develop our approach, a more flexible track assignment might yield a high profit. For example, a reinforcement learning agent may learn to open and close track assignments dynamically. Also we might employ Kalman filters on the detections in image coordinates to further stabilise the detections. Using means of Transfer Learning, we may investigate how to easily adapt our models to other situations.

Acknowledgement. This work was supported by the *DamokleS 4.0* project [5] project funded by the European Regional Development Fund (ERDF), the European Union (EU) and the federal state North Rhine Westphalia.

References

1. Amin, S., Burke, J. OpenMoves: a system for interpreting person-tracking data (2018). https://doi.org/10.1145/3212721.3212846
2. Bunte, A., et al.: Evaluation of cognitive architectures for cyber-physical production systems. CoRR abs/1902.08448. arXiv: 1902.08448. http://arxiv.org/abs/1902.08448 (2019)
3. Cao, Z., Simon, T., Wei, S.-E., Sheikh, Y.: Realtime multi-person 2D pose estimation using part affinity fields. In: CVPR (2017)
4. Chen, H. et al.: Deep transfer learning for person re-identification (2018). https://doi.org/10.1109/BigMM.2018.8499067
5. DamokleS 4.0 - IKT für Cyber Physical Systems. https://www.damokles40.eu/. Accessed 31 Oct 2018
6. Dey, A.K.: Understanding and using context. Pers. Ubiquit. Comput. **5**, 4–7 (2001). ISSN 1617–4909
7. Gómez-Silva, J.M., Izquierdo, E., de la Escalera, A., Armingol, J.M.: Transferring learning from multi-person tracking to person re-identification. Integr. Comput.-Aided Eng. 1–16 (2019)
8. Handmann, U., Hommel, S., Grimm, M., Malysiak, D.: APFel - fast multi camera people tracking at airports, based on decentralized video indexing. Science^3- -Saf. Secur. 48–55 (2014)
9. Hao, T., Wang, Q., Wu, D., Sun, J.-S.: Multiple person tracking based on slow feature analysis. Multimed. Tools Appl. **77**(3), 3623–3637 (2017). https://doi.org/10.1007/s11042-017-5218-4
10. Hasselbring, W. et al.: Industrial DevOps. CoRR abs/1907.01875. arXiv:1907.01875. http://arxiv.org/abs/1907.01875 (2019)
11. Heikkila, J., Silven, O.: A four-step camera calibration procedure with implicit image correction. In: Proceedings of the 1997 Conference on Computer Vision and Pattern Recognition (CVPR 1997), p. 1106. IEEE Computer Society, Washington, DC, USA (1997). ISBN 0-8186-7822-4. http://dl.acm.org/citation.cfm?id=794189.794489
12. Hermsen, K., et al.: Dynamic, adaptive and mobile system for context- based and intelligent support of employees in the steel industry. In: 4th ESTAD (European Steel Technology and Application Days), Düsseldorf, Germany (2019). https://www.metec-estad2019.com/files/190619_metec-estad_programmflyer_a5q_web-5.pdf
13. MathWorks: Camera Calibration. https://mathworks.com/. Accessed 23 Feb 2018
14. Nouiri, M., Trentesaux, D., Bekrar, A.: EasySched: a multi-agent architecture for the predictive and reactive scheduling of Industry 4.0 production systems based on the available renewable energy. CoRR abs/1905.12083. arXiv: 1905.12083. http://arxiv.org/abs/1905.12083 (2019)
15. Pizer, S.M., et al.: Adaptive histogram equalization and its variations. Comput. Vision Graph. Image Process. **39**, 355–368 (1987). ISSN 0734–189X
16. Prisacariu, V., Reid, I.: fastHOG - a real-time GPU implementation of HOG. Technical report 2310/09. Department of Engineering Science (2009)
17. Qasem, Z., Bons, J., Borgmann, C., Eimler, S., Jansen, M.: Dynamic, adaptive, and mobile system for context-based and intelligent support of employees in heavy industry (2018). https://doi.org/10.1109/ES.2018.00021
18. Simon, T., Joo, H., Matthews, I., Sheikh, Y.: Hand keypoint detection in single images using multiview bootstrapping. In: CVPR (2017)

19. Source code and data used in this paper. https://gitlab.hs-ruhrwest.de/nico. zengeler/detectionprocessing. Accessed 15 June 2019
20. Surinta, O., Khruahong, S.: Tracking people and objects with an autonomous unmanned aerial vehicle using face and color detection (2019). https://doi.org/ 10.1109/ECTI-NCON.2019.8692269
21. Wei, S.-E., Ramakrishna, V., Kanade, T., Sheikh, Y.: Convolutional pose machines. In: CVPR (2016)
22. Welch, G., Bishop, G., et al.: An introduction to the Kalman filter (2001)
23. Wiskott, L., Sejnowski, T.J.: Slow feature analysis: unsupervised learning of invariances. Neural Comput. 14, 715–770 (2002)
24. Zengeler, N., et al.: An Evaluation of human detection methods on camera images in heavy industry environments. In: 2019 IEEE 14th Conference on Industrial Electronics and Applications (ICIEA) (2019)

Yet a Smarter Irrigation System

Sérgio F. Lopes[1]($\boxtimes$), Rui M. S. Pereira[2], Sofia O. Lopes[2], Micael Coutinho[2],
Aureliano Malheiro[3], and Victor Fonte[4]

[1] Centro Algoritmi, University of Minho, Guimarães, Portugal
`sergio.lopes@dei.uminho.pt`
[2] Center of Physics, University of Minho, Guimarães, Portugal
`{rmp,sofialopes}@math.uminho.pt,`
`b8719@fisica.uminho.pt`
[3] CITAB, University of Trás-os-Montes e Alto Douro, Vila Real, Portugal
`amalheir@utad.pt`
[4] University of Minho and UNU-EGOV, Braga, Portugal
`vff@di.uminho.pt`

Abstract. A new type of irrigation system is being developed in the context of the research project 02/SAICT/2017-28247-FCT-TO-CHAIR. The output are irrigation plans based on optimal control theory that minimize water usage and keep crops safe. In this paper, we present the main features of the system prototype. The system uses soil moisture sensors in the field, weather forecasts and parameters that the farmer provides. This data is input to an Octave/Matlab program that implements an Optimal Control algorithm to compute the irrigation plan for the crop field. The system consists of an electronic device that interfaces the sensors in the field and a server computer. The field device reads data from any analogue sensors and uses mobile communications to upload the data to the server computer. The server provides a website for users to insert data about their crops and fields and it retrieves weather forecast data from a freely available service. Once a day the server runs the Optimal Control irrigation-planning algorithm and the result is provided on the user web page using both numerical and graphical formats. Due to the diversity of irrigation infrastructures installed in crop fields and water availability for irrigation, the system does not automatically control/actuate the irrigation. That task is left on the hands of the farmer.

Keywords: Irrigation planning · Optimal control · Internet of Things

1 Introduction

Climate change is a proven fact. In the report of 2007 from IPCC [1], one can read that global warming is an issue to be dealt with urgency. Temperature will rise, longer and more frequent drought periods will occur. One of the most affected regions will be the Iberian Peninsula. In the South of Iberia, extreme drought periods are already very frequent. Our study has Portugal in mind, but

© ICST Institute for Computer Sciences, Social Informatics and Telecommunications Engineering 2020
Published by Springer Nature Switzerland AG 2020. All Rights Reserved
H. Santos et al. (Eds.): SmartCity 360 2019, LNICST 323, pp. 337–346, 2020.
https://doi.org/10.1007/978-3-030-51005-3_28

it could easily be adapted to other parts of the world. In this scenario, it is necessary that the decision makers are able to decide on all issues related to water management.

Irrigation of crop fields consumes most of the water resources in Portugal annually. So, it becomes crucial that a proper irrigation planning is able to maximize the profits of a crop field, while spending the least water resources possible, with the highest efficiency [2]. With this paper, the authors intend to give a contribution in order to achieve such objective. A "smart irrigation" system is proposed, which is based on a mathematical model implemented in Matlab/Octave. The model uses Optimal Control theory.

Optimal control theory emerged as research topic in the 1950s, in response to problems concerning the aerospace exploration [3] of the solar system. Nowadays, optimal control is a tool acknowledged by its effectiveness, which is applied to different areas, such as robotics [4], biological systems [5], health [6], economy [7,8], agriculture [9], among many others. The goal of optimal control theory is to find a control law for a system such that a certain optimality criteria is achieved.

The proposed mathematical model is able to plan the irrigation for a given crop in such a way that water usage is minimized, while ensuring the crop is safe. The considered dynamic equation guarantees the water balance (taking into account rainfall, irrigation, humidity in the soil, evapotranspiration and losses due to infiltration), and the defined constraints ensure that crops have their water needs fulfilled. Direct methods (such as IPOPT, SQP, Active Set, etc) that guarantee a feasible solution is obtained were used in optimal control. It has been proven that mathematical models similar to the ones presented in this article obtain a solution that is a local extrema [11].

In this paper, our focus is on the integration of all the necessary technologies and know how, in order to obtain a "smart irrigation" system prototype. The paper is divided in further six sections. In Sect. 2, the mathematical model developed to generate the irrigation plan is presented. Section 3 presents the requirements of the system. Section 4 describes the proposed architecture and in Sect. 5 the behaviour of the system is presented. In Sect. 6, an initial version of the implementation of the mathematical model is shown. Section 7 presents the conclusions and future work.

2   Mathematical Model for the Irrigation Plan, and the Necessary Data

This section presents a mathematical model developed to obtain an optimal irrigation plan for a given set of data. We want to minimize the volume of water used in irrigation, knowing that the water balance equation gives the variation of water in the soil. In our optimal control problem, the trajectory is the water in the soil and the control is the amount of water introduced in the soil via its irrigation system. Our problem is formulated in its discrete version as

$$\min \sum_{i=1}^{N-1} u_i$$

$$\text{s.t.:} \quad x_{i+1} = x_i + h \, f(t_i, x_i, u_i), \text{ a.e. } i = 1, \ .., \ N-1$$

$$x_i \geq x_{\min}, \qquad\qquad i = 1, \ .., \ N \qquad\qquad (1)$$

$$u_i \geq 0, \qquad\qquad \text{a.e. } i = 1, \ .., \ N-1$$

$$x_1 = x_0,$$

where x is the trajectory, u is the control, f is balance water function, $x_{\min}$ is the hydrologic need of the crop, x_0 is the initial state (read from moisture sensors), h is the time step discretization and $N = 10/h$ (if we are using a $h = 1$ day, N=10). The dynamic equation implements the water balance in the soil, which is given by

$$f(t_i, x_i, u_i) = u_i + \text{rainfall}(t_i) - \text{evapotranspiration}(t_i) - \text{losses}(x_i), \quad (2)$$

where evapotranspiration is the evaporation of the soil and the transpiration of the crop, and losses are water losses due to the runoff and deep infiltration. Rainfall forecast for a specified number of days (i.e., the duration of the irrigation plan demanded by the user) is obtained from a meteorological web site. Evapotranspiration is calculated using Penman Monteith model [12] (that needs a set of tabulated values that characterize the soil, the crop, etc) and the losses parcel is described based upon the postulate of Horton's equation, which states that infiltration decreases exponentially with time [13]. That means the dynamical equation is

$$x_{i+1} = x_i + h(g(t_i, u_i) - \beta x_i, \quad (3)$$

where $g(t_i, u_i) = u_i + rainfall(t_i) - evapotranspiration(t_i)$. From (2) and (3), one may say $losses(t_i) = \beta x(t_i)$, where β depends on the type of soil.

3   System Requirements

An overview of the system is shown in Fig. 1 supporting the gathering of fundamental requirements in an informal way. The Optimal Irrigation Algorithm needs (1) weather forecast data that can be obtained from free services available on the internet, (2) soil moisture values that are obtained by soil moisture sensors, and (3) the characteristics of the field to be irrigated and the crop. An irrigation field has an irrigation system and its characterization consists of the land area, soil composition and crop identification. From this set of data the algorithm computes the irrigation plan for the given field, which consists in a list of water amount for each day, for a number of days.

Currently, the algorithm assumes infinite irrigation capacity, leaving the management of water resources entirely to the farmer. For this reason and also

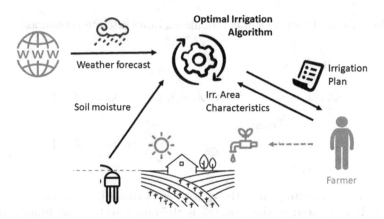

Fig. 1. Overview of system and its integration in the field.

because there are many different irrigation systems, the system does not actuate on irrigation hardware. Each irrigation area has a unique set of characteristics, most predominantly crop and soil, and naturally requires its own soil moisture sensor. To deal with variability of soil characteristics in short distances or small areas, the farmer must install the necessary sensors at appropriate places. This way the system is kept simple and flexible.

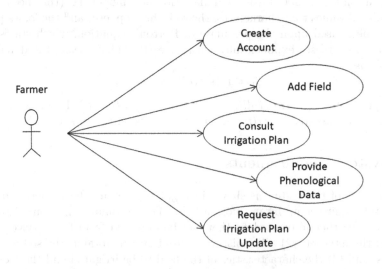

Fig. 2. UML diagram with the system's use-cases.

The usage of the system is described in the UML use-case diagram of Fig. 2, whose actors for now are farmers only. First, they need to create an user account, with usual information, and then they can add irrigation areas, including their characteristics. Afterwards, they can consult the irrigation plan that the system computes daily for each of its fields. The farmer can also provide phenological data, such as bud break and flowering date, to fine-tune the output of the system. All other inputs to the Optimal Irrigation Algorithm are either obtained automatically (e.g., soil moisture reading) or fixed parameters (e.g., soil characteristics) introduced only once. The idea is to make the system practical to use on the daily farming life.

Besides the daily plan that is scheduled, the system allows the farmer to request an update of the irrigation plan at any moment. This is important to deal with situations in which any input variable changes significantly and unexpectedly within a day. This is called re-planning (see [10] for more details) and it is likely to be useful when weather conditions deviate from the forecast.

4   System Architecture

The system is composed of Soil Moisture Measuring Devices (SMMDs), one for each field, and an Irrigation Planning Server. The hardware architecture of the former and software architecture of the latter are shown in Fig. 3. The farmer interacts with the system through a web application, which is appropriate for usage both on a smartphone in the field and on a larger computer screen at the office. The farmer web application provides the functionalities identified in Fig. 2.

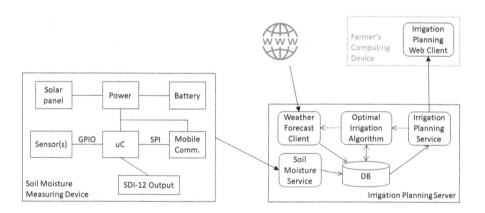

Fig. 3. System architecture

The SMMDs at the field are low power devices offering several months of operation on a battery, and a solar panel for longer power autonomy. They read the values of a set of soil moisture sensors at different depths and send the readings to the central server using mobile data communications (through a GPRS/UMTS module), following the Internet-of-Things concept. The SMMDs processing is done by a low-power micro-controller, that puts the device to sleep almost all of the time. To be compatible with standard environmental data loggers, SMMDs will also feature an SDI-12 interface. SMMDs software consists of: (1) a very simple configuration routine; and, (2) a main routine that makes moisture sensor readings and sends them to the server.

The software architecture of the Irrigation Planning Server consists of: (1) a Database storing all the data, present and historic data for analysis; (2) a Soil Moisture Service that receives the data from SMMDs and stores it in the database; (3) a client to retrieve weather forecast data from an internet service; (4) the Optimal Irrigation Algorithm; and, (5) an Irrigation planning service that serves the farmer's web client. The implementation will use modern approaches, such as REST interfaces for services, single-page application based on a framework such as Angular, and a NoSQL database (since data is mostly collections). The programming language will either be Javascript on node.js or python.

5   System Behaviour

Although the Optimal Irrigation Algorithm is executed on the server once a day by default, the SMMDs main routine sends data to the Soil Moisture Service hourly. This mechanism is important for further research analysis and also to support sporadic planning requested by the farmer.

SMMDs configuration routine is executed when the configuration button is pressed, and sends a message to the server announcing a new SMMD is available to be configured. When this happens, the farmer's web application display a new device (ID) on the view for adding new fields. Then, the farmer has only a few tens of seconds to select the device and start configuring it. After that time the new field is no longer available for configuration. Besides the introduction of the fixed parameters mentioned in Sect. 3, the configuration involves giving the field a meaningful name. If the farmer is using a device with GPS, the application automatically fills-in the coordinates of the new field, simplifying the process. Otherwise, the farmer must choose the location on a map.

The time during which a new field is available for configuration is short, but still there is a chance that two or more fields might appear at the same time. When that happens the farmer must retry until a single field appears to be positively sure that the field is hers/his. This process reassures the farmer about the correct linking between SMMDs and irrigation field in the web app.

The fields are shown on a map and on a list, respectively making them easily identifiable geographically and by name. When a field is selected, the respective most recent irrigation plan is shown. If the system does not receive data from a given sensor, the farmer is alerted that the device has failed and the respective irrigation plan is not updated.

6   Implementation and Results

Currently, the system is not yet fully implemented. We have implemented the Optimal Irrigation Algorithm in Octave/Matlab. The weather forecast data is automatically downloaded from a meteorological web site (https://www.apixu.com/) using a phyton script and it is converted to text files stored on a dropbox folder. The data consists of temperature (maximum and minimum), average wind speed and average humidity in the air, for seven days. Soil moisture data is obtained manually using a data logger and analog sensors. The tabulated values that characterize soil (ThetaFC and ThetaWP, which affect hydrologic need of the crop, x_{min} in Eq. 1, see [15]) and crop (Root height that affects x_{min} and crop's evapotranspiration, and crop ET coefficient that affects the crop's evapotranspiration, see Eq. 2) are provided by the user via a simple application developed with GUIDE from Matlab. The interface, shown in Fig. 4, allows the user to perform a new execution of the algorithm, either by changing soil or crop data, or by feeding in a new weather forecast and sensor data file. Once the plan is ready, the user may use it on the irrigation system.

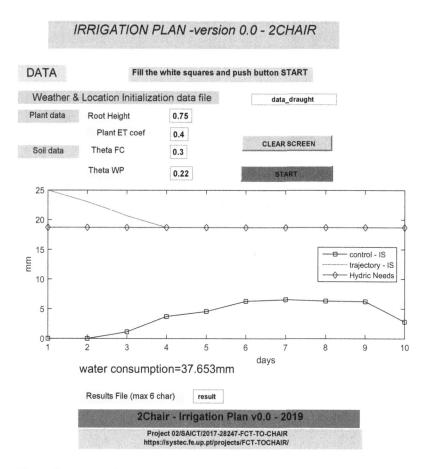

Fig. 4. Irrigation plan for a grass field in Oporto on a dry period (summer).

This enables us to experiment with the model. For example, we have executed the optimal irrigation algorithm for the same soil/location during a dry period, for two different crops, and during a rainy period. For the dry period, the resulting irrigation plan for ten days is shown in the graph of Fig. 4, showing irrigation is necessary almost everyday. The x-axis is the days ahead, "trajectory-IS" curve is the moisture in the soil, "control-IS" curve is the amount of water to be supplied by the irrigation system, and "hydric needs" is the minimum moisture the soil must have such that the crop does not die. Next, we increased the evapotranspiration coefficient of the plant. It will need more water, thus the algorithm should provide an irrigation plan with more water. Results can be seen in Fig. 5, and follow what is expected. Considering a period of rainy days, there is no need to irrigate, as shown in Fig. 6. The interface developed is easy to use and constitutes a reasonably good prototype for testing different scenarios.

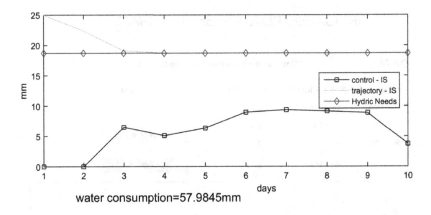

Fig. 5. Irrigation plan for a crop with higher evapotranspiration (ET coef.= 0.6) in Oporto on a dry period. The crop needs more water, consumption increases.

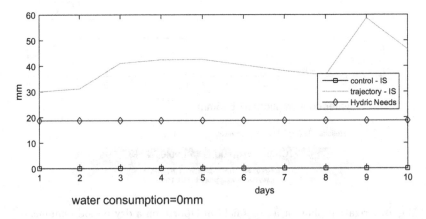

Fig. 6. Irrigation plan for a grass field in Oporto on a wet period (early spring). No irrigation is needed.

7   Conclusion and Future Work

We were able to integrate a smart irrigation system that provides the farmer with an optimized irrigation plan for a period of up to 10 days. Weather data is imported from https://www.apixu.com/, the moisture sensor provides the soil moisture that is manually uploaded to a server. This data is collected to a file that is the input to the optimization program. The rest of the data, crop and soil characteristics, is provided by the farmer. The prototype is an application developed using GUIDE (from Matlab). It is easy to use and allows a farmer to easily create scenarios by changing the input data. The output is the irrigation plan, which can be seen graphically and also in the form of a text file generated by the application.

We have also designed a system architecture to offer optimal irrigation planning to multiple users in a friendly way, namely through a web application with minimal input. Future work includes the next development stage, which is the implementation of the architecture described in this paper, and the introduction of an additional mathematical model. This model, based on Richards equation [14], is in development, and it will be able to estimate soil moisture given a reduced number of sensors. There is also the possibility to search for irrigation systems that offer an interface for external command, and include some hardware modules on the field devices to automatically actuate them.

Acknowledgements. The authors were supported by POCI-01-0145-FEDER-006933-SYSTEC, PTDC/EEI-AUT/2933/2014, POCI-01-0145-FEDER-016858 TOC-CATTA and POCI-01-0145-FEDER-028247 To Chair - funded by FEDER funds through COMPETE2020 - Programa Operacional Competitividade e Internacionalização (POCI) and by national funds (PIDDAC) through FCT/MCTES which is gratefully acknowledged. Financial support from the Portuguese Foundation for Science and Technology (FCT) in the framework of the Strategic Financing UID/FIS/04650/2013 is also acknowledged. The authors also thank SMARTEGOV Project (P2020 NORTE-45-2015-23) Harnessing EGOV for smart governance.

References

1. IPCC - Intergovernmental panel on climate Change Fourth assessement report on climate change 2007: Symthetis report - summary for policy makers; IPCC; Geneva; Switzerland. ISBN 92-9169-122-4
2. Haie, N., Pereira, R.M.S., Machado, G., Keller, A.A.: Analysis of Effective Efficiency in decision making for irrigation interventions. Water Resour. **6**, 700–707 (2012). https://doi.org/10.1134/S0097807812060097
3. Longuski, J.M., Guzmán, J.J., Prussing, J.E.: Optimal Control with Aerospace Applications. STL, vol. 32. Springer, New York (2014). https://doi.org/10.1007/978-1-4614-8945-0. ISBN 978-1-4614-8945-0
4. De Jager, B., Van Keulen, T., Kessels, J.: In Optimal Control of Hybrid Vehicles. Springer-Verlag, London (2013). ISBN 978-1-4471-5076-3
5. Lenhart, S., Workman, J.T.: In Optimal Control Applied to Biological Models. Chapman and Hall and Crc Press, Boca Raton (2007). ISBN 9781584886402

6. Schättler, H., Ledzewicz, U.: Optimal Control for Mathematical Models of Cancer Therapies. IAM, vol. 42. Springer, New York (2015). https://doi.org/10.1007/978-1-4939-2972-6. ISBN 978-1-4939-2972-6

7. Seierstad A., Sydsaeter, K.: In Optimal Control Theory with Economic Applications, North-Holland (1986). ISBN 978-0444879233

8. Ramirez, W.F.: In Application of Optimal Control Theory to Enhanced Oil Recovery. Elsevier Science, Amsterdam (1987). ISBN 9780080868790

9. Lopes, S.O., Fontes, F.A.C.C., Pereira, R.M.S., de Pinho, M.R., Ribeiro, C.: Optimal control for an irrigation planning problem: characterisation of solution and validation of the numerical results. In: Moreira, A.P., Matos, A., Veiga, G. (eds.) CONTROLO'2014 – Proceedings of the 11th Portuguese Conference on Automatic Control. LNEE, vol. 321, pp. 157–167. Springer, Cham (2015). https://doi.org/10.1007/978-3-319-10380-8_16

10. Lopes, S.O., Fontes, F.A.C.C., Costa, M.F., Pereira, R.M.S., Gonçalves, A.M., Machado, G.J.: Irrigation planning: replanning and numerical solution. In: AIP Conference Proceedings, pp. 626-629 (2013). https://doi.org/10.1063/1.4825569

11. Lopes, S.O., Fontes, F.A.C.C., Pereira, R.M.S., de Pinho, M.D.R., Gonçalves, A.M.: Optimal control applied to an irrigation planning problem. Math. Probl. Eng. 10 (2016). https://doi.org/10.1155/2016/5076879

12. Walter, I.A., Allen, R.G., Elliott, R.L., et al.: ASCE standardized reference evapotranspiration equation. In: Watershed Management and Operations Management 2000. ASCE (2000)

13. Horton, R.E.: An approach toward a physical interpretation of infiltration capacity. Soil Sci. Soc. Am. Proc 5, 300–417 (1940)

14. Cooper, L.J., et al.: Fluid flow in porous media using image-based modelling to parametrize Richards' equation. Proc. R. Soc. A 473(2207) 2017, https://doi.org/10.1098/rspa.2017.0178

15. Pereira, R., Gonçalves, M., Lopes, S., Fontes, F., Machado, G.J.: Irrigation planning: an optimal control approach. In: International Conference of Numerical Analysis and Applied Mathematics, Procedia Technology, vol. 17, pp. 699–704 (2014)

Intelligent Technologies for Interactive Entertainment

Robot Creativity: Humanlike Behaviour in the Robot-Robot Interaction

Predrag K. Nikolić[1(✉)] and Mohd Razali Md Tomari[2]

[1] School of Creativity and Art, ShanghaiTech University, 393 Huaxia Middle Road, Pudong, Shanghai 201210, China
predragnikolic@shanghaitech.edu.cn
[2] Faculty of Electrical and Electronic Engineering, Universiti Tun Hussein Onn Malaysia, 86400 Parit Raja, Batu Bahat, Johor, Malaysia
mdrazali@uthm.edu.my

Abstract. Artificial Intelligence development is mainly directed toward imitating human reasoning and performing different tasks. For that purpose, related software and program solution where artificial intelligence is used have mostly thinking abilities. However, there are many questions to answer in ongoing AI research, especially when we come to the point which is addressing humanlike behaviour and reasoning triggered by emotions. In this paper, we are presenting an interactive installation Botorikko: Machine Create State, which is part of the Syntropic Counterpoints art/research project. We are exposing AI cyber clones to some of the fundamental questions for humankind and challenge their creativity. The robots are trained by using the publications Machiavelli and Sun Tzu and confronted to the crucial questions related to moral, ethic, strategy, politics, diplomacy, war etc. We are using a recurrent neural network (RNN) and robot-robot interaction to trigger unsupervised robot creativity and humanlike behaviour on generated machine-made content.

Keywords: Artificial Intelligence · Robot-robot interaction · Machine-made content · Robot creativity · Artificial intelligence humanlike behaviour · Interactive installation

1 Introduction

Development of an Artificial Intelligence nowadays is mainly directed toward imitating human reasoning and performing different tasks in the segments of thinking and learning, problem-solving and making decisions. Therefore, most of the software and program solutions based on Artificial Intelligence implemented into robots, computers, or other related systems has thinking abilities [1]. However, there are many questions to answer in contemporary Artificial Intelligence research which are corresponding to the way AI agent are solving those tasks. Ideally, robots should be in a position to perform the different task autonomously without human control or assistance [2]. Hence, we should address important questions to human behavior and reasoning, which is not only

© ICST Institute for Computer Sciences, Social Informatics and Telecommunications Engineering 2020
Published by Springer Nature Switzerland AG 2020. All Rights Reserved
H. Santos et al. (Eds.): SmartCity 360 2019, LNICST 323, pp. 349–357, 2020.
https://doi.org/10.1007/978-3-030-51005-3_29

rational but rather triggered by emotions. What about the ethical and moral dimensions of such decisions? Furthermore, the development of such autonomous systems and devices requires more investigations toward machine consciousness, reasoning and cognition tasks performed in their judgment or decision-making [3].

Today's artificial intelligence is used in our daily lives by using it in GPS, machines for manufacturing of various products, and extensive usage in business areas such as customer service, finance, sales and marketing, administration and technical processes in various sectors. Most of the implementations mentioned could not be considered as replacement of human task but more to complement them, with the notion of giving to the people more freedom to develop their potentials and creativity [4]. But if we are developing AI agents to achieve and exceed the performances of humans, then we need to be aware of their full learning capacities and the evolution of their creativity. Furthermore, it would be interesting to explore and analyze different AI techniques capable of improving an outcome and the whole system.

In this paper, we are presenting interactive installation Botorikko: Machine Create State, which is part of the Syntropic Counterpoints art/research project. The project has the intention to expose artificial intelligence cyber clones to some of the fundamental questions for humankind and challenge their creativity [5]. Our focus will be to present how we prototype humanlike robot neck which behaves based on generated content's sentiment, as result of robot-robot interaction. Lastly, we will conclude and specify future directions of the Botorikko: Machine Create State experimental artwork.

2 Background

The most often, creativity in robotics is analyzed in the context of a robot performing behaviours that typically requires human creativity [6]. Gopinath & Weinberg [8] investigate the creative domain of musical robots and suggest a model for a robot drummer based on selected natural and expressive drum strokes that are similar to a human drummer. Schubert & Mombaur [8] created the model of motion dynamics that enables a robot to imitate creative paintings. Bird & Stokes [9] are proposed autonomy and self-novelty as a new requirement for a creative robot. Saunders, Chee, & Gemeinboeck [10] are emphasizing results of the system in particular when co-creation occurs between humans and robots. Kantosalo & Toivonen [11] are proposing a method for alternating co-creativity, where the teacher interacts with AI creative agent modifies the shared creative concept. Colin et al. [12] focus is less on producing a creative output and more of the process of creativity itself. They have introduced a hierarchy of problem spaces and represent different abstractions of the original reinforcement learning problem. Vigorito & Barto [13] are also treating creativity as a matter of creative process, rather than a creative outcome. For them, creative reasoning is a proves that emphasizes (i) sufficient variation and (ii) sufficient selection of candidate policies. Under sufficient variation, they are addressing action of representing the problem at multiple levels of abstraction. Furthermore, they propose that new behaviours can only be discovered by representing the learning problem at a sufficient abstraction. Searching for the solution on multiple levels of abstraction makes a distinction between creative robots, which produce novel output, and AI agents which are searching through space at a lower level of abstraction.

The creative act is for sure one of the most fantastic human capabilities which can be evoked in robots. The real test for artificial intelligence and new generation of robots would be to challenge their abilities in artistic domains such as dance, music, painting and drama. For anthropomorphic robots, the domain of the dance is fascinating and challenging to test their skills of replicating and embodying human movements. In that case, a creative process can replicate the mental processes involved in human creativity to generate movements by taking into account different music genres, personal artistic style, the audience evaluation [14].

Unlike the usage of artificial intelligence as a medium to support or imitate human creativity and behavioural, our approach is to liberate and explore its creative patterns through the robot's interactions. In the first Syntropic Counterpoints art installation titled "Robosophy Philosophy: Ubermensch and Magnanimous" we confronted philosophical standpoints of Aristotle (Magnanimous) and Nietzsche (Übermensch) and used their cyber clones to run debates and generate autonomously content we considered as results of AI agents creative act [5]. The artwork's cyber clones are developed as a combination of chatbot technologies and Recurrent Neural Network (RNN) models [15], enabling reinforcement learning toward the creation of artificial conversational agents with human-level performances.

3   Interactive Installation Botorikko - Machine Created State

The artwork Syntropic Counterpoints: Botorikko, Machine Created State is conceptualized as an interactive installation made of two to bicycles construction modified to carry two computer monitors and two pseudo robot manikin figures (see Fig. 1). The visitors can listen over the speakers and see on the computer monitors dialogues which are running in real-time between Machiavelli (Italian diplomat, politician, historian, philosopher, humanist, writer, playwright and poet of the Renaissance period) and Sun Tzu (general, military strategist, writer and philosopher who lived in the Eastern Zhou period of ancient China) AI clones. They are discussing strategies in politics, diplomacy, and how to deals and win in wars and conflicts. By doing that they are making a foundation for the first Machine Created State. Movement of the monitors follows the sentiments in the content created by AI clones and based on six basic emotions anger, happy, sad, fear, surprise, disgust.

Visitors can interact with the installation by pedalling bicycles which will automatically start sword fight between Machiavelli and Sun Tzu manikin figures look robots, placed at the front part of the bicycles and with the computer monitors placed instead of their heads (see Fig. 2). The installation is a unique example of human-robot-robot interaction which tends to become genuine social phenomena of our and future time.

Fig. 1. Interactive Installation Botorikko, two head mounted displays and two pseudo robots manikin figures (@copyright photo: Predrag K. Nikolic)

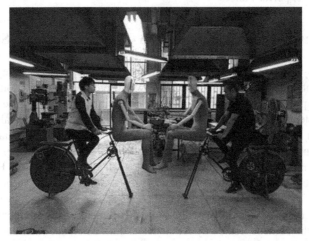

Fig. 2. Interactive Installation Botorikko, human-robot-robot interaction (@copyright photo: Predrag K. Nikolic)

4 Our Approach

In our approach, we are combining art and technology to create intelligent interactive artefacts which are trained to generate content as part of an artwork's creative concept and expression [3]. We are using two independent neural networks, one trained on books of Machiavelli and other one trained on books of Sun Tzu. The training was done with joined text of English translation of the books and use of many-to-many LSTM networks built with Keras and TensorFlow libraries, designed to generate the sequence of words based on the input sequence.

Sentiment analysis is done with Amazon Comprehend service, but other solution will be tested to find optimal results.

5   Prototyping Humanlike Behavior

5.1   BioMechanics of Human Neck

Even though each vertebrae movement range is limited, in combination off all seven joints, eventually neck can produce numerous head motions. Figure 3 visualizes human neck movements that comprise of three type range of motions based on biomechanical data [16]. Bending motions can be carried out in either forward (see Fig. 3(a)) or backward (see Fig. 3(b)) within the range of $+40°$ to $-50°$, respectively. The second motion which is lateral flexion (see Fig. 3(c)), is also known as side bending or swing can be performed by human within the range of $\pm40°$. Finally, the last motions are rotational (Fig. 3(d)) in which the left and right torsional can be executed within the range of $\pm55°$. In this project, the biomechanics information of human neck was investigated in term of its type of movements and individual range of motion to generate natural neck mechanism of robot head. Based on this finding, the designed robot head shall be capable of producing three degrees of freedom (3DOF) movements with constraints angle, as mentioned previously to reproduce natural human-like motions. Details of the robot design and mechanism will be elaborate in the next section.

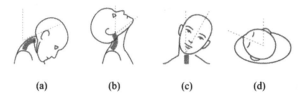

| (a) | (b) | (c) | (d) |

Fig. 3. Visualization of head movements [17]: (a) Bending forward, capped at $+40°$, (b) Bending Backward, capped at $-50°$ (c) lateral flexion, range within $\pm40°$ (d) Rotation, and range within $\pm55°$

5.2   Neck Mechanism Design

For our robotic head platform, a serial neck mechanism with three DOF was selected (seen Fig. 4) Since our total load capacity of the robot head is around one-kilogram, a serial mechanism was selected for its robustness and simplicity as compared to the parallel one. Technically, the mechanism comprises of three cube servo motors that stacked serially with various joints as in Table 1. Originally cube servo can be attached directly without any additional joints. However, for a bending motion with direct joint, such configuration will cause a non-symmetrical arrangement, and furthermore, all payload will be focused on the motor shaft only (see Fig. 5 (left)). To overcome this, combination of U-joint and rotational connect was employed in which the latter part is used to hold the motor on the opposite side of the shaft. By using this configuration, the bending motion will mainly cause by motor's body rotation and hence can hold more payload from the head.

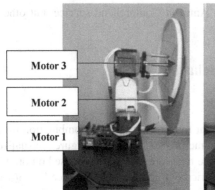

Fig. 4. Serial Neck Mechanism of robot head from side view (left) and perspective view (right)

Table 1. List of components for the robot neck.

No	Part name	Quantity	Function
1	Cube Servo G15	3	High torque DC motor with 360° angle control
2	Cube Servo Shield	1	Interpreter between controller and Cube servo
3	Arduino Uno	1	Robot controller
4	Rotatable Connect	1	Provide a freedom for Cube servo to rotate on the opposite side of the output while attaching to U Joint
5	U Joint	1	Create joint between rotation and bending motion
6	External Joint	2	Mount servo on neck's base and robot head

Fig. 5. Neck mechanism comparison of the cube servo by direct attach (left) and using U-joint attachment (right)

The first motor at the base responsible for generating rotational motion, the second motor attached with u-joint produce flexion motion and third motor with the head attached perform lateral flexion motion (see Fig. 5). All the motors are assigned unique address number and connected via a half-duplex serial communication protocol that controlled from the servo shield. The motor can perform smooth and continuous 360° rotation and can hold a stall torque up to 15 kilograms when powered with 12 V. All motors were assigned a range of motion constraint same as human neck parameters.

5.3 Control System

The control system module was designed to control the robot neck movement asynchronously. To achieve that real-time operating system (RTOS) based on ChibiOS was employed. Under such configuration, all motors can perform the task simultaneously and hence can generate smooth motion. The motors arrangement (see Fig. 4) constitutes of three servo motors. Motor 1 was responsible for rotational motion, and the control parameters were set to a positive value for a left turn and negative value for the right turn. As for motor 2 that executes the bending task, positive angle value was set for forward while negative for the backward. Finally, for the swing motion tasks that were assigned to motor 3, a positive value is for right swing and negative value for the left one. For all motors angle degree of zero is for the initial centre position.

For generating a humanlike robot's gaze emotion, the relation between the robot angle and the emotion need to be known in advance. For that reason, we use parameters that Johnson & Cuijpers were studied [18]. In their study, 44 participants were given a set of robot's head movement direction, and they need to select which emotion plausibly reflect the head direction. The summary of the robot corresponding angle set with its dominant emotion was list out in Table 2.

Table 2. List of robot emotion and its corresponding neck joints angle

No	Robot emotion	Flexion angle	Lateral flexion angle	Rotation angle
1	Anger	20	0	0
2	Happy	−30	0	0
3	Sad	20	0	0
4	Fear	20	0	−45
5	Surprise	−30	0	0
6	Disgust	20	0	−45

6 Conclusions and Future Directions

In the first part of the installation development, our focus was to improve artificial intelligence clones' performances and follow the sentiment of generated content with humanlike behaviour. For that purposes, we designed a humanlike robot neck platform capable of reacting on six basic emotions with equivalent movements. The system detects emotions from the generated content by the artificial intelligence clones. Several basic criteria we considered to achieve smooth neck imitation movements related to an emotional reaction, such as degrees of freedom, range of motion, velocities, total payload and torque requirement.

In our further research and development of the system, we will focus on created content analysis toward a better understanding of robots' creation. Furthermore, we intend to experiment with the content sentiment and challenge robot reasoning and sentiment-driven behaviour in its own creation.

Acknowledgement. We thank Marko Jovanovic, brilliant Software Engineer, who gave us a technical solution and developed the Artificial Intelligence Clones we are using in the project.

References

1. Zhang, Y., Robinson, D.K., Porter, A.L., Zhu, D., Zhang, G., Lu, J.: Technology roadmapping for competitive technical intelligence. Technol. Forecast. Soc. Change **110**, 175–186 (2016)
2. Gottfredson, L.S.: The general intelligence factor (1998)
3. Nikolic, P.K., Yang, H.: Artificial intelligence clone generated content toward robot creativity and machine mindfulness. Mob. Netw. Appl. 1–10 (2019). https://doi.org/10.1007/s11036-019-01281-z
4. Shabbir, J., Anwer, T.: Artificial intelligence and its role in near future. arXiv preprint arXiv:1804.01396 (2018)
5. Nikolić, P.K., Yang, H., Chen, J., Stankevich, G.P.: Syntropic counterpoints: art of AI sense or machine made context art. In: ACM SIGGRAPH 2018 Posters, p. 18. ACM (2018)
6. Gemeinboeck, P., Saunders, R.: Creative machine performance: Computational creativity and robotic art. In: Proceedings of the 4th International Conference on Computational Creativity, pp. 215–219 (2013)
7. Gopinath, D., Weinberg, G.: A generative physical model approach for enhancing the stroke palette for robotic drummers. Robot. Auton. Syst. **86**, 207–215 (2016)
8. Schubert, A., Mombaur, K.: The role of motion dynamics in abstract painting. In: Proceedings of the Fourth International Conference on Computational Creativity, vol. 2013. Citeseer (2013)
9. Bird, J., Stokes, D.: Evolving minimally creative robots. In: Proceedings of the Third Joint Workshop on Computational Creativity, pp. 1–5. IOS Press, Amsterdam (2006)
10. Saunders, R., Chee, E., Gemeinboeck, P.: Evaluating human-robot interaction with embodied creative systems. In: Proceedings of the Fourth International Conference on Computational Creativity, pp. 205–209 (2013)
11. Kantosalo, A., Toivonen, H.: Modes for creative human-computer collaboration: alternating and task divided co-creativity. In: Proceedings of the Seventh International Conference on Computational Creativity (2016)
12. Colin, T.R., Belpaeme, T., Cangelosi, A., Hemion, N.: Hierarchical reinforcement learning as creative problem solving. Robot. Auton. Syst. **86**, 196–206 (2016)
13. Vigorito, C.M., Barto, A.G.: Hierarchical representations of behavior for efficient creative search. In: AAAI Spring Symposium: Creative Intelligent Systems, pp. 135–141 (2008)
14. Augello, A., Cipolla, E., Infantino, I., Manfre, A., Pilato, G., Vella, F.: Creative robot dance with variational encoder. arXiv preprint arXiv:1707.01489 (2017)
15. Karpathy, A.: The unreasonable effectiveness of recurrent neural networks. Andrej Karpathy Blog (2015)

16. Panero, J., Zelnik, M.: Human Dimension and Interior Space: A Source Book of Design Reference Standards. Watson-Guptill Publications, New York (1979)
17. Penčić, M., Čavić, M., Savić, S., Rackov, M., Borovac, B., Lu, Z.: Asssitive humanoid robot MARKO: development of the neck mechanism. In: MATEC Web of Conferences, vol. 121, p. 08005 (2017)
18. Johnson, D.O., Cuijpers, R.H.: Investigating the effect of a humanoid robot's head position on imitating human emotions. Int. J. Soc. Robot. 11(1), 65–74 (2018)

A Game Informatical Analysis of Dark Chess by Game Refinement Theory

Shuo Xiong[1], Aoshuang Ye[2][(✉)], and Hiroyuki Iida[3]

[1] Huazhong University of Science and Technology, Wuhan, China
xiongshuo@hust.edu.cn
[2] Wuhan University, Wuhan, China
yasfrost@whu.edu.cn
[3] Japan Advanced Institute of Science and Technology, Nomi, Japan
iida@jaist.ac.jp

Abstract. This paper explores the evolutionary changes of Chinese chess variants such as Chinese dark chess. A computer program is created for each variant and self-play experiments are performed to collect many data such as the average number of possible moves and game length. These data are analyzed to examine the degree of game sophistication, while game refinement measure is employed for the assessment.

Keywords: Game refinement theory · Chinese dark chess · Flipping strategy

1 Introduction

Chinese chess and Chinese dark chess are all Chinese board games. These two games share similarities in aspects like pieces, rules, board size and etc. In this paper, we introduced game refinement theory as measure method to discuss the potential connections between two games. About the experiment, we focus on Chinese dark chess, which data of Chinese chess can be collected from the past research. In the Sect. 1, we introduce the Chinese dark chess and propose a variant version of it. In the Sect. 2, we introduce the game refinement theory. In the Sect. 3, we clarify the methodology about experiment which conducted on Chinese dark chess. In the discussion part, we compare the experiment data and find the possible potential links between two games [10].

1.1 Dark Chess

Chinese Dark chess has another name which was called "An Qi", "An" means dark and "Qi" means chess. In Chinese dark chess, players only use half part of the board, consists of 8×4 squares, totally 32 squares and for each player has 16 pieces and squares. The pieces as same as normal Chinese chess rule, which include one "Shuai" (means king, marked as K/k), two "Shi" (means

H. Santos et al. (Eds.): SmartCity 360 2019, LNICST 323, pp. 358–368, 2020.
https://doi.org/10.1007/978-3-030-51005-3_30

guard, marked as G/g), two "Xiang" (means Bishop, marked as B/b), two "Ju" (means rook, marked as R/r), two "Ma" (means knight, marked as N/n), two "Pao" (means cannon, marked as C/c) and five "Bing" (means pawn, marked as P/p) [1,2,6–8,10].

At the beginning of the game, all the pieces are randomly placed on the board with the chess icon facing down, so the type of the piece is unknown. When playing the game, the two players alternately move. There are two kinds of actions: first one is flip action, showing an unknown face down state; second one is moving action, moving a color displayed by yourself from the start point to the target point. For a cannon, it can skip another piece for long distance movement. An unknown fragment that is flipped is called a revealing fragment. From the above discussion, we know that the first player in Chinese Black must flip the pieces at the beginning.

With the exception of cannons, all types of debris can only move up and down in a 32 area to move or capture other fragments within one square. The cannon moves in the same way as other pieces, but when capturing pieces, like Chinese chess, they need to skip a piece to capture pieces of any distance in the same row or column [2]. The portion of the cannon that is skipped by the cannon is called a carriage. Chinese black chessboard is shown in Fig. 1.

As shown in Table 1. Each piece has a rank, A higher rank piece can capture the equal or lower rank pieces. However, there are some exceptions rules as follows:

1 Pawn is the weakest, however it can capture the strongest piece king
2 King is the most powerful but it could not capture pawn
3 Cannon cannot capture pieces directly, it has to jump over one piece

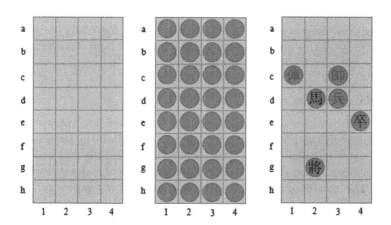

Fig. 1. Chinese dark chess board 4×8

The player wins when the opponent has no legal moves or all chips are captured. When neither player captures or reveals the piece within 40 steps, the game ends in draw. Repetition of positions also results in a draw. The state space complexity and the game tree complexity of Chinese Dark Chess were estimated to be 10^{37} and 10^{135}, respectively [2]. The game tree complexity is smaller than Chinese chess.

Table 1. Dark chess

Chinese Name	English Mark	Rank	Icon	Exception
Shuai/Jiang	King	6	帥 將	The highest rank but can't capture pawn
Shi	Guard	5	仕 士	
Xiang	Bishop	4	相 象	
Ju	Rook	4	俥 車	
Ma	Knight	2	傌 馬	
Bin/Zu	Pawn	1	兵 卒	The lowest rank but can capture King
Pao	Cannon	s	炮 砲	Capture all types of pieces by jumping over

1.2 Perfect Information Version of Dark Chess

In this part, we have imported a possible version of Chinese dark chess, which removed the flipping part from the game. Without flipping, the perfect information part of Chinese dark chess game can verify the game sophistication in another aspect. Without flipping, game strategy would be more concise. Chinese dark chess with perfect information shares every rule with the original Chinese dark chess. New version of Chinese dark chess is more like Chinese chess. In this paper, we propose this new game as intermediate version for discovering possible connection between Chinese chess-like games.

1.3 Related Works on Chinese Dark Chess

Chen et al. [2] used an alpha-beta algorithm with different display strategies in conjunction with the initial depth flip method to reduce the branching factor. They separate the opening game, the midfield game and the end game to apply different policies. Chen et al. [11] establish a database of endgames with reverse analysis. The created database is used for each first moving color, displaying up to 5 clips. They use 2 TB of memory to represent 1012 positions. The position status is stored as a win, lose or draw. Yan et al. [9] combined the chance node and Monte Carlo tree search (MCTS), then an uncertain Monte Carlo tree search model is proposed. They demonstrated a shorter simulation by adjusting three strategies called "Capture First", "Capture Stronger Piece First" and "Capture and Escape Stronger Piece First". As the decimation rate decreases, the winning rate increases and the simulation makes more sense for the MCTS.

2   Game Refinement Theory

The dynamics of decision options in the decision space has been investigated, which is a key factor in gauging game entertainment. Then, a measure of the refinement in games was proposed in 2003 year. The outcome of interesting games is always uncertain until the very end of the game. Thus, the variation in available options stays nearly constant throughout the game. In contrast to this, one player quickly dominates over the other in uninteresting games. Here options are likely to be diminishing quickly from the decision space. Therefore, the refined games are more likely to be seesaw games.

We review the early work of game refinement theory. The decision space is the minimal search space without forecasting. It provides the common measures for almost all board games. The dynamics of decision options in the decision space has been investigated and it is observed that this dynamics is a key factor for game entertainment. Thus a measure of the refinement in games was proposed.

A measure of game refinement (GR) theory is employed for assessing the degree of attractiveness of the game, which is derived from the game progress model [4]. The "game progress" is twofold. First is the game speed or scoring rate, while the other is the game information progress that emphasizes on the game outcome. Game information progress presents the degree of certainty of a game's result in time or steps. Having full information of the game progress, i.e. after its conclusion, the game progress $x(t)$ will be given as a linear function of time t with $0 \leq t \leq t_k$ and $0 \leq x(t) \leq x(t_k)$. It is assumed in the current model that the game information progress in any games is happening in our minds. We do not know yet about the physics in our minds, but it is likely that the acceleration of information progress is related to the force in mind. Hence, it is reasonably expected that the larger the value $\frac{x(t_k)}{(t_k)^2}$ is, the more the game becomes exciting due to the personal challenge faced by the players in achieving the game outcome. Thus, we apply its root square $\frac{\sqrt{x(t_k)}}{t_k}$, as a game refinement measure (denoted as GR). Generally, in board game we assume the Branching factor "B" as the $x(t_k)$ and the Depth of game "D" as the t_k. Then, Table 2 shows the measures of game refinement for three mind sports: chess, shogi and Go. It is conjectured that GR value of sophisticated mind sports varies between 0.07 and 0.08.

Table 2. Measures of game refinement for various types of games

Game	$x(t_k)$	t_k	R
Chess	35	80	0.074
Chinese chess	38	95	0.065
Shogi	80	115	0.078
Go	250	208	0.076

3   Methodology

3.1   Design of Dark Chess Engine

In past tournaments of Chinese dark chess, most of programs used the expecti-minimax tree [11]. Normal minimax tree can not simulate flipping part because it is stochastic. The expectiminimax tree combines flipping node with movement nodes. Hence, we get the method which can search both parts in same game tree. We also implement alpha-beta pruning which efficiently reduce the simulating time.

In expectiminimax tree search, a heuristic value will be given to flipping nodes. This value combines probability and weight values of pieces. In this dark chess engine, we only search one level flipping nodes. Because the weakness of the expectminimax tree search is that taking too much time on searching flipping [11]. Bacause heuristic function can not differs flipping orders which has similar location, Therefore, for flipping part, one-level searching only makes decision whether flip or not. The action is still decided by flipping function.

To improve the strength of AI, a strong flipping strategy is necessary in Chinese dark chess. Firstly, we designed a relatively weaker version of flipping strategy, which purely depends on simple board evaluation. Then, another version is designed for final version AI. In our system, flipping strategy follows one principle that AI always choose the safest way. Under this principle, there are two phases of flipping are given. In the phase 1, AI will flip the piece which can not be captured in next move to ensure absolute safety. In the phase 2, AI will evaluate all positions and give them a value. This value follows the following formula.

$$Risk = C_1 \sum_{i=1}^{n} P_i + C_2 \left(1 - \sum_{i=1}^{n} P_i\right) \tag{1}$$

In this formula, C_1 and C_2 means fixed constant. In our experiment, C_1 is 1 and C_2 is 1. P_i means the probability that covered piece could capture the target piece. A function is designed to calculate the probabilities.

Recent studies have shown that MCTS is an efficient algorithm for games of no chance [11]. And MCTS can be implemented to any game without specific knowledge. Therefore, we implemented MisirlouV3 which tied for second place in preliminary and the final fourth in the UEC-GAT tournament. Normally, MCTS highly depends on the number of simulation to improve the quality of searching. Hence, we set a thresh-hold value of winning ratio in this AI. In this paper, any move being chosen will be checked by function. If this choice is disqualified, the program will activate the sub-AI automatically. The sub-AI designed based on simple principle, which AI will find the most valuable target and move closer to it.

3.2 Resign System

Different with Chinese chess, Chinese dark chess has its own chain of capturing. On specific circumstances, Chinese dark chess can be ended before all pieces being eliminated. For example, when one player has no method to capture opponent's top rank piece, game ends. Therefore, the time after the game outcome has been determined is considered as meaningless time. Hence, we can design a system for judging these situations. We conduct 1000 self-play experiments for same level AIs to collect data. By using this data, a model based on decision tree has been established. According to this classification model, we can design a reasonable judge system for Chinese dark chess experiment to get real game length. The accuracy for this model is 80.3%.

Table 3. Statistics of 1000 self-play experiments

Type	0	1	2	3	4	5
King (Win)	170	305				
King (Lose)	423	102				
Pawn (Win)	19	100	124	118	83	31
Pawn (Lose)	72	174	114	99	52	14
Cannon (Win)	204	175	96			
Cannon (Lose)	362	139	24			

According to Table 3 and its decision tree model, first two rules for resign system is set. Other rules are set from 3–6:

1 If your number of king is 1, your number of cannon can not be 0.
2 If your number of king is 0, your number of pawn should be at least 2.
3 If your number of king is 0, your top rank should be at least same level as opponent's top rank.
4 If your number of cannon is 0, number of your top rank piece is 1, which same with your opponent. This game ends with draw. (If top rank is king, number of pawn should be 0 too)
5 If your number of king and cannon are 0, opponent's number of top rank piece is larger.
6 If your number of king is 1, your number of remaining piece is 1. Opponent's number of remaining pieces is larger than 1 and it includes king or pawn.

3.3 Choice of Search Algorithm

For constructing strong AI, we use expectminimax algorithm with alpha-beta pruning. Normal min-max tree takes too much time to simulate one turn and can not search the flipping part. Expectiminimax with alpha-beta pruning not only efficiently reduce the simulating time but also combine the strategic part and flipping part. After implementation, simulation time for one turn is approximately 6 s [3].

Alpha-Beta pruning is one the most effective pruning method for min-max tree. Alpha-Beta pruning set two bounds for min-max tree,which are alpha bound and beta bound. Alpha bound and beta bound are both stored in every node. Beta bound will be set as $+\infty$ and alpha bound is $-\infty$. Different with normal min-max tree, alpha-beta pruning always check its bounds before it obtain the value of node. As pseudo code 1 shows, for all max nodes, their alpha bounds will be updated after selection. On the contrary, for those min nodes, their beta bounds will be updated. If beta is smaller than alpha or equal to alpha, rest of branched will be excluded from the tree. Because it meaningless to search them already [5].

Algorithm 1. Alpha-beta method implemented in Chinese Dark Chess AI

```
function ALPHA-BETA(node)
    if (node is a terminal node)
        return the heuristic value from evaluation
    if (node is a max node)
        temp := −∞
        for each child in node
            temp := max(Alpha-beta(child))
            α := max(α, temp)
            if β ≤ α
            break
        return temp
    else
        temp := +∞
        for each child in node
            temp := min(Alpha-beta(child))
            β := min(β, temp)
            if β ≤ α
            break
        return temp
end function
```

---

4   Discussion

In order to promote data accuracy, we design three AIs who has tree different search depth to simulate the game process. First AI is the weakest one, which has 2 levels of search depth. Relatively, second 2 AI has 4 levels of search depth and third AI has 6 levels of search depth. Then, These three AIs fight against each other with 9 types of tournaments. Battles between two levels has been conducted for 50 times. After all the experiments, we know the average branching factor and game depth as Table 4 and 5 shows.

Table 4. Average branching factor of Chinese dark chess

B	1st		
2nd	Level 1	Level 2	Level 3
Level 1	20.2446	19.956	20.0259
Level 2	21.2534	20.4253	19.8365
Level 3	19.4695	20.0463	19.3593

Table 5. Average game length of Chinese dark chess

D	1st		
2nd	Level 1	Level 2	Level 3
Level 1	63.3	69.96	73.08
Level 2	57.4	63.56	73.2
Level 3	73.56	74.64	78.84

Table 6. The winning ratio of each level

W	1st		
2nd	Level 1	Level 2	Level 3
Level 1	48%/50%/2%	36%/60%/4%	44%/56%/0%
Level 2	64%/24%/12%	44%/56%/0%	48%/52%/0%
Level 3	60%/40%/0%	52%/48%/0%	52%/44%/4%

According to data given above, we notice the game refinement value is in zone value. This result suits for Chinese dark chess's success in the market. Comparing the data of perfect information dark chess with imperfect information dark chess, the game length get much longer after implementation of flipping. With implementation of flipping, Chinese dark chess becomes more competitive than perfect information Chinese dark chess. The game refinement value of perfect information Chinese dark chess is much higher than most of popular games, which means players can enjoy its impact. But without competition, fun of perfect information Chinese dark chess fades fast. Sophisticated players get longer game depth in experiments. Because sophisticated player could cause seesaw effect in the end of game. According to Table 6, Higher rank AI obviously get advantage in tournaments. Compare with the perfect information AI, the strong AI's advantage aren't obvious. The reason could be high quality flipping policy make up the strength rift between two version. After experiments of Chinese dark chess, we could see another result which comes from perfect information version of Chinese dark chess.

From Table 6 and 9, we notice the weaker player also can defeat stronger player with considerable possibility. On the other hand, Chinese Dark Chess is a typical imperfect information game. We conducted another set of 100 self-play experiments for Chinese dark chess to calculate more accurate game refinement value as Table 10 shows. Data of Chinese chess is also given in Table 2.

Table 7. Average branching factor of perfect information dark chess

B	1st		
2nd	Level 1	Level 2	Level 3
Level 1	16.7774	17.3665	17.377
Level 2	16.8505	17.5443	17.106
Level 3	17.123	17.0273	17.2313

Table 8. Average game length of perfect information dark chess

D	1st		
2nd	Level 1	Level 2	Level 3
Level 1	24.98	17.52	23.32
Level 2	20.92	20.52	22.32
Level 3	29.76	23.76	22.94

Table 9. The winning ratio of each level of perfect information dark chess

W	1st		
2nd	Level 1	Level 2	Level 3
Level 1	54%/46%/0%	40%/56%/4%	56%/44%/0%
Level 2	52%/48%/0%	50%/48%/2%	32%/64%/4%
Level 3	64%/36%/0%	84%/16%/0%	47%/51%/2%

Table 10. Self-play experiments

	B	D	WR	R
Chinese dark chess	20.6675	61.32	46%/49%/5%	0.074

From the table above, we notice that game refinement value of Chinese dark chess is a little lower than the zone value. This means Chinese dark chess is more competitive game than we supposed.

In order to get more sophisticated game. Almost all sophisticated games' refinement value gather in zone 0.07 ˜ 0.08. Chinese chess, and Chinese dark chess are all popular Chinese board games, which have game refinement zone value. In consideration of perfect information Chinese dark chess is a variant version we proposed. Huge difference with zone is reasonable. On one hand, flipping part not only improve the fairness in the game but also extend the game length. On the other hand, random initial place mechanism makes game length even shorter. Therefore we can see two different possible modification from Chinese chess. Chance based mechanism takes charge of the game, which makes their game refinement value higher in perfect information Chinese dark chess. From the self-play experiments, we can see that Chinese dark chess is a fair game, which has almost fifty-fifty percentage of winning.

5 Conclusion

In this paper, we designed the experiment platform for Chinese dark chess. According to the data we collected, a new possible evolution process for three Chinese board games has been proposed. In the AI tournament, we found the Chinese dark chess is a quite fair game no matter the sequence of players. Some effective change which applied in Chinese dark chess could be taken into consideration. Currently, because Chinese dark chess's chance based mechanism, professional tournament isn't suitable.

References

1. Abraham, R., Marsden, J.E., Marsden, J.E.: Foundations of Mechanics. Benjamin/Cummings Publishing Company Reading, Massachusetts (1978)
2. Chen, B.-N., Shen, B.-J., Hsu, T.: Chinese dark chess. ICGA J. **33**(2), 93–106 (2010)
3. Ding, C.H.Q., He, X., Zha, H., Gu, M., Simon, H.D.: A min-max cut algorithm for graph partitioning and data clustering. In: Proceedings 2001 IEEE International Conference on Data Mining, pp. 107–114. IEEE (2001)
4. Iida, H., Takahara, K., Nagashima, J., Kajihara, Y., Hashimoto, T.: An application of game-refinement theory to Mah Jong. In: Rauterberg, M. (ed.) ICEC 2004. LNCS, vol. 3166, pp. 333–338. Springer, Heidelberg (2004). https://doi.org/10.1007/978-3-540-28643-1_41
5. Knuth, D.E., Moore, R.W.: An analysis of alpha-beta pruning. Artif. Intell. **6**(4), 293–326 (1975)
6. Kreps, D.M.: Game Theory and Economic Modelling. Oxford University Press, Oxford (1990)
7. Rivest, R.L.: Game tree searching by min/max approximation. Artif. Intell. **34**(1), 77–96 (1987)
8. Roth, A.E.: The early history of experimental economics. J. Hist. Econ. Thought **15**(02), 184–209 (1993)

9. Yen, S.J., Chou, C.W., Chen, J.-C., Wu, I.-C., Kao, K.Y.: The art of the Chinese dark chess program DIABLE. In: Chang, R.S., Jain, L., Peng, S.L. (eds.) Advances in Intelligent Systems and Applications - Volume 1. SIST, vol. 20, pp. 231–242. Springer, Heidelberg (2013). https://doi.org/10.1007/978-3-642-35452-6_25
10. Yen, S.-J., Chou, C.-W., Chen, J.-C., Wu, I.-C., Kao, K.-Y.: Design and implementation of Chinese dark chess programs. IEEE Trans. Comput. Intell. AI Games **7**(1), 66–74 (2014)
11. Yen, S.-J., Chou, C.-W., Chen, J.-C., Wu, I.-C., Kao, K.-Y.: Design and implementation of Chinese dark chess programs. IEEE Trans. Comput. Intell. AI Games **7**(1), 66–74 (2015)

Tools of Smart Governance in Cities of the Slovak Republic

Katarína Vitálišová[1], Anna Vaňová[1], Kamila Borseková[1], Ľudmila Nagyová[2], and Dagmar Cagáňová[3]([✉])

[1] Matej Bel University in Banská Bystrica,
Tajovského 10, 975 90 Banská Bystrica, Slovak Republic
{katarina.vitalisova,anna.vanova,kamila.borsekova}@umb.sk
[2] Slovak University of Agriculture in Nitra, Trieda A. Hlinku 2, 949 76 Nitra, Slovak Republic
ludmila.nagyova@uniag.sk
[3] Faculty of Materials Science and Technology in Trnava, Slovak University of Technology in Bratislava, ul. Jána Bottu 25, 917 24 Trnava, Slovak Republic
dagmar.caganova@stuba.sk

Abstract. The aim of the paper is to define the Smart Governance and its tools from the theoretical point of view, with special attention given to the civic participation as an important part of governance. Referring to the theory review, the authors of the paper identify the tools of Smart Governance in the Slovak Republic at the local level. Consequently is demonstrated its utilization on the examples of Slovak city, Banská Bystrica, as one of the pioneers in implementation the smart city concept in Slovakia. The main source of data are the Acts of the Slovak Republic, strategical documents at the national and local level, as well as the primary research in a form of questionnaire survey carried out among citizens in 2019. The final part of the paper presents the possibilities to develop systematically civic participation in the cities with support of smart IT technologies based on inspirations from well-developed smart cities in Europe.

Keywords: Smart governance · Participation · City · Tools

1 Introduction

Nowadays, local municipalities deal with many problems resulting from increasing urbanization. The number of people living in cities is growing steadily, affecting pollution, employment, energy demand, waste production, as well as local public budgets. To tackle with these problems, the strategy of smart city has been developed that effectively interconnects and utilizes the digital, physical and social systems in public space to create a sustainable and prosperous future for the city's inhabitants. In this concept, the city has an ambition to become better place for living. It should be based on the change in city mindset by linking and activating stakeholders as its integral part of city.

H. Santos et al. (Eds.): SmartCity 360 2019, LNICST 323, pp. 369–387, 2020.
https://doi.org/10.1007/978-3-030-51005-3_31

The local stakeholders, especially citizens, should be actively involved in city governing and managing. In the smart city the governance is embodied in transparent management system that allows residents to participate easily in planning and decision-making processes of city development, as well as to provide open access to information to residents. These processes are carried out via modern information and communication technologies. In the literature, it is named as smart governance.

The issue of smart governance is rather up-to-date topic, still with great potential for research. In the first part of the paper, the authors of the paper define the basis of the smart governance and identify its tools with emphasis on the civic participation. Subsequently, there are analyzed the tools on the example of the Slovak Republic, namely Banská Bystrica city in a form of case study. In the last part, there are discussed the empirical research results and suggested the measurements how to systematically develop civic participation in the cities as a part of smart governance with inspirations from well-developed smart cities in Europe.

2 Smart Governance and Civic Participation

City is smart, if it uses participatory governance based on active involvement of relevant stakeholders, invests in human resources, social capital, traditional and modern (ICT) infrastructure and thereby ensuring sustainable economic growth, high quality of living and efficient management of natural resources (Caragliu et al. 2011; Dominici 2012). It requires also smart management approach of public administration representatives as a part of smart city governance.

Smart governance can be seen as a basis for the development of smart administration through the application of new information and communication technologies (ICT) in management of local municipalities. Smart governance with utilization of ICT improves decision-making process by better cooperation with different stakeholders and higher rate of their participation at solving public issues. It forms the public value through leadership, civic participation, partnership, accountability, responsiveness, transparency, collaboration, data sharing and its mutual linking (Osella et al. 2016).

According to Mellouli et al. (2014) the smart governance is characterized by two features, free access to information and presence of technologies. Although, ICT and technology innovations are a key element of smart governance implementation, the government in smart city aims to harmonize management, governance and policy with other factors, especially with human capital as a driving force of changes. (Lee and Lee 2014; Cagáňová 2019). Finally, it contributes to better measurement processes, data sharing among stakeholders, more efficient resources use and performance assessment what facilitates the public participation and monitoring (Maheshwari and Janssen 2014; Nam and Pardo 2014).

To the main success factors of smart governance belongs the change of organizational and administrative structure within local authority and involvement of stakeholders into the management and governing of municipality (Alawadhi and Scholl 2016). The new structure is usually more resistant and active in combination with new technologies and innovative strategies lead to better understanding of societal problems, improving government to citizen relationships, government to businesses relationships as well as to non-profit organizations (Gil-Garcia et al. 2015; Mellouli et al. 2014; Cagáňová et al. 2017; Bolívar, 2016).

To summarise the abovementioned and including the approach of Pereira et al. (2018) the main features of smart governance are as follows:

1. strong focus on government decisions aimed at improving the quality of life in cities in various dimensions (smart living, smart mobility, smart people, smart economies and smart environment);
2. widely available, user-friendly and interactive technologies that promote the involvement of citizens and other stakeholders beyond the traditional objectives to optimize and co-create services and improve the quality of life;
3. strong emphasis on citizens, recognition of their key role in co-decision making processes to increase public value creation;
4. the management of smart cities is a form of governance that allows decision-making rights to be allocated to stakeholders, especially citizens, so that their participation is effective and has an impact on decision-making processes, thereby improving the quality of living in cities.

The following authors (Borseková et al. 2018; Gil-Garcia et al. 2016; Scholl and Alawadhi, 2016; Castelnovo et al. 2015; Estevez and Janowski 2013; Picazo-Vela et al. 2012) defined various dimensions of municipality on the basis of the deeper smart governance analysis. The particular policies contribute to sustainability and resilience of the locality. The government awareness is strengthened in environmental field, that helps to prevent the environmental consequences of growth and development to improve the quality of life for next generation and to be more flexible in case of disasters and citizen emergency. Another dimension is ability to use digital technologies and smart information-processes and decision-making activities. Their integration into the administrative system transforms all kinds of interactions with stakeholders, especially with citizens and foster those by transparency, open access of data and information as well as by control processes and performance assessment. The last dimension is associated with creativity, entrepreneurship and social equality, because the concept stimulates culturally diverse citizens and the business environment and supports the decrease of social exclusion and social justice. On the other hand, there appears also a criticism of this dimension caused by digital gap excluding some categories of residents (e.g. older residents, disable persons, or with lower income).

Smart governance covers various activities supporting participation of stakeholders, especially citizens, in all stages of local policy process (Castelnovo et al. 2015; Vitálišová 2018; Szilva et al. 2017). Governments use and share data, information and knowledge to support evidence-based decision-making that allows governments to make decisions based on credible findings and improves the effectiveness of public policies and programs. The traditional activities of stakeholder's participation is a participation in decision-making processes and engagement in improving public services in the city or co-creation of public services. These activities increase the government openness, transparency, accountability and thus the quality of relationships between citizens and local governments.

In the paper, the focus is put on activities aimed at supporting participation of citizens in local policy process including also the term of civic participation. So far, in the next subchapter, the authors of the paper define the tools used within smart cities.

2.1 Tools of Smart Governance in Civic Participation

Citizens play a central role in the decision-making process and their fundamental contribution is in the formation of public values in the city. By many authors (inter alia Vaňová 2018; Pereira et al. 2018; Melouli et al. 2014; Castelnovo et al. 2015), citizens' engagement is seen as a basis for smart governance in the concept of a smart city.

According to Pereira et al. (2018) civic participation is defined as an intensity of the direct involvement of stakeholders in the decision-making process on government measures. It is important to monitor the way in which civilian meetings are organized in order to facilitate communication between government, citizens, companies, stakeholders and relevant groups directly affected by a particular decision or problem.

From the citizen point of view, they tend to be more involved when they notice that the government is open to interaction and incorporate their views into decision-making, and when they have access to useful, relevant, complete set of government information (Mellouli et al. 2014).

The traditional participation activities include public consultations, public meetings, focus groups, surveys, civic counseling or committees, referenda and initiatives.

Due to dominant role of ICT in smart cities, they are widely implemented also in all areas of civic participation with aim to increase citizens' ability to participate in governance, including public service delivery processes at various stages of preparation such as planning, decision-making, implementation and evaluation (Pérez-González and Daiz-Daiz 2015; Kleinhans et al. 2015; Castelnovo et al. 2015). In other words, city planning and management can be improved by involving citizens through new technologies in a smart city (Khan et al. 2015). It is appropriate to use ICT-based tools especially in order to increase the number of participating citizens in a public debate that were excluded from the debate or not attracted by traditional participation tools. ICT contributes to create the values of society; leads to an important transformation of government-public relations in public governance as a key aspect of smart governance. Therefore, smart governance can be defined as a form of participative governance strongly linked to a governance model that promotes communication, interaction, cooperation, participation in public administration and direct democracy (Pereira et al. 2018; Navarro-Galera et al. 2016; Misuraca and Rossel 2012).

The new phenomena in ICT tools are social media (e.g. Facebook, Twitter, Linked in, etc.). In the public sector, they have a positive impact on openness, accountability, transparency, direct democracy, as well as on new strategies for managing public consultation and public policy interactions. The result is a change in the role of citizens in policy-making. Citizens' cooperation in policy-making can increase their innovation and efficiency, leads to new forms of cooperation between government and citizens, and among citizens. (Linders 2012; Stamati et al. 2015; Diáz-Diáz and Pérez-González 2016).

To the tools of smart governance belong also the tools of e-participation and e-democracy (MacIntosh and Whyte 2002; Buchsbaum 2007; Pekárek 2008), and tools supporting the availability of open data and transparency of local municipality (Johannessen and Berntzen 2018). The list of all tools presents the Table 1.

As it is evident from the Table 1, tools of smart governance are simple, fast, and accessible with clear results and measurable benefits. They include the tools of e-participation, e-consultation, e-democracy, supporting tools in communication and information collecting from citizens, which guarantee also the transparency in local municipality. All these instruments aim to increase citizens' engagement in governance and their participation in policy-making; facilitating and promoting participation by information and communication technologies; as well as the availability of information in a clear way (MacIntosh and Whyte 2002; Bawa et al. 2016).

These tools prove to be useful with the use of modern ICT, as they offer useful information and various ways of interaction, but the challenge is a lack of knowledge and skills of users. The link between transparency and smart cities is in technology as well as in information that is rather transparent and digitized, so make them easier to

Table 1. Tools of smart governance in civic participation.

Tools of e-participation	Tools for supporting e-consultation	Tools supporting e-participation activities	Tools of e-democracy	Tools supporting transparency
Electronic petitions	Electronic advisory voting	Frequently Asked Questions (FAQ)	E-vote or e-Voting	Transparent documents (online incoming and outgoing mail records, online documents, online records of minutes, search mechanism)
Electronic referendum (SMS, electronic election kiosk, electronic voting equipment)	Decision making simulation	Webcast, webcasting of council meetings	Electronic petition	Transparent meetings (time and place of meetings, online agenda, online webcasting)
E-panel	Quick polls	Blog	Electronic Questionnaire	Transparent processes (processes description, visual tools)
Discussion forums, chat rooms	Surveys	Alerts and notification services	Mailing list, SMS notification	Transparent benchmarking (online planning documents, online annual reports, references to relevant statistical data collected by authorised offices, online survey results)
Electronic Communities (online group of citizens discussing selected political issues and making possible suggestions)		Notification Services	Electronic registers, databases and archives on the Internet	Transparency of local municipality (online list of local government members, voting records and calendar management)

(*continued*)

Table 1. (*continued*)

Tools of e-participation	Tools for supporting e-consultation	Tools supporting e-participation activities	Tools of e-democracy	Tools supporting transparency
Electronic Citizens' Councils (a group of selected people listens and communicates with experts on selected issues)				Transparent data and information publishing (questions via email, survey or social media, online (real-time) questions (net-meetings or chat), discussion forums/blogs where citizens can ask questions)

Source: MacIntosh and Whyte 2002; Johannessen and Berntzen 2018

find and use. Different categories of transparency allow citizens to use government data to create new and useful applications that are targeted at citizens to solve their problems and thus to improve city life. So digital information can help to address the objectives of a smart city for more informed and participatory citizen (Chourabi et al. 2012).

3   Materials and Methodology

The paper is dedicated to the topics of smart governance, specifically its tools in civic participation. The paper aims to explain the term smart governance and its tools from the theoretical point of view, with special attention given to the civic participation as an important part of governance. Subsequently, it researches the issue on examples of cities in the Slovak Republic. It defines generally the available obligatory and facultative tools of governance in the Slovak cities. In the next step, it demonstrates the tools exploitation in Banská Bystrica, the city in central Slovakia, belonging to the pioneers in implementation of smart city concept.

The analysis of smart governance tools in the Slovakia uses data from Slovak legislation and strategical documents. The case study of Banská Bystrica presents the data of primary research in a form of questionnaire survey among citizens realized in spring 2019. In data processing were used the methods of statistical correlation and induction, e.g. hypothesis testing, as well as the methods of descriptive statistics.

The last part of the paper discusses and summarizes the most important research findings and identifies suitable proposals to develop systematically civic participation in the cities as a part of smart governance with inspirations from Vienna and Helsinki.

4   Tools of Smart Governance in Civic Participation in Slovak Cities

Civic participation is a democratic activity in a democratically established state that includes a wide range of opportunities for citizens to express their active attitude towards public affairs and to actively pursue their interests (Kováčová 2011). By creating space for civic participation, municipalities can gain different ideas and feedback from their citizens. They can also participate in the decisions of the local government and thus eliminate possible conflicts. The civic participation enables citizens to see, understand and participate in decision-making and control decisions taken by local government (Pirošík 2005).

Citizens able to participate should be aware, able to deduce, present opinions, challenge decisions, control power, engage in dialogue, communicate with key local authorities and collaborate with various social institutions and the third sector (Višnovský 2010). To be efficient and prepared local government, the municipal authorities should be relevantly trained and handle the expertise needed to create proposals and activities. It should strengthen activities to increase citizens' participation in decision-making and to get feedback for assessment the realized activities. (Jackson 2012).

In the Slovak Republic, according to the Constitution the local municipality has the obligation to provide information on its activities in the state language in an appropriate manner. In more details this issue is regulated by Act no. 211/2000 Coll. on free access to information. The main ways of civic participation are defined by Act no. 369/1990 Coll. on municipal establishment following the Constitution as to be elected or to vote the representatives of municipal authorities, local referendum and assembly of municipal residents. These are the obligatory tools of civic participation. There belong also the possibility to be a member of advisory bodies of local parliament as well as the possibility to take part at the meeting of local parliament.

However, in practice, also the group of "voluntary" civic participation tools is evident (Staroňová and Sičáková-Beblavá 2006). Voluntary participation is based on the local government's own initiative, which aims to increase citizens' active participation and support local democracy. This group includes tools of informing and getting feedback as follows: polls, surveys, collection of comments, public commenting, information for the public in various printed forms (e.g. leaflets, brochures, etc.), complaints, local media, events for citizens, information in local newspapers, information boards and bulletin boards. The second subgroup contains various forms of communication with citizens as citizen board, citizens' advisers, hours for intercourse with the public, first contact office, public assembly, public discussion, public hearings and meetings, advisory board and action group, communication through mediators, telephone communication (Staroňová and Sičáková-Beblavá 2006; Pirošík 2005; Vaňová, Bernátová 1999 and 2000).

In the field of electronic tools for the local municipalities, there is available portal eGov to increase informing and communication between citizens and government. Citizens can not only get information, but also comment on materials and evaluate the office and members of the local parliament what helps municipalities to become more transparent (eGov 2017). As voluntary forms of participation are unlimited, its possibilities are continually being expanded mainly by modern forms that use information-communication technologies to a large range.

Some local municipalities in Slovakia use different platforms to improve e-services, as a part of smart governance. One such platform is "Digital City". The platform is divided into two parts, namely services for local municipalities and citizens. The services for municipalities include digital local parliament (planning and preparation of meetings and archive of materials and resolutions), eVoting (transparent and paperless management of negotiations and voting of local representatives), registry administration, geographic information system, electronic auctions (fast, clear and transparent look on the auctions), interactive maps (the possibility to review the zoning plans, land register and addresses), reporting and city budget. For the citizen are available - on-line forms, that help filling and checking for correctness, various submissions, decisions and reimbursement; "City" in mobile (application offers information about city activities, displays a city map), publicly available office information (obligatory published information on website – contracts, orders, invoices etc.) (Datalan news 2/2014).

In the next part of the text, the authors of the paper analyze the exploitation of various obligatory and voluntary tools of civic participation with special attention given to the new modern tools based on ICT and smart governance in a form of case study.

4.1 Case Study of Banská Bystrica

Banská Bystrica is located in the centre of Slovakia. On 1 January 1991, Banská Bystrica became an independent self-governing territorial unit of the Slovak Republic. The city consists of nineteen city districts. The municipal bodies are the mayor of the city and the city council. The city council has 31 deputies. The mayor of the city is the independent candidate Ján Nosko. The mayor of the city is a representative and supreme executive body.

The city council establishes the city board, which is an initiative, executive and control body of the city council. It also serves as an advisory body to the mayor of the city. The city council has eight members and consists of members of local parliament. The municipal authority is an executive body of the city council and the mayor. It includes municipal employees and provides services for the organisational and administrative affairs of the city council, the mayor and bodies established by the city council.

The City of Banská Bystrica has established eleven city council commissions for economic development; transport; construction and technical infrastructure; environment; education; social development, housing and health; tourism; sport, leisure and youth; modern self-government and urban areas; culture; protection of public interest in the function execution and complaints investigation. Problems of transport, security and protection are the responsibility of city police.

In addition to the tasks of self-governing, the city also performs some delegated tasks of state administration, in particular through: building office - construction, land-use planning, decision-making and building regulations; registry office - works in the area of registry, civil matters and citizens' records; education office.

Banská Bystrica is the sixth largest city in Slovakia with population of 78,484 inhabitants (Statistical Office of the SR). The number of inhabitants is decreasing annually. This is due to lower birth rates and population migration.

Most economically active people work in public administration, defense and education, retail and healthcare. The biggest employers in Banská Bystrica are from the service industry (PHSR of Banská Bystrica).

From 8 regional cities, Banská Bystrica region is on the 7th place in GDP per capita. The region is lagging behind in labour productivity and inflow of foreign direct investment. Despite this, unemployment in 2019 fell to 3.53%. (State Office of the Slovak Republic).

There is quite a good transport infrastructure in the city. There is a train station, a newly built bus station. Population transport is carried out by suburban transport and urban public transport, using buses and more environmentally friendly trolleybus. There is no network of cycling paths in the city. Sliač Airport is close to the town. The city is a crossroad to the north and south of Slovakia.

Banská Bystrica has decided to become a smart city. In the first phase of the implementation of the Smart City concept, the priority of the city became Smart Governance. The city of Banská Bystrica wants to realised Smart City concept comprehensively and focus on all areas of smart city, like a people, life, environment, mobility, economy, but nowadays it considers the change inside the office to be a key one. The city perceives the process of creating Smart City as a comprehensive solution, from sensors and data collection to complex solutions, in which citizens can also be involved through civic participation tools. At this stage of the smart city strategy, the city management puts emphasis on obtaining information, creating statistics that can focus on linking with the city's project intentions.

In terms of smart governance, the city is looking for opportunities to increase the quality of internal processes at the office. The Informatisation and Digitization Department introduced a cloud link. The aim is to centralize the entire municipal information system in one place. In this way, all municipal departments, contributory and budgetary organizations of the city will be linked. New solutions are being implemented, the use of old software that does not meet today's technological conditions is being eliminated.

Currently, the municipal authority uses the following channels and media for communication and participation (Table 2):

To evaluate the current situation in the use of modern tools of civic participation the authors of the paper carried out a questionnaire survey in the segment of Banská Bystrica citizens in spring 2019. The aim of the questionnaire was to examine the current situation of using modern forms of civic participation in Banská Bystrica and to identify the possibilities of its development.

The questionnaire was distributed electronically by e-mail and placed on social networks. For those who do not use the Internet, the authors of the paper have distributed the questionnaire in printed form. The questionnaire was made available for six weeks and its completion was anonymous. The authors of the paper have used the statistical methods to evaluate the questionnaire and then verified the hypotheses on the significance level $\alpha = 0.1$. So far, in the research participated 93 respondents - 61 were women and 32 were men. The authors of the paper have tested the representativeness of the selected sample with a Chi square test based on the population age category at a significance level of $\alpha = 0.05$. The results of Chi square test are:

Chi-Square	6.851
df	4
Asymp. Sig.	0.144

Thus, it is possible to conclude that the sample is representative based on age.

In the questionnaire survey, the authors of the paper have investigated how citizens are interested in public affairs, whether they are involved in decision-making processes, how they evaluate the possibilities of civic participation and which forms they consider to be beneficial. According to the research results, 22 respondents (23.7%) are actively involved in public affairs and 17 respondents (18.3%) are interested in public affairs, but are not actively involved. Up to 58.1% are not interested in public affairs, and only 6% of these respondents would be interested in taking decisions in the city, if something changed.

Citizens also evaluated the possibilities of civic participation. Up to 45% of respondents rated options as average (on a rating scale from 1 to 5, where 1 is an excellent score, the score was 3), 26% of respondents rated participation opportunities as good and 29% of respondents considered opportunities for civic participation as insufficient.

Consider the low level of citizen involvement; the authors of the paper were interested in the resources and channels of communication from which citizens have information about the city. The residents could choose multiple sources from which to gather information. Based on Fisher exact test and Binomial test (Table 3), the authors of the paper have found that up to 90% of the respondents receive information via information and

Table 2. Tools of smart governance in civic participation.

Applied form of civic participation	
Electronic board	Obligatory information such as draft general binding regulations, master control plan, etc.
Open data	Administrative segmentation
	Inhabitants/Population
	Self-government
	Registry of dogs
	List of tax debtors
	Contracts
	Delivery invoices, customer invoices, order
	Petitions
Electronic services	Submission of online requests and electronic communication with the municipal authority
Client centre	Electronic communication of citizens with the City Hall, free telephone lines
Purity line	A free telephone line designed to stimulate cleanliness and public order
Electronic contacting local government representatives	Contact via email and social networks
Electronic questionnaire, polls	Email and online polls
Electronic petition	Electronic petition without a guaranteed electronic signature
Video recording	Offline video from City Council meetings
Discussion forum on the city website	Discussions divided into individual thematic sections
Social networks	Official website of the city on Facebook, Instagram and site of the mayor. Participation in discussions, city events, photo and video galleries
Blog	Sources of information where volunteered city representatives contribute interesting topics from the city's current affairs
Newspaper Radničné noviny	The monthly of the city is distributed on-line on the official website and on social networks
Link to the mayor	Mobile app for city-based complaint reporting available on the Internet
Geographic Information System	Map view of the city for the possibility of viewing the greenery, cadastral map, city plan, etc.
Map guide of Banská Bystrica	Map of the location of parks, landmarks and places of interest

(*continued*)

Table 2. (*continued*)

Applied form of civic participation	
Participatory budget	A democratic instrument that enables citizens to be directly involved in the decision-making process on redistribution of financial funds. Current information is available on the website and Facebook social network

Source: own research, 2019.

communication technologies - from the city's official website (banskabystrica.sk), from social networks such as Facebook and Instagram or from other websites.

Table 3. Fisher exact test and binomial test of dominant information sources.

Responses in survey	Responses		Percent of Cases
	N	Percent	
From internet	58	25.9	64.4
From social networks	74	33	82.2
From Radničné noviny	30	13.4	33.3
From other internet sources	25	11.2	27.8
From relatives and family	34	15.2	37.8
I do not look for information	3	1.3	3.3
Total	224	100	248.9

	Category	N	Observed Prop.	Test prop.	Exact. Sig. (2-tailed)	Exact. Sig. (2-tailed)
Group 1	1	84	0.9	0.5	0.000	0.000
Group 2	0	9	0.1			
Total		93	1			

Source: own research

The Fig. 1 shows the percentage of respondents who identified individual responses for a particular source of information.

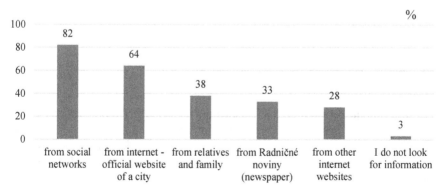

Fig. 1. Sources of information. Source: own research

The respondents rated individual modern forms of civic participation with a grade of 1- excellent up to 5 - insufficient. The authors of the paper have made the evaluation in the form of an arithmetic mean. The evaluation results are shown in the Fig. 2. The best scoring options were e-poll and questionnaire, electronic board and blog. For the sake of clarity, the authors of the paper have ranked the individual modern forms of civic participation from the best rated to the worst rated. All values in the graph are shown in the average values given by the respondents.

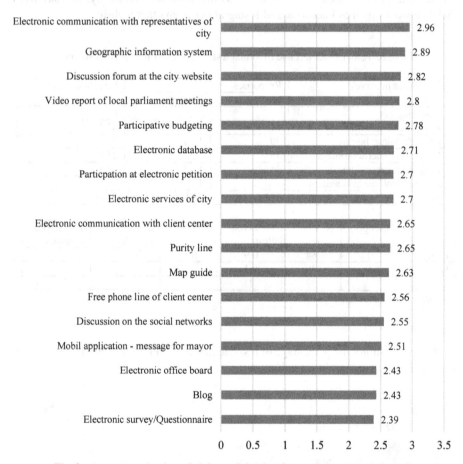

Fig. 2. Average evaluation of civic participation forms. Source: own research

However, in the research is also included the finding which modern forms of civic participation should be a part of the Smart Governance concept in Banská Bystrica. The evaluation of interest in using modern forms of civic participation was tested by a non-parametric Friedman test, which determined the continuous order of forms that the respondents are most interested in and the Wilcoxon Signed Ranks test ($\alpha = 0{,}1$), which has helped to determine the difference between the forms in their previous Friedman test. The test result was divided into three groups. According to the results, the authors of the paper can declare that the order of the tools is as follows. The first group of instruments is an electronic referendum; electronic voting or electronic voting; electronic petitions and emergency services. The second group involves the application of urban activity along with the city map; E-panel; electronic services and online forms. The last group included those instruments of civic participation that were not of great interest to citizens - electronic advisory voting; frequently asked questions; electronic citizens' councils; mailing list and SMS notifications; electronic communities and decision making. According to the results, the authors of the paper can declare that the inhabitants are interested in such modern forms of civic participation where their regular participation is not necessary. They are interested in civic participation where they express their opinion, but do not have to comment it and discuss it. The respondents were interested in receiving alerts that would keep them informed of the current city events (Table 4).

5 Discussion and Recommendations

Civic participation includes a wide range of opportunities by which a citizen can express his/her active attitude to public affairs and can actively pursue his/her interest. Citizens' participation in local government decisions can eliminate possible conflicts. The city is supposed to provide quality services and tools to ensure that public confidence in decisions is increased, thereby encouraging a responsible approach to decisions in matters of public interest. Only to create a space for people to participate is not enough, there is necessary to teach citizens how to do it. Therefore, informing citizens about opportunities for participation plays an important role. The citizen awareness and their informing as a key component of civic participation was confirmed also by research results. The authors of the paper assume that the situation is very similar in all Slovak cities, and probably in villages too. The modern age provides various possibilities how to inform and communicate with citizens, especially with support of ITC. However, it is necessary to cover by these activities the whole range of citizens, from young to older and to accustom the used tools to its abilities and age. In addition, the city of Banská Bystrica should focus on creating space for civic participation and gaining ideas and feedback from citizens, what can be currently defined as a weakness of the city by the research results.

The key precondition to develop civic participation as a part of smart governance is also close cooperation with all relevant stakeholders. In case of Slovak cities, it should include the collaboration with citizens, local companies, educational institutions, non-profit organisations and other stakeholders in the region, or coming from abroad. The main instrument how to develop smart governance systematically in context of multilateral cooperation is a smart city strategy. It should indicate the development direction of all smart city components including the smart governance. It should be linked with all other strategic documents of the city, deadlines for implementation, budgeting, defining co-workers and coordinators of these plans together with other investment projects of the city, intentions of city individual departments and individual city districts. It is also a case of Banská Bystrica. The management of Banská Bystrica is aware of the benefits of using smart solutions in urban space and is working on smart solutions, but there absent a comprehensive development document which defines the main development tendencies and priorities. Most of the planned smart solutions and tools are aimed at solving a

Table 4. Wilcoxon Signed Ranks Test of modern participative tools.

Combination of compared answers	Z	Asymp. Sig. (2-tailed)	Monte Carlo Sig. (2-tailed)			Monte Carlo Sig. (1-tailed)		
			Sig.	99% Confidence interval		Sig.	99% Confidence interval	
				Lower bound	Upper bound		Lower bound	Upper bound
9 × 1	−0.415	0.678	0.695	0.683	0.707	0.346	0.334	0.359
10 × 9	0	1	1	1	1	0.52	0.507	0.533
8 × 10	−0.769	0.442	0.458	0.445	0.471	0.229	0.218	0.239
14 × 8	1.391	0.164	0.164	0.154	0.173	0.083	0.076	0.09
2 × 14	−0.232	0.817	0.82	0.81	0.83	0.406	0.394	0.419
13 × 2	−0.022	0.982	0.983	0.98	0.986	0.494	0.481	0.506
12 × 13	−1.127	0.26	0.279	0.267	0.29	0.138	0.129	0.147
5 × 12	−1.511	0.131	0.14	0.131	0.149	0.07	0.064	0.077
7 × 5	−0.982	0.326	0.341	0.329	0.353	0.174	0.164	0.184
4 × 7	−0.602	0.547	0.56	0.547	0.572	0,277	0.266	0.289
11 × 4	−0.249	0.803	0.811	0.801	0.821	0.402	0.389	0.099
3 × 11	−0.318	0.751	0.762	0.751	0.773	0.385	0.372	0.398
6 × 3	1.286	0.199	0.201	0.191	0.211	0.099	0.091	0.106

1 Electronic survey/Questionnaire
2 Discussion forum at the city website
3 Electronic communication with representative of city
4 Participative budgeting
5 Participation at electronic petition
6 Video report of local parliament meetings
7 Blog
8 Electronic database
9 Purity line
10 Electronic communication with client center
11 Discussion on the social networks
12 Mobil application - message for mayor
13 Electronic services of city
14 Electronic office board
15 Free phone line of client center
16 Geographic information system
17 Map guide
Source: own research

particular problem in the city and are not a part of a systematic solution. The weakness of the city is a system of organization and non-involving the relevant partners, which can cause the fragmentation of civic participation tools and their inadequate exploitation in defined areas of the smart city. Another factor influencing the level of smart city concept implementation in each city are relevant competences of local authorities' employees. To be successful in the implementation process is necessary to trainee the employee in their PC skills, to teach the relevant knowledge of various tools and platforms that operate through information and communication technologies in the field of smart governance.

Because of the slow progress in implementation of new ICTs in Slovak local authorities, the possible threat is a lack of funds for smart technologies implementation. However, there is a conceptual support at the European Union's and national level (e.g. URBACT, Operational programmes, the calls of Ministry of Economy or Deputy Prime Minister of the Slovak Republic for Investments and Informatization). As a supporting institution there is established also the first Slovak Smart City Cluster in Poprad. It promotes the Smart City concept in the Slovak Republic and raises awareness of the Smart City concept; links academic and commercial spheres, supports cooperation with other organizations and associations with a similar subject of activity, as well as with state and local government authorities in preparing and commenting on relevant legal standards. The authors of the paper consider equally important also to develop the international public-private partnerships for the development of high-quality ICT services.

In tools of civic participation as a part of smart governance the social networks (e.g. facebook, Instagram, twitter, etc.) are often used. The research confirmed also the dominant role of electronic informing of public. The social networks contribute to increase the citizen awareness with relatively low costs. Citizen's informing should cover a wide range of information provided, so the city should involve also other important stakeholders from the territory to present information (e.g. secondary schools, universities, libraries, information offices, local business entities, etc.) in electronic way. For inspiration, Vienna uses as a tool to inform citizen an artificial intelligence assistant who answers questions about accessible information on the city's website. It uses a text and voice computer program based on artificial intelligence that simulates a dialogue between two people. Such a system responds to topics related to city services such as local municipality, parking, swimming pools, ticket prices, opening hours or events. Depending on the location of the user, the program can show the nearest point of interest on the map as a drinking water fountain or waste collection point. The service is also used to commemorate events that the user is interested in, such as meetings and public hearings.

The experts in the issues of smart governance, as well as the research results point out the importance of online questionnaires, polls and surveys. Their importance is significant in all stages of strategic development planning. They help to make better decisions in development activities and prepare the projects that meet the needs of the residents. This kind of platform already operates in Vienna as Vienna Digital Agenda. The platform allows the residents to provide feedback on projects at different stages of planning, thereby strengthening civic participation. Citizens can overlook and comment on several alternative plans and vote for suggestions for solution alternatives. Electronic voting is available. The user registers for the service through a functional email address and the participants must respect the ethics code. The service is monitored by an administrator for inappropriate posts. The service serves to actively exchange views between experts from the city council and citizens in the various preparatory phases. Such a process

facilitates electronic communication between the residents and officials of the municipal office. The residents can contact the competent staff directly by the subject, thereby
shortening the time for responding to the citizens' comments and hearing the public's
voice (Sag´s Wien, 2019; Smart city Vienna, 2019; WienBot-digital assistant, 2019).

Another good practice example in implementation of smart governance tools comes
from Helsinki. The city uses the European platform of D-Cent project, which develops tools for online democracy and participation. The D-CENT participatory platform
enables citizens to be informed and receive real-time notifications on issues of interest;
design solutions; cooperate in policy-making; vote for solutions that would improve
access to proposed ideas from residents to improve city life.

All the proposals can significantly improve the decision-making process within the
local policy. They effect positively all stages, from open consultation, input collecting,
creating proposals and communication (Anthopoulos 2017). This serves to increase
citizens' interest in engaging in policymaking and services, enabling the co-decision
and co-creation process using alternative instruments.

6   Conclusions

Using modern tools for civic participation as part of smart governance should become a
part of the decision-making processes in all dimensions of smart city. To do it systematically, the key step is to prepare and implement smart city strategy integrated with all
other strategical municipal documents.

Sufficient and appropriately set up opportunities for civic participation and the use
of online platforms for more transparent governance can help to increase citizens'
involvement in public affairs, and facilitate the processes inside the city authorities.

The issues of smart governance has not been deeply researched and still there are
many questions regarding its role and importance for local policy. The paper covers
partially the gaps in exploring the role of civic participation tools in a smart city, with
demonstration on the case study of Banská Bystrica, the city in the central part of
Slovakia. The case study pointed out that also cities in central European countries have
ambitions to be progressive and implement recent trends in their development. However,
only next years or even decades will show the real impacts of smart governance and
success rate in changes in civic awareness and participation in public affairs in these
countries with specific "soviet" history.

Acknowledgements. The paper has been written as a part of VEGA project Nr. 2/0077/19:
"Working competencies in the context of Industry 4.0 development", and 030STU-4/2018 KEGA
project titled "E- platform as basis for improving collaboration among universities and industrial
enterprises in the area of education" and H2020 project Nr. 873134 CALIPER "Linking science
and research for gender equality". The paper also presents the partial outputs of project VEGA
1/0213/20 Smart Governance in Local Municipalities and project VEGA 1/0380/20 Innovative
approaches to the development of small and medium-sized cities.

References

Act No. 211/2000 Coll. on free access to information

Act No. 369/1990 Coll. on municipal establishment

Anthopoulos, L.G.: Understanding Smart Cities: A Tool for Smart Government or an Industrial Trick? Public Administration and Information Technology. PAIT22. Springer, Cham (2017). https://doi.org/10.1007/978-3-319-57015-0

Bawa, M., Caganova, D., Szilva, I., Spirkova, D.: Importance of internet of things and big data in building smart city and what would be its challenges. In: Leon-Garcia, A., et al. (eds.) SmartCity 360 2015-2016. LNICST, vol. 166, pp. 605–616. Springer, Cham (2016). https://doi.org/10.1007/978-3-319-33681-7_52

Bolívar, M.P.R.: Mapping dimensions of governance in smart cities: practitioners versus prior research. In: Proceedings of the 17th International Digital Government Research Conference on Digital Government Research, pp. 312–324. ACM, New York (2016)

Borseková, K., Koróny, S., Vaňová, A., Vitálišová, K.: Functionality between the size and indicators of smart cities: a research challenge with policy implications. Cities Int. J. Urban Policy Plann. [elektronický zdroj] **78**, 17–26 (2018). ISSN 0264-2751

Buchsbaum, T.: E-democracy- The Council of Europe Recommendation, p. 23 (2007). http://www.ictparliament.org/sites/dfault/files/wepc2007_buchsbaum.pdf. Accessed 09 May 2017

Cagáňová, D., Bawa, M., Delgado Sobrino, D.R., Saniuk, A.: Internet of Things and Smart City. Uniwersytet Zielonogórski, 1. vyd. Zielona Góra 138s (2017). ISBN 978-83-65200-07-5

Cagáňová, D., Stareček, A., Horňáková, N., Ridzoňová- Hlásniková, P.: The analysis of the Slovak citizens' awareness about the smart city concept. In: ACM Mobile Netw. Appl. pp. 1–9. ISSN 1383-469X (2018: 2.390 - IF, 2 - JCR Best Q, 0.426 - SJR, Q2 - SJR Best Q); SCOPUS: 2-s2.0-85059663979. https://doi.org/10.1007/s11036-018-01210-6

Caragliu, A., Del Bo, C., Nijkamp, P.: Smart cities in Europe. J. Urban Technol. **18**(2), 65–82 (2011)

Castelnovo, A., et al.: Smart cities governance the need for a holistic approach to assessing urban participatory policy making. Soc. Sci. Comput. Rev. **34**(6), 724–739 (2015)

Chourabi et al. Understanding Smart Cities: An Integrative Framework. In: 45th Hawaii International Conference on System Sciences, pp. 2289–2297 (2012)

Data from eGov (2017)

Datalan news 2/2014 (2014)

Díaz-Díaz, R., Pérez-González, D.: Implementation of social media concepts for e-government: case study of a social media tool for value co-creation and citizen participation. J. Organ. End User Comput. **28**(3), 18 (2016)

Dominici, G.: Smart cities e communities: l'innovazione nasce dal basso (2012)

Estevez, E., Janowski, T.: Electronic governance for sustainable development—conceptual framework and state of research. Gov. Inf. Q. **30**, 94–109 (2013)

Gil-Garcia, J.R., Pardo, T.A., Nam, T.: What makes a city smart? Identifying core components and proposing an integrative and comprehensive conceptualization. Inf. Policy **20**, 61–87 (2015)

Gil-Garcia, J.R., Zhang, J., Puron-Cid, G.: Conceptualizing smartness in government: an integrative and multi-dimensional view. Gov. Inf. Q. **33**, 524–534 (2016)

Jackson, J.: Modern leadership for modern local government, In Council of Europe Centre of Expertise for Local Government Reform. p. 410 (2012). https://wcd.coe.int/com.instranet.Ins traServlet?command=com.instranet.CmdBlobGet&InstranetImage=2751082&SecMode=1& DocId=1991708&Usage=2. Accessed 20 Dec 2016

Johannessen, M.R., Berntzen, L. (eds.): Smart Technologies for Smart Governments: Transparency, Efficiency and Organizational Issues. PAIT, vol. 24. Springer, Cham (2018). https://doi.org/10.1007/978-3-319-58577-2

Khan, Z., Anjum, A., Soomro, K., Tahir, M.A.: Towards cloud based big data analytics for smart future cities. J. Cloud Comput. **4**(1), 1–11 (2015). https://doi.org/10.1186/s13677-015-0026-8

Kleinhans, R., Ham, M., Evans-Cowley, J.: Using social media and mobile technologies to foster engagement and self-organisation in participatory urban planning and neighbourhood governance. Plann. Pract. Res. **30**(3), 237–247 (2015)

Kováčová, E.: Verejná správa SR a jej súvislosti. Univerzita Mateja Bela, Banská Bystrica (2011)

Lee, J., Lee, H.: Developing and validating a citizen-centric typology for smart city services. Gov. Inf. Q. **31**(1), 93–105 (2014)

Linders, D.: From e-government to we-government: defining a typology for citizen coproduction in the age of social media. Gov. Inf. Q. **29**, 446–454 (2012)

MacIntosh, A., Whyte, A.: An evaluation framework for e-consultations? In e-Service J. (2002), https://www.researchgate.net/publication/236753459_Analysis_and_Evaluation_of_E-Con sultations. Accessed 05 Jan 2017

Maheshwari, D., Janssen, M.: Reconceptualizing measuring, benchmarking for improving interoperability in smart ecosystems: the effect of ubiquitous data and crowdsourcing. Gov. Inf. Q. **31**, 84–92 (2014)

Mellouli, S., Luna-Reyes, L.F., Zhang, J.: Smart government, citizen participation and open data. Inf. Polity **19**, 1–4 (2014)

Misuraca, G., Rossel, P.: Report of the thematic session on smart cities: sustainable urban innovation. In: ICEGOV 2012. Theory and practice of electronic governance, Albany, NY (2012)

Nam, T., Pardo, T.A.: The changing face of a city government: a case study of Philly311. Gov. Inf. Q. **31**, 1–9 (2014)

Navarro-Galera, A., Alcaraz-Quiles, F.J., Ortiz-Rodríguez, D.: Online dissemination of information on sustainability in regional governments. Effects of technological factors. Gov. Inf. Q. **33**, 53–66 (2016)

Osella, M., Ferro, E., Pautasso, E.: Toward a methodological approach to assess public value in smart cities. In: Gil-Garcia, J.R., Pardo, Theresa A., Nam, T. (eds.) Smarter as the New Urban Agenda. PAIT, vol. 11, pp. 129–148. Springer, Cham (2016). https://doi.org/10.1007/978-3-319-17620-8_7

Pekárek, A.: E-participace a její současný stav v české praxi. In: Ikaros **12**(4), pp. 1–4 (2008)

Pereira, G.V., et al.: Smart governance in the context of smart cities: a literature review. Inf. Polity **28**(2), 143–162 (2018)

Pérez-González, D., Daiz-Daiz, R.: Public services provided with ICT in the smart city environment: the case of Spanish cities. J. Univ. Comput. Sci. **21**, 248–267 (2015)

Picazo-Vela, S., Gutierrez-Martinez, I., Luna-Reyes, L.F.: Understanding risks, benefits, and strategic alternatives of social media applications in the public sector. Gov. Inf. Q. **29**, 504–511 (2012)

Pirošík, V.: Participácia v samospráve (nástroj protikorupčnej politiky). TIS, Bratislava (2005)

Sag's Wien - The app for your concerns to the city. Administration, Vienna City https://www. wien.gv.at/sagswien/index.html. Accessed 20 Mar 2019

Smart city Vienna: All participation projects at a glance, Vienna City Administration, Urban Innovation Vienna, https://smartcity.wien.gv.at/site/en/wien-gestalten-2/. Accessed 20 Mar 2019

Scholl, H.J., Alawadhi, S.: Smart governance as key to multi-jurisdictional smart city initiatives: the case of the eCityGov Alliance. Soc. Sci. Inf. **55**(2), 255–277 (2016)

Stamati, T., Papadopoulos, T., Anagnostopoulos, D.: Social media for openness and accountability in the public sector: cases in the Greek context. Gov. Inf. Q. **32**, 12–29 (2015)

Staroňová, K., Sičáková-Beblavá, E.: Verejná politika a miestna samospráva: štyri princípy spravovania: praktická príručka. Adin, Bratislava (2006)

Szilva, I., Caganova, D., Bawa, M., Pechanova, L., Hornakova, N.: Knowledge management perception in industrial enterprises within the CEE region. In: Longo, A., et al. (eds.) IISSC/CN4IoT -2017. LNICSSITE, vol. 189, pp. 66–75. Springer, Cham (2018). https://doi.org/10.1007/978-3-319-67636-4_8

Vaňová, A., Borseková, K., Hlaváčová, D.: Nové trendy v rozvoja miest a úloha inteligentnej ekonomiky. In: Kultúrna a sociálna diverzita na Slovensku VI. Signis, Banská Bystrica 276s (2018). ISBN 978-80-973146-1-3

Vitálišová, K.: Lokálne vládnutie a komunálna politika v podmienkach miest a obcí v SR. In: Kultúrna a sociálna diverzita na Slovensku VI. Signis, Banská Bystrica 276s (2018). ISBN 978-80-973146-1-3

Višnovský, E.: Občianska participácia ako problém kultúry. PLICHTOVÁ, J. Občianstvo particpácia adeliberácia na Slovensku. Bratislava: Slovenská akadémia vied, pp. 45–82 (2010). ISBN 978-80-224-1173-8

Vaňnová, A., Bernátová, M.: Marketing pre samosprávy. Komunikácia s verejnosťou. Ekonomická fakulta, Univerzita Mateja Bela 96 s. (1999). ISBN 80-8055-338-6

Vaňová, A., Bernátová, M.: Marketing pre samosprávy: príručka pre samosprávy. Ekonomická fakulta, Univerzita Mateja Bela 180 s (2000). ISBN 80-8055-337-8

WienBot - digital assistant: Vienna City Administration, https://www.wien.gv.at/bot/. Accessed 20 Mar 2019

Regional Brand in Slovak Tourism

Janka Beresecká[1], L'udmila Nagyová[2], and Dagmar Cagáňová[3(✉)]

[1] Faculty of European Studies and Regional Development, Slovak University of Agriculture in Nitra, Tr. A. Hlinku 1, 949 74 Nitra, Slovak Republic
janka.beresecka@gmail.com

[2] Faculty of Economics and Management, Slovak University of Agriculture in Nitra, Tr. A. Hlinku 2, 949 76 Nitra, Slovak Republic
ludmila.nagyova@uniag.sk

[3] Faculty of Materials Science and Technology in Trnava, Slovak University of Technology in Bratislava, ul. Jána Bottu 25, 917 24 Trnava, Slovak Republic
dagmar.caganova@stuba.sk

Abstract. After almost 20 years of the independent Slovak Republic existence in the midst of a turbulent changing Europe, the country perceives brands as a tool for expressing the company's given ability, its rapid recognition or creating a priori positive connotations associated with this extreme. Tourism brands are currently the result of cluster initiatives, support for the local economy at all levels of the national economy. The aim of the paper is to identify tourism brands, to evaluate awareness of the "Certified Rural Accommodation" brand and to point out the importance of a regional brand perceived as a guarantee of the tourism accommodation services quality that owes the creation and establishment of the market to regional public or private sector actors. The brand value was examined by both the customer and the provider. The basic research set of customer awareness research was 174 respondents addressed by an electronic questionnaire. Provisioning of brand value from the perspective of the provider was carried out for the actors representing the public and private sectors at regional and local level. The research results indicate that the brand awareness of the customer is below average, for various reasons; low promotion. Awareness is assessed by the provider as above average; a growing number of certified accommodation facilities. By predicting the basic economic indicator in tourism by 2020 using the correlation analysis with one dependent variable, the authors of the paper have pointed out the importance of establishing the tourism brand in the market.

Keywords: Brand value · Tourism brand · Innovation · Provider · Customer · Brand awareness

1 Introduction

The role of regional brands is to reach the visitor with a comprehensive, original, unambiguous concept of presenting products, services, associations, space, not only the region but also the state. In order to fulfill these tasks, it is necessary to coordinate the entire

H. Santos et al. (Eds.): SmartCity 360 2019, LNICST 323, pp. 388–411, 2020.
https://doi.org/10.1007/978-3-030-51005-3_32

labeling process from branding to brand sustainability. Not all countries are sufficiently aware of the nature, importance, seriousness and benefits of the regional brands. Our aim in the paper was to choose from a wide portfolio of brands, to choose a brand that is applied in current Slovak practice, it is unique, original, long-term established on the market, but the results indicate that awareness of this brand is low. Finding the causes of this situation is a long-term process that is conditioned by the availability of information, the scope of primary research, and the expression of the respondents' will to provide the required information. Rare sources are obtaining knowledge from a state where the position of tourism is better based on quantitative indicators. The importance of searching for these causes and even the essence of regional marking was confirmed by the quantitative results and prediction of selected economic indicator usable in tourism.

2 Tourism, Product and Services in Tourism and Current Changes

Tourism is a dynamically developing sector that has reached a mature stage of development (Goeldner and Ritchie 2014). In Slovakia it is a sector with a strong cross-sectional character, an excellent starting potential currently insufficient development (Beresecká 2012). Slovakia cannot compete with neighboring countries in the field of tourism (Krogmann et al. 2015). The problems in tourism development are insufficient utilization of potential, achieved quality of services, insufficient quality of basic and accompanying tourist infrastructure, unsatisfactory level of foreign language knowledge, insufficient quality of promotion (Meszárošová and Levický 2017).

Many entities are involved in the development of this sector - tourism service providers (businesses providing accommodation and catering services, tourism businesses (banks, insurance companies and others), service providers (professional and sectoral unions, marketing agencies, ministries, regional structures - their size, economic strength, provided services, financial resources, organizational and legal form are different but they are complementary to each other, so they cannot work without each other (Michálková 2010). Each tourism subject uses a set of techniques, tools and measures to organize tourism through which he coordinates, plans, organizes, communicates and makes decisions within tourism with a view to its sustainable development (Kratochvíl 2007). The successful development of tourism is also the result of previous development and adaptation of local government bodies to the conditions of the country's development (Gecíková and Papcunová 2014).

There is no universal organizational structure of tourism in Slovakia, it has the character of cooperative management of the destination, it is managed through a three-level organizational structure at the national, regional and local level. Public, private, nonprofit sector as well as public-private partnerships are coordinated within each level of governance. The main body of tourism is currently the Ministry of Transport and Construction of the Slovak Republic. Coordination of activities within the perspective type of tourism, namely rural tourism in Slovakia, is also within the competence of another Ministry, namely the Ministry of Agriculture and Rural Development of the SR. The marketing activities of the country are not managed by a separate contributory or budgetary organization established by the Ministry, but by a section within the organizational structures of the Ministry. Unified presentation of Slovakia abroad is ensured by the Ministry of Foreign and European Affairs of the Slovak Republic. This role arose from the program declaration of the Slovak Government for the years 2012–2016 and from the so-called. of the Competence Act. (Beresecká 2019a, b). The need for a systematic solution for the coordination of tourism development, young, small and applicable legislation serving to promote cooperation between the various actors, was addressed by the creation of various tourism associations, clusters emerging at regional level. They are geographically concentrated actors, have broadly defined membership, are sector-specific, and are established as public-private partnerships (Duman et al. 2009), generate improved service quality, increased visibility, joint marketing activities, but also joint engagement at major local events (Novelli et al. 2006). Significant attributes of clusters include synergy and cooperation, a common approach to resources, cost reduction (Staszewska 2008; Schejbal 2012), high flexibility, division of marketing information (Saxena 2005). The success of the cluster as a form of cooperation is influenced by various factors, including willingness to cooperate, open communication (formal and informal), traditions, human and social capital, creativity, but also participation in joint projects, education and promotion. Tourism clusters are becoming an important regional development element (Balog 2015).

Due to the need to make the region more attractive but also to offer the specific experience that clients seek, the services and products in tourism clusters are appropriately combined and modified with each other (Michael 2003). These attributes are significant and necessary in view of the growing competitive space in this sector as well. International tourism competition has set new rules in the global marketplace and has been looking for new, innovative, fantasy products and tourism brands that can help create a unique product offering.

Innovation is perceived through gastronomic culture (Kontis and Skoultsos 2018), product development innovations and market diversification outside the peak tourist season, (Connell et al. 2015; Cagáňová et al. 2015), changes in Internet branding (Morgan and Veloutsou 2013; Alejziak 2007), changes in the perception of satisfaction, quality, performance and various other variables that are a good predictor of customer's intended loyalty (Geng et al. 2008; Kontis and Skoultsos 2018). The policy changes also affect the difference in requirements for men and women for leisure activities and prefer holiday experiences (Chen et al. 2018), which affects the composition of the current tourism product (Xu 2010; Perri 2015). He argues that product creation is influenced by the expectations of tourists, who are currently more sophisticated, are seeking for more personalized travel experience, which is often defined as leisure travel. Changes also occur in the consumer behavior of tourists, which includes certain decisions, activities, ideas, or experiences to meet consumers' needs. The decision-making process is becoming more routine, which currently refutes the opinion of Hyde and Lawson (2003), who argued that tourist decisions include planned purchases. The tourist of the future will be demanding and will also require quality accommodation services with which he is currently not very satisfied (Beresecká and Hudáková 2019).

Nowadays, knowledge-based changes in tourism are also perceived. Silent knowledge, which can be achieved through direct experience and procedural, based on official education and training programs in this field. (Yin and Jahanshahi 2018). The combination of knowledge, perception, creativity and accidental confluence of events continually identifies opportunities for the emergence of new tourism products (Russell and Faulkner 2004), covering the whole complex of aspects and components of the product, including attitudes and expectations of quality (Ghadban et al. 2017).

2.1 Brand in Tourism

The brand in tourism began to write its history in the last decade of the 20th century. Recently, there is a growing interest in brands in tourism, as tour operators are increasingly aware that they can win the customer not only through the right price but above all through the hearts of visitors. Brands in tourism services depend on specific people and locations (country or location). Some locations have built up an image based on the brand category, others based on their location. Rich, dynamic, entertaining customers are attracted to places known for their many devices to meet their requirements. On the other hand, customers looking for rest, relaxation, peace and quiet, will seek spa spots and outdoor stays. Brand building is no longer just a concern for manufacturing and trading companies or tourist businesses, but they appear in different areas of life. The brand is used to refer to tangible products, services, people, regions or countries. Regional product brands are a phenomenon of the present period and interest in them is growing significantly in European countries (Gúčik et al. 2011; Seifertová et al. 2013; Ricz et al. 2011).

Attributes of a strong brand in tourism include a strong brand that is interested in product characteristics, convincingly offers one key advantage, speaks about the value system of the company (the company is focused on innovation, offers quality) is the image of customers who buy it, it can be attributed to human characteristics (young, mature, old brand, etc.). Brands that develop these five attributes, fulfill specific promises, through which they contribute to the creation of strong preferences (Gúčik et al. 2018) are considered to be successful.

In the field of tourism, the whole process of brand building and management can be perceived as a complex of brand building and brand management activities and brand building and brand management, which overlap and complement each other. The process of building and managing a territory brand should at least include the creation of a responsible working team with powers to manage and control the whole process, analyzing the current perception of the territory and determining the current position of the territory, identifying the main branding idea and analyzing the strengths, weaknesses, opportunities and threats, identifying and addressing the opinion leaders of the territory, analyzing various alternatives to the idea, identifying and defining target groups, visualizing branded manuals, creating a system of marketing activities to promote the brand to customers (Vaňová et al. 2017).

In tourism, sustainability is associated with the notion of satisfaction. The mpirical results of the study have been published in the scholarly literature, providing information on how important the analysis of image-satisfaction-loyalty relationships is. Image - Awareness is modified and supplemented by any new information, stimulus, own experience or experience of acquaintances, friends and family and participates in the creation of a diversified, detailed and realistic picture of the destination. Tourists tend to rely on this model of decision-making on the choice of destination leading to satisfaction. Therefore, destinations must pay due attention to the creation of a positive image through the quality of services and products that influence the satisfaction and behavior of visitors. Tourists are willing to re-visit the destination and disseminate positive information about it. The study pointed to a relationship between loyalty and repeated visits. For these reasons, it is essential to ensure a high level of tourist satisfaction in order to develop appropriate tourist behavior, improve sustainability and target competitiveness (Geng et al. 2008). Brand awareness (Matlovičová 2015) can be measured through memories (which product brands the customer remembers), first memory (which brand was the first customer spontaneously remembered), dominance (the customer remembered the brand as the only one), identification (the customer has ever met the brand).

In tourism, the sustainability of a brand is significantly perceived through the use of a virtual communication environment, through electronic marketing. Electronic marketing is considered to be a more efficient way of communicating on the market compared to traditional means of communication. Maráková (2016) states that "the Internet can do without marketing, modern marketing without the Internet does not". E-marketing tools include websites, online advertising, email and webcasting, mobile marketing, Internet communities (Web 2.0., Web 3.0., Wiki systems, Flickr, Blogs, Facebook, You tube, Pinterest, Twitter, TripAdvisor, etc.) and mashups.

3 Materials and Methodology

The aim of the paper is to identify tourism brands, to evaluate the awareness of the brand "Certified Rural Accommodation" and to point out the importance of a regional brand perceived as a guarantee of the quality of tourism accommodation services in which regional public and private sector actors are involved.

Primary and secondary sources were used to process the paper. Secondary sources have become the starting point for the analysis of theoretical bases and identification of tourism brands used in practice of the Slovak Republic. The source of statistical data was the database belonging to the Statistical Office of the Slovak Republic and Internal Records in the Office of the Nitra Self-Governing Region.

Primary brand awareness research was carried out through quantitative and qualitative methods. The quantitative research was carried out when researching brand awareness by the customer. The basic research set of customer awareness research was 174 respondents addressed by an electronic questionnaire. The collection of the primary data in obtaining the customer's view of the brand's performance was realized by the method of inquiry, electronic communication at one-off frequency, with a monothematic focus. The questionnaire consisted of 15 questions in order to get an answer why? What is brand awareness? Provider awareness of the brand, searching for causes and relationships will be carried out by a questioning method where the target group will be the individual and the experts, using a personal way of communication, direct questioning, degree of standardization - non-standardized, one-off frequency of questions, with multi-topic/omnibus focus. For the purposes of primary research, the authors of the paper perceive the provider dual, that is, as the primary provider of accommodation services and the holder of the Certified Rural Accommodation brand. Provisioning of brand value from the perspective of the provider was carried out for actors representing the public and private sectors at regional and local level.

Research question: Is awareness of the 'Certified Rural Accommodation' brand on the tourism market sufficient? resulted in the following hypotheses, which the authors of the paper will subsequently verify by the proposed procedures and methods.

H0: According to the results of field research, customer awareness of the 'Certified Rural Accommodation' brand is below average.
H1: Awareness of the 'Certified Rural Accommodation' brand is above average according to customer field research.
H2: Awareness of the 'Certified Rural Accommodation' brand is below average by the provider based on field research results.
H3: Awareness of the 'Certified Rural Accommodation' tag is above average by the provider according to the results of field research.

The research question and hypotheses resulted in the compilation of the graphical logical framework within the issue shown in the Fig. 1.

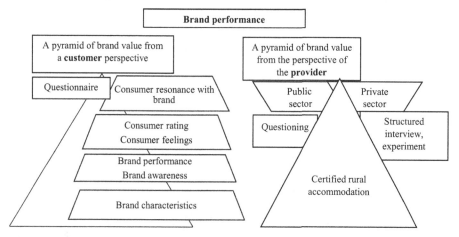

Fig. 1. Logical framework of the research question. Source: own research, (Beresecká 2019a)

In order to show the importance of establishing the tourist brand, the prediction of the basic economic indicator of tourism - the number of overnight stays was used. One-variable correlation analysis method was used. The parameters of the quadratic function P1, P2, P3, the value R - correlation index and the value R2 - correlation coefficient were used to determine the suitability of the relations used. The correlation coefficient explains how much of the total variability of the endogenous variable explains the model, that is, how much of the total variability is determined by the quantified econometric model (most commonly reported in percentage). It is a measure of reconciling the empirical values the quality of the endogenous variable with the modeled values (Beresecká 2019a).

A multi-criteria indirect method - point method was used to compare the level of the regions development. The 1–8 rating represents the regions order from the best to the worst results of the indicator.

4   Results and Discussion

Tourism has progressed progressively since the turn of the millennium. In the current period, the global growth again and has become one of the fastest growing economic sectors in the global market. Historically, the highest volume of visitors in recent years has been reached by tourism in Slovakia. Over the past three years, tourism performance in Slovakia has increased by approximately 45% (volume of visitors by 44%; revenue from tourist accommodation establishments by 48%), which significantly contributes to the creation of economic values, cultural and social development of the country, creation of local products or job opportunities.

Favorable developments from a global perspective and comparisons with neighboring countries are less satisfactory, as also shown in the Fig. 2.

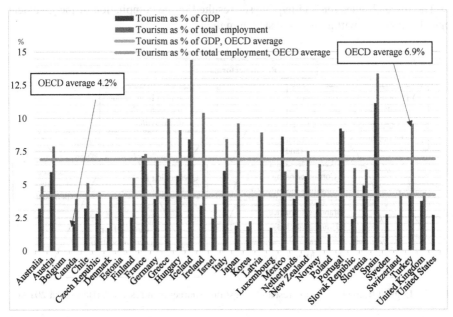

Fig. 2. OECD direct tourism contribution. Source: https://read.oecd-ilibrary.org/urban-rural-and-regional-development/oecd-tourism-trends-and-policies-2018_tour-2018-en#page28

The growth rate of tourism performance in the Slovak Republic is slowing down. This is also the case with the results achieved in the Czech Republic, as shown in the Table 1.

The year-on-year development of accommodation statistics is also changing, as in 2017 the increase in foreign visitors was 6.7% (+135 thousand visitors) but the average growth rate in Europe meant an 8.4% increase in traffic. The neighboring states of the Slovak Republic also record faster year-on-year increases, which results from foreign visitors (e.g. the Czech Republic + 870 thousand foreign visitors with growth rate + 9.4%, Poland + 695 thousand visitors with growth rate 11.4%, Hungary + 348 thousand

Table 1. Selected and compared economic indicators in tourism

Country	Tourism as % of GDP	Tourism as % of total employment	Tourism as % of GDP, OECD average	Tourism as % of total employment, OECD average
Slovak Republic	2.35	6.21	4.20	6.90
Czech Republic	2.80	4.40	4.20	6.90

Source: https://read.oecd-ilibrary.org/urban-rural-and-regional-development/oecd-tourism-trends-and-policies-2018_tour-2018-en#page28

visitors with growth rate + 6.6%, Austria + 1.3 million visitors with growth rate 4.8%). Such developments indicate stagnation and unfavorable state of dynamics of tourism development in the Slovak Republic in comparison with the boom on the global tourism market (Update of Marketing Strategy, 2019, In Beresecká 2019a, b).

The key to change and development of tourism is orientation to attractive forms of tourism, development, expansion and innovation of unique offer. In tourism, it is necessary to create an offer that corresponds to the expectations of sophisticated tourists of the present time who are looking for authentic, interactive and quality travel experiences. Focusing on the quality and level of provided services in tourism is an important tool of competition in a competitive environment and gains a stronger influence in the choice of destination or products.

Nowadays, visitors or potential tourists have a greater choice of products, destinations, but paradoxically, less and less time to choose the right product or service, so the brand becomes the focus of interest in the business environment. The following table provides an analysis of established brands in the Slovak Republic tourism.

The inclusion of the regional level marks shown in the Table 2 is carried out from the point of view of the grouping of local actors into a particular partnership, mainly Local Action Groups, which take on a regional character.

The role of the unified presentation of Slovakia abroad resulted from the legislative document. of the Competence Act. The country's "Good idea Slovakia" brand with symbolic significance works on two levels. The direction out of the country in building the social world, thus fulfilling social symbolism and inwardly serves to build its own identity. The initiator is the Ministry of Foreign and European Affairs of the Slovak Republic.

In 2014, the National Program for the Support of Agricultural Products and Foodstuffs was established, as well as brands serving to support domestic food production in a growing competitive environment after Slovakia's accession to the EU - "Quality Label SK". Products with above-standard quality parameters were marked with the "SK GOLD Quality Mark" mark (http://www.znackakvality.sk/?pl=17). These brands are initiated by the Ministry of Agriculture and Rural Development of the Slovak Republic.

Table 2. Tourism brands in the Slovak Republic

Level	Brands	Graphic representation of the brand
National level	destination / country marker	
	national products / quality label SK	
	enterprises / organization	
Regional level	regional products	
	clusters	
	tourism enterprises	

Source:http://www.ezat.sk/znaky_kvality/kriteria;   http://www.ubytovanienavidieku.sk/);
https://www.visitorava.sk/https://www.kupeledudince.sk/ospolocnosti/organizacia-cr-dudince;
http://www.systemkvalitycr.sk/sk/onas.html;   http://www.karsticum.sk/Page/ZnackaRegionalnehoProduktu;
http://www.klasterliptov.sk/;https://ochutnaj.praveslovenske.sk/znacka-kvality-sk/;   https://www.cedronnitrava.sk/;
https://obeclipove.lipove.sk/infos/novinky/Tlacova_spravaregionalna_znacka_kvality_Podunajsko.pdf;
http://www.malohont.sk/clanok.php?id=278;   http://vydra.sk/2019/06/13/regionalny-produkt-horehronie/;
https://regiongron.sk/udelenie-znacky-regionalny-produkt-pohronie/;   https://www.bystricoviny.sk/prclanky/190158/;
https://www.trnava-vuc.sk/klaster-cestovneho-ruchu-zapadne-slovensko;
http://www.klasterliptov.sk/,https://www.visitorava.sk/o-nas/;
https://www.kupeledudince.sk/o-spolocnosti/organizacia-cr-dudince); http://uksk.sk/stranka-2/stranka22/

In Slovakia, an innovative and voluntary tool "Slovak Quality System for Tourism Services" has been created for organizations active in tourism, which is able to systematically help to improve the quality of services, gain expertise and increase their competitiveness. The system is based on simple principles of quality management, based on knowing the needs of the customer and continuously improving the quality of services provided. The entire system was created under the license of the proven German Service Qualität Deutschland system, which was taken over by several countries and became the basis for the Slovak Quality System for Tourism. Currently, 18 entities hold this brand. The implementer and coordinator of the quality system is the Ministry of Transport and Construction of the Slovak Republic (https://www.mindop.sk/ministerstvo-1/cestovny-ruch-7/slovensky-system-kvality-sluzieb-v-cestovnom-ruchu/startuje-slovensky-sys tem-kvality-sluzieb-v-cestovnom-ruchu).

The system of regional labeling of products and services in Slovakia has not yet been officially represented at national level. The regional branding system is open to any region with clearly defined borders. Existing regional labels in Slovakia are mainly initiated by Local Action Groups or Public Private Partnerships operating on the LEADER principles. The National Network of Slovak Local Action Groups (NSS MAS) thus covers the national level of coordination and promotion of regional labeling in Slovakia. In each regional labeling region, there is a local regional coordinator who carries out regional labeling activities and communicates with local producers and service providers. The actors of the regional labeling agreed on a uniform design of the logotype of the local products and services labeling in Slovakia and the minimum principles for the certification of the regional product or service were adopted, which will be respected in each acceding region. In addition, each region will take into account its specificities and uniqueness in its principles. There are several important regional brands in the Slovak Republic. The regional product quality label e.g. Ponitrie received products: cow's and goat's milk, mousse, mead, oil paintings, liquid chilli pepper extract, pumpkin seeds, accommodation and catering services. The regional product brand Hont presents the regional product under the slogan: "The best of traditional rural products". The area is unique in preserving traditions and crafts: lace making, pottery and blacksmithing. Or the goal of the creation of the "Regional Product Nitrava" brand was to strengthen local business, develop the local economy in the area of production and services, support local markets, restoring wine houses, reviving old vineyards other. The importance of the regional brand lies not only in the presentation of products and services of regional entrepreneurs, but also creates space for closer cooperation, gaining new contacts and mutual experience.

Cluster organizations in tourism are an important type of clusters in Slovakia. Most cluster organizations were established as associations of legal entities. The only exception is the Balnea Cluster Dudince Tourism Association, which is a civic association (http://www.siea.sk/klastre-cestovneho-ruchu/c-323/klastre-cestovneho-ruchu). All clusters operate in specific tourist attractive microregions. Even three, Klaster Orava, Klaster Liptov and Klaster Turiec, operate within one self-governing region of Žilina. Similarly to technology cluster organizations, cluster organizations operating in the field of tourism were spontaneously created mainly from the activities of companies, cities and self-governing regions, without the support of the national government. The strongly competitive environment forced businesses to find appropriate models to face intense trans-regional but also transnational competition. Cluster organizations are focused on the promotion and development of "traditional" tourism, except for the Balneo Cluster Dudince focused on health tourism. The main activity of these cluster organizations is targeted marketing in Slovakia as well as in Central European countries (especially Hungary, Czech Republic, Poland, Austria), strengthening of partnership among cluster members and building of new cross-border partnerships. The clusters carried out development projects, various support events, building a common infrastructure (tourist information offices, prerequisites for discount cards), information and promotional activities. Like technology-oriented cluster organizations, tourism cluster organizations have the potential for further growth (Balog 2015; Cagáňová et al. 2015). Supporting the development of clusters in the Slovak Republic is partially addressed by legislation only in the case of tourism through Act No. 91/2010 Coll. on the promotion of tourism. The

Act does not explicitly mention "clusters" as actors, but defined types of associations (https://www.siea.sk/klastre-na-slovensku/).

The European - Slovak Association of Agritourism and Tourism as one of the first professional associations in Slovakia acceded to the award of the Quality Label for the tourism and agrotourism facility marked with the logo "Slovakia - Rural Holidays". The role of this brand is to ensure and guarantee the quality of services provided in rural tourism and agrotourism facilities, their prestige in competition with other facilities in the industry (http://www.ezat.sk/znaky_kvality/kriteria). Once the criteria have been met, the tourist accommodation facilities, regardless of their territorial competence within the Slovak Republic, may be the holder of this brand.

Quality label Certified accommodation in rural areas can be obtained by accommodation facilities located in one of the eight regions of the Slovak Republic, namely in the Nitra region, which also meets the minimum requirements for the award of the mark.

4.1 Certified Rural Accommodation

The system of accommodation facilities certification in the countryside was successfully established in 2013 in the Nitra region of Slovakia. The region is a predominantly rural, slowly growing region of the SR, with adequate activity and position, average degree of readiness for innovation, on average competitive outside the centers of EU development activities and with the possibility of cross-border cooperation with the Republic of Hungary. In terms of socio-economic level, the Nitra Region shows average to below-average values, while the natural, positional, economic and cultural potential of the region is higher than the level of its utilization. The natural conditions in the Nitra region as well as the character of the economy gave it a rural character. The reason for introducing the quality label in rural areas "Certified accommodation in rural areas" into practice was the long-term unfavorable position of the region in the tourism sector (Beresecká 2012), which is also evident from data in the Table 5. Development of basic economic indicators in tourism. The efforts of public sector representatives at regional level were to reverse this situation. One of the solutions was the creation of the brand perceived as a guarantee of the quality of services provided by accommodation facilities located in the countryside.

The main objective of the Rural Accommodation Certification project was and is to improve the quality of the services provided in the countryside, to guarantee and present the quality of the services to the outside, to take into account the perception of service quality by guests, to facilitate customer decision making and control. The partial objectives of creating and establishing certification are shown in the Fig. 3.

The condition for awarding the mark was fulfillment of the minimum number of points of the accommodation facility broken down according to their classification into a certain category, which are given in the Table 3.

Reviews include the following areas: location and appearance of the accommodation, availability of the accommodation, basic facilities of the accommodation, staff, information, security at the accommodation, feedback between the service provider and the guest, additional equipment of the accommodation, additional services of the accommodation. The system also uses four different forms of additional designation of

Fig. 3. Objectives for certification of rural accommodation. Source: Jarábková et al. (2013)

Table 3. Classification of requirements for the award of certified rural accommodation

Group of accommodation facilities	Certification criteria		
	Compulsory	Optional	Collectively
Hotel facilities: hotel, garni hotel, mountain hotel, congress hotel, wellness hotel, spa hotel, boutique hotel, apartment hotel, motel, botel, guest house	48 points	Min. 37 points	Min. 85 points Max. 163 points
Parahotel accommodation facilities: apartment house, hostel, cottage settlement, camping, privacy hostel (room, facility, holiday apartment)	47 points	Min. 37 points	Min. 84 points Max. 162 points

Source: own elaboration

accommodation: certified rural accommodation 'tourism', certified rural accommodation 'water stay', certified rural accommodation 'culture and education', 'multi-purpose' certified rural accommodation. Certified accommodation has the possibility to apply for inclusion in one of the groups of certified accommodation facilities, which express the narrower focus of the accommodation services on a specific target group of guests, whose requirements the accommodation can satisfy best. Assignment to the appropriate group will allow the visitor to easily navigate thematically through the accommodation search.

The first results of brand building and management in the Nitra region for specific accommodation establishments that went through the certification process appeared in 2013. This year, 13 accommodation establishments were certified. In 2014 there were 7, the year 2016 was a breakthrough, because it achieved the lowest number of certifications, namely 3, 2017 recorded a record increase in certifications in the number of 14 accommodation facilities. The spatial distribution of certified accommodation facilities is shown in Fig. 4.

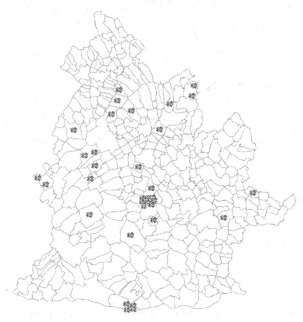

Fig. 4. Location of certified accommodation facilities of the Nitra Region. Source: own elaboration, (Beresecká 2019a)

Significant interest in the brand showed accommodation facilities allocated in the villages Štúrovo and Podhájska.

4.2 Assessment of Brand Awareness Certified Rural Accommodation

Brand awareness was assessed in two ways by customers and providers.

The basic research set of customer awareness research was 174 respondents addressed by an electronic questionnaire. From the results of quantitative research in the form of inquiries, it was found that women in a percentage of 77.6%, coming from abroad, living in the city, were predominantly involved in research on the brand awareness of Certified Accommodation in Rural Areas. They were from Slovakia, they lived mostly, 68.67% in municipalities. Respondents under the age of 25 (78.7%) with university education showed interest in the research; they are students who report income ranging from EUR 1001–1500, living mostly in a family of four (42.5%).

The Certified Rural Accommodation logo consists of two parts - a graphic element, which is based on the motif of a flower of brown-green color and the text, Certified Rural Accommodation. The following table shows the results of the primary research on brand value from a customer perspective (Table 4).

The first result of primary research is a statistical portrait of the socio-demographic profile of respondents who completed a questionnaire in order to ascertain the level of

Table 4. Brand value from the customer's perspective

	Indicator	Absolute expression	in %
Brand awareness	**Do you know this brand?**		
	Yes	17	9.8
	No	157	90.2
	Do you think the brand of certified accommodation is sufficiently promoted?		
	Yes	6	3.4
	No	168	96.6
Brand performance	**How do you like the look of this brand?**		
	1. I don't like it at all	3	1.7
	2. I don't like it anymore	23	13.2
	3. I like or dislike it	65	37.4
	4. It's pretty	67	38.5
	5 It is very pretty	16	9.2
	If so, were you satisfied with the services of certified accommodation?		
	1. I was not at all satisfied	29	16.7
	2. Rather dissatisfied	10	5.7
	3. Satisfied and dissatisfied	96	55.2
	4. Satisfied	21	12.1
	5. Very satisfied	18	10.3
Consumer feelings	**What do you think first when you see this brand?**		
	Nature	143	82.2
	Pleasure	2	1.1
	Peace	16	9.2
	Family	1	0.6
	Trust	7	4
	Quality	5	2.9
	What do you like on the brand?		
	Colour	66	37.9
	Shape	45	25.9
	Font	25	14.4
	Overall, I like it	31	17.8
	It affects me emotionally	7	4
Consumer rating	**If you have the possibility to choose an accommodation facility, would you choose a certified accommodation facility?**		
	Yes	138	79.3
	No	36	20.7
	What does the brand mean to you?		
	Quality	55	31.6
	Professionalism	24	13.8

(continued)

Table 4. (*continued*)

	Traditions	39	22.4
	Trust	33	19
	History	11	6.3
	Future	12	6.9
Brand use	**Have you used the services of certified rural accommodation?**		
	Yes	39	22.4
	No	135	77.6

Source: own research, own elaboration

awareness of the Certified Rural Accommodation brand. 9.8% of the respondents said they knew the brand, 96.6% said the brand was under-promoted, but 38.5% said it was pretty. Respondents who used the services of certified accommodation facilities could not express their satisfaction with the services provided. 55.2% said they were both satisfied and dissatisfied with the services. The brand evokes nature in the respondents and they like it in color. 79.3% stated that they would prefer certified facilities when deciding and choosing between certified and non-certified accommodation.

The identification of the brand's value from the provider's perspective was carried out by actors representing the public and private sectors at regional and local level (guarantor and holders of Certified Rural Accommodation).

The primary public sector researcher was the guarantor of the certification system, which had the right to grant, use and withdraw the aforementioned brand, namely the Tourism Department of the Nitra Self-Governing Region. The results indicate that public sector representatives are above average satisfied with the certification system. Their satisfaction is enhanced by the knowledge and the fact that the Nitra Self-Governing Region is the "first and only region", which in 2013 already tried to introduce a system that guarantees the quality of services. At present, the uniqueness and originality of this system persists. The representatives are satisfied that they have been able to create a subsidy system that in practice can guarantee the sustainability of the established brand. They perceive the value of the brand through the expressed interest in certification and the increase in the number of certified accommodation facilities.

The primary research of private sector representatives was focused on identifying attitudes towards the certification system, identifying weaknesses and strengths that would lead to a positive change in the entire certification process. The answers to the questions are:

Why did you get certified, what does such marking mean to you?
The answer to this question was unequivocal for all respondents. A strong motive was financial support, repeated with a uniform amount of EUR 1,000. *"This was strong ..., ... main ..., ... important ..., ... at the beginning the only reason not to try ..."*

What do you like about the certification system?
The respondents welcomed such activity, it was the first and is still the first in the region

in the Slovak Republic. They are satisfied that *"... some office ..."* has shown interest and wants to help them, it is not only *"... declared, but also real help ..."*. They also welcome the possibility of meetings organized by the certifying authority, seeing that the number of certified establishments is increasing, so even the first concerns *"... whether we did well"* are falling.

What do you dislike about the certification system?
The respondents commented on the complexity of certification, the disproportionate number of criteria they must meet to be certified. They currently have a problem with submitting projects, they have to submit them electronically and many of them do not have IT skills. They would welcome more training and targeted, e.g. how to work with the booking system, how to train people to achieve satisfaction and repeat attendance in their establishments. What benefits can bringing together, working together? At present, devices are perceived only through a competitive perspective.

They would welcome *"... a body to help them organize organized events to guarantee their attendance"*. On the other hand, in an area with the highest percentage of accommodation facilities as well as certified accommodation facilities, other types of accommodation facilities, which are not regulated by the Decree, would also welcome. It would also help them e.g. administration and updating of the website of the municipality, which would answer a number of questions asked by the visitors of the tourism concerning the events that are currently planned to be realized in the municipality. They expect assistance from the municipality in the professional processing of promotional materials, as they perceive their efforts for certification and its acquisition as a *"thing"* that is also presented by the municipality.

What would you change in the entire certification process?
Clearly web page. Because *"... first look at the page is about Podhájska"*. The page is missing contact information, *"..... people are asking us if it really works, why are there no names to take care of it"*, ... "do they really look at those criteria?"

The results of primary research suggest that brand value from the perspective of providers is perceived very positively, through uniqueness, originality, leadership through the creation of a quality assurance system, or a strong financial incentive factor, whether by public or private sector actors.

Results for the research question: **Is awareness of the brand of Certified rural accommodation in the tourism market sufficient?** confirm the hypotheses:

H0: Brand awareness Certified rural accommodation is below average according to customer field research, which means that brand value is low, below average because of low promotion, brand performance, but gives rise to feelings that are key to rural tourism development.

H2: Brand awareness Certified rural accommodation is above average according to the provider's field research results. The public sector representative perceives the brand's value through an increased number of certified accommodation facilities, and the private sector perceives it through subsidies. (Beresecká 2019a).

The importance of establishing the brand Certified accommodation in the countryside

On the basis of the results of qualitative research, there is a space for deeper knowledge that can be obtained by quantitative research. From the results of quantitative research, we sought the answer to the question: Is it necessary and worthwhile in the conditions of the Slovak Republic to make efforts to create and manage a brand that in some way guarantees the quality of tourism services for accommodation providers in small capacity accommodation? The results processed from secondary sources are shown in Table 5.

Table 5. Development of basic economic indicators in tourism

Indicator	Year	Territorial unit									
		SR	BA	TT	TN	NR	ZA	BB	PO	KE	Nitra order
Number of beds in accommodation facilities	2013	197 747	28 143	15 942	14 397	17 440	40 440	21 115	34 131	26 139	6
	2016	192 218	27 920	15 795	15 259	16 190	40 057	21 518	32 291	23 188	6
	2017	194 274	28 456	15 534	15 534	18 106	39 250	21 587	32 009	21 893	6
	2018	201 451	28 785	17 704	15 774	18 784	43 084	22 984	32 750	21 586	6
Number of accommodation facilities	2013	3485	233	276	246	307	882	494	701	346	7
	2016	3 489	241	267	287	303	907	508	671	305	5
	2017	3 495	234	270	279	353	892	516	662	289	4
	2018	4 007	275	295	326	388	1 063	588	728	344	4
Number of visitors	2013	4 048 505	1 073 854	263 709	238 336	238 440	819 016	400 251	700 248	314 651	7
	2016	5 023 629	1 386 283	318 524	322 020	298 829	975 536	520 895	854 528	347 014	8
	2017	5 375 475	1 447 811	366 717	371 591	324 652	1 035 225	569 164	894 173	366 142	8
	2018	5 596 407	1 460 130	365 027	370 034	335 670	1 119 677	627 660	932 121	386 088	8
Number of overnights	2013	11 486 571	2 184 586	1 076 726	972 493	612 661	2 397 984	1 335 415	2 256 759	649 947	8
	2016	14 138 420	3 000 449	1 203 899	1 274 486	828 062	2 777 136	1 614 400	2 713 587	726 401	7
	2017	14 936 766	3 103 541	1 351 121	1 374 363	977 268	2 896 764	1 680 911	2 790 308	762 490	7
	2018	15 515 083	3 082 284	1 352 397	1 454 952	970 827	3 097 483	1 825 981	2 901 080	830 079	7

Note: SR – Slovak Republic, BA – Bratislava region, TT – Trnava region, TN – Trenčin region, NR – Nitra region, ZI – Žilina region, BB – Banská Bystrica region, PO – Prešov region, KE – Košice region[1]
Source: ŠÚ SR, own elaboration

Based on the analysis of the selected economic indicators development in tourism, it can be stated that the order of Nitra region location, where the brand is established, has been fixed since 2013, i.e. since the brand was established to 2018. The number of accommodation establishments has changed positively, with a shift from 7 to 4. The state of disinterest in the region continues to remain, compared to 2013, the region fell to the last 8th place out of 8 regions. However, the tourists visiting the region will stay in the region for a longer period, as evidenced by a change in the number of overnight stays from eighth to seventh.

This deeper knowledge based on quantitative results has led us to know the near future, the prediction of economic indicators. For this purpose the indicator - number of overnight stays was chosen. The results are shown in the Fig. 5 and the Table 6.

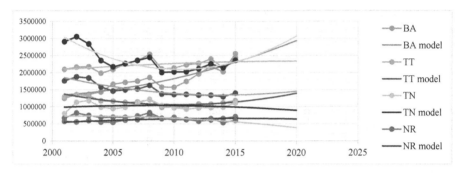

Fig. 5. Forecast of the number of overnight stays in regions of the SR. Source: own elaboration

Table 6. Number of overnights

p1	6.86E+10	1.21E+10	1.45E+10	-4086939608	-2367710352	-2507877360	1.25E+10	4.29E+10	-4.563E+09
p2	-68274703.5	-12160978.22	-14456387.55	4071424.094	2351038.781	2484095.891	-12397269.13	-42724262.3	4557703.79
p3	16994.64273	3045.194431	3595.535122	-1013.734184	-583.4587765	-614.5611267	3077.838329	10625.71254	-1137.90008
R	0.427682541	0.892283243	0.847945957	0.160351939	0.600825946	0.4801029	0.898199957	0.889895889	0.72323782
R²	0.182912356	0.796169386	0.719012346	0.025712744	0.360991817	0.230498794	0.806763163	0.791914693	0.52307294

Source: own elaboration (Beresecká, 2019a)

The following table shows the quantitative representation of the graphically represented predictions in absolute and percentage terms (Table 7).

The results show that not every region in the Slovak Republic tends to grow the selected indicator. The forecast for the number of overnight stays shows that the greatest percentage change will occur in 2020 in the Bratislava, Nitra and Žilina regions. The

Table 7. Forecast of the overnight stays number in absolute and percentage terms in regions of the SR

Area	Year 2001	Year 2015	Change 2015/2001 in %	Year 2020	Change 2020/2001 in %
SR model	11968042	11628986	−2.83	13122385	9.65
BA model	1345869	2305185	71.28	2937092	118.23
TT model	1371156	1137097	−17.07	1395081	1.74
TN model	987318	991064	0.04	896097	−9.24
NR model	548724	707945	29.01	642794	17.14
ZA model	2095152	2319410	10.70	2341118	11.74
BB model	1857498	1344112	−27.64	1453155	−21.76
PO model	3037034	2317424	−23.69	3069863	1.08
KE model	725345	555866	−23.37	387237	−4661

Source: own elaboration

worst forecast in the monitored economic indicator will be in the Košice, Banská Bystrica and Trenčín regions.

Based on the forecast, the unfavorable position of the Nitra region should change significantly, but the results will not reach the value of the indicator achieved in 2015.

Given the extent of this contribution, it is not possible to address a number of indicators that could initiate tourism development. Neither the one-member econometric model expresses several factors influencing the increasing trend. Ide, e.g. on the district's GDP, subsidies for tourism, investment development, the share of expenditures of citizens on services. It creates space for further empirical research and searching for possible causes of poor development of the country, not only in the field of tourism.

5 Discussion

Creation and use of the brands in the Slovak Republic can be characterized as a heterogeneous, uncoordinated activity caused by multi-species, multiple brands that do not have central management at national level by the public or private sector. In the Czech Republic, with which the Slovak Republic formed a common Czechoslovak state by the end of 1992, the situation is different from this point of view. The creation of regional brands in the Czech Republic was stimulated by the Natura 2000 project "People for Nature, Nature for People", funded by the European Commission, which was implemented in 2004–2006. The regional product labeling was one of the main parts of this project aimed at raising public awareness of the pan-European network of Natura 2000 protected areas. Since 2005, the rules and criteria for product labeling have been set, including the name and appearance of the brand itself and Group or Regional Development Agency. Already in the first year the first certificates were awarded to products in the Krkonoše, Beskydy and Šumava. Since 2006, the branding system has been called "Home Products". Private sector actors have shown significant interest in regional brands not only in terms of abundance but also in the scope of tourism services. Based on the demand for regional labeling, the Ministry of the Environment in 2007 created certification rules for the labeling of accommodation and catering services. In 2008, the European Flower Eco-label was awarded. This year is also significant in the Czech Republic the establishment of the Association of Regional Brands. The association logo is shown in the Fig. 6.

Fig. 6. The association logo. Source: http://www.regionalni-znacky.cz/arz/cs/o-nas/

The Association is the national coordinator of the regional labeling system, it is an association of regions with its own brand. Its activities are governed by the statutes and internal rules. The Association ensures that all brands maintain a high standard and provide space for the joint development of regional brands.

The main objective of regional labeling is to raise the profile of regions and highlight interesting products that are being created in this area. Since 2004, 27 regions have been involved in the regional branding system. In each region there is a regional coordinator who manages the brand. The product brand is awarded by an independent certification committee (independent in each region), subject to compliance with the prescribed rules. In connection with the labeling of products, in some regions the labeling is also used to support selected accommodation and catering facilities. In addition to certified products and services, experiences are also marked and certified.

The regional branding system in the Czech Republic is open to any region with clearly defined borders. The initiator of a new brand must be a local organization or institution that will act as a regional coordinator. The territorial scope of this system signs is shown in Fig. 7.

In addition to this system, there are other brands operating in the Czech Republic that are not members of the association, e.g. the brand "Tradition of the White Carpathians", "Regional Product Bohemian Paradise", but the marking is based on similar principles.

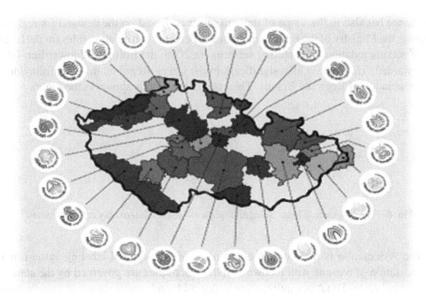

Fig. 7. Territorial scope of regional brands in the Czech Republic. Source: http://www.regionalni-znacky.cz/arz/cs/o-nas/

6 Conclusion

The paper points out some critical problems, which include the underestimated role of the state in tourism. Although the tourism industry in the global context is a sector with high development dynamics, Slovakia has not seen this trend in recent years. Based on the results of theoretical and empirical knowledge, it can be concluded that the brand process in Slovakia is not institutionalized, not coordinated by the national coordinator. Branding is initiated by regional activities, while marketing activities are fragmented, undersized, professionally unprofessionally managed. There is little awareness of the unique, original, long-term established 'Certified Rural Accommodation' brand operating in the territory of one of the eight regions used by the accommodation providers. The solution to the change in the position of tourism in the territory of the Slovak Republic would be to create a public sector body at the national level, especially for the tourism sector, which the country currently lacks. This would ensure a coordinated and integrated development of the sector, including the implementation of communication strategies.

Acknowledgements. This research was supported and funded by 030STU-4/2018 KEGA project titled "E- platform as basis for improving collaboration among universities and industrial enterprises in the area of education" and with support of 2/0077/19 VEGA project titled "Work competencies in the context of Industry 4.0" and H2020 project Nr. 873134 CALIPER "Linking science and research for gender equality".

References

Alejziak, W.: Megatrendy a výzvy rozvoja politiky národního a medzinárodného cestovného ruchu. Ekonomická revue **40**(1), 3–20 (2007)

Balog, M.: Klastrová politika v podmienkach Slovenska. 1. vyd., Bratislava: Slovenská inovačná a energetická agentúra (2015). https://www.siea.sk/materials/files/inovacie/publikacie/studia_SIEA_Klastrova_politika_web.pdf

Balog, M., Cagáňová, D., Šujanová, J.: Management of Regional Development - Promotion of Innovation Processes, p. 82. Slovak university of technology in Bratislava, Bratislava (2014). ISBN 978-80-89708-04-8

Beresecká, J.: Zlepšenie efektívnosti marketingových prístupov k rozvoju vidieckeho cestovného ruchu v Nitrianskom kraji. [Doktorská dizertačná práca], p. 177. Univerzita Konštantína Filozofa v Nitre, Nitra (2012)

Beresecká, J.: Marketingová koncepcia vidieckeho turizmu v slovenskom regióne. 1. vyd., p. 146. Slovenská poľnohospodárska univerzita, Nitra (2018)

Beresecká, J.: Povedomie o značke vo vidieckom turizme: [Habilitačná práca], p. 150. Univerzita Konštantína Filozofa v Nitre, Nitra (2019a)

Beresecká, J.: Marketingovo-komunikačná stratégia brandingu lokálneho turizmu, p. 54. Univerzita Konštantína Filozofa v Nitre, Nitra (2019b)

Beresecká, J., Hudáková, M.: Vzťah vzdelanostnej úrovne k triáde produktu vidieckeho turizmu. Aktuální problémy cestovního ruchu "Cestovní ruch – Příležitost pro venkov". Topical issues of Tourism "Rural tourism – possibility for a destanation", pp. 22–32. Vysoká škola polytechnická Jihlava, Jihlava (2019)

Bystricoviny. https://www.bystricoviny.sk/pr-clanky/190158/

Cagáňová, D., Bawa, M., Šujanová, J., Saniuk, A.: Innovation in Industrial Enterprises and Intercultural Management. 1. Vyd., p. 126. University od Zielona Góra, Zielona Góra (2015). ISBN 978-83-933843-4-1

Cedron Nitrava. https://www.cedronnitrava.sk/

Certifikované ubytovanie na vidieku. http://www.ubytovanienavidieku.sk/

Connell, J.S., Page, J., Meyer, D.: Visitor attractions and events: responding to seasonality. Tourism Manag. **46**(C), 283–298 (2015)

České regionální značky. http://www.regionalni-znacky.cz/arz/cs/o-nas/

Dovolenka na vidieku. http://www.ubytovanienavidieku.sk/

Duman, P., Balog, M., Rehák, Š., Zaušková, A., Loučanová, E.: Klastre na podporu rozvoja inovácií. Bratislava: Slovenská inovačná a energetická agentúra (2009). https://www.siea.sk/materials/files/inovacie/slovenske_klastre/Klastre-SIEA.pdf

Gecíková, I., Papcunová, V.: Využitie strategických nástrojov riadenia v podmienkach miestnej samosprávy na Slovensku v roku 2014. Procedia – Sociálne a behaviorálne vedy: Súčasné problémy v podnikaní, riadení a vzdelávaní 2013. Medzinárodná vedecká konferencia, Vilnius 14. **110**, 969–978 (2014)

Geng, Ch., Chi, Q., Qu, H.: Examining the structural relationships of destination image, tourist satisfaction and destination loyalty: an integrated approach. Tour. Manag. **29**(4), 624–636 (2008)

Ghabdan, S., Shames, M., Arrage, J.A., Fayyad, A.A.: Rural tourism in Lebanon: what does the market reveal? CEPN Working Papers 2017–19, Centre d'Economie de l'Université de Paris Nord (2017)

Goeldner, C.H. R., Richie, B.J.R.: Cestovní ruch, princípy, příklady, trendy, p. 303. Albatros Media, Praha (2014)

Gúčik, M., et al.: Marketing cestovného ruchu. 1. vyd., p. 264. Dali-B.B., Banská Bystrica (2011). https://books.google.sk/books?id=0nHB-88dd6UC&pg=PA119&lpg=PA119&dq=podnikov%C3%A1+komunikacia%C3%A1cia&source=bl&ots=G21j0bm0mO&

Gúčik, M., et al.: Marketing cestovného ruchu, p. 248. Wolters Kluwer, Bratislava (2018)

Hyde, K.F., Lawson, R.: The nature of independent travel. J. Travel Res. **42**(1), 13–23 (2003)

Chen, Y.C., King, B., Lee, H.W.: Experiencing the destination brand: behavioral intentions of arts festival tourists. J. Destination Mark. Manag. **10**, 61–67 (2018)

Jarábková, J., Fáziková, M., Beresecká, J.: Certifikácia ubytovacích zariadení na vidieku, p. 149. Slovenská poľnohospodárska univerzita, Nitra (2013)

Klastre cestovného ruchu. https://www.siea.sk/klastre-cestovneho-ruchu/

Klastre cestovného ruchu. http://www.siea.sk/klastre-cestovneho-ruchu/c-323/klastre-cestov neho-ruchu/

Klaster cestovného ruchu západné Slovensko. https://www.trnava-vuc.sk/klaster-cestovneho-ruchu-zapadne-slovensko/

Klastre na Slovensku. https://www.siea.sk/klastre-na-slovensku/

Klaster Liptov. http://www.klasterliptov.sk

Klaster Orava. https://www.visitorava.sk/

Kontis, A.-P., Skoultsos, S.: Enhancing hospitality services through the engagement of visitors in local gastronomy experiences: a marketing perspective from the supply-side. In: Katsoni, V., Velander, K. (eds.) Innovative Approaches to Tourism and Leisure. SPBE, pp. 339–349. Springer, Cham (2018). https://doi.org/10.1007/978-3-319-67603-6_26

Kratochvíl, P.: Organizace Cestovního ruchu. COT Business **9**(1), 49 (2007)

Kritériá značky kvality. http://www.ezat.sk/znaky_kvality/kriteria

Krogmann, A., Oremusová, D., Šolcová, L., Nemčíková, M.: The perception of tourism in the Podhajska resort by its visitors. In: Aktuální problémy cestovního ruchu (10. mezinárodní konference): sborník příspěvků, pp. 215–225. Jihlava, Česká republika, VŠPJ (2015)

Kúpele Dudince. https://www.kupeledudince.sk/o-spolocnosti/organizacia-cr-dudince

Maráková, V.: Marketingová komunikácia v cestovnom ruchu, p. 168. Wolters Kluwer, Bratislava (2016)

Matlovičová, K.: Značka územia. Prešovská univerzita, p. 320. Grafotlač, Prešov (2015)

Meszárošová, Z., Levický, M.: Cestovný ruch ako prostriedok na podporu rozvoja euroregiónov. Verejná správa a regionálny rozvoj **13**(1), 105–110 (2017)

Miestna akčná skupina CEDRON-NITRAVA. https://www.cedronnitrava.sk/

Miestna akčná skupina Malohont. http://www.malohont.sk/clanok.php?id=278

Ministerstvo cestovného ruchu

Tlačová správa – Miestna akčná skupina Združenie Dolný Žitný ostrov. https://obeclipove.lipove. sk/infos/novinky/Tlacova_spravaregionalna_znacka_kvality_Podunajsko.pdf

Michael, E.J.: Tourism micro-clusters. Tour. Econ. **9**(3), 133–145 (2003)

Michálková, A.: Regionálne siete v cestovnom ruchu. Ekonomická univerzita v Bratislave, Bratislava, p. 130 (2010)

Ministerstvo dopravy a výstava SR. https://www.mindop.sk/ministerstvo-1/cestovny-ruch-7/slo vensky-system-kvality-sluzieb-v-cestovnom-ruchu/startuje-slovenskysystem-kvality-sluzieb-v-cestovnom-ruchu

Morgan, T., Veloutsou, A.C.: Beyond technology acceptance: brand relationships and online brand experience. J. Bus. Res. **6**(1), 21–27 (2013)

Novelli, M., Schmitz, B., Spencer, T.: Networks, clusters and innovation in tourism: UK experience. Tour. Manag. **27**(6), 1141–1152 (2006)

Obec Lipové. http://www.malohont.sk/clanok.php?id=278

Ochutnaj pravé slovenské potraviny. https://ochutnaj.praveslovenske.sk/znacka-kvality-sk/

OECD Tourism Trends and Policies (2018), Authors OECD, p. 376. https://www.oecd-ilibrary.org/ urban-rural-and-regional-development/oecd-tourism-trends-and-policies-2018_tour-2018-en

Perri, A.: Social Networking Usage: Recommended citation 2005–2015. Pew Research Center (2015). http://www.pewinternet.org/2015/10/08/2015/Social-Networking-Usage-2005-2015/

Region Gron. https://regiongron.sk/udelenie-znacky-regionalny-produkt-pohronie/

Regionálne produkty. http://www.kopanice.regionalneprodukty.sk/

Ricz, A., et al.: South Pannon food chain network project. DETUROPE. Central Eur. J. Reg. Dev. Tour. **3**(3), 96–153 (2011)

Russell, R., Faulkner, B.: Entrepreneurship, chaos and the tourism area lifecycle. Ann. Tour. Res. **31**(3), 556–579 (2004)

Saxena, G.: Relationships, networks and the learning regions: case evidence from the Peak District National Park. Tour. Manag. **26**(2), 277–289 (2005)

Seifertová et al.: Průvodcovské činnosti Praha: Vydavatelsvo Grada, p. 204 (2013)

Schejbal, C.: Clusters in tourism. Acta Geoturistica. **3**(1), 1–7 (2012). http://geotur.tuke.sk/pdf/2012/n01/01_Schejbal_v3_n1.pdf. Accessed 24 Jan 2016

Slovenský system kvality služieb v cestovnom ruchu. https://www.mindop.sk/ministerstvo-1/cestovny-ruch-7/slovensky-system-kvality-sluzieb-v-cestovnom-ruchu/startuje-slovensky-system-kvality-sluzieb-v-cestovnom-ruchu/

Slovenský systém kvality služieb v cestovnom ruchu. http://www.systemkvalitycr.sk/sk/o-nas.html

Staszewska, J.: Úloha klastrov na trhu cestovného ruchu. Ekonomická revue cestovného ruchu **41**(1), 26–33 (2008)

Systém kvality cestovného ruchu. http://www.systemkvalitycr.sk/sk/onas.html

Štatistický úrad SR (2018). http://datacube.statistics.sk/

Ubytovanie na vidieku. http://www.ubytovanienavidieku.sk/

Únia klastrov Slovenska. http://uksk.sk/stranka-2/stranka22/

Vaňová, A., et al.: Prípadové štúdie z marketingu územia, z verejného a neziskového marketingu, p. 100. Ekonomická Fakulta, Banská Bystrica (2017)

VYDRA – Vidiecka rozvojová aktivita. http://vydra.sk/2019/06/13/regionalny-produkt-horehronie/

Výrostová, E.: Regionálna ekonomika a rozvoj. Bratislava: Iura edition, spol. s r.o., p. 352 (2010)

Značka regionálneho produktu. http://www.karsticum.sk/Page/ZnackaRegionalnehoProduktu

Značka kvality SK. http://www.znackakvality.sk/?pl=17

Značka kvality SK. https://ochutnaj.praveslovenske.sk/znacka-kvality-sk/

Xu, J.B.: Percpetions of tourism products. Tour. Manag. **31**(5), 607–610 (2010)

Yin, M., Jahanshahi, A.A.: Developing knowledge-based resources: the role of entrepreneurs' social network size and trust. Sustainability **10**(10), 3380 (2018)

Should We Share Rights and Obligations with Artificial Intelligence Robots?

Corneliu Andy Pusca[✉]

Danubius University of Galati, Galați, Romania
andypusca@univ-danubius.ro

Abstract. Technology could have impact on the public safety of humans it is not enough to simply presume it works. The social structures are already revolutionized by the introduction of artificial intelligence in the industry and society and the legal framework is not yet prepared to absorb the impact. This is why we consider that robots should have a distinctive legal status, separate from their users and owners. The role of this special issue is to define the contents of the status of the artificially intelligent agents (liability, rights, tax duties and so on) for a minimum certainty not only related to eventual damages, but also to the public safety and data protection.

Keywords: Robots · Personhood · Rights · Liability · Taxation · Control

1 Introduction

Artificially Intelligent agents are more and more present in society. They have the potential to improve our daily life and social welfare. But, the introduction of AI already provokes some technologic, industrial and regulatory challenges.

"From Mary Shelley's Frankenstein's Monster to the classical myth of Pygmalion, through the story of Prague's Golem to the robot of Karel Čapek, who coined the word, people have fantasized about the possibility of building intelligent machines, more often than not androids with human features; Humankind stands on the threshold of an era when ever more sophisticated robots, bots, androids and other manifestations of artificial intelligence ("AI") seem poised to unleash a new industrial revolution, which is likely to leave no stratum of society untouched, it is vitally important for the legislature to consider all its implications" (Parliament 2016).

The lawmakers should reform the legal frameworks in order to accommodate the presence of AI agents in society. The robots operating autonomously, without the intervention or awareness of humans will raise questions regarding attribution of rights or restrictions/ obligations for them, liability for their actions, taxation, data privacy, robotic labor replacing human labor. "In the short to medium term robotics and AI promise to bring benefits of efficiency and savings, not only in production and commerce, but also in areas such as transport, medical care, education and farming, while making it possible to avoid exposing humans to dangerous conditions, such as those faced when cleaning

H. Santos et al. (Eds.): SmartCity 360 2019, LNICST 323, pp. 412–419, 2020.
https://doi.org/10.1007/978-3-030-51005-3_33

up toxically polluted sites; whereas in the longer term there is potential for virtually unbounded prosperity;" (Parliament 2016).

The European Commission recently funded RoboLaw ("Regulating Emerging Robotic Technologies in Europe: Robotics facing Law and Ethics"), a project with the objective to analyze ethical and legal issues raised by robotic application and to suggest if new regulation is needed. The conclusion of the project are included in a report titled "Guidelines on Regulating Robotics" (Palmerini 2014).

There are still a lot of confusion and lack of information around the terms of robotics and the artificial intelligence incorporated into robots. The European Parliament passed a resolution with recommendations to the European Commission on civil law rules on robotics (Parliament 2016). Among the proposals it was highlighted the desire to establish ethical principles for developing and using AI-based robotics and solving the numerous liability issues. In this context, The Parliament is calling the European Commission to consider introducing a specific legal status for intelligent robots, to establish a European agency for robotics and artificial intelligence, in order to provide technical, ethical and regulatory expertise required to meet the challenges and opportunities arising from the development of robotics (Hauser 2017).

Human safety, privacy, integrity, dignity, autonomy, data ownership are the main topics of a proposal for the establishment of a "Charter on Robotics" which aims at setting up an ethical framework for the design and use of robots. The principles contained in the Charter are very broad defined and require top researchers in the field of robotics which should comply with the principles of beneficence (robots should act in the best interests of humans), non-maleficence (robots should not harm a human), autonomy (the capacity to make an informed, un-coerced decision about the terms of interaction with robots) and justice (Parliament 2016).

2 Robots and Artificial Intelligence

Robots are not only walking and talking machines. The terms robots and artificial intelligence are used with minimum rigor.

The robot is defined as a machine capable of conducting a series of actions automatically a computer – capable of carrying out a complex series of actions automatically. It is closely linked to the "robotic process automation". This concept encompasses the software computer and programs that have the purpose of replacing human activity that require repetitive rules-based tasks, not necessary conducted by psychical machines. But for sure machines that perform simple tasks, such as heating food or shredding paper, dependent on human initiative, are not part of this concept (Alexandre 2017).

The word robot can refer to both physical robots and virtual software agents, but the latter are usually referred to as bots. Robots tend to possess some or all of the following abilities and functions: accept electronic programming, process data or physical perceptions electronically, operate autonomously to some degree, move around, operate physical parts of itself or physical processes, sense and manipulate their environment, and exhibit intelligent behavior, having computers mimic the behavior of people or animals.

There are many types of robots: mobile robots, industrial robots (manipulators), service robots, educational robots, modular robots, collaborative robots. *Mobile robots* have the capability to move around in their environment and are not fixed to one physical location. An example of a mobile robot that is in common use today is the automated guided vehicle or automatic guided vehicle (AGV). *Industrial robots* are defined as "an automatically controlled, reprogrammable, multipurpose, manipulator programmable in three or more axes, which may be either fixed in place or mobile for use in industrial automation applications." A *service robot* is "a robot which operates semi or fully autonomously to perform services useful to the well-being of humans and equipment, excluding manufacturing operations." Modular robotic technology is currently being applied in hybrid transportation, industrial automation, duct cleaning and handling. Many research centers and universities have also studied this technology, and have developed prototypes. A *collaborative robot* or cobot is a robot that can safely and effectively interact with human workers while performing simple industrial tasks (https://en.wikipe dia.org/wiki/Robot).

Robots can generally be distinguished by their appearance (humanoids, animaloids), by application (industrial, domestic, military, medical, entertainment), by shape, size and locomotion (legged/wheeled, nanorobots) or by operating environment (UAV/drones, space robots, underwater robots) (Ballas and Konstantakopoulos 2017).

Artificial intelligence (AI) is harder to define. Generally speaking it refers to the intelligence exhibited by machines. But considering that its only one, *per se*, and it is accessed by humans and machines, the question is are the human intelligence and machine intelligence the same?

Alan Turing, in his famous paper *Computing machinery and Intelligence* suggested that the question should be if a machine can convince a human that it can think, rather than to ask or to try to determine if it can think or not. This is why the Turing test consist in a communication between a human and a machine, the human being not aware that is communicating with a machine (Turing 1950). Despite some other similar tests, the Turing test remains a mark in the AI existence assessing.

The Artificial Intelligence development nowadays is very related with the machine learning concept and its new age of "deep learning", in which computers learn from experience and improve their performance over time using algorithms that have the ability to "learn" (Surden 2014). *Active learning* algorithms access the desired outputs (training labels) for a limited set of inputs based on a budget, and optimize the choice of inputs for which it will acquire training labels. It is considered that unsupervised learning is the true artificial intelligence "where the learning algorithm is let loose on the data with no restrictions and permitted to draw whichever connections it wishes (Zimmermman 2015). Given unlimited information resources currently available and combined with constantly computing power we can predict that machines using unsupervised learning will develop skills of comprehension that will revolutionize the way decision are made (Zimmermman 2015).

Instead of a definition of Artificial Intelligence (literature hold multiple definitions) we prefer to provide examples of traits associated with the concept of AI: *language processing, learning, perception, planning, reasoning, manipulation of objects, motion, social intelligence, solving problems* (Kurzweil 1999). Not all of these traits should exist in each agent, just enough in order to justify a human intelligence comparison.

3   Types of Artificial Intelligence

The intelligence itself it is accessed by all kind of lively species, in nature. Animals, plants, not necessary using logic or reasoning have a small capacity of problem solving. Not depending of the container, the artificial intelligence also may manifest itself with a different degree of intensity. Considering this, we may classify AI in four categories: reactive machines, limited memory, theory of mind and self-awareness (http://theconversation.com/understanding-the-four-types-of-ai-from-reactive-robots-to-self-aware-beings-67616).

The Reactive machines have no memory, no ability of using past experience, hence it behaves in the same way every time they encounter the same situation. For example, the Google's Alpha Go, IBM's Deep Blue chess-playing supercomputer, which beat international grandmaster Garry Kasparov in the late 1990s are reactive machines which means they cannot function beyond the specific tasks they were programmed.

Machines with limited memory have the ability of looking into the past by identifying certain objects and monitoring them over time. For example, self-driving cars are able to observe other cars' speed and direction and use this information to decide when to change lanes, in order to avoid cutting off another driver or being hit by a nearby car. Personal assistant is another example.

The Theory of mind machines understand that people, creatures and objects in the world can have thoughts and emotions that affect their own behavior. They understand how humans formed societies and have social interactions. C-3PO and R2-D2 from the Star Wars saga, for example, were able to form representations about the world, adjusting their behavior according to their understanding of others' feelings, expectations, motivations and intentions (Alexandre 2017).

Self-awareness describe the ultimate stage of artificially intelligence: systems able to form representation about themselves, conscious, sentient and able to understand others' feelings, not only knowing what they want, but also understanding that they want and why they want. Eve from Ex Machina it's a good example and all the hosts from HBO's TV series Westworld which makes the beautiful distinction between theory of mind and self-aware agents.

4   Not Enough Legislation

As humans we are already sharing the society with the artificial intelligence and it is presumed that in the future more and more AI agents will be prepared to interact with us. But, as we know, the society is based on rules and the legal field makes social relations possible. Is the legal framework prepared to contain this reality or should we make some adjustments?

For example (Allgrove 2004) if a person (Andy) is negotiating a supply contract for his business using an intelligent software system who can measure the stock levels, compare terms of different suppliers and place orders, and the acceptant (Emma) is doing the process also using an AI system, who are the authors of the contract, knowing that the agreement and even the delivery was made before humans in charge with the contracting process were aware of its existence (maybe during night sleep)? Does the contract respect the present legal framework, as we know it?

One possible answer is that the contract is considered signed by the humans. A conservative approach will probably say that the machines cannot be parties to an agreement, hence, the contract would not exist. However, we may consider that, in the same evening, after noticing that his stock was running low, Andy logged in to his computer and noticed that the system had placed an order which had been received and accepted by a supplier (Emma). Feeling assured, Andy went home and had an unconcerned night of sleep. Andy ignores whether Emma is using a system to manage her orders or not. Does Andy have a reasonable expectation to be supplied with the goods?

If Andy had placed the order himself, would Emma be excused from performance because the order was accepted by her system instead of herself manually? On the contrary, Emma had accepted the order manually, would she be excused from performance because the order was placed by Andy's system? Or is it reasonable to excuse Emma from performance because both parties in the communications were the systems, despite the fact that Andy ignores the existence of Emma's system? In every case, even for the most conservative minds, the answer seems to be negative. But then, how to frame this contract in light of the current legal framework?

One possible approach is to consider the system as a mere *tool* for contracting or for communicating. Under this approach, the contract directly be celebrated between Andy and Emma. This approach offers the advantage of being easily introduced in the legal framework without the need for any major changes, (Allen and Widdison 1996) either by legislation, case law or doctrinal consideration On the hand, it relies on the fiction that anything issuing from the computer really issues directly from its human controller, completely ignoring any autonomy that the system may have. Furthermore, by presuming a consensus among parties which might not even be aware that the contract was celebrated or that the other party exists, this approach deprives the formation of the contract of its single most important element: the meeting of wills.

Another approach for this case is to consider the conduct of the system the conduct of a *person* (employee). Under this approach, the contract would be celebrated between one of Andy's legal agents and one of Emma's legal agents. In the party's eyes, what difference does it make if there is an employee operating the counterparty's computer or if it is operating itself? The advantage of this approach is that it does not rely on any presumption or bend the contract formation principles. Furthermore, it enables Andy and Emma to resort to any defenses they might have in case one of their employees did, indeed, celebrating the contract rather than considering them direct parties to the agreement. However, this approach implies taking a legislative option in favor of considering Andy and Emma's systems as separate legal entities from their owners and users.

We aimed at demonstrating that, with the proliferation of artificial intelligence, questions will rise and the legal framework will inevitably need to adapt. We believe that "the more autonomous robots are, the less they can be considered simple tools in the hands of other actors" (Parliament 2016).

5 Conceiving an Electronic Person

The Europeean Parliament in its Civil Law Rules on Robotics (draft report) introduced a request for "creating a specific legal status for robots, so that at least the most sophisticated autonomous robots could be established as having the status of electronic persons with specific rights and obligations, including that of making good any damage they may cause, and applying electronic personality to cases where robots make smart autonomous decisions or otherwise interact with third parties independently" (Parliament 2016).

The concept of legal personality itself was not an immutable reality throughout history. The origins of the concept of legal personality date back to the 13th Century and are attributed to Pope Innocent IV, who founded the persona ficta doctrine, allowing monasteries to have a legal existence apart from monks (Rosen et al. 2017). The term electronic person was first coined in a 1967 article for LIFE magazine.

The concept of legal personality itself was not an immutable reality throughout history. As years went by and legal doctrine progressed, several other realities would end up being considered as separate legal entities from its owners or users. In the international legal system, this is the case of sovereign states and of various international and intergovernmental organizations, such as the United Nations or the European Union. In national jurisdictions, virtually every country applies this reasoning to companies and other forms of business associations. Specific jurisdictions even extend it to much more farfetched cases. In India, courts have attributed legal personality to Hindu idols, considering them capable of having rights and duties (namely, owning property and paying taxes) and, in New Zealand, the Whanganui River was granted legal personality in March 2017 because the Whanganui Māori tribe regard the river as their ancestor. It is also common for ships to be considered separate legal entities under Maritime Law and for animals to have their own legal status under various national jurisdictions (Alexandre 2017).

The legal status of persons, animals, objects and other realities (such as rivers and companies) varies from jurisdiction to jurisdiction and, over the course of time, even within the same jurisdiction and regarding the same reality. This observation enables us to conclude that a separate legal status or a legal personality does not derive from the quality of natural person, but it is the result of legislative options, which are based on moral considerations, that attempt to reflect social realities in the legal framework or that simply were made out of legal convenience. Hence, since no principle dictates when the legal system must recognize an entity as a legal person, or when it must deny legal personality, and no guidance derives from the study of the history of the institute, it is then relevant to ascertain whether artificially intelligent agents are morally entitled to be considered separate legal entities, whether doing so would reflect a social reality or whether it would be a convenient option from a legal point of view.

The question whether artificially intelligent agents are morally entitled to be considered separate legal entities needs to be preceded by the following interrogations: which realities are morally entitled to it and what characteristic or characteristics do they possess that supports such consideration? In our view, those realities are natural persons and animals and those characteristics are the capacities to act autonomously and to have subjective experiences. As for artificially intelligent agents, the same rationale may apply: they would be morally entitled to a separate legal status provided they possess the capacities to act autonomously and to have subjective experiences (Alexandre 2017).

The artificially intelligent agents should be held *liable* for damages they cause? Is it even possible to hold these agents liable? How to achieve such possibility? The Draft

Report with Recommendations to the Commission on Civil Law Rules on Robotics of the European Parliament's Committee on Legal Affairs goes even further and suggests that "the insurance system should be supplemented by a fund in order to ensure that damages can be compensated for in cases where no insurance cover exists" to which all parties (designers, owners and users) would "contribute in varying proportions".

The eventual use of public services or infrastructures by an artificially intelligent agent does not translate into a benefit for the agent, but for the user or designer who instructed him to take the action that implied the use of such service or infrastructure. In fact, since artificially intelligent agents are designed to directly or indirectly contribute to the welfare of humans, a human will always be the ultimate beneficiary of the public services or infrastructures that the agent uses while carrying out its purpose. Hence, it does not seem correct to say that it would be fair for artificially intelligent agents to be taxed because they benefit from public investment. *Taxes*, however, may also be justified by necessity. This is the case of taxes that aim at modifying patterns of consumption or employment within the economy, by making some classes of transaction more or less attractive.

Artificial intelligence has an unprecedented potential to disrupt the *labor markets*, as machines will be able to replace workers in a variety of cognitive and creative tasks and in tasks that employ manual labor but could not have been automated so far due to technologic constraints (such as driving). Even if, so far, markets have balanced themselves by moving a slice of labor towards more cognitive-oriented tasks, the fact that artificial intelligence will be able to replace jobs in virtually every tier of the pyramid is generating concerns that jobs will be eliminated faster than new ones can be created. Furthermore, even in the event that artificial intelligence results in net job creation, it is unlikely that current methods of workforce retraining are able to accompany its pace. Some authors even claim that machine learning may empower artificially intelligent agents to take on the new jobs created as a consequence of their own development. Under any of these scenarios, such events will directly result in loss of revenue for governments due to a reduction in tax collections since capital income is taxed at much lower rates than labor income. In addition to this, the replacement of human labor by automated labor may translate in major growths of social security expenses since social security systems are designed to provide unemployment insurance to workers who lose their jobs. These increased expenses, combined with the loss of fiscal revenue, are generating concerns as to the sustainability of current social security systems.

6 Conclusion

The purpose of this article is to demonstrate the need for a separate legal status for the artificially intelligent agents. Defining the contents of that status: liability, rights and potential taxation duties, allows for minimum certainty as to the consequences of the introduction of those new intelligent agents in society. This will contrast with the large amount of unknown. This is why the risks still need to be addressed and mitigated as they are not only related to eventual damages, but also to the protection of personal data and public safety itself.

Making machines that are more and more autonomous, it might be difficult for humans to ensure that such machines do not become too autonomous. Losses of control may occur due to malfunctions, security breaches, the superior response time of computers compared to humans' or conscious or unconscious flawed programming, namely, regarding a fragile distributional shifting, unsafe exploration, unscalable oversight, negative side effects.

Designing robots that could impact the safety or wellbeing of humans, it is not enough to simply presume that it works. We believe that if designers cannot achieve justified confidence that an agent is safe and controllable, so that deploying it does not create an unacceptable risk of negative consequences, then the agent cannot and should not be deployed. Nevertheless, we also believe that artificial intelligence has the potential to place mankind on the path to prosperity and ultimately free Men from the burden of labor, giving us the opportunity to focus on tasks where creativity and passion play bigger roles. As Stephen Hawking once put it, with current and near- future technology "everyone can enjoy a life of luxurious leisure if the machine-produced wealth is shared, or most people can end up miserably poor if the machine-owners successfully lobby what they have prescribed, or any others which are recommended or adopted, shall, at every moment, be susceptible to adjustment in order to strike a balance between guaranteeing the wellbeing of our species and the freedom towards innovation. Artificial intelligence is not something to be afraid of, but rather to embrace. And, by pro-actively discussing the challenges this technology may comport, we are a few steps closer to prevent any potential downside while still fully reaping its benefits."

References

Alexandre F.M.: The Legal Status of Artificially Intelligent Robots. Tilburg (2017)

European Parliament: Draft Report with recommendations to the Commission on Civil Law Rules on Robotics. Committee on Legal Affairs (2016)

Palmerini, E.: RoboLaw: Regulating Emerging Robotic Technologies in Europe: Robotics facing Law and Ethics (2014). http://www.robolaw.eu/

Ballas, G., Konstantakopoulos, T.: Robot law - Greece Chapter. In: Bensoussan, A., Bensoussan, J. (eds.) Comparative Handbook: Robotic Technologies Law, Larcier, Lexing, pp. 133–166. New Technologies & Law (2017)

Hauser, M.: Do robots have rights? The European parliament addresses artificial intelligence and robotics (2017)

Turing, A.: Computing Machinery and Intelligence (1950)

Surden, H.: Machine Learning and Law. Washington Law Review (2014)

Zimmermman, E.J.: Machine minds: frontiers in legal personhood. SSRN 43 (2015)

Kurzweil, R.: The Age of Spiritual Machines. Penguin Goup, New York (1999)

Allgrove, B.D.: Legal Personality for Artificial Intellects: Pragmatic Solution or Science Fiction? University of Oxford, Oxford (2004)

Allen, T., Widdison, R.: Can computers make contracts? Harv. J. Law Techol. **9**, 25 (1996)

Rosen, C., Nilson, N. Bertram, R.: Shakey. LIFE (2017)

Crossing Sensory Boundaries with Creative Productions

Predrag K. Nikolić[1]([⊠]) [iD] and Nancy L. Russo[2]

[1] School of Creativity and Art, ShanghaiTech University, 393 Huaxia Middle Road,
Pudong, Shanghai 201210, China
predragnikolic@shanghaitech.edu.cn
[2] Faculty of Technology and Society, Malmö University,
Nordenskiöldsgatan 1, 211 19 Malmö, Sweden
nancy.russo@mau.se

Abstract. We seek to investigate possibilities of extending the emotional and cognitive experience of using products or services through the cross-modality of vision with other senses (synesthesia). Through multi-sensory, interactive environments, consumers become more engaged in the use of a product or service and may, in fact, participate as co-creators of their own experiences. To achieve the highest level of spontaneity and provoke human activation to enable us to study this, we suggest an experimental context based on interactive technologies, aesthetics and design. For this purpose, we use an artistic environment in the form of an interactive installation. Two examples of such experimental interactive art installations, Art Machine: Mindcatcher and Re-Digital, are described in this paper.

Keywords: Synesthesia · Cross-modal experience · Interactivity · Interaction design · Multisensory interface design · User experience · Product design · Service design

1 Introduction

Synesthesia is a combination of several senses simultaneously. It is psychological phenomena where stimuli on one particular physical sensory can produce additional sensory experiences for which sensory inputs which do not exist [1]. It is an unusual condition which gives rise to a merging of the senses. For example, smells may trigger the experience of shapes, or letters may give rise to the perceptual experience of color or may cause the experience of any combination of tastes, smells, shapes or sensations [2]. One of the most reported types of synesthesia is audio-visual (AVS) [3], where sound stimuli can evoke the visual experience and vice versa. In particular, sound such as middle note 'C' can induce red color experience but the same note three octaves higher can become green [4]. Likewise, we can have different varieties of the sense responses on sensory stimulation such as; taste a particular food (gustatory) can associate us to the visual appearance of the food [5]; when we hear a certain sound (auditory) can induce smell of a specific food (olfactory) [6]. Despite early skepticism, contemporary research in the

© ICST Institute for Computer Sciences, Social Informatics and Telecommunications Engineering 2020
Published by Springer Nature Switzerland AG 2020. All Rights Reserved
H. Santos et al. (Eds.): SmartCity 360 2019, LNICST 323, pp. 420–427, 2020.
https://doi.org/10.1007/978-3-030-51005-3_34

field shows that synesthesia exists, moreover it has potential to manifests as a conscious phenomenon and involve robust qualitative phenomenology [7]. Often, syncsthesia is misunderstood as simple metaphor people are addressing to different emotional or perceptual phenomena, such as color perception (e.g., most of the people will address anger to red color). In fact, it is unique type of phenomenal experiences triggered without direct sensory stimulation [1]. Perhaps these misunderstandings are why the phenomenon was considered as unreliable for over a century after its discovery by Francis Galton [8]. In the last decade we can follow increased interest in the cross-sensory experiences and raising interest in synesthesia as its correlated phenomena [9, 10] especially because people can generate rich mental images for the other senses as well, beside the most commonly though visual experience. For example, multisensory advertising approach uses different combination of senses to stimulate consumers' other sensory perceptions related to product or service [11]. In line with that, the design experience has become a sensual fusion of the human and the product, a form of interaction that is dependent upon the user's presence and bodily actions [12].

2   Interactivity and Strategy of Participation

Interactivity has a long history as an essential conceptual component of the field of arts and design. Theorist and writer Jack Burnham were one of the first who pointed on interactivity as a conceptual approach in art. He related it to two-way communication between artwork and visitors seen as kind of premature attempts in happenings, kinetic art, and luminous art [13]. Unfortunately, in those cases the individual is physically passive, unable to affect the work, interaction is happening on an only psychological level. Roy Ascott's 1959 Change Painting is an early example of an artwork which had the tendency to involve the audience in a directly physical way. Furthermore, in his work, he empathizes the correlation between the act of changing and elicited aesthetic experience in the participant. As a result of his early conceptual ideas, in 1966 he coined a new term Behaviourist Art [14]. This concept represents the possibility of using a system such as in Change Painting as an interface between the author and the audience. Between the late 1960 s and early'70 s, the concept of Ascott's Behavior Art highly reflected on the work of British artist Stephen Willats. He created a new form of art conceptually inspired by techniques of cybernetics and the behavioural social sciences [15]. Willats believed that the main purpose of art is to change human understanding and behaviour. His artistic strategy involved usage of market research, social survey and feedback methods to involve different social groups in the act of interaction with the artworks [16].

Furthermore, the concept of creative interaction evolved throughout time and embraced any project based on an interactive strategy of participation [17]. This means that the participant is invited to take part in a product prototype under rules and constraints which are part of a designed system and not the interactive process itself. In our research practice, we consider redefining the users as a creative source as one of the fundamental purposes of interactive art [18]. When users become a creative source, they are not simply consumers of the product of the artistic or design process but instead become co-creators (along with the artist, designer, and even other users) through interaction with the prototype. In some of the previous researches has been specified that in interactive systems psychological outcomes associated with digital interaction includes cross-modal correspondences perceived by multisensory modalities [19], enhanced learning, entertainment, and persuasive effects [20, 21].

3   Re-Thinking the Interface Toward Multisensory Products

The way we feel and understand the world around us through our senses. They are many studies who are exploring phenomena of perception and relationship between the usage of multiple sensory modalities and its effect on user experience. The more stimuli engaged at the same time can evoke the richer experiences, higher impact and make it more memorable across different senses [22–24]. Likewise, the higher number of sensory inputs in a virtual environment could increase people's sense of presence as well as improve awareness related to virtual objects placement [25]. In such cases, we are using different types of a multisensory interface as a medium between us and non-physical, virtual space we are interacting and abstract world we are experiencing. Such interfaces can offer significant advantages, not only to already mentioned online adverting but even more important to synesthetic repertoire of assistive products capable to help people with disabilities such as blindness [26].

With the only screen, mouse, keyboard and tactile gestures we are becoming limited in controlling, changing and responding to a variety of new digital inputs. In such situation available physical repertoire of body actions have the potential to respond to raising new interaction design needs. This interface design conceptual approach leads us to several questions important to answer such as: How to diminish the isolation between person and interface and to make the interface disappear? How to extend an interface more widely into human life? How to create a understandable interactive sensing and vocabulary of human actions such as motion, gesture, touch, gaze, speech, and interactions with physical objects?

In the interactive installation Art Machine: MindCatcher our goal was to investigate different qualities of multisensory user experience achieved through the usage of body movement-based interface and audio-visual sound response and to relate them to visitor perception. Like Monika Fleischmann in her work Rigid Waves [27], we explored through artwork innovative interfaces such as immersive virtual reality touch, balance, and motion or like Rafael Lozano-Hemmer who explored in his installation Re: Positioning Fear integrated physical and virtual spaces by motion and gestures [28].

The Art Machine: Mindcatcher installation was conceptualized on the usage of audio-visual digital outputs as an incentive for users' interactions and creative actions. The outputs consisted of three colours; red, blue, yellow (visually), three tones C, G, E (auditory), three sized circles (Fig. 1), and a touch-sensitive floor (tactile) as the interactive medium between artwork as a paradigm of product and participant as a consumer. By pressing differently lightened switches on the interactive floor interface visitors were capable of achieving multisensory experience within the installation space. (Figure 2). The digital outputs could have been controlled and modulate based on switch sensor choice and foot pressure duration on it.

A second experimental project, Re-Digital was designed in two parts: one is exposed in public space as garbage cans and the second part is a web location where

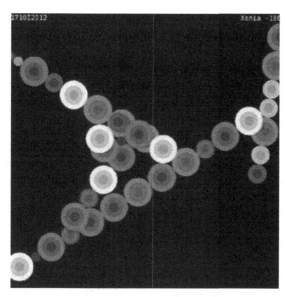

Fig. 1. Art Machine: MindCatcher Visualization (photo copyrights: Predrag K. Nikolic) (Color figure online)

Fig. 2. Art Machine: MindCatcher Floor Interface (photo copyrights: Predrag K. Nikolic)

everyone can upload files - "digital garbage" - and make it available for recycling. The public space (external) consists of three garbage cans for three types of files; text, video, images (visually). Visitors can search and preview content on a recycled 14-inch monitor and old PC computer, and by reaching deep into the garbage cans they can download it on USB or mobile phone. An important conceptual part is to join a specific smell (olfactory), metaphorically connected with garbage smell, to an abstract form (computer files). Our intention is to add one more dimension of being to virtual products such as digital photos, digital video, or in the future to software applications and digital media services by collecting sensory information which will evoke memories or associations to objects or situations. Based on that in both of our experiments we focused on:

- production of multisensory experience as more consistent over time;
- creation of environment as an extremely important factor which could direct multisensory integration and perception;
- redefining the users as a creative source;

to achieve that we build two multi-sensory interfaces. In the case of the Art Machine: MindCatcher based on motion, touch, sound and vision and in the case of Re-Digital on vision and smell. Important part for our experiment was to alter users into creative sources, we found interactive art as interesting tool to provoke such transformation [19]. As such, we found the interactive installation to be a proper environment for sensory integration. This was important because stimuli that appear to originate from the same spatial location are more likely to be attributed to a single multisensory source rather than to separate sources [20].

In the interactive installation Art Machine: MindCatcher we tested multisensory experience within twenty participants randomly selected for a contextual in-depth interview. According to their responses, 80% of them described having a creative experience through which they felt they were contributing to the creation of a human being. They were able to visualize 3D shapes based on generated two dimensional representations projected on the screen. The result of the multisensory experience was, as some of them said, "Creative DNA Code" (Fig. 3) where they joined the molecular structure of the body they created to DNA pieces created by other participants (Fig. 4). The fact that they could return and continue their creative act gave them an opportunity to refresh memories of previous sessions and associations to objects done by themselves or others.

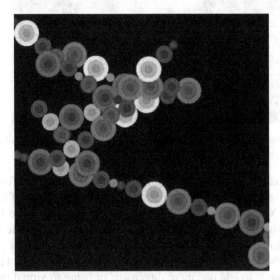

Fig. 3. Art Machine: MindCatcher Individual Creative Sessions

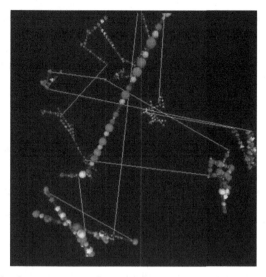

Fig. 4. Art Machine: MindCatcher Group Creative Sessions

In the installation Re-Digital we are focused on merging visual with olfactory experience for long-term perceptual transformation and attribution to new quality of meanings. The experiment is in the phase of collecting relevant data from the different user groups.

4   Conclusion and Future Directions

We believe that interactions between people and various sensory attributes in different modalities could increase structural connectivity and be more consistent over time, if experienced through creative interaction, contribution and aesthetic experience. Our research aims to understand the relationship between interactions, sensory stimuli and product perception with special attention to psychological mechanisms of synesthesia and opportunity to use it in cross-modal user experience design. Synesthesia may help us to understand how combine interaction design concepts and brain capabilities to merge different sensory information into new approach to future multisensory service design.

The projects Art Machine: MindCatcher and Re-Digital are intended to contribute to the field of research where product design utilizes interactive multimodal environments and technologies to involve the user in co-creative activities and better product or service acceptance. The general idea behind that is to explore opportunities to respond to great variety of human perceptions and as such to move the design process into much wider and deeper realms of life. For example, moving away from conventional interfaces mostly designed for screen based interactive products, we consider as a significant product conceptualization change as well as cultural event worth investigating. Also, we suggest that aesthetical experience could play a significant role in the methodological approach. Still, digital media industry does not incorporate enough usage of different sensory modalities in their new products ideation and design. They do not make full use of the multisensory potential of the products that they market/produce, although it plays important role in a consumer's interactions with the environment [29, 30]. We believe that product and service design strategies lead by multisensory and synesthetic experience logic can take us to more effective interactions between users, products and services and better stimulation of consumer's senses and more pleasurable and memorable brand experience.

References

1. van Leeuwen, T.M., Singer, W., Nikolić, D.: The merit of synesthesia for consciousness research. Front. Psychol. **6**, 1850 (2015)
2. Simner, J.: Defining synaesthesia. Br. J. Psychol. **103**(1), 1–15 (2012)
3. Afra, P., Anderson, J., Funke, M., et al.: Neurophysiological investigation of idiopathic acquired auditory–visual synesthesia. Neurocase **18**(4), 323–329 (2012)
4. Ginsberg, L.: A case of synaesthesia. Am. J. Psychol. **34**, 582–589 (1923)
5. Cytowic, R.E.: The Man Who Tasted Shapes: A Bizarre Medical Mystery Offers Revolutionary Insights Into Reasoning, Emotion, and Consciousness. Putman, New York (1993)
6. Beeli, G., Esslen, M., Jäncke, L.: Synaesthesia: when coloured sounds taste sweet. Nature **434**(7029), 38 (2005)
7. O'Callaghan, C.: Synesthesia vs. crossmodal illusions (2017)
8. Jewanski, J., Simner, J., Day, S.A., Ward, J.: The development of a scientific understanding of synesthesia from early case studies (1849–1873). J. History Neurosci. **20**(4), 284–305 (2011)
9. Ramachandran, V.S., Hubbard, E.M.: The phenomenology of synaesthesia. J. Conscious. Stud. **10**(8), 49–57 (2003)
10. Wu, Y.L., Chen, P.C.: The Synesthesia effects of Online Advertising Stimulus Design on Word-of-Mouth and Purchase Intention: From the Perspective of Consumer Olfactory and Gustatory (2016)
11. Rich, A.N., Bradshaw, J.L., Mattingley, J.B.: A systematic, large-scale study of synaesthesia: implications for the role of early experience in lexical-colour associations. Cognition **98**(1), 53–84 (2005)
12. Stenslie, S.: Virtual touch: a study of the use and experience of touch in artistic, multimodal and computer-based environments (2010)
13. Burnham, J.: The aesthetics of intelligent systems. https://monoskop.org/images/0/02/Burnha mJack1970TheAestheticsofIntelligentSystems.pdf. Accessed 02 Oct 2019
14. Ascott, R.: Telematic Embrace: Visionary Theories of Art, Technology, and Consciousness. University of California Press, Berkeley (2007)
15. Willats, S.: Art and Social Function, Batsford (2002)
16. Walker, J.A., Phillpot, C.: Glossary of Art, Architecture and Design Since 1945. Library Association Publishing, Chicago (1992)
17. Giaccardi E.: Interactive strategies of network art. relationships and agency. In: CADE 1999: Third Conference on Computers in Art & Design Education. Citeseer (1999)
18. Gonzales, A., Finley, T., Duncan, S.: Interactive art: effects on user identity user satisfaction. In: CHI 2009 Proceedings of the 27th International Conference on Human Factors in Computing Systems (2008)
19. Spence, C.: Audiovisual multisensory integration. Acoust. Sci. Technol. **28**(2), 61–70 (2007)
20. Tao, C.C., Bucy, E.P.: Conceptualizing media stimuli in experimental research: psychological versus attribute-based definitions. Hum. Commun. Res. **33**(4), 397–426 (2007)
21. Vorderer, P., Knobloch, S., Schramm, H.: Does entertainment suffer from interactivity? The impact of watching an interactive tv movie on viewers' experience of entertainment. Med. Psychol. **3**(4), 343–363 (2001)

22. Bahrick, L.E., Lickliter, R.: Intersensory redundancy guides attentional selectivity and perceptual learning in infancy. Dev. Psychol. **36**(2), 190 (2000)
23. Spence, C.: The report on the secret of the senses. The Communication Group, London (2002)
24. Stein, B.E., Meredith, M.A.: The Merging of the Senses. The MIT Press, Cambridge (1993)
25. Washburn, D.A., Jones, L.M., Satya, R.V., Bowers, C.A., Cortes, A.: Olfactory use in virtual environment training. Model. Simul. **2**(3), 19–25 (2003)
26. Ferreira, A.A., Brito, G., Silva, L.N.D., Mouzinho, J.V., Morais, R., Pereira, J.R.: Synesthesia vision integration with Recife's public transport. In: Proceedings of the 16th Web For All 2019 Personalization-Personalizing the Web, p. 15. ACM, May 2019
27. Fleischmann, M., Strauss, W., Bohn, C.A.: Liquid views: rigid waves. In: ACM SIGGRAPH 98 Electronic Art and Animation Catalog. ACM, p. 21 (1998)
28. Hayes, S.C., Strosahl, K.D., Wilson, K.G.: Review of acceptance and commitment therapy: an experiential approach to behavior change (2002)
29. Schifferstein, H.N., Spence, C.: Multisensory product experience. In: Product Experience, pp. 133–161. Elsevier (2008)
30. Sense, L.M.B.: Build Powerful Brands Through Touch, Taste, Smell. Sight, and Sound New York. Free Press (2005)

Lightweight Neural Network for Sketch Recognition on Mobile Phones

Ni Kong[(✉)], Hong Hou, Zhe Bai, and Xiaoqun Guo

Northwest University, Xi'an, China
kongni929@163.com, katarina.vitalisova@umb.sk, hhong66@sina.com,
17782609482@163.com, guoxiaoq@nwu.edu.cn

Abstract. With the popularity of smart terminals, people tend to draw simple sketches to express emotions and ideas in communication, which means the era of reading pictures is coming. Therefore, in the field of sketch recognition, the application of deep network models in mobile devices is an irreversible trend. However, most existing works with good performance has a large number of parameters by using deep learning method. In order to further improve recognition speed and ensure the accuracy, we propose a lightweight neural network architecture to recognize sketch object. Specifically, we apply depthwise separable convolution into the network to reduce parameters and adjust the network effectively for the sparsity of sketch. Outperforming the state-of-the-art approaches, we achieves 85.3% and 83.7% on TU-Berlin and QuickDraw benchmarks respectively. Furthermore, the number of parameters is reduced to a large extent, which are 5% and 20% of the amount of Sketch-A-Net and MobileNets. We also develop a sketch recognition application for mobile phones to demonstrate the proposed scheme.

Keywords: Sketch recognition · Lightweight networks · Depthwise separable convolution

1 Introduction

In recent years, the popularity of touch-based smart phones has largely changed the way people communicate with each other. Due to the intuitiveness and simplicity of sketch, people tend to draw sketches at any time and send interesting stick figures to express emotions and ideas (Li et al. 2017a). Thus, an effective means of social intercourse is provided by sketch for people with different culture and language. For better human-computer interactions, research on sketch so far includes sketch recognition, sketch-based image retrieval and sketch synthesis (Eitz et al. 2012; Song et al. 2017; Li et al. 2017b).

The goal of sketch recognition is to identify the object category of an input sketch. Traditional works mainly extracted hand-crafted features which were coupled with Bag-of-Words to yield a final feature representations for sketch. But the accuracy is lower than human recognition because these features constructed by natural image are not suitable

H. Santos et al. (Eds.): SmartCity 360 2019, LNICST 323, pp. 428–439, 2020.
https://doi.org/10.1007/978-3-030-51005-3_35

for sketch. Recent years, researchers built networks aimed at hand-drawn sketch using deep learning methods, and the accuracy was improved obviously compared to traditional methods. However, these existing approaches have more parameters and recognition speed is slow. With the promotion of smart phones, the networks model should be refined to improve recognition speed while ensuring accuracy. In order to identify sketch using network models on mobile phones, it is meaningful to study lightweight networks.

In this work, we propose a lightweight neural network for sketch recognition which achieves good accuracy on the QuickDraw-10 M and TU-Berlin benchmarks. Furthermore, the amount of network parameters is greatly reduced and recognition speed is improved. Finally, we apply the lightweight framework in the sketch recognition application for mobile phones.

The contributions of our work are as follows.

1. We apply the depthwise separable convolutions firstly for sketch recognition and the parameters of our network is only 0.85 MB which is 20% of the amount of MobileNets.
2. Our method achieves 85.3% and 83.7% accuracy on QuickDraw-10 M datasets and TU-Berlin benchmarks, which outperforms the state-of-the-art approaches.
3. We develop a sketch recognition application for smart devices using the lightweight neural network.

2 Related Work

2.1 Sketch Recognition Method

Most prior works used traditional image classification methods and extracted shallow hand-crafted features for sketch recognition. Li constructed a multi-kernel learning framework by combining several local features to represent sketch completely (Li et al. 2015). A new shape context descriptor was designed by Cao named symmetric-aware flip invariant sketch histogram to refine the sketch shape context function (Cao et al. 2013). However, these features were subjective and uncertain. Therefore the recognition accuracy was far inferior to human performance.

Advancement in deep learning has significantly influenced image recognition since 2012. Firstly, Sarvadevabhatla tested AlexNet and LeNet on sketch and AlexNet performed better than LeNet (Sarvadevabhatla and Babu 2015). The ground-breaking work of Yu, for the first time, beat human on sketch recognition task by constructing a convolutional neural network namely Sketch-a-Net until 2015 (Yu et al. 2015). The same team tried to improve the performance by designing data augmentation techniques (Yu et al. 2017). Zhao combined convolutional neural network and recurrent neural network to perform the task (Zhao et al. 2016; Zhao et al. 2016). Leveraging the inherent sequential nature of sketch, Sarvadevabhatla addressed the problem as sequence learning task (Sarvadevabhatla et al. 2016). These works improved the performance to some extent. Yet these models are relatively large due to using deep neural network. Moreover, the recognition task consumes more time and the speed is slow. Our focus is to address the problem by designing a lightweight deep neural network which takes recognition accuracy and speed into consideration.

2.2 Sketch Recognition Applications

With the popularization of touch screen devices, people tend to interact directly with intelligent machines to gain more knowledge and fun. In addition, the sketch has become a new way of communication in network because of its convenient and interesting features. Therefore, some sketch recognition and retrieval algorithms for smart devices have begun to develop. In 2017, Google released an AI experiment application called Quick! Draw, which uses recurrent neural network to guess the sketches that users draw in 20 s based on strokes (Ha and Eck 2017). And, Xiao introduced the PPTLens system to convert sketch images captured by smart phones to digital flowcharts in PowerPoint and they proposed an effective stroke extraction strategy (Xiao et al. 2015). In our work, the sketch recognition application we built on mobile phones is a new attempt. We use the proposed lightweight neural network for sketch recognition to speed up recognition while ensuring accuracy.

3 Methodology

3.1 LW-Sketch-Net

Our lightweight neural network (LW-Sketch-Net) ensure recognition accuracy by applying depthwise separable convolutions and adjusting the network for the spasity of the sketch. Meanwhile, the recognition speed is improved to a large extent. Figure 1 illustrates our overall framework.

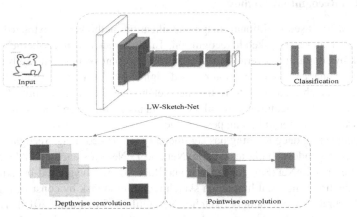

Fig. 1. LW-Sketch-Net architecture Source: own research

Depthwise Separable Convolutions. LW-Sketch-Net applies the depthwise separable convolutions proposed by Google. In a standard convolution, both filters and channels input into a new set of outputs in one step. But the depthwise separable convolutions split the operation into two layers, a separate layer for filtering and another layer for combining channels. Specifically, the depthwise convolution learns the spatial feature on each channel of the input sketch and then the pointwise convolution combines channels features. The decomposition can simplify training models and reduce network parameters. Figure 2 shows the detailed steps of two convolutions.

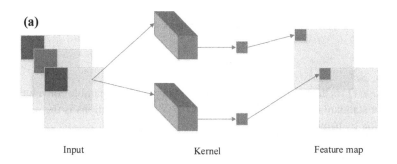

(a)

Input   Kernel   Feature map

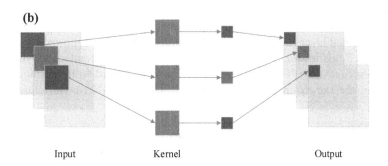

(b)

Input   Kernel   Output

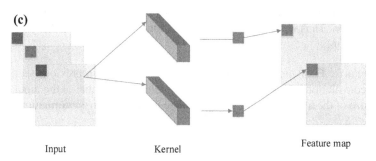

(c)

Input   Kernel   Feature map

Fig. 2. (a) Detailed steps for standard convolutions (b) Detailed steps for depthwise convolutions (c) Detailed steps for pointwise convolutions Source: own research

A convolutional layer takes as input a W × H × IC feature map and produces W × H × OC feature maps, where W and H is the spatial width and height of input feature map, IC and OC are the number of input and output channels. The convolution kernel K of size K × K, standard convolutions have the computational combining features and channels. The computational cost of convolution is listed as follows.

$$W \times H \times IC \times K \times K + W \times H \times IC \times OC \times 1 \times 1 \tag{1}$$

$$W \times H \times IC \times OC \times K \times K \tag{2}$$

$$1/OC + 1/K^2 \tag{3}$$

Equation (1) is the total computational cost of depthwise separable convolutions and Eq. (2) for standard convolutions. The ratio of two above equations is the reduction in computation by using the new convolution form as listed in (3).

LW-Sketch-Net Structure. The LW-Sketch-Net structure is built on depthwise separable convolutions as mentioned in the previous section. The specific network architecture is shown in Table 1.

There are some commonalities between LW-Sketch-Net and other sketch-oriented convolutional network architectures. As the common forms in neural networks, depthwise convolutional layers and pointwise convolutional layers are followed by a batchnorm and ReLU nonlinearity with the exception of the final fully connected layer which feeds into a softmax layer for classification. However, combined with the unique characteristics of the sketch, more unique aspects in LW-Sketch-Net architecture are as follows.

Larger First Convolutional Layer Filters. The size of the filters in the first convolutional layer is a relatively sensitive parameter since all subsequent processing depend on the output of this layer. Generally, the size in most neural networks is 3 × 3. But we find that larger filters are more appropriate for sketch through experiments because more contextual information can be captured. The sketches stored in the computer are sparse, and the usual convolution filters size is too small for each convolution operation to learn valid information. Thus we set the size of the first convolution filters to 9 × 9 to capture more information.

Larger Depthwise Convolutional Layer Filters. As mentioned in previous section, the depthwise convolutions aim to learn spatial feature on each channel of the input sketch. When the size of the filters is small, it is difficult to obtain effective information because

Table 1. LW-Sketch-Net architecture.

Layer	Type	Filter size	Filter num	Output size
	Input			64 × 64 × 3
L1	Conv	9 × 9	64	64 × 64 × 64
L2	Conv_1 dw Conv_1 pw	9 × 9 9 × 9	64 64	64 × 64 × 64 64 × 64 × 64
L3	Conv_2 dw Conv_2 pw	9 × 9 9 × 9	128 128	32 × 32 × 64 32 × 32 × 128
L4	Conv_3 dw Conv_3 pw	9 × 9 9 × 9	128 128	32 × 32 × 128 32 × 32 × 128
L5	Conv_4 dw Conv_4 pw	9 × 9 9 × 9	256 256	16 × 16 × 128 16 × 16 × 256
L6	Conv_5 dw Conv_5 pw	9 × 9 9 × 9	256 256	16 × 16 × 256 16 × 16 × 256
L7	Conv_6 dw Conv_6 pw	9 × 9 9 × 9	512 512	8 × 8 × 256 8 × 8 × 512
L8	Conv_7 dw Conv_7 pw	9 × 9 9 × 9	512 512	8 × 8 × 512 8 × 8 × 512
L9	Global Average Pooling			1 × 1 × 512
L10	Soft max			1 × 1 × 340/250

Source: own research

sketch is too sparse in the computer compared to the natural image. Thus, a natural intuition would be: is it possible if we can enlarge the size of filters in each depthwise convolutional layer. So avoiding the computational complexity during training and obtaining more information between sketch categories, we use 9×9 filters size in each depthwise convolutional layers.

Fewer Convolution Filters per Layer. In the training of natural image, the first convolutional layer filter of the deep convolutional network mainly extracts information such as image edges and chromatic aberrations. In order to obtain more complete information, the number of filters is generally 64 and the last layer is up to 1024. The sketch lacks color and texture information, so the number of filters used for natural image recognition is too redundant for sketch recognition task. Moreover, the edge information learned by some filters is repeated, so reducing the number of filters in the sketch recognition network has no significant impact on the acquisition of information. Based on the above reasons, we reduce the number of filters in each layer, respectively 64, 128, 256 and 512, to reduce the amount of network parameters.

3.2 Sketch Recognition Application for Smartphones

We design and implement sketch recognition application to provide users with a simple tool. The illustration is shown in Fig. 3.

Fig. 3. Illustration of sketch recognition application Source: own research

As shown in the Fig. 3, we conduct a mobile sketch application and a web sketch service respectively, which communicate and transfer data to each other. Specifically, the mobile sketch application mainly provides the user with the function of drawing a sketch, then saves and uploads the image to the server. The sketch service identifies the received sketches through our LW-Sketch-Net model and then returns the identified results to the mobile sketch application. Finally, the mobile sketch application presents the recognition result to the user through the interface.

The sketch recognition application is a scenario for the framework we propose. Due to the small amount of parameters in our LW-Sketch-Net, the web service can get recognition results faster, which further improves the recognition speed.

4   Methodology

4.1   Datasets and Settings

We evaluate our model on the QuickDraw datasets and the TU-Berlin datasets. The first datasets collected by Google in 2017 consists of 50 million hand-drawn sketches with 345 categories which is the first large-scale sketch datasets. Experience has shown that 20,000 sketches are enough to represent a sketch category. So we randomly select 30,000 sketches in each category, where 20,000, 5000 and 5000 are used for training, verification and testing respectively. A total of 10,200,000 sketches are used in our experiments, which we call Quickdraw-10 M.

TU-Berlin datasets presented by the Technical University of Berlin in 2012 which is the commonest benchmark in existing researches. It is divided into 250 categories which includes 80 sketches and it included 20,000 sketches totally. Due to the small scale, data augmentation is commonly with deep convolutional neural networks (CNNs) to avoid over-fitting. We replicate sketches with a number of transformations. Specifically, for each input sketch, we do rotation in the range [50, 130, −50, −130] degrees and the total of training instances is 100,000. We rescale all sketches to 64 × 64 pixels.

4.2   Competitors

We have compared with popular CNNs baselines because our model uses convolutional neural networks. Specifically, we have compared: (1) AlexNet, a deep network with five convolutional and three fully-connected layers (Krizhevsky and Sutskever 2012), (2) VGGNet-16 with 16 convolutional layers (Simonyan and Zisserman 2015), (3) ResNet-50, with 50 layers (He et al. 2016), and (4) MobileNets, a light weight deep neural networks, based on a streamlined architecture that uses depthwise separable convolutions (Howard et al. 2017).

To prove the effectiveness of our architecture, we have studied several other alternatives which tested on the TU-Berlin benchmark. Here we briefly describe these methods. Sketch-A-Net is the first CNNs framework for sketch recognition (Yu et al. 2015). Deep-Sketch and deep-CRNN-sketch are based on CNNs and recurrent neural networks (RNNs) (Zhao et al. 2016; Zhao et al. 2018). AlexNet-FC proposes a combined architecture with AlexNet and RNNs for sketch recognition task (Sarvadevabhatla et al. 2016). DVSF uses ensemble of networks to learn the visual and temporal properties of the sketch (He et al. 2017).

4.3   Results and Discussions

Effect of Unique Aspects of LW-Sketch-Net. To evaluate the effect of the size of the first layer filters, we conduct six experiments by changing the size from 3 to 15. The results are listed in Table 2. The accuracy on two datasets is 83.3% and 83.5% respectively when size is 9 × 9, which outperform the accuracy when size is 3 × 3. It is worth noting that the accuracy is not greatly improved when the size is 15 × 15. The convolution filter is larger, the receptive field will be larger, so that the more picture information is seen and the better the features obtained. However, the larger convolution filters lead to the more the parameters. As shown in Table 2, the increase of the parameter amount is greater than the improvement of the accuracy rate, so we select the convolution filter size is 9 × 9. Thus, it is necessary to balance accuracy and parameter quantity when selecting the optimal size.

Table 2. Effect of larger first convolutional layer filters.

Datasets	Filters size	Accuracy (%)	Parameters(MB)
QuickDraw-10 M	3 × 3	82.9	2.47
	9 × 9	**83.3**	**2.49**
	15 × 15	83.4	2.52
TU-Berlin	3 × 3	79.8	2.38
	9 × 9	**83.5**	**2.40**
	15 × 15	83.8	2.42

Source: own research

We have performed four experiments on two benchmarks to validate the effect of depthwise convolutional layer filters size when the first layer filters size is 9 × 9. The results are shown in Table 3. More sketch information have be learned by the larger size of depthwise convolutional filters. It achieves 85.1% accuracy on the QuickDraw-10 M datasets and 86.2% accuracy on the TU-Berlin benchmarks, more than 1.8% and 2.7% improvement compared to the situation when the size is 3 × 3.

Table 3. Effect of larger depthwise convolutional layer filters.

Datasets	Filters size	Accuracy (%)	Parameters(MB)
QuickDraw-10 M	3 × 3	83.3	2.49
	9 × 9	**85.1**	**2.69**
TU-Berlin	3 × 3	83.5	2.40
	9 × 9	**86.2**	**2.54**

Source: own research

Additionally, we have compared the normal number of filters per layer with the special situation that half number of filters every layer. It is noted that the size of first layer and depthwise convolutional layers are 9 × 9. The detailed results are listed in Table 4. The recognition accuracy is 83.7% and 85.3% respectively on two datasets. Furthermore, the ratio of filter reduction is significantly larger than the ratio of the accuracy reduction. In terms of the amount of parameters, the number of filters in the entire network is reduced by half, and the parameter amount is 30% of the total when the number of filters is not reduced.

Table 4. Effect of fewer convolutional filters per layer.

Datasets	Filters num	Accuracy (%)	Parameters(MB)
QuickDraw-10 M	64-128-256-512-1024 64-64-128-256-512	85.1 **83.7**	2.69 **0.85**
TU-Berlin	64-128-256-512-1024 64-64-128-256-512	86.2 **85.3**	2.54 **0.79**

Source: own research

Comparison Against Competitors. We report the sketch recognition results of our LW-Sketch-Net on QuickDraw-10 M datasets, compared to state-of-the-art works in Table 5. The following observations can be made: (1) LW-Sketch-Net outperforms the state-of-the-art photo-oriented CNNs model on the large-scale datasets. AlexNet obtains only 64.5% which has the worst performance among all deep models due to its rough and simple structure. ResNet-50 and VGGNet-16 outperform AlexNet because there are more layers involved in networks. The appropriate number of network layers helps to capture more sketch features, (2) our model obtains the accuracy by a significant margin, with 3.2% improvement over the performance of RNN&CNN + CEL + SCL, only a method designed for sketch on QuickDraw datasets (Xu et al. 2018). Furthermore, the accuracy of the Sketch-A-Net is 11.5% lower than the LW-Sketch-Net. The results show that our network has good recognition ability on large-scale datasets, and (3) LW-Sketch-Net is superior to MobileNets while there is much smaller 20% of the total number of parameters. The parameters amount of our network are the least among all networks while maintaining accuracy. It is clear that our network is required for sketch recognition task.

Table 5. Recognition accuracy on QuickDraw-10 M datasets.

Model	Accuracy (%)	Parameters(MB)
AlexNet	64.5	60
ResNet-50	66.8	25
VGGNet-16	68.3	138
Sketch-A-Net	72.2	17
MobileNets	77.3	4.2
RNN&CNN + CEL + SCL	80.5	123
LW-Sketch-Net	**83.7**	**0.85**

Source: own research

Most of the previous research on sketch recognition was based on TU-Berlin benchmark. Our work achieves 85.3% recognition accuracy and clearly outperforms other methods as Shown in Table 6. Specifically, Deep-Sketch and Sketch-A-Net only apply CNNs to recognize sketch, which achieves 69.2% and 74.9% accuracy. Compared to

CNN-based methods, the sequential features of the strokes can be captured by RNNs. The recognition accuracy of deep-CRNN-sketch obtains 71.8% which combined the CNNs and RNNs based on Deep-Sketch. DVSF models the visual and sequential patterns of the strokes and achieves 79.6% accuracy. AlexNet-FC which poses the sketch recognition task as a sequence modeling using gated recurrent unit achieves 85.1%.

Table 6. Recognition accuracy on TU-Berlin datasets.

Model	Accuracy (%)
Deep-Sketch	69.2
deep-CRNN-sketch	71.8
Human	73.1
Sketch-A-Net	74.9
Sketch-A-Net	77.9
DVSF	79.6
AlexNet-FC	85.1
LW-Sketch-Net	**85.3**

Source: own research

Generally, our LW-Sketch-Net outperforms over the performance of competitors, not only the CNN-based methods but also combined CNN and RNN frameworks. It should also be noted that our method has fewer parameters by a significant margin. Our network parameters are only 0.85 MB, which is much less than the parameters of the CNN-only method, let alone the method of combining CNNs and RNNs.

5 Conclusions

In this work, we propose a lightweight neural network architecture by using depthwise separable convolutions for sketch recognition and develop a sketch recognition application for mobile devices. Leveraging on a large-scale QuickDraw-10 M and TU-Berlin benchmarks, we explore the LW-Sketch-Net with fewer parameters, which is understudied in prior works. The experiments demonstrate that our model outperforms other methods. In the field of sketch recognition, our research provides the effective directing for the combination of deep neural networks and mobile terminals.

References

Li, H.Y., Hou, H., Guo, X.: The exploration on global village language: harmony. In: ICSCA 2017 Proceedings of the 6th International Conference on Software and Computer Applications, pp. 171–175 (2017a)

Eitz, M., Hays, J., Alexa, M.: How do humans sketch objects? ACM Trans. Graph. (TOG) **31**(4), 1–10 (2012)

Song, J., Song, Y.Z., Xiang, T., Hospedales, T.M.: Fine-grained image retrieval: the text/sketch input dilemma. In: BMVC (2017b)

Li, Y., Song, Y.Z., Hospedales, T.M., Gong, S.: Freehand sketch recognition using deep features. In: IJCV 122–169 (2017)

Li, Y., Hospedales, T.M., Song, Y.Z., Gong, S.: Free-hand sketch recognition by multi-kernel feature learning. Comput. Vis. Image Underst. **137**, 1–11 (2015)

Cao, X.C., Zhang, H., Liu, S., Guo, X.J., Liang, L.C.: SYM-FISH: a symmetry-aware flip invariant sketch histogram shape descriptor. In: ICCV 2013, pp. 313–320 (2013)

Sarvadevabhatla, R.K., Babu, R.V.: Freehand sketch recognition using deep features. Comput. Sci. (2015)

Yu, Q., Yang, Y., Song, Y.Z., Xiang, T., Hospedales, T.M.: Sketch-a-net that beats humans. In: BMVC (2015)

Yu, Q., Yang, Y., Liu, F., Song, Y.Z., Xiang, T., Hospedales, T.M.: Sketch-a-net: a deep neural network that beats humans. IJCV **3**(122), 411–425 (2017)

Zhao, P., Wang, F., Liu, H.T., Yao, S.: Sketch recognition using deep learning. J. Sichuan Univ. (2016)

Zhao, P., Wang, F., Liu, H.T., Yao, S.: A sketch recognition method based on deep convolutional-recurrent neural network **2**(30) (2018)

Sarvadevabhatla, R.K., Kundu, J., Babu, R.V.: Enabling my robot to play pictionary: re-current neural networks for sketch recognition. ACMMM (2016)

Ha, D., Eck, D.: A neural representation of sketch drawings (2017)

Xiao, C., Wang, C., Zhang, L.: PPTLens: Create Digital Objects with Sketch Images (2015)

Howard, A.G., Zhu, M., Chen, B.: MobileNets: Efficient Convolutional Neural Networks for Mobile Vision Applications (2017)

Krizhevsky, A., Sutskever, I., Hinton, G.E.: Imagenet classification with deep convolutional neural networks. In: NIPS 2012, pp. 1097–1105 (2012)

Simonyan, K., Zisserman, A.: Very deep convolutional networks for large-scale image recognition (2015)

He, K., Zhang, X., Ren, S.: Deep residual learning for image recognition. In: IEEE Conference on Computer Vision and Pattern Recognition (CVPR) (2016)

He, J., Wu, X., Jiang, Y., Zhao, B., Peng, Q.: Sketch recognition with deep visual-sequential fusion model. In: Proceedings of the 25th ACM International Conference on Multimedia, pp. 448–456 (2017)

Xu, P., Huang, Y., Yuan, T.: SketchMate: Deep Hashing for Million-Scale Human Sketch Retrieval (2018)

User Experience of Gamified Virtual Reality (VR) in Sport: A Review

Nurshamine Nazira Nor[1,2(✉)], Mohd Shahrizal Sunar[1,2], and Azyan Yusra Kapi[1,2,3]

[1] School of Computing, Faculty of Engineering,
Universiti Teknologi Malaysia, 81310 Johor Bahru, Malaysia
shaminenazira95@gmail.com, shahrizal@utm.my, azyanyusra@gmail.com
[2] Media and Game Innovative Centre of Excellence, Institute of Human Centered Engineering,
Universiti Teknologi Malaysia, 81310 Johor Bahru, Malaysia
[3] Universiti Teknologi MARA, 81700 Pasir Gudang, Johor, Malaysia

Abstract. Virtual Reality (VR) technology has evolved widely over the previous few years. VR Head Mounted Display (HMD) of various complexities are created for the commercial market and have been used much further than just entertainment games: education, museums, marketing and a broad variety of healthcare problems are now partially covered by VR applications. This paper's primary aim is summarized as follows: 1) to analyze the element of gamification in sports; 2) to analyze the user experience of VR in sports applications; 3) identify aspect of gamified virtual reality recognized by respondents. The input to this assessment is to analyze the aspect of gamification and the component of VR which is not being implemented or which may result in user experience failure.

Keywords: Virtual reality · Gamification · Sports

1 Introduction

Virtual reality (VR) technology has evolved widely over the previous few years. In the past literature, recent advancements in VR can be seen from desktop displays to a virtual reality 360 [1] and Head Mounted Display (HMD). Advanced complexities in HMDs were designed and built for the commercial market and the purpose is far more than just an entertainment game. Education, marketing [2] and a large range of healthcare are now partly covered by VR applications [3]. VR has achieved surprising upgrades and it is also expected to have an enormous influence on daily life. People in everyday life are often attracted by short-term incentives rather than long-term rewards. The attraction to the short-term incentives occasionally drives people to neglect attitude that would be beneficial and subsequently cause individual to lose focus, skip practice, smoke, and overconsume, for instance [4]. In attempting to break these patterns, powerful self-control alone is not enough, and thus people are actively looking for new approach of motivation. In previous literature, gamification is one of the approaches to master and practice self-motivation. Hence, this paper will provide a review as reference [test] and

H. Santos et al. (Eds.): SmartCity 360 2019, LNICST 323, pp. 440–449, 2020.
https://doi.org/10.1007/978-3-030-51005-3_36

will describe gamification and VR terms and the relation between both terms which specifically focusing on VR's user experience in sports. This paper's primary aim is summarized as follows: to analyze the gamification's element in general context of sports and secondly, the user experience in VR's sports applications. Then, it aims to identify the aspect of gamified virtual reality experienced by the respondents in VR's sports applications. The outcome of this study will lead to an analysis that identify the elements of gamification in sports and the component of VR, which is not being implemented. Furthermore, existing factors that contribute to poor VR's user experience will also be discovered. The following section will discuss the theory basis, and these are accompanied by the parts of the literature review and followed by gamification and VR's trends. Conclusion and future work will be presented in the final section.

1.1 Theory Foundation

There has been a growing number of literatures on gamification and VR in recent years. Both terms will be explained further with the definition of sports as the direction of this study.

Gamification

Gamification has become a point of conversation across media [5] and one of the possible answers to "Is there a better method of helping people to work hard?". Gamification has been described as the method of user engagement, problem solving, game thinking and game mechanics [6]. Game classification can be described where there is an interactive and objective-oriented interaction in which players can interfere to play with each other's active agents. Examples of game design components typically involve scoring schemes such as points, achievements and showing progress using rates and experience points. In addition, loyalty programs such as frequent flyer points are also implemented as a component of game design for the air travel industry. These component of gamification schemes will enhance a service's use and alter the user's composition as they perform towards external benefits [5]. Reference in [5] indicated seven main aspects in a gamified scheme: points, levels, rankings, badges, challenges or quests, on-board loops and social commitment. In today's popular gamification facilities, sport and fitness are one of the most popular gamification areas and will be the focus of this study.

Virtual Reality (VR)

VR relates to a computer-simulated environment that seeks to cause a feeling of being present in another location mentally or physically [7]. VR technology is primarily presented as an immersive and hierarchical desktop technology that can enhance the perception of reality [8]. VR systems can be categorized into three main categories. There are non-immersive, immersive and semi-immersive dependent on one of the essential aspects of VR [9]. VR was first introduced to sport studies in the 1990s. In sports applications, VR technology can offer a platform for people who may not be able to participate in various sport training courses [10]. One of the VR's main advantages is that digital content sharing can resulted in further representative sampling and comprehensive duplication [11]. Reference in [11] also pointed out that, there are numerous opportunities for fans in the sport industry to discover VR technology material that enables fans to get closer than ever before in the field. However, limited researches have been done to study how modern VR technologies could improve the practice of applied sport psychology [12].

Sports

Sports typically involve physical activity that refers to any type of body motion that eventually leads towards a rise in one's energy consumption and is conducted in different situations such as work, daily routines and recreation time [13]. In sports and fitness, motivation is the basis of all athletic activity and achievement. Contrarily, it appears to be an area in which individuals find it difficult to get motivated. In recent studies, the alternatives to promote involvement in everyday physical activity have received more attention. VR environments are used to improve imaging practice in sport areas as an approach to a real environment [14]. Since motivation is also considered as the basis of gamification, this study proposes to analyze user experience of gamified VR in sports training setting.

User Experience (UX)

Some UX concepts include the user's qualitative experience of engaging with the product [15]. UX is a dynamic process that is taking place in the real world, reshaping the experience and future growth of the user [16]. With such a comprehensive view of UX, researchers are encouraged to understand a global UX viewpoint that incorporates the role of the product in the users' life [16]. The value of UX varies based on the type of product and its intended uses. Several products are produced without the intention of creating a good customer relationship, while others are planned to provide an excellent UX [16]. In brief, UX involves the responses and reactions of the consumer during the engagement with the product, from the moment they are presented with it to the moment they are used in a certain way.

2 Literature Review

The digital databases for this review were searched and visited on 19 May 2019. Gamification AND ("virtual reality" OR sport fitness) were used as a search string or keyword in the paper selection. Twenty-four papers were found after the preliminary searches to narrow down the selections that align with the goals of this study. In the literature review, the selected papers were examined to investigate the characteristics of gamification in wide context of sports (Sect. 2.1). Moreover, user experience in VR's sport application will be identified (Sect. 2.2), and the combination of gamification and VR in sport applications (Sect. 2.3).

2.1 Gamification in Sport

A complete Gamification Framework called Octalysis (2013) [17] is introduced by Yu-kai Chou. In his perspective, gamification is a model that prioritize on human motivation in the cycle [17]. Essentially, it is a Human-Focused Design. The method is focusing on an octagon design with eight-core drives for each side: epic meaning and calling, development and accomplishment, creativity and feedback, ownership and possession, social influence and relatedness, scarcity and impatience, unpredictability and curiosity as well as loss and avoidance (Fig. 1) [17]. The Octalysis Framework is structured so that the Core Drives, which concentrate on creative self-expression and social dynamics, are grouped on the right side of the octagon or it termed as Right-Brain Core Drives (Intrinsic). The Core Drives that are most commonly associated with logic, analytical thought, and ownership are measured on the left side of the Octagon and are termed as Left-Brain Core Drives (Extrinsic). Extrinsic motivation is a motivation that originates from a goal, purpose, or reward. The goal does not have to be intriguing or attractive, but due to the goal or reward, people are driven and motivated to accomplish the task.

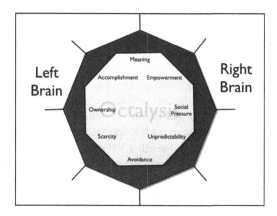

Fig. 1. Left brain vs right brain core drives [17].

Based on the Left Core drives (Extrinsic) in Octalysis framework, gamification elements have been collected and found in the studies into 8 different of gamification elements. Table 1 focused on extrinsic gamification element that are mostly used in sport context. The overall results indicate that among the game elements tested in the study, points [18–21], leaderboard [18, 19, 21, 22] and challenges [18–20, 22] has highest number of effects on the participants. However, based on the results conclude that different people experience gamification in different ways and that personal characteristics such as exercise habits and sports technology attitudes influence the way gamification affects exercise motivation [22].

2.2 Virtual Reality in Sport

As discussed before, VR systems can be divided into three major groups, which are fully immersive, non-immersive and semi-immersive [9]. The immersive VR system is the most expensive and offers the highest level of immersion [9]. This gives the user the impression that they are in the real environments. Non-Immersive VR system, or also defined as Desktop VR system or Window on World system, is the less immersive and cheapest VR system [9]. This enables users to communicate with a 3D environment via a stereo screen monitor and glasses [9]. Semi-immersive VR system, also known as

Table 1. Gamification element

Extrinsic gamification element	Included in the study	#
Points	[18–21]	4
Leaderboards	[18, 19, 21, 22]	4
Achievements/badges	[20, 21]	2
Challenges	[18–20, 22]	4
Avatars	[18]	1
Rewards	[18]	1
Quest	[20]	1
Play mode	[22]	1

hybrid systems [1], generates a high rate of immersion while maintaining the ease of the VR desktop [9]. It has shown that the results are influenced by several features of the VR display and the level of Virtual Reality system. Table 2 provides a description of the study based on user experiences in VR sports. As shown, the use of HMD was fully immersive [23–27] compared to the other VR display. The use of more immersive virtual environment during sport can improved motivation and participants' cycling velocity [21]. Based on the table below, user is able to experience fully immersive environment when they are using HMD as the VR display. HMDs can create the most immersive experiences, that can be achieved through an advanced positional tracking, motion controllers and high frame rates [28]. A bigger display or the combination of more multimodal environmental components will enhance the feeling of immersion in the virtual globe and this may affect efficiency.

Table 2. Level of virtual reality system based on user experience

VR Display	Level of VR system based on user experience		
	Non immersive	Semi immersive	Fully immersive
Cave Automatic Virtual Environment (CAVE)		[25, 28]	
Head Mounted Display (HMD)			[23–27]
Laptop screen	[29, 30]		
Projected	[31, 32]		

2.3 Gamified Virtual Reality in Sport

Gamification of Virtual Reality in sport have been recognized nowadays. To produce a good user experience (UX), the products must be able to fulfill users' requirement or able to attract the user to engage with the product [16]. Thus, the element of gamification has been used in order to increase the user motivation and to engage user with the systems. Not to forget, the immersive level of the environment is also one of the main points for the user to perceive the system as real environment and to attract them to continuously playing or staying with the system [16]. Table 3 shows the combination from the Table 1 and 2. Immersion is linked to the feeling of being inside a virtual environment [16]. Based on the Table 3 below, it shows that fully immersive have the highest number of studies compared to the other level of VR system based on UX [33–37]. Besides that, adding on challenges [33, 34, 36, 37] and avatars [33–36] as the gamification element has the highest number of studies in fully immersive level of VR system. It is because challenges are essential for the experience, as the user's primary goal is no longer a dull practice, but a challenge within a match that offers greater incentive to complete the activity [33]. Furthermore, the existence of an avatar can be an efficient way of increasing VR exercise concentration [34].

Table 3. Characteristic of gamified VR in sport

Extrinsic gamification element	Level of VR system based on user experience		
	Non immersive	Semi immersive	Fully immersive
Points	[35, 38]	[39, 40]	[33, 36, 37]
Leaderboards	[38, 41]	[40]	
Achievements/badges			[33]
Challenges	[35, 38, 41]	[39]	[33, 34, 36, 37]
Avatars	[38, 41]		[33–36]
Rewards		[40]	[33, 37]
Quest			[33]
Play mode			[34]

3 Trends

3.1 Improvements of Gamification in Design Practice

One appropriate criticism of the present gamified procedures was the narrow viewpoint on game design, leveraging only a limited amount of design components, mostly aimed at acquiring an instant commitment by conveying extrinsic motivations and behavioral reactions [42]. For instance, Chittaro and Buttussi (2018) begin with the issue of developing a serious game for mobile devices to help in the changing of attitudes in aviation security [43]. They realize that, gamification schemes and serious games are always based on real-world scenario simulations that incorporate points, badges and leader boards to benefit the user, while distinct and more complicated design aspects that create enjoyable games are seldom used [43]. The use of components from the arcade game tradition, such as rigid time limits, avoiding barriers and enemies, and a game framework have been organized around levels of difficulty to assist users in conceptual learning on how to act during the evacuation of aircraft [43].

3.2 Visualization of 3D Scenarios

Several techniques to visualize a virtual or real situation have been introduced in the recent year. Some techniques reflect the real state of fresh developments due to being cited among the frequently adopted techniques as the most interesting by customers. There are Immersive (IV), Nomadic (NV) and Head Mounted Displays (HMD) [44]. A few immersive video techniques that enable navigation in a video have been created [44]. The user can discover the situation in all angles as the video plays. HMDs need to be adapted. Nevertheless, specialists do not suggest the use of HMD at the aged of fifteen and below because of the overly stimulating imagery is hazard to adolescents whose brains are still developing [44].

4 Conclusion and Future Work

This review recognized research studies that explored the use of VR in sport, gamification in sport, and the combination of VR and gamification in sport. A VR based training and involvement scheme has some benefits, such as the ability of athletes to training despite the weather conditions and the ability of individuals to feel the real condition of the environment. Besides, gamification can increase individual motivations where it utilizes a system of goals and accomplishments in boosting the organization's efficiency. Individual satisfaction and performance are increased by implementing gamified elements. In this study, the use of gamification methods to help physical exercise in the immersive VR setting have been studied. Through the outcomes of a user experience, it can prove that gamification components are boosting the pleasure of the user throughout the physical activity and provide a set of rules to encourage the athlete or user to perform better. However, in order to analyze the generality of impacts with VR and gamification in sports, future study is needed. Findings need more varied populations, particularly elements, athletes, kids, and elderly people.

Acknowledgement. Deep appreciation to Universiti Teknologi Malaysia (UTM) for supporting our ongoing research under UTM Transdisciplinary Research Grant (Q.J130000.3509.05G07) that will allow us to identify gamification of VR in sport based on user experience. Based on the analysis of the studies, it will give ideas to boost user motivation and to attract user attention to continuously perform better in sport. Moreover, it able to increase athlete's quality performance in sports field as well as experiencing the real environment without having weather limitation for example.

References

1. See, Z.S., Sunar, M.S., Kusnayat, A., Aziz, K.A.: Interactive panorama VR360 for corporate communications: an industrial scenario case study. Int. J. Integr. Eng. **10**(6), 169–177 (2018)

2. Tomi, B., et al.: Dynamic body circumference measurement technique for a more realistic virtual fitting room experience. In: 2018 IEEE Conference on e-Learning, e-Management e-Services, IC3e 2018, pp. 56–60 (2019)
3. Bastug, E., Bennis, M., Medard, M., Debbah, M.: Toward interconnected virtual reality: opportunities, challenges, and enablers. IEEE Commun. Mag. **55**(6), 110–117 (2017)
4. Ainslie, G.: Specious reward: a behavioral theory of impulsiveness and impulse control. Psychol. Bull. **82**(4), 463–496 (1975)
5. Zichermann, G., Cunningham, C.: Gamification by design: implementing game mechanics in web and mobile apps (2011)
6. Version, E., et al.: The Art of Computer Game Design (2003)
7. Baños, R.M., Botella, C., Garcia-Palacios, A., Villa, H., Perpiña, C., Alcañiz, M.: Presence and reality judgment in virtual environments: a unitary construct? CyberPsychol. Behav. **3**(3), 327–335 (2002)
8. Zhou, Y., Wang, S.Y.: Study on the application of VR technology in sport reality shows. In: Proceedings of 2018 1st International Cognitive Cities Conference IC3 2018, pp. 200–201 (2018)
9. Bamodu, O., Ye, X.M.: Virtual reality and virtual reality system components, vol. 765–767 (2013)
10. Bird, J.M.: The use of virtual reality head-mounted displays within applied sport psychology. J. Sport Psychol. Action **11**, 1–14 (2019)
11. Li, B.J., Bailenson, J.N., Pines, A., Greenleaf, W.J., Williams, L.M.: A public database of immersive VR videos with corresponding ratings of arousal, valence, and correlations between head movements and self report measures. Front. Psychol. **8**, 2116 (2017)
12. Neumann, D.L., et al.: A systematic review of the application of interactive virtual reality to sport. Virtual Real. **22**(3), 183–198 (2018)
13. Tu, R., Hsieh, P., Feng, W.: Walking for fun or for 'likes'? The impacts of different gamification orientations of fitness apps on consumers' physical activities. Sport Manage. Rev. **22**(5), 682–693 (2018)
14. Bideau, B., Multon, F., Kulpa, R., Fradet, L., Arnaldi, B., Delamarche, P.: Using virtual reality to analyze links between handball thrower kinematics and goalkeeper's reactions. Neurosci. Lett. **372**(1–2), 119–122 (2004)
15. McCarthy, J., Wright, P.: Technology as experience. Interactions **11**(5), 42–43 (2004)
16. Rebelo, F., Noriega, P., Duarte, E., Soares, M.: Using virtual reality to assess user experience. Hum. Factors **54**(6), 964–982 (2012)
17. Chou, Y.-K.: Actionable gamification: beyond points, badges, and leaderboards. Octalysis Med. 1–151 (2016)
18. Menéndez-Ferreira, R., Torregrosa, J., Maldonado, A., Ruiz-Barquin, R., Camacho, D.: A gamification approach to promote sports values. In: CEUR Workshop Proceedings, vol. 2166 (2018)
19. Sevinç, D., Çolak, M.: The effect of electronic body protector and gamification on the performance of taekwondo athletes. Int. J. Perform. Anal. Sport **19**(1), 110–120 (2019)
20. Jurgens, D., McCorriston, J., Ruths, D.: An analysis of exercising behavior in online populations. In: Proceedings of ICWSM, pp. 630–633 (2015)
21. Tóth, A., Lógó, E.: The effect of gamification in sport applications. In: 9th IEEE International Conference on Cognitive Infocommunications, CogInfoCom 2018 - Proceedings, no. CogInfoCom, pp. 69–74 (2019)
22. Kari, T., Piippo, J., Frank, L., Makkonen, M., Moilanen, P.: To gamify or not to gamify? Gamification in exercise applications and its role in impacting exercise motivation. In: BLED 2016 Proceedings on 29th Bled eConference Digital Economy, pp. 393–405 (2016)

23. Shepherd, J., Carter, L., Pepping, G.-J., Potter, L.-E.: Towards an operational framework for designing training based sports virtual reality performance simulators. In: Proceedings, vol. 2, no. 6, p. 214 (2018)

24. Arndt, S., Perkis, A.: Using Virtual Reality and Head-Mounted Displays to Increase Performance in Rowing Workouts, pp. 45–50 (2018)

25. Schmidt, S., et al.: Impact of virtual environments on motivation and engagement during exergames. In: 2018 10th International Conference on Quality of Multimedia Experience QoMEX 2018 (2018)

26. Katsigiannis, S., Willis, R., Ramzan, N.: A QoE and simulator sickness evaluation of a smart-exercise-bike virtual reality system via user feedback and physiological signals. IEEE Trans. Consum. Electron. 65(1), 119–127 (2019)

27. Petri, K., et al.: Training using virtual reality improves response behavior in karate kumite. Sport. Eng. 22(1), 1–12 (2019)

28. Vogt, T., Herpers, R., Scherfgen, D., Strüder, H.K., Schneider, S.: Neuroelectric adaptations to cognitive processing in virtual environments: an exercise-related approach. Exp. Brain Res. 233(4), 1321–1329 (2015)

29. Anderson-Hanley, C., et al.: Exergaming and older adult cognition: a cluster randomized clinical trial. Am. J. Prev. Med. 42(2), 109–119 (2012)

30. Oliveira, B.R.R., Deslandes, A.C., Nakamura, F.Y., Viana, B.F., Santos, T.M.: Self-selected or imposed exercise? A different approach for affective comparisons. J. Sports Sci. 33(8), 777–785 (2015)

31. Baños, R.M., et al.: Using virtual reality to distract overweight children from bodily sensations during exercise. Cyberpsychol. Behav. Soc. Netw. 19(2), 115–119 (2016)

32. Murray, E.G., Neumann, D.L., Moffitt, R.L., Thomas, P.R.: The effects of the presence of others during a rowing exercise in a virtual reality environment. Psychol. Sport Exerc. 22, 328–336 (2016)

33. Tuveri, E., Macis, L., Sorrentino, F., Spano, L.D., Scateni, R.: Fitmersive games. In: International Working Conference on Advanced Visual Interfaces - AVI 2016, no. June, pp. 212–215 (2016)

34. Farrow, M., Lutteroth, C., Rouse, P.C., Bilzon, J.L.J.: Virtual-reality exergaming improves performance during high-intensity interval training. Eur. J. Sport Sci. 19(6), 1–9 (2018)

35. Parton, B.J., Neumann, D.L.: The effects of competitiveness and challenge level on virtual reality rowing performance. Psychol. Sport Exerc. 41(August 2017), 191–199 (2019)

36. Bolton, J., Lambert, M., Lirette, D., Unsworth, B.: PaperDude: a virtual reality cycling exergame. In: Proceedings of the Extended Abstracts of the 32nd Annual ACM Conference on Human Factors in Computing systems - CHI EA 2014, pp. 475–478 (2014)

37. Kharbach, S., Ahmad, S.S., Ahmed, N.M.H., Fetais, N.: Virtual reality falconry: simulation of a traditional qatari sport methodology and techniques. In: 2018 International Conference on Computer and Applications (ICCA) ICCA 2018, pp. 12–17 (2018)

38. Zhang, M., Xu, M., Han, L., Liu, Y., Lv, P., He, G.: Virtual network marathon with immersion, scientificalness, competitiveness, adaptability and learning. Comput. Graph. 36(3), 185–192 (2012)

39. Sigrist, R., Rauter, G., Marchal-Crespo, L., Riener, R., Wolf, P.: Sonification and haptic feedback in addition to visual feedback enhances complex motor task learning. Exp. Brain Res. 233(3), 909–925 (2014)

40. Nagendran, A., Pillat, R., Adam, K., Welch, G., Hughes, C.: Measuring spatial presence: introducing and validating the pictorial presence SAM. Presence Teleoper. Vir. Environ. 23(2), 109–132 (2013)

41. Matthews, T., Carter, S., Pai, C., Fong, J.: Evaluating a mobile transcription tool for the deaf. Behaviour 4206(August), 2006 (2015)

42. Rapp, A.: Drawing inspiration from world of warcraft: gamification design elements for behaviour change technologies. Interact. Comput. **29**(5), 648–678 (2017)
43. Chittaro, L., Buttussi, F.: Exploring the use of arcade game elements for attitude change: two studies in the aviation safety domain. Int. J. Hum Comput Stud. **127**, 112–123 (2019)
44. Ali, N.S., Nasser, M.: Review of virtual reality trends (previous, current, and future directions), and their applications, technologies and technical issues. ARPN J. Eng. Appl. Sci. **12**(3), 783–789 (2017)

CitySkin: Which Color Is Your City?

Isabel Paiva[1]([⊠]) and Tiago Fernandes[2]

[1] Faculdade de Ciências e Tecnologia, Universidade Nova de Lisboa, Almada, Portugal
isabelpaiv@gmail.com
[2] Faculdade de Engenharia da Universidade de Porto, Porto, Portugal

Abstract. Mobile phones are becoming ubiquitous machines with increasing processing power. This paper will focus in discussing an experimental application, CitySkin, which relies on mobile phones for data retrieval with mapping purposes. This mobile visual system provides an accessible mean to design an invisible skin of a city (an output map) following a user point of view at a given moment in time. This project explores relations between subjectivity and raw data by combining hard data with visual mapping. Cities and their intrinsic diversity can be compared. Slightly different input variables can present greater changes in a recurrent path. CitySkin records the mood of a specific derive discussing the cultural implications on computing and the design of its ubiquity.

Keywords: Data visualization · Mapping · Ubiquitous computing · Digital art · GPS referencing

1 Introduction

According to Weiser and Brown the concept of Ubiquitous Computing (U.C.) aims to create "a calm computing" achieved by having computers disappear (Weiser and Brown 1996). This is made possible by conveying computing surrounding humans as part of environments. U.C offers a perspective that emphasizes human and social aspects, presenting computation as an open definition (Denning 2011) challenging its terms, significance and appearance.

U.C. discussion is translated into projects that combine research and life. For instance, contributions can be observed given by the progressive miniaturization of sensors and actuators, as to the exploration of smart materials (Coelho and Zigelbaum 2010) but also by applying natural structures to design (Oxman 2010) as well as Maeda's bits, atoms and crafts research (Maeda 2018). These relations inspire hybrids of several form and nature. Moreover, some authors (Kim and Symonds 2010) defend that we are fully living in a UC era, considering that this ubiquity of computation is made real with the use smartphones. CitySkin research project acknowledges this last statement and aims to contribute with a proposal that tackles the hybridization of art with science.

In the last decade, mobile phones became a common tool for communication in a post-industrialized world (Castells et al. 2006) but also in developing countries. When analyzing the spread of mobile phones use in a globalized world, the appeal lies on

© ICST Institute for Computer Sciences, Social Informatics and Telecommunications Engineering 2020
Published by Springer Nature Switzerland AG 2020. All Rights Reserved
H. Santos et al. (Eds.): SmartCity 360 2019, LNICST 323, pp. 450–462, 2020.
https://doi.org/10.1007/978-3-030-51005-3_37

Fig. 1. CitySkin image output: driving for 33 min.

the emotional tie and social implication given by a personal object. But on the other hand, it is relevant to the context of CitySkin project, to mention the iniquity on existent access to different features provided by mobiles phones, but also the network coverage quality, factors that are definitive to better define the audience. It is relevant to say that smartphones are still a "first world" tool, which translates to context CitySkin in terms of accessibility.

Smartphones are used as a tool. They combine their computing, mobility, and mapping possibilities. Smartphones beyond having an exponential computing power, commonly have features as WI-FI, 4G and 5G network connection, GPS, accelerometer, high quality camera, commonly in people's pockets. These particular features offer a realm of possible combinations.

In addition, CitySkin project, addresses consequences of digitalization of information and big data. Tools such as smartphones have created an exponential ability to collect and store massive amounts of information. On one hand, this massive amount of information generation brought forward the need to improve their readability. The exponential growth of information has found in graphic visualization a model to simplify the interpretation of data complexity. Data visualization not only improves reading, as creates rich aesthetic experiences, adding new perspectives to visual and cultural discussion while conveying digital information. All these solutions have been made possible by mutual contributions arising from computer science and art. Examples of these prevailing collaborations can be found in current definition of design made by institutions such as NY MoMA, in the Design and the Elastic Mind (MoMA 2008), Talk To Me (MoMA 2011) and Design and Violence (MoMA 2015) exhibitions commissioned by Antonelli or in the Linz's Ars Electronica (Ars Electronica 2019) a festival where, since the 70's, science and art collaboration is discussed and celebrated. However Data Visualization is also a prevailing visual experience distributed in Internet under several categories and by a myriad of authors.

CitySkin's conceptual design is inspired by these approaches, and uses computation to measure and visualize routes inside the city. It references mapping, data visualization, and digital art critic (Crampton 2009; Tufte 2006; Hall 2006) but also makes a contribution for the shifting concepts on computing. Cityskin draws a visualization to hard data by proposing a literal and psychogeographic journey, considering human subjectivity, in an implicit invitation for derive, surprise and improvisation (Debord 1958).

2 Related Work

Background of experimental mobile applications is found in the context of digital art. Since the beginning of the public internet that terms like "internet art" attributed to extended nomadic networks have emerged and have been explored by digital artists. In this context, the particular designation of "software art", coined work that referenced formal outputs given by computational instructions.

Since the 90's, artists like Golan Levin have presented work that rely on software features. Golan Levin created interactive software that allowed manipulating visuals and sounds in real time. Telesymphony is a project that extends Golan's work to nomadic devices. Sound is generated by the ringtones of audience's mobile devices (Paul 2008).

Mapping is an excellent conceptual tool to understand and cope with urban landscape information. Considering U.C. and Data Visualization strategies, cities that dwell with interchange of massive information, are becoming progressively U-Cities (Hwang 2008), this meaning, Ubiquitous Cities. MIT SENSEable City Lab ("MIT Senseable City Lab" 2019) has contributed to U-Cities research with several projects. One of these projects, trash track ("trash track" 2018) attaches sensors to discarded objects and maps its path until the dump. The output map gives awareness to the existence of long trails, as opposed to a more efficient proximity system, indicating waste of resources in an immediate way. Projects like Pedro Cruz and Machado (2016), Lisbon blood vessels uses veins in circulatory system as a metaphor to visualize, with aesthetics appeal, Lisbon's traffic flow. This method can also give real-time valuable information to drivers.

A growing number of designers and researchers are using data visualization technics for artistic expression, but also the particular features on mobile phones as survey machines. GPS, wi-fi, embedded camera, computation, in addition to mobility, are presently used and mixed in different approaches. MobiSpray by Jürgen Scheible uses mobile phones as an artistic toll to paint digital graffiti. Scheible created a client server application that uses mobiles as gesture-control (Scheible 2009). Mobiles are used as pointing mechanism drawing on a video-projection, thus, creating digital public art. Large scale drawing using mobile devices is another example of the GPS use for artistic expression, and a concept presented by several artists ("gpsdrawing" 2018).

Travelling inside a city deals with relations between time and space, i.e. geography, time measurement and a less obvious category, a degree of fun. Enjoyment is the one addressed by Mark Shepard's in experimental mobile application Serendipitor (Shepard 2011). The same is expressed by Atau Tanaka and Petra Gemeinboeck in "Net derives" (Tanaka and Gemeinboeck 2006). Serendipitor is part of a broader project, Sentient City, which tackles with design of the city of the future. Serendipitor is an i-phone application that invites the user to explore different paths in a city map. It calculates alternative ways to get to a particular part of the city, with inherent proposals to diverge. "Net derive", also follows the concept of derive, transforming the city in an instrument. Mobile phones, using GPS position, camera and microphone, exchange information between spectators in a gallery and three participants in the streets of a city. Sounds and pictures from the streets become information to visualize and sonificate locations.

Finally, two experimental mobile applications from Japanese company Aircord, show how playfulness can be aesthetically relevant and simple (Aircord 2018) The first virtual free runner is an animated man that reacts to accelerometer with a tap to jump button, to be used with a projector.

3   Design Principles

3.1   Art Concept

Describing time visually has always been a concern with clear practical implications in life from the beginning of times. Current time measurements have implicit computations based in sky observations. It is relevant to look into history of science and math. These time divisions originated from computations made in the beginning of civilization, 4000 years ago, in Mesopotamia. Surviving Babylonians' clay tablets records show cumulative data from sky observations that throughout time allowed predicting celestial phenomenon with precision. For instance, it was an ancient civilization that gave 7 days to the week.

The number seven had a mystical significance to Babylonians. It was associated with the seven heavenly bodies: the sun, Mars, Mercury, Jupiter, Venus and Saturn. As such, the measurements of the week that are still in use today are based in astronomical observations made in ancient past.

Mesopotamians' great mathematics put forward a 60 base system, which allowed defining the sixty minutes in the hour, and the 360° of the circle (Fara 2009). The sexagesimal system is useful to measure angles, geographic coordinates, and time. Mesopotamian representation of time was created from a circle division, having different attributions to year, month and day. These divisions of time were also based in astronomical observations. For instance, the month division correlates with the observation of the moon. To some extent, and considering some alterations, this system created by ancient mathematicians is still used embedded in our high tech life, and use in the apps in our mobiles phones.

This leap in time, and historical background gives understanding of cultural implications of time division, but also indicate a clear relation to direct observation of natural elements. These divisions depend on interpretation and record of celestial moving objects and therefore have an implicit design (Fig. 2). CitySkin is also inspired by this convention of time measurement that relies on observation. Using mobile cameras as a metaphor of the eye, and giving direct relation with geographic space, by GPS location recording,

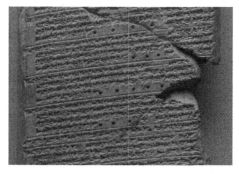

Fig. 2. Part of a clay tablet, 3 pieces, Neo-Assyrian. A copy of the so-called Venus Tablet of Ammisaduqa (detail) The British Museum, retrieved from https://www.britishmuseum.org/res earch/collection_online/collection_object_details.aspx?objectId=314745&partI

CitySkin provides visual maps of travels that connect locations and time. It uses a pre-defined computational model (based in the number 60 as a direct quote of Babylonian measurements). The result is a graphic map that will give an impression of a particular city at a given time.

3.2 Prototyping

The prototyping studies began by physically travelling the city by car, and defining a path. First trial was a crossing over Tagus River, from the South bank, the city of Almada, to Lisbon, in the North Bank (Fig. 3). The journey took 33 min.

Fig. 3. Prototyping the journey between Almada and Lisbon

Throughout this travelling, one photo was taken roughly each of the 33 min using a mobile phone (Fig. 4).

These photos were used to output map studies, by stretching, adding filters, and searching for a visual result that was focused on color. Mainly, creating a map of colors predominance within a specific trip (Fig. 5 and Fig. 6).

Fig. 4. Prototyping: taking one photo each minute

Fig. 5. Output color map number 1 test using photos from Fig. 4. (Color figure online)

Fig. 6. Output color map number 2 test using photos from Fig. 4. (Color figure online)

3.3 Design

The application design follows the prototyping results. The final graphic map (skin) results from photos taken during an up to 60-min journey, by foot or in a vehicle. Cityskin takes a photo each minute and has its location recorded. The difference between position

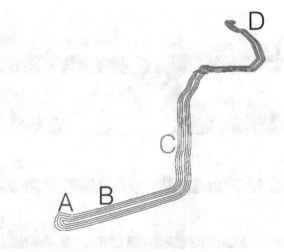

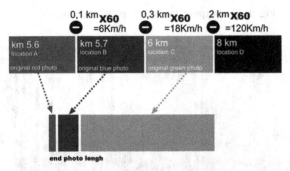

Fig. 7. Image length computation

A and B will define the velocity and this value determines each photo final length (Fig. 7). A median filter is applied to each photo, in order to emphasize color, and its length is compressed or stretched according to the velocity variables. These images are lined horizontally, and a white space is kept between them. The white space adds readability to each picture, but also becomes an editable input text space.

GPS coordinates are presented as default text between stripes. The users are allowed to substitute this geographic information by editing their own text labeling in each white line (Fig. 8). The final map results from a representation of hard data and open variables related to movement and color – visual impressions, time, type of transportation and user input.

The final map will be presented as a stripe of colors, showing long stripes when the user is moving faster, and narrower stripes when the user is moving slower.

3.4 Technology

The first implementation test was made for iOS. CitySkin output corresponds to a single JPG image file (Fig. 1 and Fig. 11), containing the GPS coordinates of each of the

Fig. 8. U.I. input text screen

images captured, with photos taken each minute. The final image directly represents the path taken by the user, synthesizing the user perspective and the particular variables associated to the travel.

This final skin output can be shared. The jpg format image is aimed to either be published in socials networks or sent via e-mail.

3.5 Designing Relations: Objective Derive

Quotidian journeys are often a routine experience where landscapes blur into oblivion. CitySkin can provide insights about different layers of perception, and a singular perspective. The application invites the user to find different maps around the known but also unknown places.

The measurement method is inspired by Babylonian direct observation of celestial phenomena. As such, Cityskin is offering an interpretation on data given from visual cues. CitySkin can visualize and find interesting differences, coincidence or patterns on journeys maps.

It becomes possible to compare visuals from different cities, but also the subjective variables given by an individual journey. These changes can be given by time spent in different locations, or even provoked by the user's imagination.

CitySkin was designed considering that identical paths would provide completely different maps accordingly to the use, emphasizing the differences around the experience found in routine.

3.5.1 Sharing Images

Fig. 9. User Interface: share screen

One of the main features of CitySkin application (Fig. 9) is the ability to share output. This feature is designed to support a ritual of communication, this being, according to Mikko Villi (2010) often more important than the photographic quality itself. Also, it has been noticed that photo sharing rituals are followed by text message practices, i.e. often images do not substitute texting.

CitySkin combines image and texting, and opens directions and opportunity for experimentation concerning the combined use of image and texting, as a common way of communication.

4 Issues and Solutions

4.1 Human Variables and Algorithm

CitySkin's visual variations depend on velocity, which determines each stripe picture's length. This variation, however, brought the necessity to distinguish walking from a vehicle journey, because velocity has implications in the final design (Fig. 10). Accessing two different algorithms solved the issue, accordingly to user input determination of velocity, either walking or travelling in a vehicle.

Fig. 10. U.I. drive or walk screen

4.2 Identifying Location

CitySkin's computation depends on a correct identification of location (Fig. 11), using GPS by default. As noted by several authors (Kerr 2019; Liao et al. 2006) GPS referential location has problems. It is common for mobile phones to lose signal indoor, making GPS based projects only suitable for outdoors. The lack of accuracy is also observable.

CitySkin invite users to test the application in excellent conditions. When that is impossible, the geographic information can be manually inputted as referenced. In the absence of the user labeling, CitySkin will use an average measurement.

Fig. 11. GPS default graphic aspect – CitySkin in Helsinki (GPS: 60.173294, 24.936304)

5 Future Work

CitySkin is a work-in-progress project. Next steps will include system evaluation aiming to refine the user experience. Also it will be made accessible to other platforms, as Android and Windows. Also we aim to integrate the distribution of Cityskin's output in the website.

6 Conclusion

Cityskin project tests relations between computation and art, acknowledging the incremental computation ubiquity allowed by mobile phones. Ubiquitous Computing is addressed by this application, considering cities intelligence. In a broad sense proposes to test playfulness and a sense of discovery, thus, giving focus on the user experience. CitySkin produces outputs which give visibility to invisible layers present in the quotidian life, thus, adding a cultural impression to design and computation.

Each image reflects the point of view of a user along a path. There will be differences in colors and distortion on the output image (skin). Each skin will be unique and will reflect the singular point of view of the user's time, place and playfulness.

CitySkin also provides a mean to compare and experiment with different times of the day or year of a specific place, but also between different cities. Furthermore, this application allows recognizing patterns of time. Finally, the information presented in the final map, can give the user, a visual and immediate way to evaluate activities that relate to routine and movement. This information presentation benefit from a comparative evaluation, like for instance physical activities or by visualizing traffic jams. Cityskin is a tool to measure the quotidian qualitatively and quantitatively.

Capturing this life's time, that has periods perceived as blanks or non-places, is ultimately one the useful contribution of this application. Is this case, the challenge is to re-capture the perception of fleeting time, specifically showing variables that are not obvious to the user. Thus, add a sense of wonder or fun, to an often called draining, empty experience that is commuting, or even register layers of perception while travelling un/familiar places. Finally. CitySkin suggest to slow down, and embrace contemplation.

References

Aircord (2018). https://www.aircord.co.jp/en/

Antonelli, P., Museum of Modern Art (New York N.Y.): Design and the elastic mind. New York London: Museum of Modern Art; Thames & Hudson distributor (2008). http://www.moma.org/interactives/exhibitions/2008/elasticmind/index.htm

Talk to me (2011). http://wp.moma.org/talk_to_me/

Design and violence (2015). https://www.moma.org/interactives/exhibitions/2013/designandviolence/

Ars electronic (2019). http://new.aec.at/prix/en/einreichdetails/preise/

Castells, M., et al.: Mobile Communication and Society: A Global Perspective. MIT Press (2006)

Coelho, M., Zigelbaum, J.: Shape changing interfaces. Pers. Ubiquit. Comput. (2010). https://doi.org/10.1007/s00779-010-0311-y

Crampton, J.: Mapping: A Critical Introduction to Cartography and GIS. John Wiley, Hoboken (2009)

Cruz, P., Machado, P.: Pulsing blood vessels: a figurative approach to traffic visualization. IEEE Comput. Graph. Appl. 36(2), 16–21 (2016)

Debord, G.: Theory of the Dérive (1958). http://www.bopsecrets.org/SI/2.derive.htm

Denning, P.J.: What have we said about computation? In: Ubiquity Symposium closing argument. ACM (2011)

Fara, P.: Science a four thousand year history: Oxford University Press, Oxford (2009)

Gpsdrawing (2018). http://www.gpsdrawing.com/

Hall, P.: Else/Where: Mapping New Cartographies of Networks and Territories, University of Minnesota Design Institute (2006)

Hwang, J.S.: U-City: the next paradigm of urban development. In: Handbook of Research on Urban Informatics: The Practice and Promise of the Real-Time City, pp. 367–378 (2008). https://doi.org/10.4018/978-1-60566-152-0.ch025

Kerr, J., et al.: Several Best Practices in Data Reduction & Analysis of GPS Data University of California [ppt], San Diego (2019). http://docplayer.net/18521965-Best-practices-in-data-reduction-analysis-of-gps-data.html

Kim, T., Symonds, J.: Planning for knowledge cities in ubiquitous technology spaces. Ubiquit. Pervasiv. Comput. 1613–1625 (2010). https://doi.org/10.4018/9781599048383.ch013

Liao, L., Patterson, D.J., Fox, D., Kautz, H.: Building personal maps from GPS data. Ann. New York Acad. Sci. 1093, 249–265 (2006). https://doi.org/10.1196/annals.1382.017

Maeda, J.: Maeda studio (2018). https://maedastudio.com/

MIT Senseable City Lab. MIT Senseable City Lab, 21 January 2019. http://senseable.mit.edu/

Oxman, N.: Material-based design computation, Ph.D. Thesis, MIT (2010). http://dspace.mit.edu/handle/1721.1/59192

Paul, C.: Digital Art (World of Art), Thames & Hudson (2008)

Scheible, J.: MobiSpray: mobile phone as virtual spray can for painting big anytime anywhere on anything. Leonardo J. Int. Soc. Arts Sci. Technol. **42**(4), 332–341(2009)

Shepard, M.: Serendipitor, Sentient City: Ubiquitous Computing, Architecture, and the Future of Urban Space (2011). http://serendipitor.net/site/

Tanaka, A., Gemeinboec, P.: Net derives: Participative Locative Media work (2006). http://www.ataut.net/site/IMG/pdf/Tanaka-Net_Derive-score.pdf

Tufte, E.: Beautiful Evidence. Graphics Press (2006)

Villi, M.: Visual Mobile Communication Camera Phone Photo Messages as Ritual Communication and Mediated Presence. Aalto University, School of Art and Design (2010)

Weiser, M., Brown, J.: The Coming Age of Calm Technology. Xerox Park (1996). https://pdfs.semanticscholar.org/23a6/cdc72fa2a59d62ea94aa68cfe484982cf2b8.pdf

Increasing the Representation of People with Disabilities in Industry 4.0: Technopreneurship, Malaysia Perspectives

Ruhiyati Idayu Abu Talib[1,2(✉)], Mohd Shahrizal Sunar[1,2],
and Ruzimi Mohamed[1]

[1] Media and Game Innovation Centre of Excellence (MaGICX),
Institute of Human Centered Engineering (iHumEn),
Universiti Teknologi Malaysia (UTM), Johor, Malaysia
ruhiyati.magicx@gmail.com
[2] School of Computing, Faculty of Engineering,
Universiti Teknologi Malaysia, Johor Bahru, Malaysia
shahrizal@utm.my
http://ihumen.utm.my/magicx/

Abstract. In this paper, we argue that the advancement of technology in Industry 4.0, which covers growth areas such as big data and machine learning, cybersecurity, digital currencies, blockchain and the Internet of Things (IoT), with expected creations of new job opportunities in the areas of Cyber Security, Data Analytics, Network & Infrastructure and Software Development that can easily be done at home, has produced an ideal scenario in the context of job opportunities for People with Disabilities (PWDs). Under the Eleventh Malaysia Plan (2016–2020), more programs are currently being implemented to empower productive PWDs. These also include greater accessibility to basic education and skills training, one of it being entrepreneurship, to build relevant skills among PWDs so that they are able to compete in the open market either as employees, self-employed individuals or entrepreneurs.

Keywords: Industry 4.0 · Person with disabilities · Technology entrepreneur · Technopreneur · Entrepreneur · Information technology · Empower

1 Introduction

Based on the World Health Organization's (WHO) estimates, in developing countries, the number of people with disabilities range between 5% and 10% [1]. Based on the total population of 32 million in 2018, if the estimate of the WHO is taken into account, the number of people with disabilities in Malaysia should

Supported by Malaysia Technology Development Corporation(MTDC) and Universiti Teknologi Malaysia (UTM).

© ICST Institute for Computer Sciences, Social Informatics and Telecommunications Engineering 2020
Published by Springer Nature Switzerland AG 2020. All Rights Reserved
H. Santos et al. (Eds.): SmartCity 360 2019, LNICST 323, pp. 463–473, 2020.
https://doi.org/10.1007/978-3-030-51005-3_38

be between 1.6 to 3.2 million. A study conducted by the Institute for Public Health, Ministry of Health Malaysia in 2015, to supplement existing data and provide data for monitoring and evaluation of health programs implemented by the Ministry of Health, found that the prevalence of disability among adults in Malaysia was 11.8%, based on a sample survey of 19,959 healthy adults with ages between 18 to 50 years [5]. This survey supported WHO's estimate of the number of disabilities in Malaysia.

Using the 2017 Ministry Of Education data [2], estimating that at least 50% of the inclusive education students will choose to continue their studies in higher institutions (Fig. 1), we are looking at the labor market with at least 15,000 productive PWDs. There is an urgent need to create a future in which they participate more actively in society, a future which increases their independence and in which they are able to make decisions about their lives and futures, by offering them opportunities for employment and access to essential services. The

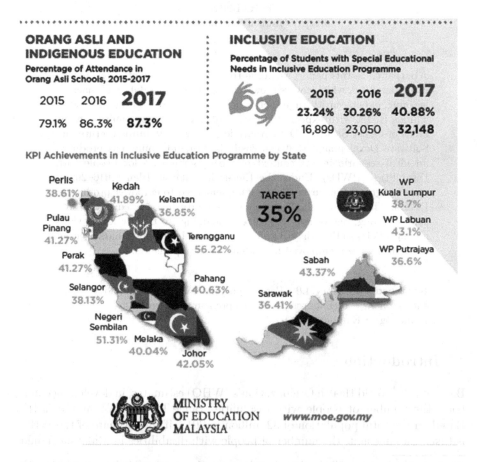

ORANG ASLI AND INDIGENOUS EDUCATION
Percentage of Attendance in Orang Asli Schools, 2015-2017

2015	2016	**2017**
79.1%	86.3%	**87.3%**

INCLUSIVE EDUCATION
Percentage of Students with Special Educational Needs in Inclusive Education Programme

	2015	2016	**2017**
	23.24%	30.26%	**40.88%**
	16,899	23,050	**32,148**

KPI Achievements in Inclusive Education Programme by State

Perlis 38.61%
Kedah 41.89%
Kelantan 36.85%
Pulau Pinang 41.27%
Terengganu 56.22%
Perak 41.27%
Pahang 40.63%
Selangor 38.13%
Sarawak 36.41%
Negeri Sembilan 51.31%
Melaka 40.04%
Johor 42.05%
Sabah 43.37%

TARGET 35%

WP Kuala Lumpur 38.7%
WP Labuan 43.1%
WP Putrajaya 36.6%

MINISTRY OF EDUCATION MALAYSIA   *www.moe.gov.my*

Fig. 1. Inclusive education: percentage of students with special educational needs in inclusive education programme. Source from: Ministry of Education [9]

World Bank estimated that the total national income losses ranged from US$ 1,370 billion to US$ 1,940 billion worldwide, due to the exclusion of people with disabilities from mainstream society [15].

2 Employment, Self-employment and Entrepreneurship for People with Disabilities

There are a number of literature studies discussing the challenges for PWDs regarding their job opportunities in the labor force [16,28,29]. Among the challenges are [12]:

- Inaccessible transportation
- Inaccessible buildings
- Negative attitudes by employers
- Low self-esteem
- Overprotective families

Lack of appropriate transportation facilities is a major barrier to PWD employment. Secondly is the stigma and prejudice of employers and society to PWDs. The Labor Force's 2017 report showed that there are a total of 303,000 PWDs outside the labor force, which translate into total national income losses ranging from US$ 1.18 billion to US$ 1.68 billion according to the World Bank estimate [15] (Fig. 2).

Reasons for not seeking work	('000)		(%)	
	2016	2017	2016	2017
Total	6,987.6	7,042.9	100.0	100.0
Schooling	3,002.8	3,008.8	43.0	42.7
Homework/family responsibilities	2,906.5	2,905.0	41.64	41.2
Going for further studies	155.3	153.3	2.2	2.2
Disabled	274.1	303.2	3.9	4.3
Not interested	88.2	75.8	1.3	1.1
Retired	560.7	597.7	8.0	8.5

Fig. 2. Source from: Statistic Department of Malaysia [24]

From 1999 to 2001, a total of 4,017 disabled workers were registered with the Labor Department. Out of these 4,017, a total of 2,529 people with disabilities were placed in various job sectors. Khor (2010) noted that despite the 1% quota, the public sector employed only 581 people and the private sector employed less than 5,000 people with disabilities [15]. To mitigate the problems, the Ministry of Woman Family and Community Development (MWFCD) led the "Project to Support Disability Participation" [13] with a joint collaboration with the Japan International Cooperation Agency (JICA), which resulted in the creation of a specific job tittle called "Job Coach". A Job Coach is a job mediator between employers and PWDs. A Job Coach is responsible for promoting employment for PWDs and maintaining their retention rates. Based on the outcome of the project, having in-house job coaches in workplaces helped to increase job placements and opportunities for PWDs. In 2012, the Labor Department registered 13,339 PWDs, out of which 9,074 were successfully employed.

Under the Eleventh Malaysia Plan (2016–2020)[3], more programs are currently being implemented to empower productive PWDs; including greater accessibility to basic education and skills training, one of which is entrepreneurship, to build relevant skills among PWDs so that they can be employed by the relevant private and public sectors. There are a total of 3,782 PWDs working in the public sector as of September 2018. The Ministry of Education has the highest number of such staff at 1,477. Currently the goal is to reach a number of 12,811 [18]. While it is an increase from 2,623 in 2014, it is still less than 1% of the quota allocated by the government. Other solutions to the problems of unemployment among PWDs include increasing the number of PWD entrepreneurs and self-employed individuals. Since the terms self-employed and entrepreneur are closely linked [27], we refer to the following definitions and will continue to use both terms synonymously:

Self-employment: Those who work for profit or fees in their own business, profession, trade or operate a farm [6].

Entrepreneurship: A combination of the activities discovery, evaluation and exploitation of opportunities to introduce e. g. goods and services, processes and organization structures that were not existent before [23].

3   Definition of Technopreneurship

An Entrepreneur is a person who finds a gap in the market and develops new products or services to address the gap. *A Technopreneur*, on the other hand, is one of the major extensions of entrepreneurship, based on the U.S. legal definition [30]. A Technopreneur is a new age entrepreneur who uses technology to make innovations and comes out with something new. Technopreneurs operate differently from those in the current economic order, by optimizing the use of technology to innovate new products and services that create a marketplace disruption. For example, Uber's founders thought (Idea) of a different way of calling a cab (market gap), used the power of technology (built an integrated GPS app) and changed the taxi/cab industry's economy completely.

3.1 Role of Technology and Mastering Technology Competency for PWDs

To compete in today's global landscape, it is essential to use state-of the-art technologies such as computer systems, including software and hardware, or manufacturing processes. However, the efficient and successful use of ordinary technology subject to the context, requires specific capabilities. Typical requirements include, the ability to perceive technology, the ability to work with technology, and the ability to understand technology.

People with higher education level would generally imply a greater ability to use technology [19]. However, people with disabilities such as physical or cognitive impairments, are often limited with respect to these capabilities, even if they are highly educated. In most cases, this is due to inadequate technologies that do not meet PWDs requirements. Therefore, PWDs are often unable to make efficient use of technology. This means that PWDs have disadvantages in obtaining independent individuality (perspective of individuals) as well as information necessary for entrepreneurship (perspective of information society), in addition to overcoming barriers in order to organize their businesses in a competitive manner (perspective of business organization).

3.2 Technoprenuership and PWDs

Being an entrepreneur affords individuals with a certain degree of independence [26], which is crucial for PWDs as they are very unique individuals that require a certain type of environment to thrive in. At the same time, entrepreneurship demands from its entrepreneurs a tenacity and strong self-motivation to succeed [22].

According to the Flow Theory of Csikszentmihalyi, motivation can be achieved or maintained if the capabilities of a person are sufficient to meet the requirements of a particular situation. If the capacity of a person is insufficient for the task, it is more likely to be abandoned by the individual [7]. PWDs are often at a disadvantage when it comes to handling a complex situation such as entrepreneurship. The task for PWDs is much more difficult and at times even impossible, compared to people without disabilities. They lack specific capabilities due to their disability, e.g., visual or mobile capabilities, which worsen their chance to compete in the market.

Data from the Malaysian Ministry of Education (2017)[8] showed that there were about 2,139 disabled students enrolled into Malaysian public universities, which comprised of a total student enrolment of 119,558 in 2017. This showed that PWDs are still lagging behind in education systems in Malaysia, thereby placing them at a disadvantage in terms of job opportunities in the open market. Educational inferiority can easily reduce self-motivation, which could also result in damaged self-esteem [25].

Technology is an important factor in achieving and maintaining self-motivation and self-esteem for PWDs, and it also helps them in participating in the social environment [11]. Assistive technologies (AT), accessible websites and accessible applications make it possible for PWDs to become part of the society [4, 20]. For instance, artificial limbs, retina implants or screen readers that enhance inclusion and self-esteem set important conditions for starting businesses for PWDs. Additionally, technology is also a critical factor in today's business startups.

The OECD report provides a better understanding of the complexity of this multifaceted topic, with specific recommendations for policy actions in order to promote the self-employment of people with disabilities [31]. The first suggestion that can be derived from this article concerns the need for IT accessibility laws to be regulated and tightened, particularly for public institutions. Secondly, the policy requires an accessible educational framework to ensure that more students with disabilities are able to complete their college degrees and thus build a proper basis for self-employment. Thirdly, it is strongly recommended that the AT market be consolidated and standardized to ensure the high-quality supply and dissemination of suitable AT and innovative services for people with disabilities to help them start their own businesses. Ultimately, by advertising and funding such R&D projects, policies can attract attention and efforts, which can help in developing and evaluating accessible technologies for disabled entrepreneurs [31].

In Fig. 3, we illustrate our points in these sections about disabled entrepreneurship for clearer understanding.

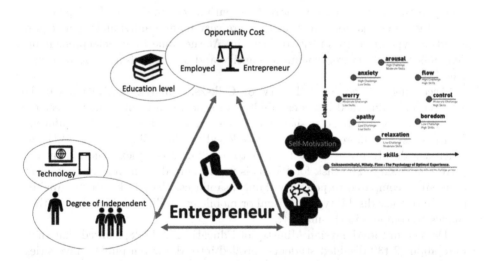

Fig. 3. Technology, self-motivation and entrepreneurship

4 Government vs Private Sector Initiatives

4.1 Government Initiatives

There has been a paradigm shift in Malaysia over the years when it comes to dealing with PWD issues. Before the PWDs Act was enacted in 2008, the approach taken by Malaysia in dealing with PWD issues was more about a Charity Model Disability [14], that had no specific plan and policy aimed at improving their quality of life and well-being. In 2010, Malaysia signed the United Nations Convention on the Rights of Persons with Disabilities (UNCRPD) and in November 2012, Malaysia and other members of the United Nations Economic and Social Commission for Asia and the Pacific (UNESCAP) adopted the "Making the Right Real" strategy for PWDs in Asia and the Pacific, which included 10 goals and 62 indicators. This was to serve as part of Malaysia's strategy for moving forward towards building a stronger policy framework for mainstream disabled people and ensuring their effective participation in the society. UNCRPD defined disability in accordance with the Social Model Disability [21], that recognized disability as an evolving concept and also noted that disability was the result of interactions between people with disabilities, and attitudinal and environmental barriers that impede their full and effective participation in society on an equal footing with people without disabilities. The responsibilities of implementing a national plan and policy regarding PWD fall under the jurisdiction of the National Council for Persons with Disabilities (NCPWD), chaired by the Ministry of Women, Family and Community Development (MWFCD). NCPWD recognized that a collective effort through multi-sectoral and multi-agency collaboration with other relevant agencies was needed to achieve comprehensive and holistic results.

There are a number of government agencies that cater to the matter of entrepreneurship. For example, Majlis Amanah Rakyat (MARA) or The Trust Council for Bumiputera, a statutory agency, has been given the government's mandate to develop successful and innovative Bumiputera entrepreneurs who are empowered with global human capital and integrity, and who contribute to increased equity ownership in return. MARA has a dual role to play in the development of education and entrepreneurship. MARA has successfully implemented its educational transformation in Technical and Vocational Education and Training (TVET) in line with its slogan, "Entrepreneurship and Global Education", combining with the ethos of entrepreneurship to develop "glocal" technoprenuers. Although MARA has successfully developed and implemented technoprenuer syllabus for their entrepreneurs, this is only for the those non-disabled. We can hardly get data from them about the number of disabled entrepreneurs due to the low numbers they have and to their inconsistency in keeping records of PWD entrepreneurs.

There are very few government agencies that provide specific initiatives for PWD entrepreneurs. One of that is the Malaysia Welfare Department which has introduced a grant scheme to enable eligible PWDs to expand their businesses; known as "Skim Galakan Perniagaan Orang Kurang Upaya (SB-OKU)". A total of RM 16 million has been budgeted for this scheme, which has benefited a total of 1,563 PWDs as of 2014. Analysis of the current government infrastructure for PWDs showed that it is an extension of existing infrastructure available to ordinary people or people with no disabilities. The existing approach to PWD issues is close the gap between normal people and PWDs through a lens of a non-disabled people's perspectives. But if we agree that disability is a direct result of a hostile environment (Social Disability Model) rather than physical and mental disability (Medical Disability Model), then we must change our approach by trying to close the gap between PWDs and normal people, through PWDs perspective. For example, looking at the situation from a blind person's perspective might help us ask questions like - What if we live in a world without light? How will we do business? How can we create a non-visually dependent business environment? What kind of skills are needed to survive in that alternate world? Eight years after the government introduced inclusive development as the national agenda, the results were found, and the data was not encouraging.

4.2   Private Sector Initiatives

Although there is an increasing awareness of the demand to have more PWD entrepreneurs in the market, the private sector has been very slow on the uptake. Currently, only the Maybank Foundation has developed a holistic entrepreneur ecosystem that specifically targets minorities in Malaysia [10].

Reach Independent and Sustainable Entrepreneur (R.I.S.E) program is designed to train, coach and mentor participants to develop their entrepreneurial skills, resulting in higher income levels, and thus improving their overall standard of living. The key features of the program include; Practical entrepreneurship training, Effective mentoring and focus on income improvement, and Large-scale involvement of Maybank employees. Currently R.I.S.E is in phase 2 and has successfully trained 1,080 PWDs with the top 40% result for the initial 280 participants involved in the pilot project in Malaysia. This pilot project was started in September 2014, and has an average income increase as highlighted below:

- Per participants in RISE is 411.7
- Income Increase from RM 462.50 to RM 2,366.47;
- Average Income Increase RM 1,903.97

The R.I.S.E. programme starts with a three-day training on entrepreneurship and financial management. This is followed by three to six months of mentoring with a special focus on motivating participants. After the programme, participants continue to be guided and introduced to business opportunities. Their income-generation ability is also monitored. Maybank does not provide special loans to the R.I.S.E. participants but supports them to become eligible for standard loans. The training has enabled participants to build innovative sales strategies into their business ideas, enhance business management skills and augment client acquisition and retention, resulting in greater financial independence and increased resilience in businesses.

The fourth industrial revolution is changing the global economic landscape, covering growth areas such as big data and machine learning, cybersecurity, digital currencies, blockchain and the Internet of Things (IoT), with an expected creation of 30,000 jobs by 2020. New areas like Cyber Security, Data Analytics, Network & Infrastructure and Software Development will replace legacy areas or make the traditional workforce obsolete [9]. Emerging job positions such as digital content creators, programmers, social media managers, which can easily be done at home, are ideal positions in the context of job opportunities for PWDs.

5   Conclusion

Disabled people experience higher unemployment rates, economic inactivity and lack of social protection compared to their non-disabled peers. Research shows that there are economic and business benefits for PWDs inclusion. These include the benefits for economies as a whole, for companies that adopt various practices, and for people with disabilities themselves. In the era of the fourth industrial, the constraints of physical impairment should no longer applies due to the divergent of technology available. Technologies enable a more flexible working environment, better involvement in PWD's workforce and a range of new jobs [17].

Referring to a report from OECD, it is seen that for PWDs in parts of Europe, self-employment or entrepreneurship appears to be a viable opportunity [31].

Our research shown that the Technopronuership ecosystem for PWDs in Malaysia is almost non-existant. It should be developed further for them, and should be guided by the underlying principle that in all actions involving persons with disabilities, their interests and needs should be taken into account; whether undertaken by individuals, public or private social welfare institutions, courts of law, administrative authorities or legislative bodies or entities; recognizing that inclusion and mainstreaming should be promoted and specialized.

Acknowledgement. Deepest gratitude to Malaysia Technology Development Corporation (MTDC) and Universiti Teknologi Malaysia (UTM) for supporting our ongoing research that will allow us to identify suitable technopreneur skills that PWDs need and the level of their knowledge that will give them the opportunity to participate actively in Industry 4.0 movement and taking advantages of an advancement in technology to change how they are interacting with the society.

References

1. Disability and health. https://www.who.int/news-room/fact-sheets/detail/disabil ity-and-health, Accessed 09 May 2019
2. file. https://www.moe.gov.my/index.php/menumedia/media-cetak/penerbitan/terb itan/buku-informasi/1587-quick-facts-2018-malaysia-educational-statistics-1/file, Accessed 09 May 2019
3. Rmke-11   book.pdf.   https://www.talentcorp.com.my/clients/TalentCorp_2016_ 7A6571AE-D9D0-4175-B35D-99EC514F2D24/contentms/img/publication/ RMKe-11%20Book.pdf, Accessed 20 May 2019

4. Ahmad, F.K.: Use of assistive technology in inclusive education: making room for diverse learning needs. Transcience **6**(2), 62–77 (2015)
5. Na, A., et al.: Prevalence and determinants of disability among adults in malaysia: results from the national health and morbidity survey (NHMS) 2015. BMC Public Health **17**(1), 756 (2017)
6. Becker, E.H.: Self-employed workers: an update to 1983. Monthly Lab. Rev. **107**, 14 (1984)
7. Csikszentmihalyi, M., Csikszentmihalyi, I.S.: Optimal Experience: Psychological Studies of Flow in Consciousness. Cambridge University Press, Cambridge (1992)
8. Ministry of Education: Kpt - 4. statistik pendidikan tinggi 2017 - bab 2 : Universiti awam. https://mohe.gov.my/muat-turun/awam/statistik/2017-3/470-statistik-pendidikan-tinggi-2017-bab-2-universiti-awam, Accessed 13 May 2019
9. Ministry of Education: Malaysia education blueprint 2013–2025 : 2017 annual report (2017). https://www.padu.edu.my/wp-content/uploads/2018/07/AR2017-English-PPPM-.pdf, Accessed 16 May 2019
10. Maybank Foundation: Sustainability reports (2017). https://maybankfoundation.com/index.php/media-center/sustainability-reports, Accessed 13 May 2019
11. Halabisky, D.: Entrepreneurial activities in Europe-entrepreneurship for people with disabilities (2014)
12. Heron, R., Murray, B.: Assisting Disabled Persons in Finding Employment: A Practical Guide (2003)
13. Japan International Cooperation Agency (JICA): Baseline survery : The project to support participation of persons with disabilities, May 2010. http://www.jobcoachmalaysia.com/pdf/BaseLineSurveryFinalEnglish24052010.pdf, Accessed 09 May 2019
14. Kanter, A.S.: The Development of Disability Rights Under International Law: From Charity to Human Rights. Routledge, Abingdon (2014)
15. Khor, H.: Turning disability into a national asset. Penang Econ. Mon. 16–20 (2010)
16. Lee, M.N., Abdullah, Y., Mey, S.C.: Employment of people with disabilities in Malaysia: drivers and inhibitors. Int. J. Special Educ. **26**(1), 112–124 (2011)
17. Meager, N., Higgins, T.: Disability and skills in a changing economy. UK Commission for Employment and Skills, Briefing Paper Series (2011). http://www.oph.fi/download/140962_equality-disability.pdf
18. Menon, P.: Hannah: Govt pushing ministries to hire oku as example to private sector-metro news—the star online, November 2018. https://www.thestar.com.my/metro/metro-news/2018/11/17/govt-pushing-ministries-to-hire-oku-as-example-to-private-sector/, Accessed 13 May 2019
19. Pick, J.B., Azari, R.: Worldwide digital divide: influences of education, workforce, economic, and policy factors on information technology. In: Proceedings of the 2007 ACM SIGMIS CPR conference on Computer personnel research: The global information technology workforce, pp. 78–86. ACM (2007)
20. Ringland, K.E., Wolf, C.T., Boyd, L.E., Baldwin, M.S., Hayes, G.R.: Would you be mine: appropriating minecraft as an assistive technology for youth with autism. In: Proceedings of the 18th International ACM SIGACCESS Conference on Computers and Accessibility, pp. 33–41. ACM (2016)
21. Shakespeare, T., Watson, N.: The social model of disability: an outdated ideology? In: Exploring theories and expanding methodologies: Where we are and where we need to go, pp. 9–28. Emerald Group Publishing Limited (2001)
22. Shane, S., Locke, E.A., Collins, C.J.: Entrepreneurial motivation. Human Resource Manage. Rev. **13**(2), 257–279 (2003)

23. Shane, S.A.: A General Theory of Entrepreneurship: The Individual-Opportunity Nexus. Edward Elgar Publishing, Cheltenham (2003)
24. Department of Statistic Malaysia: Labour force survey report, malaysia, 2017 (2017). https://www.dosm.gov.my/v1/index.php?r=column/pdfPrev&id=aEdIelhlVTBtOHhjOUxqcXhyc2pCUT09, Accessed 16 May 2019
25. Steele, C.M.: Stereotypes and the fragility of academic competence, motivation, and self-concept. In: Handbook of competence and motivation, p. 436 (2013)
26. Stephan, U., Hart, M., Mickiewicz, T., Drews, C.C.: Understanding motivations for entrepreneurship. BIS Res. Pap. **212** (2015)
27. Szaban, J., et al.: Self-employment and entrepreneurship: a theoretical approach. J. Manage. Bus. Adm. Central Europe **26**(2), 89–120 (2018)
28. Ta, T.L., Leng, K.S.: Challenges faced by Malaysians with disabilities in the world of employment. Disabil. CBR Inclusive Dev. **24**(1), 6–21 (2013)
29. Ta, T.L., Wah, L.L., Leng, K.S.: Employability of people with disabilities in the northern states of peninsular malaysia: employers' perspective. Disabil. CBR Inclusive Dev. **22**(2), 79–94 (2011)
30. USLegal, Inc.: Technopreneur law and legal definition. https://definitions.uslegal.com/t/technopreneur/, Accessed 09 May 2019
31. Vaziri, D., Schreiber, D., Wieching, R., Wulf, V.: Disabled entrepreneurship and self-employment: the role of technology and policy building (2014)

Author Index

Printed in the United States
By Bookmasters